A Teacher's Guide to Education La  W9-CPE-347
Fourth Edition

This clearly written text, which is adapted from its parent volume, *Education Law, 4e*, provides a concise introduction to topics in education law that are most relevant to teachers. The greater the likelihood of litigation or error in a particular area of professional practice the more extensive the discussion. Topics concerning teacher relationships with their students include: student rights, discipline, negligence, discrimination, and special education. Topics concerning teacher relationships with their employers include: teacher rights, hiring and firing, contracts, unions, collective bargaining, and tenure. Key features include the following:

- **Presentation**—To aid comprehension, technical terms are carefully explained when first introduced and discussions of complex topics move logically from overview to elaboration of important details to summary of key topics and principles.
- **Flexibility**—Because it is concise and affordable, *A Teacher's Guide to Education Law* can be used in a variety of courses or in professional seminars dealing with teachers and the law.
- **New Material**—All chapters have been updated to include the case law and legislation of the past five years. About half have undergone major revision. The index contains almost 200 more entries than in the third edition.

This text is suitable for any course within a teacher education program that is devoted solely or partly to the legal issues that concern teachers.

Michael Imber (Ph.D., Stanford University) is Professor of Educational Leadership and Policy Studies in the School of Education at the University of Kansas.

Tyll van Geel (Ed.D., Harvard University; J.D., Northwestern University) is Taylor Professor of Education Emeritus in the Graduate School of Education, University of Rochester.

A Teacher's Guide to Education Law
Fourth Edition

Michael Imber
University of Kansas

and

Tyll van Geel
University of Rochester

Routledge
Taylor & Francis Group

NEW YORK AND LONDON

First edition published 1992 by McGraw-Hill
Second edition published 2000 by Lawrence Erlbaum Associates, Inc.
Third edition published 2004 by Lawrence Erlbaum Associates, Inc.

This edition published 2010
by Routledge
270 Madison Avenue, New York, NY 10016

Simultaneously published in the UK
by Routledge
2 Park Square, Milton Park, Abingdon, Oxon OX14 4RN

Routledge is an imprint of the Taylor & Francis Group, an informa business

Typeset in Sabon by Swales & Willis Ltd, Exeter, Devon

Printed and bound in the United States of America on acid-free paper by
Edwards Brothers, Inc.

Library of Congress Cataloging in Publication Data
Imber, Michael.
A teacher's guide to education law / Michael Imber and Tyll van Geel.—4th ed.
    p. cm.
    Includes bibliographical references and index.
    1. Educational law and legislation—United States. 2. Teachers—Legal status,
    laws, etc.—United States. I. Van Geel, Tyll. II. Title.
       KF4119.85.I46 2010
       344.73'07—dc22

                                                                    2009043756

ISBN 10: 0–415–87577–3 (hbk)
ISBN 10: 0–415–99463–2 (pbk)
ISBN 10: 0–203–85988–X (ebk)

ISBN 13: 978–0–415–87577–6 (hbk)
ISBN 13: 978–0–415-99463–7 (pbk)
ISBN 13: 978–0–203-85988–9 (ebk)

We dedicate this book to our families:
Jane, Molly, and Jake Imber
Katy, Alix, and Tap van Geel

And we dedicate the 4th edition
to the newest members of our families:
Michael Imber's granddaughter, Alice
Tyll van Geel's grandchildren,
Max, Kira, and Sam

Contents in Brief

Contents

Preface

Many aspects of the law of education have changed during the fifteen years since the first edition of *A Teacher's Guide to Education Law* was published. This fourth edition has been extensively updated and revised to reflect the changes, but its goal remains the same: to provide public school teachers with the legal knowledge necessary to do their jobs.

The text is organized to reflect the variety of legal problems that elementary and secondary school teachers actually face. The focus is on the law relating to students, teachers, and school programs. The greater the likelihood of litigation, legal controversy, or error in a particular area of professional practice, the more extensive the discussion. Topics that have been added or significantly expanded or revised since the book was first published include (among many others): the No Child Left Behind Act, student rights especially in the areas of free speech and search and seizure, employment discrimination, racial and sexual harassment of students and school employees, affirmative action and voluntary school integration, issues relating to the use of the Internet, and the law relating to special student populations. The Table of Cases of this fourth edition contains about 1000 more entries than in the first edition.

Every effort has been made to make the book comprehensible to readers with little or no background in law. The text is written in a style that teacher should find familiar. When technical legal terms are used, their meaning is explained. Discussions of particularly complex topics begin with an overview, and subsequent sections provide additional detail. The last section of each chapter provides a summary of the most significant topics and principles discussed. The first chapter is devoted to providing a foundation for understanding the remainder of the book, including a thorough explanation of the system of legal citations employed.

One of the difficulties of producing a comprehensive treatment of education law designed for teachers throughout the United States is that legal principles and interpretations can vary significantly from state to state. No attempt has been made to review the laws of each state exhaustively. Rather, the text focuses on generally applicable principles, noting areas where the specifics of state law vary. In these areas, readers may want to supplement the material presented with statutes and cases from their own state.

One final word of caution. Anyone who expects unambiguous answers to all legal questions is in for disappointment. Some legal issues are well settled, and they are presented as such. However, by its very nature, the law is often complex and uncertain. New issues and new perspectives on old issues arise continually; questions that once seemed settled are reexamined as notions about government and law evolve. Even experts often cannot agree on the application of a legal principle to a particular situation. Thus, in some instances, we can only pose issues and present a range of less-than-definitive answers for contemplation.

We hope you learn from and enjoy the book and that your study of the law of education is successful and rewarding.

—*Michael Imber*
—*Tyll van Geel*

1 Understanding Education Law

Teachers perform their duties within a network of law—law that both empowers and constrains. The law creates local school districts and gives school boards the authority to raise taxes and borrow money, buy property, construct buildings, hire and fire teachers, purchase supplies, determine the curriculum, and discipline pupils. At the same time, the law limits the exercise of all these powers. The law protects the free speech rights of students and teachers; guarantees them procedural protections when they are disciplined or fired; and prohibits policies that wrongfully discriminate on the basis of race, national origin, gender, disability, or religion. The law provides an orderly way for students, parents, teachers, and taxpayers to seek a remedy when they believe the school has treated them unjustly.

This chapter introduces the forms of law that affect the operation of schools, the role of the courts in making and interpreting education law, and the judicial systems of the federal government and the states. In preparation for the cases and commentary that comprise the rest of the book, the chapter concludes by describing the elements of a court decision and explaining the standard system of legal citations.

1.1 FORMS OF LAW

The network of education law is woven of constitutional provisions, statutes, regulations, policies, and common law. These various forms of law are designed to complement one another, but at times they may conflict. To further complicate matters, rules of law originate at the federal and state levels and sometimes with local school boards. Thus, in a legal sense, school officials serve many masters.

The Federal Constitution

The Constitution of the United States is the fundamental law of the nation. The Constitution establishes the three branches of the federal government—executive, legislative, and judicial; describes the relationship among the three branches; forms the union of the states; dictates the relation between the federal government and the states; and provides for the protection of individual rights. The Constitution both legitimates and limits the actions of government. It controls the relationship between the government and individual citizens but does not regulate interactions among private persons. Thus, the Constitution regulates the actions of government-run public schools and the relationship between the government and private schools. However, except under certain unusual circumstances, the Constitution does not limit the actions of private schools or control the relationships between private schools and their students or employees.

Although it mentions neither education nor schools, the Constitution has been interpreted as empowering Congress to raise money for education and to adopt certain types of legislation affecting schools. However, the Tenth Amendment limits the federal role in governing education: "The powers not delegated to the United States by the Constitution, nor prohibited by it to the States, are reserved to the States respectively, or to the people." Because the Constitution does not delegate to the United States or prohibit from the states the power to create and operate schools, the amendment allows states to perform these functions if they choose. Thus, the United States is one of the few countries without a centralized system of educational governance and policy-making. The resulting system of state and local control of education complicates the study of education law because rules often vary from state to state and even within states.

The remainder of the federal Constitution is relevant to education, nevertheless, in that no state education law, school district policy, or public school practice may be inconsistent with any article or amendment to the Constitution. Many of the important legal conflicts in education involve statutes, policies, or practices alleged to violate constitutional provisions. Most often cited in those allegations are those constitutional provisions that guarantee certain rights and freedoms of citizenship by limiting the power of the government to control individual behavior. These include the First Amendment guarantees of freedom of speech and freedom of religion, the Fourth Amendment protection against unreasonable search and seizure, and the Fourteenth Amendment requirements that states not violate their citizens' rights to "due process" and "equal protection of the laws."

State Constitutions

In keeping with the Tenth Amendment, the basic power to control education devolves upon the states. However, the U.S. Constitution does not require the states to exercise this power, and for several decades following the adoption of the Constitution the states did not use their inherent authority. However, as the nineteenth century progressed, the people of each state adopted a state constitution requiring their legislatures to establish a system of free public schooling for all children.

Typically, state constitutions contain vague language stating that there shall be schools and other educational activities and describing in general terms the way schools shall be governed and funded or the purposes for which they shall exist. For example, Article VIII, Section 1 of the Indiana Constitution states:

> Knowledge and learning, generally diffused throughout a community, being essential to the preservation of a free government; it shall be the duty of the General Assembly to encourage, by all suitable means, moral, intellectual, scientific, and agricultural improvement; and to provide by law, for a general and uniform system of Common School, wherein tuition shall be without charge, and equally open to all.

Thus, in Indiana, as in all states, the state legislature is charged with establishing and maintaining a system of free public schools. Many state constitutions also create state boards of education or state superintendencies and a few give these agencies powers independent of the legislature.

Most state constitutions contain provisions mirroring the federal Constitution, such as those prohibiting the establishment of religion and guaranteeing the equal protection of the laws. In fact, these state constitutional provisions may be more protective of individual rights than the U.S. Constitution. State constitutions may extend individual rights beyond those protected by the U.S. Constitution, but they may not contradict the U.S. Constitution or permit government practices that it prohibits.

State and Federal Statutes

The U.S. Congress and state legislatures execute their powers and duties through the enactment of statutes. Federal statutes must be consistent with the U.S. Constitution, and state statutes may not contradict either their own state's constitution or any federal law. A majority of the statutes controlling the operation of the public schools are enacted by state legislatures, but federal statutory law providing aid to schools and prohibiting various forms of discrimination are also significant.

Although the specifics vary greatly, most state legislatures have enacted statutes that:

* Dictate who may and who must attend school.
* Create local public school districts and boards and the means for their alteration and dissolution.
* Designate the qualifications for public school teachers and educational administrators.
* Prescribe the curriculum that the public schools must offer.
* Establish minimum requirements for high school graduation.
* Create a system for raising and distributing funds for education.
* Establish certain limited powers for schools to discipline students and employees.
* Fix the selection process, duties, powers, and limitations of local boards of education.
* Regulate certain aspects of the program of private schools.
* Delegate authority to regulate and oversee certain aspects of education to state agencies and officers.

In every state, the laws governing education are organized by topic and published either as an education code or as a section of the general laws of the state.

Despite the Tenth Amendment, Congress can exercise great influence over schools by virtue of its ability to control the allocation of federal funds and by exercising its power to regulate interstate commerce. Federal statutes are particularly influential because, unlike state laws, they apply throughout the United States. However, unlike state legislatures, Congress historically has been reluctant to pass laws that regulate schools. In recent decades, this reluctance has abated as Congress has attached many conditions to the use of federal funds and enacted general laws that apply to schools, including, for example, laws prohibiting discrimination in employment and protecting persons with disabilities. The two most significant federal statutes in terms of their effects on the programs of local public schools are the Individuals with Disabilities Education Act (see sec. 6.3) and the No Child Left Behind Act (see sec. 2.6).

Regulations

Regulations differ from both constitutions and statutes. Most regulations are created by public departments, agencies, or bureaus that in turn are created by statutes. Regulations are designed to implement the goals and fill in the details of legislation. A regulation must meet three requirements: it must have been adopted according to a procedure prescribed in a statute, its substance must be consistent with the statute the regulation is intended to implement, and the statute itself must be constitutional.

Many of the specifics of education law are found in regulations issued by state departments of education, the U.S. Department of Education or its predecessors, and other state and federal agencies. For example, most of the rules governing the treatment of students with disabilities under the Individuals with Disabilities Education Act are contained in regulations created by the Department of Education. States also have extensive sets of regulations that provide further specifics concerning the required treatment of pupils with disabilities. Educators are as legally bound by these regulations as by the statute itself.

Common Law

Constitutions are adopted by the people, statutes by legislatures, regulations by agencies, and the common law is created by courts. Hence, in common law cases, courts invent the relevant legal rules and apply them to the case at hand. By contrast, in constitutional and statutory cases, the court is only interpreting and applying a law created by another authority.

As it originally came to the United States from Great Britain the common law had two main branches: civil and criminal. Today in the United States the criminal branch has for the most part been superseded by statutes. For educators, the civil branch of the common law is the more important. This branch is divided into contracts and torts. Contract law establishes the conditions under which an exchange of promises creates binding obligations (see chap. 9). Tort law deals with a variety of matters including negligent behavior that results in an injury, intentional injuries, libel and slander, and injuries resulting from defects in buildings or land (see chap. 10). Each state has its own system of common law with some mostly minor variations among the states.

School Board Policies

Subject to the scope of authority delegated to them by the state legislature, school boards may issue their own rules and regulations. All of their enactments must conform to the limitations of relevant constitutional provisions, statutes, regulations, and common law. When a school board acts in accordance with these requirements, its own rules and regulations are binding on itself. For example, if a board adopts a set of procedures to be used before a student is suspended from school, it and the district's employees may be legally required to adhere to them.

1.2 THE COURTS AND EDUCATION LAW

Courts perform three overlapping functions of importance to school officials whether or not they are personally involved in litigation. First, courts resolve conflicts by applying constitutional provisions, legislation, and regulations to specific situations. Second, courts rule on the constitutional validity of statutes, policies, and actions. For example, courts determine whether a statute is consistent with the Constitution or the expulsion of a student violates a constitutional right. Third, courts provide the official interpretation of the federal and state constitutions, statutes, regulations, and common law.

In performing these functions, courts must frequently deal with broad, ambiguous, and even vaguely worded rules of law. Often the meaning of a law is at the heart of a legal dispute. It is one thing to know, for example, that the Fourteenth Amendment to the U.S. Constitution requires "equal protection of the laws" for all persons and quite another to determine whether an affirmative action program that gives preference to some people because of their race or gender is consistent with this requirement.

Interpreting rules of law raises difficult and unsettled issues. Some argue that constitutional interpretation should be based solely on the intent of the framers and ratifiers, whereas others believe the Constitution must evolve in response to new conditions and problems. Similarly contentious issues arise concerning the interpretation of statutes and common law precedent.

Regardless of the theory of interpretation employed, the decisions rendered by courts form a body of law known as case law. Some case law is constitutional law, some is statutory law, and some is common law. The study of education law or any subject area of law is primarily a study of cases because case law provides the authoritative interpretation of constitutional provisions, statutes, and common law. We study cases to find out who prevailed in a particular legal dispute and to learn why. By studying the rulings of courts, we hope to learn to conduct ourselves lawfully in related situations.

Decisions in prior cases similar to the one under consideration are referred to as **precedents**. If a precedent comes from a court with jurisdiction in the area of a current dispute, it is called a **mandatory** precedent. If it comes from a different area of jurisdiction, it is called a **persuasive** precedent. Mandatory precedents make law and bind the actions of government in a particular area of jurisdiction, whereas persuasive precedents merely show how courts in other jurisdictions view a particular question.

Even when a mandatory precedent exists, it still may not govern the outcome of a current dispute. Because no two cases are ever factually identical, the precedent may only provide partial guidance or a critical difference may make the precedent **distinguishable** and thus inapplicable to a current case. Whether an otherwise binding precedent is distinguishable is frequently a matter of dispute in a lawsuit. A mandatory precedent from a higher court must be followed, but courts may decline to follow their own previous rulings. Courts are not bound to follow persuasive precedents, but they may choose to unless there is a contradictory mandatory precedent.

1.3 THE JUDICIAL SYSTEM

There are both federal and state courts. Both systems are organized into three levels: trial courts, intermediate courts of appeal, and one highest court (or in a few states, two). Federal and state courts vary in the kinds of cases they may decide but, in both systems, courts at all levels are limited to dealing with cases that someone brings before them. A court cannot, for example, declare that a newly enacted statute is unconstitutional until a case comes before the court that depends on the constitutionality of the statute. In most instances, cases can only be initiated by someone with a direct stake in the outcome of the dispute. Such an individual is said to have **standing**.

Federal Courts

The federal court system deals almost exclusively with cases involving federal constitutional or statutory issues. Only in certain limited and exceptional circumstances will the federal courts deal with conflicts regarding the interpretation of state constitutions, state statutes, or common law. Nevertheless, the decisions of federal courts have had a tremendous impact on local schools.

There are ninety-five federal trial courts called **district** courts. Each state has at least one federal district court and heavily populated states may have several, each with jurisdiction over a different region of the state. These courts hear evidence in order to build the factual record of cases brought before them. Their primary function, once the facts are determined, is to apply the law as found in the Constitution, federal statutes, and relevant higher court precedent. Trial judges rarely get involved in reinterpreting the law.

The intermediate appellate courts in the federal system are the **circuit courts of appeals**. There are thirteen federal circuit courts—eleven with jurisdiction over a group of states,

Table 1.1 Jurisdiction of Federal Circuit Courts of Appeals

Circuit	Jurisdiction
1st	Maine, Massachusetts, New Hampshire, Puerto Rico, Rhode Island
2nd	Connecticut, New York, Vermont
3rd	Delaware, New Jersey, Pennsylvania, Virgin Islands
4th	Maryland, North Carolina, South Carolina, Virginia, West Virginia
5th	Louisiana, Mississippi, Texas
6th	Kentucky, Ohio, Michigan, Tennessee
7th	Illinois, Indiana, Wisconsin
8th	Arkansas, Iowa, Minnesota, Missouri, Nebraska, North Dakota, South Dakota
9th	Alaska, Arizona, California, Guam, Hawaii, Idaho, Montana, Nevada, Northern Mariana Islands, Oregon, Washington
10th	Colorado, Kansas, New Mexico, Oklahoma, Utah, Wyoming
11th	Alabama, Florida, Georgia
D.C.	Washington, D.C.
Federal	Washington, D.C. (specialized courts)

one for the District of Columbia, and one consisting of three specialized federal courts. Table 1.1 indicates the jurisdiction of each circuit.

The function and procedures of both the intermediate and highest appellate courts differ greatly from trial courts. These multimember courts conduct no trials and hear no new evidence. Their sole function is to review the records of lower courts to determine if errors of law have been committed. Errors of law come in many forms, including incorrect instructions to juries, wrongful applications of rules of evidence, procedural mistakes, and misinterpretations of the Constitution, relevant statutes, or other rules of law.

After considering both written and oral arguments from both sides of the case, the panel of judges votes, reaches a decision, and begins the process of opinion writing. This may entail some bargaining among the judges regarding the rationale for the decision and the legal rules and principles to be announced. If an appellate court decides that an error of law has been made, it has two basic options: to declare a new final judgment or to remand the case for retrial by the lower court in accordance with the appellate court's new ruling.

The highest federal court, the **Supreme Court**, hears appeals from the federal circuit courts and from any of the state highest courts in cases involving issues of federal law. (In rare instances, not usually relevant to education, the Supreme Court may also conduct trials.) The Court is not obligated to hear every case appealed to it and decides with full opinion only about 100 of the 7,000 cases brought to it each year. The Court is so selective regarding the cases it chooses to hear because its primary purpose is not simply to correct the mistakes of the lower courts. As the only court whose rulings are binding throughout the country, the Supreme Court serves as the final arbiter of the meaning of federal statutes and the U.S. Constitution. As such, the Court endeavors to hear cases that will resolve inconsistent rulings among the federal circuit courts, that raise an especially important or novel point of law, and that have potentially widespread consequences.

Supreme Court justices and all other federal judges are appointed by the president with Senate approval and serve for life unless removed for committing a crime. Because the Supreme Court has nine members, it takes the agreement of five to form a **majority opinion** of the Court. Precedent is created only if at least five justices agree on the outcome of a case and the rationale for the decision. Justices who disagree with the decision may issue **dissenting opinions** but only majority opinions have the force of law. Similarly, justices agreeing with the outcome but disagreeing with the rationale may issue separate, nonbinding, **concurring opinions**.

Even when there is no majority agreement on the rationale for a decision the outcome of the case is still decided by majority vote. There may be a **plurality opinion** supported by a majority of the justices on the winning side and one or more concurring and dissenting opinions. If the Court is split badly enough, there may not even be a plurality opinion, only a brief unsigned *per curiam* opinion stating the outcome of the case and a group of concurring and dissenting opinions. In any case, none of the various opinions issued when there is no majority opinion creates precedent. When the Court is deadlocked on even the outcome of a case, with one judge not participating, the judgment of the circuit court is affirmed and no precedent is created.

State Courts

State courts hear cases involving state constitutional law, state statutes, and common law and may also hear cases involving federal issues. Cases raising both state and federal questions are heard in state court. Many education cases are decided in state courts because they raise no federal legal questions. For example, cases of alleged negligence by school officials are usually heard in state courts.

The structure of state judiciaries mirrors the federal system: trial courts, intermediate appellate courts, and usually a single highest court. Although state courts at all levels are known by a variety of names, in the majority of states the highest court is the supreme court. State trial courts usually cover a relatively small geographical area, whereas intermediate courts hear appeals from more than one trial court jurisdiction. As in the federal system, the opinions of intermediate courts are binding only within their jurisdiction so it is possible for different intermediate courts within the same state to reach conflicting legal conclusions. One of the roles of a state's highest court is to reconcile discrepancies in lower court opinions. The highest court's decisions are binding on all other courts within its state court system but not on federal courts or the courts of other states.

1.4 ELEMENTS OF A JUDICIAL DECISION

Trial courts sometimes, intermediate courts often, and highest courts usually conclude their proceedings by issuing a written opinion. Judicial opinions are comprised of a set of components or elements that provide the information necessary to understand a court's decision concerning who won the case and why. A standard opinion contains the following elements: the case name, a review of the facts, a restatement of the claims and arguments of both sides, a review of the case's procedural history, a statement of the issue(s), a ruling on the issue(s), a justification for each ruling, and the disposition.

Case Name

Almost all cases are named for the adversaries or **parties** to the case. The person who brings a suit to trial is called the **plaintiff** or sometimes the **complainant**, and the person or governmental unit against whom the suit is brought is the **defendant** or **respondent**. In trial court opinions, the name of the case is in the form *Plaintiff v. Defendant* (e.g., *McLaughlin v. Central School District No. 21*). If the case is appealed, the initiator of the appeal (the loser of the previous round) is called the **appellant** or the **petitioner** and the other party, the **appellee** or **respondent**. In the federal system and most other courts, the case name now lists the appellant first and the appellee second (e.g., *Central School District No. 21 v. McLaughlin*).

Facts

A court's statement of the facts of the case recounts who did what to whom, when, where, how, and why. The court describes the conflict between the parties as determined from the evidence presented at trial. Although sometimes these descriptions are human dramas of high emotion, often the facts are merely descriptions of laws or policies adopted by a governmental entity and a discussion of their effects.

Claims

The opinion may next review the objectives or goals of the two parties and the arguments offered in support of their claims. For example, if the parties disagree about the correct interpretation of a statute, the decision will reprint the part of the statute in dispute and discuss the contentions of the parties regarding the meaning of the statute.

Procedural History

Opinions usually include a review of the motions, counter-motions, and other legal maneuvers of the parties as well as the previous decisions of lower courts in the case. For example, a decision of a state's highest court may indicate that the trial court ruled for the plaintiff and why and that the intermediate appellate court reversed the decision and why.

Issues

In every case, the parties disagree about the facts or on the proper application of the law to the facts. The questions raised by these disagreements are the issues of the case. The outcome depends on the court's answers to the issues. Some cases raise both issues of fact and issues of law. For example, a case may turn on the following two questions: whether the teacher was present in the room when the student was hurt, and what level of supervision the law requires a teacher to give students. Some opinions explicitly state the issues as the court sees them, but others are less forthcoming and leave it to the reader to work out the issues.

Often courts assist their analysis by dividing a large complex issue into a series of smaller ones. These smaller issues may be organized in a logical sequence analogous to a flow chart. For example, a court may first decide whether the actions of the plaintiff are of the type protected by the Free Speech Clause of the Constitution. If the answer is yes, then it must next determine whether the defendant met the appropriate standard for controlling protected speech.

Rulings and Justification

The main body of the opinion contains the answers to the issues and the rationale or reasoning supporting each ruling. There may not be a clear separation of rulings and justifications, so again sorting these out may be up to the reader.

Rulings are also referred to as **holdings, findings,** or **conclusions of law**. A brief statement encapsulating the material facts and major conclusions of law may also be referred to as the holding of the case. Rulings interpreting a constitutional provision or other law may provide **principles, rules, standards,** or **doctrine** to guide the application of the law in related situations.

Courts arrive at their rulings through deductive reasoning with the relevant facts and rules of law as premises. The deductive argument also provides the justification for the decision. A simple example:

Premise 1 (factual finding): X was driving at 40 mph on Main St.

Premise 2 (rule of law): The speed limit on Main St. is 30 mph, and exceeding this speed limit is the legal wrong of speeding.

Conclusion (ruling): X has committed the legal wrong of speeding.

The cases in this book, however, are never so simple because, although the facts may be well known, the application of the relevant legal rules, principles, or tests is not clear-cut. For example, if the legal rule required that drivers maintain a reasonable speed rather than specifying a precise speed limit, the issue of whether X was speeding would be more diffi-cult to decide.

Disposition

Having determined the winner of a legal dispute and explained its rationale, the court con-cludes its opinion with an order dictating what must be done consistent with the holdings in the case. If the defendant wins a trial, the trial court will simply dismiss the case and per-haps order the plaintiff to pay court and legal fees. If the plaintiff wins, the trial court will fashion a remedy for the injustice the plaintiff has suffered. Depending on the type of case, the law may permit various forms of remedy including payment of money damages, issuance of an injunction or order requiring public officials to cease prohibited practices or perform mandated duties, or other relief specifically fashioned to undo the wrong. In some cases, the court may order further proceedings to decide on an appropriate remedy. An appellate court can conclude a case by affirming or upholding the trial court decision, modifying it in some respect, or reversing the trial court. In the latter case, the court may either issue an order of its own or remand the case back to the trial court for additional proceedings consistent with its ruling. Many cases are remanded for procedural reasons with the outcome no longer in doubt.

* * *

Interpreting judicial opinions is a subtle and imprecise act. Lawyers and judges in later cases argue over the meaning of precedents just as they argue over the meaning of statutes and constitutional provisions. For example, a court may have ruled against start-ing the school day with an organized prayer, but does this ruling preclude a moment of silence?

One common pitfall is to confuse the holdings of a court with the **dicta** that surround it. Dicta, which may be defined as "side comments," are parts of an opinion not necessary to the outcome. Opinions often include commentaries concerning issues and hypotheticals related to the case under consideration. For example, the opinion in a speeding case might say: "Although a life and death emergency might justify exceeding the speed limit, there was no emergency here." This is dicta and concluding that drivers are authorized to exceed the speed limit in life and death emergencies would be wrong.

1.5 LEGAL CITATIONS

Citations to judicial opinions are in the form of a series of numbers and abbreviations following the case name that indicate where the opinion may be found. The books that report court decisions, known as case reporters, are generally found only in law libraries and other specialized locations. Additionally, the full text of published federal and state court decisions as well as federal and state statutes and regulations of government agencies can be found at various sites on the Internet. A good starting point for locating cases and other legal research is www.findlaw.com. Other useful sites include: www.supremecourtus. gov; www.farislaw.com; www.ed.gov; www.law.cornell.edu; www.law.stanford. edu/library; www.brennancenter.org; and www.aclu.org. State department of education web sites are a good source for state statutes and regulations.

Case citations all follow the same basic format. An example of a citation for a U.S. Supreme Court opinion with each of its elements identified is as follows:

Keyishian v. Board of Regents,	385	U.S.	589	(1967)
Name of Case,	Volume	Case Reporter	Page	(Year Decided)

This case is found on page 589 of volume 385 in the set of books known as *United States Reports*, always abbreviated "U.S." in case citations (see Table 1.2). Although the year is given, the case can be found without it. *United States Reports* is the official government publication of Supreme Court opinions. Several private case reporters also publish Supreme Court opinions. The most commonly cited of these is the *Supreme Court Reporter* (S. Ct.). For example, the *Keyishian* case may be cited as 87 S. Ct. 675, indicating that the opinion may be found on page 675 of volume 87. The *United States Reports* citation should be used unless it is not yet available.

Citations to lower federal courts give the same information as Supreme Court citations and give the abbreviated name of the specific circuit or district court in parentheses before the date (although this information is not necessary to find the case). An example of a federal circuit court of appeals decision from the Fifth Circuit is:

Tomkins v. Vickers, 26 F.3d 603 (5th Cir. 1994).

An opinion from the district court of the Northern District of Illinois would be:

Olesen v. Board of Education, 676 F. Supp. 820 (N.D. Ill. 1987).

Citations to lower federal court decisions may also include additional information about the subsequent actions of higher courts. For example, in *Uzzell v. Friday*, 547 F.2d 801 (4th Cir. 1977), *cert. denied*, 446 U.S. 951 (1980), the last part of the citation indicates that the Supreme Court "denied certiorari," meaning it refused to review the case. The

Table 1.2 Reporters for Federal Court Decisions

Abbreviation	Title	Courts Reported	Publisher
U.S.	United States Reports	Supreme Court	U.S. government
S. Ct.	Supreme Court Reporter	Supreme Court	West Publishing Co.
F.3d	Federal Reporter, third series	Circuit Courts	West Publishing Co.
F. Supp. 2d	Federal Supplement, second series	District Courts	West Publishing Co.

official denial is reported in *United States Reports* as cited. (Some textbooks, including this one, omit the *cert. denied* citation unless it is considered particularly important.) Other citations might include a notation that the decision was subsequently affirmed (*aff'd*) or reversed (*rev'd*).

State case citations follow the same format, but they have their own case reporters. Although some states publish their own case reporters, the most readily available source of state appellate court decisions is the regional reporters published by West Publishing Company. Seven regional reporters cover groups of states (see Table 1.3). The information in parentheses indicates the state and year for cases heard in the states' highest courts or a more complete court name for other cases. Some sources employ a double ("parallel citation") also listing the official state-published reporters, but, in keeping with current standard style, this volume only uses the citation to the regional reporter.

Statutory citations are similar to cases, but a section (§) number is given instead of a page. Federal statutes may be cited to the *United States Code* (U.S.C.), the preferred source; to the *Statutes at Large* (Stat.); or to the *United States Code Annotated* (U.S.C.A.). For example, 42 U.S.C. § 2000d (1981) refers to section 2000d in volume 42 of the edition of *United States Code* published in 1981. Some case books and textbooks, including this one, omit the years from statute citations because the volume and section numbers are the same in every edition of statutes. A federal statute might also be referred to by its popular name, such as the "Individuals with Disabilities Education Act," followed by the citation.

Each state has its own specialized notation for citations to state statutes, but most follow a format similar to federal. In some states there is more than one possible source and citation for the same statute.

Federal regulations are published in the *Code of Federal Regulations* (C.F.R.) and in the *Federal Register* (Fed. Reg.). Citations give the volume, abbreviation, section or page, and (sometimes) year of publication, such as 34 C.F.R. 106.12 (1996) or 62 Fed. Reg. 12,038 (1997).

Complete information concerning legal citations may be found in *The Bluebook: A Uniform System of Citation* (18th edition), published by the Harvard Law Review Association in 2005. New editions are published about every five years. Information concerning legal citations is also available online at www.law.cornell.edu/citation.

Table 1.3 Regional Reporters

Abbreviation	Title	States
A.2d	Atlantic Reporter, second series	Connecticut, Delaware, District of Columbia, Maine, Maryland, New Hampshire, New Jersey, Pennsylvania, Rhode Island, Vermont
N.E.2d	North Eastern Reporter, second series	Illinois, Indiana, Massachusetts, New York, Ohio
N.W.2d	North Western Reporter, second series	Iowa, Michigan, Minnesota, Nebraska, North Dakota, South Dakota, Wisconsin
P.3d	Pacific Reporter, third series	Alaska, Arizona, California, Colorado, Hawaii, Idaho, Kansas, Montana, Nevada, New Mexico, Oklahoma, Oregon, Utah, Washington, Wyoming
S.E.2d	South Eastern Reporter, second series	Georgia, North Carolina, South Carolina, Virginia, West Virginia
S.W.3d	South Western Reporter, third series	Arkansas, Kentucky, Missouri, Tennessee, Texas
So. 2d	Southern Reporter, second series	Alabama, Florida, Louisiana, Mississippi

1.6 SUMMARY

The law plays a part in everything that educators do. Some practices are required by law, some are prohibited, and the rest are permitted. The law of education comes in a variety of forms: constitutional provisions, statutes, regulations, common law, and policies. Some of the law originates at the federal level, some at the state, and some policies are formulated by local school boards with authority delegated by the state.

Regardless of the origin of a law, it falls to the courts to interpret it and apply it to specific disputes. Courts also resolve inconsistencies between laws and rule on the validity of laws that might contradict higher authority. Ultimately, case law provides the official meaning of laws.

There is a federal judiciary, and each state has its own judicial system. The organization of the judicial systems at both levels consists of trial courts and two levels of appellate courts, intermediate and highest. In the federal system, these are known as district courts, circuit courts of appeal, and the Supreme Court. Trial courts hear evidence, determine facts, and apply the law, whereas appellate courts correct errors of law at lower levels. Appellate courts, especially the highest courts, focus on issues of broad significance. Their majority opinions make law within their area of jurisdiction.

Most written court decisions contain certain common elements. The facts of the case are the events and actions that created the dispute under consideration, and the issues are the disputed questions of law or fact. The holdings of a court explain and justify its decisions. Holdings set precedent for future cases. Published court decisions as well as laws and regulations are cited according to a uniform system of legal notation.

2 Curriculum

The primary responsibility of teachers is to promote the educational goals of their state, school district, and school. Their primary function is to participate in the delivery of the school's program or curriculum. This chapter considers the legal origins of the curriculum, focusing on the power of the local, state, and federal government to determine what will be taught in public schools.

In every state, parents and children are subject to laws requiring young people to attend public schools or a state-approved alternative. The most legally troublesome outcome of compulsory attendance laws is that some children find themselves in public schools where they are exposed to teachings that violate their parents' or their own basic beliefs. The public school curriculum is society's primary method of attempting to structure its future. Because of the perceived potential of schools to promote cultural, political, ideological, and even religious attitudes and behaviors, debate over curriculum is pervasive, ongoing, and acrimonious. To control curriculum is to decide how the young are to be instructed, what we as a society would have them know and value, and ultimately, what we would have them believe.

As the U.S. becomes ever more pluralistic, pressures mount to ensure that the public school provides its diverse population with a common educational experience. Equally strong are demands that schools respect and even promote the various cultures into which the school population was born. In short, society is faced with many questions: Will the public school curriculum be a smorgasbord or a melting pot? Will public schools offer an array of culturally, politically, ideologically, educationally, and linguistically diverse experiences from which parents or students may choose? Will there be separate schools and programs for, among others, Black males, Spanish-speaking children, fundamentalist Christians, and those who want to study the arts? Or will the schools provide all students with a common experience? If a common experience is provided, will it be multicultural or focused primarily on the dominant culture? Whichever option is chosen, how and by whom will the curriculum be developed? Will its ultimate goal be to promote diversity or to create a uniform U.S. culture and creed?

Overlaying these debates are conflicting views over the role and impact of standardized, high-stakes tests in promoting student learning and school accountability. Simply put, some people claim that properly designed tests effectively promote and measure what students ought to learn. Others argue these tests inevitably distort what true education should be about.

This chapter explores the legal issues that arise out of these disputes. Section 2.1 presents an overview of the shared legal authority for the creation and control of the school program focusing primarily on the role of the state. Sections 2.2–2.5 examine a variety of constitutional challenges to the power of the state and local school boards to set curriculum, select materials, and structure the activities of public schools. Most of these challenges are based on the religion or speech clauses of the First Amendment or other constitutional provisions. Section 2.6 addresses the No Child Left Behind Act and other federal statutes affecting the program of schools.

2.1 AUTHORITY TO CONTROL THE PUBLIC SCHOOL PROGRAM

Legal authority over the school curriculum is shared among various levels and agencies of government. As a consequence of the Tenth Amendment (see sec. 1.1) basic authority over schooling is a reserved to the states. Thus, historically, state legislatures have been the primary source of the law that shapes the curriculum. The state legislatures in varying degrees have chosen to share the authority to formulate curriculum with local school districts within boundaries established by a state department of education and the legislature itself. At the school district level, the school board has primary legal authority over the curriculum, but in several states power has been further delegated to individual school councils.

Overlaying this complex authority structure are statutes of the federal government, which increasingly limit state and local options. The primary mechanisms of federal control are categorical aid, money provided with programmatic requirements attached, and various antidiscrimination statutes (see chaps. 5 and 6). By far the most influential of the categorical aid programs in affecting the program of public schools are the Individuals with Disabilities Education Act (see chap. 6) and the No Child Left Behind Act (see sec. 2.6). Finally, the judiciary, primarily through its constitutional interpretations of the religion clauses of the First Amendment, also has a significant effect on the program of public schools.

Although some state constitutions contain brief references to subjects that must be taught, the primary legal authority for specifying the curriculum of the public schools rests with the state legislatures. (In a few states, by constitutional provision, this power is shared between the state legislature and the state board of education.) The state legislature may, if it wishes, prescribe the basic course of study down to the last detail, select all books and materials, determine graduation requirements, prescribe standardized testing requirements, and even establish the methods of instruction.

In practice no legislature has gone this far. All of them, to varying degrees, voluntarily share control of the curriculum with their state boards of education and, most importantly, with local school boards. Historically, the primary state mechanisms of curriculum control were laws and regulations requiring local schools to teach specified courses and topics, creating pupil classification systems by age and grade, and setting minimum course and credit requirements for high school graduation, and these mechanisms are still important today. About half the states also have a system of statewide textbook adoption, usually involving a legislatively authorized commission with the power to select an array of acceptable books from which school boards may choose.

In recent years, all states have adopted mandated school accountability systems based on the administration of standardized tests to assess student achievement. These testing programs have the effect of significantly increasing the degree of state influence over both the allocation of curricular time and the content of courses. Although they may not be mandated to do so by law, many districts now base their curriculum on the topics that are contained on the tests. In states with minimum competency tests that students must pass in order to be promoted from grade to grade or receive a high school diploma, schools typically devote significant instructional time to preparing students to take the tests. In many schools, this process of curricular "alignment" has led to significant modification of the previous program.

Nevertheless, state laws requiring or authorizing local school districts to offer a particular course usually leave it to the school board to develop its own syllabus and choose its own instructional methods. The major exception is sex education. A number of states both mandate the teaching of sex education and specify topics or instructional approaches that may or may not be used. At least half a dozen states require that abstinence be taught as the best way to avoid pregnancy and sexually transmitted disease.[1] Several states prohibit courses that discuss or promote the "homosexual lifestyle."[2] Illinois requires teaching and honoring "respect for monogamous heterosexual marriage."[3] Louisiana prohibits the distribution of contraception or counseling or advocating abortion and specifies that the instruction "shall not include religious beliefs, practices in human sexuality, nor the subjective moral and ethical judgments of the instructor or other persons."[4] Missouri prohibits the use of materials relating to human sexuality provided by a provider of abortion services.[5] A number of states, including Oklahoma, give parents the right to inspect sex education materials.[6] Idaho requires parental and community involvement in the development of sex education curricula.[7] Some states, Alabama and Kansas among them, give parents the right to have their children excused from sex education classes.[8]

A number of states have enacted statutes requiring that students be taught only in English.[9] These laws have the effect of making the use of bilingual instruction illegal except as required by federal law (see sec. 6.5). California's statute specifically prohibits the use of state funds or resources for instruction in any English dialect such as Black (or African-American Vernacular) English. California's law also specifically authorizes parents to sue for enforcement of the law and for actual damages and attorney fees. A school board member, administrator, or teacher who repeatedly violates the law can be held personally liable.

A mostly older, but still valid, body of case law involves the claim that a local school board lacks the state-delegated authority to implement a particular course or program. School boards have prevailed in almost all these cases. For example, in 1886, the Supreme Court of Indiana ruled that local boards had the legal authority to require their pupils to study and practice music.[10] Similarly, the Arizona Supreme Court ruled in 1927 that physical education could be included in the curriculum.[11] Much more recently, a California court upheld the authority of a local school board to enter into a contract with a private company in which the school received video equipment in exchange for showing its students a daily ten-minute current-events program designed to appeal to teenagers. Plaintiffs objected to the agreement because the programs included two minutes of commercial advertising; however, the court disagreed because the contract and the programs had a valid educational purpose and because individual students could be excused from watching if they wished.[12] Even without the opt-out provision, it is probable that the program would have been approved because the statutory authority of local school boards to offer or require courses of their own choosing is well-settled.

Parents have been successful, however, in litigation to force a school to offer a particular course or program when their claim was supported by a specific state statute. Some states require the school board to maintain a kindergarten or provide a foreign language or other course on petition of a specified number of parents or students. In Massachusetts, for example, twenty pupils or 5 percent of the students enrolled in a high school, whichever is less, may demand that a course be taught.[13] In a number of states, parents have a statutory right to examine the school curriculum.[14]

In some places, legal authority over certain aspects of the public school program has been further decentralized by state-mandated creation of local school councils with authority over certain aspects of the school's program. In Kentucky, school-site councils now enjoy a range of powers that include control of the curriculum, instructional practices, textbooks, and instructional materials.[15] The Chicago School Reform Act created Local School Councils that have the power to appoint the principal, approve school improvement plans, and make recommendations regarding textbooks and other curricular matters.[16] Even in states where local school councils are not mandated, some school boards have chosen to create them.

Charter schools are legal entities created by the legislatures of about forty states. In some states, they are state-approved, not-for-profit, nonreligious private schools that control their own programs and receive state funding for each pupil they attract. Some states also permit existing public schools to apply to become charter schools at the initiation of local parents and teachers. Charter schools are released from many of the requirements of their state and local school board, thereby freeing them to develop their own policies and programs. For example, Connecticut permits up to one-half of the teachers in charter schools to be non-certified.[17] However, there are other regulations with which charter schools must comply, such as antidiscrimination requirements, labor laws, reporting, and even open meeting law requirements.[18]

Outside the formal governance process of education, many extralegal influences affect the curriculum, such as textbook manufacturers, teacher unions and professional associations, parents, and a variety of special interest groups. Teachers and school administrators also may have a great deal of control over the programs of their own classrooms and schools. This control may be viewed as delegated either explicitly by the school board or implicitly by the failure of state and local authorities to act. This chapter focuses on the legal authority to control the curriculum rather than on the political and educational mechanisms of curriculum development.

2.2 OBJECTIONS TO RELIGIOUS OBSERVANCES IN PUBLIC SCHOOLS

The past sixty years have seen almost no constitutional litigation challenging the right of states or schools to teach the basic subjects. Although some parents probably oppose the teaching of grammar, music, or physical education for psychological, pedagogical, or idiosyncratic reasons, these parents seem content either to accept the state's authority to control the program of the public schools or to opt for a private or home school whose program they find more acceptable.

This does not mean that states and their schools now enjoy the freedom to offer or require any program without fear of parental complaint. When school programs concern value-laden issues about which there is no consensus within the community, some parents are sure to object. If the objection can be framed in constitutional terms, litigation often results. In cases when a public school's curriculum is found to conflict with federal or state constitutional principles, a court will prohibit its use.

By far the most common constitutional objection raised against a school program is that it fails to respect the wall of separation between church and state. In the early years of U.S. public schooling, the wall of separation was often crossed. Bible readings, organized prayers, the celebration of religious holidays, and a variety of other religious observances and ceremonies were common features of school programs in most places. In addition, public schools generally offered a kind of pan-Protestant curriculum that many Catholics and non-Christians found offensive. In fact, objections to the strongly Protestant flavor of the public school curriculum led to the founding of the Catholic schools, by far the largest private school system in the United States.

School Prayer

By the mid-twentieth century, those who objected to overt religious practices in public schools began looking to the courts for relief. In 1962, in *Engel v. Vitale*,[19] the Supreme

Court prohibited the organized recitation of a nondenominational prayer especially composed by the state to avoid offending any religious group. The following year, the issue of organized Bible readings in school reached the Court in *School District of Abington Township v. Schempp*.[20]

In *Schempp*, the Court simultaneously considered two cases in which students and their parents objected to the reading "without comment" of Bible verses and the Lord's Prayer as part of the schools' morning exercises. The plaintiffs argued that the exercises violated the First Amendment's prohibition against the government's "establishment of religion." The schools defended their practices by pointing out that the readings were not designed to promote any particular religion (various versions of the Bible were utilized) and that students were not compelled to participate in the exercises and could even leave the room if they wished, and by arguing that to eliminate the readings would violate the right of free exercise of religion of those who wished to hear them.

The *Schempp* Court based its findings in favor of the plaintiffs on its understanding of the intentions underlying the adoption of the Establishment Clause. Quoting from an earlier opinion, the Court declared:

> The [First] Amendment's purpose was not to strike merely at the official establishment of a single sect, creed, or religion, outlawing only a formal relation such as had prevailed in England and some of the colonies. Necessarily it was to uproot all such relationships. But the object was broader than separating church and state in this narrow sense. It was to create a complete and permanent separation of the spheres of religious activity and civil authority by comprehensively forbidding every form of public aid or support for religion.

Based on this understanding, the *Schempp* Court developed a framework for evaluating claims that school programs and curricula conflict with the Establishment Clause. The Court declared that for a public school program to withstand a challenge based on the Establishment Clause, both its **purpose** and its **primary effect** must be secular. These two requirements have since been combined with a third criterion called **entanglement** (designed to prohibit either the reality or the appearance of situations in which government and religious activity cannot be distinguished from one another) to form a three-part test that is now used to adjudicate all cases involving an alleged violation of the Establishment Clause. Known as the *Lemon* test after the case in which it was first employed,[21] the test holds that a government policy or practice violates the Establishment Clause if (a) its purpose is to endorse or disapprove of religion, or (b) its primary effect is to advance or inhibit religion, or (c) it creates excessive administrative entanglement between church and state. The test prohibits any action of government that serves either to advance or to inhibit one religion compared to another or religion in general.

Applying the framework to the facts of the *Schempp* case, the Court concluded that government-sponsored prayers and readings from holy books, even if arguably nondenominational, had both the purpose and primary effect of advancing religion in general. Even when participation was voluntary, the Court recognized that state sponsorship of religious exercises signals approval and, in the context of the public school, tends to encourage conformity to prevailing practice and belief.

The Court rejected the argument that removing organized prayer from school was an expression of hostility toward religion or that it established a "religion of secularism." Nor did prohibiting schools from formally organizing and supporting prayers infringe on the free exercise of religion of those who wished to pray. Nothing prevented students from praying voluntarily before or after school or even silently during the school day.

Since the 1960s, federal courts have relied on the analyses in *Schempp* and *Vitale* and on the *Lemon* test to decide a number of other cases concerning prayer and religious texts in schools. In 1980, in *Stone v. Graham*,[22] the Supreme Court disallowed a Kentucky statute requiring schools to display copies of the Ten Commandments purchased with private funds. The Court noted that this was not a case "in which the Ten Commandments are integrated into the school curriculum, where the Bible may constitutionally be used in an appropriate study of history, civilization, ethics, comparative religion, or the like. Posting of religious texts on the wall serves no such educational function." Similarly, in a 1993 Michigan case, a federal district court found that the posting of a two-foot by three-foot picture of Jesus at a busy intersection in the school's hallways violated the Establishment Clause.[23]

In *Karen B. v. Treen*,[24] the Fifth Circuit disallowed an opening exercise in which a student voluntarily selected and read a prayer. Likewise, in *Collins v. Chandler Unified School District*,[25] the Ninth Circuit prohibited the practice of allowing a student to lead a school assembly in prayer even if attendance at the assembly was voluntary. The Court further ruled that prohibiting the practice did not violate the free exercise rights of students who wished to pray.

In 1985, a federal district court in Michigan rejected the argument that academic freedom protects a teacher's right to pray and read the Bible in class.[26] In 1989, the Eleventh Circuit banned the practice of coaches leading their players in prayer before an athletic event,[27] and in 1992, in *Lee v. Weisman*,[28] the Supreme Court resolved a disagreement in the lower courts by ruling that opening prayers at graduation ceremonies are unconstitutional. The Court noted that such "state-sponsored and state-directed religious exercise[s]" create "subtle coercive pressures" for participation and conformity of belief. Both the Fifth and Sixth Circuits have barred local school boards from opening their public meetings with prayers. Both opinions emphasized the presence of students at the meetings.[29]

In response to *Lee v. Weisman*, some school districts have sought ways to include prayers at school-sponsored public events such as football games and graduation ceremonies without running afoul of the Establishment Clause. These efforts have sought to take advantage of the fact that students themselves enjoy First Amendment free speech protection (see chap. 3). Thus, if a prayer could be considered the private speech of a student rather than "school-sponsored" speech, it might survive an Establishment Clause challenge.

To this end, the Santa Fe Independent School District revised its former policy of having a "Student Chaplain" deliver prayers at football games. Under the new policy, the student body was empowered to vote each year, under the advice and direction of the school principal, on whether to have a student speaker at football games "deliver a brief invocation and/or message [to] solemnize the event." If a majority agreed, then a second election would be held to choose the student speaker from a list of volunteers; the chosen student could "decide what message and/or invocation to deliver consistent with the goals and purposes of this policy."

In *Santa Fe Independent School District v. Doe*,[30] the Supreme Court struck down the new policy. The Court rejected the claim that the invocations were "private speech" in the context of a governmentally created forum. Rather, said the Court, the invocations were authorized by a government policy whose purpose was to preserve the past practice of opening the games with a prayer. The process would almost inevitably result in the selection of a student who would choose an invocation consisting of a prayer. Indeed, the very word "invocation" suggests the use of a prayer. Under the circumstances, concluded the Court, "an objective Santa Fe High School student will unquestionably perceive the inevitable pregame prayer as stamped with her school's seal of approval." The fact that much of the audience at the football game was not required to attend did not alter this conclusion.

In *Cole v. Oroville Union High School District*,[31] the Ninth Circuit added another dimension to the meaning of the *Santa Fe* decision. In *Cole*, two students—one who was elected by the students to give an invocation and another who was a co-valedictorian—wanted to use their opportunity to speak at the school's graduation ceremony to deliver, respectively, a sectarian prayer and proselytizing Christian talk. The principal of the school denied both students permission to present the material they had prepared. In response to the students' claim that their free speech rights had been violated, the court ruled that the circumstances under which the two presentations were to be made was sufficiently like that of *Santa Fe*—the principal had the authority to review all speeches and invocations and had the final say regarding their content—that if they had been permitted to use their material, the school would have violated the Establishment Clause. In other words, not only was the school permitted to prohibit the students from speaking as they wished, but it also was constitutionally obligated to do so.

Shortly after *Lee v. Weisman* but before *Santa Fe*, the Fifth Circuit reconsidered a challenge to a school's policy of allowing seniors to choose student volunteers to deliver "nonsectarian, nonproselytizing" prayers at their graduation ceremony. The court approved the policy, finding that its secular purpose was to "solemnize the occasion," that there was little likelihood that its primary effect would be to advance religion, and that there was no official endorsement of religion since the decision of whether to have prayers was left to the students.[32] However, both the Third and Ninth Circuits came to the opposite conclusion in pre-*Santa Fe* cases: student-initiated prayers at graduation ceremonies violated both the purpose and primary effect tests and were therefore unconstitutional.[33]

Following *Santa Fe*, in *Adler v. Duval County School Board*,[34] the Eleventh Circuit concluded that student-initiated graduation prayers may be constitutionally permissible. The court found the policy in *Adler* distinguishable from *Santa Fe* because there was no official supervision of the selection of the speaker or the content of the speech. Also, the policy authorized only an "opening and closing message" without reference to an invocation or prayer. The *Adler* court refused to read *Santa Fe* as saying that speech is state-sponsored simply because it is authorized by government policy and takes place on government property. Only state control over the content of the message turns private speech into state speech. The Eighth Circuit used a similar line of reasoning in ruling against a parent who claimed that the Establishment Clause had been violated when another parent, who was also a school board member, delivered a prayer at graduation. No other school official had prior knowledge of what the parent/school board member planned to say.[35]

In 1999, the Fifth Circuit considered the constitutionality of a school-based counseling program called "Clergy in the Schools." Under the program, local clergy who volunteered to participate were invited to the school to meet with groups of students to discuss issues relating to "civic virtues" such as "violence, peer pressure, racial issues, . . . divorce . . . [and] drugs," but not "sex and abortion." The clergy were told not to discuss religion, quote religious materials, provide information about church services, identify their specific religious affiliation, or wear distinctive religious garb. School officials selected the students to take part in the counseling sessions, and students were told that they could decline to participate if they chose. School officials including the principal also attended the sessions. The court found that the program violated both the primary effect and entanglement prongs of the *Lemon* test and that it failed to meet the requirement that government programs be religiously neutral. Wrote the court,

By adopting a counseling program specifically designed for volunteer clergymen only, then underscoring its exalted position by taking students out of academic classes at special times during the school day to participate in this project, these public school officials unmistakably endorse religion in a constitutionally impermissible way.

Citing *Lee v. Weisman*, the court also concluded that despite the opt-out provision, students were subjected to impermissible coercive pressure to attend the sessions. The program, said the court, was not really voluntary because the student's choice was "either to participate in the Program against his wishes or decline at the risk of becoming a pariah."[36]

Moments of Silence

In response to rulings against organized prayer in public schools, some states and school districts have incorporated moments of silence into their programs. In *Wallace v. Jaffree*,[37] the Supreme Court considered the issue of whether an Alabama law authorizing public schools to incorporate "a period of silence for 'meditation or voluntary prayer' is a law respecting the establishment of religion within the meaning of the First Amendment." Based on the specific wording of this moment of silence statute and the legislative history of its adoption, the Court concluded that the law had no secular purpose. The law's sponsor had said that it was an "effort to return voluntary prayer to the schools." The specific mention of prayer in the law indicated that the state intended to characterize prayer as a favored practice. Wrote the Court, "Such an endorsement is not consistent with the established principle that Government must pursue a course of complete neutrality toward religion." Of great interest in the opinion, however, is the implication that a state statute that only authorized a moment of silence—without any reference to prayer—might be constitutional.

Other federal courts have found formally organized moments of silence unconstitutional if their purpose was to encourage prayer.[38] The Fourth Circuit, however, upheld a Virginia statute that required schools to establish a "minute of silence" so that "each pupil may, in the exercise of his or her individual choice, meditate, pray, or engage in any other silent activity which does not interfere with, distract, or impede other pupils in the like exercise of individual choice."[39] Despite the reference to prayer in the statute, the court concluded that it did not have a religious purpose because the text of the statute was religiously neutral. The law served the secular purposes of permitting nonreligious meditation and of accommodating religion, which the court said was a "secular purpose in that it fosters the liberties secured by the Constitution." The legislative history of the statute also indicated the secular purpose of providing a transitional moment to enable students to compose themselves and focus on the day ahead. Based on a similar line of reasoning, a federal district court upheld a Texas statute requiring schools to "provide for the observance of one minute of silence" during which "each student may, as the student chooses, reflect, pray, meditate, or engage in any other silent activity that is not likely to interfere with or distract another student." Although the statute was an amended version of a previous law that did not refer to prayer, the court concluded that a reasonable observer "would not find the addition of the word 'pray' to operate as an endorsement of religion or prayer in the classroom."[40]

Bible Study

The *Schempp* opinion includes the statement that the study of the Bible is permissible "when presented objectively as part of a secular program of education." This statement has tempted some schools to use Bible study as a ruse for the promotion of religion. Courts have consistently declared unconstitutional programs of Bible instruction in which the hiring and supervision of teachers and the selection of materials were controlled by a private religious group.[41] Instructors for a course that studies the Bible may not be hired on the basis of their religious belief and religious tenets cannot be advanced in the course. If religious materials are merely used as examples of a type of literature or as part of a study of secular history, world cultures, or comparative religion, then the Constitution has not been violated.[42] Thus, a federal district court in New Jersey rejected a challenge to a school's posting of calendars that recognized a variety of national, cultural, ethnic, and religious holidays.[43] In fact, the systematic deletion of all religious materials from the curriculum would raise a constitutional problem if motivated by hostility toward religion.

School officials sometimes permit or even encourage outside organizations, such as the Gideons, to distribute free Bibles to students on school grounds. In 1977, the Fifth Circuit prohibited a Bible distribution program, citing three other cases that reached the same conclusion. In reaching its decision, the court stressed that the school's distribution program was not neutral; rather, it favored the Gideon movement and religion generally.[44] In similar, more recent decisions, both the Seventh Circuit and Eighth Circuits blocked Bible distribution programs within fifth grade classrooms.[45] However, in other cases, Bible distribution has been permitted in school hallways or grounds where access has been granted to other outside organizations such as the Boy Scouts and where students are free to accept Bibles or not.[46]

Religious Holidays and Music

Is it permissible to close schools for religious holidays? Although there has not been litigation specifically addressing the ubiquitous practice of closing school on and around Christmas, it seems likely that it would be judged constitutionally permissible because, in addition to its religious significance, Christmas has become an important secular celebration in the United States and much of the world.[47] That it would be impossible to provide a safe school environment on Christmas because so many teachers would be absent provides an additional justification for closing the school. The same reasoning might apply to Easter, but the issue is moot because schools are closed on Sundays anyway.

Structuring the school calendar around other religious holidays is more problematic. The safe-environment argument might apply to any holiday that most teachers would take anyway. Also, closing school on any day that the state has declared a legal holiday is probably permissible. A federal district court in Hawaii upheld a state law that made Good Friday a legal (and school) holiday, saying that Good Friday had the same constitutional standing as Thanksgiving and Christmas.[48] However, the Seventh Circuit reached the opposite conclusion and specifically rejected the argument that Good Friday was like Thanksgiving and Christmas. Good Friday, said the court, "is a day of solemn religious observance, and nothing else, for believing Christians, and no one else."[49]

Despite, or perhaps because of, its dual status as a religious and secular holiday, Christmas creates difficult legal and political problems when it is celebrated at school. What symbols of Christmas and the Christmas season may a school display? The confusion of constitutional doctrine in this area was evident in *County of Allegheny v. ACLU, Greater Pittsburgh Chapter*[50] when a fragmented Supreme Court prohibited the display of a crèche in a courthouse, but upheld the display of a menorah and Christmas tree outside another public building. What acknowledgments of the origins and meaning of Christmas are permissible in school? When does a "holiday pageant" become too much like a religious service to be allowed?

In *Florey v. Sioux Falls School District, 49–5,*[51] the Eighth Circuit considered the constitutionality of a set of policies and rules adopted by a school district to regulate the religious content in school programs and holiday celebrations. The plaintiffs objected to rules permitting activities like the singing of Christmas carols and other "observations" of religious holidays. After examining the history of the adoption of the policy, the court accepted the district's claim that the purpose of the policy was "to advance the students' knowledge and appreciation of the role that our religious heritage has played in the social, cultural and historical development of civilization." Noting that the rules specifically prohibited any devotional activities and required that any religious content be "presented objectively as part of a secular program of education," the court further agreed with the district that the primary effect of the policy would be to accomplish the policy's stated purpose, not to advance or inhibit religion. Finally, the court found that the policy would not foster excessive entanglement between church and school.

Based on its understanding of the *Lemon* test, the Eighth Circuit found the policy evaluated in *Florey* and the activities that it permitted not to be in violation of the Establishment Clause. Most courts would probably agree that the Constitution does not require the removal from the school program of all activities that have any association with the celebration of religious holidays. However, schools and individual teachers are prohibited from sponsoring programs or activities that have a purpose or primary effect of promoting (or discouraging) religious belief.

The study and performance of religious music raises particularly tricky issues. Much of the music regularly used in many public schools was originally written to promote religion and continues to play a part in religious observances. However, some of the same music is part of the secular U.S. culture. Certainly, as the *Florey* opinion suggests, a school's music program should not have the appearance of a religious ceremony, even a nondenominational one. However, schools need not avoid all songs that mention religious holidays or symbols or even music with liturgical origins.

In 1997, the Tenth Circuit rejected a challenge to a Salt Lake City high school's performance of "many" pieces of religious music and to its presentation of concerts in churches and other religious venues.[52] In another case, the Fifth Circuit approved the use of a piece entitled, "The Lord Bless You and Keep You," as the theme song of a high school choir.[53] These cases indicate that the use of religious music is generally permissible as long as it is part of a secular program of music instruction and performance.

2.3 RELIGIOUS AND MORAL OBJECTIONS TO COURSE CONTENT AND MATERIALS

The last section considered objections to the inclusion of prayer and other religious practices in school programs and activities. This section addresses the issues raised by the teaching of courses, theories, or topics and the use of materials claimed to promote or denigrate religious beliefs or practices. Plaintiffs may argue that a school has violated the Establishment Clause by shaping the curriculum in accordance with religious doctrine, for example, by prohibiting the teaching of evolution or requiring creation science, or by selecting materials alleged to promote "secular humanism." Other plaintiffs rely on the Free Exercise Clause or the right of parents to direct the upbringing of their children to seek exemption from unwanted topics and materials.

Evolution and Creationism

In *Epperson v. Arkansas,*[54] the Supreme Court considered the constitutionality of an Arkansas law that made it illegal for a public school teacher "to teach the theory or doctrine that mankind ascended or descended from a lower order of animals," that is, the theory of evolution. The case was brought by a biology teacher who was placed in an untenable position when her school district adopted a biology textbook containing a chapter on evolution. Thus, she was both required to and prohibited from teaching the theory. Although affirming the general right of the state "to prescribe the curriculum for its public schools," the Court pointed out that the state's power over curriculum is limited by the mandates of the Establishment Clause. To determine whether the First Amendment had been violated, the Court considered the origin and purpose of the law:

> In the present case, there can be no doubt that Arkansas has sought to prevent its teachers from discussing the theory of evolution because it is contrary to the belief of some that the Book of Genesis must be the exclusive source of doctrine as to the origin of man. No suggestion has been made that Arkansas' law may be justified by considerations of state policy other than the religious views of some of its citizens. It is clear that fundamentalist sectarian conviction was and is the law's reason for existence. . . .

> Arkansas' law cannot be defended as an act of religious neutrality. Arkansas did not seek to excise from the curricula of its schools and universities all discussion of the origin of man. The law's effort was confined to an attempt to blot out a particular theory because of its supposed conflict with the Biblical account, literally read.

Having found no secular purpose to support the antievolution law, the Court resolved the teacher's dilemma by finding the law unconstitutional.

Epperson has been the basis of several lower court opinions blocking school boards from accommodating the religious preferences of parents by removing materials, topics, or courses from the curriculum.[55] However, at least one circuit court decision affirms the legitimacy of permitting all people, even those with religious motivations, to have the opportunity to influence educational policy. The case involved a challenge to a school board rule, adopted against a background of local church opposition to social dancing, that barred the use of school facilities for dancing. Plaintiffs claimed that the no-dancing rule was religiously motivated, but the court concluded that there was insufficient proof that the rule had been adopted for religious reasons:

> The mere fact a governmental body takes action that coincides with the principles or desires of a particular religious group, however, does not transform the action into an impermissible establishment of religion. . . . We simply do not believe elected governmental officials are required to check at the door whatever religious background (or lack of it) they carry with them before they act on rules that are otherwise unobjectionable under the controlling *Lemon* standards. In addition to its unrealistic nature, this approach to constitutional analysis would have the effect of disenfranchising religious groups when they succeed in influencing secular decisions.[56]

Because *Epperson* effectively prevented legislatures from barring the teaching of evolution, several fundamentalist groups have attempted to use judicial means to eliminate its instruction. In *Wright v. Houston Independent School District*,[57] the plaintiffs claimed that the uncritical teaching of evolution, ignoring the biblical account of creation, established the religion of secularism. The district court disagreed, saying it was "not the business of the government to suppress real or imagined attacks upon a particular religious doctrine. Teachers of science in the public schools should not be expected to avoid the discussion of every scientific issue on which some religion claims expertise."[58]

The unsuccessful effort to obtain legislative or judicial elimination of evolution from the public school curriculum has prompted a different strategy; namely, to get the state legislature to require the teaching of scientific creationism as an alternative theory. These "balanced treatment" laws have required, for example, that if evolution is taught, then scientific creationism also must be taught. However, the courts have nullified balanced treatment laws because, as the Supreme Court explained in *Edwards v. Aguillard*,[59] their purpose was "to advance the religious viewpoint that a supernatural being created humankind" and thus, to promote religion. The Court summarized its conclusion as follows:

> [T]he Purpose of the Creationism Act was to restructure the science curriculum to conform with a particular religious viewpoint. Out of many possible science subjects taught in the public schools, the legislature chose to affect the teaching of the one scientific theory that historically has been opposed by certain religious sects.

Disappointed with the outcome of *Edwards*, a school board in Louisiana adopted a policy that required its teachers to read the following "disclaimer" every time evolution was mentioned in one of its classrooms:

> It is hereby recognized by the Tangipahoa Board of Education that the lesson to be presented, regarding the origin of life and matter, is known as the Scientific Theory of Evolution and should be presented to inform students of the scientific concept and is not intended to influence or dissuade the Biblical version of Creation or any other concept.

In *Freiler v. Tangipahoa Parish Board of Education*,[60] the Fifth Circuit found that the disclaimer policy violated the Establishment Clause. The policy had the purpose and effect, not as the board claimed of promoting critical thinking, but of protecting and maintaining religious belief.

After *Freiler* a Georgia school district with the stated purpose of promoting critical thinking required that its science textbooks bear the following sticker:

> This textbook contains material on evolution. Evolution is a theory, not a fact, regarding the origin of living things. This material should be approached with an open mind, studied carefully, and critically considered.

Although it acknowledged that unlike the *Freiler* disclaimer, the sticker did not refer to any religious theory, a federal district court nevertheless ruled the requirement unconstitutional on the grounds it had the effect of endorsing religion. The court found that the sticker endorsed the view of Christian fundamentalists that evolution was a "problematic theory," mislead students as to the status of evolution in the scientific community by using the term "theory" in the colloquial (not the scientific) understanding of the term to mean "questionable opinion or hunch," and targeted only evolution as a topic to be approached with an open mind. Thus, the court concluded "that an informed, reasonable observer would interpret the Sticker to convey a message of endorsement of religion. That is, the Sticker sends a message to those who oppose evolution for religious reasons that they are favored members of the political community, while the Sticker sends a message to those who believe in evolution that they are political outsiders."[61]

In 2005, a federal district court in Pennsylvania undertook a particularly thorough consideration of the legal issues raised by a school district's policy regarding the teaching of evolution. The case, *Kitzmiller v. Dover Area School District*,[62] garnered a great deal of national attention. Like *Freiler*, it involved a statement adopted by a school board to be read by teachers in conjunction with the study of evolution. The statement informed students that "Darwin's Theory of Evolution" was being taught because it was included in the state-mandated academic standards and on the state assessments, that the theory was "not a fact" and contained "gaps . . . for which there is no evidence," and that "Intelligent Design" was an alternative theory that students might want to explore on their own and discuss with their families. After a trial that lasted about a month, the court concluded that the board's policy constituted an endorsement of religion and thus violated the Establishment Clause. The court found that despite being packaged somewhat differently, intelligent design was another name for creationism, that the re-naming was in part a strategic response to court rulings excluding creationism from the curriculum, and that intelligent design insofar as it relies on "forces acting outside the natural world, forces we cannot see, replicate, control or test" was not a science but a theological argument. The court noted that evolution was the only scientific theory that the board had chosen to challenge, that the only alternative offered was inherently religious, and that statements by board members indicated that their purpose had been to promote religion in the classroom.

Secular Humanism, Atheism, and Freedom of Religion

Some plaintiffs have argued that a public school's program violates the Establishment Clause by promoting the religion of secular humanism. In *Smith v. Board of School Commissioners of Mobile County*,[63] a group of parents challenged the constitutionality of using home economics textbooks that they claimed implied that moral decisions could be made without reference to God and history books said to "uniformly ignore the religious aspect of most American culture." The plaintiffs argued that the primary effect of these books was to promote secular and atheistic beliefs. They demanded that the school provide their children with alternative materials consistent with their religious beliefs.

In rejecting the plaintiffs' claims and demands, the court pointed out that nearly everything taught at school inevitably will be either consistent or inconsistent with some religious belief. For example, the teaching that murder is wrong is consistent with the belief of many religions. However, the Establishment Clause does not require schools to avoid teaching about or even taking a position on issues about which some religion may have also taken a stand. It is only required that schools remain separate and neutral relative to religion.

Closely related to the issue raised in *Smith* is the question of whether it is permissible for schools to display images and symbols of fictional or hypothetical supernatural beings or to read materials concerning magic, fantasy, and the supernatural. Courts have uniformly rejected claims by parents that such activities as posting Halloween symbols at school, using a "Blue Devil" as a school mascot, and reading stories about witches and sorcerers were violations of the Establishment Clause.[64] Despite these rulings, some school boards and schools have adopted policies banning all mention of the supernatural in the classroom. Such a ban may be legally impermissible if its purpose is to make the curriculum consistent with religious beliefs.

The question becomes more complex if students are asked not merely to read, but to participate in ceremonies or rituals. One federal district court concluded the Establishment Clause was violated when as part of an "Earth Day Ritual" students were asked to construct a structure that the court said was equivalent to an altar and to participate in a ceremony at which the teacher said, "We came from the earth, we are part of the earth, we are all involved in this cycle. One day we will become dead; then we'll go back to the earth." The district court found that the ceremony promoted the religion of Gaia. However, the Second Circuit reversed the ruling, concluding that the Earth Day ceremonies were only intended to promote conservation and respect for the earth. State law, the court noted, required schools to engage pupils in exercises that encouraged interest in, knowledge of, and protection of the planet. The ceremony did not promote the belief that the earth possessed supernatural powers or should be worshiped, and the "altar" was a tepee. Relying on Supreme Court precedent, the court noted that the Establishment Clause is not violated merely because a statement either is in agreement with or is in disagreement with a given religious tenet.[65]

Not all religious objections to school programs are based on the Establishment Clause. In *Mozert v. Hawkins County Board of Education*,[66] the Sixth Circuit considered a claim by students and parents that being forced to participate in programs designed to promote critical thinking, tolerance, and moral development and to read material that exposed them to ideas and values that contradicted their religious beliefs violated their right to free exercise of religion. Plaintiffs argued that the school had an obligation to provide their children with an alternative program consistent with their religious beliefs, but the court found that the plaintiffs had not shown that the school's programs and materials placed a burden on their religious practices or beliefs. Exposure to contrary views, explained the court, is not the same as compulsion to believe. As *Mozert* implies, courts are unlikely to grant religion-based exemptions to school programs designed to teach tolerance or other secular community values.

Sex Education

Sex education has been a frequent target of parental objection. In *Cornwell v. State Board of Education*,[67] parents argued that a program of "family life and sex education" violated the Establishment Clause. The court disagreed: ". . . [T]he purpose and primary effect here is not to establish any particular religious dogma or precept, and the [program] does not directly or substantially involve the state in religious exercises or in the favoring of religion or any particular religion." Whereas the *Cornwell* plaintiffs sought complete elimination of sex education from the school program, other parents have tried to exempt only their own children. (Recall that some states give parents a statutory right to exempt their children from sex education [see sec. 2.1].) In *Valent v. New Jersey State Board of Education*,[68] the court rejected the argument that required instruction in sex education violated plaintiffs' free exercise rights. Even condom distribution programs have survived claims that they violated parents' free exercise rights; however, parents have sometimes prevailed when they argued that condom distribution programs violated their right to direct the upbringing of their child or to be informed of the medical care offered to their child.[69]

A 1995 case involved an "AIDS awareness program" that included frank and graphic discussions of various sexual and other bodily functions and an emphasis on "safe sex" rather than abstinence. Parents objected both on free exercise grounds and on the grounds that exposing their children to the program without their permission violated their Fourteenth Amendment right to control their children's upbringing, but the court disagreed: "If all parents had a fundamental constitutional right to dictate individually what the schools teach their children, the schools would be forced to create a curriculum for each student whose parents had genuine moral disagreements with the school's choice of subject matter."[70] In another case the parent failed to convince the court of a parental right to have their child exempted from a curriculum that encouraged students to "to under-stand and respect gays, lesbians, and the families they sometimes form in Massachusetts, which recognizes same-sex marriage."[71] In *Fields v. Palmdale School District*[72] the court rejected a claim by parents that the distribution to elementary school students of a questionnaire containing questions about sex violated parents' substantive due process and privacy rights.

* * *

Is there any way to calculate the net effect of the cases discussed in this section? Do these opinions require that secular humanism be taught in the public schools? Do they eliminate all traces of the United States' religious heritage from the public schools? The answer to the latter two questions is no. On the one hand, schools may not tailor their programs in accordance with religious beliefs, offer religious instruction or theistic moral training, or endorse the Bible as the only true source of knowledge. On the other hand, schools may not systematically purge the curriculum of all mention of religion or ideas that are consistent with religious belief, endorse atheism, or declare that science is the only real source of knowledge or that the Bible is not true. Thus, the Constitution excludes from the classroom both proreligion bias and the antireligion sentiments of some secular humanists.

Schools are free to teach the importance of critical thinking, reasoning, and the need for personal inquiry and choice. They may teach tolerance, open-mindedness, and receptivity to different cultures and values. (Although some may see these views as secular, notice that they are consistent with the teachings of many religions.) Schools are also free to teach much of the agenda of many traditional religious groups, such as patriotism, family values, and the duty to obey the law. Concerning sex education, the Constitution permits a range of choices: states may require schools to instruct their pupils in contraception and the prevention of AIDS, offer a program that discourages all extramarital sex, or teach that individuals must make their own choices in matters of sex. In the absence of state guidelines, local schools are free to adopt any of these options or to exclude sex education from their program.

Inevitably, some of what is taught in public schools will violate the personal and moral convictions of some parents. Parts of the public school curriculum will be consistent with the beliefs of some religions and parts will contradict religious doctrine. Parents have no constitutional right to insist that their children be exempt from participation in educational programs that are inconsistent with their personal or religious convictions; however, no curriculum may be selected because it agrees with or opposes any religious or antireligious belief.

2.4 FREE SPEECH AND RELATED OBJECTIONS TO PROGRAMS AND POLICIES

Although the religion clauses have been the primary basis for constitutional challenges to school programs, the First Amendment's guarantee of freedom of speech also has been the basis of several significant attacks. In these cases, the Free Speech Clause is used in an atypical way. Rather than assert a right to express their own ideas, plaintiffs claim either a right not to be forced to express a particular idea (i.e., a right not to speak) or a right to be exposed to the ideas of others (i.e., a right to hear or to know). (See chap. 3 for a general discussion of the rights of students to express themselves and chap. 7 regarding the free speech rights of teachers.)

The Right Not To Speak

The first Supreme Court case to apply the constitutional guarantee of freedom of speech to students at school was *West Virginia State Board of Education v. Barnette*,[73] in which the Court prohibited the state from compelling the students in its schools to recite the Pledge of Allegiance. In doing so, the Court specifically reversed a ruling it had made only three years earlier.[74]

Although *Barnette* was brought by a group of Jehovah's Witnesses who objected to the Pledge of Allegiance requirement on religious grounds, the Court based its ruling on free speech. The Court noted that the state has every right to adopt a curriculum designed to "inspire patriotism and love of country" by such traditional educational methods as teaching about the constitutional guarantees of civil liberties. The Court wrote:

> Here, however, we are dealing with a compulsion of students to declare a belief. . . . To sustain the compulsory flag salute, we are required to say that a Bill of Rights, which guards the individual's right to speak his own mind, left it open to public authorities to compel him to utter what is not in his mind.

Moreover, the Court noted that, "the power of compulsion is invoked without any allegation that remaining passive during a flag ritual creates a clear and present danger. . . ." Thus, concluded the Court, although the state's purpose in requiring a flag salute was valid, its methods overstepped constitutional bounds:

> If there is any fixed star in our constitutional constellation, it is that no official, high or petty, can prescribe what shall be orthodox in politics, nationalism, religion, or other matters of opinion or force citizens to confess by word or act their faith therein. If there are any circumstances which permit an exception, they do not now occur to us.

This principle of freedom of thought and expression is so important, said the Court, that it has been given a special status outside of the democratic decision process:

> The very purpose of a Bill of Rights was to withdraw certain subjects from the vicissitudes of political controversy, to place them beyond the reach of majorities and officials and to establish them as legal principles to be applied by the courts. One's right to life, liberty, and property, to free speech, a free press, freedom of worship and assembly, and other fundamental rights may not be submitted to vote; they depend on the outcome of no elections. . . .

Finally, the Court rejected the idea that because they are dealing with minor students, schools and educators should be exempt from the restrictions of the Bill of Rights: "That they are educating the young for citizenship is reason for scrupulous protection of Constitutional freedoms of the individual, if we are not to strangle the free mind at its source and teach youth to discount important principles of our government as mere platitudes."

Since *Barnette*, schools have been prohibited from insisting that students participate in flag salutes or other patriotic ceremonies. Students may not be forced to stand during the ceremony or to leave the room if they choose not to participate.[75] In 2003 the Third Circuit affirmed a lower court ruling that a statute requiring schools to notify parents if their child refused to participate in the flag salute violated the child's right of free speech.[76]

Whether it is permissible to include a flag salute in a school's daily program, as many schools do and some states require, has long been controversial. Several courts have upheld school-sponsored recitation of the Pledge against the claim that its reference to God (which was not in the Pledge when *Barnette* was decided) violates the Establishment Clause.[77] In 2002 the Ninth Circuit concluded that the use of the Pledge in public schools does violate the Establishment Clause. The court found that the phrase "under God" had both the purpose and primary effect of promoting religion and that, in a school setting, there was inevitable coercion to participate in the flag-salute ceremony. The court noted that President Eisenhower when signing the bill amending the Pledge to include the phrase "under God" said, "From this day forward the millions of children will daily proclaim in every city and town, every village and rural schoolhouse, the dedication of our Nation and our people to the Almighty."[78]

In 2004 the Supreme Court reversed the Ninth Circuit's decision on the technical grounds that the parent who brought the suit did not have standing because he was not the custodial parent.[79] Other suits challenging the Pledge on the same grounds have since been brought. In 2005 the Fourth Circuit Court ruled that a state statute requiring daily, voluntary recitation of the Pledge was constitutional. The court found that inclusion in the Pledge of the words "under God" did not alter its nature as a patriotic activity: "Even assuming that the recitation of the Pledge contains a risk of indirect coercion, the indirect coercion is not threatening to establish religion, but patriotism."[80]

Barnette has often been cited by the Supreme Court when prohibiting government practices that have the effect of forcing people to espouse a political belief, support a candidate, or display a political slogan against their will.[81] However, except for the prohibition against compelled recitation of the Pledge, the right not to speak has had little effect on the program of schools.

In a 1993 case, the Third Circuit rejected a claim based on *Barnette* that a school's program of compulsory community service required students to embrace and express a belief in the value of altruism. The court concluded that

> There is no basis in the record to support the argument that the students who participate in the program are obliged to express their belief, either orally or in writing, in the value of community service. Nor was evidence produced that people in the community would perceive their participation in the program as an intended expression of a particularized message of their belief in community service and altruism.[82]

Community service requirements have also prevailed against the argument that they violate parents' rights to control the upbringing of their children and against the novel argument that they violate the Thirteenth Amendment's prohibition of involuntary servitude.[83]

Arguably, *Barnette* might prohibit teachers from insisting that students give "ideologically correct" answers on an examination. Students might object to payment of a fee used to support a newspaper or speakers whose politics they oppose. Although neither of these issues has been litigated in the context of public schools, similar cases involving public colleges suggest that the latter argument might succeed.[84]

Despite *Barnette*, schools remain free to promote patriotic beliefs and community values. Nothing in the Constitution prohibits schools from urging students to support the country or its policies, but students must not be required or coerced to say that they will do so.

The Right To Hear

Courts have taken a variety of positions on whether and to what extent the Constitution places limits on the school board's authority to reject or eliminate books and other materials from the curriculum or school library. A California court avoided reaching a constitutional decision by ruling that the local school board did not have statutorily delegated authority to remove books it judged socially unacceptable. The board was, however, found to have authority to remove books judged obscene for minors.[85] In *President's Council v. Community School Board, No. 25*,[86] the Second Circuit found that removal from the school library of a book judged "offensive" by the school board raised no substantial constitutional issue. The court reasoned that removal of books was an academic decision and that, although it was sure to be controversial at times, the judiciary should avoid "intrusion into the internal affairs of school." However, in *Minarcini v. Strongsville City School District*,[87] the Sixth Circuit found that the students' First Amendment "right to know" prohibited removal of books based on the "social and political tastes of school board members."

In *Zykan v. Warsaw Community School Corp.*,[88] the Seventh Circuit developed a set of guidelines for determining whether a school board's removal of curricular materials overstepped constitutional bounds. The court found that although school boards generally enjoy wide latitude to determine what material may be used in their schools, they may not "substitute a rigid and exclusive indoctrination for the mere existence of their prerogative to make pedagogic choices regarding matters of legitimate dispute," impose "religious or scientific orthodoxy or . . . a desire to eliminate a particular kind of inquiry generally," or "exclude a particular type of thought, or even . . . some identifiable ideological preference."

In 1981, the Supreme Court addressed the issue of a school board's censorship of library books in *Board of Education v. Pico*.[89] The case was brought by a group of students who claimed that their free speech rights were violated when the school board, at the urging of a politically conservative lobbying organization, ordered nine books removed from the school library. Although a committee convened by the board to consider the matter had recommended retaining most of the books, the school board justified its actions by declaring that the books were "anti-American, anti-Christian, anti-Sem[i]tic, and just plain filthy."

Pico produced no majority opinion. Although five of the nine justices agreed that the Constitution placed some limits on a school board's authority to remove books from its schools' libraries, they could not agree on an appropriate test for determining those limitations. The plurality opinion sought to balance the authority of the school board to attempt to prepare students for adult citizenship by inculcating them with democratic values with the students' right to receive ideas. The right to receive ideas, said the opinion, "follows ineluctably from the *sender's* First Amendment right to send them." The plurality emphasized that unlike participation in the classroom curriculum, use of the library was completely voluntary and offered the students an opportunity for self-education and individual enrichment. Whereas the plurality felt that the library's unique role required tolerating a broader spectrum of opinion than was necessary in other aspects of the curriculum, the dissenting justices believed that the school board should be free to remove books that conflicted with their social, political, or moral views from any aspect of the school's program, including the library.

The Court's plurality opinion (recall that plurality opinions do not create precedent as majority opinions of the Supreme Court do) advocated a motivational test:

> [School authorities] rightly possess significant discretion to determine the content of their school libraries. But . . . [o]ur Constitution does not permit the official

suppression of *ideas*. Thus whether petitioners' removal of books from their school libraries denied respondents their First Amendment rights depends upon the motivation behind petitioners' actions. If petitioners *intended* by their removal decision to deny respondents access to ideas with which petitioners disagreed, and if this intent was the decisive factor in petitioners' decision, then petitioners have exercised their discretion in violation of the Constitution. . . . On the other hand, . . . an unconstitutional motivation would not be demonstrated if . . . petitioners . . . decided to remove the books at issue because those books were pervasively vulgar [or] based solely upon the "educational suitability" of the books . . .

In addition to its failure to establish precedent, the usefulness of *Pico* is limited by the plurality's insistence that its reasoning applied only to the removal of books from the school library and not to the purchase of books or removal of classroom materials. Furthermore, recent decisions on related matters suggest that today's Supreme Court has moved closer to the position of the *Pico* dissenters: school boards enjoy broader discretion in controlling all aspects of the curriculum than the *Pico* plurality would have allowed (see discussion of *Hazelwood School District v. Kuhlmeier* in sec. 3.3).

This approach is reflected in *Virgil v. School Board of Columbia County*.[90] In *Virgil*, the Eighth Circuit upheld the decision of a school board to remove from the curriculum an anthology that had been used as the textbook in a high school humanities course. The board had taken its action against the advice of the district's textbook review committee because of concerns over "sexually explicit content" and "excessive vulgarity" in selections such as *Lysistrata* and *The Miller's Tale*. Although the court questioned the wisdom of the school board's action, it concluded that the school board had acted within its authority because the removal was "reasonably related to legitimate pedagogical concerns." Whether the *Virgil* court would have ruled the same way if the school board had removed the books because it disagreed with their political and social viewpoints (e.g., the antiwar message of *Lysistrata*) is not clear.

School boards undoubtedly have broad leeway to control all aspects of their curricula as long as they act on the basis of legitimate pedagological concerns. In particular, all courts seem to agree with *Virgil* that books judged obscene, vulgar, or sexually offensive may be removed from the classroom or library. Likewise, the prohibition of school theatrical productions considered vulgar or age-inappropriate has generally been allowed.[91] However, no court has yet rejected the *Pico* plurality's view that "If a Democratic school board, motivated by party affiliation, ordered the removal of all books written by or in favor of Republicans, few would doubt that the order violated the constitutional rights of the students denied access to these books." In fact, even the main dissenting opinion in *Pico*, written by Justice Rehnquist, affirmed this dictum.

In 2006 the Dade County school board ordered removal from a school library of a travel book about Cuba following a complaint from a parent that the book did not accurately portray life under the Castro regime. The board removed the book even after several committees had recommended retention of the book based on fifteen criteria that the board itself had established for deciding such cases. The board's order extended to all books in the same series as the offending book even though none of the other books in the series had received any complaints or gone through the review process. Applying the approach of the plurality opinion in *Pico* the court barred removal of the books. Despite the school board's claim that the books contained "inaccuracies," the court found that the books were content neutral and were not written to "discuss issues of government with respect to any of the countries [covered by the series] . . . The emphasis was on things people share in common, not what divides and drives them apart." Thus the school board members' concern with "inaccuracies" was but a "guise and pretext for 'political ortho-doxy,'" namely, the view of the board regarding the "true evil of Castro's government and the oppression of the Cuban people."[92]

A few courts have imposed procedural due process requirements on school boards desiring to censor books. One court said the board could remove books from the library only by following preestablished, non-vague guidelines.[93] Another court ruled that the Due Process Clause of the Fourteenth Amendment was violated when the board failed to follow its own procedures for the removal of books.[94] However, not all courts concur in these judgments.[95] Whether constitutionally required or not, the establishment of and adherence to a definite set of procedures for dealing with requests to censor books seems a sound policy.

The desire of educators and legislators to make the Internet available to students at school but to limit their access to certain types of materials has created new legal issues. The Children's Internet Protection Act (CIPA)[96] permits schools to receive federal finan-cial assistance in obtaining Internet access if the school agrees to use filtering software that blocks all access to legally obscene material and child pornography and to bar children from access to material that is "harmful to minors." In *United States v. American Library Association*,[97] the Supreme Court ruled that placing these conditions on the availability of federal funds is not a violation of free speech. The decision further suggests that schools and public libraries have the right to place the same kind of restrictions on their collection of printed materials. Despite this case, schools are not permitted to enforce limitations on access to Internet sites (or printed materials), except those sanctioned by CIPA, because of official disagreement with ideas expressed on the sites. Control of access to web sites must be based on legitimate pedagogical concerns.

2.5 OBJECTIONS TO DISCRIMINATORY MATERIAL

Only a few courts have dealt with claims that methods of curriculum development, mate-rials selection, or a curriculum itself violates the Equal Protection Clause by being racially or sexually biased. In *Loewen v. Turnipseed*,[98] plaintiffs challenged the book selection policy of a statewide textbook commission. Although it had authority to approve up to five books, the commission selected only one, *Your Mississippi*, for use in a required state history course. The authors and publishers of a competing book, *Mississippi: Conflict and Change*, together with parents, students, and local officials, charged that the approved book deprecated Blacks and championed White supremacy and that that the commission had acted for racial reasons. The district court agreed that the rating process had been racially motivated. The vote was split along racial lines, with the commission's five White members refusing to rate *Conflict and Change* despite its having received favorable reviews and the two Black members supporting its adoption. Comments of the White members also indicated that they opposed *Conflict and Change* for racial reasons. The court ordered that both books be listed as approved and eligible for adoption by local school districts.

The *Loewen* court avoided confronting the most difficult issues that could arise in this kind of case: whether a particular book or course is itself racially, sexually, or ethically biased and, if so, whether public schools are prohibited by the Constitution from offering a curriculum biased against a racial or gender group. It is far from clear what standards would govern these issues. Take, for example, Mark Twain's classic novel, *Huckleberry Finn* with its repeated use of the term "nigger." Is it a candidate for judicial censure on the ground that the use of such a term in public schools carries a message of racial inferiority in violation of the Equal Protection Clause? Consider another example: the portrayal of

Shylock in William Shakespeare's *The Merchant of Venice*. The use of this play and Charles Dickens' novel *Oliver Twist* was in fact the subject of a legal challenge on the ground that these books projected an invidious image of Jews.[99] In a nonconstitutional decision, the court ruled that the play and book could be used because there was no evidence that the authors' intentions were antisemitic. Would the court have banned the works if antisemitic intentions had been discovered?

What of books and plays that have only male heroes—are they discriminatory toward women? Or what of history books that contain few references to Native Americans? What of Black literature critical of Whites and feminist writings critical of males—are these to be banned on the ground that they discriminate against one group or another? It is doubtful that courts will address these concerns except perhaps in the most blatant cases. One court has ruled that a school's use of materials expressing a racially biased point of view does not violate either the Equal Protection Clause of the Constitution or Title VI of the Civil Rights Act of 1964 (see sec. 5.8) unless done with an intent to discriminate.[100]

In the absence of judicial guidelines, the responsibility for the provision of an unbiased and sound curriculum rests with state and local education decision makers. For example, because in all likelihood courts will neither prohibit the use of *Huckleberry Finn* nor block its removal from the school, education officials are faced with the choice of requiring students to read the book, making it available to those who want it without requiring it, or not even having it available. Although neither the law nor education theory mandates a particular course of action, this and all other curricular decisions should be made after reflective deliberations on the literary, social, and historical significance of the books, materials, and topics under consideration and not in panicked response to the demands of small groups of parents, students, or patrons.

2.6 FEDERAL STATUTORY RESTRICTIONS ON SCHOOL PROGRAMS

A variety of federal statutes control aspects of the programs that schools offer and the way they treat their students. These laws generally operate either by offering federal funding to schools that follow requirements specified in the law or threatening the loss of federal funding to schools that fail to comply with the law. Several federal laws are designed to assure equity in schools' treatment of racial and ethnic minorities and gender groups. These laws are examined in Chapter 5. Other federal laws regulate the education that states and school districts must provide to children with disabilities and those with limited English proficiency. These laws are examined in detail in Chapter 6. Another federal law, the Equal Access Act, is designed to promote school recognition of student rights of free association and speech. It is discussed in Section 3.6. Still another federal law, the Family Education Rights and Privacy Act, regulates the way schools keep and disseminate student records. It is considered in Section 10.3.

Three additional federal statutes bear directly on the school's authority to control its own program and materials: the No Child Left Behind Act, the Copyright Act, and the Hatch Amendment. By far the most influential of these laws in terms of its effects on school programs is the No Child Left Behind Act. These three laws are discussed in this section.

The No Child Left Behind Act and the Curriculum

The federal statute known as the No Child Left Behind Act (NCLB)[101] is the 2001 revision of the Elementary and Secondary Education Act (ESEA) first passed in 1965. NCLB is a complex statute that combines a grant program (the former Title I program) directed toward schools with high concentrations of students in poverty; a new assessment, accountability, and reform system; and a number of other provisions that affect many aspects of school operations. The grant program and accountability component together are designed to promote improvement in high-poverty schools and to ensure all students access to "scientifically-based instructional strategies" and challenging academic content. The ultimate goal is to bring all students to a state-specified level of proficiency by 2014. This section reviews the aspects of NCLB that affect the general school curriculum. Other aspects of NCLB are addressed throughout the book (see index).

The assessment, accountability, and school-improvement system that is a requirement for the receipt of grant money under NCLB represents a far-reaching expansion of federal control over public education. The assessment and accountability systems include requirements that states and school districts:

- Administer tests "aligned" with the state-adopted "standards" annually to all students in grades 3–8 and at least once during high school to assess student "proficiency" in mathematics, and reading or language arts. Science must also be tested, at least once during grades 3–5, once during grades 6–9, and once during grades 10–12. The assessment of any student who has attended school in the United States for three or more consecutive years must be in English. (On a case-by-case basis individual students may be exempted from this requirement.) The English proficiency of students of limited English speaking ability must also be assessed annually.
- Adopt Annual Measurable Objectives (AMOs)—the percentage of student who must be assessed as "proficient" on the state tests each year in order for a school or district to be making "adequate yearly progress" (AYP). AMOs are required for the student body of each school and school district as a whole and there must be separate AMOs for disadvantaged students, students from specified racial and ethnic groups, students with disabilities, and students with limited English proficiency. AYP requires that the percentage of students rated as proficient each year increases incrementally in order to meet the goal of 100 percent proficient by 2014. There are some exceptions to this requirement (so-called "safeharbor" provisions), and some states that have been allowed to adopt somewhat different AYP requirements based on a so-called "growth model." The growth model allows a school to receive credit for students who are making progress toward eventual proficiency even if they are not yet proficient.
- Issue various reports detailing the assessment results, including: a report on each student for parents and teachers; assessment results disaggregated by gender, major racial and ethnic groups, English proficiency, migrant status, disability, and status as economically disadvantaged; and school, school district, and state report cards.
- Continue to participate in the biennial National Assessment of Education Progress of reading and math for students in the 4th and 8th grades.

A school that fails to meet AYP for two consecutive years must be identified as needing improvement. The district and state must provide technical assistance to the school, and its pupils must be allowed to participate in a public school choice plan by the next school year. Schools that fail to meet AYP for three consecutive years must offer low-income families the opportunity to receive instruction from a "supplemental services provider" of their choice. Schools that fail to meet AYP for four consecutive years must take one or more of a specified series of corrective actions, including replacing school staff, implementing a new curriculum, decreasing management authority at the school level, appointing an outside expert to advise the school, extending the school day or year, and changing the school's internal organizational structure. Schools that fail to meet AYP for five consecutive years must be "restructured." Restructuring may include reopening the school as a charter school, replacing all or most of the school's staff, or state takeover of school operations. Analogous requirements apply to districts that fail to meet AYP including, after four years, the possibility that students will be allowed to transfer to a higher-performing district.

The school-improvement provisions of NCLB include requirements that all teachers of core academic subjects be "highly qualified" as defined by state standards and that poor and minority children are not disproportionately taught by unqualified, inexperienced, or out-of-field teachers. Professional development programs must be provided to increase the number of highly qualified teachers. Districts must see to it that all paraprofessionals complete two years of study at an institution of higher education. Parents have a legal right to receive information concerning the qualifications of their children's teachers if they request it.

Section 7906 of NCLB[102] provides that none of the funds authorized under the law shall be used:

(1) to develop or distribute materials, or operate programs or courses of instruction directed at youth, that are designed to promote or encourage sexual activity, whether homosexual or heterosexual;

(2) to distribute or to aid in the distribution by any organization of legally obscene materials to minors on school grounds;

(3) to provide sex education or HIV-prevention education in schools unless that instruction is age-appropriate and includes the health benefits of abstinence; or

(4) to operate a program of contraceptive distribution in schools.

Section 7904 of NCLB[103] specifies that districts must "certify in writing to the State educational agency involved that no policy of the local educational agency prevents, or otherwise denies participation in, constitutionally protected prayer in public elementary schools and secondary schools," as detailed in the "Guidance" written by the Secretary of Education. Failure to comply with the Guidance can mean the loss of federal funds. The Guidance referred to in the law is a statement issued in February 2003 by the Secretary of Education that provides the Department of Education's interpretation of Supreme Court opinions reviewed in this chapter.[104]

It provides that:

- Students may pray when not engaged in school activities or instruction, subject to the same rules designed to prevent material disruption of the educational program that are applied to other privately initiated expressive activities. Among other things, students may read their Bibles or other scriptures, say grace before meals, and pray or study religious materials with fellow students during recess, the lunch hour, or other non-instructional time to the same extent that they may engage in nonreligious activities.

- Students may organize prayer groups and religious clubs and these groups must be given the same access to school facilities as other groups.

- When acting in their official capacities as representatives of the state, teachers, school administrators, and other school employees are prohibited by the Establishment Clause from encouraging or discouraging prayer, and from actively participating in such activity with students. Teachers may, however, take part in religious activities where the overall context makes clear that they are not participating in their official capacities.

- If a school has a "minute of silence" or other quiet periods during the school day, students are free to pray silently, or not to pray, during these periods of time. Teachers and other school employees may neither encourage nor discourage students from praying during such time periods.
- It has long been established that schools have the discretion to dismiss students to off-premises religious instruction, provided that schools do not encourage or discourage participation in such instruction or penalize students for attending or not attending. Similarly, schools may excuse students from class to remove a significant burden on their religious exercise, where doing so would not impose material burdens on other students. For example, it would be lawful for schools to excuse Muslim students briefly from class to enable them to fulfill their religious obligations to pray during Ramadan.
- Students may express their beliefs about religion in homework, artwork, and other written and oral assignments free from discrimination based on the religious content of their submissions. Such home and classroom work should be judged by ordinary academic standards of substance and relevance and against other legitimate pedagogical concerns identified by the school. Thus, if a teacher's assignment involves writing a poem, the work of a student who submits a poem in the form of a prayer (for example, a psalm) should be judged on the basis of academic standards (such as literary quality) and neither penalized nor rewarded on account of its religious content.
- Student speakers at student assemblies and extracurricular activities such as sporting events may not be selected on a basis that either favors or disfavors religious speech. Where student speakers are selected on the basis of genuinely neutral, evenhanded criteria and retain primary control over the content of their expression, that expression is not attributable to the school and therefore may not be restricted because of its religious (or antireligious) content.
- School officials may not mandate or organize prayer at graduation or select speakers for such events in a manner that favors religious speech such as prayer. Where students or other private graduation speakers are selected on the basis of genuinely neutral, evenhanded criteria and retain primary control over the content of their expression, however, that expression is not attributable to the school and therefore may not be restricted because of its religious (or antireligious) content.
- School officials may not mandate or organize religious (baccalaureate) ceremonies. However, if a school makes its facilities and related services available to other private groups, it must make its facilities and services available on the same terms to organizers of privately sponsored religious baccalaureate ceremonies.

The Copyright Act

The Copyright Act of 1976[105] is of particular importance to teachers because it regulates the duplication of materials for classroom use. A copyright gives its owner a property interest in the copyrighted materials in much the same way one might own a house or a car. A copyright owner enjoys a set of "exclusive rights," including the right to reproduce the work, to sell copies, and to perform or display the work publicly. Thus, the excessive duplication of copyrighted materials without permission can violate the law. However, under certain circumstances, the law does allow teachers to make copies of copyrighted materials for classroom use. The circumstances under which duplication is permitted are known as "fair use."

The Copyright Act states that "the fair use of a copyrighted work . . . for purposes such as criticism, comment, news reporting, teaching (including multiple copies for classroom use), scholarship, or research is not an infringement of copyright." To determine whether the use in any particular case is fair, four factors are considered:

1. The "purpose" and character of the use, including whether such use is of a "commercial nature" or is "for nonprofit educational purposes." Copying for commercial purposes is more strictly controlled than copying for educational purposes.
2. The "nature" of the copyrighted work. Certain types of materials such as newspaper articles and materials that are out of print lend themselves to fair use duplicating.
3. The "amount and substantiality of the portion used" in relation to the work as a whole. The more one takes from the copyrighted material and the more closely the taken portion represents the heart of the work, the greater the likelihood of copyright infringement. (This factor is discussed further later.)
4. The effect of the use upon the "potential market for or value of" the copyrighted material.

In order to clarify these factors, a congressional committee has developed additional guidelines that, although not binding, have been taken into account by the courts.[106] These guidelines state that, for research or teaching purposes, teachers may make single copies of a chapter from a book, an article from a periodical or newspaper, a short story, short essay, or short poem, a chart, graph, diagram, or cartoon. A teacher may make multiple copies for classroom use only if the copying meets the tests for brevity, spontaneity, and cumulative effect.

"Brevity" is defined to mean 250 words of a poem or not more than two pages of poetry; a complete article, story, or essay of fewer than 2,500 words; an excerpt of 10 percent of a work or 1,000 words; or one graph or one cartoon. Copying is "spontaneous" when done at the inspiration of an individual teacher and when it occurs so close in time to the use of the work that it would be unreasonable to expect the teacher to obtain permission to copy. The "cumulative effect" limitation is violated if the copying is for more than one course in the school; more than one poem, story, or article or two excerpts are copied from the same author; more than three items are taken from a collective work or periodical volume during one class term; or if a teacher uses multiple copies more than nine times in one course during one class term.

All copying of copyrighted material must also conform to the following rules: (a) copies may not be used to create anthologies or other collective works; (b) consumable materials such as workbooks, tests, and answer sheets may not be copied; (c) copying may not be substituted for purchasing, be "directed by higher authority," or be repeated with the same item by the same teacher from term to term; (d) students may only be charged for the actual costs of duplication; and (e) each copy must include a notice of copyright.

An additional set of guidelines applies to the copying of music. Music may be copied to replace purchased copies that are not immediately available for an imminent performance provided that purchased copies are substituted in due course. For academic purposes other than a performance, it is permissible to make one copy per student consisting of up to 10 percent of a whole work, provided the copied portion does not constitute a "performable unit." A teacher may make a single copy of a sound recording for the purpose of constructing aural exercises or examinations. A single copy of a performance of copyrighted materials by students may be made for evaluation or rehearsal purposes. Finally, purchased or printed copies may be edited or simplified as long as the fundamental character of the work is not distorted or any lyrics altered or added.

The Hatch Amendment

The Hatch Amendment,[107] also known as the Protection of Pupils Rights Act, has two main provisions. The first requires that all instructional materials used by schools in connection with research or experimentation be available for parental inspection. The second prohibits subjecting any student to psychiatric or psychological testing or treatment when the primary purpose is to obtain information concerning such matters as political affiliation; psychological problems; sexual behavior or attitudes; or illegal, antisocial, self-incriminating, or demeaning behavior. A school's failure to comply with the law could result in the loss of federal funds. The law contains many undefined terms that make its interpretation difficult, and as a practical matter it seems to have little effect on most schools.

2.7 SUMMARY

The state's power over the program of public schools is subject to few legal restrictions. Nevertheless, in practice, the states have chosen to delegate some of their power over curriculum to local school boards. To some extent, the federal government has also become involved, mostly through categorical aid programs and restrictions attached to federal funds. Thus, decisions concerning standards, graduation requirements, mandated subjects, course content and perspectives, instructional methods, and materials are made through a complex process involving multiple levels of government.

Most challenges to state and local school board authority over the public school program are based on the religion clauses of the First Amendment. These cases are of two types. In one type, the plaintiffs rely on the Establishment Clause to object to organized prayers, Bible readings, moments of silence, dissemination of religious writings, and religious ceremonies in school. Many of these plaintiffs have succeeded. Using the *Lemon* test, courts prohibit the provision of any program whose purpose or primary effect is religious rather than secular.

In the second type of case, the plaintiffs object to course content or materials alleged to inhibit or advance religion. Some of these plaintiffs have won, as when the Supreme Court nullified an Arkansas law prohibiting the teaching of evolution. The Court found that the law's only purpose was to prevent the teaching of a scientific theory that contradicted fundamentalist Christian belief. However, most Establishment Clause objections to course content and materials have failed. Mere agreement or disagreement of a curriculum with the teachings of any particular religion or with religion in general is not an Establishment Clause violation as long as the curriculum has a secular purpose. In particular, plaintiffs arguing that curricula devoid of religious content, failing to mention God, or contradicting religious teachings establish a religion of secularism or secular humanism have not been successful. Similarly, when plaintiffs have claimed a free-exercise-based right not to be exposed to teachings that contradict their religious beliefs or their moral convictions, courts have generally rejected their claims.

Two types of free speech objections have been brought against school programs. In one, the plaintiffs claim a right not to be forced to espouse a political view against their will. The main application of this principle within the context of the public school is to prohibit requiring students to participate in a flag salute ceremony. The same principle might also prohibit requiring ideologically correct responses on an assignment or exam. The second type of free speech case is based on an alleged right to hear or to know. Most of these cases involve objections by student plaintiffs to school board decisions to remove books from the classroom or school library. Some library cases succeed when the court finds that the board's only motivation is a desire to suppress a disfavored political idea or theory. In general, however, courts give school boards broad latitude in selecting and discarding curricular materials, especially those judged obscene, vulgar, sexually offensive, or age inappropriate. Some courts do require that decisions to censor books be reached by applying preexisting, nonvague procedures. Schools' regulation of Internet use by their students is subject to constitutional and federal statutory restrictions.

A final type of constitutional objection to school programs involves courses or materials alleged to discriminate against one or more racial, ethnic, or gender groups. Little case law exists in this area and courts are not likely to get involved in any but the most blatant cases, such as when biased materials are used with an intent to discriminate against a racial or ethnic minority. In general, decisions concerning the political and social perspectives of the curriculum are more issues of educational policy than law.

Several federal laws place restrictions on state and local control of school programs. Of these laws, the most potentially significant is the No Child Left Behind Act, which includes a number of assessment, accountability, and school improvement requirements that may have far-reaching consequences for many schools.

NOTES

1 CODE OF ALA. § 16–40A-2; LA. REV. STAT. ANN. 17:281; MISS. CODE ANN. § 37–13–171; N.J. STAT. § 18A:35–4.20; R.I. GEN. LAWS § 16–22–18; 70 OKLA. STAT. § 11–105.1; CODE OF ALA. § 16–40A-2; MO. REV. STAT. § 170.015.
2 ARIZ. REV. STAT. § 15–716; S.C. CODE ANN. § 59–32–30.
3 § 105 ILCS 5/27–9.1
4 LA. REV. STAT. ANN. 17:281; Coleman v. Caddo Parish Sch. Bd., 635 So. 2d 1238 (La. Ct. App. 1994); *see also* S.C. CODE ANN. § 59–32–30.
5 § 170.015 MO. REV. STAT.
6 OKLA. STAT. tit. 70, § 11–1–5.1.
7 IDAHO CODE § 33–1610.
8 ALA. CODE § 16–40A-2.
9 CAL EDUC. CODE § 305; ARIZ. REV. STAT. ANN. § 15–751.
10 State *ex rel.* Andrews v. Webber, 8 N.E. 708 (Ind. 1886).
11 Alexander v. Phillips, 254 P. 1056 (Ariz. 1927).
12 Dawson v. East Side Union High Sch. Dist., 34 Cal. Rptr. 2d 108 (Cal. App. 6 Dist. 1994).
13 Johnson v. Sch. Comm. of Brockton, 358 N.E.2d 820 (Mass. 1977); *see also* State *ex rel.* Mueller v. Common Sch. Bd. of Joint Sch. Dist. No. 2 of Princeton, 242 N.W. 574 (Wis. 1932); State *ex rel.* Thayer v. Sch. Dist. of Neb. City, 156 N.W. 641 (Neb. 1916).
14 *See, e.g.*, MINN. STAT. ANN. § 15. 141137.
15 KEN. REV. STAT. ANN. §§ 160.345(2)(I)I, 160.345(2)(I)(6), 160.345(2)(g).
16 ILL. COMP. STAT. ANN. § 5/34–2.1 et seq.
17 CONN. GEN. STAT § 10–66dd.
18 *See, e.g.*, MICH. COMP. LAWS ANN. § 380.501 et seq.
19 370 U.S. 421 (1962).
20 374 U.S. 203 (1963).
21 Lemon v. Kurtzman, 403 U.S. 602 (1971).
22 449 U.S. 39 (1980).
23 Washegesic v. Bloomingdale Pub. Sch., 813 F. Supp. 559 (W.D. Mich. 1993), *aff'd*, 33 F.3d 679 (6th Cir. 1994).
24 653 F.2d 897 (5th Cir. 1981), *aff'd*, 455 U.S. 913 (1982).
25 644 F.2d 759 (9th Cir. 1981).
26 Breen v. Runkel, 614 F. Supp. 355 (W.D. Mich. 1985).
27 Jager v. Douglas County Sch. Dist., 862 F.2d 824 (11th Cir. 1989).
28 505 U.S. 577 (1992).
29 Doe v. Tangipahoa Parish Sch. Bd., 473 F.3d 188 (5th Cir. 2006); Coles v. Cleveland Bd. of Educ., 171 F.3d 369 (6th Cir. 1999).
30 530 U.S. 290 (2000).

31 228 F.3d 1092 (9th Cir. 2000); *see also* Lassonde v. Pleasanton Unified Sch. Dist., 320 F.3d 979 (9th Cir. 2003).
32 Jones v. Clear Creek Indep. Sch. Dist., 977 F.2d 963 (5th Cir. 1992).
33 Am. Civil Liberties Union of N.J. v. Black Horse Pike Reg'l Bd. of Educ., 84 F.3d 1471 (3d Cir. 1996); Harris v. Joint Sch. Dist. No. 241, 41 F.3d 447 (9th Cir. 1994), *vacated*, 515 U.S. 1154 (1995).
34 250 F.3d 1330 (11th Cir. 2001).
35 Doe *ex rel*. Doe v. Sch. Dist. of City of Norfolk, 340 F.3d 605 (8th Cir. 2003).
36 Doe *ex rel*. Doe v. Beaumont Indep. Sch. Dist., 173 F.3d 274 (5th Cir. 1999).
37 472 U.S. 38 (1985).
38 Doe v. Sch. Bd. of Ouachita Parish, 274 F.3d 289 (5th Cir. 2001); May v. Cooperman, 780 F.2d 240 (3d Cir. 1985), *appeal dismissed*, 484 U.S. 72 (1987); Walter v. W. Va. Bd. of Educ., 610 F. Supp. 1169 (S.D. W. Va. 1985); *but see* Gaines v. Anderson, 421 F. Supp. 337 (D. Mass. 1976).
39 Brown v. Gilmore, 258 F.3d 265 (4th Cir. 2001).
40 Croft v. Governor of Texas, 530 F. Supp. 2d 825 (N.D. Tex. 2008).
41 Doe v. Porter, 370 F.3d 558 (6th Cir. 2004).
42 Herdahl v. Pontotoc County Sch. Dist., 933 F. Supp. 582 (N.D. Miss. 1996); Hall v. Bd. of Sch. Comm'rs of Conecuh County, 656 F.2d 999 (5th Cir. Unit B Sept. 1981), *modified*, 707 F.2d 464 (11th Cir. 1983); Doe v. Human, 725 F. Supp. 1499 (W.D. Ark. 1989), and 725 F. Supp. 1503 (W.D. Ark. 1989), *aff'd*, 923 F.2d 857 (8th Cir. 1990); Crockett v. Sorenson, 568 F. Supp. 1422 (W.D. Va. 1983); Wiley v. Franklin, 474 F. Supp. 525 (E.D. Tenn. 1979).
43 Clever v. Cherry Hill Township Bd. of Educ., 838 F. Supp. 929 (D.N.J. 1993).
44 Meltzer v. Bd. of Pub. Instruction of Orange County, 548 F.2d 559 (5th Cir. 1977), *rev'd in part*, 577 F.2d 311 (5th Cir. 1978) (en banc).
45 Berger v. Renselaer Cent. Sch. Corp., 982 F.2d 1160 (7th Cir. 1993); Doe v. South Iron R-1 Sch. Dist., 498 F.3d 878 (8th Cir. 2007).
46 Peck v. Upshur County Bd. of Educ., 941 F. Supp. 1465 (N.D. W. Va. 1996); Schanou v. Lancaster County Sch. Dist. No. 160, 863 F. Supp. 1048 (D. Neb. 1994), *vacated*, 62 F.3d 1040 (8th Cir. 1995).
47 Koenick v. Felton, 190 F.3d 259 (4th Cir. 1999).
48 Cammack v. Waihee, 673 F. Supp. 1524 (D. Haw. 1987), *aff'd*, 932 F.2d 765 (9th Cir. 1991).
49 Metzl v. Leininger, 57 F.3d 618 (7th Cir. 1995).
50 492 U.S. 573 (1989); *see also* Capitol Square Review Bd. v. Pinette, 515 U.S. 753 (1995).
51 619 F.2d 1311 (8th Cir. 1980).
52 Bauchman v. W. High Sch., 132 F.3d 542 (10th Cir. 1997).
53 Doe v. Duncanville Indep. Sch. Dist., 70 F.3d 402 (5th Cir. 1995).
54 393 U.S. 97 (1968); *see also* Scopes v. State, 289 S.W. 363 (1927) (for historical background).
55 Pratt v. Indep. Sch. Dist. No. 831, 670 F.2d 771 (8th Cir. 1982); Hopkins v. Hamden Bd. of Educ., 289 A.2d 914 (Conn. C.P. 1971).
56 Clayton v. Place, 884 F.2d 376 (8th Cir. 1989).
57 366 F. Supp. 1208 (S.D. Tex. 1972), *aff'd*, 486 F.2d 137 (5th Cir. 1973).
58 *See also* Daniel v. Waters, 515 F.2d 485 (6th Cir. 1975).
59 482 U.S. 578 (1987); *see also* McLean v. Ark. Bd. of Educ., 529 F. Supp. 1255 (E.D. Ark. 1982).
60 185 F.3d 337 (5th Cir. 1999).
61 Selman v. Cobb County Sch. Dist., 390 F. Supp. 2d 1286 (N.D.Ga.2005).
62 400 F. Supp. 2d 707 (M.D. Pa. 2005).
63 655 F. Supp. 939 (S.D. Ala.), *rev'd*, 827 F.2d 684 (11th Cir. 1987).
64 Kunselman v. W. Reserve Local Sch. Dist., 70 F.3d 931 (6th Cir. 1995); Brown v. Woodland Joint Unified Sch. Dist., 27 F.3d 1373 (9th Cir. 1994); Fleischfresser v. Dirs. of Sch. Dist. 200, 15 F.3d 680 (7th Cir. 1994); Guyer v. Sch. Bd. of Alachua County, 634 So. 2d 806 (Fla. Dist. Ct. App. 1994).
65 Altman v. Bedford Cent. School Dist., 245 F.3d 49 (2d Cir. 2001).
66 827 F.2d 1058 (6th Cir. 1987).
67 314 F. Supp. 340 (D. Md. 1969), *aff'd*, 428 F.2d 471 (4th Cir. 1970).
68 274 A.2d 832 (N.J. Sup. Ct. Ch. Div. 1971); *see also* Leebaert *ex rel*. Leebaert v. Harrington, 193 F. Supp. 2d 491 (D. Conn. 2002).
69 Curtis v. Falmouth Sch. Comm., 652 N.E.2d 580 (Mass. 1995); Alfonso v. Fernandez, 606 N.Y. S.2d 259 (N. Y. App. Div. 1993).

70 Brown v. Hot, Sexy & Safer Prod., Inc., 68 F.3d 525 (1st Cir. 1995).

71 Parker v. Hurley, 474 F. Supp. 2d 261 (D. Mass. 2007); *but see* Stanley v. Carrier Mills-Stonefort Sch., 459 F. Supp. 2d 766 (S.D. Ill. 2006).

72 427 F.3d 1197 (9th Cir. 2005); *see also* C.N. v. Ridgewood Bd. of Educ., 430 F.3d 159 (3d Cir. 2005).

73 319 U.S. 624 (1943).

74 Minersville Sch. Dist. v. Gobitis, 310 U.S. 586 (1940).

75 Lipp v. Morris, 579 F.2d 834 (3d Cir. 1978); Goetz v. Ansell, 477 F.2d 636 (2d Cir. 1973); Banks v. Bd. of Pub. Instruction of Dade County, 450 F.2d 1103 (5th Cir. 1971).

76 Circle Sch. v. Phillips, 270 F. Supp. 2d 616 (E.D. Pa. 2003), *aff'd*, Circle Sch. v. Pappert, 381 F.3d 172 (3d Cir. 2004).

77 Sherman v. Cmty. Consol. Sch. Dist. 21, 758 F. Supp. 1244 (N.D. Ill. 1991), *modified*, 980 F.2d 437 (7th Cir. 1992); Smith v. Denny, 280 F. Supp. 651 (E.D. Cal. 1968), *appeal dismissed*, 417 F.2d 614 (9th Cir. 1969).

78 Newdow v. United States Congress, 292 F.3d 597 (9th Cir. 2002), *cert. denied*, 124 S. Ct. 383 (2003), *rev'd on other grounds*, Elk Grove Unified Sch. Dist. v. Newdow, 542 U.S. 1 (2004).

79 Elk Grove Unified Sch. Dist. v. Newdow, 542 U.S. 1 (2004).

80 Myers v. Loudoun County Pub. Schs., 418 F.3d 395 (4th Cir. 2005).

81 Abood v. Detroit Bd. of Educ., 431 U.S. 209 (1977); Wooley v. Maynard, 430 U.S. 705 (1977).

82 Steirer v. Bethlehem Area Sch. Dist., 987 F.2d 989 (3d Cir. 1993).

83 Herndon v. Chapel Hill-Carrboro, 89 F.3d 174 (4th Cir. 1996); Immediato v. Rye Neck School District, 73 F.3d 454 (2d Cir. 1996).

84 Uzzell v. Friday, 547 F.2d 801 (4th Cir. 1977); Galda v. Rutgers, 772 F.2d 1060 (3d Cir. 1985).

85 Wexner v. Anderson Union High Sch. Dist. Bd. of Trustees, 258 Cal. Rptr. 26 (Cal. Ct. App. 1989).

86 457 F.2d 289 (2d Cir. 1972).

87 541 F.2d 577 (6th Cir. 1976).

88 631 F.2d 1300 (7th Cir. 1980).

89 457 U.S. 853 (1981).

90 862 F.2d 1517 (11th Cir. 1989).

91 Seyfried v. Walton, 668 F.2d 214 (3d Cir. 1981); Bell v. U-32 Bd. of Educ., 630 F. Supp. 939 (D. Vt. 1986); *but see* Bowman v. Bethel-Tate Bd. of Educ., 610 F. Supp. 577 (S.D. Ohio 1985).

92 American Civil Liberties Union of Florida v. Miami-Dade County Sch. Bd., 439 F. Supp. 1242 (S.D. Fla. 2006).

93 Sheck v. Baileyville Sch. Comm., 530 F. Supp. 679 (D. Me. 1982).

94 Salvail v. Nashua Bd. of Educ., 469 F. Supp. 1269 (D.N.H. 1979).

95 Bicknell v. Vergennes Union High Sch. Bd. of Dir., 638 F.2d 438 (2d Cir. 1980).

96 47 U.S.C. § 247.

97 539 U.S. 194 (2003).

98 488 F. Supp. 1138 (N.D. Miss. 1980).

99 Rosenberg v. Bd. of Educ. of City of N.Y., 92 N.Y.S.2d 344 (N.Y. App. Div. 1949).

100 Grimes v. Cavazos, 786 F. Supp. 1184 (S.D.N.Y. 1992).

101 20 U.S.C. §§ 6311–6322.

102 20 U.S.C. § 7906.

103 20 U.S.C. § 7904.

104 *Guidance on Constitutionally Protected Prayer in Public Elementary and Secondary Schools*, 68 Fed. Reg. 9,648 (Feb. 28, 2003).

105 17 U.S.C. §§ 101–1101.

106 Marcus v. Rowley, 695 F.2d 1171 (9th Cir. 1983).

107 20 U.S.C. § 1232h.

3   Student Freedom of Expression

Chapters 3 and 4 consider legal issues relating to the school's control of student conduct. A theme that runs through both chapters is the tension between the school's need to maintain an orderly environment and students' rights as citizens and human beings. Specifically, this chapter examines the extent and limitations of students' constitutional right to freedom of expression in light of the school's need to maintain order and execute its mission. Chapter 4 considers the school's proper response when students misbehave.

In the not-too-distant past, the school's authority over its students was subject to few limitations. Courts commonly viewed the school as operating in the place of parents (in loco parentis), a doctrine that justified all manner of regulation, just as true parenthood confers broad powers. Until the latter part of the twentieth century, children, much less students, did not enjoy the protections of the Bill of Rights and the Fourteenth Amendment except in a few specialized contexts. Accordingly, only statute and common law restrained the authority of educators. Law relating to student behavior was scant, dealt primarily with the type and severity of permissible punishment, and allowed educators to decide what acts could be prohibited.

Thus, a popular education law textbook published by Madaline Remmlein in 1962 devotes only ten of its 346 pages to issues relating to the control of student conduct.[1] It notes that "[p]upils have the responsibility of obeying the school laws and rules and regulations of the state and local governing officials," and "the duty of submitting to orders of their teachers and other school authorities." Only two limitations on the school's authority are discussed: Statutory and common law are said to limit the severity of corporal punishment, and expulsions are supposed to be based on rules that are reasonable, although no case law findings against unreasonable school rules are presented. With the exception of the Supreme Court's ban against a required flag salute in *West Virginia State Board of Education v. Barnette* (see sec. 2.4), Remmlein mentions no constitutional limitations on the school's authority over its pupils.

Although Remmlein's treatment of this topic was complete for its time, two developments of the past six decades render it outdated. First, courts have recognized that, although children's legal status is not identical to adults', a child is nevertheless entitled to constitutional protection.[2] The state is now expected to provide strong justification for the differential treatment of children, particularly where fundamental rights are involved. Second, the doctrine of in loco parentis has been largely abandoned. Courts have come to realize that for most purposes it is more appropriate to view the school as an arm of the state rather than as a substitute parent. Therefore, courts are willing to extend the protection of the Bill of Rights and Fourteenth Amendment to students.

This does not mean that schools no longer have the authority (and duty) to control their pupils. On the contrary, the basic premise of Remmlein's chapter still holds: Students have a responsibility to obey the law, school rules, and the commands of their teachers.

However, for its part, the school must be governed by the limitations that the law places on state regulation of its citizens. The school is expected to afford its pupils the full protection of their constitutional rights as defined by the courts.

3.1 FREEDOM OF EXPRESSION: AN OVERVIEW

The clauses of the First Amendment that deal with freedom of expression state: "Congress shall make no law . . . abridging the freedom of speech, or the press, or the right of the people peaceably to assemble, and to petition the Government for redress of grievances." As already discussed, these limitations apply to the actions of state government by virtue of the Due Process Clause of the Fourteenth Amendment.

Freedom of expression is a cornerstone of personal freedom and democracy. Four major themes emerge from among the many reasons given by political theorists and courts for its steadfast protection:

1. Freedom of expression is essential to the effective operation of a system of self-government. People are unlikely to reach reasoned decisions unless they are free to debate the issues confronting them.
2. Without freedom of expression, uncovering and challenging false ideas is extremely difficult, thereby drastically reducing the possibility of learning the truth and impeding personal and political improvement.
3. Freedom of expression fosters self-realization and achievement.
4. Freedom of expression operates as a social and political safety valve permitting people to dissipate anger without resorting to violence.

Courts typically extend broad-based, vigorous protection to freedom of speech. At the same time, they recognize that no right can be absolute. Some forms of speech are so damaging that to protect them would do more harm than good. Probably the best-known example is that the state may outlaw crying "fire" in a crowded theater when there is no fire because of the tremendous potential for harm to people and property. Thus, in interpreting the freedom of expression clauses, the courts have developed extensive doctrine designed to protect both the essential values underlying the First Amendment and those other legitimate interests that speech can damage. Drawing the appropriate lines has produced an extensive body of cases involving a complex set of definitions, tests, and rules.

Definition of Speech

Almost any action can be considered to have some expressive content. But, because the First Amendment specifically prohibits government action that abridges the freedom of "speech," many cases raise the issue of whether a particular expressive act falls into the category of speech. For example, punching someone in the nose can certainly be seen as a form of expression, but is it speech? Under most if not all circumstances, the answer would be no, so government regulation of nose punching—although arguably subject to other constitutional restraints—is not subject to the restraints imposed by the First Amendment.

Drawing the line between speech and other forms of expressive conduct is not always so easy. For example, is sleeping in a park speech? In one case involving people sleeping in a park as part of a demonstration to protest the plight of the homeless, the Supreme Court said that it was.[3] Similarly, the Court has declared that flag burning in conjunction with a political demonstration is a speech act, the regulation of which must conform to strictures of the First Amendment.[4] The Court wrote: "In deciding whether particular conduct possesses sufficient communicative elements to bring the First Amendment into play, we have asked whether '[a]n intent to convey a particularized message was present, and [whether] the likelihood was great that the message would be understood by those who viewed it.'" This then is the test for determining if a specific act is speech for First Amendment purposes.

Schools' desire to regulate the appearance of their students often raises the issue of whether hairstyles or clothing constitute speech for First Amendment purposes. Some courts have accepted the contention that a student's hairstyle is speech, but others have disagreed.[5]

As for clothing, courts sometimes do not consider a general style of dress or the selection of a type of apparel or adornment to be speech. Thus, one court ruled that the wearing of one earring was not speech even though the students wore the earring as a gang symbol, and another court ruled that wearing sagging pants was not speech although it too indicated gang affiliation.[6] However, not all courts have reasoned this way. The Fifth Circuit ruled that a school district's requirement that students wear a uniform did raise a free speech question because a student's choice of clothing style had "communicative content" in that it may symbolize ethnic heritage, religious beliefs, and political and social views. Despite reaching this conclusion the court upheld the school's uniform policy.[7] Courts are in agreement that a school's desire to regulate clothing because of the message or logo printed on the clothing raises an issue of freedom of speech and decide these cases based on the constitutional doctrines discussed in this chapter.[8]

Categories of Speech

Most types of speech receive strenuous first amendment protection, but there are some that receive only limited protection and some that receive no protection at all. The categories of speech that have been determined by the courts not to be deserving of First Amendment protection include obscenity, fighting words, threats, and defamation of private citizens. If a specific set of words or other expressive act falls into one of these categories it does not enjoy the protection of the First Amendment whether or not it causes disruption or harm. Legally, obscenity is expression that meets three conditions: (a) the average person applying contemporary community standards would find that, taken as a whole, it appeals to prurient interests; (b) the publication depicts or describes in a patently offensive way sexual conduct specifically defined in state law; and (c) taken as a whole, the work lacks serious literary, artistic, political, or scientific value.[9] Fighting words are those that by their very utterance inflict injury or tend to incite an immediate breach of the peace.[10] A threat is a statement that a reasonable speaker would expect to be interpreted as a serious expression of an intent to harm.[11] Defamation is a complex concept that for present purposes may be defined as a false statement made to a third party that subjects a person to contempt, ridicule, or similar harm (see sec. 10.2). Because these forms of speech are not protected by the First Amendment, government may, if it wishes, prohibit them and punish those who engage in them. Thus, the Eighth Circuit permitted a school to expel a student for writing a composition that his ex-girlfriend reasonably interpreted as a threat to rape and murder her.[12]

The categories of speech that receive only limited First Amendment protection include commercial speech, offensive or indecent speech, and defamation of public figures. To receive any protection, commercial speech—advertisements—must not be about an illegal activity or be misleading. For commercial speech that meets these criteria, government may still impose regulations if: (a) its interest in regulating is substantial, (b) the regulation directly advances that interest, and (c) the regulation is narrowly tailored to achieve the objective.[13] The law regarding offensive speech—speech dealing with excrement or sexual activity in a vulgar or indecent way—is not completely settled, but regulation appears permissible when such speech would be accessible to children.[14]

Speech outside the categories listed previously receives the highest level of protection. Courts are particularly vigilant in protecting political speech, speech that concerns issues of public controversy and concern. But even the most highly protected categories of speech may be regulated and even prohibited when the justification is sufficiently strong.

Forums of Speech

The law recognizes four different forums where speech may occur on government property. A traditional public forum is a place such as a public street or park that has customarily been open to the public for purposes of assembly, demonstrations, speeches, and other expressive activities. Speech in traditional open forums may only be regulated if the regulations are necessary to achieve a compelling state interest and narrowly drawn to achieve that end. Viewpoint and speaker-based regulation are prohibited although reasonable, content-neutral regulations of time, place, and manner may be enforced. A designated public forum is a place that has not traditionally been open to public assembly and speech, but which the government by explicit policy or longstanding practice has voluntarily opened to the general public. A school auditorium during nonschool hours may qualify as a designated open forum if it is customarily available for meetings by nonschool groups. If the government has created such a forum, then the same rules apply as in the traditional public forum. A limited public forum is created when the government has voluntary opened a place for speech activities but has limited the expressive activities to certain kinds of speakers or certain subjects. In these places the government may enforce reasonable, viewpoint-neutral regulations of the content of the speech, for example, not permitting an auditorium devoted to stage productions to be used for a political campaign rally. A non-public forum is a place neither traditionally nor by designation opened to the general public for expressive activities. A school auditorium that is never loaned or rented to nonschool groups may qualify as a non-public forum. Regulation of access to the non-public forum for speech activities need only be reasonable and viewpoint-neutral. The government may employ a selective-access policy requiring prospective users to obtain permission to use the forum.[15]

Regulation of Protected Speech

Government may wish to regulate speech for a number of different reasons: disagreement with the viewpoint expressed by the speech, objection to the subject matter of the speech, desire to silence a specific speaker, concern over the possible disruptive or other adverse effects of the speech, and desire to limit the types and topics of speech that may occur at a given time and place. Each of these reasons raises different legal issues.

Regulation of speech based solely on the **viewpoint** that is being expressed (for example, allowing pro-government but not anti-government ideas to be expressed) is strictly prohibited by the First Amendment. As the Supreme Court has stated, "If there is a bedrock principle underlying the First Amendment, it is that the government may not prohibit the expression of an idea simply because society finds the idea offensive or disagreeable."[16] Regulation of speech based on **subject matter** (for example, allowing some topics to be written about in a newspaper while prohibiting others) is generally also impermissible unless the suppression occurs in a limited-public forum or a non-public forum. Regulation based on subject matter in a traditional public forum or public forum-by-designation must satisfy the strict scrutiny test: The regulation must be necessary to serve a compelling governmental interest. Regulation based on the identity of the **speaker** is usually viewed by courts as equivalent to suppression based on viewpoint and is thus prohibited. In some cases, however, courts apply the rules of subject-matter regulation to speaker-based regulation.

Desire to avoid predicted **adverse effects,** for example the panic that might ensue if someone falsely shouts "fire" in a crowded theater, is a common rationale for regulation of speech. Schools often wish to prohibit speech that they fear might cause students to engage in dangerous or illegal behaviors like fighting or drug use. When government seeks to block speech because of its predicted adverse effects, it bears the burden of showing that the prediction is valid. To satisfy its burden, the government may seek to show that a prohibited act of speech was "directed to inciting or producing imminent lawless action and . . . likely to incite or produce such action."[17] A well known, older version of this test allowed for the prohibition of speech that created a clear and present danger of an evil the government had a right to try to prevent.[18] Government, however, may not identify as an adverse effect the mere fact the people may change their minds and believe the viewpoint being expressed. Finally, government may seek to regulate the **time,** the **place,** or the **manner** of the speech. For example, the use of a loudspeaker truck may be limited to certain hours and the loudness of the sound emitted may be limited to a certain decibel level. Content-neutral regulations like these are permissible if they further an important or substantial governmental interest and if the restriction of speech is no greater than is essential to further that interest.[19]

Applying the relevant free speech doctrine to specific situations is not always easy. Consider, for example, the **heckler's veto.** What if a speaker's views are so unpopular that the audience threatens violence toward the speaker? Is the speech then considered fighting words? Has it inspired imminent lawless action? Can the speaker therefore be punished? If so, then a hostile audience may negate the right to speak freely. These issues are not entirely settled.[20]

Freedom of Expression and Students

When dealing with issues concerning the free speech rights of students, courts look first to general free speech principles. However, courts do not simply take these principles and apply them directly to students. Rather, the law defining student free speech rights is based on general principles of free speech considered and often modified in light of the special status of students and public schools.

The landmark 1969 case, *Tinker v. Des Moines Independent Community School District*,[21] marked the first general acceptance by the Supreme Court of the principle that students do not "shed their constitutional rights to freedom of speech or expression at the schoolhouse gate." *Tinker* granted school officials the power to prohibit only student speech that was materially and substantially disruptive to the legitimate educational mission of the school. In the years following *Tinker*, the doctrine of material and substantial disruption stood as the basic rule regarding the regulation by school officials of all manner of student speech regardless of how and where the speech occurred. But because the doctrine was in several respects vague and ambiguous (e.g., what exactly is material and substantial disruption?), it spawned a series of lower court decisions that were inconsistent in the degree to which they afforded students free speech protection. Section 3.4 explores the *Tinker* case and its interpretation by the lower courts.

Beginning in the decade of the 1980s, a more conservative Supreme Court began cutting back on the protections afforded by *Tinker*. The Court limited the sweep of *Tinker* by identifying two circumstances when the material-and-substantial-disruption rule does not apply. First, it ruled that in a school-sponsored context, such as a school assembly or a school-operated student newspaper, the leeway that school officials have to control student expression is greater than in other contexts. Section 3.3 examines the law concerning school-sponsored student speech. Second, following a line of reasoning first applied in several lower court decisions, the Supreme Court recognized that there is at least one category of speech that does not enjoy the protection of the First Amendment in the schools. Section 3.2 explores the categories of student speech that may be excluded from First Amendment protection.

3.2 UNPROTECTED CATEGORIES OF STUDENT SPEECH

School officials are free to prohibit student speech that falls into one of the categories of speech that receive no First Amendment protection: obscenity, fighting words, threats, and defamation of private citizens (see sec. 3.1). In addition, there are several categories of student expression that at least some courts have excluded from First Amendment protection: speech that is offensive, lewd, vulgar, or "obscene-as-to-minors." In 2007, in *Morse v. Frederick*,[22] the Supreme Court considered the issue of whether school officials violated a student's right to freedom of expression when they prohibited him from advocating the use of illegal drugs.

The *Morse* Case

Morse, the principal of a high school in Juneau, Alaska, permitted the students and staff of her school to leave the building during the school day to observe the Olympic Torch Relay, which was passing in front of the school. Students were permitted to stand in designated areas on both sides of the street adjacent to the school, where teachers and administrators monitored their actions. Frederick, a senior, arrived late to school and joined his fellow students across from the school to watch the Relay.

The Supreme Court described the subsequent relevant events as follows: "As the torch-bearers and camera crews passed by, Frederick and his friends unfurled a 14-foot banner bearing the phrase: "BONG HiTS 4 JESUS." The large banner was easily readable by the students on the other side of the street." Principal Morse immediately crossed the street and demanded that the banner be taken down. Everyone but Frederick complied. Morse confiscated the banner and told Frederick to report to her office, where she suspended him for ten days. Morse later explained that she told Frederick to take the banner down because she thought it encouraged illegal drug use, in violation of established school policy.

Frederick objected to the suspension and appealed to the district superintendent, who upheld the punishment. In explaining his decision, the superintendent noted that Frederick had displayed his banner "in the midst of his fellow students, during school hours, at a school-sanctioned activity." He further explained that Frederick "was not disciplined because the principal of the school 'disagreed' with his message, but because his speech appeared to advocate the use of illegal drugs. . . . The common-sense understanding of the phrase 'bong hits' is that it is a reference to a means of smoking marijuana."

Frederick next brought suit against the school on the grounds that it had violated his First-Amendment right to freedom of speech. He argued that the school had no authority to control his actions because he had not been at school when they occurred and that, in any case, his speech could not be prohibited because it did not pose a danger of material and substantial disruption to the school. The Ninth Circuit found in Frederick's favor, and the school appealed to the Supreme Court.

The Supreme Court rejected Frederick's first claim, that the school lacked authority over his actions, because although not on school grounds, they occurred in the context of a school-sponsored "social event or class trip." The Court agreed with the school that, Frederick cannot "stand in the midst of his fellow students, during school hours, at a school-sanctioned activity and claim he is not at school."

Frederick's second claim, that the school could not prohibit his speech because it did not pose a danger of material and substantial disruption, was the basis of the Ninth Circuit's decision in his favor. In reversing the Ninth Circuit's decision, the Supreme Court noted that although there were several possible meanings of the phrase "bong hits 4 Jesus," it was reasonable for the principal to interpret it as promoting illegal drug use and not as political speech or speech that expressed an opinion on an issue of "national debate"; that drug use among students was a serious problem that both schools and various braches of government at all levels were attempting to combat; and that the free-speech rights of students at school are not always identical to those of citizens in other contexts. Based on these factors, the Court concluded that the school's actions were permissible:

> School principals have a difficult job, and a vitally important one. When Frederick suddenly and unexpectedly unfurled his banner, Morse had to decide to act—or not act—on the spot. It was reasonable for her to conclude that the banner promoted illegal drug use—in violation of established school policy—and that failing to act would send a powerful message to the students in her charge, including Frederick, about how serious the school was about the dangers of illegal drug use. The First Amendment does not require schools to tolerate at school events student expression that contributes to those dangers.

As Justice Alito wrote in his concurring opinion, *Morse*

> goes no further than to hold that a public school may restrict speech that a reasonable observer would interpret as advocating illegal drug use . . . [but] it provides no support for any restriction of speech that can plausibly be interpreted as commenting on any political or social issue, including speech on issues such as the wisdom of the war on drugs or of legalizing marijuana for medicinal use.

Justice Alito further cautioned that "The opinion of the Court does not endorse the broad argument . . . that the First Amendment permits public school officials to censor any student speech that interferes with a school's 'educational mission.'" Nor does *Morse* authorize school officials to proscribe speech that is, as the Court put it, "plainly 'offensive'" or "that could fit under some definition of 'offensive.'" Therefore, schools may only prohibit offensive student speech, even speech that offends a targeted racial, ethnic, or gender group in accordance with the *Tinker* rule, that is, if the speech is materially and substantially disruptive to the need for order and discipline within the school (see sec. 3.4).

Applying *Morse*

In a case decided prior to *Morse* the Sixth Circuit upheld a school's ban of the wearing of a T-shirt that the court described as follows:

> The front of the T-shirt depicted a three-faced Jesus, accompanied by the words "See No Truth. Hear No Truth. Speak No Truth." On the back of the shirt, the word

"BELIEVE" was spelled out in capital letters, with the letters "LIE" highlighted. Marilyn Manson's name (although not his picture) was displayed prominently on the front of the shirt . . .

Because Marilyn Manson, described by the court as a "Goth" rock musician with a ghoulish persona, was associated with drug use, the court said the prohibition was permissible because the T-shirt was an implicit attack on the school district's mission.[23] After *Morse* this case could only be decided the same way if the court concluded that the T-shirt, which made no explicit reference to drugs, could reasonably be interpreted as advocating illegal drug use. In another case decided prior to *Morse*, the Fourth Circuit allowed school officials to prohibit the distribution of a newspaper that carried an advertisement for a "head shop," a store specializing in the legal sale of paraphernalia used for illegal drug consumption.[24] A court relying on *Morse* might make the same decision after concluding that this advertisement advocated the use of illegal drugs. Suppression of speech advocating the use of alcohol or tobacco is also likely to be permitted under *Morse* because alcohol and tobacco are drugs whose use by minors is illegal.[25]

Threats

As previously noted, threats are not protected by the First Amendment either in or out of school. A threat is a statement that a reasonable speaker would expect to be interpreted as a serious expression of intent to harm. Note that the person making the threat does not actually have to harbor an intent to harm. Nor does the actual speaker have to expect that the threat will to be interpreted as such. All that is necessary is that a hypothetical "reasonable" speaker would anticipate that the statement would be interpreted as threatening. It is also not necessary that the speaker communicate the threat to the person being threatened. Courts may uphold the punishment of students who communicate a threat to a third party. Even so, and perhaps not surprisingly, courts have sometimes had difficulty in deciding whether a particular expression constituted a threat. And in some cases, courts have relied on *Tinker* (see sec. 3.4) or *Fraser* (see sec. 3.3) to permit punishment of students for statements that did not fit the definition of "threat" but contained depictions of violence.[26]

In response to several highly publicized school shootings in the late 1990s, many schools have become very concerned with the issue of school safety. In order to lessen the potential for violence, schools sometimes wish to suppress not just threatening speech, but any speech containing violent themes. In *LaVine v. Blaine School District*,[27] the Ninth Circuit ruled that a principal did not violate a student's free speech rights when the principal expelled him on an emergency basis after he showed his teacher a poem he had written that was filled with imagery of violent death, suicide, and the shooting of fellow students at school. The court noted that in addition to the poem, the principal had considered the student's previous suicidal ideation, disciplinary history, family situation, recent break-up and subsequent stalking of his former girlfriend, and a recent school shooting in a nearby city. The court further noted that the school allowed the student to return as soon as he was evaluated by a psychiatrist in whose opinion the student was not a threat to himself or others.

In another case, Adam at age fourteen drew a picture in the privacy of his home that depicted his high school soaked in gasoline alongside an individual with a torch and missile. The picture also showed two students with guns and a student throwing a brick at the principal while saying "shut the f— up faggot." A racial expletive was also included in the picture. Adam showed the sketch to three people at his home. Two years after he completed the drawing, Adam's younger brother, Andrew, showed the picture to his school-bus driver who confiscated it and gave it to the principal. Andrew was suspended and Adam was expelled in part because of the drawing. Adam and Andrew brought suit claiming among other things that their First Amendment rights had been violated. The court rejected the claim on various grounds, finding that the drawing did constitute a true threat "to cause injury or even death to others or to cause damage to the school's facilities." Thus despite the fact Adam never himself brought the picture to school or showed the picture to anybody at the school, and despite the fact the picture was two years old when it ended up in the hands of the principal, the Court found that it constituted a threat and did not enjoy First Amendment protection.[28]

In another case, a teacher confiscated a student's private notebook containing an entry entitled "Dream," which described the student's day dream of shooting a teacher. Following her suspension from school for ten days, the plaintiff claimed her First Amendment rights had been violated. In ruling in favor of the school district the Eleventh Circuit said a student's right to freedom of expression "should not interfere with a school administrator's professional observation that certain expressions have led to, and therefore could lead to, an unhealthy and potentially unsafe learning environment for the children they serve." School officials, said the court, must have flexibility to control student speech "even if such speech does not result in a reasonable fear of immediate disruption." The court claimed, debatably, that these principles were affirmed by the Supreme Court in *Morse*. The concurring opinion would have limited the "inquiry in this case to whether [the plaintiff's] story and the circumstances surrounding it would cause school officials to reasonably anticipate a substantial disruption of or material interference" with the work of the school or the rights of other students.[29]

As these cases indicate, recent courts have shown a propensity to allow school officials to prohibit speech depicting school violence even if the speech does not meet the legal definition of "threat." But there have been some exceptions. In *Ponce v. Socorro Independent School District* a student wrote in his private diary a story he titled "My Nazi Diary Based on a True Story" in which he described a pseudo-Nazi group's plan to commit an attack on his high school. After the student showed another student some of the contents of the diary, that second student informed a teacher, which ultimately led to a search of the writer's backpack, which turned up the diary. After reviewing the content of the diary overnight, the assistant principal suspended the plaintiff for three days for issuing a "terroristic threat." The court found the record devoid of any facts to establish that the story was a terroristic threat or anything other than a work of fiction.[30]

Lewdness, Vulgarity, and Obscenity-as-to-Minors

The Supreme Court has ruled that when student speech can be considered *school-sponsored*, the school is free to prohibit speech that is "indecent, lewd, and offensive to modesty and decency" (see sec. 3.3). Speech that fits the legal definition of obscenity (see sec. 3.1) may also be prohibited at school because obscenity is not protected speech. The Supreme Court has also recognized that speech that falls outside the legal definition of obscenity may be obscene-as-to-minors,[31] and schools are free to prohibit such speech. In order to be classified as obscene-as-to-minors, material must (1) appeal to the prurient interest of minors, (2) violate prevailing standards in the adult community of suitability for minors, and (3) lack any serious artistic, literary, political, or scientific value for minors.

Courts have also given schools considerable leeway to regulate speech that, although not legally obscene or obscene-as-to-minors, can be considered lewd, vulgar, or "plainly offensive."[32] Thus in *Pyle v. South Hadley School Committee*,[33] a federal district court upheld the decision of school officials to bar students from wearing T-shirts that bore the messages "Coed Naked Band; Do It To The Rhythm," and "See Dick Drink. See Dick Drive. See Dick Die. Don't Be A Dick." Another court upheld the suppression of a T-shirt that read "Drugs Suck."[34] In another, arguably aberrant, case a student was suspended for 2.5 days and had her grades lowered 2 percent for each class missed for violating the school rule that "prohibited profane or inappropriate language on school property." The student was overheard in the school's office saying "shit" to herself upon receiving a note that her mother could not pick her up, a note she received too late for her to catch the school bus.[35] The court saw the issue in the case as: can the school constitutionally ban "profane or inappropriate language" anywhere on school property?" It based its decision on the principle that "A school's authority to condemn indecent language is not inconsistent with a student's right to express his views." In a higher education case, the Supreme Court prohibited a university from expelling a student for distributing an independent newspaper with an offensive, but not obscene, political cartoon and the headline "M—— f—— Acquitted" on the front page. The cartoon depicted a policeman raping the Statue of Liberty.[36] It is doubtful that the Court would reach the same conclusion in the context of a high school. But school officials must bear in mind the Supreme Court's caution in *Morse* that they do not have the authority to suppress speech merely because it is "offensive" under "some definition" of the term.

3.3 SCHOOL-SPONSORED SPEECH

Sections 3.3 and 3.4 consider student speech that does not fall into one of the unprotected categories of student speech discussed in Section 3.2. Section 3.4 considers independent student speech, what the *Tinker* Court referred to as "personal intercommunication among students." This section considers student speech that is not "independent," but rather takes place as part of the student's participation in the school's curriculum or other activity under the school's sponsorship and control. School officials have much greater leeway to regulate speech in these contexts.

Hazelwood v. Kuhlmeier

Hazelwood School District v. Kuhlmeier,[37] involved a high school principal's deletion from the school newspaper, prior to publication, of articles concerning "students' experiences with pregnancy," and "the impact of divorce on students at the school." The newspaper was produced by the students as part of a regularly scheduled course and was funded primarily by the district. The regular practice at the school was for the journalism teacher to submit the page proofs of each issue to the principal for his review prior to publication. The principal's reasons for deleting the articles included a concern over possible embarrassment to students and parents identified or identifiable in the stories, a belief that "references to sexual activity and birth control were inappropriate for some of the younger students at the school," and a concern that the student journalists had not followed proper journalistic procedures because parents mentioned in the divorce article had not been given an opportunity to respond. The student editors and writers claimed that the principal's actions violated their right to freedom of the press.

The court of appeals cited *Tinker* in finding in favor of the students, but the Supreme Court reversed the decision. The lower court felt that the student newspaper was a public forum, "intended to be and operated as a conduit for student viewpoint." As such, it believed that the school could only censor the paper to avoid material and substantial disruption of education or to prevent an invasion of the rights of others. But, according to the lower court, neither of these conditions obtained: It was unlikely that the articles would cause educational disruption, and, in a legal sense, the articles did not constitute libel or invasion of privacy or breach of any other right.

The Supreme Court's basic disagreement with the court of appeals was that the Supreme Court did not view the newspaper as a public forum. Although the school had usually permitted the students to control the content of the paper, the Court nevertheless found that the primary purpose of the newspaper was as a laboratory to teach the principles of proper journalism. Thus, reasoned the Court, *Hazelwood* presented a far different question from *Tinker*. The Court explained the difference as follows:

> The question whether the First Amendment requires a school to tolerate particular student speech—the question that we addressed in *Tinker*—is different from the question whether the First Amendment requires a school affirmatively to promote particular student speech. The former question addresses educators' ability to silence a student's personal expression that happens to occur on the school premises. The latter question concerns educators' authority over school-sponsored publications, theatrical productions, and other expressive activities that students, parents, and members of the public might reasonably perceive to bear the imprimatur of the school. These activities may fairly be characterized as part of the school curriculum, whether or not they occur in a traditional classroom setting, so long as they are supervised by faculty members and designed to impart particular knowledge or skills to student participants and audiences.

Having established this distinction, the Court went on to explain that the school's function relative to a school newspaper or school play is not just as the place where these activities happen to take place, but rather is a role analogous to the publisher of a newspaper or the producer of a play. As such, the school can legitimately regulate student speech appearing to "bear the imprimatur of the school" for a variety of reasons. These might include a desire to impart an educational message; for example, by excluding poorly written or researched or biased material, to disassociate the school from values it does not share, or to shield other students from age-inappropriate information, "which might range from the existence of Santa Claus in an elementary school setting to the particulars of teenage sexual activity in a high school." In fact, concluded the Court, any reason that is designed to advance the school's legitimate educational goals will suffice: "[E]ducators do not offend the First Amendment by exercising editorial control over the style and content of student speech in school-sponsored expressive activities so long as their actions are reasonably related to legitimate pedagogical concerns."

Applying *Hazelwood*

Following *Hazelwood*, student free speech cases depend on the following issues: Did the speech occur as part of the curriculum or in a situation where it might be perceived as having the endorsement of the school? If not, the case will be resolved based on the *Tinker* test and other principles explained in Section 3.4. If so, did school policy, either explicitly or implicitly by longstanding practice, indicate that the school-sponsored publication or event is a designated public forum (see sec. 3.1)? If the answer is yes (e.g., a school-sponsored newspaper traditionally operated as a forum for students to express their own ideas on topics of their own choosing), the *Tinker* doctrine again applies. If, as in *Hazelwood*, the answer to the second question is no, that is, if the school publication has been maintained as a non-public forum, then the doctrine announced in *Hazelwood* applies. Then the relevant question is whether the actions of school officials in restricting student speech were "reasonably related to legitimate pedagogical concerns." If so, then the restrictions are allowed. But if the censorship had "no valid educational purpose," the First Amendment rights of students have been violated.

Whether a particular activity constitutes a designated public forum or a school-sponsored curricular activity has sometimes been controversial. In one case, a school invited students to paint murals on plywood panels temporarily erected in its halls to block off a construction project. When school officials required that some religiously themed murals be painted over, the free speech case the students brought forced the court to consider whether the panel-painting was a curricular activity. The court announced two guidelines for deciding the issue: expressive activities were curricular if they were (1) supervised by faculty members, and (2) designed to impart particular knowledge or skills to student participants. The court concluded that the activity was curricular because there was faculty supervision and the point of the project was to promote appreciation for art and school spirit. Suppression of the religious murals was permissible because it was not based on the viewpoint expressed by the mural but rather on "content."[38]

In *Walz ex rel. Walz v. Egg Harbor Township Board of Education*,[39] a parent argued that a party in a pre-kindergarten class was a public forum because the students were allowed to exchange gifts. When a student was prohibited from distributing gifts with religious messages, the parents claimed that the prohibition violated their child's free speech rights. The court rejected the claim finding that the party was a highly regulated curricular event with the clearly defined curricular purpose of teaching social skills and respect for others in a festive setting. "At no point during the holiday parties did the school solicit individual views from the young students about the significance of the holiday to them personally." The student, said the court, had ignored the rules of a structured classroom activity with the intention of promoting an unsolicited message. "[T]he school's restrictions on this expression were designed to prevent proselytizing speech that, if permitted, would be at cross-purposes with its educational goal and could appear to bear the school's seal of approval."

Nevertheless, not all activities that occur at school can be classified as school-sponsored. One court rejected a school's argument that the speech of a student club was school-sponsored because the club met on school grounds, had access to the school's daily bulletin, and was allowed to put up posters, use the auditorium, and meet at the flagpole for prayers before the state of the school day. Because the school did not actively or substantively participate in any of the club's activities, the court rejected the school's argument. Wrote the court,

> To adopt the [school district's] definition of "school-sponsored" would devoid that term of any helpful meaning, as nearly every student group activity happening to occur on school grounds can, in some tenuous sense, be described as using school facilities and as designed to impact some sort of knowledge upon its members. Rather for expressive activity to be school-sponsored, the school needs to take affirmative steps in promoting the particular speech.[40]

It is possible for a graduation ceremony to be operated as a designated or limited open forum if the school exercises no control over what is said—either by the way graduation speakers are selected or by vetting speeches in advance.[41] If, as is probably true in the majority of cases, the school retains at least some authority over the substance of graduation speeches, the ceremony is school-sponsored and may be regulated as a non-public forum. The school would be free to exercise control over the content of speeches provided it has a legitimate pedagogical concern. In speeches given at a graduation ceremony that is a school-sponsored forum, the school would be obligated by the Establishment Clause to prohibit prayer, proselytizing, and religious themes in order to avoid giving the impression of government endorsement of religion.[42]

The *Hazelwood* Court's concept of "legitimate pedagogical concern" has also been the subject of litigation. A federal district court concluded that a school had no legitimate pedagogical concern in blocking the publication in the school newspaper of an article about a lawsuit pending against the district.[43] Another court said a school had no legitimate pedagogical reason for preventing a student who was participating in an event in which students developed and sold their own products from selling candy-canes made from pipe cleaners with a card with a religious message.[44]

Bethel School District No. 403 v. Fraser[45] is a pre-*Hazelwood* case that provides an example of both a type and context of student speech that can be regulated by school officials. The case involved a student punished for using "sexual innuendo" in a nominating speech for a fellow student at a school assembly. The student had been warned in advance by teachers not to make the speech, and some of the audience had responded to the speech by yelling, "graphically simulating the sexual activities pointedly alluded to in [Fraser's] speech," or appearing "bewildered and embarrassed."

The lower courts cited *Tinker* in finding the school's actions in violation of the student's free speech rights, but the Supreme Court found important distinctions between the cases. Whereas the school officials in *Tinker* had acted to suppress a disfavored idea (viewpoint discrimination), the Bethel school administrators objected only to the manner of Fraser's speech. The Court felt that it was perfectly appropriate for the school to enforce rules prohibiting "the use of vulgar and offensive terms in public discourse." In fact, the Court believed that such rules would serve the educational purpose of teaching students that "even the most heated political discourse in a democratic society requires consideration for the personal sensibilities of the other participants and audiences." Also mentioned was that, unlike *Tinker*, Fraser's speech occurred as part of a "school-sponsored activity."

The Court summarized its findings as follows:

> We hold that petitioner School District acted entirely within its permissible authority in imposing sanctions upon Fraser in response to his offensively lewd and indecent speech. Unlike the sanctions imposed on the students wearing armbands in *Tinker*, the penalties imposed in this case were unrelated to any political viewpoint. The First Amendment does not prevent the school officials from determining that to permit a vulgar and lewd speech such as respondent's would undermine the school's basic educational mission. A high school assembly or classroom is no place for a sexually explicit monologue directed towards an unsuspecting audience of teenage students. Accordingly, it was perfectly appropriate for the school to disassociate itself to make the point to the pupils that vulgar speech and lewd conduct is wholly inconsistent with the "fundamental values" of public school education . . .

Courts have relied on *Fraser* and *Hazelwood* to permit censorship of student speeches at assemblies, provided the action was based on "legitimate pedagogical concerns." Thus, in *Poling v. Murphy*,[46] the court upheld the punishment of a student whose campaign speech included "rude" and "discourteous" remarks about an assistant principal. The court noted that local officials should be given wide latitude to determine legitimate pedagogical concerns for their schools. In this case, the action was justified by the desire to teach "the art of stating one's views without indulging in personalities and without unnecessarily hurting the feelings of others."

In another case, the Eighth Circuit relied upon *Hazelwood* in concluding that a school could deny a student the right to hold student office because he distributed condoms to underscore his campaign slogan that he was the "safe choice." The school could legitimately block condom distribution in order to avoid the impression that it had given its imprimatur to teenage sexual activity. The court rejected the argument that punishment of the student amounted to improper viewpoint suppression when other candidates were permitted to distribute candy:

> The distribution of condoms is qualitatively different from the handing out of candy or gum. The one can be read to signify approval or encouragement of teenage sexual activity. The other constitutes the traditional bestowing of a de minimis gratuity not associated with any social or political message.[47]

In reaching this decision the court avoided the issue of whether *Hazelwood* allows educators to make viewpoint-based decisions regarding speech in school-sponsored contexts. On this crucial question the circuit courts are split. For example, would it be permissible for a school to permit a student to present a speech at a school assembly outlining the scientific consensus on the causes of global warming while preventing another student from offering a particular religion's differing perspective on the same issue? The First, Third, and Tenth Circuits have concluded that *Hazelwood* permits viewpoint-based suppression of speech as long as the restriction is reasonably related to legitimate pedagogical concerns.[48] However the Second, Sixth, Ninth, and Eleventh Circuits have said that *Hazelwood* requires viewpoint neutrality even in the face of legitimate pedagogical concerns.[49]

In response to *Hazelwood*, several state legislatures have passed Student Freedom of the Press laws requiring that students be given editorial control of their own school newspapers and relieving schools, administrators, and teacher-advisors from any liability for what students write. Where these laws exist, educators may not censor the content of or viewpoint expressed in school newspapers, but only advise students of possible legal, moral, or journalistic problems with their work.[50]

Even in states without Student Freedom of the Press laws, if a school newspaper has been operated as a designated public forum, content and viewpoint neutrality requirements apply. In *Zucker v. Panitz*,[51] a pre-*Hazelwood* case, the court enjoined the principal from barring publication of an advertisement expressing opposition to the Vietnam War. Because the paper was at least a designated public forum, the discriminatory exclusion of the disfavored viewpoint was not permissible. The same result was reached in another case when a school newspaper that had run advertisements for the military refused advertisements for an organization advocating alternatives to military service.[52]

Nevertheless, *Hazelwood* ensures that teachers have ample authority to pursue their educational goals by controlling student speech in the context of course activities and assignments. Several courts have cited *Hazelwood* when affirming the right of teachers to prevent students from selecting a religious topic as the subject of a term paper.[53] However, the *Hazelwood* Court's emphasis on "valid educational" purposes does not authorize school officials to act on personal whim or subjective preferences. The U.S. Department of Education position on religious content in schoolwork is consistent with this principle (see sec. 2.7):

> Students may express their beliefs about religion in homework, artwork, and other written and oral assignments free from discrimination based on the religious content of their submissions. Such home and classroom work should be judged by ordinary

academic standards of substance and relevance and against other legitimate pedagogical concerns identified by the school.

A school may not prevent a student from selecting a religious (or nonreligious) topic when the topic is relevant to the course and work assigned (e.g., write a paper describing the most meaningful event in your life), but it may penalize students who select topics, religious or not, that are not relevant the work assigned (e.g., a student assigned to write a paper on the "Darwinian theory of evolution" who insists on writing about the Biblical theory of creation or the Lamarckian theory of inheritance instead).

Several courts have been willing to expand the implications of *Fraser* and *Hazelwood* beyond the context in which they were decided. One court relied on *Fraser* to permit a principal to suppress displays of a school symbol that Black students and parents found offensive. The court noted that, by its very nature, a "school mascot or symbol bears the stamp of approval of the school itself," and that the desire to avoid insulting a segment of the student body is a legitimate concern.[54] An Arizona court cited *Hazelwood* when approving a school's mandatory dress code on the somewhat novel theory that the students' dress might be perceived by outsiders as having the approval of the school.[55] Basing its reasoning on *Fraser*, a federal district court in Georgia concluded that school officials could, without violating a student's right not to speak, force the student to issue a public apology for her behavior.

If the "school board" can determine "what manner of speech" is inappropriate in the classroom . . . it can also dictate what speech is proper when fulfilling its "charge to inculcate the habits and manners of civility" . . . especially where the prescribed utterance does not touch upon the student's other protected freedoms.[56]

Another court cited *Fraser* in permitting a school to discipline a student for referring to central-office administrators as "douchebags" on a publicly accessible blog affiliated with the school.[57]

The Marilyn-Mason-T-shirt case discussed in Section 3.2 is another example of a court willing to extend the bounds of *Hazelwood* to cover speech that would not normally be considered school-sponsored. The court upheld the authority of school officials to ban Marilyn Manson T-shirts because the "message" of the shirts was inconsistent with the basic educational mission of the school. The court wrote that the T-shirts sported symbols and words that promoted values (e.g., drug use) that were so patently contrary to the school's educational mission that the school had the authority to prohibit them even though there was no proof of disruption.[58]

Not all courts have been willing to expand the implications of *Hazelwood* and *Fraser*, however. In 1992, the Ninth Circuit considered a case in which students claimed a violation of their free speech rights when school officials required them to remove buttons critical of replacement teachers hired during a strike of regular teachers. School officials claimed the buttons were disruptive, but a replacement teacher confirmed that there had been no disruption in her class. In deciding the case, the court declined to rely on *Fraser* because the buttons, which bore such slogans as "I'm not listening to scabs" and "Do scabs bleed?," were not lewd, vulgar, or plainly offensive. *Hazelwood* did not apply either, said the court, because this was not the kind of speech that the public was likely to believe carried the imprimatur of the school. Thus, basing its ruling solely on *Tinker*, the court ruled in favor of the students because school officials had been unable to prove that the buttons were disruptive: "The passive expression of a viewpoint in the form of a button worn on one's clothing is certainly not in the class of those activities which inherently distract students and break down the regimentation of the classroom."[59]

3.4 INDEPENDENT STUDENT SPEECH

The first Supreme Court case to consider the issue of student free speech rights was *Tinker v. Des Moines*. As the cases considered in the previous two sections repeatedly affirm, *Tinker* is still the precedent that controls the regulation of student speech that does not fall into one of the unprotected categories of speech examined in Section 3.2 and is not school-sponsored as discussed in Section 3.3. *Tinker* controls the regulation of what the Court referred to as "independent student speech."

The *Tinker* Case

The *Tinker* case involved a group of students who decided along with their parents to wear black armbands to indicate their objections to the Vietnam War. The administrations of the students' schools became aware in advance of the planned protest and passed a rule forbidding the wearing of armbands at school under penalty of suspension. The students wore the armbands to school, refused to remove them when asked by their principals, and were suspended until the end of their planned protest period, when they returned without armbands.

In order to decide whether the schools had violated the First Amendment rights of the suspended students, the Court had to consider a number of issues. The first issue was whether the constitutional right to freedom of speech applies to students at school. The Court had little trouble deciding this issue in the affirmative because the Constitution is the fundamental law of the land; it applies in all circumstances although sometimes our understanding of it may be modified by special circumstances. "It can hardly be argued," declared the Court, "that either students or teachers shed their constitutional rights to freedom of speech and expression at the schoolhouse gate." At the same time, the Court recognized that "the special characteristics of the school environment" may create one of those circumstances that require modification of the way freedom of speech is understood and applied. "Our problem," wrote the Court, "lies in the area where students in the exercise of First Amendment rights collide with the rules of the school authorities."

The second issue that the Court had to consider was whether the students had in fact engaged in speech. After all, the students had not been punished for speaking, but rather for wearing black bands on their arms. Here again, the Court had little trouble concluding that this type of behavior was an expressive act, "akin to pure speech," as the Court put it, that did fall under the protection of the First Amendment. Freedom of speech serves to protect not only actual talking, but also a variety of activities whose main purpose and effect is to express an idea.

The next and much more difficult issue for the *Tinker* Court was to determine the extent to which school officials are justified in curtailing student speech in accordance with the special circumstances of the school. The Court recognized that the public schools are entrusted with the role of educating the vast majority of children, that this role is crucial to the well-being of society, and that unfettered student speech can sometimes interfere with the accomplishment of the school's educational mission. But the Court also recognized that although any expression of an idea that differs from another person's has the potential to lead to a disturbance, freedom of speech is so important that even schools must endure some risk of disturbance in order to protect the expression of ideas. Based on these principles, the Court concluded that schools are justified in regulating student speech only if and to the extent that regulation is necessary to prevent "material and substantial" disruption of the educational process or to protect the rights of others within the school community.

With these issues decided, the Court's final task was to apply its analysis to the facts at hand. Although the administration claimed that its motivation in banning the armbands had been to prevent disruption of the schools, it was clear to the Court that the real motivation was disagreement with the idea that the students wished to express. After all, the administrations had decided in advance to prohibit the armbands before there was any hint of disruption. There was also evidence that other forms of potentially disruptive symbolic speech, including the wearing of Nazi medallions, had been permitted at the schools and that any disruption actually associated with the wearing of the armbands was extremely minor. Thus, the Court determined that the administrations had overstepped their constitutional bounds and found in favor of the students.

By declaring that students do not leave their right to freedom of speech at the schoolhouse gate, *Tinker* opened the school to the expression of a wide variety of ideas, even those disfavored by school officials or society in general. Although not prohibiting the school from trying to inculcate students in the political values and beliefs of society (see chap. 2), the Court did find that the Constitution requires the school to operate as a marketplace of ideas in which students retain the right to disagree, to formulate their own positions, and, in independent speech, to express their dissent to others. The *Tinker* Court viewed the school as a microcosm of a democratic society with students enjoying a right to freedom of expression strongly analogous to the right of citizens in society at large. At the same time, the *Tinker* Court recognized that school officials have a legitimate interest in maintaining an orderly environment so the school can accomplish its educational mission and that they must sometimes regulate speech in order to do so.

In striking a balance between student free expression rights and the school's legitimate needs, the Court formulated a rule for determining when school officials lawfully may regulate student speech. The *Tinker* test says that school officials may only prohibit student speech that causes, or reasonably could be expected to cause, material and substantial disruption of the school's operations or that "invades" the rights of others.

Applying the *Tinker* Test

The most important implication of the *Tinker* test is that school officials may not punish or prohibit speech merely because of a disagreement with the ideas expressed. Nor may they act to suppress or punish speech because of a generalized fear of disruption. But when school officials can reasonably forecast that a student's speech will disrupt the school's pursuit of its educational mission, they may prohibit the speech. Thus, one court refused to issue an injunction against the long-term suspension of a student who published instructions on how to hack into the school's computer system in an underground newspaper. The court noted that *Tinker* does not require school officials to tolerate speech that has the potential to cause "substantial harm."[60]

Tinker also authorizes schools to enforce reasonable regulations limiting the **time, place, and manner** of student expression even in traditional public forums as long as the regulations are necessary for the school to perform its educational function:

> But conduct by the student, in class or out of it, which for any reason—whether it stems from time, place, or type of behavior—materially disrupts classwork or involves substantial disorder or invasion of the rights of others is, of course, not immunized by the constitutional guarantee of freedom of speech.

Time, place, and manner regulations are designed not to impede the expression of ideas but only to ensure an orderly and efficient use of facilities. Examples include allowing distribution of student-written literature before or after school but not during school hours (time), permitting students to post notices on some bulletin boards but not others (place), and allowing student-initiated speech during lunchtime but prohibiting the use of amplification devices (manner). To be constitutionally permissible, such regulations must meet four criteria: (a) the regulation must be content-neutral (i.e., not based on the subject matter or content of the speech), (b) the regulation must serve a significant governmental purpose such as safety or the allocation of resources among competing uses, (c) the regulation must be narrowly tailored (i.e., not substantially broader than necessary to achieve its purpose), and (d) the regulation must leave ample alternative means to reach the target audience.[61] The Supreme Court has said that a restriction of speech may be justified "if it furthers an important or substantial governmental interest; if the governmental interest is unrelated to the suppression of free expression; and if the incidental restriction on . . . First Amendment freedoms is no greater than is essential to the furtherance of that interest.[62]

Based on these principles, a state court upheld a school rule limiting student rallies and demonstrations to specific locations and times. The purpose of the rule was to ensure the orderly use of school facilities.[63] If the purpose of the rule had been to prevent students from expressing disagreement with school policy, the outcome of the case probably would have been different. A federal district court struck down a rule that only allowed students to distribute literature before and after school. The court noted that the regulation was not necessary to prevent material and substantial disruption of the school.[64] Another court struck down as "not narrowly tailored to serve [the school's] interests" a rule that prohibited the distribution of literature if the literature served "no school purpose."[65]

Regulation of expression can be a legitimate way to allocate a given space to competing uses but should not be used as a subterfuge to censor speech activities because of their content. Whereas it is perfectly legal, perhaps even desirable, to prohibit students from making political speeches during math class, except under very unusual circumstances, it is not permissible to prohibit political speech at times when students are normally free to discuss topics of their own choosing, such as during lunch period.

Political Speech

The *Tinker* test is relevant to the regulation of all manner of independent student speech: unofficial publications including underground newspapers, pamphlets, and questionnaires; clothes, accessories, and buttons bearing messages; symbols of all sorts, including symbols of gang membership and of religious affiliation or belief; and student demonstrations and criticisms of school officials. One court even ruled that one gay male taking another male to the prom was an expressive activity that could only be regulated according to the *Tinker* test.[66]

As in *Tinker*, courts are particularly vigilant in protecting the rights of students to criticize government policy and government officials. Thus, at least two cases have found against schools that prohibited students from wearing T-shirts calling President Bush a chicken hawk, drug addict, and an "international terrorist."[67] The schools involved in these cases were unable to show that the T-shirts were or were likely to become materially and substantially disruptive to the need for discipline and order within the school.

Many cases have arisen out of school attempts to suppress expression that is offensive to a segment of the student body or to the school's desire to impart values like tolerance and respect for diversity. Courts generally permit schools to prohibit students from wearing or otherwise displaying the Confederate flag in school when there are racial tensions in the school that provide a basis for forecasting disruption.[68] Similarly, in *Madrid v. Anthony*[69] the court upheld a school's prohibition of T-shirts that read "We Are

Not Criminals" and "Border Patrol" each of which addressed different sides of an on-going dispute among Hispanic, African-American, and Caucasian students regarding immigration.

In the *Castorina* ex el. *Rewt v. Madison County School Board*,[70] the school did not pre-vail in an attempt to ban Confederate-flag shirts because there was no showing of disruption from the shirts and the school had permitted other students to wear clothing venerating Malcolm X. But what if the situation had been different and there was proof of disruption caused by the Confederate flag T-shirts but not from the Malcolm X clothing? Could the school in that circumstance act to bar the T-shirts while permitting the wearing the Malcolm X clothing? In other words, can a school engage in viewpoint discrimination if the statement of one view creates material and substantial disruption but a statement of the opposing view does not? There is a strong indication in the *Tinker* opinion that view-point discrimination is not permissible. Yet the Court's statement on this point is ambigu-ous: "Clearly, the prohibition of expression of one particular opinion, at least without evidence that it is necessary to avoid material and substantial interference with school-work or discipline, is not constitutionally permissible."

A Ninth Circuit case, *Harper v. Poway Unified School District*[71] involved a student who on a day devoted to the teaching of tolerance wore a T-shirt with statements condemning homosexuality as contrary to God's will. When he refused to remove the T-shirt, the school required him to spend the day in a school conference room doing his homework. No other disciplinary action was taken. The court rejected the claim that the student's free speech rights had been violated, relying on *Tinker's* statement that school officials may prohibit speech which impinges on the rights of other students. In a broad reading of that ruling, the court said students have a right to be free from

> psychological attacks that cause young people to question their self-worth and their rightful place in society . . . Speech that attacks high school students who are members of minority groups that have historically been oppressed, subjected to verbal and physical abuse, and made to feel inferior, serves to injure and intimidate them, as well as to damage their sense of security and interfere with their opportunity to learn.

The court noted that disagreements may justify social or political debate "but they do not justify students in high schools assaulting their fellow students with demeaning state-ments." More generally, the court said, schools may prohibit "the wearing of T-shirts on high school campuses and in high school classes that flaunt demeaning slogans, phrases or aphorisms relating to a core characteristic of particularly vulnerable students and that may cause them significant injury." In sharp contrast to *Harper*, some other courts have protected students' rights to display anti-gay sentiments and slogans attacking the beliefs and practices of other students including in one case a T-shirt that read "INTOLERANT Jesus said . . . I am the way, the truth and the life. John 14:6" and "Homosexuality is a sin! Islam is a lie! Abortion is murder! Some issues are just black and white!" The court found that the fact that the school included students and staff members who were Muslims and homosexuals and some who had had abortions was an insufficient basis to anticipate that there would be disruption.[72]

Hate Speech

Cases like *Harper* that involve **hate speech** pose very difficult legal problems. Some speech that casts racial, religious, and gender groups in a negative light, no matter how invidious, is clearly political ("Only White men should be President"), and some is designed solely to give offense ("Jews suck"). Many examples of hate speech such as the T-shirts described in the previous paragraph do express some sort of political or religious sentiment but in a manner designed to provoke, attack, or offend. Hate speech that falls into the unprotected categories of threat or fighting words may be banned, but political or religious hate speech may only be regulated according to the principles of *Tinker*.

The Supreme Court, in *R.A.V. v. City of St. Paul*,[73] has ruled that cities and states may not suppress speech that gives offense to a racial, ethnic, religious, or gender group merely because of disagreement with the hateful viewpoint being expressed. *Tinker* also prohibits the regulation of student speech merely because of disagreement with the viewpoint expressed but permits regulation of speech that is materially and substantially disruptive or invasive of the rights of others. The latter standard has not been extensively explored in case law but presumably it permits, at a minimum, suppressing and punishing speech that invades the privacy (see sec. 10.3) of or defames (see sec. 10.2) another member of the school community. But speech is not defamatory just because it expresses negative or even hateful opinions of an individual or group. As a practical matter, hate speech within the context of a diverse school will often be materially and substantially disruptive. This fact coupled with an acceptance of the school's legitimate goal of opposing racial discrimination led one federal court to conclude that the principles of the *R.A.V.* decision do not apply to the regulation of independent student speech.[74] In addition, there are federal statutes that require schools to prevent student-on-student racial or sexual harassment (see sec. 5.9).

Drafting regulations that prohibit hate speech without being unconstitutionally vague or overbroad can be very difficult. A rule is impermissibly vague if people "of common intelligence must necessarily guess at its meaning and differ as to its application."[75] An example would be a school rule against "speaking in an irritating manner." A rule is impermissibly overbroad if its effect is to prohibit not only speech that the government is permitted to regulate but also speech that is protected by the First Amendment.[76] An example would be a school rule against speech that makes another person "feel uncomfortable." While this rule could be applied (permissibly) to prohibit lewd talk, threats, and slander, it could also be used (impermissibly) to suppress dissenting opinions on sensitive political issues. (See sec. 4.1 for a more thorough discussion of vagueness and overbreadth.)

One case ruled that the phrase "ill will" in a school's anti-racial-harassment policy was overbroad and probably vague as well. The court noted that the Supreme Court has stated that "the mere fact that expressive activity causes hurt feelings, offense, or resentment does not render the expression unprotected."[77] Another case found against a school's anti-harassment policy that prohibited "verbal . . . conduct . . . which offends, denigrates or belittles an individual because of . . . actual or perceived race, religion, color, national origin, gender, sexual orientation, disability, or other personal characteristics." Citing *Fraser*, *Hazelwood*, and *Tinker*, the court found that the policy would impermissibly allow the school to prohibit student speech that was not lewd, school-sponsored, or disruptive and to engage in viewpoint discrimination. The court noted that school rules whose effect is to prohibit only speech that is defined by federal law as racial harassment (see sec. 5.9) may be permissible.[78]

Heckler's Veto

Whether by word or symbol, the expression of any unpopular idea amidst a hostile audience may produce disruption. Thus, the issue arises whether school officials must protect the maker of a controversial speech or the wearer of a provocative symbol and control the audience or whether they may seek to limit disruption by censoring the expression. More generally, can a hostile audience nullify the free speech rights of the speaker by threatening to be disruptive? Neither *Tinker* nor any other school case addresses the question of the "heckler's veto." Presumably, the initial response of school officials must be to protect the speaker, but a determination of when this may be deemed impractical and steps taken to silence the speaker must await further litigation.

Expression also has the potential to be psychologically disruptive to an unreceptive audience. This was part of the *Harper* court's rationale for allowing the school to suppress anti-gay sentiments, and it is part of the reason that threats and fighting words may be prohibited. In formulating the "material and substantial disruption" standard, the *Tinker* Court was primarily concerned with physical disturbance. But, as in *Harper*, some courts have broadened the notion to include the potential to produce psychological stress in other students. In *Trachtman v. Anker*,[79] the court permitted a school to ban the distribution by high school journalists of a questionnaire eliciting "rather personal and frank information about [other] students' sexual attitudes, preferences, knowledge and experience." School officials had instituted the rule because they feared that students asked to complete the questionnaire might be harmed psychologically. At the trial, some psychologists supported the administration's position and others contradicted it. The court ruled as it did even though no one was forced to fill out the questionnaire and students were alerted to the subject matter of the questionnaire before reading it. The danger of the *Trachtman* courts reasoning is that like the heckler's veto, it has the potential to abrogate the rights granted in *Tinker* by allowing schools to ban any speech that another student might find upsetting.

Protests against the School

Protests against school policies and personnel fall into the category of political speech. Courts generally give students broad latitude to criticize the policies and practices of their schools as well as teachers and school officials. In *Depinto v. Bayonne Board of Education*,[80] fifth-grade students wore buttons with a photograph of a Hitler Youth group to protest their school's mandatory uniform policy. The photograph depicted rows and rows of young men facing in the same direction and wearing the same outfit but without any Nazi symbols visible. The court found that the students had a First Amendment right to wear the button. The court rejected the contentions that the photograph was lewd, vulgar, indecent, or plainly offensive; that the speech could be viewed as school-sponsored; that the speech was likely to cause disruption; and that the *Tinker* test should be interpreted in a more lenient manner in grade schools. With regard to the last issue, a few other courts have given school's broader latitude to control the speech of elementary students than older students.[81]

In *Seamons v. Snow*,[82] a student-athlete, after having been cruelly humiliated by teammates, reported the incident to school officials including the football coach. The coach then brought the student-athlete before the team, accused him of betraying the team by reporting the incident, and when the student-athlete refused to apologize, dismissed him from the team. Among other issues raised in the case was whether the student-athlete had a First Amendment right to file the complaint. The court ruled that under *Tinker* the student-athlete's filing of the complaint was not disruptive, hence protected speech. Another case found a student's free speech rights had been violated when he was suspended for writing a demeaning commentary on the physique of a school official including such statements as: "Because of his extensive gut factor, the 'man' hasn't seen his own penis in over a decade," and "If it is wasn't for his gut, it would still take a magnifying glass and extensive searching to find it." The commentary was contained in an e-mail message that was subsequently brought to school by another student, but there was no evidence that it was disruptive.[83]

At the same time, courts recognize that student protests and demonstrations can sometimes be materially and substantially disruptive to the school and its programs. In *Lowery v. Euverard*,[84] three football players circulated a petition expressing hatred of their coach and a desire not to play for him. When the school found out about the petition, the three players were dismissed from the team. The court ruled in favor of the school. There was a reasonable forecast of disruption from the petition in the form of damage to team cohesion and morale. In another case, members of a basketball team signed a petition asking for the resignation of a coach who had been verbally abusive. Just before a game, the players refused to participate, forcing the school to use junior varsity players. The protesting players were permanently suspended from the team. The court found that the petition itself was protected speech. But the court also concluded that that the students' refusal to play the game—assuming for the sake of argument it was "expressive conduct"—was disruptive so the suspension was upheld.[85] The Eighth Circuit also upheld the dismissal of a student-athlete for circulating a letter to her teammates that called on the other students to "stand up for what we believe in." The court interpreted the letter as "suborning insubordination."[86]

Religious Speech

Religious speech receives vigorous First Amendment protection, but religious speech by students can create tricky problems for school officials. The "Guidance" issued by the Department of Education pursuant to the No Child Left Behind Act (see sec. 2.6) states that schools should not prohibit private student religious speech based on its content. Students who wish to discuss their religious views among themselves during their free time have a right to do so. But what of students who wish to publicize and promote their religious views among their schoolmates? Does freedom of speech protect the right to proselytize at school? Does the Establishment Clause require the school to prohibit this form of speech? Do other students have a right to be protected from being proselytized at school? Is there a conflict between freedom of speech and freedom of religion?

In *Thompson v. Waynesboro Area School District*,[87] the court found in favor of students who had been prohibited from distributing in their school's hallways religious literature written by an outside group. The school had argued that it had a duty to protect other students from receiving religious literature possibly in opposition to their own beliefs and to avoid the appearance that the school endorsed the religious viewpoint of the literature. However, the court concluded on the basis of testimony by the school's principal that "the restrictions . . . were at least to some extent content based" in violation of the students' freedom of speech. The school had permitted the distribution of other types of literature even if written by outside groups and the students' time, place, and manner of distribution had been nondisruptive. After employing the *Lemon* test (see sec. 2.2), the court further declared that allowing distribution of the religious literature would not violate the Establishment Clause.

Other courts have made rulings similar to *Thompson*.[88] A federal court ruled in favor of a third-grade student who had been prohibited from distributing religious literature to other students during noninstructional time. The court noted that the school had permitted the distribution of other literature at the same time and that there was no evidence that the distribution would be disruptive. Allowing the distribution would not pose an Establishment Clause problem, said the court, because it would be apparent that the materials were the personal expression of the student and were not endorsed by the school.[89] In *Adler v. Duval County School Board*,[90] the Eleventh Circuit ruled that the delivery of a religious graduation speech by a student selected by vote of the student body and permitted to decide what to say without supervision from school officials did not violate the Establishment Clause since this was private student speech and not official school sponsorship of religion. This ruling implies that private religious speech by students can only be regulated in accordance with the *Tinker* test. Note, however, that if the school had a significant role in selecting the graduation speaker or deciding what was said, a religious graduation speech would violate the Establishment Clause.[91]

In *Chalifoux v. New Caney Independent School District*,[92] a federal district court in Texas concluded that school officials had failed to present sufficient evidence of disruption to justify their refusal to let students wear rosaries for purely religious reasons. The district claimed that because rosaries were gang symbols for some students, a rule banning the wearing of rosaries for any reason was justified. In rejecting the district's argument, the court found that there had been only one instance on school grounds of students who claimed to be gang members wearing rosaries and that when the plaintiffs in the case wore their rosaries, there was no evidence that they attracted the attention of other students. The court also found that the school's rule against "gang-related apparel" was unconstitutionally vague (see sec. 4.1).

Not all courts have been protective of student religious speech activities. One court ruled that it was permissible to prohibit students from distributing religious literature and otherwise proselytizing in the hallways. The court found that the goal of avoiding any endorsement of religion was important and that the restriction was not a serious infringement on the rights of students because they could distribute their literature off school grounds.[93] The danger of this position is that all student free speech rights could be eliminated on the basis that students could always conduct their speech activities off campus.

Dress Codes and School Uniforms

As noted in Section 3.1, some courts consider choice of clothing to be a form of expression and others do not. For courts that do view a student's choice of clothing as a form of expression, a requirement that students wear a school uniform becomes a restriction on speech in that it prevents student from expressing themselves through their clothes. The Fifth Circuit took this position in dealing with two separate cases challenging school uniform policies on free speech grounds. Finding that the regulations were content-neutral, the court employed the tests used to decide the constitutionality of content-neutral regulations of speech: whether the regulations served an important government purpose and whether they were narrowly tailored to serve that purpose. In ruling in favor of the school districts, the court found that the uniform policies served the important purposes of promoting decorum, decreasing tensions, reducing gang-related activity, reducing discipline problems, and reducing the likelihood that students would be able to bring weapons to school concealed in their clothing. The regulations were narrowly tailored in that any First Amendment infringement was temporary because students could choose what to wear after school. One district's policy also included an opt-out provision for students and parents with bona fide religious or philosophical objections.[94]

The Sixth Circuit took a similar approach in dealing with a middle school dress code that prohibited among other things, visible body piercing, unnaturally colored hair, pants and skirts that are not solid colors, hats, scarves and sweatbands, clothing with holes, platform shoes, flip-flops, stretch knit pants, form fitting or baggy shirts, and tops with writing and logos larger than the size of a quarter. The court found that the code served several

important purposes including bridging socio-economic gaps, focusing attention on learning, increasing school unity and pride, promoting safety, reducing discipline problems,
and improving self-respect. The court also rejected the claim that the code was overbroad,
noting that it applied only during school hours and that students retained other outlets for
expression such as wearing buttons and through school assignments.[95]

The Fourth Circuit in *Newsom* ex rel. *Newsom v. Albemarle County*,[96] concluded that
a school dress code that prohibited students from wearing "messages on clothing, jewelry,
and personal belongings that related to drugs, alcohol, tobacco, weapons, violence, sex,
vulgarity, or that reflect adversely upon persons because of their race or ethnic group" was
overbroad insofar as it barred messages relating to weapons. (The case did not address
other aspects of the code.) The code was so broad in this respect, the court noted, that it
would prevent a student from wearing the state seal of Virginia, which depicts a women
standing with one foot on a vanquished tyrant holding a spear, and other common and
benign athletic and military insignias.

Prior Review

May school officials insist on reviewing student-initiated written materials prior to their
distribution on school grounds? May officials prohibit the distribution of material that
fails to meet specified criteria and, if so, under what circumstances? The Supreme Court
has not considered these issues, and federal circuit courts have given differing answers.

In a 1971 case, *Eisner v. Stamford Board of Education*,[97] the Second Circuit affirmed
the constitutionality of a system of prior review that meets the following criteria: standards for determining whether a publication may or may not be distributed cannot be
vague or overbroad (see sec. 4.1); there must be clear specification of when prior approval
is required and to whom publications are to be submitted; a definite, brief period (say two
to three days) must be established for conducting the review and it must be clearly stated
that distribution may proceed if the school fails to respond within the stated time period;
and students must be made aware of an appeals process in cases of adverse decisions.
Based on these criteria, a federal district court struck down a school's prior-review system
because it lacked clear standards. The system permitted a school official to prohibit distribution of literature that not serve "school purposes" or did not address student needs
or interests. The system also lacked a specific time period for conducting the review.[98] The
Seventh Circuit applied a somewhat different set of criteria in striking down a system of
prior review found to be "per se unreasonable."[99]

In a 1988 case, *Burch v. Barker*,[100] the Ninth Circuit specifically rejected the *Eisner*
court's conclusion and prohibited the school from enforcing any system of prior review.
The case concerned the punishment of students who distributed a nonschool-sponsored
newspaper in violation of a requirement of prior review. School officials "testified that in
their view a predistribution censorship policy was necessary for the safe operation of the
school, to avoid distractions, hurt feelings and career damage to the faculty, to further
parental and community expectations and to avoid potential school liability." However,
the court pointed out that there had been no incidents of disruption relating to the distribution of this or any other publication at the school, that even "[t]he defendants' expert
admitted that he knew of no studies nor any statistics showing that school districts without a system of predistribution review and censorship of student-written communication
experience educational disruption as a result of underground newspapers," and that
"[t]here was no evidence that anyone familiar with [the independent newspaper] confused
it with any school-sponsored publication or believed its contents reflected the view of the
school administration."

Thus, concluded the court, the prior-review rule was based on exactly the sort of "undifferentiated fear or apprehension of disturbance" that the *Tinker* court rejected as a justification for limitations on speech. The court reasoned that the school had no more need to know in advance the content of independent student writing than it had to know in advance the content of independent student talking. "Interstudent communication does not interfere with what the school teaches," wrote the court; "it enriches the school environment . . ." The court was careful to point out that the school did retain the right to stop further distribution of libelous, obscene, and materially and substantially disruptive publications after it had begun and to punish those who distribute such material. But, explained the court, a system of subsequent punishment is far less dangerous than a system of prior review, also called prior restraint:

> A system of prior restraint is in many ways more inhibiting than a system of subsequent punishment: it is likely to bring under government scrutiny a far wider range of expression; it shuts off communication before it takes place; suppression by a stroke of the pen is more likely to be applied . . .; the system allows less opportunity for public appraisal and criticism; the dynamics of the system drive toward excesses, as the history of all censorship shows.

It is likely that some courts would follow the *Burch* decision and others might follow *Eisner* or formulate their own restrictions on prior review. At a minimum, it can be said that because prior review has the potential to discourage expression, the school bears the burden of showing that any system it employs meets First Amendment requirements.

3.5 OFF-CAMPUS SPEECH

Off-campus behavior means behavior that does not occur at school or at a school-sponsored activity. In general, the authority of school officials to control off-campus behavior is limited by state statutes unless the behavior has direct bearing on the operation of the school (see sec. 4.1). When constitutional rights like free speech are involved, the authority of school officials is further limited.

Thomas v. Board of Education[101] concerned a group of students punished by their school for producing and distributing a satirical magazine entitled *Hard Times*, characterized by school officials as "morally offensive, indecent, and obscene." The magazine was written, produced, and sold off-campus and contained a request that the magazine not be brought to school. However, some copies did find their way into the school. In finding that the school had overstepped its constitutional bounds by punishing the magazine's writers, the court reasoned that the school had no legitimate educational purpose that would justify this kind of intrusion into students' off-campus expression. The court's position was that once students leave the school, what they say or write is no business of the school. Otherwise, students' free speech rights could be significantly and impermissibly curtailed by the taste and views of school officials and the patrons of the school district.

Because the students published their newspaper off campus, the *Thomas* court rejected the use of the *Tinker* test. But the court implicitly applied the test, noting that the publication of the newspaper did not create any disruption within the school. The court did not indicate what if any level of school disruption might permit the school to act. Although *Thomas* was decided before *Hazelwood*, the outcomes are consistent. *Hazelwood* might permit school officials to control the contents of an independent newspaper or web site produced in such a manner that it would appear to the community to have the imprimatur of the school. However, in *Thomas*, the student editors of *Hard Times* had taken steps to separate their work from the school and followed the suggestions of school officials regarding this issue.

The *Thomas* case emphasizes the danger of allowing school officials too much latitude to control off-campus student speech. But when student off-campus speech is directly detrimental to a school's ability to perform its educational function, punishment may be allowed. Thus, when a student provided instructions for hacking into a school's computer in an underground newspaper, the court ruled in favor of the school.[102] In *J.S. ex rel. H.S. v. Bethlehem Area School District*,[103] the highest state court in Pennsylvania upheld the expulsion of a student who, in a web site produced off-campus, wrote insulting and probably defamatory statements about teachers and the principal, depicted one teacher with her head cut off, and offered to pay a hit man $20 to kill her. Although the court concluded that the statements did not constitute true threats, it found that the web site caused psychological stress in the staff that was sufficiently disruptive to justify the expulsion. In another case a school was permitted to discipline a student for sending an instant message that included a crudely drawn image of a gun firing a bullet into a person's head with blood splattering. Beneath the drawing were the words "Kill Mr. VenderMolen." The court said that whether or not the message constituted a true threat, it was reasonable for school officials to foresee the risk of material and substantial disruption.[104]

In a 1976 case, a federal court upheld the suspension of a student who made loud, insulting remarks about a teacher at a local shopping mall. The court ruled that the student's comments, "There's Stear . . . He's a prick," were "fighting words," a category of speech that does not receive First Amendment protection (see sec. 3.1) and that failure to discipline the student "could lead to devastating consequences in the school."[105] But students have prevailed in most recent cases involving student off-campus speech that was insulting or demeaning to teachers or other students. In *Klein v. Smith*[106] the court protected a student from suspension after he had made a vulgar gesture with his middle finger at a teacher near a restaurant after school hours. The court wrote,

> Any possible connection between his act of "giving the finger" to a person who happens to be one of his teachers and the proper and orderly operation of the school's activities is, on the record here made, far too attenuated to support discipline against Klein for violating the rule prohibiting vulgar or discourteous conduct toward a teacher. The gesture does not constitute "fighting words" which might justify stripping the communicative aspects of the gesture of a protected status under the First Amendment.

In *Beussink v. Woodland R-IV School District*, a student won a preliminary injunction barring his suspension for the content of his homepage, which was

> highly critical of the administration at Woodland High School. Beussink used vulgar language to convey his opinion regarding the teachers, the principal and the school's own homepage. Beussink's homepage also invited readers to contact the school principal and communicate their opinions regarding Woodland High School.[107]

Another case protected a student from discipline for creating a web site containing "crude and juvenile" materials and describing a number of other students as "losers."[108]

The *Thomas* court refused to view the student-produced newspaper as on-campus speech even though a small ("insignificant," said the court) amount of its production had occurred at school and even though some copies were stored at school. The line between on- and off-campus speech has become somewhat blurred in recent years because electronic communications often make student expression available in school regardless of where it is initiated. In general, courts consider speech to be off campus unless it is initiated at school or the speaker specifically transmits it to school, such as by distributing copies of an underground newspaper at school or posting on a school's official web site. One court found in favor of a student disciplined for sending an e-mail containing vulgar insults concerning school officials to friends who printed the e-mail and distributed it on school grounds.[109] But some courts have allowed schools more leeway to punish speech initiated off campus if the student should have realized that the speech was communicated in a way that it was likely to come to the attention of school authorities.[110]

The mere fact that a student publishes information or opinions about a school or its administrators, teachers, or students does not transform off-campus speech into on-campus speech. Students have the right to publish—either by traditional or electronic means—the information that they attend a particular school and to disseminate facts, information, and opinions about their school.

3.6 FREEDOM OF ASSOCIATION AND USE OF SCHOOL FACILITIES

By organizing associations and speaking as a group, individuals can amplify their voices. Although freedom of association is not explicitly guaranteed by the First Amendment, the Supreme Court has recognized it as a corollary of free speech. As such, the Court in *Healy v. James*[111] has said that public colleges may not deny official recognition to student political organizations or bar them from campus except by application of the *Tinker* test.

Freedom-of-association cases at the high school level generally follow *Healy* in prohibiting schools from banning student groups because they embrace disfavored ideas. For example, in *Dixon v. Beresh*,[112] the court found unconstitutional a principal's refusal to grant recognition as a school organization to a student-organized "Young Socialist Alliance." The principal was acting under a board of education policy forbidding recognition of any group "advocating controversial ideas" or "stressing one side of issues." The court reasoned that the effect of the policy was to suppress the expression of ideas and that there was no legitimate forecast of "material and substantial disruption as required by *Tinker*."

Dixon is consistent with the general free speech doctrine prohibiting schools from engaging in viewpoint discrimination in their regulation of speech. Recall that viewpoint discrimination is impermissible in all forums of speech, including limited public (also called "limited open") forums (see sec. 3.1). In *East High School Prism Club v. Seidel*, a student club obtained an injunction prohibiting the school from denying the club access to the limited open forum created for curriculum-related student clubs. The club "sought to serve as a prism through which historical and current events, institutions, and culture could be viewed in terms of the impact, experience and contributions of gays and lesbians." The school in denying recognition to the group had applied its own rules inconsistently and based the exclusion on the viewpoint it espoused.[113] Similarly, the Third Circuit found that impermissible viewpoint discrimination had occurred when a Bible club was denied the opportunity to meet in an "activity period" that served as a limited open forum.[114]

Whether schools may deny use of school facilities to groups that discriminate on the basis of race, gender, religion, sexual orientation, or other grounds is a very difficult legal question. The Supreme Court has recognized that any law or policy that forces a group with a point of view (referred to by the Court as an "expressive association") to accept members it does not desire has the potential to impair the organization's free speech rights.

The law or policy can only be upheld if it serves a compelling state purpose and is narrowly tailored to achieve that purpose.[115] Based on this doctrine, the Seventh Circuit in *Christian Legal Society v. Walker*[116] granted an injunction prohibiting a university from refusing to recognize a student organization that prevented active homosexuals from becoming voting members or officers. The injunction was granted because the "university's interest in preventing discrimination against homosexuals did not outweigh [the] organization's interest in expressing its disapproval of homosexual activity . . ." A similar result was reached by the Second Circuit in a case in which the school district refused to recognize a religious club because the constitution of the club specified that the club's officers must be Christians. This case was not decided on constitutional grounds but rather on the basis of a federal statute known as the Equal Access Act (see next subsection).[117]

Despite these cases, there are at least two grounds that might in some cases permit schools to deny recognition to organizations that discriminate. First, denial would probably be permissible if it were necessary in order to avoid violating the school's obligations under laws that prohibit schools from maintaining or tolerating a racially or sexually hostile environment (see sec. 5.9). Second, denial would be permissible if an organization's speech activities were materially and substantially disruptive to the order and discipline of the school.

The Equal Access Act

The federal Equal Access Act (EAA)[118] complements the freedom-of-association rights granted to students by the First Amendment. The EAA states in part:

> It shall be unlawful for any public secondary school which receives Federal financial assistance and which has a limited open forum to deny equal access or a fair opportunity to, or discriminate against, any students who wish to conduct a meeting within that limited open forum on the basis of the religious, political, philosophical, or other content of the speech at such meetings.

Schools are not required by the Act to grant recognition to non-curricular clubs. A school might legitimately decide not to recognize any student group for administrative ease or to reserve its resources for school-sponsored purposes.[119] But if a school provides an opportunity for even one noncurricular student group to use school premises during noninstructional time, a limited open forum requiring nondiscriminatory access in accordance with EAA has been created.[120]

The statute further specifies that:

> Schools shall be deemed to offer a fair opportunity to students who wish to conduct a meeting within its limited open forum if such school uniformly provides that—
>
> (1)   the meeting is voluntary and student-initiated;
> (2)   there is no sponsorship of the meeting by the school, the government, or its agents or employees;
> (3)   employees or agents of the school or government are present at religious meetings only in a nonparticipatory capacity;
> (4)   the meeting does not materially and substantially interfere with the orderly conduct of educational activities within the school; and
> (5)   nonschool persons may not direct, conduct, control, or regularly attend activities of student groups.

In *Board of Education of the Westside Community Schools v. Mergens*,[121] the Supreme Court defined "noncurricular related student group" to mean:

> any student group that does not directly relate to the body of courses offered by the school. In our view, a student group directly relates to a school's curriculum if the subject matter of the group is actually taught, or will soon be taught, in a regularly offered course; if the subject matter of the group concerns the body of courses as a whole; if participation in the group is required for a particular course; or if participation in the group results in academic credit. We think this limited definition of groups that directly relate to the curriculum is a commonsense interpretation of the Act that is consistent with Congress' intent to provide a low threshold for triggering the Act's requirements.
>
> For example, a French club would directly relate to the curriculum if a school taught French in a regularly offered course or planned to teach the subject in the near future. A school's student government would generally relate directly to the curriculum to the extent that it addresses concerns, solicits opinions, and formulates proposals pertaining to the body of courses offered by the school. If participation in a school's band or orchestra were required for the band or orchestra classes, or resulted in academic credit, then those groups would also directly relate to the curriculum. The existence of such groups at a school would not trigger the Act's obligations.
>
> On the other hand, unless a school could show that groups such as a chess club, a stamp collecting club, or a community service club fell within our description of groups that directly relate to the curriculum, such groups would be "noncurriculum related student groups" for purposes of the Act. The existence of such groups would create a "limited open forum" under the Act and would prohibit the school from denying equal access to any other student group on the basis of the content of that group's speech. Whether a specific student group is a "noncurriculum related student group" will therefore depend on a particular school's curriculum, but such determinations would be subject to factual findings well within the competence of trial courts to make.

Based on this definition, the Court ruled that denial of recognition to a student-initiated "Christian Club" by a school that recognized a variety of other noncurriculum-related student groups violated the EAA. The Court also rejected the contention that the Act itself violates the Establishment Clause. Other courts have relied on *Mergens* in ruling that a drama club is noncurricular even if the school has a course devoted to the study, but not performance of plays[122] and that a Key Club (student service organization) was noncurricular.[123] In general, for a club to be curricular, there must be a significant connection between the club's focus and a school course, not just a tangential connection or overlap.[124]

EAA only applies when noncurricular clubs are given access to school facilities during "noninstructional time," but the distinction between instructional and noninstructional time is not always obvious. Two circuit courts have issued conflicting rulings. The Third Circuit ruled that a school's "activity period" when students were free to go to club meetings, study hall, or student government meetings, take make-up tests, or attend tutoring was noninstructional time. The fact that the activity period fell within the school day when attendance was mandatory did not make the period instructional time.[125] The Ninth Circuit ruled that a time called "student/staff time" was instructional time because student attendance in the school was required despite the fact that no formal classroom instruction took place except on a voluntary basis.[126] In a different case, the Ninth Circuit held that a lunch period was noninstructional time since no instruction took place during this time and students were not required to remain on campus.[127]

EAA prohibits a school from conditioning access to its facilities for an organization protected by the Act on the organization changing its name, refraining from talking about sex[128] or other controversial topics, or modifying its membership rules. Qualifying clubs must also be given the same access to student publications such as the yearbook, equipment, services, and even financial support as other clubs.[129]

EAA does permit schools to exclude a club if its presence would substantially disrupt the school. But one court made clear that exclusion is only justified if the club itself behaves disruptively. When segments of the community threw the district into turmoil over the possible recognition of a gay-student club, the court ruled that this community-generated disruption did not justify non-recognition of the club.[130] Put another way, students cannot lose their rights under EAA as a result of a heckler's veto (see sec. 3.4).

Use of School Facilities by Outside Groups

Community organizations, camps, Scouting groups, and churches and other religious organizations often wish to meet in schools, distribute materials on campus or in school buildings or through a school's internal mail system, and otherwise take advantage of school facilities to communicate their messages. As with student groups, some of the most difficult issues arise with regard to outside groups that wish to use school facilities for religious purposes. Does a school district's permitting a church or religious study group to use its facilities constitute support or promotion of religion in violation of the Establishment Clause? Does the denial of permission constitute a violation of the religious group's free speech or free exercise rights? Is there a conflict between the Establishment-Clause requirement that schools remain neutral relative to religion and the Free-Speech-Clause requirement that schools not engage in viewpoint discrimination.

The 1993 Supreme Court decision in *Lamb's Chapel v. Center Moriches Union Free School District*[131] involved a New York state law authorizing local school boards to adopt reasonable regulations for the use of school property for ten specific purposes. The list included social, civic, recreational, and entertainment but not religious purposes. Pursuant to the law, a local school district adopted a policy permitting the use of its facilities after school hours for a variety of civic and political purposes provided that "the school premises shall not be used by any group for religious purposes." Based on this policy, the district denied permission to Lamb's Chapel, a local evangelical organization, to show a six-part film series that featured lectures by psychologists who advocated that "Christian family values [be] instilled at an early stage." The district explained that the series appeared "church related."

The Supreme Court unanimously ruled that the district's rule was unconstitutional as applied to the film series. The Court acknowledged that the district, like a private owner of property, could have preserved its property for the use to which it was dedicated and need not have permitted any after-hours use of its property. However, once the district voluntarily made its facilities available for use by after-hours groups, it could not enforce rules designed to exclude expression of specific points of view. The Court explained its ruling as follows:

> That all religions and all uses for religious purposes are treated alike under [the rule] does not answer the critical question of whether it discriminates on the basis of viewpoint to permit school property to be used for the presentation of all views about family issues and child-rearing except those dealing with the subject matter from a

religious viewpoint. There is no suggestion [that] a lecture or film about child-rearing and family values would not be a use for social or civic purposes otherwise permitted by [the] Rule. That subject matter is not one that the District has placed off-limits to any and all speakers. Nor is there any indication . . . that the application to exhibit the particular film involved here was or would have been denied for any reason other than the fact that the presentation would have been from a religious perspective. In our view denial on that basis was plainly invalid . . . "although a speaker may be excluded from a nonpublic forum if he wishes to address a topic not encompassed within the purpose of the forum . . . or if he is not a member of the class of speakers for whose special benefit the forum was created" . . . the government violates the First Amendment when it denies access to a speaker solely to suppress the point of view he espouses on an otherwise includible subject.

The Court further concluded that to permit Lamb's Chapel to use the facilities would not violate the Establishment Clause because it would have neither the purpose nor primary effect of advancing or inhibiting religion and would not foster excessive entanglement with religion.

In 2001, in *Good News Club v. Milford Central School*,[132] the Supreme Court once again ordered a school district to make its facilities available to an outside group. In this case, the school district had refused to permit a private Christian organization to hold weekly after-school meetings for elementary school students at which the students sang religious songs, received Bible lessons, memorized scripture, and were instructed in Christian religious doctrine. Although the dissenting opinion characterized the meetings as "evangelical service(s) of worship," the majority found that the only difference between the activities in *Lamb's Chapel* and in this case was that the Good News Club chose to teach Christian moral lessons through live story telling and prayer, whereas in *Lamb's Chapel*, lessons were taught through films. The Court assumed that the school had created only a nonpublic or limited forum, yet the exclusion was still unconstitutional viewpoint discrimination. The Court also rejected the claim that the Establishment Clause was violated as students could attend only with parental permission so there could be no coercion to participate. Furthermore, said the Court, the Establishment Clause does not foreclose

private religious conduct during nonschool hours merely because it takes place on school premises where elementary school children may be present. [W]e decline to employ Establishment Clause jurisprudence using a modified heckler's veto, in which a group's religious activities can be proscribed on the basis of what the youngest members of the audience might misperceive.

Central to the decision in *Good News Club* was the majority's conclusion that "the club's activities do not constitute mere religious worship, divorced from any teaching of moral values." This suggests that under some circumstances, it would be possible to exclude religious services from a limited open forum based on content rather than viewpoint.[133]

Schools sometimes wish to raise money by selling access to school resources and facilities to outside groups for communicative purposes. Some examples are selling advertisements in school publications or on school buildings and commemorative tiles and bricks to be erected on school walls or grounds. If a school carries out a program like this in a manner that creates a designated public forum (that is, it opens the forum for indiscriminate use by the general public or some segment of the public), then it may not decide to exclude a particular message based on its content. If, as is more often the case, the program creates only a limited open forum (the school clearly maintains editorial control over subject matter), the school may regulate based on content but not on viewpoint.[134]

Schools may also maintain non-public forums of expression in which all speech is school-sponsored. In school-sponsored forums, the school is permitted to limit access to designated speakers and to maintain control of content as long as its actions are based on legitimate pedagogical concerns. The school would, for example, be permitted (and also required by the Establishment Clause) to ban any speech that promotes or denigrates religion. Speech is only school-sponsored if a reasonable observer would view it as emanating from the school. In two cases, courts rejected claims that messages composed by parents on bricks they purchased for permanent placement on school grounds and pamphlets placed in student mailboxes pursuant to a school policy that gave access to the mailboxes to outside groups were school-sponsored speech.[135]

The Fourth Circuit rejected the claim that a district had turned its website and e-mail systems into public forums by including information from third parties and even links to third party web pages. The court found that these vehicles for communicating with the public were designed exclusively to promote the school district's opposition to a bill pending in the state legislature; that the links to other web sites were selected exclusively by the district to support is own message; and that none of the links or other materials were placed in the web site or e-mail at the initiative of the owners of the third party web sites. The district also "disclaimed" the contents of any linked web site, thus emphasizing that only that which appeared on its own web site should be taken as the school district's speech.[136]

The Ninth Circuit rejected a claim by Planned Parenthood that its free speech rights were violated when it was denied the opportunity to purchase advertising in school publications. Basing its ruling on *Hazelwood*, the court upheld the school's position that it may properly prohibit all discussion of controversial topics in its publications and seek to avoid the impression that it approves of Planned Parenthood's position. The court found that the school's policy of excluding advertising relating to birth control products and information was viewpoint-neutral.[137]

Some of the other courts that have considered issues relating to the regulation of school-sponsored speech have required viewpoint neutrality, but some have not.[138] In *Hills v. Scottsdale Unified School District*[139] the court ruled that preventing a religious summer camp from availing itself of the opportunity extended to other nonprofit organizations to distribute literature that was not commercial, political, or religious was viewpoint discrimination. Advertisements of summer camps were generally permitted; hence "if an organization proposes to advertise an otherwise permissible type of extracurricular event, it must be allowed to do so, even if the event is obviously cast from a particular religious viewpoint (so long as all such viewpoints are treated evenhandedly)."

To promote healing after the massacre in Columbine High School, the school invited students, family members of victims, and rescue workers to make glazed tiles that would be installed in the halls of the high school. The court applied *Hazelwood* and interpreted that case not to require viewpoint neutrality. Hence the court upheld the restriction the school imposed that prohibited, among other things, references to the shooting, and religious symbols. The court found these restrictions were reasonably related to the legitimate pedagogical concerns of avoiding "divisiveness and disruption cause by unrestrained religious debate on the walls." The exclusion of references to the shooting helped to foster a positive learning environment and was permissible even though the school itself had posted references to the shooting in several places around the school.[140]

The No Child Left Behind Act (see sec. 2.6) addresses the issue of access to school facilities by Boy Scout groups and other similar organizations:

> Notwithstanding any other provision of law, no public elementary school, public secondary school, local educational agency, or State educational agency that has a designated open forum or a limited public forum and that receives funds made available through the Department shall deny equal access or a fair opportunity to meet to, or discriminate against, any group officially affiliated with the Boy Scouts of America, or any other youth group listed in title 36 of the United States Code (as a patriotic society), that wishes to conduct a meeting within that designated open forum or limited public forum, including denying such access or opportunity or discriminating for reasons based on the membership or leadership criteria or oath of allegiance to God and country of the Boy Scouts of America or of the youth group listed in title 36 of the United States Code (as a patriotic society).

Failure to comply with this requirement could result in the loss of federal funds. However, schools are not required to sponsor organizations covered by the law.[141]

NCLB also requires that secondary schools (except those with a "verifiable" religious objection to military service) "shall provide military recruiters the same access to secondary school students as is provided generally to post secondary educational institutions or to prospective employers of those students."[142] This requirement would seem to mean that military recruiters must be allowed to participate in school "job fairs" and "college nights." *Searcey v. Harris*[143] suggests that a school that makes its facilities available to military recruiters will also be constitutionally required to make its facilities equally available to groups that oppose military service. In *Searcey*, a case that predated NCLB, a peace group wanted to participate in a school's job fair in order to discourage students from entering the military but the school refused. Although the court agreed that the fair was not a public forum in that it was not open to any group that wanted to discuss any topic, the peace group still won the suit because the refusal was solely and impermissibly based on the district's disapproval of the group's point of view.

3.7 SUMMARY

Freedom of speech is a bedrock principle of American law. But almost nothing in law is absolute. Over time, courts have developed an extensive set of doctrines that explicate the extent and limitations of the individuals right to free speech and the extent and limit of the government's power to regulate speech. In general, government may regulate speech only when necessary to achieve a compelling state purpose, and regulations of speech may be no more extensive than necessary to achieve the purpose.

By their very nature, schools are places where students often wish to express their ideas through speech and other means. Inevitably, school officials will disagree with some student ideas and disapprove of some of their means of expression. However, the time has long past when schools could simply order students to keep their opinions to themselves. Like all members of society, students have a constitutional right to freedom of speech and expression even when they pass through the schoolhouse gate. Like all arms of government, the public school must honor this right. But general principles of the law of free speech are to be understood and applied in light of the special circumstances of the school.

There are certain categories of speech including obscenity, threats, fighting words, and defamation of private citizens that receive no constitutional protection. Governments and their agencies including schools, may prohibit or regulate these categories of speech as much as they wish. There are additional categories of speech including lewd, vulgar, and obscene-as-to-minors speech and speech that advocates illegal drug use that are similarly unprotected in the context of the school. Schools may prohibit speech that falls into any of theses categories.

Schools also have a good deal of authority to regulate speech occurring as part of their curriculum or in any situation where speech appears to have the endorsement of the school. In these situations, regulation is permissible as long as it is "reasonably related to legitimate educational concerns." The school may control the content and style of the official school newspaper for various reasons, such as to teach journalism lessons, may limit the topics that students may consider in classroom discussions or assignments, and may prohibit lewd and insulting campaign speeches at school assemblies. However, even in school-sponsored situations, prohibition of speech because of a disagreement with the viewpoint being expressed is legally questionable.

Student speech that does not fall into one of the unprotected categories and is not school-sponsored receives the highest level of legal protection. In *Tinker v. Des Moines*, the Supreme Court ruled that independent student speech may only be prohibited if it materially and substantially disrupts the school's legitimate educational purpose or if it invades the rights of others. Reasonable regulation of the time, place, and manner of speech designed to accommodate competing demands for facilities is permitted, but regulation of independent student speech based on its content or viewpoint is rarely justified. Even rarer are situations in which schools are justified in regulating student speech that occurs off campus.

The free speech principles discussed in this chapter can be extremely complex. Student speech can be tasteless, obnoxious, and seemingly without value. No doubt there are times when school officials are tempted to prohibit students from expressing themselves without worrying too much about the legality of their actions. At such times school officials should bear in mind that a central educational purpose of public schools is to prepare citizens to understand and exercise the right of free speech. This can best be accomplished by letting students exercise free speech rights at school to the greatest extent consistent with the school's other educational needs.

NOTES

1 MADALINE REMMLEIN, SCHOOL LAW (2d ed. 1962).

2 *In re* Gault, 387 U.S. 1 (1967).

3 Clark v. Cmty. for Creative Non-Violence, 468 U.S. 288 (1984).

4 Texas v. Johnson, 491 U.S. 397 (1989).

5 Bishop v. Colaw, 450 F.2d 1069 (8th Cir. 1971); Gfell v. Rickelman, 441 F.2d 444 (6th Cir. 1971).

6 Olesen v. Bd. of Educ. of Sch. Dist. No. 228, 676 F. Supp. 820 (N.D. Ill. 1987); Bivens v. Albuquerque Pub. Schs., 899 F. Supp. 556 (D.N.M. 1995).

7 Canady v. Bossier Parish Sch. Bd., 240 F.3d 437 (5th Cir. 2001); *see also* Long v. Bd. of Educ. of Jefferson County, 121 F. Supp. 2d 621 (W.D. Ky. 2000).

8 Sypniewski v. Warren Hills Reg'l Bd. of Educ., 307 F.3d 243 (3rd Cir. 2002); Boroff v. Van Wert City Bd. of Educ., 220 F.3d 465 (6th Cir. 2000).

9 Miller v. California, 413 U.S. 15 (1973).

10 Chaplinsky v. New Hampshire, 315 U.S. 568 (1942).

11 Lovell v. Poway Unified Sch. Dist., 90 F.3d 367 (9th Cir. 1996).

12 Doe *ex rel.* Doe v. Pulaski County Special Sch. Dist., 306 F.3d 616 (8th Cir. 2002); *compare*, J.S. *ex rel.* H.S. v. Bethlehem Area Sch. Dist., 807 A.2d 847 (Pa. 2002).

13 Bd. of Trustees of State Univ. of N.Y. v. Fox, 492 U.S. 469 (1989); Cent. Hudson Gas & Elec. Corp. v. Pub. Serv. Comm'n, 447 U.S. 557 (1980).

14 FCC v. Pacifica Found., 438 U.S. 726 (1978); *but see* Cohen v. California, 403 U.S. 15 (1971).

15 Perry Educ. Ass'n v. Perry Local Educators Ass'n, 460 U.S. 37 (1983); Ark. Educ. Television Comm'n v. Forbes, 523 U.S. 666 (1998); Cornelius v. NAACP Legal Def. & Educ. Fund, Inc.,

473 U.S. 788 (1985); Lamb's Chapel v. Center Moriches Union Free Sch. Dist., 508 U.S. 384 (1993).

16 Texas v. Johnson, 491 U.S. 397 (1989).

17 Brandenburg v. Ohio, 395 U.S. 444 (1969).

18 Schenck v. United States, 249 U.S. 47 (1919).

19 United States v. O'Brien, 391 U.S. 367 (1968).

20 *Compare* Edwards v. South Carolina, 372 U.S. 229 (1963), *with* Feiner v. New York, 340 U.S. 315 (1951).

21 393 U.S. 503, see sec. 3.4.

22 551 U.S. 393 (2007).

23 Boroff v. Van Wert City Bd. of Educ., 220 F.3d 465 (6th Cir. 2000).

24 Williams v. Spencer, 622 F.2d 1200 (4th Cir. 1980).

25 *See* McIntire v. Bethel Indep. Sch. Dist. 804 F. Supp. 1415 (W.D. Okla. 1992).

26 Doe *ex rel.* Doe v. Pulaski County Special Sch. Dist., 263 F.3d 833 (8th Cir. 2001); Doe *ex rel.* Doe v. Pulaski County Special Sch. Dist., 306 F.3d 616 (8th Cir. 2002); J.S. v. Bethlehem Area Sch. Dist., 807 A.2d 847 (Pa. 2002); S.G. *ex rel.* A.G. v. Sayreville Bd. of Educ., 333 F.3d 417 (3d Cir. 2003).

27 257 F.3d 981 (9th Cir. 2001).

28 Porter *ex rel.* Leblanc v. Ascension Parish Sch., 301 F. Supp. 2d 576 (M.D. La. 2004).

29 Boim v. Fulton County Sch. Dist., 494 F.3d 978 (11th Cir. 2007). *See also* Finkle v. Bd. of Educ. of Syosset Cent. Sch. Dist., 386 F. Supp. 2d 119 (E.D.N.Y. 2005).

30 Ponce v. Socorro Independent Sch. Dist., 432 F. Supp. 2d 682 (W.D. Tex. 2006). *See also* In re George T., 93 P.3d 1007 (Cal. 2004).

31 Ginsberg v. New York, 390 U.S. 629 (1968).

32 Chandler v. McMinnville Sch. Dist., 978 F.2d 524 (9th Cir. 1992).

33 861 F. Supp. 157 (D. Ma. 1994), *modified*, 55 F.3d 20 (1st Cir. 1995).

34 Broussard v. Sch. Bd. of City of Norfolk, 801 F. Supp. 1526 (E.D. Va. 1992).

35 Anderson v. Milbank Sch. Dist. 25–4, 2000 DSD 49 (S.D. 2000).

36 Papish v. Bd. of Curators of Univ. of Mo., 410 U.S. 667 (1973).

37 484 U.S. 260 (1988).

38 Bannon v. Sch. Dist. of Palm Beach County, 387 F.3d 1208 (11th Cir. 2004).

39 342 F.3d 271 (3d Cir. 2003).

40 Westfield High Sch. L.I.F.E. Club v. City of Westfield, 249 F. Supp. 2d 98 (D. Mass. 2003).

41 Adler v. Duval County Sch. Bd., 250 F.3d 1330 (11th Cir. 2001).

42 Cole v. Oroville Union High Sch. Dist., 228 F.3d 1092 (9th Cir. 2000).

43 Dean v. Utica Cmty. Schs., 345 F. Supp. 2d 799 (E.D. Mich. 2004).

44 Curry *ex rel.* Curry v. Sch. Dist. of the City of Saginaw, 452 F. Supp. 2d 723 (E.D. Mich. 2006).

45 478 U.S. 675 (1986).

46 872 F.2d 757 (6th Cir. 1989).

47 Henerey *ex rel.* Henerey v. St. Charles, 200 F.3d 1128 (8th Cir. 1999).

48 Fleming v. Jefferson County Sch. Dist. R-1, 298 F.3d 918 (10th Cir. 2002); C.H. *ex rel.* Z.H. v. Oliva, 195 F.3d 167 (3d Cir. 1999), *vacated*, 197 F.3d 63 (3d Cir. 1999) (en banc), *aff'd in part and rev'd in part*, 226 F.3d 198 (3d Cir. 2000) (en banc); Ward v. Hickey, 996 F.2d 448 (1st Cir. 1993).

49 Kincaid v. Gibson, 191 F.3d 719 (6th Cir. 1999), *rev'd on other grounds*, 236 F.3d 342 (6th Cir. 2001) (en banc); Planned Parenthood v. Clark County Sch. Dist., 941 F.2d 817 (9th Cir. 1991); Searcey v. Harris, 888 F.2d 1314 (11th Cir. 1989); *compare* Downs v. Los Angeles Unified Sch. Dist., 228 F.3d 1003 (9th Cir. 2000); Peck v. Baldwinsville Cent. Sch. Dist., 426 F.3d 617 (2d Cir. 2005).

50 KAN. STAT. ANN. §§ 72.1504–72.1506.

51 299 F. Supp. 102 (S.D.N.Y. 1969).

52 San Diego Comm. Against Registration & the Draft v. Governing Bd. of Grossmont Union High Sch. Dist., 790 F.2d 1471 (9th Cir. 1986).

53 Settle v. Dickson County Sch. Bd., 53 F.3d 152 (6th Cir. 1995); Duran v. Nitsche, 780 F. Supp. 1048 (E. D. Pa. 1991), *vacated*, 972 F.2d 1331 (3d Cir. 1992).

54 Crosby v. Holsinger, 852 F.2d 801 (4th Cir. 1988).

55 Phoenix Elementary Sch. Dist. No. 1 v. Green, 943 P.2d 836 (Ariz. Ct. App. 1997).

56 Kicklighter v. Evans County Sch. Dist., 968 F. Supp. 712 (S.D. Ga. 1997), *aff'd*, 140 F.3d 1043 (11th Cir. 1998).

57 Doninger v. Niehoff, 527 F.3d 41 (2d Cir. 2008).

58 Boroff v. Van Wert City Bd. of Educ., 220 F.3d 465 (6th Cir. 2000).

59 Chandler v. McMinnville Sch. Dist., 978 F.2d 524 (9th Cir. 1992).

60 Boucher v. Sch. Bd. of Sch. Dist. of Greenfield, 134 F.3d 821 (7th Cir. 1998).

61 Ward v. Rock Against Racism, 491 U.S. 781 (1989); Clark v. Cmty for Creative Non-Violence, 468 U.S. 288 (1984).

62 United States v. O'Brien, 391 U.S. 367 (1968).

63 Lipkis v. Caveney, 96 Cal. Rptr. 779 (Cal. Ct. App. 1971).

64 Raker v. Frederick County Pub. Schs., 470 F. Supp. 2d 634 (W.D. Va. 2007).

65 M.B. *ex rel.* Martin v. Liverpool Cent. Sch. Dist., 487 F. Supp. 2d 117 (N.D.N.Y. 2007).

66 Fricke v. Lynch, 491 F. Supp. 381 (D.R.I. 1980); *but see* Harper v. Edgewood Bd. of Educ., 655 F. Supp. 1353 (S.D. Ohio 1987).

67 Guiles v. Marineau, 461 F.3d 320 (2d Cir. 2006); Barber v. Dearborn Pub. Sch., 286 F. Supp. 2d 847 (E.D. Mich. 2003).

68 Scott v. Sch. Bd. of Alachua County, 324 F.3d 1246 (11th Cir. 2003); Denno v. Sch. Bd. of Volusia County Florida, 218 F.3d 1267 (11th Cir. 2000); West v. Derby Unified Sch. Dist. No. 260, 206 F.3d 1358 (10th Cir. 2000); Melton v. Young, 465 F.2d 1332 (6th Cir. 1972).

69 510 F. Supp. 2d 425 (S.D. Tex. 2007).

70 246 F.3d 536 (6th Cir. 2001).

71 445 F.3d 1166 (9th Cir. 2006); *see also* Governor Wentworth Reg. Sch. Dist. v. Hendrickson, 421 F. Supp. 2d 410 (D.N.H. 2006); Bar-Navon v. Sch. Bd. of Brevard County, 2007 U.S. Dist. LEXIS 82044 (M.D. Fla. 2007).

72 Nixon v. Northern Local Sch. Dist. Bd. of Educ., 383 F. Supp. 2d 965 (S.D. Ohio, E.D. 2005); *see also* Chambers v. Babbit, 145 F. Supp. 1068 (D. Minn. 2001).

73 505 U.S. 377 (1992).

74 Sypniewski v. Warren Hills Reg'l Bd. of Educ., 307 F.3d 243 (3d Cir. 2002).

75 Connally v. General Constr. Co., 269 U.S. 385 (1926).

76 Gooding v. Wilson, 405 U.S. 518 (1972).

77 Sypniewski v. Warren Hills Reg'l Bd. of Educ., 307 F.3d 243 (3d Cir. 2002); *but see* West v. Derby Unified Sch. Dist. No. 260, 206 F.3d 1358 (10th Cir. 2000).

78 Saxe v. State College Area Sch. Dist., 240 F.3d 200 (3d Cir. 2001).

79 563 F.2d 512 (2d Cir. 1977).

80 514 F. Supp. 2d 633 (N.J. 2007).

81 S.G. *ex rel.* A.G. v. Sayreville Bd. of Educ., 333 F.3d 417 (3d Cir. 2003); Walz *ex rel.* Walz v. Egg Harbor Township Bd. of Educ., 342 F.3d 271 (3d Cir. 2003); Muller *ex rel* Muller v. Jefferson Lighthouse Sch., 98 F.3d 1530 (7th Cir. 1996).

82 84 F.3d 1226 (10th Cir. 1996).

83 Killion v. Franklin Regional Sch. Dist., 136 F. Supp. 2d 446 (W.D. Pa. 2001); see sec. 4.5 regarding regulation of speech initiated off campus.

84 497 F.3d 584 (6th Cir. 2007).

85 Pinard v. Clatskanie Sch. Dist., 467 F.3d 755 (9th Cir. 2006), *amended opinion.*

86 Wildman v. Marshalltown Sch. Dist., 249 F.3d 768 (8th Cir. 2001).

87 673 F. Supp. 1379 (M.D. Pa. 1987).

88 Slotterback v. Interboro Sch. Dist., 766 F. Supp. 280 (E.D. Pa. 1991); Rivera v. E. Otero Sch. Dist., R-1, 721 F. Supp. 1189 (D. Colo. 1989); Nelson v. Moline Sch. Dist. No. 40, 725 F. Supp. 965 (C.D. Ill. 1989).

89 M.B. *ex rel.* Martin v. Liverpool Cent. Sch. Dist., 487 F. Supp. 2d 117 (N.D. 2007).

90 250 F.3d 1330 (11th Cir. 2001).

91 Cole v. Oroville Union High Sch. Dist., 228 F.3d 1092 (9th Cir. 2000).

92 976 F. Supp. 659 (S.D. Tex. 1997).

93 Hemry v. Sch. Bd. of Colo. Springs Sch. Dist. No. 11, 760 F. Supp. 856 (D. Colo. 1991).

94 Littlefield v. Forney Indep. Sch. Dist., 268 F.3d 275 (5th Cir. 2001); Canady v. Bossier Parish Sch. Bd., 240 F.3d 437 (5th Cir. 2001); *see also* Long v. Bd. of Educ. of Jefferson County, 121 F. Supp. 2d 621 (W.D. Ky. 2000).

95 Blau v. Fort Thomas Pub. Sch. Dist., 401 F.3d 381 (6th Cir. 2005).

96 354 F.3d 249 (4th Cir. 2003). *See also* Griggs *ex rel.* Griggs v. Fort Wayne Sch. Bd., 359 F. Supp. 2d 731 (N.D. Ind. 2005).

97 440 F.2d 803 (2d Cir. 1971).

98 M.B. *ex rel.* Martin v. Liverpool Cent. Sch. Dist., 487 F. Supp. 2d 117 (N.D. 2007); *see also* Westfield High Sch. L.I.F.E. Club v. City of Westfield, 249 F. Supp. 2d 98 (D. Mass. 2003).

99   Muller v. Jefferson Lighthouse Sch., 98 F.3d 1530 (7th Cir. 1996); *see also* Sullivan v. Houston Indep. Sch. Dist., 475 F.2d 1071 (5th Cir. 1973).

100   861 F.2d 1149 (9th Cir. 1988); *see also* Fujishima v. Bd. of Educ., 460 F.2d 1355 (7th Cir. 1972).

101   607 F.2d 1043 (2d Cir. 1979).

102   Boucher v. Sch. Bd. of the Sch. Dist. of Greenfield, 134 F.3d 821 (7th Cir. 1998).

103   807 A.2d 847 (Pa. 2002).

104   Wiseniewksi v. Weedsport Cent. Sch. Dist., 494 F.3d 34 (2d Cir. 2007).

105   Fenton v. Stear, 423 F. Supp. 767 (W.D. Pa. 1976).

106   635 F. Supp. 1440 (D. Me. 1986).

107   30 F. Supp. 2d 1175 (E.D. Mo. 1998).

108   Coy v. Bd. of Educ. of North Canton City Schs., 205 F. Supp. 2d 791 (N.D. Ohio 2002)

109   Killion v. Franklin Reg'l Sch. Dist., 136 F. Supp. 2d 446 (W.D. Pa. 2001). *See also* Layshock *ex rel.* Layshock v. Hermitage Sch. Dist., 496 F. Supp. 2d 587 (W.D. Pa. 2007).

110   Wiseniewksi v. Weedsport Cent. Sch. Dist., 494 F.3d 34 (2d Cir. 2007).

111   408 U.S. 169 (1972).

112   361 F. Supp. 253 (E.D. Mich. 1973).

113   95 F. Supp. 2d 1239 (C.D. Utah 2000); *see also* Gay Lib v. Univ. of Mo., 558 F.2d 848 (8th Cir. 1977); Gay Student Serv. v. Tex. A&M Univ., 737 F.2d 1317 (5th Cir. 1984).

114   Donovan v. Punxsutawney Area Sch. Bd., 336 F.3d 211 (3d Cir. 2003).

115   Boy Scouts of America v. Dale, 530 U.S. 640 (2000).

116   453 F.3d 853 (7th Cir. 2006).

117   Hsu v. Roslyn Union Free Sch. Dist. No. 3, 85 F.3d 839 (2d Cir. 1996).

118   20 U.S.C. § 4071.

119   Student Coalition for Peace v. Lower Merion Sch. Dist. Bd. of Sch. Dirs., 776 F.2d 431 (3d Cir. 1985).

120   High Gay/Straight Alliance v. Bd. of Educ. of Salt Lake City Sch. Dist., 81 F. Supp. 2d 1166, 1184 (D. Utah 1999).

121   496 U.S. 226 (1990).

122   Boyd County High Sch. GSA v. Bd. of Educ. of Boyd County, 258 F. Supp. 2d 667, 690–91 (E.D. Ky. 2003).

123   Pope v. East Brunswick Bd. of Educ., 12 F.3d 1244 (3d Cir. 1993).

124   Colin *ex rel.* Colin v. Orange Unified Sch. Dist., 83 F. Supp. 2d 1135 (C.D. Cal. 2000).

125   Donovan v. Punxsutawney Area Sch. Bd., 336 F.3d 211 (3d Cir. 2003).

126   Prince v. Jacoby, 303 F.3d 1074 (9th Cir. 2002).

127   Ceniceros v. Board of Trustees, 106 F.3d 878, 880 (9th Cir. 1997).

128   Colin *ex rel.* Colin v. Orange Unified Sch. Dist., 83 F. Supp. 2d 1135 (C.D. Cal. 2000).

129   Prince v. Jacoby, 303 F.3d 1074 (9th Cir. 2002).

130   Boyd County High Sch. GSA v. Bd. of Educ. of Boyd County, 258 F. Supp. 2d 667 (E.D. Ky. 2003).

131   508 U.S. 384 (1993).

132   533 U.S. 98 (2001).

133   *See* Bronx Household of Faith v. Bd. of Educ., 331 F.3d 342 (2d Cir. 2003).

134   *See* Hills v. Scottsdale Unified Sch. Dist. No. 48, 329 F.3d 1044 (9th Cir. 2003); Seidman v. Paradise Valley Unified Sch. Dist. No. 69, 327 F. Supp. 2d 1098 (Ariz. D. 2004); DiLoreto v. Downey Unified Sch. Dist. Bd. of Educ., 196 F.3d 958 (9th Cir. 1999).

135   Rusk v. Clearview Local Schs., 379 F.3d 418 (6th Cir. 2004); Demmon v. Loudon County Pub. Schs., 342 F. Supp. 2d 474 (E.D. Va. 2004).

136   Page v. Lexington County Sch. Dist. One, 531 F.3d 275 (4th Cir. 2008).

137   Planned Parenthood v. Clark County Sch. Dist., 941 F.2d 817 (9th Cir. 1991) (en banc).

138   Seidman v. Paradise Valley Unified Sch. Dist. No. 69, 327 F. Supp. 2d 1098 (Ariz. D. 2004); *contra* Fleming v. Jefferson County Sch. Dist. R-1, 298 F.3d 918 (10 Cir. 2002).

139   329 F.3d 1044 (9th Cir. 2003).

140   Fleming v. Jefferson County Sch. Dist. R-1, 298 F.3d 918 (10th Cir. 2002).

141   20 U.S.C. § 7908.

142   20 U.S.C. § 7905.

143   888 F.2d 1314 (11th Cir. 1989).

4   Student Discipline

Most school administrators are all too familiar with activities designed to control student conduct. Indeed, the duties of school administrators have always included tasks that, in society at large, are the province of legislators, police, courts, and penal systems. This chapter provides the legal basis for the performance of these tasks. The chapter considers the formulation of school codes of conduct, the investigation of suspected misconduct, and the assignment and enforcement of punishment.

The always complex job of maintaining order in school and disciplining students when they misbehave has become a very high profile function in recent decades. Parents consistently place school safety at or near the top of their list of educational concerns. Highly publicized incidents of shootings and other serious criminal acts at schools have led to public and legislative pressure to rid schools of violence, weapons, and drugs. Researchers have concluded that when the atmosphere of the school leads students to feel unsafe, learning decreases, thereby further emphasizing the need to maintain an orderly environment.

These sociological and psychological trends have been accompanied by significant changes in the law. These changes have both empowered school officials to deal with disruptions and increased the legal threat to school officials if they fail to deal with violence and crime adequately. Some states' constitutions actually give students the right to safe schools.[1] The federal No Child Left Behind Act requires that any student who attends a "persistently dangerous public school" or who becomes a victim of a violent crime at school must be allowed to transfer to a safe public school or charter school within the district. States are required to determine which schools are to be classified as persistently dangerous in consultation with school districts.[2]

Most states have adopted so called Safe School Acts that impose on school boards a duty to adopt disciplinary policy review committees and student codes of conduct and require school administrators to report to law enforcement officials whenever they believe that certain specified categories of criminal activity have occurred at school. School officials who fail to comply with these requirements may face liability for negligent indifference to dangerous school conditions. This statutory liability supplements the preexisting common law duty (discussed in chap. 10) that all school officials have to provide adequate supervision in schools and to protect students from violence by other students. Some Safe School Acts also make the perpetrator of violence liable to the victim for double or even treble damages and make parents accountable for the harmful behavior of their children. Criminal penalties have also been increased for students possessing guns or drugs or committing violence in school.

Many states' statutes authorize schools to employ specialized security personnel, often referred to as "school resource officers" or "SROs," to assist with the effort to combat crime and misbehavior within the school. The authorizing statutes vary significantly from state to state as to the circumstances and conditions under which SROs may be employed, the status of the officers, the extent of their law enforcement authority, and whether they are permitted to carry weapons.[3] Clearly, society places a high priority on the provision of a safe and orderly school.

At the same time, school officials who are overly zealous in carrying out their disciplinary responsibilities face possible legal liability for violating the rights of their students under federal and state law. A federal law known as Section 1983 makes it possible for students to collect monetary damages from school officials who violate their clearly established constitutional or statutory rights (see sec. 10.10). School officials who conduct very invasive searches of students in violation of constitutional guidelines or who impose impermissibly harsh or cruel punishment on students are especially vulnerable.

School officials thus must walk a narrow path. The law demands, communities expect, and students deserve a vigorous effort to maintain a safe and orderly school environment. Yet, in all functions relating to student discipline, the law demands that the rights of students as persons under federal and state constitutions be protected. At the same time, the law recognizes that the school's need for an orderly environment and the special status of students as children justify more control than the society at large exercises over adults. Many of the most difficult questions in education law concern the conflict between the individual rights of students and the corporate needs of the school.

The basic principle of lawful student discipline is that schools can justify only as much rule-making, policing, adjudicating, and punishing as is necessary to promote their legitimate goals. Schools should utilize all lawful means to control student behavior when control is necessary to protect persons or property, promote learning, or prevent disruption of the educational process; however, gratuitous control of students is not justifiable. The law will support school officials when they act reasonably to promote safety and order, but care must be taken not to suppress or punish unpopular behavior when there is no legitimate reason to do so.

4.1 CODES OF CONDUCT

Primary responsibility for the formulation of student codes of conduct rests with local school boards, but both federal and state statutes impose some requirements. The federal Gun-Free Schools Act[4] mandates that any state receiving federal funds (all do) enact a law requiring local educational agencies to expel or suspend for not less than a year any student who brings a firearm to school. Federal statutes also require schools to adopt and enforce rules prohibiting racial and sexual harassment (see sec. 5.9).

Some states have statutes requiring schools to suspend students for certain specified acts. California's list of offenses mandating suspension includes attempting or threatening the use of force, possession of a controlled substance, theft, commission of an obscene act, and intimidating witnesses in a school disciplinary hearing, among others.[5] A number of states also have statutes requiring districts to adopt policies addressing bullying, harassment, and intimidation.[6]

State legislatures have delegated to local school boards, usually in broad and general terms, the authority to maintain discipline and order in the schools.[7] Once, most school boards executed their delegated disciplinary authority without a large number of expressly stated written rules of student conduct. Students were simply ordered not to misbehave, and it was left to administrators and teachers to decide whether misbehavior had occurred and what to do about it. This system—mirroring the internal processes of the family—was consistent with the view of educators as surrogate parents. Just like parents, educators had broad latitude in evaluating and responding to the behavior of the children in their charge.

Discipline without rules has certain advantages, especially when the disciplinarian is thoughtful and well-meaning. The absence of preestablished regulations and procedures can promote the creative resolution of disciplinary problems, whereas rigid regulation can promote conflict, with students and school officials behaving like opposing lawyers seeking strategic advantage through the exploitation of loopholes. An excessive reliance on rules can change the relationship between students and teachers from familiar to estranged.

However, discipline without a formal written set of rules has important disadvantages. Broad discretion almost inevitably leads to the inequitable application of standards and punishment on the basis of race, sex, social class, personal dislike, or negative reputation. Moreover, in the absence of a formal system of rules, students may remain confused and uncertain about the limits of acceptable behavior.

In the terminology of constitutional law, an authority system that operates without explicit rules raises an issue of due process. The Fourteenth Amendment prohibits states from depriving persons of life, liberty, or property without due process of law. One of the implications of this requirement is that people may be convicted and punished for criminal acts only on the basis of laws that were adopted prior to the commission of the acts. The idea is that fairness demands that people be notified in advance of behavior that is unacceptable so that they may conform their behavior to required standards. In addition, the existence of preestablished rules helps avoid the problem of different law enforcement officials taking different views as to what is allowable.

Sensitive to the dangers of interjecting the formal requirements of adult criminal law into the schools, the courts have struck a compromise. On the one hand, punishment of flagrantly disruptive and destructive behaviors that ordinary students can reasonably be expected to realize are prohibited, such as fighting and vandalism, is permitted even without prior announcement of rules.[8] On the other hand, most courts do require preestablished rules for the punishment of conduct that many students would not realize as a matter of common sense is prohibited. A few courts go so far as to require on constitutional grounds that the rules be written,[9] and state statutes may also require written rules. Additionally, some courts require published rules when speech activities are prohibited or when penalties are particularly severe.[10] Even if courts do not always demand it, many schools wisely choose to develop a written code of student conduct to encourage compliance and avoid unfairness, confusion, and potential litigation.

School boards generally have broad powers to control student conduct delegated to them by the legislature[11] that they in turn may delegate to their professional employees. However, some rules go beyond the scope of the school's authority. *Neuhaus v. Federico*[12] involved a challenge by a group of boys to a high school's rule regulating the length of male students' hair. The rule had been adopted by a committee of students, parents, and teachers and approved by a vote of the student body as part of a dress code. The school defended the rule as authorized by a state statute allowing school boards to "establish rules for the government of the schools and pupils." Interpreting the statute as authorizing only rules that "have some reasonable connection to the educational process," the court ruled in favor of the students. The school could present no credible evidence that long hair on boys was likely to cause disruption or pose a health and safety risk or in any way interfere with the operation of the school. Furthermore, the court was concerned that the rule impermissibly and arbitrarily regulated off-campus behavior because, unlike clothing, hair length could not be modified upon returning home. Finally, although the court commended the school for allowing students to develop their own dress code, it pointed out that the school could not enforce a rule that was beyond its scope of authority regardless of the origin of the rule.

Several other, but not all, courts have agreed with *Neuhaus* that hair regulations are beyond the statutory authority of the school.[13] However, most cases attacking rules governing the length of students' hair are based on state or federal constitutional protections of free speech, free exercise of religion, or equal protection. Cases based on free speech often fail because many courts do not consider hair length a form of expression.[14] Likewise, free exercise claims usually fail unless the plaintiff can show that the regulation requires violating an important and clearly established tenet of religion, not just custom or preference.[15] In one case, Native-American students were able to use the Free Exercise Clause in conjunction with other constitutional principles to bar enforcement of a rule that boys' hair should be no longer than the top of a standard dress collar. The plaintiffs presented expert testimony that long hair was an aspect of Native-American religious life, that it had important symbolic meaning (i.e., it was a form of speech), and that the right of parents to control the upbringing of their children would be compromised by enforcement of the rule. The school was unable to prove that the hair regulation was necessary to maintain order in the school.[16]

Fourteenth Amendment-based challenges to hair regulation often invoke the right of privacy, a liberty interest protected by the Due Process Clause.[17] Plaintiffs have succeeded in the First, Second, Fourth, Seventh, and Eighth Circuits,[18] but the Third, Fifth, Sixth, Ninth, Tenth, and Eleventh Circuits have upheld the regulations.[19] In a case based on its state constitution, the Texas Supreme Court concluded that minors do not have the same constitutional rights under the Texas Constitution as adults. Hence, a school's restrictions on hair length and the wearing of earrings did not raise a state constitutional issue.[20] It is questionable whether most other state high courts would endorse this reasoning.

The authority of school officials to regulate what students wear has also been challenged on statutory and constitutional grounds. For the most part, courts have affirmed the statutory authority of schools to enforce reasonable clothing regulations. For example, in *Fowler v. Williamson*,[21] the court allowed the school to prohibit the wearing of jeans to graduation. However, several courts have concluded that school officials exceeded their authority when they barred female students from wearing pants or culottes without proof that wearing these garments caused disruption, endangered the safety of students, harmed instructional effectiveness, or injured student morals.[22]

In evaluating a constitutionally based challenge to a school's dress code, the court in *Wallace v. Ford*[23] concluded that although students do enjoy a constitutional right to govern their appearance, the school may nevertheless enforce rules designed to promote its educational mission. The court noted that less justification is needed for clothing regulations than hair regulations because the latter also control students' appearance away from school, but the former do not. Based on this approach, the court upheld regulations prohibiting excessively tight skirts or pants and skirts more than six inches above the knee, but disallowed regulations prohibiting frayed trousers, tie-dyed clothing, and longer skirts. Another court disallowed a rule prohibiting the wearing of jeans.[24] Generally, school dress codes are constitutionally permissible when necessary to avoid distraction or disruption of the educational process. (See discussion of school uniforms in sec. 3.4.)

The once-common practice of excluding married students from school was found to exceed the district's authority in *Carrollton-Farmers Branch Independent School District v. Knight*;[25] however, several courts have allowed rules excluding married students from extracurricular activities.[26] Even if they are within the school's statutory authority, rules that discriminate against married students might violate their constitutional right of privacy.[27]

When schools seek to regulate off-campus behavior, their authority may be challenged. A number of mostly older decisions affirm the school's authority to prohibit such conduct as drinking, drug use, fighting, and patronizing certain stores and events, but they are of questionable validity today. Most recent cases only permit regulation of off-campus conduct that "has a direct and immediate effect on the discipline or general welfare of the school."[28] Thus, although disciplining a student for attacking a teacher off school grounds is definitely permissible, most out-of-school behavior is beyond the school's power. (See sec. 3.5 regarding regulation of off-campus speech.)

School rules may be challenged on constitutional grounds if they are arbitrary or unreasonable. "Zero-tolerance" policies; that is, rules requiring that students be expelled for possession of drugs or weapons, may be vulnerable to such challenges when applied in an arbitrary manner (see sec. 4.5).[29] In *Price v. New York City Board of Education*,[30] students claimed that a school rule banning the possession as opposed to the use of cell phones on school property was unreasonable, but the court concluded that the rule had a rational basis:

> Any enforcement system focusing on use, rather than possession, requires teachers, rather than only security personnel at the school door, to observe and enforce the ban and become involved in confronting students and punishment decisions, in detriment of their pedagogical mission, both by reducing their time teaching and by increasing their perception as an adversary to students.

The court noted a number of other ways in which cell-phone possession might be disruptive to the school's educational mission such as by ringing at inappropriate times or being used to facilitate cheating and that the alternative, less restrictive rules suggested by the student-plaintiffs required the school to expend significant resources. The court also rejected the claim that the ban unconstitutionally interfered with the right of parents to control the upbringing of their children.

School rules may also be challenged on the constitutional grounds of vagueness or overbreadth. **Vague** rules violate the Due Process Clause of the Fourteenth Amendment because, like no rules at all, they fail to provide adequate notice of what is impermissible and they invite uneven, biased, and variable application. In criminal law a rule is unconstitutionally vague if persons "of common intelligence must necessarily guess at its meaning and differ as to its application."[31] Courts do not require that school rules be as precisely crafted as criminal laws, but courts nevertheless insist that rules give students a reasonable opportunity to know and understand what they may and may not do.

Thus, one court blocked the enforcement of a regulation that stated that "Gang related activities such as display of 'colors,' symbols, signals, signs, etc. will not be tolerated on school grounds." The Eighth Circuit found the regulation impermissibly vague because the term "gang related activities" was not defined and left students unclear about what was not allowed and gave school officials too much discretion to decide what constituted a gang symbol. The court noted that the rule could have been used to punish students for wearing cross earrings or baseball caps or if their shoes were untied.[32] Other examples of school rules found to be impermissibly vague are:

- A prohibition of the use of alcohol or drugs "prior to" coming on school grounds.[33]
- A rule against "misconduct."[34]
- A rule forbidding "inappropriate actions" or "unacceptable behaviors."[35]
- A requirement that students be "neatly dressed and groomed, maintaining standards of modesty and good taste conducive to an educational atmosphere."[36]

However, in *Alex v. Allen*,[37] the court disagreed with students who claimed that rules against "flagrant disrespect of teachers," "loitering in the heavy areas of traffic," "rowdy behavior or running in the building," "locker misuse," "extreme dress or appearance which is disruptive to class," and "hand-holding and other displays of affection" were impermissibly vague. The court pointed out that schools should have more flexibility in making rules than legislatures do in writing criminal statutes. The court felt that the challenged rules were directed at conduct that "clearly disrupts the educational process," and that they spelled out in "sufficient detail the conduct that is forbidden."

The *Alex* court also rejected the claim that the challenged rules were overbroad. An **overbroad** rule does more than necessary to achieve the desired ends and in so doing infringes on constitutionally protected rights. The issue of overbreadth arises most often in connection with the regulation of speech.[38] Rules are unconstitutionally overbroad not because they prohibit a specific constitutionally protected act but because they could be applied to other constitutionally protected behavior. For example, a student punished for distributing obscene literature at school in violation of a school rule banning distribution of all literature could object to the overbreadth of the rule. The distribution of obscene material is not constitutionally protected, but many of the behaviors that the rule might inhibit are. Rules prohibiting "hate speech," that is, speech that attacks or offends particular racial, ethnic, or gender groups, may raise the issues of vagueness and overbreadth (see sec. 3.4).

In addition to the constraints of the Constitution, federal statutes may limit the school's authority to formulate rules. For example, the school could not enforce rules prohibiting students from engaging in meetings that are their right under the Equal Access Act (see sec. 3.6). Federal law also regulates the disciplining of students with disabilities (see sec. 6.3).

4.2 THE USE OF FORCE TO CONTROL STUDENTS

This section considers the law relating to the use of force by school officials to enforce school rules and prevent injury, damage, or disruption. Examples include forcibly conducting a misbehaving student to the principal's office, physically seizing fighting students to pull them apart, and force in self-defense. Corporal punishment, the deliberate inflicting of physical pain to punish misbehavior, is considered separately in Section 4.5.

Both the federal Constitution and state common law and statute bear on the authority of school officials to use force to maintain order in the school. The relevant provisions of the Constitution are the Fourth Amendment protection against "unreasonable . . . seizures" and the Due Process Clause of the Fourteenth Amendment. The Seventh Circuit has ruled that a teacher or administrator violates the Fourth Amendment by physically controlling a student "only when the restriction of liberty is unreasonable under the circumstances then existing and apparent." Based on this principle, the court concluded that a teacher did not violate a student's Fourth Amendment right when the teacher grabbed the student first by the wrist and subsequently by the elbow to speed her exit from the classroom. The student had engaged in a verbal altercation that had the potential to erupt into violence.[39]

In *Ramirez v. Hsu*[40] a federal district court upheld the detention of a student for three hours after school officials had received numerous reports from other students that the plaintiff had drugs in her possession and had used drugs that day. The court found the seizure was reasonably related to three objectives: (1) preventing the disruption that could occur if she were allowed to return to class; (2) disciplining the plaintiff to impress on her that drug possession and use were a serious matter; and (3) preventing plaintiff from using or distributing drugs. However, in another case, the Eleventh Circuit concluded that the a nine-year-old student's Fourth Amendment rights had been violated when a school resource officer handcuffed her "to help persuade her to rid herself of her disrespectful attitude" and "to impress upon her the serious nature of committing crimes that can lead to arrest, detention or incarceration." The court found the officer's actions not to be reasonable since at the point of the handcuffing there was no potential threat to anyone's safety, and the student was not engaging in any disruptive behavior even though earlier she had resisted a coach's order by threatening to hit him in the head.[41]

The Fourth, Fifth, Sixth, Ninth, and Tenth Circuits have recognized that the Due Process Clause's protection of bodily integrity and security applies to students. The Ninth Circuit has outlined a set of criteria for deciding whether this right has been violated when a school official forcibly controls a student: (a) the need for the use of force, (b) the relation between the need and the action, (c) the extent of harm to the student, and (d) whether the action was taken in good faith or for the purpose of causing harm. The court used these factors to find against a high school principal who, with little provocation, punched, choked, and slapped three different students.[42] These doctrine and decisions indicate that using force to control students is constitutionally permissible when necessary to maintain order as long as the force used is proportional to the need.

In *Heidemann v. Rother*,[43] the Eight Circuit ruled that a school did not violate the substantive due process rights of nine-year-old, nonverbal student with mental and physical disabilities when, on the advice of a licensed physical therapist, school officials tightly wrapped the student for as much as an hour and a half at a time to restrain and calm her. The court was not willing to conclude that the wrapping "represented a substantial departure from accepted professional judgment, practice, or standards" and since it was within those standards the Fourteenth Amendment had not be violated.

State common law, both civil and criminal, and state criminal statutes generally prohibit the use of force by one person against another with certain exceptions. Parents, school officials, and other adults with charge over children may use reasonable force to maintain order and discipline. The reasonableness of the force directed at a child is determined by a number of factors including its purpose, the age, sex, and physical and mental condition of the child; the nature of the offense; the influence of the child's behavior on other children; the extent of the harm inflicted; and whether the force was disproportionate to the offense or was unnecessarily degrading.[44] In general, school officials may use force to enforce school rules when it is necessary and reasonable under the circumstances. (See secs. 10.1 and 10.9 for a discussion of tort claims that may result from unreasonable uses of force that cause harm to a student.)

4.3 THE INVESTIGATION OF MISCONDUCT

When school officials suspect a violation of a school rule or that a criminal act has been committed by a student at school, they may want to investigate. When the safety of other students or personnel is involved, they may have a duty to investigate (see sec. 10.4 on the duty to maintain a safe environment). Investigations can take many forms, including surveillance, questioning, and searching students, their possessions, or their lockers.

Anybody even vaguely familiar with the controversies surrounding police investigations will realize that these investigations can and do implicate important constitutional rights. The Fifth Amendment rights not to be a witness against oneself, to be protected from a coerced confession, and to receive a *Miranda* warning and the Fourth Amendment right not to be subjected to a search without probable cause are vigorously protected in the adult criminal law. In their dealings with the police, children enjoy many of the same constitutional protections although sometimes in modified form.[45]

The major question of this section is the extent to which these protections extend into schools. Do these same rights protect students when they are investigated at school? Must school-based investigations observe the same constitutional guidelines as police investigations in society at large? The answer depends in part on whether the investigation is a police investigation or a school investigation. When police investigations extend into schools, they must follow the same guidelines as at other times, but the law holds school investigations to different and generally more lenient standards.

The distinction between a police investigation and a school investigation is not always obvious. It depends primarily on the status of those who initiate and conduct the investigation, whether they are police officers or school officials, and the motivation for the search. In a North Carolina case, a county deputy sheriff who was assigned to a full-time, permanent position in a school, conducted a search of a student that yielded a bag of marijuana. After conviction as a delinquent, the student appealed claiming the evidence was found as a result of an illegal search. In rejecting the claim, the court decided that the deputy was not an "outside officer"; nor did he conduct the search at the behest of an "outside officer." The deputy, the court said, "was exclusively a school resource officer, who was present in the school hallways during school hours and was furthering the school's educational related goals when he stopped the juvenile." Thus the more the lenient constitutional guidelines applicable to school officials applied and under those guidelines the search was constitutionally permissible.[46]

In *In re D.E.M.*,[47] school officials searched a student after receiving a tip from the police that the student might be carrying a gun. The student claimed that police-search standards should have applied because the school officials had acted as "agents" of the police. To decide the issue, the court looked at the totality of the circumstances including who initiated the search, the purpose of the search, and whether the police "acquiesced in" or "ratified" the search. The court concluded that the mere fact that school officials cooperated with the police did not establish that the police acquiesced in or ratified the search. School officials conducted the search under their duty to assure a safe school. The police did not request or "in any way participate" in the search, nor did the police "coerce, dominate, or direct" the actions of the school officials. However in *F.P. v. State*,[48] the court found that a search conducted by a school official had to satisfy the constitutional rules applicable to police officers because the school official had acted on a tip from a police officer who was interested in investigating the student's possible involvement in the crime of car theft.

In *People v. Overton*[49] a police officer and a school official went together to a locker after a student seemingly confessed to having marijuana in his locker. Finding that the school official had not been coerced by the officer into opening the locker, the court concluded that the search was not a police search since the school official was merely carrying out his duty to keep illegal substances out of the school. The court ruled as it did despite the fact that, after the school official opened the locker, it was the police officer who searched the jacket in the locker and found the marijuana cigarettes. In *Cason v. Cook*[50] a police "liaison officer" was present but not in uniform when a school official initiated a search of a student. After the school official's search yielded evidence of criminal conduct, the officer conducted a pat-down search of the student. The court refused to apply police-search standards, finding that the officer's involvement had been only "marginal."

In a more difficult case, a student had been called to the office after a tipster informed school officials that the student was dealing drugs. He refused to allow himself to be searched until a deputy sheriff entered the office, told the student it would be better to cooperate, and asked him to empty his pockets. In refusing to apply police-search standards to the case, the court noted that the deputy had not developed the facts that promoted the search, nor ordered that the student be detained, nor made the initial effort to search the student.[51]

In *Miranda v. Arizona*,[52] the Supreme Court said that the Fifth Amendment's protection against being forced to be a witness against oneself requires that suspects taken into custody be informed of their right to remain silent and to consult an attorney and of certain other rights. Interrogations may only proceed with strict procedural safeguards against forced self-incrimination. Some student-plaintiffs have argued that the same protections should be afforded to students under investigation by school officials, but courts have concluded that when an interrogation is conducted entirely by school officials with no police involvement, students do not have the right to remain silent and the school officials are not required to give the student a *Miranda* warning.[53] One court ruled that a student's rights were not violated when a school official interrogated the student for twenty minutes about a bomb threat after two other students had implicated him.[54] Another case ruled against a student who claimed that his *Miranda* rights were violated when school officials continued to question him after police had already arrived on the scene. The court ruled that the school officials acted independently and not as agents of the police.[55]

The Fourth Amendment prohibits the government from subjecting an individual to an unreasonable **search**. But not all investigations constitute searches for Fourth Amendment purposes. To determine if an investigation is a search, courts ask whether the person allegedly searched had an expectation of privacy and, if so, whether the expectation was one that society recognizes as reasonable.[56] Consider, for example, an item left in "plain view" on the front seat of an automobile parked in a school's parking lot. A school official or police officer who looks into the car and sees the item has not conducted a search because leaving the item on the front seat of the car indicates that the owner had no expectation of privacy or that any claimed expectation of privacy is not reasonable.[57] Nor does the examination of garbage disposed of in a public receptacle or the videotaping of individuals in public places constitute a search. Similarly, there is no expectation of privacy if someone loses a purse or backpack. Thus, if school officials look through a lost purse for identification and find controlled substances, the controlled substances are considered to have been in plain view.[58] Surveillance, even surreptitious surveillance through a two-way mirror, of areas normally open to inspection, such as classrooms, school yards, and even public areas of a washroom, is not a search.[59] On the other hand, more intrusive measures like pat-downs and drug testing and intrusions into areas that could not normally be perceived by the senses such as by metal detectors and electronic eavesdropping are searches.

Locker investigations by school officials are not regarded by some courts as searches. These courts commonly reason that because the locker is jointly controlled by the student and the school, the student does not have a reasonable expectation of privacy, at least against school officials.[60] In these jurisdictions, school officials are free to conduct random, unannounced locker searches for any reason or no reason. They must be careful, however, not to select lockers for examination on the basis of race, gender, or other discriminatory criteria. And to avoid misunderstanding, it is probably wise for schools in these jurisdictions to make clear to students that their lockers may be searched.[61]

In some states, courts have taken the opposite view: students do have an expectation of privacy with respect to their lockers against school officials.[62] In these states, school officials may not search lockers unless the criteria announced in the *T.L.O.* case (discussed later in this section) are met. One court has ruled that, even if students do have an expectation of privacy, school officials may still search lockers without cause if they have informed students in advance of the possibility of random searches.[63] Another court reached the opposite conclusion.[64]

Whether or not the locker itself receives Fourth Amendment protection, the examination of the contents of the locker may be protected.[65] In jurisdictions where random locker searches are not permitted, school officials who meet the *T.L.O.* criteria would in most instances also be permitted to search the contents of the locker. In jurisdictions where random locker searches are permitted, it may still be impermissible to randomly search backpacks and other containers found in lockers.[66]

Whether a **sniff by a dog** trained to detect drugs is a search is only partially settled. The Supreme Court has said that a dog sniff of luggage at an airport is not a search.[67] However, the use of drug-sniffing dogs at school raises different issues. In *Horton v. Goose Creek Independent School District*,[68] the Fifth Circuit Court of Appeals ruled that dog sniffing of cars or lockers is not a search, but that sniffing of students themselves is a search for Fourth Amendment purposes. The court explained that the odors emanating from cars or lockers are left open to public perception. Their examination poses little threat of embarrassment or discomfort to innocent students. Officials are free to use dogs to enhance their perception just as they are free to use binoculars to enhance their perception of objects left in plain sight. However, the examination of bodily odors is different, explained the court:

> [T]he intensive smelling of people, even if done by dogs, [is] indecent and demeaning. Most persons in our society deliberately attempt not to expose the odors emanating from their bodies to public smell. In contrast, where the Supreme Court has upheld limited investigations of body characteristics not justified by individualized suspicion, it has done so on the grounds that the particular characteristic was routinely exhibited to the public. Intentional close proximity sniffing of the person is offensive whether the sniffer be canine or human. One can imagine the embarrassment which a young adolescent, already self-conscious about his or her body, might experience when a dog, being handled by a representative of the school administration, enters the classroom specifically for the purpose of sniffing the air around his or her person.
>
> We need only look at the record in this case to see how a dog's sniffing technique—i.e., sniffing around each child, putting his nose on the child and scratching and manifesting other signs of excitement in the case of an alert—is intrusive.

If a student gives voluntarily **consent** to a search, the Fourth Amendment imposes no constraints, whether the search is conducted by school officials or the police. However, waivers of constitutional rights are valid only when freely given by someone who fully comprehends the options.[69] This standard requires more than acquiescence or failure to resist; there is a strong presumption that an individual would not knowingly waive a constitutional right when doing so would reveal evidence of wrongdoing. The court in *Tarter v. Raybuck*[70] phrased the doctrine as follows:

> We are not convinced that David Tarter knowingly and intelligently waived his constitutional rights when he "consented" to be searched, and we are inclined to resolve this case on the basis of consent. The burden would be upon defendants to demonstrate such a voluntary relinquishment of constitutional rights by plaintiff. There is a presumption against the waiver of constitutional rights. That he may have acquiesced in the initial search does not necessarily demonstrate the relinquishment of his rights to challenge his initial search. In fact, David Tarter's testimony was that he only submitted to the search because he was afraid. Furthermore, there is no indication he even was aware that he might have had a constitutional right to object to a search.

Thus, the student who empties pocket or purse after being ordered to do so has not consented to the search. Nor would consent be seen as voluntary if school officials use tactics of intimidation or coercion: "If you agree to empty your pockets, I won't call the police." The age and intelligence of the student are also relevant to the validity of consent. In one case, a federal district court concluded that a student had not voluntarily consented to a strip search because he never explicitly said that he consented to the search but merely said several times that he had nothing to hide, he was not specifically asked to consent to a strip search, the extensiveness of the search was not explained to him, he was not given a chance to talk with an advocate, and generally it was a situation in which the plaintiff, a special education student with ADHD, could perceive he had no options.[71]

The best policy is never to search students on the basis of their consent alone but only when the criteria set down in *New Jersey v. T.L.O.*[72] (explained later in this section) are met. Even if a student refuses voluntarily to consent to a search, school officials may continue to question the student. The student's response to the questions may provide sufficient justification for a subsequent search.[73]

In *Webb v. McCullough*,[74] the Sixth Circuit held that school officials are not limited by the Fourth Amendment when chaperoning school-sponsored trips with parental consent. In this situation the authority of school officials was found to be analogous to that of parents who have wide latitude to search their children. It is probable that not all courts would reach the same conclusion. In *Kuehn v. Renton School District No. 403*,[75] the court prohibited the searching of the luggage of all members of a band as a precondition for participation in a concert trip.

The objections students raise to school searches are typically prompted by a desire to invoke the exclusionary rule. The **exclusionary rule** requires the suppression of evidence seized in violation of Fourth Amendment guidelines.[76] The courts are in general, but not unanimous, agreement that evidence illegally seized by school officials may not be used against students in a criminal or juvenile delinquency hearing.[77] Courts are split regarding whether the exclusionary rule applies in school disciplinary hearings.[78] The highest court in New York ruled that a weapon discovered in a student's possession by an illegal search and thus excluded from use in a juvenile delinquency hearing could nevertheless be used in a school disciplinary proceeding.[79]

Another motivation for objecting to searches is that a federal statute[80] makes it possible for students to seek monetary damages from school officials who violate their Fourth Amendment or other constitutional rights.[81] In theory, monetary damages are possible against both the school district and the offending officials personally, but in practice damages have proved difficult to obtain (see sec. 10.10).[82]

The *T.L.O.* Case

Determining whether an investigation by a school official constitutes a search is only the first step in determining whether the investigation is permissible. The Fourth Amendment prohibits only "unreasonable" searches, so the question is: Under what circumstances are searches of students by school officials reasonable? After many years of conflicting lower court decisions, the Supreme Court addressed this question in 1985.

The case, *New Jersey v. T.L.O.*,[83] involved a student, T.L.O., seen smoking by a teacher in the girls' bathroom in violation of the rules of the school. The teacher escorted T.L.O. to the principal's office, where, under questioning, T.L.O. denied that she had been smoking or that she smoked at all. The principal then demanded to see T.L.O.'s purse. Opening the purse, the principal found a pack of cigarettes that he removed as evidence that T.L.O. was lying. As he did so, he saw a pack of rolling papers in the purse. This caused the principal to suspect that T.L.O. might possess marijuana. He then proceeded to search the rest of the purse and found marijuana as well as other evidence implicating T.L.O. in the selling of illegal drugs. This evidence was turned over to the police and used to convict T.L.O. of delinquency in juvenile court. T.L.O. challenged the conviction, claiming that the search of her purse was impermissible under the Fourth Amendment and that the evidence thus obtained should be suppressed.

In order to evaluate T.L.O.'s claim, the Court first had to determine "the proper standard for assessing the legality of searches conducted by public school officials." In other words, the Court had to adopt a rule or procedure to determine when an educator's search of a student is reasonable under the Fourth Amendment. The Court noted that some lower courts had previously held, on the basis of the doctrine of *in loco parentis*, that school officials were exempt from the limitations of the Fourth Amendment, but this idea was rejected as being "in tension with contemporary reality and the teachings of the Court." Conversely, the Court also rejected the view of some lower courts that educators should be required to show "probable cause," that is, very great likelihood that a search would reveal evidence of a crime, in order to satisfy the Fourth Amendment. In so doing, the Court recognized that although educators are not their students' parents, neither are they police officers.

Instead, the Court fashioned a compromise in keeping with the wording of the Fourth Amendment itself: School officials may search a student only if they have **reasonable cause** to believe that the search will reveal evidence of a crime or the violation of a school rule. Thus, the Supreme Court formulated a rule designed to accommodate the school's need to keep order while at the same time recognizing the students' right to be free from unreasonable searches.

Applying this analysis to the facts in *T.L.O.*, the Court found that the principal had satisfied the requirement of reasonableness. Looking in the purse for cigarettes was directly related to the question of the credibility of T.L.O.'s denial that she ever smoked. Once the initial search for the cigarettes had incidentally revealed the rolling papers, the suspicion of drug possession was also reasonable, thus justifying the remainder of the search. For this reason, T.L.O.'s appeal was denied.

Applying the *T.L.O. Guidelines*

Declining to view school administrators as analogous to either parents or police for Fourth Amendment purpose, *T.L.O.* limits searches to the following situations: A school official must have reasonable grounds to believe that a search of a specific individual will produce relevant evidence that the individual has violated a specific school rule or law. *T.L.O.* also places limits on the scope or nature of the search.

School officials may search only on the basis of reasonable grounds. Officials must have evidence that makes it reasonable to believe that the search is likely to be fruitful. Although it is impossible to state a precise definition of reasonable grounds, courts are unlikely to accept vague suspicion unsupported by evidence pointing to a specific act of wrongdoing. Thus, in *Matter of Pima County Juvenile Action*,[84] a student was seen near bleachers where students congregated for various reasons including drug use. The student previously had been mentioned in a staff meeting in a discussion of drug use, but the principal had no personal knowledge regarding the student's conduct, no prior reports of drug use or sale, and no other reason to suspect he had drugs in his pockets. The court concluded that the principal did not have reasonable grounds to search the student. However, in a similar case, a search of two boys found without passes in a restroom known as a haven for drug use and sale was upheld.[85] A Massachusetts court upheld as reasonable the search of a student who violated an order not to return to school without his parent, bypassed a metal detector, and was found in an unauthorized area of the school.[86] In another case, a federal district court said a school official accompanying students on a field trip was justified in searching a student's hotel room when he smelled marijuana outside the room.[87] Another federal district court upheld a search based on the observation that the student "looked stoned."[88]

In *DesRoches v. Caprio*,[89] the Fourth Circuit ruled that school officials had reasonable individualized suspicion that a student was the culprit in the theft of shoes sufficient to justify a search after a search of the other eighteen suspects had not turned up the missing shoes. The plaintiff was the last student to be designated for searching because he alone among the nineteen had refused to consent to be searched. In another case, New York's highest court held that it was permissible for a school official to feel the outside of a book bag after the bag emitted an unusual metallic thud when the student put it down; having felt the outline of a gun, it was then reasonable to search the bag.[90] But a federal district court ruled that a strip search was not reasonable at its inception merely because the students were the last ones in a locker room prior to $60 being reported missing from the locker room.[91]

In *Cales v. Howell Public Schools*,[92] a security guard caught a student ducking behind cars in the school parking lot. The student also gave a false name when questioned. In finding the search in this case illegal, the court wrote:

> It is clear that plaintiff's conduct created reasonable grounds for suspecting that some school rule or law had been violated. . . . Plaintiff's conduct was clearly ambiguous. It could have indicated that she was truant, or that she was stealing hubcaps, or that she had left class to meet a boyfriend. In short, it could have signified that plaintiff had violated any of an infinite number of laws or school rules. This Court does not read *TLO* so broadly as to allow a school administrator the right to search a student because that student acts in such a way so as to create a reasonable suspicion that the student has violated *some* rule or law.

However, in a related case involving the successful search of a student's automobile for cigarettes, the court concluded that the search was justified at its inception because in addition to the student's being out of class without a pass, there was a history of students smoking in the parking lot where the student was found, and the student had lied about going to his car to retrieve an art project.[93]

Sometimes statements by another student—for example, one who witnesses a crime—can form the basis of the reasonable suspicion necessary to justify a search.[94] Often the issue depends on the trustworthiness of the student informant under the circumstances. One court declared that information supplied by a student informant may be the basis for a search "[a]bsent information that a particular student informant may be untrustworthy."[95] In another case, an informant who had established a good working relationship with the school staff by working as an office aide was deemed reliable when the informant's tip was specific as to what would be found and its location.[96] But the Ninth Circuit concluded that a search was not justified at its inception when school officials relied on a tip from a friend of the searched student who said that the illegal pills found on her person had been given to her by the student. The court found that the informant was not reliable and was trying to shift attention away from herself.[97] In another case, a school's failure to check whether student informants were trustworthy—the informants were in fact students who had a possible motive to falsely accuse the searched student of carrying drugs—led the court to conclude that the search (which turned up no drugs) was illegal.[98]

Whether the school official who actually conducts the search must have been the original recipient of the tip from the informant and must know the identity of the informant was addressed in *In re Juvenile 2006–406*.[99] On two separate occasions, a teacher reported to the vice principal information that students, whom the teacher did not name, had reported that another student possessed drug paraphernalia. The court concluded the search was reasonable at its inception because, while the vice principal did not know the tipsters, he did know the teacher.

The reasonable grounds or suspicion must generally be directed at the specific individual or individuals to be searched. Although *T.L.O* itself says nothing about sweep searches of all students in the hope of turning up incriminating evidence, a number of other courts have declared this practice to be impermissible.[100] There are a number of exceptions to this rule such as certain instances of random drug testing of pupils and the use of metal detectors (both discussed later). In addition, some courts have upheld sweep searches of students when school officials believed that one among a number of students was carrying a weapon. The necessity of keeping the school free of weapons was found to justify these searches even in the absence of individualized suspicion.[101]

The requirement of individualized suspicion is enforced with the greatest vigor in connection with strip searches. The more intrusive the search, the more likely that the courts will insist that school officials have good reasons to suspect the student.[102] The Sixth Circuit allowed a strip search based on a tip from an informant only after the court had satisfied itself that the school official had questioned the informant to make sure the tip was not motivated by malice.[103] In finding a strip search impermissible the Second Circuit wrote, "[A]cceptance of one student's accusatory statement to initiate a highly intrusive search of another students—with no meaningful inquiry or corroboration—concerns us."[104]

The point of the search must be to uncover relevant evidence that would help to establish that a student did in fact violate a specific school rule or law. In *T.L.O.*, the search began with a view toward showing that T.L.O. had smoked. In the process of that search, evidence of drug use came into plain view. This justified continuing the search, in effect a second search, for additional relevant evidence of drug use or drug dealing. Note, however, that, for example, even a strong suspicion that a student had phoned in a false bomb threat would not justify a search of the student's pockets.

Even if a search is justified at its inception, *T.L.O.* places limits on the scope of the search. A school search must not be excessive in light of the age and sex of the student searched and, most importantly, the nature of the infraction suspected. As noted earlier, school officials may be personally sued for actual and even punitive damages under federal law, as well as under state tort law, for violations of students' Fourth Amendment rights (see sec. 10.10). The danger of losing such a suit is particularly high with regard to strip searches because the scope of these searches often cannot be justified under the criteria established in *T.L.O.* and subsequent lower court decisions and the harm caused by unjustified strip searches can be significant.[105]

In one case, a school official had reasonable grounds to believe a student was carrying a knife. He opened the student's purse and, not seeing the knife, proceeded to also open a small zippered pocket inside the purse that had no bulge in it. He felt inside the pocket, found no knife but felt a plastic bag, which he could feel contained no knife. Nevertheless, he removed the bag, which contained rock cocaine. The court ruled that the scope of this search exceeded the *T.L.O.* guidelines: "While school safety may readily justify a basic search for weapons, the student's interest in privacy should preclude a scavenger hunt after the basic search has produced no weapons. . . . These drugs were discovered during a search extended by simple curiosity rather than suspicion."[106] In another case, the Supreme Court of West Virginia held that a strip search of a student suspected of stealing $100 was excessive in light of the nature of the crime being investigated. Even though the money was found in the student's underwear, the court said that the student's "suspected conduct did not pose the type of immediate danger to others that might conceivably necessitate and justify a warrantless strip search."[107] Similarly, another court concluded that strip searching two eight-year-olds twice to find $7 that was allegedly stolen was unreasonable. "*T.L.O.*," said the court, "forbids school officials from undertaking the most intrusive of searches where the infraction is relatively minor and presents no threat of imminent danger. . . ."[108] And a federal district court refused to sanction a strip search for $60 which involved requiring two female students to strip naked in front of each other, and then to shake out their gym clothes.[109]

Despite these cases, courts will permit even a very intrusive search when conditions are exigent enough and when steps are taken to make sure the search is no more intrusive and embarrassing than necessary under the circumstances. In general, intrusive searches for drugs or weapons are more likely to pass constitutional muster than searches for missing money or goods. A federal district court upheld a very intrusive search of a student who, when he was questioned about the possession of marijuana, appeared stoned and smelled of marijuana. The strip search was undertaken only after a search of the student's pockets, shoes, and socks did not yield drugs. The court found the search permissible in scope because the plaintiff was not nude during the search, no women were present, his genitals were not examined and he was not "touched inappropriately." The assistant principal only ran his hands around the interior of the boxer shorts to make sure nothing was hidden inside, but the student was not asked to remove his shorts.[110] Another court ruled in favor of school officials who strip searched a sixteen-year-old student who was perceived to have an unusual bulge in the crotch and whose name had been associated several times with drug dealing and use.[111]

In 2009, the Supreme Court in *Safford Unified School Dist. No. 1 v. Redding*,[112] issued a ruling with important implications for the issues under discussion. Reversing the Ninth Circuit, the Court ruled against school officials who conducted a strip search of a thirteen-year-old student after another student claimed she had received a prescription ibuprofen pill from her. Characterizing strip searches as "degrading," "embarrassing," "frightening," and "humiliating," the Court found that "both subjective and reasonable societal expectations of personal privacy support the treatment of such a search as categorically distinct, requiring distinct elements of justification on the part of school authorities for going beyond a search of outer clothing and belongings." The decision stopped short of saying that strip searches of students can never be constitutionally permissible, but it does indicate the necessity of an extremely strong justification, including significant danger or other exigent circumstances and focused suspicion that the evidence sought is hidden inside the student's underwear. Regardless of the constitutionality of strip searches, some state's statutes and the regulations of some school districts including New York City categorically prohibit them.[113]

Heightened concern over the dangers posed by student possession of weapons and use of drugs has led some schools to implement programs of relatively nonintrusive searches without the particularized suspicion required by *T.L.O.* "Wanding" students and requiring them to walk through **metal detectors** are searches. But the few courts that have considered the constitutionality of these searches have upheld them, noting the need to achieve a safe school, the nondiscriminatory nature of the searches, and the minimal infringement of the students' privacy.[114] Not so with programs of random suspicionless searches of pockets and backpacks. The Eighth Circuit wrote,

> While the [district] has expressed some generalized concerns about the existence of weapons and drugs in its schools, it conceded . . . that there is nothing in the record regarding the magnitude of any problems with weapons or drugs that it has actually experienced. All schools surely have an interest in minimizing the harm that the

existence of weapons and controlled substances might visit upon a student population, but public schools have never been entitled to conduct random, full-scale searches of students' personal belongings because of a mere apprehension.[115]

Similarly, the Supreme Court of Washington struck down a district's policy of requiring students going on a band concert tour to submit to a pre-departure luggage search.[116]

There are, however, circumstances when courts have upheld suspicionless searches of groups of students. The Eighth Circuit allowed the search of pockets and shoes of all male students in grades 6 to 12 after there were reports of a knife in the school, and a school bus seat that day had been slashed.[117] In another case, a California court upheld the search of five students when, after school officials stopped a potential fight, one student pointed to the five and said "Don't pick on us; one of those guys has a gun."[118] In the absence of the great danger posed by the likely presence of deadly weapons, group searches are much less likely to be approved. A number of cases have prohibited elementary schools from strip searching whole classes of students to look for missing money even after less intrusive measures had failed.[119]

Drug Testing

Courts will permit the required drug testing of a particular student if the individualized reasonable suspicion requirement of *T.L.O.* is met. In one case the Third Circuit found that a school had the authority to insist on a drug test for a student who was flushed; had glassy eyes, dilated pupils, and high blood pressure; manifested unusual behavior for her; and had difficulty remembering her parents' daytime phone numbers. The student's speech was not slurred and she did not smell of either alcohol or drugs.[120] But in another case, the court concluded that there simply was not enough of a proven connection between fighting and drug use to justify requiring a drug test of a student who was in a fight.[121]

In *Vernonia School District 47J v. Acton*,[122] the Supreme Court considered the constitutionality of a school's program of random or suspicionless drug testing of student athletes. In upholding the program, the Court noted that random drug testing may be justified in situations where drug use is especially prevalent or dangerous, the purpose of the testing is to assist rather than to punish the students, the testing system is reliable and the results confidential, and in situations such as competitive sports where continued drug use carries more than the usual dangers.

After the *Vernonia* decision, some school districts initiated programs of suspicionless drug testing of all students engaged in competitive extracurricular activities including such activities as choir and debate. The Supreme Court addressed the constitutionality of this more expansive policy in *Board of Education of Independent School District No. 92 of Pottawatomie County v. Earls*.[123] After considering the specifics of the district's drug-testing policy, the "nature and immediacy" of the school's concerns about drug use among its students, "and the efficacy of the Policy in meeting" the school's concerns, the Court found that the policy was reasonable and therefore permissible under the Fourth Amendment.

That random drug-testing programs were approved in *Earls* and *Vernonia* should not be taken to mean that random drug testing of all students would be constitutional. Both these cases involved testing only students who voluntarily participated in extracurricular programs involving physical activities and travel that, if undertaken under the influence of drugs, could result in injury to the drug user and others. The drug-testing procedures used in both cases were carried out in a manner designed to minimize embarrassment, and the drug-testing records were confidential. In neither case were the results turned over to law enforcement authorities; nor did a positive test lead to the imposition of school discipline. Both districts were experiencing a "drug problem" when they instituted their policies. It is likely that drug-testing programs that do not meet most or all of these conditions would not pass constitutional muster.[124] In 2003, the Supreme Court of New Jersey approved a school's random drug-testing program of students engaged in extracurricular activities or possessing a parking permit. The school only implemented this policy after other anti-drug efforts—dog-sniffing sweeps and locker searches—had failed and after an anonymous survey of students conducted by an outside company indicated widespread drug use and drinking among students.[125] Even random drug-testing programs that are permissible under the federal Constitution may not be permissible under some state constitutions.

School officials contemplating the creation of a random drug-testing program should recognize that such programs raise both constitutional and educational issues. A major point raised by the four dissenting judges in the *Earls* case is that unjustified random searches send a message that conflicts with the school's educational mission:

> In regulating an athletic program or endeavoring to combat an exploding drug epidemic, a school's custodial obligations may permit searches that would otherwise unacceptably abridge students' rights. When custodial duties are not ascendant, however, schools' tutelary obligations to their students require them to "teach by example" by avoiding . . . measures that diminish constitutional protections.

School officials should also be aware that the specific design of random drug-testing programs is likely to be subjected to scrutiny especially with regard to issues of student privacy. One court ruled that a policy that required students to reveal in advance of being tested for illegal drugs all the prescription drugs they were taking—even if the prescription was one that could not affect the test—was a privacy violation under the state constitution. However, the same court concluded that a policy that gave a student who tested positive the opportunity to submit evidence that lawfully prescribed medications accounted for the positive results was constitutional.[126]

"Seizure" of Students Suspected of Wrongdoing

Like unreasonable searches, unreasonable "seizures" are prohibited by the Fourth Amendment. In evaluating a claim that a school unreasonably seized a student in the course of an investigation, courts employ a framework similar to the one formulated by the Supreme Court in *T.L.O.* to evaluate claims of unreasonable searches. A seizure is permissible if it is, first, justified at its inception; and, second, justified in its scope, that is, if the length of detention is reasonable under the circumstances. Using this approach, the Tenth Circuit upheld a twenty minute seizure of a student for questioning in connection with the investigation of an anonymous bomb threat. The seizure was justified at its inception because other students had implicated the plaintiff in making the threat, and was justified in its length given the seriousness of the problem.[127]

In *Shuman v. Penn Manor School District*,[128] after a student was accused by another student of sexual misconduct, school officials held him in a conference room from 10 a.m. until 2 p.m. during which time he did homework, and was allowed to eat lunch in the cafeteria and to get a drink of water. The court agreed that the plaintiff had been "seized" since a reasonable person in his position would believe he was not free to leave. The court then noted that the constitutionality of seizures in public schools had to be examined in light of the goals and responsibilities of public schools. Relying on a standard of reasonableness that had also been adopted by the Fifth, Seventh, Ninth and Tenth Circuits, the Third Circuit upheld the detention as reasonable under the circumstances. The serious nature of the allegation, and the need to investigate it coupled with the accommodations afforded the student supported the reasonableness of the detention.

In *Milligan v. City of Slidell*,[129] the Fifth Circuit upheld as reasonable the removal of a student from class in order to question him about rumors that a fight, possibly involving the use of weapons, was to take place after school. The court balanced the student's interest in privacy against the school's interest in preventing violent misconduct. Helping to tip the scale in favor of the school was the court's conclusion that, "Students at school . . . have a significantly lesser expectation of privacy in regard to the temporary 'seizure' of their persons than does the general population."

4.4 THE ADJUDICATION OF GUILT

In U.S. society, the judgment of people accused of crimes is guided by certain fundamental principles. The process begins with a presumption of innocence and the government bearing the burden of proving guilt. Whatever the accusation, the defendant has the right to a fair and impartial trial. Extensive procedural safeguards and rules of evidence maximize the likelihood of a just verdict while respecting basic human rights and dignity. Even when a person is found guilty, the Constitution places limits on permissible punishments, no matter what the crime.

These same principles apply to government-controlled, noncriminal accusatory proceedings like school disciplinary actions. Both the Constitution and state statutes impose procedural and substantive requirements designed to ensure fairness and minimize error. Although they vary somewhat, state statutes generally incorporate and in some cases expand on the constitutional rights discussed later. States are free to grant accused students more procedural safeguards than the Constitution requires, but never fewer. (See also sec. 6.3 regarding federal statutes that regulate the disciplining of students with disabilities.)

The **Due Process Clause** of the Fourteenth Amendment says that the state shall not "deprive any person of life, liberty, or property without due process of law." Although the concept of due process has never been fully defined, it embodies a philosophy of justice that requires evenhanded deliberation prior to acting. In its procedural sense, due process means the right to be heard. At the minimum, it requires that individuals not be punished or deprived of their rights by the state without first being given a chance to tell their side of the story. Another important due process principle is that the greater the contemplated punishment, the more extensive are the procedures necessary to guard against an unjust verdict.

Historically, public schools had broad authority to discipline students unfettered by due process requirements. In the early 1960s, federal courts began to require some due process for students expelled from public schools.[130] By the early 1970s, most, but not all, federal courts were applying the Due Process Clause to all cases of exclusion from school, although the terms of the requirements varied considerably from court to court. The law was particularly unsettled with regard to suspensions of short duration.

The *Goss* Case

In 1975, the Supreme Court did much to clarify the issue with its decision in *Goss v. Lopez*.[131] *Goss* concerned a group of students suspended for ten days by an Ohio high school for participating in "disturbances" during a period of "widespread student unrest." Some of the students denied wrongdoing, but none of them was given a hearing prior to suspension, only notified of their punishment. The suspensions were carried out in accordance with an Ohio law authorizing suspension without a hearing, but the students argued that their due process rights had been violated by the school's action.

Because the Fourteenth Amendment requires due process only in cases where a state seeks to deprive an individual of life, liberty, or property, the first issue that the Court had to face was whether attendance at school is a property right. The state argued that it wasn't because there is no right to attend school granted by the U.S. Constitution. The Supreme Court rejected this argument, nothing that whereas Ohio had no obligation to provide schooling to its children, it had chosen to do so. In so doing, it had created a property right to school attendance; the students then possessed the right to be in school just as they possess tangible property or anything else to which they have legal entitlement. (Note, that in making this ruling, the Supreme Court was not saying that school attendance is a constitutional right. In fact, the Court specifically ruled in *San Antonio Independent School District v. Rodriguez*[132] that there is no constitutional right to education.) Not only do students possess a property right to school attendance, but they also possess a liberty interest in the maintenance of a good reputation, one that is implicated in cases where school suspensions are noted on a student's permanent record.

Having established the relevance of the Due Process Clause to punitive exclusion of students from school, the Court next faced the task of developing a framework that would work in the school context. Noting as always the urgent need of the school for the maintenance of discipline, the Court recognized that schools could not and should not be expected to conduct themselves like courts. They must be able to act quickly and to get on with the business of education. However, even a short-term exclusion from school is a "serious event in the life of the suspended child," one that should not be allowed to take place without at least some procedural safeguards. Therefore, the Court ruled that short-term suspensions, like the ones in *Goss*, could take place only after students were afforded some kind of hearing. Thus, the suspensions without a hearing and the Ohio law that permitted them were unconstitutional.

Goss resolved the major questions concerning the application of the Due Process Clause in public schools. Any nontrivial deprivation of a student's liberty or property interests requires due process. Liberty interests include freedom from restraint and, as in *Goss*, the maintenance of one's reputation. Property interests can arise by ownership or by state action as when statutes grant the right to attend public school. Because deprivation of even one day of schooling is "a serious event in the life of the suspended child," and therefore not trivial, suspensions of any length require due process.

Once it has been determined that due process applies in a particular case, it becomes necessary to determine what process is due. *Goss* indicates that, except under emergency circumstances, a hearing should precede a child's exclusion from school. For short-term suspensions, defined by the court as ten days or less, *Goss* requires notice of the charges and case against the student followed by an opportunity to refute them. Little time need elapse between the student's notification of the alleged violation and the hearing. For example, an accusing teacher might notify a student of alleged misconduct and immediately accompany the student to the school office where the principal listens to teacher and student, makes a judgment, and, if necessary, assigns a suspension of ten days or less. There are not any specific procedural requirements about where or how the hearing is to be conducted. One court ruled that the hearing requirement was satisfied when a principal spoke to a disruptive student and then to her parent on the telephone after the student had been removed from school.[133] Thus, *Goss* attempts to accommodate both the student's right to fair treatment and the school's need to act quickly without undue expenditure of resources.

Post-*Goss* Issues

Although *Goss* provides the framework for applying the Due Process Clause to school disciplinary cases, as always the lower courts have needed to resolve a variety of specific issues. These issues fall into four groups: besides short-term suspension, what punishments require due process or can be given without a hearing; are suspensions without a hearing ever permissible; under what circumstances may a hearing be held after exclusion from school rather than before; and when punishment goes beyond short-term suspension, what additional procedures are required.

Most courts do not require hearings for punishments that do not involve exclusion from school. Other punishments are either not considered deprivations of liberty or property or are considered trivial. For example, in *Dickens v. Johnson County Board of Education*,[134] temporary placement in a "time out" area was considered too inconsequential to trigger due process. Although students have a statute-given property right to a public education, they have no property right to any of its components. Thus, courts have said that denying a student a place on an extracurricular sports team, a role in a play, a place in the band, or admission to the academic honor society or an advanced placement course does not require a hearing.[135] Other courts have denied the due process claims of students whose grades were reduced for academic (as opposed to disciplinary) reasons[136] or who were prohibited from attending graduation ceremonies.[137] The Supreme Court itself has ruled that no hearing is required prior to corporal punishment.[138]

On the other hand, courts may require due process for punishments that entail a significant decrease in the opportunity to learn or diminish a student's future prospects even if no actual suspension is involved. This is particularly likely when, for disciplinary reasons, students are deprived of significant benefits to which they are otherwise entitled. In *Cole v. Newton Special Municipal Separate School District*,[139] the court ruled that a hearing was required for an in-school suspension because the student was deprived of instruction. Likewise, in *Laney v. Farley*,[140] the Sixth Circuit said that in-school suspension might require due process if it isolates a student from educational opportunities or is long enough to damage a student's reputation. But in the case before the court, due process was not required because the suspension for was for one day in the school office and the student was marked present and required to complete her schoolwork. In *Warren v. National Association of Secondary School Principals*,[141] the court mandated a hearing for a student expelled from the National Honor Society. In *State* ex rel. *Yarber v. McHenry*, the court ruled that grade reduction for disciplinary reasons, such as failure to comply with the school's attendance policy, requires due process.[142]

The only situation in which the courts seem willing to allow suspension without a hearing is when the student freely admits guilt. Confession can be seen either as a waiver of the right to a hearing or as demonstrating that there is no practical need for one.[143]

The Court in *Goss* suggested that there were occasions when a student could be suspended with notice and hearing to follow "as soon as practicable": Students "whose presence poses a continuing danger to persons or property or an ongoing threat of disruption to the academic process may be immediately removed from the school." Although not much litigation has addressed this point, the exception appears to apply best to violent or destructive students unwilling or unable to control themselves long enough to participate in a brief hearing. In *White v. Salisbury Township School District*,[144] the court agreed with the school district that a police accusation of smoking marijuana on school grounds justified a suspension prior to a hearing. The decision is hard to understand, because after they learned of the infraction from the police, school officials told the student he could remain in school for the rest of the day but was not to report to classes the next day, with the hearing to follow.

The wording of the *Goss* opinion indicates that school disciplinary procedures must conform to the general due process doctrine that more severe punishments require more elaborate procedures. Lower courts have unanimously interpreted *Goss'* focus on suspensions of ten days or less as signaling that more extensive due process is required prior to long-term suspension or expulsion.[145]

It is important to remember that due process requirements are not directly related to the seriousness of the student's misconduct; rather the requirements are determined by the nature and weight of the contemplated punishment. Any punishment that is by nature a deprivation of liberty or property creates a need for some procedural due process. The greater the weight of the contemplated deprivation, the more due process required. Thus, using a series of short-term suspensions for the same offense is not a permissible way to avoid the more extensive due process of long-term suspension.

However, courts generally judge the weight of a suspension by its length, not by the severity of its impact. For example, in *Lamb v. Panhandle Community Unit School District No. 2*,[146] a student was suspended for the last three days of the school year. As a result, he missed final examinations, failed three courses, and could not graduate. The student claimed that he should have been afforded extensive due process because of the great effect the punishment had on his life. The court disagreed and ruled that a suspension of three days was short-term regardless of when it occurred.[147]

Long-Term Suspension

Courts are in agreement that exclusion from school for more than ten days requires formal notice of specific charges. The notice should specify the time and place of the hearing far enough in advance to permit preparation of a defense.[148] The hearing itself should be before an impartial tribunal, which may be and often is the board of education itself.[149] The accused student should have the opportunity to present evidence and refute adverse evidence.[150] A finding of guilt must be based on substantial evidence with the district bearing the burden of proof. Less demanding than the "beyond a reasonable doubt" standard used in criminal proceedings, substantial evidence requires a showing that guilt is more likely than innocence or, as one court put it, "such relevant proof as adequate to support a conclusion of ultimate fact."[151] To suspend a student based on an unreliable drug test would violate this requirement.[152]

The following issues of due process for long-term suspension must be viewed as unsettled because courts have taken conflicting positions:

- The provision of a list of witnesses prior to the hearing. The majority of the courts have held that this is not required.[153]
- The right to confront and question adverse witnesses. A number of courts permit testimony in the form of anonymous affidavits, but others do not.[154] Some courts have said that students do not have the right to cross-examine adverse witnesses.[155] (But denial of the right to cross-examine may lead a court to question the sufficiency of evidence.[156])
- The admissibility of hearsay with most courts permitting it.[157]
- Whether impartiality is compromised when the school board's own attorney presents the case against the student. The courts are about evenly split on this question.[158]
- The right to be represented by an attorney. Once again, the courts are split.[159]
- The right to a recording or transcript of the hearing. Most courts do not recognize this right.[160]
- The right to a written statement of the reasons explaining the decision to suspend, also not required by most courts.[161]

Given the uncertainties in the law, the prudent course is to provide extensive due process in cases where long-term exclusion from school is contemplated. Schools should endeavor to fairly apply preestablished standardized disciplinary procedures to avoid the appearance of prejudice, minimize the potential for litigation, and, most important, prevent unjust punishments. This means, for example, not allowing the individual presenting the case against the student to attend the tribunal's private deliberations because this practice allows new evidence to be introduced without refutation and gives the impression that the tribunal is giving serious attention to only one side of the case. Similarly, extensive use of hearsay should be avoided for the same reason it is excluded from criminal courts: Second-hand testimony tends to be unreliable and difficult to refute. If the school's case is presented by an attorney, the student should be permitted to have one as well. In short, as a matter of sound education policy, sound administrative practice, and simple fairness, schools should endeavor to employ evenhanded disciplinary procedures designed to ascertain the truth.

4.5   THE ASSIGNMENT OF PUNISHMENT

The assignment of punishment is the last phase of student discipline, and, as a practical matter, the one that matters most. Severe punishments have the potential to adversely affect students' life prospects, whereas lenient punishments may fail to instruct students as to the severity of their infractions and leave others vulnerable to the students' continued wrongdoing. In a sense, the assignment of punishment also has the greatest potential to bring litigation of any aspect of student discipline. Students may bring lawsuits objecting to the wording of school rules, they may claim that evidence of their wrongdoing was gathered unlawfully or that due process protections were not scrupulously observed, but whatever the official cause of action, often their real complaint is that they are being punished. In recent years, lawsuits directly challenging the school's authority to impose a particular punishment in response to a particular offense or to impose a particular punishment at all have become more common. With so much at stake, morally, educationally, and legally, attention to fairness, to the needs of offending students and others in the school community, and to the legal limits on the school's authority to punish is crucial.

Federal and state constitutions and statutes as well as the common law all bear on the authority of schools to punish their students. The Fourth Amendment protection against "unreasonable . . . seizures" has been used to challenge punishments that confine a student in a so-called "time-out" room or isolate a student to prevent further disruption of an activity.[162] Generally, these suits will not succeed provided the punishment is "reasonably related to [its] objectives . . . and not excessively intrusive in light of the age and sex of the student and the nature of the infraction." Suits challenging punishments that violate this principle may be successful. In one case, a federal district court refused to dismiss a suit involving the use of a time-out room where: the room could be used at the absolute discretion of the teacher, the locking of the room violated the fire code, the use of a time-out room had not been written into the individual educational plan for this student with a disability, the use of the time-out room was without parental consent, and although teachers could look into the room through a peep hole, the student could not look out.[163] Two students who were disciplined by being locked for a day in a small, dirty janitor's closet without lunch or bathroom breaks successfully brought a substantive due process case against the school.[164]

After being paddled twenty times with a wooden paddle two feet in length, three to four inches wide and one-half inch thick, James Ingraham brought suit arguing that his Eighth Amendment right to be free from cruel and unusual punishment had been violated. The

Supreme Court rejected this claim in *Ingraham v. Wright*,[165] finding that the Eighth Amendment was only applicable to criminal proceedings. In any event, said the Court:

> Public school teachers and administrators are privileged at common law to inflict only such corporal punishment as is reasonably necessary for the proper education of the child; any punishment going beyond the privilege may result in both civil and criminal liability. As long as the schools are open to the public scrutiny, there is no reason to believe that the common-law constraints will not effectively remedy and deter excesses such as those alleged in this case.

The Court also concluded that the Due Process Clause did not require notice and a hearing prior to the imposition of corporal punishment. Although the Eighth Amendment does not apply to corporal punishment in the context of public schools, the Fourteenth Amendment does. Thus, students who are physically punished by school officials may seek redress by claiming that their right to bodily integrity as protected by the Due Process Clause of the Fourteenth Amendment has been violated. This is a different sense of due process from the procedural requirements discussed earlier in the chapter. As the Fifth Circuit explained, "Corporal punishment is a deprivation of **substantive due process** when it is arbitrary, capricious, or wholly unrelated to the legitimate state goal of maintaining an atmosphere conducive to learning."[166] Whether or not school officials may be held constitutionally liable for excessive force depends, according to the Fourth Circuit, on the severity of the injury caused by the punishment, the proportionality of the punishment to the need for it, and whether the punishment was motivated by malice or sadism and was shocking to the conscience.[167] Most other circuit courts have adopted similar tests for addressing claims that a specific instance of corporal punishment violates substantive due process.[168]

When the *Ingraham* case was decided, only two states banned corporal punishment; today, at least twenty states do either by statute or regulation.[169] Many school boards in states that permit corporal punishment have banned the practice or severely limited its use. As the earlier quote from *Ingraham* suggests, state laws and local policies permitting corporal punishment do not immunize educators from legal problems connected with its use. Educators who employ corporal punishment improperly or violate school board procedures may face dismissal.[170] They may also face civil or even criminal liability for excessive physical punishment resulting in harm. In deciding whether a particular instance of corporal punishment is improper, a court will consider the age and physical condition of the student; the seriousness of the misconduct; the specific details and severity of the punishment including part of the body hit, number of blows, implement and force employed, and the injury resulting; the past behavior of the student; the frame of mind of the disciplinarian including whether there was anger or malice; the availability of less severe but equally effective means of discipline; and whether the school's own regulations concerning corporal punishment were followed.[171] (See also the discussion of assault and battery in sec. 10.1.) Schools using corporal punishment should, therefore, at the very least, adopt and abide by a rigid set of self-restrictions designed to ensure that punishment is neither excessive nor otherwise unlawful. One sound practice would be to require the presence of a second educator as a witness whenever a student is hit.

The Due Process and Equal Protection Clauses of the Fourteenth Amendment have also been used to challenge school punishments other than corporal punishment. One student claimed that expulsion violated his implicit right to an education under the U.S. Constitution. A federal district court disagreed and ruled that there is no such right and, therefore, that expulsion is proper if rationally related to a legitimate governmental purpose.[172] Likewise, students arguing that exclusion from school without provision of an alternative educational program violates their state constitutional right to an education generally have not met with success. Students do have a right to a state-funded education, say the courts, but the right can be forfeited by violating school rules.[173] However, the West Virginia Supreme Court upheld the constitutionality of long-term suspensions only after noting that the suspended students would still have "reasonable state-funded basic educational opportunities and services available."[174]

In general, whether an excluded student must be given an alternative program is a statutory rather than a constitutional issue. Similarly, the maximum length of permissible suspension, whether permanent expulsion is allowed, and what offenses may result in suspension or expulsion are also determined by state statute.[175] For example, Kansas statutes authorize "any certified employee" to "suspend or expel" a student for violation of any rule "published" by the school or "approved" by the board, "conduct which disrupts, impedes or interferes with the . . . school," "conduct which substantially impinges upon or invades the rights of others," conduct that has resulted in a conviction for any state or federal crime, or disobeying an order of a teacher or other school authority." Although this list seems to give the school very wide discretion to exclude students, the law goes on to state that, "an expulsion may be for a term not exceeding 186 school days," so permanent exclusion is not allowed.[176]

Sometimes, statutes may require that a particular punishment be applied to a particular offense. The Gun-Free Schools Act of 1994[177] requires that states receiving federal education funds (that is, all states):

> shall have in effect a State law requiring local educational agencies to expel from school for period of not less than one year a student who is determined to have brought a weapon to a school under the jurisdiction of local educational agencies in that State, except that such State law shall allow the chief administering officer of such local educational agency to modify such expulsion requirement for a student on a case-by-case basis.

The Act goes on to say that states may, if they wish, permit school districts to provide alternative "educational services" to excluded students. Many states have modified their own statutes to comply with this federal mandate.[178] Some state laws also mandate exclusion from school under other specified circumstances. In Massachusetts, for example, principals are required to suspend pupils they deem a threat to other students and staff.[179]

"Zero-Tolerance"

Zero-tolerance policies (i.e., rules requiring that students be expelled for possession of drugs or weapons) are vulnerable to constitutional challenges when applied in an arbitrary manner.[180] For example, suppose a student was expelled for having a knife in his backpack that another student put there without his knowledge. The student might argue that the expulsion violated his Fourteenth Amendment right to substantive due process in that he was deprived of his liberty and property interest in school attendance for reasons that were entirely unconnected to any legitimate educational goal of the school. In *Colvin v. Lowndes County, Mississippi School District*,[181] the court overturned the zero-tolerance-policy-based one-year suspension of a sixth-grade student with a disability for possession of a small knife. The court found that rigid adherence to the zero-tolerance policy without consideration of the individual circumstances of the case violated the student's due process rights. The court noted that, "Individualized punishment by reference to all relevant facts and circumstances regarding the offense and the offender is a hallmark of our criminal justice system."

Academic Penalties

Academic penalties for unexcused absences have often been challenged in court with mixed results. Some courts have said that schools have the authority to lower grades for nonattendance, but others have disagreed.[182] Challenges claiming that the lowering of grades in a particular situation was arbitrary have sometimes succeeded particularly if the policy was not applied evenhandedly.[183] In *Slocum v. Holton Board of Education*[184] the policy of lowering grades when a student failed to make up missed days by attending study sessions was found not to be arbitrary. In *Barno v. Crestwood Board of Education*[185] the court ruled that a district policy that led to the denial of a diploma was unreasonable and contrary to state law. The policy required a 93 percent attendance rate and no more than thirteen days of absence. Here the student was absent eighteen days, but all but two of the absences were excused. In *State* ex rel. *Yarber v. McHenry*,[186] the court struck down on due process grounds a policy that cost a student a semester's worth of credit because he failed to meet the school's attendance policy by not attending four make-up classes. The court noted that the policy involved taking away previously earned credit, thus depriving the student of a property interest without a hearing. The court in *Knight v. Board of Education*[187] rejected a substantive due process claim attacking the loss of one-letter grade for the quarter for unexcused absences. A Kentucky court found that a school's policy of reducing grades for days missed while suspended exceeded the school's authority,[188] but other courts have upheld such policies challenged under state law.[189]

Cases challenging the lowering of grades and other academic penalties for misbehavior have also produced mixed results. In *Smith v. School City of Hobart*,[190] the court rejected on due process grounds a school's policy of lowering grades for nonacademic misconduct. Said the court, "Reducing grades unrelated to academic conduct results in a skewed and inaccurate reflection of a student's academic performance." But in a case in which a student was expelled for the term for violating a school's drug policy and stripped of all credit earned, the court found that punishment not to be unconstitutionally excessive.[191] In *Katzman v. Cumberland Valley School District*,[192] a school suspended a student for five days, expelled her from the cheerleading squad and National Honor Society, excluded her from all school activities, and reduced her grades by 10 points for the entire term because she ordered a glass of wine while on a field trip. The court concluded that the lowering of grades was an "illegal application of the Board's discretion." But the court in *South Gibson School Board v. Sollman*[193] upheld a zero-tolerance policy that required that the student be expelled and lose all credit for the semester, even credit already earned, when drug-sniffing dogs found a small amount of marijuana in his truck.

Equal protection cases may be brought against schools whose disciplinary policies discriminate on the basis of race, religion, gender, or national origin, such as by punishing students of one race more severely than another for the same offense.[194] Federal statutes also prohibit racial or gender discrimination in education including the assignment of punishment (see sec. 5.5) and place significant limitations on the punishment of students with disabilities (see sec. 6.3). Students singled out for more severe punishment than other wrongdoers for reasons other than race, religion, gender, or national origin can also bring equal protection cases, but the school will prevail as long as it has a rational basis for the differential treatment.[195] For example, applying a more severe punishment to a ringleader or to a repeat offender will probably be upheld.[196]

A final constitutional issue of potentially great significance to students who commit criminal acts at school is the question of whether being punished in a school proceeding and later by a court of law constitutes double jeopardy. The Fifth Amendment states: "[N]or shall any person be subject for the same offence to be twice put in jeopardy of life or limb." After all, students have argued, both schools and courts are agencies of the state. However, courts have rejected the argument that being punished at school precludes being punished again in court for the same offense and vice versa.[197]

Thus, students have tried to rely on a wide variety of federal constitutional principles to challenge school punishments, mostly without success. As long as punishments are reasonable in light of the student's infraction and the purpose for which they are given, as long as punishments are not so severe as to shock the conscience, and as long as punishments are not applied in a discriminatory manner, the federal Constitution will not interfere with the judgment of educators concerning the appropriateness of punishment. At the same time, the constitutions and statutes of many states and the policies of some school boards place important limitations on the authority of school officials to assign punishment. School officials who ignore these limitations place themselves and their schools at risk of litigation and place their jobs in jeopardy.

4.6 SUMMARY

Schools are permitted by statute and common law to regulate the conduct of their students. In matters of rule making, investigation of misconduct, determination of guilt, and assignment of punishment, schools generally have broad latitude. However, both state statutes and the Constitution constrain the performance of all these functions. The overriding constraint is that a school may only limit the behavior of its students in ways that are reasonably related to the promotion of legitimate educational goals.

Schools are free to create and enforce almost any rule that meets this general constraint. However, rules with no significant educational purpose and most regulation of off-campus behavior are beyond the statutory authority of the school board. Although it is not necessary to base all disciplinary action on specific preexisting rules, courts may object on due process grounds to enforcement of standards announced only after the fact. This is particularly likely when a school seeks to punish behaviors that common sense does not indicate are impermissible. The most common constitutional objection to a school rule is that it is vague. Although school rules may be more general than criminal statutes, most courts nevertheless insist that they be specific enough to permit the average student to distinguish between allowable and prohibited conduct.

When investigating possible student misconduct, school officials may employ any surveillance technique that does not intrude on a reasonably held expectation of privacy. Some courts permit searches of a student's locker without permission because the locker is controlled jointly by the student and school. Officials may question students without allowing them an attorney or alerting them to their privilege against self-incrimination. However, in order to search a student's pocket, purse, or other personal belongings, a school official must have reasonable grounds to believe that the search will produce evidence of a violation of a specific school rule or law. The suspicion must be directed at the specific student to be searched. Even so, the scope of the search must be reasonable considering the rule allegedly violated, the evidence sought, and the intrusiveness of the investigation. Certain random searches, such as required drug screening for athletes or metal detectors for everyone entering a school, may be permissible, especially if the purpose is to protect and educate rather than to punish.

The Due Process Clause of the Fourteenth Amendment requires that students be given an opportunity for a hearing prior to exclusion from school for disciplinary reasons. In *Goss v. Lopez*, the Supreme Court ruled that minimum due process for short-term suspensions of up to ten days consists of notification of the charges and an opportunity to refute them. An informal hearing may take place right after the infraction, and punishment may then be assigned. Suspensions lasting more than ten days require more elaborate due process. The accused student must be given advance notice of the charges and time and place of the hearing. Some, but not all, jurisdictions enforce other procedural protections and rules of evidence, such as the right to counsel, to cross-examine adverse witnesses, and to exclude hearsay testimony. The overriding requirement is that the tribunal be fair and impartial, with the student having adequate opportunity to present evidence and refute the opposing case. However, no hearing is required for corporal punishment or most mild classroom and school penalties.

Most constitutional challenges to schools' authority to punish their students for wrongdoing have not succeeded. However, state statutes generally set the limits of allowable punishment such as the maximum length of exclusion from school. Except where prohibited by statute or board policy, school officials may employ corporal punishment, although excessive or improper use of force or corporal punishment may lead to firing and civil or criminal penalties. School officials may also use reasonable force to keep order, to prevent harm to others or damage to property, or to defend themselves. Besides corporal punishment, the most controversial school penalty is grade reduction, but most courts have upheld academic penalties for truancy or work missed while under disciplinary suspension.

NOTES

1 Philip Leon M. v. Greenbrier County Bd. of Educ., 484 S.E.2d 909 (W. Va. 1996).
2 20 U.S.C. § 7912(a).
3 *See, e.g.*, 24 P.S. § 7–778; Nev. Rev. Stat. Ann. § 280.287; Tex. Educ. Code § 37.081; O.C.G.A. § 20–8–5.
4 20 U.S.C. § 7151.
5 Cal. Educ. Code § 48900.
6 Conn. Gen. Stat. § 10–222d; Or. Rev. Stat. § 339.356; Tenn. Code Ann. § 49–6–1016; 14 Del. C. § 4112D; N.J. Stat. § 18A:37–15; Iowa Code § 280.28; S.C. Code Ann. § 59–63–140; S.C. Code Ann. § 59–63–140; R.I. Gen. Laws § 16–21–26; A.C.A. § 6–18–514; W. Va. Code § 18–2C–3.
7 *See, e.g.*, N.Y. Educ. Code § 3214.3-a.
8 Richards v. Thurston, 424 F.2d 1281 (1st Cir. 1970); Shanley v. Northeast Indep. Sch. Dist., Bexar County, 462 F.2d 960 (5th Cir. 1972).
9 Dillon v. Pulaski County Special Sch. Dist., 468 F. Supp. 54 (E.D. Ark. 1978).
10 Nitzberg v. Parks, 525 F.2d 378 (4th Cir. 1975); Leibner v. Sharbaugh, 429 F. Supp. 744 (E.D. Va. 1977).
11 *In re* Suspension of Huffer, 546 N.E.2d 1308 (Ohio 1989).
12 505 P.2d 939 (Or. Ct. App. 1973).
13 Indep. Sch. Dist. No. 8 of Seiling v. Swanson, 553 P.2d 496 (Okla. 1976).
14 Jackson v. Dorrier, 424 F.2d 213 (6th Cir. 1970); *but see* Bishop v. Colaw, 450 F.2d 1069 (8th Cir. 1971).
15 Hatch v. Goerke, 502 F.2d 1189 (10th Cir. 1974); New Rider v. Bd. of Educ., 480 F.2d 693 (10th Cir. 1973); Moody v. Cronin, 484 F. Supp. 270 (C.D. Ill. 1979).
16 Alabama & Coushatta Tribes of Texas v. Big Sandy Indep. Sch. Dist., 817 F. Supp. 1319 (E.D. Tex. 1993), *remanded*, 20 F.3d 469 (5th Cir. 1994).
17 Griswold v. Connecticut, 381 U.S. 479 (1965).
18 *E.g.*, Massie v. Henry, 455 F.2d 779 (4th Cir. 1972).
19 *E.g.*, King v. Saddleback Junior Coll. Dist., 445 F.2d 932 (9th Cir. 1971).
20 Barber v. Colo. Indep. Sch. Dist., 901 S.W.2d 447 (Tex. 1995).

21 251 S.E.2d 889 (N.C. Ct. App. 1979), and 448 F. Supp. 497 (W.D.N.C. 1978).

22 Johnson v. Joint Sch. Dist. No. 60, 508 P.2d 547 (Idaho 1973).

23 346 F. Supp. 156 (E.D. Ark. 1972).

24 Bannister v. Paradis, 316 F. Supp. 185 (D.N.H. 1970).

25 418 S.W.2d 535 (Tex. Ct. App. 1967).

26 Bd. of Dir. of the Indep. Sch. Dist. of Waterloo v. Green, 147 N.W.2d 854 (Iowa 1967).

27 Griswold v. Connecticut, 381 U.S. 479 (1965).

28 Bd. of Educ. of Millbrook Cent. Sch. Dist. v. Ambach, 465 N.Y.S.2d 77 (N.Y. App. Div. 1983).

29 *See* Seal v. Morgan, 229 F.3d 567 (6th Cir. 2000); J.M. v. Webster County Bd. of Educ., 534 S.E.2d 50 (W. Va. 2000).

30 837 N.Y.S. 2d 507 (Sup. 2007); *aff'd*, 855 N.Y.S.2d 530 (N.Y. 1st A.D. 2008).

31 Connally v. Gen. Constr., 269 U.S. 385 (1926).

32 Stephenson v. Davenport Cmty. Sch. Dist., 110 F.3d 1303 (8th Cir. 1997).

33 Claiborne v. Beebe Sch. Dist., 687 F. Supp. 1358 (E.D. Ark. 1988).

34 Soglin v. Kauffman, 295 F. Supp. 978 (W.D. Wis. 1968), *aff'd*, 418 F.2d 163 (7th Cir. 1969).

35 Galveston Indep. Sch. Dist. v. Boothe, 590 S.W.2d 553 (Tex. Ct. App. 1979).

36 Crossen v. Fatsi, 309 F. Supp. 114 (D. Conn. 1970).

37 409 F. Supp. 379 (W.D. Pa. 1976).

38 Bd. of Airport Comm'rs of Los Angeles v. Jews for Jesus, Inc., 482 U.S. 569 (1987); Broadrick v. Oklahoma, 413 U.S. 601 (1973).

39 Wallace v. Batavia Sch. Dist. 101, 68 F.3d 1010 (7th Cir. 1995).

40 404 F. Supp. 2d 1195 (C.D. Cal. 2005).

41 Gray *ex rel.* Alexander v. Bostic, 458 F.3d 1295 (11th Cir. 2006).

42 P.B. v. Koch, 96 F.3d 1298 (9th Cir. 1996).

43 84 F.3d 1021 (8th Cir. 1996).

44 Sansone v. Bechtel, 429 A.2d 820 (Conn. 1980).

45 *In re* Gault, 387 U.S. 1 (1967).

46 *In re* S.W., 614 S.E.2d 424 (N.C. App. 2005). *See also* People v. Dilworth, 661 N.E. 2d 310 (Ill. 1996).

47 727 A.2d 570 (Pa. Super. 1999).

48 528 So. 2d 1253 (Fla. App. 1988).

49 249 N.E.2d 366 (N.Y. 1969).

50 810 F.2d 188 (8th Cir. 1987).

51 Martens v. Dist. No. 220, 620 F. Supp. 29 (N.D. Ill. 1985); *see also* Myers v. State, 839 N.E.2d 1154 (Ind. 2005).

52 384 U.S. 436 (1966).

53 Boynton v. Casey, 543 F. Supp. 995 (D. Me. 1982).

54 Edwards v. Rees, 883 F.2d 882 (10th 1989).

55 People v. Pankhurst, 848 N.E.2d 628 (Ill. App. 2d Dist. 2006).

56 Katz v. United States, 389 U.S. 347 (1967) (Harlan, J. concurring).

57 State v. D.T.W., 425 So. 2d 1383 (Fla. Dist. Ct. App. 1983); Speake v. Grantham, 317 F. Supp. 1253 (S.D. Miss. 1970), *aff'd*, 440 F.2d 1351 (5th Cir. 1971).

58 State v. Johnson, 530 P.2d 910 (Ariz. Ct. App. 1975).

59 Stern v. New Haven Cmty. Sch., 529 F. Supp. 31 (E.D. Mich. 1981).

60 *In re* Patrick Y., 746 A.2d 405 (2000); People v. Overton, 229 N.E. 2d 596 (N.Y. 1967), and 249 N.E. 2d 366 (N.Y. 1969); Zamora v. Pomeroy, 639 F.2d 662 (10th Cir. 1981).

61 Commonwealth v. Cass, 709 A. 2d 350 (Pa. 1998).

62 State v. Jones, 666 N.W.2d 142 (Iowa 2003); State v. Joseph T., 336 S.E.2d 728 (W. Va. 1985); S.C. v. State, 583 So. 2d 188 (Miss. 1991); Commonwealth v. Snyder, 597 N.E.2d 1363 (Mass. 1992).

63 Commonwealth v. Cass, 709 A.2d 350 (Pa. 1998).

64 *In re* Adam, 697 N.E.2d 1100 (Ohio Ct. App. 1997).

65 S.C. v. State, 583 So. 2d 188 (Miss. 1991).

66 *See* Commonwealth v. Carey, 554 N.E.2d 1199 (Mass. 1990); Isiah B. v. State, 500 N.W.2d 637 (Wis. 1993); *but see In re* Patrick Y., 746 A.2d 405 (Md. 2000).

67 United States v. Place, 462 U.S. 696 (1983).

68 690 F.2d 470 (5th Cir. 1982).

69 Anable v. Ford, 653 F. Supp. 22 (W.D. Ark. 1985).

70 742 F.2d 977 (6th Cir. 1984).

71 Fewless *ex rel.* Fewless v. Bd. of Educ. of Wayland, 208 F. Supp. 2d 806 (W.D. Mich. 2002).

72 469 U.S. 325 (1985).
73 DesRoches v. Caprio, 974 F. Supp. 542 (E.D. Va. 1997), *rev'd.*, 156 F.3d 571 (4th Cir. 1998).
74 828 F.2d 1151 (6th Cir. 1987).
75 694 P.2d 1078 (Wash. 1985).
76 Mapp v. Ohio, 367 U.S. 643 (1961).
77 People v. Scott D., 315 N.E.2d 466 (N.Y. 1974); *but see* State v. Young, 216 S.E.2d 586 (Ga. 1975).
78 Thompson v. Carthage Sch. Dist., 87 F.3d 979 (8th Cir. 1996); James v. Unified Sch. Dist. No. 512, 899 F. Supp. 530 (D. Kan. 1995); Jones v. Latexo Indep. Sch. Dist., 499 F. Supp. 223 (E.D. Tex. 1980); Morale v. Grigel, 422 F. Supp. 988 (D.N.H. 1976).
79 Juan C. v. Cortines, 679 N.E.2d 1061 (N.Y. 1997).
80 42 U.S.C. § 1983.
81 Williams v. Ellington, 936 F.2d 881 (6th Cir. 1991); Bellnier v. Lund, 438 F. Supp. 47 (N.D.N.Y. 1977).
82 Jenkins v. Talladega City Bd. of Educ., 115 F.3d 821 (11th Cir. 1997) (en banc).
83 469 U.S. 325 (1985).
84 733 P.2d 316 (Ariz. Ct. App. 1987).
85 *In re* Bobby B., 218 Cal. Rptr. 253 (Cal. Ct. App. 1985).
86 Commonwealth v. Smith, 889 N.E.2d 439 (Mass. App. Ct. 2008).
87 Rhodes v. Guarricino, 54 F. Supp. 2d 186 (S.D.N.Y. 1999).
88 Rinker v. Sipler, 264 F. Supp. 2d 181 (M.D. Pa. 2003).
89 156 F.3d 571 (4th Cir. 1998).
90 *In re* Gregory, 82 N.Y.2d 588 (N.Y. 1993).
91 Carlson *ex rel.* Stuczynksi v. Bremen High Sch., 423 F. Supp. 2d 823 (N.D. Ill. 2006).
92 635 F. Supp. 454 (E.D. Mich. 1985); *see also* State v. Pablo R. 137 P.3d 1198 (N.M. App. 2006).
93 Anders *ex rel.* Anders v. Fort Wayne Cmty. Schs., 124 F. Supp. 2d 618 (N.D. Ind. 2000).
94 New Mexico v. Michael G., 748 P.2d 17 (N.M. Ct. App. 1987).
95 In the Interest of S.C. v. State, 583 So. 2d 188 (Miss. 1991).
96 Phaneuf v. Cipriano, 330 F. Supp. 2d 74 (D. Conn. 2004).
97 Redding v. Safford Unified Sch. Dist. No. 1, 531 F.3d 1071 (9th Cir. 2008)(en banc).
98 Fewless *ex rel.* Fewless v. Bd. of Educ. of Wayland, 208 F. Supp. 2d 806 (W.D. Mich. 2002); *see also In re* Doe, 91 P.3d 485 (Hawaii 2004).
99 931 A.2d 1229 (N.H. 2007).
100 Burnham v. West, 681 F. Supp. 1160 (E.D. Va. 1987); Bellnier v. Lund, 438 F. Supp. 47 (N.D.N.Y. 1977); Kuehn v. Renton Sch. Dist. No. 403, 694 P.2d 1078 (Wash. 1985); Horton v. Goose Creek Indep. Sch. Dist., 690 F.2d 470 (5th Cir. 1982); *but see* DesRoches v. Caprio, 156 F.3d 571 (4th Cir. 1998).
101 Thompson v. Carthage Sch. Dist., 87 F.3d 979 (8th Cir. 1996); *In re* Alexander B., 270 Cal. Rptr. 342 (Cal. Ct. App. 1990).
102 Cornfield v. Consol. High Sch. Dist. No. 230, 991 F.2d 1316 (7th Cir. 1993); Kennedy v. Dexter Consol. Sch., 955 P.2d 693 (N.M. Ct. App. 1998).
103 Williams v. Ellington, 936 F.2d 881 (6th Cir. 1991).
104 Phaneuf v. Fraikin, 448 F.3d 591 (2d Cir. 2006).
105 Bell v. Marseilles Elementary Sch., 160 F. Supp. 2d 883 (N.D. Ill. 2001); Kennedy v. Dexter Consol. Sch., 10 P.3d 115 (N.M. 2000). *Compare* Thomas *ex rel.* Thomas v. Roberts, 261 F.3d 1160 (11th Cir. 2001), *cert. granted, vacated*, 536 U.S. 953 (2002), *on remand*, 232 F.3d 950 (2003).
106 T.J. v. State, 538 So. 2d 1320 (Fla. Dist. Ct. App. 1989).
107 West Virginia *ex rel.* Galford v. Mark Anthony B., 433 S.E. 2d 41 (W.Va. 1993).
108 Jenkins v. Talladega City Bd. of Educ., 95 F.3d 1036 (11th Cir. 1996).
109 Carlson *ex rel.* Stuczynksi v. Bremen High Sch., 423 F. Supp. 2d 823 (N.D. Ill. 2006).
110 Rinker v. Sipler, 264 F. Supp. 2d 181 (M.D. Pa.).
111 Cornfield v. Consol. High Sch. Dist. No. 230, 991 F.2d 1316 (7th Cir. 1993).
112 129 S. Ct. 2633 (2009).
113 § 167.166 MO. REV. STAT; New York City Dept. of Educ., Reg. No. A-432, p. 2 (2005).
114 In the Interest of S.S., 680 A.2d 1172 (Pa. Super. Ct. 1996); In the Interest of F.B., 658 A.2d 1378 (Pa. Super. Ct. 1995); New York v. Dukes, 580 N.Y.S.2d 850 (N.Y. Crim. Ct. 1992); Illinois v. Pruitt, 662 N.E.2d 450 (Ill. App. Ct. 1996).
115 Doe *ex rel.* Doe v. Little Rock Sch. Dist., 380 F.3d 349 (8th Cir. 2004).

116 Kuehn v. Renton Sch. Dist. No. 403, 694 P.2d 1078 (Wash. 1985).

117 Thompson v. Carthage Sch. Dist., 87 F.3d 979 (8th Cir. 1996).

118 *In re* Alexander B., 270 Cal. Rptr. 342 (Ct. App. 2d Dist. 1990).

119 Thomas *ex rel.* Thomas v. Roberts, 261 F.3d 1160 (11th Cir. 2001); Beard v. Whitmore Lake Sch. Dist., 402 F.3d 598 (6th Cir. 2005).

120 Hedges v. Musco, 204 F.3d 109 (3d Cir. 2000).

121 Willis v. Anderson, 158 F.3d 415 (7th Cir. 1998).

122 515 U.S. 646 (1995).

123 536 U.S. 822 (2002).

124 *Compare* Theodore v. Delaware Valley Sch. Dist., 761 A.2d 652 (Pa. Commw. 2000) (striking down random drug testing), *and* Linke v. Northwestern Sch. Corp., 763 N.E. 2d 972 (Ind. 2002) (upholding random drug testing).

125 Joye v. Hunterdon Cent. Reg'l High Sch., 826 A.2d 624 (N.J. 2003).

126 Weber v. Oakridge Sch. Dist., 76, 56 P.3d 504 (Or. Ct. App. 2002).

127 Edwards v. Rees, 883 F.2d 882 (10th Cir. 1989).

128 422 F.3d 141 (3d Cir. 2005).

129 226 F.3d 652 (5th Cir. 2000).

130 Dixon v. Ala. State Bd. of Educ., 294 F.2d 150 (5th Cir. 1961).

131 419 U.S. 565 (1975).

132 411 U.S. 1 (1973).

133 C.B. v. Driscoll, 82 F.3d 383 (11th Cir. 1996).

134 661 F. Supp. 155 (E.D. Tenn. 1987).

135 Seamons v. Snow, 84 F.3d 1226 (10th Cir. 1996); Mazevski v. Horseheads Cent. Sch. Dist., 950 F. Supp. 69 (W.D.N.Y. 1997); Hebert v. Ventetuolo, 638 F.2d 5 (1st Cir. 1981); Bernstein v. Menard, 557 F. Supp. 90 (E.D. Va. 1982), *appeal dismissed*, 728 F.2d 252 (4th Cir. 1984); *but see* Duffley v. N.H. Interscholastic Athletic Ass'n, 446 A.2d 462 (N.H. 1982).

136 Campbell v. Bd. of Educ. of New Milford, 475 A.2d 289 (Conn. 1984).

137 Swany v. San Ramon Valley Unified Sch. Dist., 720 F. Supp. 764 (N.D. Cal. 1989); Fowler v. Williamson, 448 F. Supp. 497 (W.D.N.C. 1978); Dolinger v. Driver, 498 S.E.2d 252 (Ga. 1998).

138 Ingraham v. Wright, 430 U.S. 651 (1977).

139 676 F. Supp. 749 (S.D. Miss. 1987), *aff'd*, 853 F.2d 924 (5th Cir. 1988).

140 501 F.3d 577 (6th Cir. 2007).

141 375 F. Supp. 1043 (N.D. Tex. 1974).

142 915 S.W.2d 325 (Mo. 1995) (en banc).

143 Keough v. Tate County Bd. of Educ., 748 F.2d 1077 (5th Cir. 1984); Coffman v. Kuehler, 409 F. Supp. 546 (N.D. Tex. 1976).

144 588 F. Supp. 608 (E.D. Pa. 1984).

145 *See, e.g.*, Gonzales v. McEuen, 435 F. Supp. 460 (C.D. Cal. 1977).

146 826 F.2d 526 (7th Cir. 1987).

147 *See also* Keough v. Tate County Bd. of Educ., 748 F.2d 1077 (5th Cir. 1984).

148 Strickland v. Inlow, 519 F.2d 744 (8th Cir. 1975); *but see* Walker v. Bradley, 320 N.W.2d 900 (Neb. 1982).

149 Sullivan v. Houston Indep. Sch. Dist., 475 F.2d 1071 (5th Cir. 1973).

150 Dixon v. Ala. State Bd. of Educ., 294 F.2d 150 (5th Cir. 1961).

151 Mandell v. Bd. of Educ., 662 N.Y.S.2d 598 (N.Y. App. Div. 1997); Washington v. Smith, 618 N.E.2d 561 (Ill. App. Ct. 1993).

152 Anable v. Ford, 653 F. Supp. 22 (W.D. Ark.), *modified*, 663 F. Supp. 149 (W.D. Ark. 1985).

153 Keough v. Tate County Bd. of Educ., 748 F.2d 1077 (5th Cir. 1984).

154 Newsome v. Batavia Local Sch. Dist., 842 F.2d 920 (6th Cir. 1988); Brewer v. Austin Indep. Sch. Dist., 779 F.2d 260 (5th Cir. 1985).

155 Bogle-Assegai v. Bloomfield Bd. of Educ., 467 F. Supp. 2d 236 (D. Conn. 2006); B.S. *ex rel.* Schneider v. Bd. of Sch. Trustees, 255 F. Supp. 2d 891 (N.D. Ind. 2003).

156 Rigau v. Dist. Sch. Bd. of Pasco County, 961 So. 2d 382 (Fla. App. 2 Dist. 2007).

157 Tasby v. Estes, 643 F.2d 1103 (5th Cir. Unit A Apr. 1981).

158 Gonzales v. McEuen, 435 F. Supp. 460 (C.D. Cal. 1977); Alex v. Allen, 409 F. Supp. 379 (W.D. Pa. 1976).

159 Givens v. Poe, 346 F. Supp. 202 (W.D.N.C. 1972); Gonzales v. McEuen, 435 F. Supp. 460 (C.D. Cal. 1977).

160   Jaksa v. Regents of Univ. of Mich., 597 F. Supp. 1245 (E.D. Mich. 1984) *aff'd*, 787 F.2d 590 (6th Cir. 1986).

161   Jaksa v. Regents of Univ. of Mich., 597 F. Supp. 1245 (E.D. Mich. 1984) *aff'd*, 787 F.2d 590 (6th Cir. 1986).

162   Hassan v. Lubbock Indep. Sch. Dist., 55 F.3d 1075 (5th Cir. 1995).

163   Rasmus v. Arizona, 939 F. Supp. 709 (D. Ariz. 1996).

164   Orange v. County of Grundy, 950 F. Supp. 1365 (E.D. Tenn. 1996).

165   430 U.S. 651 (1977).

166   Woodard v. Los Fresnos Indep. Sch. Dist., 732 F.2d 1243 (5th Cir. 1984).

167   Hall v. Tawney, 621 F.2d 607 (4th Cir. 1980).

168   Johnson v. Newburgh Enlarged Sch. Dist., 239 F.3d 246 (2d Cir. 2001); Neal *ex rel.* Neal v. Fulton County Bd. of Educ., 229 F.3d 1069 (11th Cir. 2000), *reh'g & reh'g en banc denied*, 244 F.3d 143 (11th Cir. 2000); London v. Dirs. of DeWitt Pub. Schs., 194 F.3d 873 (8th Cir. 1999); Saylor v. Bd. of Educ. of Harlan County, 118 F.3d 507 (6th Cir. 1997); P.B. v. Koch, 96 F.3d 1298 (9th Cir. 1996); Metzger v. Osbek, 841 F.2d 518 (3d Cir. 1988); Wise v. Pea Ridge Sch. Dist., 855 F.2d 560 (8th Cir. 1988); *compare* Moore v. Willis Indep. Sch. Dist., 233 F.3d 871 (5th Cir. 2000); Fee v. Herndon, 900 F.2d 804 (5th Cir. 1990).

169   CAL. EDUC. CODE § 49001; N.Y. COMP. CODES R. & REGS. tit. 8, § 19.5.

170   Bott v. Bd. of Educ., Deposit Cent. Sch. Dist., 360 N.E.2d 952 (N.Y. 1977).

171   P.B. v. Koch, 96 F.3d 1298 (9th Cir. 1996); Thompson v. Iberville Parish Sch. Bd., 372 So. 2d 642 (La. Ct. App. 1979); B.L. v. Dep't of Health & Rehabilitative Serv., 545 So. 2d 289 (Fla. Dist. Ct. App. 1989); People v. Wehmeyer, 509 N.E.2d 605 (Ill. App. Ct. 1987); Rolando v. Sch. Dir. of Dist. No. 125, County of LaSalle, 358 N.E.2d 945 (Ill. App. Ct. 1976); Calway v. Williamson, 36 A.2d 377 (Conn. 1944).

172   Craig v. Selma City Sch. Bd., 801 F. Supp. 585 (S.D. Ala. 1992).

173   Doe v. Superintendent of Sch. of Worcester, 653 N.E.2d 1088 (Mass. 1995); Kolesnick v. Omaha Pub. Sch. Dist., 558 N.W.2d 807 (Neb. 1997); D.B. v. Clarke County Bd. of Educ., 469 S.E.2d 438 (Ga. Ct. App. 1996).

174   Cathe v. Doddridge County Bd. of Educ., 490 S.E.2d 340 (W. Va. 1997).

175   Spencer v. Omaha Pub. Sch. Dist., 566 N.W.2d 757 (Neb. 1997).

176   KAN. STAT. ANN. §§ 72–8901–02.

177   20 U.S.C. § 8921.

178   *See, e.g.*, W. VA. CODE § 18A–5–1a.

179   Doe v. Superintendent of Sch. of Worcester, 653 N.E.2d 1088 (Mass. 1995).

180   *See* Seal v. Morgan, 229 F.3d 567 (6th Cir. 2000); J.M. v. Webster County Bd. of Educ., 534 S.E.2d 50 (W. Va. 2000).

181   114 F. Supp. 2d 504 (N.D. Miss. 2000).

182   Campbell v. Bd. of Educ. of New Milford, 475 A.2d 289 (Conn. 1984); Bitting v. Lee, 564 N.Y.S.2d 791 (N.Y. App. Div. 1990) (ruling for school); Gutierrez v. Sch. Dist., 585 P.2d 935 (Colo. Ct. App. 1978) (ruling for student).

183   Ochsner v. Bd. of Trustees, 811 P.2d 985 (Wash. Ct. App. 1991).

184   429 N.W. 2d 607 (Mich. Ct. App. 1988).

185   731 N.E.2d 701 (Ohio Ct. App. 1998).

186   915 S.W.2d 325 (Mo. 1955) (en banc).

187   348 N.E.2d 299 (Ill. App. Ct. 1976); *see also* Raymon v. Alvord Indep. Sch. Dist., 639 F.2d 257 (5th Cir. 1981).

188   Dorsey v. Bale, 521 S.W.2d 76 (Ky. Ct. App. 1975).

189   Donaldson v. Bd. of Educ., 424 N.E.2d 737 (Ill. Ct. App. 1981).

190   811 F. Supp. 391 (N.D. Ind. 1993); *see also* Hamer v. Bd. of Educ., 383 N.E.2d 231 (Ill. Ct. App. 1978).

191   Fisher v. Burkburnett Independent Sch. Dist., 419 F. Supp. 1200 (N.D. Tex. 1976); *see also* New Braunfels Indep. Sch. Dist. v. Armke, 658 S.W.2d 330 (Tex. Ct. App. 1983).

192   479 A.2d 671 (Pa. Commw. Ct. 1984).

193   768 N.E.2d 437 (Ind. 2002).

194   Hawkins v. Coleman, 376 F. Supp. 1330 (N.D. Tex. 1974).

195   Smith v. Severn, 129 F.3d 419 (7th Cir. 1997).

196   *See* Reed v. Vermilion Local Sch. Dist., 614 N.E.2d 1101 (Ohio Ct. App. 1992).

197   Matter of C.M.J., 915 P.2d 62 (Kan. 1996); Clements v. Bd. of Trustees of Sheridan County Sch. Dist., 585 P.2d 197 (Wyo. 1978).

5 Equal Educational Opportunity
Race and Gender

Chapters 5 and 6 deal with issues of equity in education. This chapter looks at legal efforts to end discrimination based on race and gender. The litigation and legislation it examines challenge a variety of discriminatory practices including forced segregation of the races, gender-based denial of educational opportunity, racial and gender discrimination in school discipline and athletics, and racial and sexual harassment. Chapter 6 examines equity issues relating to student populations with special needs: For students with disabilities or who are limited-English speaking, equality of opportunity may require an educational program that is different and in some cases even separate from the majority of students. A third set of equity issues, relating to the way public education is funded, is not considered in this text because it has less direct bearing on the work of teachers.

For more than fifty years, the search for equality of opportunity has been the subject of more influential litigation than any other educational issue. Even after all this time, however, the meanings of terms like equity and equality of opportunity have not been fully clarified. Does equity mean providing the same education to everyone or does it mean providing all pupils with an education tailored to their particular characteristics and needs? Does equity require spending the same amount on each student or more on some than others or should equity be viewed in terms of outcomes? For example, should everyone be given whatever education is necessary to reach a certain level of achievement? Issues like these play a central role in the cases and principles discussed in Chapters 5 and 6.

Historically, Blacks were the first group to bring serious legal challenge to the notion that states are free to provide whatever education they choose to whomever they wish. The case that dispelled this notion forever was *Brown v. Board of Education*.[1] The claims of the various other groups discussed and the litigation they have brought, although different in important respects, can be viewed as descended from *Brown*.

5.1 THE EQUAL PROTECTION CLAUSE AND RACIAL DISCRIMINATION

The legal foundation of *Brown* and of the quest for equality of opportunity in education generally is the Equal Protection Clause of the Fourteenth Amendment of the Constitution, which states: ". . . [N]or shall [any State] deny to any person within its jurisdiction the equal protection of the laws."

Over the years, the Supreme Court repeatedly has been called upon to define and interpret these simple-sounding words. In rough terms, to deny equal protection means to treat a person or group differently from others without sufficient reason. The Fourteenth Amendment permits the classification and differential treatment of individuals by the government if there exists an adequate justification, but prohibits discrimination when no satisfactory reasons exist.

Governments create distinctions among people in almost everything they do. For example, some individuals are classified as criminals and sent to jail, whereas others remain free. Some are issued driver's licenses but others are denied them. In the realm of education, some, but not all, people are compelled to attend school. Clearly, people are treated differently, but there may be adequate justification based on criminal behavior (incarceration), physical capacity (driver's licenses), or age (compulsory schooling). Other bases of classification such as race, religion, or gender may not be adequate to legitimate the same differential treatment. How do courts determine if the justification for a particular classification is adequate? How are equal protection cases decided?

A typical equal protection case begins with an individual or group complaining that they have been denied a benefit or suffered a burden unfairly. In most cases, the criterion used by the government to allocate or deny benefits or to impose burdens selectively is overt. This was the case in the south in the early 1950s when schools were segregated: Race was the openly used criterion for assigning students to schools.

Sometimes, however, differential treatment occurs, but the criterion of classification is not openly acknowledged. This may occur in education when, for example, a school board uses a "freedom of choice" or an "open-enrollment" policy as a ruse to maintain segregated schools.[2] In cases like these, the Supreme Court has placed the burden of establishing the actual basis of the differential treatment on the plaintiffs. For example, when racial discrimination is claimed but not acknowledged, plaintiffs must prove that government policies were in fact driven by considerations of race.

Once the criterion of classification has been established, it must next be determined whether the plaintiff or the government bears the burden of proving the adequacy of the justification for differential treatment and whether the differential treatment is in fact justified. With regard to both these issues, the Supreme Court has decided that the answers shall depend in part on the criterion of classification used. When race is the criterion, the burden of proof is on the government to provide an extremely strong justification for its law or policy. In effect, race-dependent classification is presumed unconstitutional, and unless the government can overcome the presumption by providing a truly extraordinary justification, the policy is unconstitutional.

In imposing this heavy burden of proof, courts employ a test known as **strict scrutiny**. Under this test, a law or policy is presumed unconstitutional unless the government can show that it is necessary to achieve a compelling state interest. Government actions subjected to strict scrutiny will be declared unconstitutional unless they are found essential to the attainment of a legitimate and extremely important goal.

As shown later in this chapter and in subsequent chapters, courts do not impose the ultimate burden of persuasion on the government in all equal protection cases nor do they always require such a strong justification for differential treatment. Courts do impose this heavy burden on the government in race cases because all branches and levels of government have now acknowledged that U.S. history is marked by many instances of invidious and unjustified racial discrimination. Accordingly, when a court sees a policy formulated on the basis of race, it suspects that racial discrimination may again be occurring and it wants strong and convincing assurances from the government that this is not the case. Strict scrutiny is a court's way of demanding the necessary assurances. Strict scrutiny promotes the goal of equal protection of all races by imposing a burden that the government is rarely able to meet. (Strict scrutiny is also used in cases involving fundamental rights—not normally relevant to education cases.[3])

5.2 HISTORICAL PERSPECTIVE: EQUAL PROTECTION PRIOR TO *BROWN v. BOARD OF EDUCATION*

The Fourteenth Amendment was adopted in 1868 in the aftermath of the Civil War to protect the legal and political rights of newly freed slaves. Twelve years later, the Supreme Court, in *Strauder v. West Virginia*,[4] used the amendment for the first time to strike down a law barring Blacks from serving on juries. The case was easy because the law was clearly and overtly discriminatory. As the Court said, the Fourteenth Amendment protected Blacks from "legal discriminations, implying inferiority in civil society, lessening the security of their enjoyment of rights which others enjoy, and discriminations which are steps toward reducing them to the condition of a subject race."

In 1886, the Court for the first time recognized the existence of racial discrimination in the application of a facially neutral law.[5] The facts of the case were that all non-Chinese seeking waivers of a law prohibiting the operation of laundries in wooden buildings were approved, but none of the 200 Chinese applicants received waivers. The Court said this was a form of racial discrimination. A law may be fair on its face, but when administered "with an evil eye and an unequal hand" so as to make unjust discriminations between persons, it is unconstitutional. "The discrimination is admitted. No reason for it is shown, and the conclusion cannot be resisted, that no reason for it exists except hostility to the race and nationality to which the petitioners belong, and which in the eye of the law is not justified."

However, in 1896, in *Plessy v. Ferguson*,[6] the Court upheld a Louisiana statute requiring "equal but separate accommodations for the white and colored races" on trains. This decision might at first seem inconsistent with *Strauder*, but the Court saw a distinction between the two cases: The law in *Strauder* clearly gave different rights to Blacks and Whites, but the *Plessy* law treated Blacks and Whites the same. The Court rejected the claim that the Louisiana statute had a stigmatizing effect on Blacks and endorsed the legally enforced separation of the races as constitutionally permissible. The *Plessy* Court did not employ the strict scrutiny test because it had not yet been developed for use in any kind of case. Rather the Court placed the burden of proof on the plaintiff to show that the law was without adequate justification. Ultimately, however, the Court found many social justifications for the law and rejected the plaintiff's claim of its harmful effects.

In 1938, in a nonrace case, the Court took its first step toward adopting the strict scrutiny test. In *United States v. Carolene Products Co.*,[7] the Court said that the usual presumption that laws and policies are constitutional may be weakened in cases where: (a) the legislation concerns matters specifically prohibited by the Bill of Rights, (b) the legislation affects the right to vote or to disseminate information or interferes with political organizations, or (c) the legislation is directed toward religious or racial minorities. Regarding the last point, the Court specifically suggested that there would be a need for more "searching judicial inquiry" when "prejudice against discrete and insular minorities curtails the normal political processes ordinarily to be relied upon to protect" them. With these dicta, the Court signaled that it would use something like strict scrutiny to deal with legislation designed to disadvantage a particular race.

Another 1938 case, *Missouri ex rel. Gaines v. Canada*,[8] involved racial discrimination in education directly. The plaintiff challenged a policy of the University of Missouri Law School denying admission to Blacks. Missouri had no separate law school for Blacks, but the state offered to pay the plaintiff's tuition at an out-of-state school. The Court declared that Missouri's policy of providing a law school for Whites but none for Blacks violated the Equal Protection Clause even under the separate-but equal doctrine.

Gaines provided the basis for a sustained assault, led by the National Association for the Advancement of Colored People (NAACP), on the segregated higher education systems of several states. In *Sweatt v. Painter*,[9] the plaintiff claimed that Texas' separate Black law school was unequal both in tangible and intangible ways. The Court agreed that the White and Black law schools were unequal in such intangibles as reputation of the faculty, experience of the administration, position and influence of the alumni, standing in the community, traditions, and prestige. Thus, Texas had not met the full requirements of separate but equal, and the Court ordered the admission of the Black plaintiff to the White law school.

In *McLaurin v. Oklahoma State Regents*,[10] decided the same year as *Sweatt*, the Black plaintiff had been allowed to attend the University of Oklahoma but was segregated from the White students. He was assigned to a desk in an anteroom of the classroom, confined to the mezzanine of the library, and required to eat at a separate table in the cafeteria. The Court rejected this arrangement saying that McLaurin was

> handicapped in his pursuit of effective graduate instruction. Such restrictions impair and inhibit his ability to study, to engage in discussion and exchange views with other students, and, in general, to learn his profession. . . . The removal of the state restrictions will not necessarily abate individual and group predilections, prejudices and choices. But at the very least, the state will not be depriving appellant of the opportunity to secure acceptance by his fellow students on his own merits.

None of the cases directly overturned the doctrine of separate but equal but they were steps toward its elimination. Neither did these cases embrace the use of the strict scrutiny test in race cases. Yet, the Court in fact had used that test in 1944 in a noneducation case, *Korematsu v. United States*.[11] The case challenged a military order excluding all persons of Japanese ancestry from significant areas of the West Coast following the attack on Pearl Harbor. The Court wrote: ". . . all legal restrictions which curtail the civil rights of a single racial group are immediately suspect. That is not to say all such restrictions are unconstitutional. It is to say that courts must subject them to the most rigid scrutiny." However, in applying the strict scrutiny standard, the Court concluded that the military order was justified by concerns of national security. This is one of the few race cases employing the strict scrutiny test that the government has won.

During this same period, no such evolution was occurring in the Court's application of the Equal Protection Clause to cases not involving race. In *Goesaert v. Cleary*,[12] the plaintiff challenged a Michigan law denying bartender's licenses to women except wives or daughters of bar owners. The Court began by stating that historical tradition justified regulating the work of women in bars: "The Fourteenth Amendment did not tear history up by the roots, . . . the vast changes in the social and legal position of women . . . [do] not preclude the states from drawing a sharp line between the sexes, certainly in such matters as the regulation of the liquor traffic."

Regarding the exception for relatives of bar owners, the Court wrote, "While Michigan may deny to all women opportunities for bartending, Michigan cannot play favorites among women without rhyme or reason." However, the Court was satisfied that Michigan had a sufficient reason: It wished to protect women whose husbands or fathers were not present in the bar. This justification was accepted even though women were permitted to work as waitresses in bars, just not bartenders. Said the Court: "A statute is not invalid under the Constitution because it might have gone farther than it did, or because it may not succeed in bringing about the result that it tends to produce."

In contrast to strict scrutiny, the test used in *Goesaert* is known as **rational basis**. This test places the burden of proof on the plaintiff to show that the government's policy does not serve a legitimate purpose or that the classification is not connected in any reasonable way to a legitimate goal. Thus, in most nonrace equal protection cases, the plaintiff carries the burden of overcoming the presumption that the law is constitutional. The presumption can be overcome only by showing that the legislature was pursuing illegitimate purposes in creating the law or that its method of achieving a legitimate purpose was irrational or unreasonable. This can rarely be accomplished.

In sum, when *Brown v. Board of Education* reached the Supreme Court in 1954, the equal protection doctrine had three dimensions: (a) in racial segregation in higher education cases, separate but equal was being enforced in a way that was forcing some institutions to integrate; (b) in other race cases, the Court was moving toward the use of the strict scrutiny test; and (c) in nonrace cases, the Court was bending over backward to avoid rejecting any law by using the rational basis test.

5.3 RACIAL SEGREGATION

Encouraged by the success of its challenges to government-enforced segregation in public higher education, the NAACP turned its attention to the lower schools. The original plan was to pursue the same strategy as in the graduate and law school cases. Suits would be brought in various parts of the country designed to demonstrate that separate public schools were in fact unequal. The plan was not to attack directly the separate-but-equal doctrine itself but to use the doctrine to force upgrading of woefully underfinanced segregated Black schools. Then, in midstream, the NAACP changed its strategy to one of attacking the separate-but-equal doctrine directly. Thus, the argument made to the Supreme Court in *Brown v. Board of Education* and its companion case, *Bolling v. Sharpe*,[13] was that *Plessy* should be overruled and the separate-but-equal doctrine rejected.

Brown considered the constitutionality under the Fourteenth Amendment of state and city school districts that separated their students by race. *Bolling* considered the constitutionality under the Fifth Amendment of racial segregation in the federally operated Washington, D.C., schools. For purposes of the lawsuits, the plaintiffs stipulated that the facilities, textbooks, and other tangibles provided in the Black schools were equal to those in the White. In this way, they forced the Court to consider the issue of separate but equal directly. It would not be possible simply to order that conditions in Black schools be improved.

The *Brown* Court framed the issue for its consideration as follows: "Does segregation of children in public schools solely on the basis of race, even though the physical facilities and other 'tangible' factors may be equal, deprive the children of the minority group of equal educational opportunities?" To decide the issue, the Court relied heavily on evidence derived from social science, a procedure that had little precedent at the time. The testimony of psychologists and other scholars convinced the Court that

> [t]o separate [Black children] from others of similar age and qualifications solely because of their race generates a feeling of inferiority as to their status in the community that may affect their hearts and minds in a way unlikely ever to be undone . . .
>
> Segregation of white and colored children in public schools has a detrimental effect upon the colored children. The impact is greater when it has the sanction of the law; for the policy of separating the races is usually interpreted as denoting the inferiority of the negro group. A sense of inferiority affects the motivation of a child to learn. Segregation with the sanction of law, therefore, has a tendency to [retard] the educational and mental development of negro children and to deprive them of some of the benefits they would receive in a racial[ly] integrated school system.

Based on this reasoning, the Court concluded, as the plaintiffs had hoped they would, that "in the field of public education the doctrine of 'separate but equal' has no place." Schools segregated by race were unconstitutional.

De jure segregation is separation of the races by law. By contrast, **de facto** segregation is racial separation that occurs for other reasons. *Brown I* (so called because it was the first in a series of *Brown* decisions) rejected only de jure segregation of schools. Although the decision did not refer explicitly to the strict scrutiny test, the *Bolling* decision issued at the same time did: "classifications based solely upon race must be scrutinized with particular care, since they are contrary to our traditions and hence constitutionally suspect." *Bolling* indicates that de jure segregation would be unconstitutional even if the Equal Protection Clause did not exist. "Segregation in public education," wrote the Court, "constitutes an arbitrary deprivation of . . . liberty in violation of the Due Process Clause."

The Supreme Court in *Brown I* and *Bolling* reasoned that given the social and political conditions of the United States, de jure segregated schools were inherently unequal. The Court found that schools segregated by law could not be equal because even if the physical facilities and other resources were similar, segregation in and of itself had deeply harmful effects on Black students. It wasn't long before the same reasoning was employed to bar de jure segregation in public places of all kinds.[14]

Though it was clear following *Brown I, Bolling,* and related cases that mandated segregation by law was unconstitutional, questions concerning the scope of the ruling remained unsettled: Did *Brown I* and *Bolling* prohibit only segregation brought about by statute, or is segregation accomplished covertly by government policy also unconstitutional? Would the Court reject only de jure discrimination or would it also strike down statutes and policies that had as an unintended by-product a discriminatory impact on racial minorities?

It took a long time, many cases, and much confusion for answers to these questions to emerge. To make a long and complex story brief, today the Equal Protection Clause prohibits both overt and covert forms of discrimination. Intentional discrimination is unconstitutional whether enacted in a statute or accomplished through administrative policies. The Equal Protection Clause does not prohibit policies that have a discriminatory or segregative impact purely as an unintended by-product. All intentional government discrimination, whether or not overtly incorporated into law, is de jure and therefore unconstitutional, but unintended discrimination is de facto and de facto discrimination is not unconstitutional.[15]

Segregation that arises entirely as a result of private, nongovernment decisions or as a result of social conditions outside the government's control is not unconstitutional. This explains why so many schools remain racially segregated more than five decades after *Brown* outlawed de jure segregation: Most students are assigned to schools in their neighborhood, and many neighborhoods are racially segregated by factors other than intentional government action.

Intent to Discriminate

Proving intent to discriminate is the key to many racial discrimination cases. Legislative or administrative awareness of the discriminatory consequences of a policy by itself is not enough to prove intent to discriminate. A policy will not be found intentionally discriminatory if adopted in spite of a discriminatory impact, but a policy will be found intentionally discriminatory if adopted because of a discriminatory impact.[16]

However, to be successful, plaintiffs are not required to prove directly that the government tried to subject them to inferior treatment. If overt intentions cannot be established, an intent to discriminate may be inferred from a pattern of actions whose only foreseeable consequences were segregative or otherwise discriminatory. The adoption of a law or policy that a rational decision maker should have known would have a discriminatory effect is evidence of intent to discriminate. When foreseeability is combined with other corroborating evidence, intent to discriminate may be inferred.

Among the kinds of evidence that may assist in a showing of intent to discriminate are the historical background and specific series of events leading to a policy decision, departures from normal policy-making procedures, contemporaneous statements by policy makers, minutes of meetings and reports, and statements of officials at trial.[17] Plaintiffs may also be assisted in their effort to prove that a school board engaged in intentional segregation district wide by two presumptions: (a) where it has been shown that a district engaged in intentional segregation affecting a substantial portion of its schools, a finding that the entire district is intentionally discriminatory is warranted absent a showing that the district is divided into clearly unrelated units; and (b) even if the district is subdivided into unrelated units, proof of intentional discrimination in one unit is evidence of an intent to discriminate in others.[18] A persistent pattern of activity with a segregative impact by a school board may also lead to a finding of intent to discriminate.

The plaintiff need not prove that the intent to discriminate was accompanied by a desire to harm. People may take discriminatory actions out of benevolent or paternalistic motives. For example, some people believed that slavery was in the best interest of those enslaved. Rather, all that needs to be established is that "but for" the consideration of race, the decision would have been different.[19] The question has been formulated this way: "[S]uppose the adverse effects of the challenged governmental decision fell on whites instead of blacks. . . . Would the decision have been different? If the answer is yes, then the decision was made with discriminatory intent." This has been called the "reversing of groups test": Would government have made the same decision if the races of those affected had been reversed?[20] If not, the court will find the policy unconstitutional unless it can survive strict scrutiny.

Diaz v. San Jose Unified School District[21] is a case where the outcome depended on whether the school board had intended to create and maintain a segregated system of education. The alleged criterion of segregation was ethnicity. Courts view segregation by ethnicity the same way as segregation by race.

The school board in *Diaz* admitted that it had "maintained ethnically imbalanced schools" and even that it had "omitted courses of action that would have reduced the imbalance," but it claimed that the segregation resulted from adherence to a "neighborhood school" policy and thus was de facto. In finding that the board had intentionally segregated the district, the court noted that over a period of years, the board had been faced with many decisions that would affect the level of segregation in the district. These decisions concerned such matters as the creation and modification of attendance areas, the building of new schools, faculty assignments, and the provision of transportation. In virtually every instance, the board chose the "more segregative alternative," even when the other alternative would have been cheaper or more efficient. Furthermore, segregative decisions continued to be made after the board had been ordered by the state to reduce the level of segregation of its schools and despite the board's full knowledge that its policies were having exactly the opposite effect.

Even with all this evidence, no single action of the board was enough to support the conclusion that the board intended to foster segregation within its schools. Rather, as the court explained:

> An inescapable conclusion that the Board intended segregation emerges from a view of the evidence as a whole. The pattern of Board choices that consistently maintained or intensified segregation is apparent. Although many of the available alternatives

would have presented an incomplete solution, each could have contributed incrementally toward reducing ethnic imbalance. In almost every instance, the Board chose to "turn toward segregation" rather than away from it. We are left with the firm conviction that the Board did . . . act with segregative intent. . . .

Thus, the segregation was found to be de jure and therefore unconstitutional even though neither the school board nor any other government authority had an explicit policy of maintaining segregated schools.

In case like *Diaz*, the strict scrutiny test is often employed implicitly without being discussed. Proof of intent to discriminate also establishes that the government has no adequate justification for its actions. The government cannot meet its burden of proof under strict scrutiny because the reason for its policy was to separate or distinguish between the races. If it had a compelling reason for its policies, the government would have articulated it in the first place, rather than deny that its intention was to segregate.

School districts with no history of de jure segregation need not take affirmative steps to change policies that create de facto segregation. But school districts that have been found to be de jure segregated do have an affirmative obligation to disestablish their dual systems, undo the effects of segregation, and prevent an increase in segregation.[22] Failure to take these positive steps is itself proof of an intent to discriminate.

Although only de jure segregation violates the U.S. Constitution, some state constitutions may prohibit even de facto segregation. In *Sheff v. O'Neill*,[23] the highest court of Connecticut was presented with a pattern of racial imbalance in the state's schools that was typical of many urban areas throughout the United States. Although statewide the school population was 25.7 percent minority, the schools of Hartford were 92.4 percent minority. In the suburbs surrounding Hartford, only seven of twenty-one districts had minority school populations greater than 10 percent. In deciding whether this situation violated the Connecticut Constitution, the court noted that the state has an "affirmative constitutional obligation to provide all public school children with substantially equal educational opportunity." However, concluded the court, "[e]xtreme racial and ethnic isolation . . . deprives schoolchildren of a substantially equal educational opportunity. . . . Racial and ethnic segregation has a pervasive and invidious impact on schools, whether the segregation results from intentional conduct or from unorchestrated demographic factors." Thus, the court declared that the school districting system in the state was unconstitutional and ordered the trial court to develop an "appropriate remedy."

This conclusion seems consistent with the psychological evidence discussed in the original *Brown* decision. Why should the effects of segregation on minority students be any less damaging if the segregation results from state school districting practices, district pupil assignment policies, and White flight than if it results directly from state law? Why would de facto separate but equal be any more possible than de jure separate but equal?

5.4 REMEDYING DE JURE SEGREGATION

After its declaration in *Brown I* that de jure segregation in education violated the Constitution, the Supreme Court had to face the practical question of what remedy to order. Clearly, it was too much to expect that states with dual education systems and long histories of social separation of the races would simply create an integrated school system because of a constitutional interpretation by the Supreme Court. A year after *Brown I*, the Court issued another opinion, *Brown II*,[24] ordering state and local educational authorities under the supervision of federal district courts to formulate and implement plans for racial desegregation of the public schools "with all deliberate speed." The brief opinion contains few specifics, but requires the defendants to comply in "good faith" with the court's mandate in a way that takes account of local conditions and of "public and private needs."

In hindsight, the vague, open-ended remedy announced in *Brown II* seems overly timid, especially when compared to the broad philosophical vision of *Brown I*. Essentially *Brown II* reasserts the ruling that de jure segregation is illegal and orders local authorities to make a "good faith" effort to "carry out the ruling" at the "earliest practicable date." Lower federal courts are charged with supervising the desegregation effort, but warned that in doing so they must pay attention to "varied local school problems" and the importance of "reconciling public and private needs." Perhaps the Court believed that the lower federal courts could formulate specific remedies that would take into account both constitutional requirements and local social conditions. Perhaps it was further hoped that acknowledging the need for a transition period would eventually foster peaceful compliance with the Constitution. However, regardless of the Court's intention, the next years brought very little movement toward desegregation and little further involvement by the Court itself. In the decade following *Brown*, the Supreme Court issued only three additional opinions dealing with the most blatant cases.[25]

Although it accomplished little desegregation at first, *Brown* and the resistance it engendered did much to galvanize an active and vocal civil rights movement. In turn, the work of this movement led to the adoption of the most sweeping civil rights legislation since Reconstruction, the Civil Rights Act of 1964.[26] This law, among other things, prohibited racial discrimination in programs receiving federal financial assistance and barred discrimination in employment on the basis of race, gender, and religion. Based on this law, a vigorous federal effort began to dismantle segregated school systems. For the first time, opponents of de jure segregation had a potent practical weapon: States refusing to desegregate faced a total cutoff of federal education funds.

Post-Brown Decisions

Following the passage of this new Civil Rights Act, the Supreme Court, perhaps because it finally had vigorous allies in Congress and the executive branch of government, decided that it had waited long enough for the states to comply with *Brown*. In *Green v. County School Board of New Kent County*,[27] the Court invalidated a "freedom of choice" attendance plan allowing each pupil the choice of attending either a formerly Black or a formerly White school within the district. In practice, virtually all the district's pupils were attending the same school as before the plan was adopted. Although neutral on its face, the plan was unacceptable because it served to perpetuate the segregated school system. What the Court now wanted from these dual schools systems was a pupil attendance plan that would integrate the schools, a plan that would eliminate Black schools and White schools and create "just schools." "The burden on the school board today," wrote Justice Brennan, "is to come forward with a plan that promises realistically to work now."

The Court underscored its more aggressive stance a year later in a per curiam opinion in which it said that the *Brown II* era "of all deliberate speed" was over.[28] All schools that had ever been segregated by law were now on notice that only desgregation plans that worked well and fast would be acceptable.

These decisions, however forceful, still left lower federal courts, state legislatures, and school boards with important unanswered questions: Exactly what kind of desegregation plans should and could be ordered by the lower courts? What must be done, what can be done, and what cannot be done to accomplish the mandate of *Brown*? The answers to these questions have been provided in a series of Supreme Court opinions during the past four decades.

Swann v. Charlotte-Mecklenburg Board of Education[29] was a 1971 case involving a large southern school district formerly segregated by law. In 1969, after several years of operating under a district court-approved desegregation plan, the school district still had more than 50 percent of its Black pupils attending schools that were more than 99 percent Black. Responding to the mandate of the *Green* case, the district court imposed a new and more aggressive program of desegregation. The plan involved the grouping of inner-city mostly Black schools with outlying White schools within the district into common attendance zones with some busing of pupils in both directions. The school district challenged the district court's power to impose such a plan.

In ruling against the school district and upholding the plan, the Court declared: (a) that it was permissible for the district court to adopt as a target for individual schools a racial balance similar to the district as a whole as long as the target did not function as a rigid quota; (b) that it is possible as a result of segregated living patterns for a school district under a desegregation order to maintain some one-race schools, but the school district bears the "burden of showing that such school assignments are genuinely non-discriminatory"; (c) that court-ordered grouping of schools and gerrymandering of school attendance zones is permissible as a remedy for intentional segregation; (d) that mandatory within-district busing of pupils is also a permissible remedy as long as the time or distance of travel is not "so great as to either risk the health of the children or significantly impinge on the educational process"; and (e) that once the district had achieved full compliance with a desegregation order, it would be declared "unitary" at which point no further remedies would be authorized. Even if a formerly de jure segregated school district becomes de facto segregated, "[n]either school authorities nor district courts, are constitutionally required to make year-by-year adjustment to the racial composition of student bodies once the affirmative duty to desegregate has been accomplished and racial discrimination through official action is eliminated from the system."

In several cases following *Swann*, the Supreme Court developed doctrines that made it easier for plaintiffs to prove both that school authorities had engaged in de jure segregation and that their wrongful policies extended throughout the school district, not just a portion of it. A practical consequence of these doctrines was to make it easier for the courts to order district-wide busing.[30]

The remedies approved in *Swann* were potentially effective methods of desegregation in school districts with racially mixed student populations (overall, Charlotte-Mecklenburg's students were about 70 percent White and 30 percent Black). However, no amount of redrawing of school attendance areas and busing of students could result in racially mixed student populations in predominantly Black school districts. Unless, of course, predominantly White school districts were combined with predominantly Black districts for purposes of implementing a *Swann*-like plan.

In *Milliken v. Bradley (Milliken I)*,[31] the district court attempted to impose just such an interdistrict remedy. The case involved the public schools of the Detroit metropolitan area. Like many large urban areas, Detroit had a mostly Black city school district surrounded by a number of mostly White suburban districts. The city school district had been found to be de jure segregated but the surrounding districts had not. Nevertheless, the district court reasoned that a desegregation plan involving only the city district could not succeed because only about one third of the city pupils were White and because any plan that aggressively distributed the White pupils throughout the district would result in significant "White flight" to the suburbs. Therefore, the district court sought to include the suburban districts in the desegregation plan. The district court reasoned that because school district boundaries are "no more than arbitrary lines on a map 'drawn for political convenience,'" there was no reason that they could not be redrawn to achieve the constitutional mandate of desegregation.

In rejecting the district court's plan, however, the Supreme Court declared that before a district court may impose

> a cross-district remedy, it must first be shown that there has been a constitutional violation within one district that produces a significant segregative effect in another district. Specifically it must be shown that racially discriminatory acts of the state or local school districts, or of a single school district have been a substantial cause of inter-district segregation. Thus an inter-district remedy might be in order where the racially discriminatory acts of one or more school districts caused racial segregation in an adjacent district, or where district lines have been deliberately drawn on the basis of race. In such circumstances an inter-district remedy would be appropriate to eliminate the inter-district segregation directly caused by the constitutional violation. Conversely, without an inter-district violation and inter-district effect, there is no constitutional wrong calling for an inter-district remedy.

Because there had been no such showing in Detroit, the district court could not impose the cross-district plan. The goal of desegregation would be to create racial balance in individual schools similar to the racial makeup of the district as a whole.

If interdistrict remedies are not permitted, what, besides creating a more even distribution of the races, may district courts do to remedy de jure segregation in school districts like Detroit? In its next consideration of *Milliken v. Bradley* (*Milliken II*),[32] the district court fashioned a series of remedies designed to assure that the Black students of Detroit would not suffer educationally from the vestiges of de jure segregation. The major components of the plan were a "remedial reading and communications skills program," "an in-service training program for teachers and administrators to train [them] to cope with the desegregation process" and to ensure future equitable treatment of all pupils, a nonbiased testing program, and a "counseling and career guidance" program. This time, the Supreme Court approved the district court's plan, reasoning that in creating a desegregation plan, it is "essential to mandate educational components where they are needed to remedy effects of past segregation, to assure a successful desegregative effort and to minimize the possibility of resegregation." Even though the original constitutional violation consisted of assigning students to schools based on race, the remedy need not be limited to nondiscriminatory reassignment.

> [D]iscriminatory student assignment policies can themselves manifest and breed other inequalities built into a dual system founded on racial discrimination. Federal courts need not, and cannot, close their eyes to inequalities, shown by the record, which flow from a longstanding segregated system. . . .
>
> Children who have been . . . educationally and culturally set apart from the larger community will inevitably acquire habits of speech, conduct, and attitudes reflecting their cultural isolation. They are likely to acquire speech habits, for example, which vary from the environment in which they must ultimately function and compete, if they are to enter and be a part of that community. This is not peculiar to race; in this setting, it can affect any children who, as a group, are isolated by force of law from the mainstream.

Missouri v. Jenkins[33] further clarified the limits of a district court's power to include "educational components" in a desegregation remedy. In *Jenkins*, the district court ordered a costly plan that included upgrading and modifying substandard facilities in Kansas City, Missouri, to create a system of magnet schools. In order to make it possible for the school district to pay for the plan, the court mandated a property tax increase to a higher level than state law allowed. The Supreme Court found that the lower court had overstepped its authority in directly raising taxes; however, the district court was allowed to achieve the same result by ordering the local government to raise taxes beyond the state statutory limit. The Supreme Court said that this approach better served to protect the integrity of local institutions and placed the responsibility for the remedy on those who created the problem.

A magnet school-based desegregation plan was approved in *Jenkins*, as in several previous cases, even though racial quotas were employed in admitting students to schools.[34] However, in its last consideration of *Jenkins*,[35] the Supreme Court held that the district court could not continue to order salary increases for instructional personnel and extensive remedial education programs simply because "student achievement levels were still at or below the national norms at many grade levels." The ordered salary increase was simply "too far removed from an acceptable implementation of a permissible means to remedy previous legally mandated segregation." Also, improvement in test scores was "not necessarily required for the State to achieve partial unitary status as to the quality of education programs." Many factors other than de jure segregation affect student test scores. "So long as the [other] factors are not the result of segregation, they do not figure in the remedial calculus. . . . Insistence upon academic goals unrelated to the effects of legal segregation unwarrantably postpones the day when the [district] will be able to operate on its own."

Based on the Supreme Court's pronouncements in these and related cases,[36] the lower federal courts may mandate and authorize a variety of techniques for ending racial segregation. These techniques include, but are not limited to, mandatory busing, redrawing attendance zones, integration of faculties, magnet schools, magnet programs within schools, majority-to-minority pupil transfer programs, urban–suburban voluntary transfer programs (when no interdistrict violation has been proved), and when interdistrict violations have occurred, school district consolidations and metropolitan busing plans.

"Unitary" School Districts

Desegregation is an illusive goal in many large metropolitan areas where, after decades of White flight, a large majority of Black children continue to attend racially identifiable schools. Given pervasive de facto segregation, continuing resistance to desegregation in some places, and constantly changing demographics and living patterns, the question arises of when has a school district succeeded in complying with a desegregation order. When, if ever, should the courts declare a case at an end and permit the school district to design its own pupil assignment plans without judicial supervision? The Supreme Court first addressed these issues in *Pasadena City Board of Education v. Spangler*.[37] The Court noted that Pasadena had implemented a court-approved plan to achieve racial neutrality in student attendance. That being the case, the district court could not require the district to

> rearrange attendance zones each year so as to ensure that the racial mix was maintained in perpetuity. . . . For having once implemented a racially neutral attendance pattern in order to remedy the perceived constitutional violations . . . the District Court had fully performed its function of providing the appropriate remedy for previous racially discriminatory patterns.

The *Pasadena* decision did not fully define the scope of the district courts' authority to order the continuation of desegregation plans. Despite *Pasadena*, it was unclear when a school district could be declared a unitary district in which all the effects of the former dual system had been eliminated. The Supreme Court addressed this question in *Board of Education of Oklahoma City Schools v. Dowell*.[38] The Court noted that judicial supervision of a local school district was intended only as a temporary measure designed to eliminate racial discrimination and ensure compliance with a court desegregation order. It ruled that a formerly segregated school district should be considered unitary if "the board had complied in good faith with a desegregation decree" for a significant period of time and if "the vestiges of past discrimination had been eliminated to the extent practicable." In making the latter determination, a court should look "not only at student assignments, but to every facet of school operations—faculty, staff, transportation, extracurricular activities and facilities." In other words, once the effects of de jure segregation have been eliminated, a district must be considered unitary even in the face of persisting de facto segregation. The district courts may not require school districts to rearrange attendance zones and bus students in perpetuity to ensure that the integration desired by the court is maintained in the face of demographic changes.

In *Freeman v. Pitts*,[39] the Supreme Court authorized district courts to partially withdraw from control of a school district when a particular aspect of a desegregation order has been met. If, for example, all traces of segregation have been eliminated from a school district's pupil assignment procedures, the court may cease its oversight of that aspect of the district's operations while continuing to monitor other aspects of a mandated desegregation plan. The school district would, in effect, be declared unitary a piece at a time.

Despite *Freeman, Pasadena*, and *Dowell*, judicial supervision of school districts can continue for decades. For example, it was more than forty years after the original *Brown* decision when the courts stopped supervising pupil assignment plans in Topeka, Kansas.[40] And it was thirty years after *Swann v. Charlotte-Mecklenburg* (the case that authorized busing to promote desegregation) that the school district was finally declared unitary.[41] Many other formerly dual systems have also been declared unitary, including Delaware, Boston, Atlanta, and Houston.[42]

Five decades after *Brown*, overt de jure racial segregation in education has largely been eradicated, but many related problems of educational law and policy remain. Most large urban school districts now enroll a predominantly minority student population (much more so than fifty years ago), a significant percentage of whom are poor. Although the racial and social class isolation that marks these districts is usually classified as de facto segregation, debate continues regarding whether, at least in some cases, it should be viewed as de jure; whether this form of de facto segregation is a violation of Title VI of the Civil Rights of 1964 (see sec. 5.8); whether, even if ending this form of segregation is not mandated by law, states as a matter of sound educational policy ought to take aggressive steps to do so; and what those steps might be (see sec. 5.6). One attempted solution that has been tried in a small number of cities is an educational voucher plan. The No Child Left Behind Act represents another attempt to bring improved education to students in high minority, low socioeconomic-status districts and districts marked by low educational achievement (see sec. 2.6). Efforts to reform state school finance systems through litigation represent a third approach.

5.5 OTHER FORMS OF RACIAL DISCRIMINATION

De jure segregation is not the only form of racial discrimination prohibited by the Equal Protection Clause. Students may claim racial discrimination in standardized testing, tracking and ability grouping, disciplinary policies, or other areas of school policy and practice. Even in-class pupil grouping policies can violate the Equal Protection Clause. In a Seventh Circuit case, a teacher deliberately assigned a Black student to a group of four students that included another Black student because, as she explained in court, "I think in my education training sometimes we were told that African-American students need a buddy, and sometimes it works well if they have someone else working with them because they view things in a global manner." The court ruled that because the grouping was based on race, it could only be justified if the strict scrutiny test were satisfied. Strict scrutiny was not satisfied because the grouping rested on a stereotypical (not scientifically validated) view of Black students.[43]

Regardless of the context or form of the alleged racial discrimination, to prove a violation of the Equal Protection Clause, plaintiffs must prove that school officials acted with an intent to discriminate. It is not enough that a school policy or practice happens to have a disproportionate effect on a particular race or ethnic group. For example, standardized tests to assign pupils to ability groups may have the effect of disproportionately assigning one race to the lowest track. Or a school basketball team's try-out procedures may have the effect of excluding all members of one race from the team. Use of the IQ test or try-out procedure is unconstitutional only if done because of, rather than in spite of, its disproportionate effect.[44] Thus, a federal court refused to block the use of a nonculturally biased minimum competency exam even though a higher percentage of Blacks than Whites failed the test. The exam's purpose was to ensure that all students reach a certain level of knowledge and skill before receiving a diploma.[45]

In *Thomas County Branch of N.A.A.C.P. v. City of Thomasville School District*,[46] students objected to a tracking system that had the effect of isolating a disproportionate number of Black students in lower track classes. The court agreed that the district's so-called "ability tracking" system created a lower track that was disproportionately Black and an upper track that was disproportionately White. The court also agreed that the district's practices often worked to the detriment of the Black students confined to the lower track:

> Tragically, it appears that for many of these children, the "die is cast" as early as kindergarten. These children do not appear to be reevaluated (and thus potentially "re tracked") during their progression through the system. The inevitable result therefore is that they remain on the "lower ability" track for the duration of their educational careers . . .

However, the court found that the imbalance and its detrimental effects were created not as a result of any of discriminatory intentions or actions on the part of the district, but rather as a result of nondiscriminatory application of legitimate placement criteria and socio-economic conditions over which the district had no control:

> When the racial makeup of a community correlates directly with poverty and when poverty correlates with perceived academic readiness, as it does in Thomasville, this "ability tracking" inevitably leads to ability groups that are racially imbalanced. Although the Court finds that the District's tracking system has had the effect of creating racially imbalanced classes within the District's schools, the Court finds that it was not the intention of the tracking system to segregate students based upon race. Moreover, the Court finds that the District does not manipulate the ability tracking system in order to track students based upon their race.

The court noted that although tracking is controversial, it is a legitimate educational method supported by some experts and that it is not the job of courts to determine how a school district should organize its educational program.

Statistics showing that the burden of a particular policy or practice falls disproportionately on one race may be part of a showing of unconstitutional discrimination, but, as in *Thomas County*, they are not sufficient without supporting evidence of discriminatory intent. In *Hawkins v. Coleman*,[47] plaintiffs succeeded in proving intent to discriminate in the way a school district administered its disciplinary program. Statistics showed that Black students were suspended from school and subjected to corporal punishment significantly more frequently than White students. But the deciding factor in the case was expert testimony as well as the admissions of school officials themselves indicating that at least some of the disproportionate suspensions and corporal punishment given to Black students were the result of cultural insensitivity and bias. The discrimination was ruled intentional even though there was no evidence that school officials had set out to punish Black students more frequently than Whites.[48]

Another disproportionate impact case arose in connection with a school district's attempt to desegregate. The district adopted a "majority to minority" transfer program allowing students to transfer out of their regular attendance area provided the transfer would move the racial balance of the student's new school closer to that of the district as a whole. Fearful that coaches in the predominantly White schools would use the transfer provision to recruit Black athletes, the district adopted a rule requiring transferring high school students to sit out a year before becoming eligible to play. Black students forced to choose between not transferring and sitting out claimed that the rule violated the Equal Protection Clause, but the court disagreed. Although the burden of the policy might fall disproportionately on Blacks, the court concluded that this result was not intentional. The policy had been adopted at the request of Black school board members in order to prevent illegal and exploitative recruiting of Black athletes and help the predominantly Black schools retain student leaders and the positive effects of successful athletic teams.[49]

5.6 AFFIRMATIVE ACTION AND VOLUNTARY RACIAL INTEGRATION

As Section 5.4 shows, race may—in fact, must—be taken into consideration when fashioning remedies for proven de jure racial segregation. But because de facto segregation is not illegal, the question of whether race may be taken into consideration when, in the absence of proven de jure segregation, a school board voluntarily seeks to integrate its schools raises a very different issue. For example, may a school employ different admissions standards for students of different races—a so-called affirmative-action plan—in order to increase diversity within its student body? Two 2003 Supreme Court decisions concerning affirmative action in public universities provide a framework for deciding such questions.

The more significant of the two decisions, *Grutter v. Bollinger*,[50] was an extremely contentious case (even by Supreme Court standards) that produced a five-justice majority opinion and four fully or partially dissenting opinions. Collectively, the dissenting opinions vigorously disagreed with virtually every significant finding of the majority.

The case involved a challenge to the affirmative action admission plan of the University of Michigan Law School. Michigan's highly ranked law school annually admitted approximately 10 percent of 3,500 applicants. In selecting among the applicants, the school relied heavily on the applicants' undergraduate GPA and Law School Admission Test scores but also considered personal statements, letters of recommendation, and essays in which applicants described the way they would contribute to the life and diversity of the law school. The aim was to select the most capable students and those who would make the best lawyers, while at the same time achieving a diverse student body "which has the potential to enrich everyone's education and thus make the law school class stronger than the sum of its parts."

Various forms of diversity were sought, in particular "the inclusion of students from groups which have been historically discriminated against, like African-Americans, Hispanics and Native Americans, who without this commitment might not be represented in [the school's] student body in meaningful numbers." Certain minority groups (e.g., Asian-Americans) were not covered by the policy because the law school believed members of those groups were being admitted in significant numbers without special consideration. The ultimate goal was to realize the educational benefits associated with diversity: cross-racial understanding; decrease in racial stereotyping; livelier, more spirited and enlightening classroom discussion; better preparation for employment in a diverse workforce; development of skills needed in an increasingly global marketplace; and elimination of the belief that minority students consistently express a characteristic minority viewpoint. These educational benefits, the law school said, could only be accomplished if there was a "critical mass" of underrepresented minority students. "Critical mass" was defined as "meaningful numbers" or "meaningful representation," which meant sufficient numbers so that minority students were encouraged to participate in the classroom and not feel isolated. Minority students, the school said, should not be so limited in number that they feel they are the spokespersons for their race.

Although the admissions staff was not directed to admit a particular percentage of minority students, they did pay close attention to race. Analysis by an expert witness showed that membership in the targeted minority groups was in fact an extremely strong factor but not the predominant factor in acceptance. Thirty-five percent of the minority applicants were admitted; if race had not been considered, only 10 percent of the minority applicants would have been admitted, the same percentage as majority applicants. If race had not been considered, the entering classes would have been 4 percent minority instead of over 14 percent.

In considering the Equal Protection Clause challenge of a disappointed White applicant to these admissions policies, the Court employed the strict scrutiny test. Strict scrutiny would not be satisfied, said the Court, if the goal of the admission system were to reduce the historic deficit of traditionally disfavored minorities in a professional school, to remedy societal discrimination, or to increase the number of minority attorneys. However, based on the law school's judgment that diversity is essential to its educational mission, the Court found that the goal of achieving a diverse student body could provide the compelling state interest necessary to satisfy strict scrutiny. But, said the Court, in seeking this goal, the school could not employ a quota, could use race as only one element among others in realizing a diverse student body, could not unduly harm the members of any racial or ethnic group, and could only employ a selection process that was "narrowly tailored" to meet the goal.

Applying these principles, the Court concluded that the law school's policies did in fact serve the compelling state interest in creating a diverse student body and that they were narrowly tailored to meet that goal. Narrow tailoring, said the Court, did not require exhaustion of every conceivable race-neutral alternative that might achieve a diverse student body. In any event, the law school did sufficiently consider race-neutral alternatives such as a lottery or simply lowering admission standards, but it had valid reasons for rejecting these alternatives. Nor, said the Court, did the policies amount to a quota system. The school engaged in a "highly individualized, holistic review of each applicant's file, giving serious consideration to all the ways an applicant might contribute to a diverse educational environment. Race operated only as a plus factor in the context of individualized consideration of each and every applicant."

While there was a goal—"critical mass"—there was not a certain fixed number or proportion of seats reserved for minority groups. Some attention to numbers did not transform a flexible admissions system into a rigid quota system and race never led to automatic acceptance or rejection. The school also gave substantial weight to diversity factors besides race:

> Because the Law School considers "all pertinent elements of diversity," it can (and does) select nonminority applicants who have greater potential to enhance student body diversity over underrepresented minority applicants. . . . The Law School frequently accepts nonminority applicants with grades and test scores lower than underrepresented minority applicants (and other nonminority applicants) who are rejected.

The decision concludes with the stipulation that race-conscious policies must be limited in time:

> [R]acial classifications, however compelling their goals, are potentially so dangerous that they may be employed no more broadly than the interest demands. . . . We expect that 25 years from now, the use of racial preferences will no longer be necessary to further the interest approved today.

The majority did not explain why it expected that the conditions justifying the affirmative action plan in 2003 would not be present in 2028.

The second higher education affirmative action case, *Gratz v. Bollinger*,[51] rejected the undergraduate admissions policies of the University of Michigan. Admission decisions from among more than 13,000 applicants were based on a point system, with points being awarded for, among other things, grade point average, test scores, special talents, alumni relationship, in-state residency, leadership, and race. Applicants received twenty points, one-fifth of the points needed to guarantee admission, for membership in an underrepresented racial or ethnic minority group.

Employing the principles announced in *Grutter*, the *Gratz* decision concluded that, unlike the law school policy, the undergraduate system was "not narrowly tailored to achieve the interest in educational diversity." The difficulty was that this approach did not provide the kind of individualized consideration that was the hallmark of the admission process in *Grutter*. The automatic assignment of twenty points had the

> effect of making "the factor of race . . . decisive" for virtually every minimally qualified underrepresented minority applicant. . . . By comparison a non-minority student with artistic talent that rivaled that of Picasso would receive at most five points. Neither the minority nor nonminority student received truly individualized consideration to determine how they would benefit the university. And the fact that providing individualized consideration to thousands of applications would create "administrative challenges" does not render constitutional an otherwise problematic system.

The *Grutter* and *Gratz* decisions have important implications for public elementary- and secondary-school pupil assignment, transfer, and admission plans designed to promote cultural diversity and integration. In *Parents Involved in Community Schools v. Seattle School District No. 1*,[52] the Supreme Court referred extensively to these precedents in considering the case of two school districts that voluntarily adopted student-assignment plans:

> In each case, the school district relies upon an individual student's race in assigning that student to a particular school, so that the racial balance at the school falls within

a predetermined range based on the racial composition of the school district as a whole. Parents of students denied assignment to particular schools under these plans solely because of their race brought suit, contending that allocating children to different public schools on the basis of race violated the Fourteenth Amendment guarantee of equal protection.

By a 5–4 margin, the Court agreed that the plans violated the Fourteenth Amendment. Because under both plans race alone determined whether or not a student could attend a particular school, the Court viewed the case as much more analogous to *Gratz* than to *Grutter*. The districts were unable to show that differential treatment of students by race was necessary to the achievement of any compelling state purpose.

Discerning the significance of *Parents Involved* is a delicate task. Like *Grutter*, *Parents Involved* was an extremely contentious case. Chief Justice Roberts's opinion announcing the 5–4 decision contained key sections that do not set precedent because they received support from only a plurality of the Court. The case also produced two concurring and two dissenting opinions that disagreed on many aspects of the decision.

Justice Breyer's dissenting opinion, joined by three other justices, argues that the decision conflicts with a number of previous cases that have "consistently and unequivocally approved both voluntary and compulsory race-conscious measures to combat segregated schools." The plurality opinion, wrote Justice Kennedy,

> announces legal rules that will obstruct efforts by state and local governments to deal effectively with the growing resegregation of public schools, it threatens to substitute for present calm a disruptive round of race-related litigation, and it undermines *Brown*'s promise of integrated primary and secondary education that local communities have sought to make a reality.

Nothing in the history of desegregation efforts over the past fifty years, said the dissenters, gives any reason to believe that any other less race-based method than the approach employed in *Parents Involved* could effectively deal with the resegregation of schools that is currently occurring in many districts. If the dissenting judges had prevailed, school districts would have been permitted to employ race as an explicit factor in student assignment with the goal of promoting racial balance and diversity within their schools.

Justice Thomas's concurring opinion claimed that the Equal Protection Clause establishes the doctrine of "color-blindness." He would prohibit any student-assignment policy that considers race at all unless narrowly tailored to remedy past intentional segregation or discrimination.

Justice Kennedy's concurring opinion takes a much different position:

> This Nation has a moral and ethical obligation to fulfill its historic commitment to creating an integrated society that ensures equal opportunity for all of its children. A compelling interest exists in avoiding racial isolation, an interest that a school district, in its discretion and expertise, may choose to pursue. Likewise, a district may consider it a compelling interest to achieve a diverse student population. Race may be one component of that diversity, but other demographic factors, plus special talents and needs, should also be considered. Thus when individual students are assigned to schools, districts must use a multi-factor individualized decision process. What the government is not permitted to do, absent a showing of necessity not made here, is to classify every student on the basis of race and to assign each of them to schools based on that classification.

Justice Kennedy also suggested that school districts may seek to promote diversity in their student bodies by means other than race-based assignment including:

> strategic site selection of new schools; drawing attendance zones with general recognition of the demographics of neighborhoods; allocating resources for special programs; recruiting students and faculty in a targeted fashion; and tracking enrollments, performance, and other statistics by race. These mechanisms are race conscious but do not lead to different treatment based on a classification that tells each student he or she is to be defined by race, so it is unlikely any of them would demand strict scrutiny to be found permissible.

School districts are prohibited by *Parents Involved* from promoting racial diversity in their schools by "classify[ing] every student on the basis of race and . . . assign[ing] each of them to schools based on that classification." But the views of Justice Kennedy and the dissenting justices suggest that, contrary to Justice Thomas's position, school districts wishing to adopt policies that promote diversity in their student bodies still have at least two options. One is to employ a "multi-factor individualized process" for assigning students to schools in which race is one, but not the dominant, factor. The other is to adopt "mechanisms [that] are race conscious but do not lead to different treatment based on a classification that tells each student he or she is to be defined by race." Whether specific programs of voluntary integration can survive after *Parents Involved* remains to be seen.[53]

5.7 THE EQUAL PROTECTION CLAUSE AND GENDER DISCRIMINATION

As we saw in the *Goesaert* female-bartender case (see sec. 5.2), rational basis was the traditional test for adjudicating cases of alleged sex discrimination. However, in 1973, the Court, in a plurality opinion, seemed to decide to employ strict scrutiny instead. In *Frontiero v. Richardson*,[54] the plurality wrote that classifications based upon sex, like those based on race, were "inherently suspect and must therefore be subjected to close judicial scrutiny." Then, in 1976, the Court retreated partway from the use of strict scrutiny in gender cases, adopting instead a new test known as **substantial relation** or the **middle-level test**. This test is far stricter than rational basis but still more lenient than strict scrutiny.

To trigger the use of the substantial-relation test, the plaintiff must first establish the existence of either overt gender discrimination (e.g., when a statute or other rule explicitly treats males and females differently) or covert gender discrimination (e.g., unadmitted preferential treatment of one gender) in the administration of government policies or practices. Once this has been accomplished, the burden of proof shifts to the government to establish that its policy serves a purpose that is both legitimate and important and that treating males and females differently is substantially related to that purpose.[55] The law will be declared unconstitutional if the government fails to meet its burden.

Courts will employ the middle-level test to evaluate equal protection challenges to school policies or practices that classify students according to gender, from single-sex schools to sex-segregated sports teams. The constitutionality of a sex-segregated high school has been addressed in only one case, *Vorchheimer v. School District of Philadelphia*.[56] In *Vorchheimer*, a teenage girl sought admission to Central High School, an all-male program with high academic standards. Philadelphia also had an all-female high school, Girls High, of equal quality and prestige, as well as a number of coed high schools. The plaintiff's reasons for seeking admission to Central were outlined by the court as follows:

As to Girls High, she commented, "I just didn't like the impression it gave me. I didn't think I would be able to go there for three years and not be harmed in any way by it." As to Central she said, "I liked the atmosphere and also what I heard about it, about its academic excellence." She was somewhat dissatisfied with her education at George Washington High School because of her belief that the standard which the teachers set for the students was not high enough.

Nevertheless, the court, relying on the middle-level test, rejected the constitutional challenge and upheld the sex-segregated school:

> The gravamen of the plaintiff's case is her desire to attend a specific school based on its particular appeal to her. She believes that the choice should not be denied her because of an educational policy with which she does not agree.
>
> We are not unsympathetic with her desire to have an expanded freedom of choice, but its costs should not be overlooked. If she were to prevail, then all public single-sex schools would have to be abolished. The absence of these schools would stifle the ability of the local school board to continue with a respected educational methodology. It follows too that those students and parents who prefer an education in a public, single-sex school would be denied their freedom of choice. The existence of private schools is no more an answer to those people than it is to the plaintiff.

The dissenting judge argued that Philadelphia had failed to meet its burden of proof under the middle-level test:

> Some showing must be made that a single-sex academic high school policy advances the Board's objectives in a manner consistent with the requirements of the Equal Protection Clause. . . .
>
> The Board, as the district court emphasized, did not present sufficient evidence that coeducation has an adverse effect upon a student's academic achievement. Indeed, the Board could not seriously assert that argument in view of its policy of assigning the vast majority of its students to coeducational schools. Presumably any detrimental impact on a student's scholastic achievement attributable to coeducation would be as evident in Philadelphia's coeducational comprehensive schools which offer college preparatory courses as the Board suggests it would be in its exclusively academic high schools. Thus, the Board's single-sex policy reflects a choice among educational techniques but not necessarily one substantially related to its stated educational objectives. One of those objectives, in fact, is to provide "educational options to students and their parents." . . . The implementation of the Board's policy excluding females from Central actually precludes achievement of this objective because there is no option of a coeducational academic senior high school.

Litigation since *Vorchheimer* suggests that the dissenting judge's position may have been correct. In *Mississippi University for Women v. Hogan*,[57] the male plaintiff objected to the female-only admissions policy of a state nursing school. The state defended its policy by noting that it offered coeducational nursing programs at other public universities and arguing that the single-sex program served the important purpose of compensating for past discrimination against women. However, the Supreme Court found the state's position deficient on both criteria of the middle-level test. The single-sex admission policy served no important government purpose and was not even substantially related to the purpose proposed by the state:

It is readily apparent that a State can evoke a compensatory purpose to justify an otherwise discriminatory classification only if members of the gender benefited by the classification actually suffer a disadvantage related to the classification. . . . In sharp contrast, Mississippi has made no showing that women lacked opportunities to obtain training in the field of nursing or to attain positions of leadership in that field.

On the contrary, said the Court, rather than compensating for discrimination, the admissions policy perpetuated the stereotyped view of nursing as an exclusively woman's job. That the school permitted men to audit its classes undermined its claim that the presence of men would adversely affect the performance of female students or change teaching styles and that men would dominate the classroom.

United States v. Virginia[58] was another Supreme Court case that considered the constitutionality of a state-sponsored single-sex institution of higher education. Again employing the middle-level test, the Court placed the burden on the state to come up with an "exceedingly persuasive justification" for the categorical exclusion of women from the Virginia Military Institute (VMI). The state's first argument was that offering a single-sex option contributed to the goal of making available a diversity of educational options. But the Court concluded that this goal was not served by offering a unique educational benefit only to males. The state's second argument was that the admission of women would "destroy" the VMI program, thus denying both men and women the opportunity to benefit from it. But the Court disagreed: "The notion that admission of women would downgrade VMI's stature, destroy the adversative system and, with it, even the school, is a judgment hardly proved, a prediction hardly different from other 'self-fulfilling prophecies' once routinely used to deny rights or opportunities." The Court noted that the same sorts of arguments had been made to deny women access to law and medical schools. Surely, said the Court, "the State's great goal [of educating citizen soldiers] is not substantially advanced by women's categorical exclusion, in total disregard of their individual merit, from the State's premier 'citizen-soldier' corps."

In *Garrett v. Board of Education of School District of City of Detroit*,[59] a case that raised a variety of legal and educational issues, a federal district court issued an injunction prohibiting the opening of Detroit's planned all-male "Academies," elementary schools specially designed for at-risk urban boys. The Academies planned to "offer special programs including a class entitled 'Rites of Passage,' an Afrocentric (Pluralistic) curriculum, futuristic lessons in preparation for 21st century careers, an emphasis on male responsibility, mentors, Saturday classes, individualized counseling, extended classroom hours, and student uniform." Although the court agreed that addressing "the crisis facing African-American males manifested by high homicide, unemployment and drop-out rates" was an important government purpose, it nevertheless found that the proposed Academies failed to meet the requirements of the middle-level test: "While these statistics underscore a compelling need, they fall short of demonstrating that excluding girls is substantially related to the achievement of the Board's objectives." The court noted that the proposed program ignored what the school board itself admitted was an "equally urgent and unique crisis" facing urban girls. The court also concluded that the single-sex academies violated Title IX as it was then interpreted by the Department of Education. As discussed in Section 5.8, today single-sex schools may be permissible under both Title IX and the Equal Protection Clause provided certain conditions are satisfied.

The most common gender discrimination cases in elementary and secondary schools involve sex segregation in sports or occasionally, in student organizations. Female plaintiffs have their strongest chance of winning a case under the Equal Protection Clause when they have been totally excluded from playing a sport because of the absence of a girls' team. For example, in *Force v. Pierce R-VI School District*,[60] the court employed the middle-level test in ruling in favor of a girl who wished to try out for her junior high football team. Noting that even the smallest and frailest boys were allowed to try out for the team, the court rejected the school's contention that excluding girls from football was substantially related to the goal of ensuring the safety of the players. The court explained its conclusion as follows:

> Nichole Force obviously has no legal entitlement to a starting position on the Pierce City Junior High School eighth grade football team, since the extent to which she plays must be governed solely by her abilities, as judged by those who coach her. But she seeks no such entitlement here.
>
> Instead she seeks simply a chance, like her male counterparts, to display those abilities. She asks, in short, only the right to try.
>
> I do not suggest there is any such thing as a constitutional "right to try." But the idea that one should be allowed to try—to succeed or to fail as one's abilities and fortunes may dictate, but in the process at least to profit by those things which are learned in the trying—is a concept deeply engrained in our way of thinking, and it should indeed require a "substantial" justification to deny that privilege to someone simply because she is a female rather than a male. I find no such justification here.

When a comparable girls' team is available, a girl's chance of winning the right to try out for the boys' team is diminished if the sport involves contact.[61] In cases involving noncontact sports, girls have a good chance of winning, especially if a girls' team is not available.[62] But some courts have upheld the notion of separate but equal even for noncontact sports.[63]

The legal situation is even less clear regarding boys seeking to participate in noncontact girls' sports. When there is no boys' team available, male plaintiffs have met with mixed results.[64] Some courts have been persuaded that girls' teams are important for ensuring girls a fair opportunity to participate in sports. One court rejected both the constitutional and statutory arguments of a boy seeking to play on a girls' field hockey team.[65]

In *Communities for Equity v. Michigan High School*,[66] the plaintiffs brought an equal protection challenge to the Michigan High School Athletic Association's (MHSAA) policy of scheduling five girls' sports—basketball, volleyball, soccer, swimming and diving and tennis—in the spring whereas the comparable boys' sports were scheduled in the fall, the more customary season for these sports. The court agreed with the plaintiffs that as a consequence of this schedule, the girls suffered a number of disadvantages including decreased ability to be nationally ranked and recruited, exclusion from the excitement of "March Madness," and being forced to play on frozen or snow-covered fields. The MHSAA argued that the difference in treatment maximized opportunities for participation "'by creating optimal use of existing facilities and coaches, thereby permitting more teams in a sport or more spots on a team.'" But the court concluded that this argument did not justify imposing on the girls all the disadvantages of the schedule; nor was there evidence that the data showing high sport participation by boys and girls was the result of the discriminatory schedule.

5.8 FEDERAL ANTIDISCRIMINATION STATUTES

Several federal statutes supplement the Equal Protection Clause by prohibiting various forms of discrimination. This section considers two of these statutes as they pertain to the treatment of students by schools: Title VI of the Civil Rights Act of 1964, which deals with race and ethnicity, and Title IX of the Education Amendments of 1972, which deals with gender discrimination. (See chap. 7 for a discussion of federal statutes prohibiting discrimination in employment.)

Title VI (section 601) of the **Civil Rights Act of 1964**[67] provides: "No person in the United States shall, on the grounds of race, color, or national origin, be excluded from participation in, be denied the benefits of, or be subjected to discrimination under any program or activity receiving Federal financial assistance." The Department of Education regulations implementing Title VI state that a school district may not provide different or separate treatment or services or segregate on the grounds of race, color, or national origin.[68] A school district that violates this law faces the loss of all its federal funds. Title VI applies to everything a school does even if only one program or activity receives federal funds. Thus, for example, if a school receives federal support for its lunch program, it must comply with Title VI in all of its activities.

Title VI supplements the Equal Protection Clause in three ways. First, although the Equal Protection Clause can be enforced only through a suit brought by parents or students directly affected by discrimination, Title VI can be enforced by the attorney general of the United States,[69] by any federal department or agency that awards federal funds to school districts,[70] or through litigation brought by an individual.[71] Although this issue has not been decided, it seems possible that courts may use Title VI to award compensatory and punitive damages to individual victims of discrimination by school districts.[72] Second, unlike the Equal Protection Clause, proof of intent to discriminate may not be necessary under Title VI. If a federal agency has promulgated regulations implementing Title VI, and the regulations interpret Title VI to prohibit policies having a discriminatory impact, then proof of a discriminatory impact alone will be sufficient to prove a Title VI violation.[73] Thus, unintentional discrimination may sometimes be remedied through Title VI. But the remedy must be one sought by the Department of Education because the Supreme Court has ruled that private individuals may not sue to enforce disparate-impact regulations under Title VI.[74] That a policy has a discriminatory impact may not necessarily mean that Title VI has been violated if the policy is consistent with educational necessity. For example, a school might defend the use of a standardized test that one race fails at a higher rate than another by showing that the test is reliable and valid and that there is no less discriminatory measure available.[75] Third, unlike the Equal Protection Clause, Title VI applies to private as well as public schools provided they receive federal funds.

Title IX of the Education Amendments of 1972[76] closely parallels Title VI: "No person in the United States shall, on the basis of sex, be excluded from participation in, be denied the benefits of, or be subjected to discrimination under any education program or activity receiving Federal financial assistance."

Federal law makes it clear that Title IX applies to everything a school does even if only one activity or program receives federal funds.[77] Thus, a school's athletic program is subject to Title IX regulations even if the school's only federal funds are for special education. Like Title VI, Title IX permits lawsuits by both federal agencies and individuals[78] and applies to any private or public school that gets federal funds.

Student victims of gender discrimination may use Title IX to seek a court order ending the discrimination. Student victims of intentional gender discrimination may also be awarded monetary damages from the offending school district but not from individual perpetrators of discrimination.[79] The courts are split on whether victims of gender discrimination may use another federal law, known as Section 1983 (see sec. 10.10), to seek monetary damages from individual perpetrators of discrimination.[80] The courts are also split on the issue of whether Title IX prohibits unintentional gender discrimination.[81] One court rules that Title IX prohibited a state from using a seemingly-gender-neutral examination to award college scholarships because it had a discriminatory impact on female candidates.[82] Although the Supreme Court has not ruled on this issue, if its interpretation of Title VI were applied to Title IX, some unintentional gender discrimination could be prohibited.[83]

In *Jackson v. Birmingham Board of Education*,[84] the Supreme Court ruled that "indirect victims" of gender discrimination are protected from retaliation when they report violations of Title IX. In this case the coach of a girls' basketball team complained to the school board about unequal funding; the school district failed to remedy the problem and also dismissed the coach. The Supreme Court said that it would be a violation of Title IX if the coach could prove he was dismissed because he complained of sex discrimination: "Reporting incidents of discrimination is integral to Title IX enforcement and would be discouraged if retaliation against those who report went unpunished. Indeed, if retaliation were not prohibited, Title IX's enforcement scheme would unravel."

The extensive regulations issued to enforce Title IX prohibit the following:

- Admission tests that disproportionately affect one sex, unless they can be validated as reliable predictors of educational ability and as the least prejudicial means of prediction.[85]
- Codes of student conduct that treat males and females differently.[86]
- Counseling materials that discriminate on the basis of gender, for example, by encouraging different courses or occupations for different sexes.[87]
- Rules concerning marriage or pregnancy that treat students differently on the basis of sex. Thus, students may not be denied educational benefits because they are pregnant.[88]

With some exceptions, Title IX regulations also prohibit sex-segregated programs and refusing to allow participation in a program on the basis of sex. Exceptions include contact sports and ability grouping in physical education classes, sex education classes, and choruses based on vocal range. In a 1991 case, a federal judge relied partly on Title IX regulations to prohibit the opening of all-male elementary school "academies" in the city of Detroit.[89] But more recent changes in Title IX regulations permit sex-segregated classes and extracurricular activities and even single-sex schools under certain specified conditions. To be permissible, single-sex programs must be undertaken to improve educational achievement, meet identified educational needs, and be voluntary. "Substantially equal" single-sex programs must be offered to the excluded sex, and substantially equal coeducational programs must also be provided. (In the case of a single-sex charter school, there is no requirement that a substantially equal school be provided.) The school district must periodically evaluate the single-sex program to be sure it is based on genuine educational justifications and not on "overly broad generalizations about the different talents, capacities, or preferences or either sex and that any single-sex classes or extracurricular activities are substantially related to the achievement of the important objectives for the classes or extracurricular activities."[90] Even if a single-sex program is permissible under Title IX, it might still run afoul of the Equal Protection Clause.[91]

The following Title IX regulation, Section 106.41, has had a profound effect on schools:

ATHLETICS

(a) *General.* No person shall, on the basis of sex, be excluded from participation in, be denied the benefits of, be treated differently from another person or otherwise be discriminated against in any interscholastic, intercollegiate, club or intramural athletics offered by a recipient, and no recipient shall provide any such athletics separately on such basis.

(b) *Separate teams.* Notwithstanding the requirements of paragraph (a) of this section, a recipient may operate or sponsor separate teams for members of each sex where selection for such teams is based upon competitive skill or the activity involved is a contact sport. However, where a recipient operates or sponsors a team in a particular sport for members of one sex but operates or sponsors no such team for members of the other sex, and athletic opportunities for members of that sex have previously been limited, members of the excluded sex must be allowed to try-out for the team offered unless the sport involved is a contact sport. For the purposes of this part, contact sports include boxing, wrestling, rugby, ice hockey, football, basketball and other sports the purpose or major activity of which involves bodily contact.

(c) *Equal opportunity.* A recipient which operates or sponsors interscholastic, intercollegiate, club or intramural athletics shall provide equal athletic opportunity for members of both sexes. In determining whether equal opportunities are available the Director will consider, among other factors:

  (1)   Whether the selection of sports and levels of competition effectively accommodate the interests and abilities of members of both sexes;
  (2)   The provision of equipment and supplies;
  (3)   Scheduling of games and practice time;
  (4)   Travel and per diem allowance;
  (5)   Opportunity to receive coaching and academic tutoring;
  (6)   Assignment and compensation of coaches and tutors;
  (7)   Provision of locker rooms, practice and competitive facilities;
  (8)   Provision of medical and training facilities and services;
  (9)   Provision of housing and dining facilities and services;
  (10) Publicity.

Unequal aggregate expenditures for members of each sex or unequal expenditures for male and female teams if a recipient operates or sponsors separate teams will not constitute non-compliance with this section, but the Assistant Secretary may consider the failure to provide necessary funds for teams for one sex in assessing equality of opportunity for members of each sex.

These regulations have created some confusion. Section 106.41 allows sex-segregated teams in the following circumstances: contact sports regardless of whether there is a team available for the excluded sex, noncontact sports selected on a competitive basis when there is a team available for each sex, and noncontact sports selected on a competitive basis when only one team is available provided that athletic opportunities for the excluded sex have not previously been limited, such as by inferior funding or facilities. Thus, the regulations seem to permit separation when some of the constitutional decisions discussed in Section 5.7 would not. For example, as in the *Force* case, female athletes have sometimes employed the Equal Protection Clause to gain the right to try out for male teams even in contact sports. At least in those jurisdictions where these decisions have occurred, the conflicting federal regulations may not be implemented because the Constitution takes precedence over all other laws and regulations.

A "Policy Interpretation" issued by the Department of Education states that a school sponsoring an intercollegiate athletic program may meet the requirement of "equal athletic opportunity for members of both sexes" in any of three ways: "(1) the percent of male and female athletes is substantially proportionate to the percent of male and female students enrolled at the school; or (2) the school has a history and continuing practice of expanding participation opportunities for the underrepresented sex; or (3) the school is fully and effectively accommodating the interests and abilities of the underrepresented sex."[92] Whether these same principles apply to elementary and secondary schools has not been tested.

In addition to federal law, some states have constitutional provisions, statutes, and regulations that also prohibit various forms of discrimination. State law may, and in some states does, impose stricter antidiscrimination requirements than federal law. For example, state law may ensure greater opportunities for female students to try out for male teams than federal law.[93]

5.9 RACIAL AND SEXUAL HARASSMENT

Racial and sexual harassment were first recognized as legally impermissible forms of discrimination in the context of employment law. The implementing regulations of Title VII of the Civil Rights Act of 1964 proclaim that an employee may not be subjected to a racially or sexually hostile, intimidating, or offensive work environment. In addition to hostile-environment harassment, the regulations also recognize another form of sexual harassment known as "quid pro quo." In quid-pro-quo harassment, an employee is asked to exchange sex for job benefits (see sec. 7.4).

Students also look to the law for protection against racial or sexual intimidation and improper sexual advances while at school. Courts in recent decades have become increasingly sympathetic to the contention that students have a right not to be subjected to racial or sexual harassment by school employees or even by other students. Both hostile-environment racial or sexual harassment and quid-pro-quo sexual harassment against students are recognized as legal wrongs.

Students may base an objection to racial or sexual harassment on a number of different laws. The Equal Protection Clause applies only when the offender is a school official, not a fellow student,[94] and only when the victims can show that the offending conduct was intentionally discriminatory against their race or gender. In one case, a gay male student won an equal protection suit against school officials who had a policy of protecting female students from sexual harassment, but who for years had refused to protect the student from physical assault. The gay student was taunted, urinated upon, and even kicked so forcefully that he sustained internal injuries, but despite repeated protests to school officials nothing was done. The peer harassment itself was not an Equal Protection Clause violation, but the discriminatory protection policy was.[95] The Due Process Clause also may be used to object to sexual harassment when there has been a significant violation of bodily integrity and again only when the offender is a school official. Thus, one student successfully brought a due process suit against a teacher who repeatedly had sexual intercourse with her.[96] Where there has been threatened or actual bodily harm or violation (e.g., sexual intercourse), the racial or sexual harassment may constitute assault or battery under state civil and criminal law (see sec. 10.1). Some states have statutes that provide protection from harassment based on gender, race, and a variety of other factors.[97]

In most cases, the most effective protection for students against racial or sexual harassment at school is found in federal statutes. In recent years, the Department of Education (ED) and the courts have come to view racial harassment of a student as a violation of Title VI and sexual harassment of a student as a violation of Title IX. The idea is that students who experience racial or sexual harassment are being denied the benefits of their school's program on the basis of race or gender so harassment is a form of discrimination.

According to ED guidelines, racial[98] or sexual[99] harassment occurs when because of race or gender a student experiences conduct "by an employee, by another student, or by a third party that is sufficiently severe, persistent, or pervasive to limit a student's ability to participate in or benefit from an education program or activity, or to create a hostile or abusive educational environment." The guidelines provide a list of factors to be used in determining whether racial or sexual harassment has occurred including the type, frequency, and duration of the conduct; the number of individuals involved; and whether the victim suffered falling grades or psychological distress. One court ruled that Black students repeatedly being called "nigger" and other racial slurs and being subjected to racial slurs written in graffiti around the school constituted racial harassment.[100]

Because there has been more litigation over sexual than racial harassment in schools, the law regarding sexual harassment is far more developed. The ED guidelines state that "[s]exually harassing conduct . . . can include unwelcome sexual advances, requests for sexual favors, and other verbal and nonverbal, or physical conduct of a sexual nature." The more severe the conduct, the less it need be persistent to constitute a violation: "Indeed, a single or isolated incident of sexual harassment may, if sufficiently severe, create a hostile environment." However, Title IX does not prohibit nonsexual touching or other nonsexual conduct. "For example, a high school athletic coach hugging a student who made a goal or a kindergarten teacher's consoling hug for a child with a skinned knee will not be considered sexual harassment." Similarly, "[a] kiss on the cheek by a first grader does not constitute sexual harassment." Nor is harassment or bullying based on animosity or bad blood covered by Title IX. One court ruled that threats, acts of intimidation, and name calling (including "sexual names, such as bitch, pussy, and slut") directed by male members of a gang toward a female student and her brother were not actionable under Title IX because they were based on "personal animus rather than gender."[101] But, "[a] teacher's repeatedly hugging and putting his or her arms around students under inappropriate circumstances could create a hostile environment." Thus, a school employee who on several occasions touched a student's breast, buttocks, and thigh and made sexual comments to her was found to have committed wrongful sexual harassment.[102]

In general, sexual conduct directed at a student by an adult school employee constitutes harassment even if the student does not object or appears to welcome the conduct. ED guidelines state that the younger the student, the less likely the student will be deemed to have the legal capacity to consent to sexual conduct. The Seventh Circuit ruled that a thirteen-year-old plaintiff did not need to establish in a Title IX suit that she did not welcome the sexual advances—suggestive notes, phone calls, touching, and kissing—of a teacher.[103] For older high school students, ED guidelines create a rebuttable presumption that a sexual relationship with an adult school employee is not consensual. The Supreme Court has stated that sex between a student and a school employee usually constitutes sexual harassment even if the student consents.[104]

Sexual conduct by one student toward another may constitute harassment if the conduct is unwelcome and persistent or severe. One court concluded that a student had been subjected to hostile-environment harassment when another student persistently touched her, brushed up against her, and made sexual comments to her.[105] The Supreme Court has indicated that in general a single act of student-on-student harassment will not be considered sufficient to constitute a Title IX violation:

> Although, in theory, a single instance of sufficiently severe one-on-one peer harassment could be said to have such an effect, we think it unlikely that Congress would

have thought such behavior sufficient to rise to this level in light of the inevitability of student misconduct and the amount of litigation that would be invited by entertaining claims of official indifference to a single instance of one-on-one peer harassment.[106]

One court ruled that a forced act of anal sex and a request for oral sex by one male student of another was not sufficiently severe and pervasive to constitute sexual harassment.[107]

Even if severe and persistent, not all student-on-student harassment is sexual. In one case, a high school football player's upper-class teammates subjected him to an incident of sadistic treatment including binding his genitals with adhesive tape. The student reported the incident to school authorities who punished the wrongdoers and forced the team to forfeit a scheduled play-off game. The victim was then subjected to nonsexual hostile acts by team members who blamed him for the forfeit. The court ruled that the hostile environment subsequent to the initial incident was not covered by Title IX.[108] Similarly, in an elementary-school case, the court ruled that a boy's pushing and teasing, and grabbing of a girl's leg, and one incident of inappropriate touching was "nothing more than the sort of mean-spirited teasing that troublesome little boys inflict from time to time on little girls who seem vulnerable."[109]

Even if offensive behavior is sexual, Title IX is not violated unless the behavior is sufficiently severe to deny the victim access to or the benefit of an educational program. In one case a boy harassed a kindergarten girl by jumping on her back, leaning against her while holding his crotch, unzipping and lowering his pants, and kissing, groping, and inappropriately touching her. But despite the fact she was under psychological counseling, since neither the girl's attendance nor her grades suffered, the court ruled she had not been denied educational opportunities.[110] The Eleventh Circuit found no denial of access in a case in which second grade girls were chased on the playground, jumped on, rubbed against, had their breasts touched, and were subjected to efforts to look up their skirts and spoken with about sexual acts.[111]

The Department of Education with support from court decisions has stated that Title IX does not protect students from harassment based on their sexual orientation.[112] A number of cases have found, however, that Title IX does protect students from harassment based on their perceived lack of conformity to stereotypical gender behaviors.[113] As a practical matter, it may be difficult to determine whether a student is being harassed because of sexual orientation or failure to conform to a gender stereotype. Title IX also protects students from same-sex sexual harassment and both Title IX and the Equal Protection Clause prohibit a school district from providing greater protection from harassment to lesbians than gay males. Some state's statutes may protect students from harassment based on actual or perceived sexual orientation.[114]

ED guidelines state that quid-pro-quo harassment occurs when a

> school employee explicitly or implicitly conditions a student's participation in an education program or activity or bases an educational decision on the student's submission to unwelcome sexual advances, requests sexual favors, or other verbal, nonverbal, or physical conduct of a sexual nature. . . . Quid pro quo harassment is equally unlawful whether the student resists and suffers the threatened harm or submits and thus avoids the threatened harm.

For example, one court ruled that quid-pro-quo sexual harassment occurred when a teacher allowed a third grade student to copy answers from materials on the teacher's desk while the teacher sexually touched the student.[115]

When racial or sexual harassment occurs at school, who may be held responsible and what sort of compensation may be awarded? Because Title VI and Title IX only apply to "programs . . . receiving federal financial assistance," neither individuals who commit racial or sexual harassment nor their supervisors may be sued directly under these laws.[116] Employees who racially or sexually harass students in violation of Title VI or IX (or the Equal Protection Clause[117]) may be sued and forced to pay money damages under another federal statute known as Section 1983 if certain conditions are met (see sec. 10.10).[118] Peer harassers may not be sued under Section 1983. The Federal Circuit Courts are split on whether Title IX permits Section 1983 suits against principals and other supervisors of either employee or peer harassers even if they themselves did not commit harassment.[119] The Sixth Circuit has said that supervisors can only be held liable under Section 1983 if they "at least implicitly authorized, approved or knowingly acquiesced" to the harassment or displayed "deliberate indifference."[120] The Ninth Circuit has held that "liability is imposed against a supervisory official in his individual capacity for his own culpable action or inaction in the training, supervision, or control of his subordinates, . . . for his acquiescence in the [legal] deprivation, . . . or for conduct that showed reckless or callous indifference to the rights of others."[121]

In *Franklin v. Gwinnett County Public Schools*,[122] the Supreme Court held that victims of gender discrimination under Title IX, including sexual harassment, may sue their school district for money damages. Presumably, the same would hold true for victims of racial harassment under Title VI. It is not clear whether damages are limited to compensation or whether punitive damages may be awarded.[123]

Two Supreme Court decisions deal with the question of the conditions under which a school may be held liable for the harassment of a student by a district employee or another student. In *Gebser v. Lago Vista Independent School District*,[124] the Supreme Court ruled that a school district cannot be held responsible for sexual harassment of a student by an employee

> unless an official who at a minimum has authority to address the alleged discrimination and to institute corrective measures on the [school's] behalf has actual knowledge of discrimination in the [school's] programs and fails adequately to respond. . . . [M]oreover, the response must amount to deliberate indifference to discrimination . . . . The premise, in other words, is an official decision by the [school district] not to remedy the violation.

Applying these principles to the case at hand the Court noted that the student-victim had not reported her sexual intimacy with the teacher to the school principal and that the only warning signs the principal had were complaints from other parents regarding sexually suggestive comments by the teacher in class. When the school did finally learn of the sexual relationship, the teacher was fired and lost his teaching license. Thus, the facts did not prove that the principal or the district had actual knowledge of the discrimination and failed to respond.

Regarding peer harassment, the Supreme Court in *Davis v. Monroe County Board of Education*[125] ruled that a school district can be held liable for student-on-student sexual harassment when four conditions are met. First, the plaintiff must establish that the peer sexual harassment was so severe, pervasive, and objectively offensive that it undermined and distracted the plaintiff's educational experience to the point that the plaintiff was denied equal access to the school's resources and opportunities. The Court noted that simple acts of teasing and name-calling by students, even when these comments draw distinctions based on gender, would not create district liability. Nor would a single instance of severe one-on-one peer harassment expose a district to liability. Also, the Court stated that a drop in grades by itself would not be sufficient to prove the severity of the harassment. Second, the harassment must occur in a context with regard to which the district has substantial control over both the harasser and the context in which the harassment occurs; for example, during school hours and on school grounds. Third, the school district must have actual knowledge of the harassment. The Court did not specify, however, who must know about the harassment; arguably it would be sufficient if a single teacher knew. Fourth, there must be proof that the school district was deliberately indifferent to the known acts of peer sexual harassment. The district's obligation is to respond in a manner that is not clearly unreasonable. A total failure to respond or a response that exhibited discrimination in the enforcement of the school's rules—for example, protecting girls but not boys or Whites but not Blacks from harassment—are two examples of unreasonable responses. The Court acknowledged it would be reasonable for an institution to refrain from disciplinary action that would itself expose it to constitutional or statutory claims.

Following *Gebser* and *Davis*, there has been considerable litigation over the concepts of "actual knowledge" and "deliberate indifference" as employed in the decisions. The issue of whether a school district had **actual knowledge** of harassment turns on what was known, when, and by whom. In two cases, repeated complaints to a principal by a parent that their daughter was being harassed and to the principal by the victim and other students about the harassers' behavior were enough to satisfy the requirements.[126] The Fourth Circuit found that a school district was not liable for sexual harassment of a student by a teacher in a case where the principal had only "constructive," that is, inferential, knowledge of the harassment, not the required "actual" knowledge (the harassment had been reported to the principal by third parties, but her own investigation had failed to confirm it) and because the principal had "no independent authority to suspend, reassign, or terminate" the teacher. The principal was found personally liable because she had constructive knowledge of the abuse and failed to respond and because of her "desultory efforts at 'monitoring'" the teacher.[127] In another case, the Eight Circuit concluded that the actual-knowledge requirement was not satisfied when the only information school officials had was that a teacher was spending a lot of time with a student, that the student was excessively absent and tardy, and that his grades were falling.[128] The Fifth Circuit also found that the actual-knowledge requirement was not satisfied when a third grade student complained about harassment to administrative staff in the principal's office but not to the principal directly.[129]

A school district cannot be deliberately indifferent to an act of harassment prior to having actual knowledge of the harassment.[130] Once it has actual knowledge, a school district is **deliberately indifferent** if it takes no steps to investigate, to admonish or punish the harassers, and to prevent recurrence. The school's response does not have to be the one demanded by the victim's parents.[131] Nor is the reasonableness of a school's response to harassment determined solely by whether in hindsight the response was effective.[132] But the Sixth Circuit has said a school district's efforts "to remediate must be improved upon if the first steps are to no avail. When a district knows its first efforts are ineffective it must do more. Repeatedly doing the same thing which does not actually remediate the problem is not enough."[133]

To satisfy their moral and legal duty to their students and minimize their risk of legal liability, schools should adopt, publish, and abide by formal antidiscrimination and antiharassment policies. ED Title IX guidelines state that schools are required "to adopt and publish grievance procedures providing for prompt and equitable resolution of sex discrimination complaints, including complaints of sexual harassment and to disseminate a policy against sex discrimination."[134] Title VI guidelines specify that once a [school] has notice of a racially hostile environment, the [school] has a legal duty to take reasonable steps to eliminate it. . . . In evaluating a [school's] response to a racially hostile environment, [ED] will examine disciplinary policies, grievance policies, and any applicable anti-harassment policies.[135]

5.10 SUMMARY

The Equal Protection Clause of the Fourteenth Amendment to the Constitution prohibits the government from treating individuals or groups differently without adequate justification. This prohibition has been the basis of numerous lawsuits attacking segregation and other forms of discrimination in public schools. The Supreme Court has fashioned three separate tests for deciding equal protection cases:

1. **Strict scrutiny.** When government admits or a plaintiff successfully demonstrates that the criterion of classification and differential treatment is race or ethnicity, courts employ the strict scrutiny test. This test requires that the government justify its policy of differential treatment by showing that it is necessary to the accomplishment of a compelling state purpose. Except regarding certain affirmative action policies, this is a requirement that government can virtually never meet.
2. **Substantial relation.** When it is admitted or demonstrated by a plaintiff that government is classifying on the basis of gender, courts employ the substantial relation or middle-level test. This test, although not nearly as stringent as strict scrutiny, still places the burden for justifying the policy of differential treatment on the government. Gender-based classifications will be upheld only if the government can demonstrate that they are substantially related to the achievement of an important government purpose.
3. **Rational basis.** Classifications based on characteristics other than race, ethnicity, or gender (with several minor exceptions not usually relevant to education cases) are evaluated using the least stringent test. Rational basis places the burden on the plaintiff to show that differential treatment by the government is wholly unrelated to any legitimate state goal. Under this test, classifications that in any way foster or promote any legitimate goal of the government will be upheld.

As a practical matter, the Equal Protection Clause prohibits any policy or practice that intentionally segregates students on the basis of race or ethnicity or intentionally provides a racial or ethnic minority group with an inferior education. A policy or practice will be viewed as intentionally segregative or otherwise discriminatory if it purposely seeks to separate or otherwise disadvantage a minority group. Thus, any conscious decision by an educational policy maker or practitioner to separate students by race will not pass constitutional muster. Actions may also be viewed as discriminatory if a rational decision maker should have realized that the major result of the action would be to disadvantage or segregate a minority group. However, policies that have an accidental or unforeseeable disadvantageous effect on a particular racial group do not violate the Equal Protection Clause.

Beginning in 1954 with *Brown v. Board of Education*, many school districts have been found guilty of intentional racial segregation and discrimination. Federal courts are authorized to order a variety of remedies for de jure segregation, including redrawing of attendance areas, busing, magnet schools, and remedial educational programs. Courts may not, however, transfer pupils into or out of districts that have not been found de jure segregated in order to desegregate adjacent districts. Many formerly segregated districts have fully complied with court-ordered desegregation and been declared unitary, and others continue to be supervised by the courts.

School districts that have not been found guilty of intentional racial discrimination and those that have been declared unitary are prohibited from assigning students to schools on the basis of race in order to promote integration and racial diversity in their schools.

The Equal Protection Clause also prohibits educational practices that disfavor either gender unless there is very strong justification. Most programs that intentionally separate the sexes are prohibited. The major exception is athletics, but there is some uncertainty in the law.

In addition to the Equal Protection Clause, Title VI of the Civil Rights Act of 1964 and Title IX of the Education Amendments of 1972 prohibit discrimination in education on the basis of race and gender, respectively. These statutes supplement the Constitution in a number of ways, most importantly by providing remedies for discrimination not available under the Equal Protection Clause. Title VI and Title IX also provide a great deal of specificity concerning prohibited discriminatory practices. Title IX requires equity in school athletic programs. The statutes also define racial and sexual harassment as impermissible forms of discrimination and require that schools adopt and enforce a program designed to prevent racial and sexual harassment of students by school employees or fellow students. Failure to do so may leave the school and, in some cases, individual educators vulnerable to lawsuits for monetary damages.

Legal issues aside, schools should avoid policies of classification based on race, ethnicity, or gender without strong justification. Except in extraordinary circumstances, sound educational practice dictates treating Blacks the same as Whites and males the same as females. Thus, to avoid violating the Equal Protection Clause and antidiscrimination statutes with regard to race and gender, school officials need only exercise sound educational judgment and common sense.

NOTES

1 347 U.S. 483 (1954).
2 Green v. County Sch. Bd. of New Kent County, 391 U.S. 430 (1968).
3 San Antonio Indep. Sch. Dist. v. Rodriguez, 411 U.S. 1 (1973).
4 100 U.S. 303 (1879).
5 Yick Wo v. Hopkins, 118 U.S. 356 (1886).
6 163 U.S. 537 (1896).
7 304 U.S. 144 (1938).
8 305 U.S. 337 (1938).
9 339 U.S. 629 (1950).
10 339 U.S. 637 (1950).
11 323 U.S. 214 (1944).
12 335 U.S. 464 (1948).
13 347 U.S. 497 (1954).
14 Gayle v. Browder, 352 U.S. 903 (1956); Holmes v. Atlanta, 350 U.S. 879 (1955); Mayor of Baltimore v. Dawson, 350 U.S. 877 (1955).
15 Keyes v. Sch. Dist. No. 1, Denver, 413 U.S. 189 (1973); Washington v. Davis, 426 U.S. 229 (1976).
16 Personnel Adm'r of Massachusetts v. Feeney, 442 U.S. 256 (1979).
17 Arlington Heights v. Metro. Hous. Dev. Corp., 429 U.S. 252 (1977).
18 Keyes v. Sch. Dist. No. 1, Denver, 413 U.S. 189 (1973).
19 Arlington Heights v. Metro. Hous. Dev. Corp., 429 U.S. 252 (1977).
20 David A. Strauss, *Discriminatory Intent and the Taming of Brown*, 56 U. CHI. L. REV. 935, 957 (1989).
21 733 F.2d 660 (9th Cir. 1984).
22 Columbus Bd. of Educ. v. Penick, 443 U.S. 449 (1979); Dayton Bd. of Educ. v. Brinkman, 443 U.S. 526 (1979).
23 678 A.2d 1267 (Conn. 1996).

24 Brown v. Bd. Of Educ., 349 U.S. 294 (1955).

25 Cooper v. Aaron, 358 U.S. 1 (1958); Goss v. Bd. of Educ. of Knoxville, 373 U.S. 683 (1963); Griffin v. Sch. Bd. of Prince Edward County, 377 U.S. 218 (1964).

26 42 U.S.C. § 2000(d) et seq.

27 391 U.S. 430 (1968).

28 Alexander v. Holmes County Bd. of Educ., 396 U.S. 19 (1969).

29 402 U.S. 1 (1971).

30 Keyes v. Sch. Dist. No. 1, Denver, 413 U.S. 189 (1973); Columbus Bd. of Educ. v. Penick, 443 U.S. 449 (1979); Dayton Bd. of Educ. v. Brinkman, 443 U.S. 526 (1979); United States v. Scotland Neck Bd. of Educ., 407 U.S. 484 (1972).

31 418 U.S. 717 (1974).

32 433 U.S. 267 (1977).

33 495 U.S. 33 (1990) and 515 U.S. 70 (1995).

34 Davis v. E. Baton Rouge Parish Sch. Bd., 721 F.2d 1425 (5th Cir. 1983); Morgan v. Kerrigan, 530 F.2d 401 (1st Cir. 1976).

35 515 U.S. 70 (1995).

36 *See* Keyes v. Sch. Dist. No. 1, Denver, 413 U.S. 189 (1973); Columbus Bd. of Educ. v. Penick, 443 U.S. 449 (1979); Dayton Bd. of Educ. v. Brinkman, 443 U.S. 526 (1979); United States v. Scotland Neck Bd. of Educ., 407 U.S. 484 (1972).

37 427 U.S. 424 (1976).

38 498 U.S. 237 (1991).

39 503 U.S. 467 (1992).

40 Brown v. Unified Sch. Dist. No. 501, 56 F. Supp. 2d 1212 (D. Kan. 1999).

41 Belk v. Charlotte-Mecklenburg Bd. of Educ., 269 F.3d 305 (4th Cir. 2001).

42 Coalition to Save Our Children v. Bd. of Educ., 90 F.3d 752 (3d Cir. 1996); Morgan v. Nucci, 831 F.2d 313 (1st Cir. 1987); Calhoun v. Cook, 522 F.2d 717 (5th Cir. 1975); Ross v. Houston Indep. Sch. Dist., 699 F.2d 218 (5th Cir. 1983).

43 Billings v. Madison Metro. Sch. Dist., 259 F.3d 807 (7th Cir. 2001).

44 Larry P. v. Riles, 793 F.2d 969 (9th Cir. 1984).

45 Debra P. v. Turlington, 564 F. Supp. 177 (M.D. Fla. 1983), *aff'd*, 730 F.2d 1405 (11th Cir. 1984).

46 299 F. Supp. 2d 1340 (M.D. Ga. 2004), *aff'd*, Holton v. City of Thomasville Sch. Dist., 490 F.3d 1257 (11th Cir. 2007).

47 376 F. Supp. 1330 (N.D. Tex. 1974).

48 *See also* Lora v. Bd. of Educ. of N.Y., 456 F. Supp. 1211 (E.D.N.Y. 1978), *vacated*, 623 F.2d 248 (2d Cir. 1980); Rhyne v. Childs, 359 F. Supp. 1085 (N.D. Fla. 1973), *aff'd*, 507 F.2d 675 (5th Cir. 1975).

49 Young v. Montgomery County Bd. of Educ., 922 F. Supp. 544 (M.D. Ala. 1996).

50 539 U.S. 306 (2003).

51 539 U.S. 244 (2003).

52 551 U.S. 701 (2007).

53 *See* Tuttle v. Arlington County Sch. Bd., 195 F.3d 698 (4th Cir. 1999); Eisenberg *ex rel.* Eisenberg v. Montgomery County Pub. Sch., 197 F.3d 123 (4th Cir. 1999); McLaughlin v. Boston Sch. Comm., 938 F. Supp. 1001 (D. Mass. 1996).

54 411 U.S. 677 (1973).

55 Craig v. Boren, 429 U.S. 190 (1976).

56 532 F.2d 880 (3d Cir. 1976), *aff'd by an equally divided Court*, 430 U.S. 703 (1977).

57 458 U.S. 718 (1982).

58 518 U.S. 515 (1996).

59 775 F. Supp. 1004 (E.D. Mich. 1991).

60 570 F. Supp. 1020 (W.D. Mo. 1983).

61 O'Connor v. Bd. of Educ. of Sch. Dist. 23, 545 F. Supp. 376 (N.D. Ill. 1982), and 449 U.S. 1301 (1980).

62 Brenden v. Indep. Sch. Dist. 742, 477 F.2d 1292 (8th Cir. 1973); Gilpin v. Kansas State High Sch. Activities Ass'n, 377 F. Supp. 1233 (D. Kan. 1973).

63 Bucha v. Illinois High Sch. Ass'n, 351 F. Supp. 69 (N.D. Ill. 1972).

64 Clark v. Arizona Interscholastic Ass'n, 695 F.2d 1126 (9th Cir. 1982); Petrie v. Illinois High Sch. Ass'n, 394 N.E.2d 855 (Ill. App. Ct. 1979); *but see* Gomes v. Rhode Island Interscholastic League, 469 F. Supp. 659 (D.R.I.), *vacated as moot*, 604 F.2d 733 (1st Cir. 1979).

65 Williams v. Sch. Dist. of Bethlehem, 998 F.2d 168 (3d Cir. 1993).

66 377 F.3d 504 (6th Cir. 2004).

67 42 U.S.C. § 2000d.

68 34 C.F.R. § 1003 (b).

69 42 U.S.C. § 2000c-6.

70 42 U.S.C. § 2000d-1.

71 Alexander v. Choate, 469 U.S. 287 (1985); Guardians Ass'n v. Civil Serv. Comm., 463 U.S. 582 (1983).

72 *Compare* Franklin v. Gwinnett County Pub. Sch., 503 U.S. 60 (1992).

73 Guardians Ass'n v. Civil Serv. Comm'n, 463 U.S. 582 (1983).

74 Alexander v. Sandoval, 532 U.S. 275 (2001).

75 *See* Bd. of Educ. of Sch. Dist. of New York. v. Harris, 444 U.S. 130 (1979); *see also* Elston v. Talladega County Bd. of Educ., 997 F.2d 1394 (11th Cir. 1993); Larry P. v. Riles, 495 F. Supp. 926 (N.D. Cal. 1979), *aff'd in part*, 793 F.2d 969 (9th Cir. 1984).

76 20 U.S.C. §§ 1681–1686.

77 20 U.S.C. § 1687.

78 Cannon v. Univ. of Chicago, 441 U.S. 677 (1979).

79 Franklin v. Gwinnett County Pub. Schs., 503 U.S. 60 (1992).

80 *See e.g.*, Pfeiffer v. Marion Center Area Sch. Dist., 917 F.2d 779 (3d Cir. 1990); Williams v. Sch. Dist. of Bethlehem, 998 F.2d 168 (3d Cir. 1993) (Title IX preempts use of § 1983); *contra* Seamons v. Snow, 84 F.3d 1226 (10th Cir. 1996); Lillard v. Shelby County Bd. of Educ., 76 F.3d 716 (6th Cir. 1996).

81 Cannon v. Univ. of Chicago, 648 F.2d 1104 (7th Cir. 1981); NAACP v. Medical Ctr. Inc., 657 F.2d 1322 (3d Cir. 1981).

82 Sharif v. New York State Educ. Dep't, 709 F. Supp. 345 (S.D.N.Y. 1989).

83 Guardians Ass'n v. Civil Serv. Comm'n, 463 U.S. 582 (1983).

84 544 U.S. 167 (2005).

85 34 C.F.R. § 106.21(b)(2).

86 34 C.F.R. § 106.31(b)(4).

87 34 C.F.R. § 106.36.

88 34 C.F.R. § 106.40.

89 Garrett v. Bd. of Educ. of Sch. Dist. of City of Detroit, 775 F. Supp. 1004 (E.D. Mich. 1991).

90 34 C.F.R. §106.34.

91 Garrett v. Bd. of Educ. of Sch. Dist. of City of Detroit, 775 F. Supp. 1004 (E.D. Mich. 1991); see sec. 5.7.

92 *U.S. Department of Education Athletic Guidelines, Title IX of the Education Amendments of 1972, A Policy Interpretation, Title IX and Intercollegiate Athletics*, 44 Fed. Reg. 71,413, 71,423 (1979); Office for Civil Rights, United States Department of Education, *Additional Clarification of Intercollegiate Athletics Policy: Three-Part Test – Part Three*, March 17, 2005; *see also*, Cohen v. Brown University, 991 F.2d 888 (1st Cir. 1993) and 101 F.3d 155 (1st Cir. 1996).

93 Darrin v. Gould, 540 P.2d 882 (Wash. 1975) (en banc).

94 DeShaney v. Winnebago County Dep't of Social Serv., 489 U.S. 189 (1989).

95 Nabozny v. Podlesny, 92 F.3d 446 (7th Cir. 1996); *see also* Murrell v. Sch. Dist. No. 1, 186 F.3d 1238 (10th Cir. 1999).

96 Doe v. Claiborne County, 103 F.3d 495 (6th Cir. 1996).

97 MCLS § 37.2102; CAL. EDUC. CODE § 231.5; OR. REV. STAT. § 342.700; TEX. EDUC. CODE § 37.083; REV. CODE WASH. (ARCW) § 28A.640.020.

98 59 Fed. Reg. 11447.

99 62 Fed. Reg. 12033.

100 Monteiro v. Tempe Union High School Dist., 158 F.3d 1022 (9th Cir. 1998).

101 Burwell v. Pekin Cmty. High Sch. Dist. 303, 213 F. Supp. 2d 917 (C.D. Ill. 2002).

102 Seneway v. Canon McMillan Sch. Dist., 969 F. Supp. 325 (W.D. Pa. 1997); *see also* Oona R.-S. v. Santa Rosa City Sch., 890 F. Supp. 1452 (N.D. Cal. 1995), *aff'd*, 143 F.3d 473 (9th Cir. 1997).

103 Mary M. v. N. Lawrence Cmty. Sch. Corp., 131 F. 3d 1220 (7th Cir. 1997).

104 Gebser v. Lago Vista Indep. Sch. Dist., 503 U.S. 60 (1998).

105 Davis v. Monroe County Bd. of Educ., 74 F.3d 1186 (11th Cir. 1996), *vacated*, 91 F.3d 1418, *aff'd*, 120 F.3d 1390 (11th Cir. 1997) (en banc), *rev'd*, 526 U.S. 629 (1999); *see also* Rowinsky v. Bryan Indep. Sch. Dist., 80 F.3d 1006 (5th Cir. 1996).

106 Davis v. Monroe County Bd. of Educ., 526 U.S. 629 (1999).

107 Wilson v. Beaumont Indep. Sch. Dist., 144 F. Supp. 2d 690 (E.D. Tex. 2001).
108 Seamons v. Snow, 84 F.3d 1226 (10th Cir. 1996).
109 Manfredi v. Mount Vernon Bd. of Educ., 94 F. Supp. 2d 447 (S.D.N.Y. 2000).
110 Gabrielle M. v. Park Forest-Chicago Heights, Illinois. Sch. Dist. 163, 315 F.3d 817 (7th Cir. 2003).
111 Hawkins v. Sarasota County Sch. Bd., 322 F.3d 1279 (11th Cir. 2003).
112 62 Fed. Reg. 12034, March 13, 1997.
113 Theno v. Tonganoxie Unified School Dist. No. 464, 394 F. Supp. 2d 1299 (D. Kan. 2005); Montgomery v. Indep. Sch. Dist. No. 709, 109 F. Supp. 2d 1081 (D. Minn. 2000); Ray v. Antioch Unified Sch. Dist., 107 F. Supp. 2d 1165 (N.D. Cal. 2000).
114 L.W. v. Toms River Reg'l Schs. Bd. of Educ., 915 A.2d 535 (N.J. 2007).
115 Does v. Covington County Sch. Bd. of Educ., 969 F. Supp. 1264 (M.D. Ala. 1997).
116 Smith v. Metro. Sch. Dist. of Perry Twp., 128 F.3d 1014 (7th Cir. 1997).
117 Murrell v. Sch. Dist. No. 1, 186 F.3d 1238 (10th Cir. 1999).
118 Oona R.-S. v. Santa Rosa City Sch., 890 F. Supp. 1452 (N.D. Cal. 1995), *aff'd*, 143 F.3d 473 (9th Cir. 1997); *but see* Does v. Covington County Sch. Bd. of Educ., 930 F. Supp. 554 (M.D. Ala. 1996), and 969 F. Supp. 1264 (M.D. Ala. 1997).
119 *Title IX preempts availability of Section 1983*: Bruneau v. South Kortright Cent. Sch. Dist., 163 F.3d 749 (2d Cir. 1998); Waid v. Merrill Area Pub. Schs., 91 F.3d 857 (7th Cir. 1996); Pfeiffer v. Marion Center Area Sch. Dist., 917 F.2d 779 (3d Cir. 1990). *Title IX does not preempt availability of Section 1983*: Crawford v. Davis, 109 F.3d (8th Cir. 1997); Seamons v. Snow, 84 F.3d 1226 (10th Cir. 1996); Lillard v. Shelby County Bd. of Educ., 76 F.3d 716 (6th Cir. 1996).
120 Doe v. Claiborne County, 103 F.3d 495 (6th Cir. 1996); *see also* Doe v. Taylor Indep. Sch. Dist., 15 F.3d 443 (5th Cir. 1994).
121 Larez v. Los Angeles, 946 F.2d 630 (9th Cir. 1991); *see also* Baynard v. Malone, 268 F.3d 228 (4th Cir. 2001) (en banc).
122 503 U.S. 60 (1992).
123 Doe v. Oyster River Co-Op Sch. Dist., 992 F. Supp. 467 (D.N.H. 1997).
124 524 U.S. 274 (1998).
125 526 U.S. 629 (1999).
126 Vance v. Spencer County Pub. Sch. Dist., 231 F.3d 253 (6th Cir. 2000); Davis v. Monroe County Bd. of Educ., 526 U.S. 629 (1999).
127 Baynard v. Malone, 268 F.3d 228 (4th Cir. 2001) (en banc).
128 P.H. v. Sch. Dist. of Kan. City, 265 F.3d 653 (8th Cir. 2001).
129 Doe v. Dallas Indep. Sch. Dist., 220 F.3d 380 (5th Cir. 2000); *see also* Jane Doe A. v. Green, 298 F. Supp. 2d 1025 (D. Nev. 2004).
130 Davis v. DeKalb County Sch. Dist., 233 F.3d 1367 (11th Cir. 2000).
131 Fitzgerald v. Barnstable Sch. Comm., 504 F.3d 165 (1st Cir. 2007).
132 Proto v. Town of Tewksbury, 488 F.3d 67 (1st Cir. 2007).
133 Vance v. Spencer County Pub. Sch. Dist., 231 F.3d 253 (6th Cir. 2000).
134 62 Fed. Reg. 12040.
135 59 Fed. Reg. 11451.

6 Students with Special Needs

The last chapter showed that the Equal Protection Clause prohibits most race- and gender-based classifications by public schools and that classification based on other characteristics may be justified if it is rationally related to legitimate government goals. Chapter 6 considers some criteria that do justify differential educational treatment: various types of disabilities, limited English proficiency, age, and educational ability. Unlike race and gender, these characteristics may be related to an individual's need for and ability to benefit from education, and, to the extent that they are, they may be the basis for determining the educational program that an individual receives.

This does not mean, however, that schools are free to provide whatever education they choose to students who vary with regard to these characteristics. Both the Constitution and extensive federal legislation and regulations demand that even though the programs offered to special-needs students may differ from the norm, they must, nevertheless, satisfy the requirement of equality of educational opportunity for all. In fact, with regard to students with disabilities or limited English proficiency, equality of opportunity may require that a different and perhaps more extensive program be offered.

Furthermore, under the terms of the No Child Left Behind Act (see sec. 2.6), a school may be assessed in part on whether students with disabilities and students of limited English proficiency are making adequate yearly progress (AYP) toward a state-defined standard of proficiency. If an insufficient percentage of students in either of these subgroups is making AYP, the school can be subjected to a series of corrective actions even if all other groups of students and the student body as a whole are making AYP.

All this can get very complex: How much education are children with disabilities entitled to? May disruptive students with disabilities be excluded from school? What kinds of programs satisfy the school's obligation to non-English speaking students? Do exceptionally bright students have a constitutional right to start school early or to skip a grade? This chapter addresses questions like these.

6.1 HISTORICAL PERSPECTIVE: THE EDUCATION OF CHILDREN WITH DISABILITIES

In 1970, there were about eight million children with disabilities in the United States. Three million of these children were not receiving an appropriate education and another million were wholly excluded from public education. Exclusion of children with disabilities was legally possible because many states' laws excused those children from compliance with compulsory education laws. State courts generally upheld policies of excluding children with disabilities from the public schools, sometimes on the grounds that their presence would have a detrimental effect on the education of the other students.[1]

In the early 1970s, the exclusion of children with disabilities from public schooling became the target of a number of federal lawsuits, most notably *Pennsylvania Association for Retarded Children (PARC) v. Commonwealth of Pennsylvania*[2] and *Mills v. Board of Education*.[3] Although the cases differed somewhat, the major findings of both courts were similar: (a) children were excluded from the public schools because they had disabilities, (b) the effect of this policy was wholly to deprive these children of access to a publicly funded education, (c) the government's purpose in excluding them was to save money, (d) excluding children with disabilities from school was not rationally related to the goal of saving money (or to any other legitimate state goal) because uneducated people (with disabilities or not) were likely to become a much greater financial burden on the state than if they had been educated, and therefore (e) exclusion of children with disabilities from public schools violated the Equal Protection Clause.

The opinions concluded by laying down both substantive and procedural requirements. Children with disabilities must be admitted to the public schools and provided adequate or appropriate educational services suited to their individual needs. Schools must follow certain procedures when they classify students with disabilities, decide on their appropriate educational placements, reclassify, or change placement.

The *Mills* and *PARC* cases were part of a nationwide campaign that included not only lawsuits but also political efforts to get better educational services for children with disabilities through legislation. This campaign has resulted in four major federal statutes designed to ensure effective education and equitable treatment for children with disabilities:

- The Rehabilitation Act of 1973,[4] often called "RHA," "Section 504," or, most commonly, "504."
- The Americans with Disabilities Act[5] of 1990 (ADA).
- The Individuals with Disabilities Education Act[6] (IDEA), originally passed in 1975 and extensively modified and amended since. IDEA was originally called the Education for All Handicapped Children Act (EAHCA) and also was known at one time as the Education of the Handicapped Act (EHA). In 2004, the name was officially changed to the Individuals with Disabilities Education Improvement Act (IDEIA), but it is still commonly referred to as IDEA.
- The No Child Left Behind Act[7] (NCLB).

Together with related state laws and extensive federal and state regulations, these laws provide the legal framework for the education of students with disabilities. The constitutional rights of children with disabilities have not been fully explored by the courts because as a practical matter the statutes seem to satisfactorily address the demands of parents of such children for educational services at public expense.[8]

Although the IDEA is the most well known of the statutes regulating the education of students with disabilities, 504 and ADA are significant as well. IDEA is a funding program with requirements that extend only to states that accept funds under the Act. If it were not for the similar requirements imposed by 504 and ADA, states could choose to avoid their IDEA-imposed obligations by declining to accept the funds.[9] Additionally, as discussed in the next section, the scope of 504 and ADA is in some ways broader than that of IDEA. 504 and ADA extend protection to students and other individuals who are not covered by IDEA, impose obligations on schools and in situations that IDEA does not reach, and prevent forms of disability-based discrimination beyond the scope of IDEA. Nevertheless, both as a matter of law and as a practical matter, IDEA is by far the most influential statute in controlling the education of children with disabilities. NCLB adds a new dimension to federal regulation of the education offered to students with disabilities requiring emphasis on academic achievement and imposing the threat of sanctions to schools if a sufficient percentage (eventually 95 percent) of students with disabilities do not achieve the standard of proficiency set by the state for all students.

6.2 THE REHABILITATION ACT (504) AND THE AMERICANS WITH DISABILITIES ACT

The heart of the Rehabilitation Act is **Section 504**:[10] "No otherwise qualified individual with handicaps . . . shall solely by reason of her or his handicap, be excluded from the participation in, be denied the benefits of, or be subjected to discrimination under any program or activity receiving Federal financial assistance. . . ." The Act applies to all public and private schools that receive federal financial assistance and protects not just students with disabilities but *any person* "who (i) has a physical or mental impairment which substantially limits one or more of such person's major life activities, (ii) has a record of such an impairment, or (iii) is regarded as having such an impairment." Thus, 504, unlike IDEA, regulates a school's relationship not only with qualifying students but also with qualifying teachers and other employees (see sec. 7.6). Under certain circumstances, even qualifying parents may be covered. For example, the Second Circuit has ruled that 504 requires a school to provide a sign-language interpreter at district expense to deaf parents of hearing children at school-initiated activities related to the academic or disciplinary aspects of their children's education. The school's obligation, however, does not include providing an interpreter at school extracurricular activities.[11]

504 defines "major life activities" to include "caring for one's self, performing manual tasks, walking, seeing, hearing, speaking, breathing, learning and working." Thus, unlike IDEA, which only covers students who currently need special education, 504 protects children with a wide range of "impairments," those with a history of life-limiting impairments, and even those who are regarded as having such an impairment. For example, students with epilepsy or physical disabilities or attention deficit hyperactivity disorder (ADHD) are covered by 504 even though some of them may not qualify for special education under IDEA. All students who qualify for services under IDEA are also protected by 504 and ADA.

Like 504, the ADA[12] covers all persons with physical or mental impairments that substantially limit major life activities, those with a record of such impairments, and those who are regarded as having such impairments. The basic mandate of the ADA is that "no qualified individual with a disability shall, by reason of such disability, be excluded from participation in or be denied the benefits of services, programs or activities of a public entity, or be subjected to discrimination by any such entity." The term "qualified individual with a disability" means an individual with a disability who, with or without "reasonable modifications" to rules, policies, or practices; the removal of architectural and communication barriers; or the provision of auxiliary aids and services, meets the essential eligibility requirements for the receipt of services or participation in the program.

Whereas 504 regulates only entities that receive federal financial assistance, ADA applies to all "public entities" and "places of public accommodation." This includes any public or private business or agency providing goods or services to the public, including virtually all public and private schools except private religious schools, which are explicitly excluded. Where there is overlap between the two laws, the requirements of ADA are the same as 504.

Among the five main titles of ADA, Titles II and III are directly relevant to the treatment of students. Title II protects individuals with disabilities from discrimination in the provision of services by public agencies such as schools. Title II requires that public schools be made accessible to individuals with disabilities such as by modification or removal of "architectural, communication or transportation barriers" or the "provision of auxiliary aids and services." Title III prohibits discrimination by private entities that do business with the public. Private schools at all levels, except private religious schools, are specifically included. In general, ADA places the same requirements on public school programs as 504 and IDEA, and public school programs that satisfy the requirements of 504 and IDEA also satisfy ADA.

Eligibility

Students seeking to convince a court that they should be afforded the protection of 504 or ADA must demonstrate that they have a "mental or physical impairment" that "substantially limits" a "major life activity" or that they have a history of or are regarded as having such an impairment. According to the Second Circuit, the impairment does not have to relate to the activity "in which the defendants are engaged." Thus, a student with chronic fatigue syndrome that did not impair her ability to learn still qualified for protection under ADA at school because her condition "substantially limited her in the major life activities of walking, exerting herself, and attending classes. . . ."[13] The laws specifically exclude coverage to individuals because they are homosexuals, transvestites, current smokers, or users of illegal drugs or have a temporary condition such as a broken arm. ADA also excludes individuals whose presence in a program "poses a direct threat to the health or safety of others." The term "direct threat" is defined as "a significant risk to the health or safety of others that cannot be eliminated by a modification of policies, practices, or procedures or by the provision of auxiliary aids or services."

The Supreme Court has ruled that the law protects people with contagious diseases (e.g., tuberculosis), even if the disease does not incapacitate them, because they are regarded as having an impairment of a major life activity.[14] Some individuals with contagious diseases might be excluded from coverage because their conditions were temporary or because they posed a direct threat to the health of others. The Fourth Circuit ruled that a student suffering from depression was covered and that a school excluding her from an extracurricular activity violated ADA.[15] On the other hand, the Eighth Circuit ruled that a student who was having some academic difficulties but advancing from grade to grade did not have an impairment that substantially limited the major life activity of learning. Despite the fact that her band instructor had called her "retarded," "stupid," and "dumb," the court concluded that the evidence did not support the claim that she was regarded as having such an impairment.[16] A medical student with test anxiety regarding math and chemistry was ruled as not covered; to be covered said the Tenth Circuit, the plaintiff had to establish that his anxiety extended to a wide variety of courses.[17] A student with a heart condition was not covered because his condition only limited his ability to play basketball, which the court said was not a major life activity.[18]

504 protects **"otherwise qualified** individuals with handicaps." The issue of what constitutes an "otherwise qualified" individual was addressed by the Supreme Court in *Southeastern Community College v. Davis*.[19] The case concerned a woman denied admission to a nurse's training program because her hearing disability prevented her from benefiting sufficiently from the program or performing the tasks of the profession. The Court ruled against the woman, saying that an "otherwise qualified" person with a disability was "one who is able to meet all of a program's requirements in spite of his handicap," not

one "who would be able to meet the requirements of a particular program in every respect except as to limitations imposed by their handicap."

Purposeful Discrimination

Both the 504 and ADA prohibit both purposeful discrimination and also actions having the unintentional effect of discriminating against those covered by the laws. Plaintiffs claiming purposeful discrimination under 504 bear the initial burden of establishing that (a) they are a handicapped person under the law; (b) they are otherwise qualified and can participate in the program with or without reasonable accommodation; (c) they have been or are being excluded from participation in, or being denied the benefits of, or being subjected to discrimination under the program solely by reason of their handicap; and (4) the relevant program or activity is receiving federal financial assistance.[20] Once the plaintiff has met this burden of proof, the burden then shifts to the defendant to show either that the plaintiff was not otherwise qualified, or that the defendant based its actions on reasons other than the plaintiff's handicap. If the defendant meets this burden of proof, the plaintiff can still win by showing that the defendant acted based on discriminatory reasons or on misconceptions or unfounded factual conclusions, or that the reasons articulated for the rejection encompass unjustified consideration of the handicap itself. The Eighth Circuit ruled that the plaintiff must also establish that the defendant's actions showed bad faith or gross misjudgment.[21]

Several courts have ruled that under 504 it is discrimination for a school to prohibit for paternalistic reasons a student with one kidney or one eye from competing in contact sports such as wrestling and football.[22] Failure of a school district to protect a child with a disability from harassment also constitutes discrimination under 504[23] and may be a violation of IDEA as well. Courts may view harassment of students protected by 504 as analogous to racial or sexual harassment[24] (see sec 5.9) and schools officials who are "deliberately indifferent" to such harassment may be vulnerable to lawsuits for damages under the federal law known as Section 1983 (see sec. 10.10).

ADA defines discrimination broadly to include:

- Using eligibility criteria that screen out individuals with disabilities from goods, services, facilities, privileges, advantages, and accommodations.
- Failing to make reasonable modifications in policies and practices to assure that individuals with disabilities are afforded goods, services, facilities, privileges, advantages, and accommodations. However, modifications and adjustments are not required if they would fundamentally alter the goods, services, facilities, privileges, advantages, or accommodations provided. Also, the removal of architectural or communication barriers is required only if removal is "readily achievable."
- Failing to provide auxiliary aids and services to assure that individuals with disabilities are not excluded from goods, services, facilities, privileges, advantages, and accommodations.

At the heart of 504 and the ADA is the requirement that people with disabilities not be treated differently solely by reason of their disability. Regulations prohibit imposing a surcharge on students with disabilities for attending after-school programs or on parents with disabilities for making school functions accessible to them such as by provision of a sign-language interpreter. A school may not exclude a student from equal services because the student has an association with someone with a known disability; for example, excluding a child from sports because a sibling is HIV-positive is prohibited.

Unintentional Discrimination

A number of students with disabilities have attempted to rely on 504 and ADA's prohibition against actions having the unintended effect of discriminating against students with disabilities to object to academic or other eligibility requirements for school sports teams; however, courts have usually found that eligibility requirements that serve a valid purpose and apply equally to students with or without disabilities do not violate the law. Both the Sixth and Eighth Circuits have upheld rules setting a maximum age for participation in interscholastic sports. The rules had the effect of excluding some students who because of their disability were in school beyond the usual graduation age. The Sixth Circuit said that an exclusion based on age is not an exclusion based on disability, and that absent their disabilities, the plaintiffs would still have failed to satisfy the age requirement.[25] The Eighth Circuit said that age was an essential eligibility requirement designed to promote safety for all participants. Because the plaintiff could not meet the requirement, he was not "otherwise qualified" unless "reasonable accommodation" could enable him to meet the requirement. Waiving the age requirement would not be a "reasonable accommodation," but rather a "fundamental alteration" of the sports program.[26]

Several other courts have ruled that 504 and ADA require that the application of age-eligibility requirements to students with disabilities be done on an individual basis. In one case the plaintiff was a nineteen-year-old student with Down's Syndrome who spent four rather than three years in middle school and then for three years was a member of the high school swim team. When he turned nineteen, he was no longer eligible for the swim team. Based on 504 and the ADA the student asked for and obtained an order from the court granting him a waiver of the age rule. The court wrote, "It would be an anathema to the goals of the Rehabilitation Act to decline to require an individualized analysis of the purposes behind the age requirement as applied to [this student]. Failure to perform such an analysis would exalt the rule itself without regard for the essential purposes behind the rule." The court further noted that the student would have no competitive advantage as he was always the slowest swimmer in the pool; there was no risk to the plaintiff or others since this was not a contact sport; and his education had not been delayed to gain a competitive advantage. Finally the court said that exclusion of the plaintiff because of his age amounted to an exclusion based on disability since it was because of his disability that he was in school at nineteen.[27]

On a related issue, the Sixth Circuit concluded that the ADA was not violated by a rule that prohibited students from participating in athletics after more than nine semesters of enrollment. The student with a disability in this suit had been enrolled in school for more than the permitted number of semesters but had been academically ineligible for part of the time as a result of his disability. The court found that a waiver of the rule was not required by ADA because it would fundamentally alter interscholastic sports. Furthermore, reasoned the court, alteration of the rule was undesirable from a policy standpoint because it would encourage redshirting—the practice of delaying academic advancement for the sake of athletics.[28]

In another case, the Seventh Circuit considered the application to a student with a disability of a rule limiting a student's athletic eligibility to the first eight semesters following the student's enrollment in ninth grade. The plaintiff started the ninth grade but then left school because of academic problems related to his learning disability. The court found that waiving the rule was a reasonable accommodation required by ADA. The court reasoned that the rule in question did not serve any academic purpose, that the prospect of participation in athletics had actually inspired the plaintiff to improve his academic performance, and that the rule did "not appear to add anything to the protections provided by the [athletic association's] age limit rule, which generally limits the size, strength and athletic maturity of student athletes."[29] On another related issue, in a suit attacking grade-point-average and credit eligibility requirements, the student with a disability lost.[30]

Accommodation

504 and ADA require modifications to school programs and other "reasonable accommodations" as necessary so that students with disabilities are not because of their disability denied the benefits they would otherwise receive.[31] ADA regulations require that schools "shall make reasonable modifications in policies, practices, or procedures when the modifications are necessary to avoid discrimination on the basis of disability, unless the [school] can demonstrate that making the modifications would fundamentally alter the nature of the service, program, or activity."[32] RHA regulations require that public elementary and secondary schools provide a program that is designed to meet "individual educational needs of handicapped persons as adequately as the needs of nonhandicapped persons are met."[33]

Brookhart v. Illinois State Board of Education[34] considered the legality under 504 of requiring students with disabilities to pass a minimum competency test (M.C.T.) in order to graduate from high school. Said the court:

> Plaintiffs in this case have no grounds on which to argue that the contents of the M.C.T. are discriminatory solely because handicapped students who are incapable of attaining a level of minimum competency will fail the test. Altering the content of the M.C.T. to accommodate an individual's inability to learn the tested material because of his handicap would be a "substantial modification," as well as a "perversion" of the diploma requirement. A student who is unable to learn because of his handicap is surely not an individual who is qualified in spite of his handicap. Thus denial of a diploma because of inability to pass the M.C.T. is not discrimination under the RHA.
>
> However, an otherwise qualified student who is unable to disclose the degree of learning he actually possesses because of the test format or environment would be the object of discrimination solely on the basis of his handicap. It is apparent . . . that "to discover a blind person's knowledge, a test must be given orally or in braille." . . . [504] requires administrative modification to minimize the effects of plaintiffs' handicaps on . . . examinations.

Brookhart illustrates well the meaning of "otherwise qualified" and of "reasonable accommodation." To exempt students with disabilities from the requirement of demonstrating the requisite level of knowledge before being awarded a diploma would negate the essential educational purpose of minimum competency testing. Conversely, to deny a student with a disability the opportunity to demonstrate the requisite knowledge in a modified format, for example, by giving written or signed rather than oral test instructions to deaf students, is to discriminate on the basis of disability.

One court invoked the reasonable-accommodation principle in saying that a school district had to permit a student with a disability to bring her service dog to school.[35] In another case, *Cave v. East Meadow Union Free School District*,[36] the plaintiffs also claimed that a school should be required to accommodate their hearing-impaired child by permitting him to bring a service dog to school. Relying on Second Circuit precedent, the court said a reasonable accommodation was "one that gives the otherwise qualified [student] with disabilities 'meaningful access' to the program or services [of the school]." The court further noted that the school is not obligated to provide students with every accommodation they request as long as the accommodations that are provided are reasonable. In this case, the court found that the accommodations provided including, among others, a sign-language interpreter, an FM transmitter, and a student note-taker, were reasonable. The court went on to consider the consequences of permitting the dog, including the fact that one teacher was allergic and that the accommodation would in various ways detrimentally affect the student's academic program. The court concluded that the requested accommodation was not a legal requirement.

Bercovitch v. Baldwin School, Inc.[37] involved a severely disruptive sixth grade student at a private school. Having made numerous unsuccessful attempts to accommodate and modify the student's behavior, the school now sought, in effect, to expel the student. The child's parents claimed that the expulsion was impermissible under ADA because a psychologist had diagnosed the child as afflicted with ADHD. The parents argued that except for the behaviors arising out of his disability, the child was "otherwise qualified" to participate in the school's educational program and that the reasonable accommodation principle required extensive modification of the school's code of conduct as applied to the child. However, the First Circuit disagreed on both counts. The child was not otherwise qualified because he could not meet the school's behavioral requirements even with reasonable accommodations. The requested modification of the code of conduct amounted to a "significant alteration of a fundamental requirement of the school." ADA did not require "a school to suspend its normal codes of conduct in order to tolerate disruptive and disrespectful conduct when that behavior impaired the educational experience of other students and significantly taxed the resources of the faculty and other students."

Access to Facilities

Both 504 and the ADA require that school facilities be accessible to students and their parents; however, schools need not make every part of a facility accessible as long as their programs and activities when viewed in their entirety are readily accessible. Also, alterations that would fundamentally alter a program or activity or result in an undue financial and administrative burden need not be undertaken. The regulations implementing ADA list the types of alterations that should be made, including installing ramps, reconfiguring toilet facilities, and providing a reasonable number of wheelchair spaces dispersed throughout seating areas.

Educational Program

The educational program requirements of 504 generally parallel those of IDEA but with less detail. Qualifying students must be provided with an individualized educational program designed to meet their needs as adequately as the program provided to other students meets their needs. Both academic and nonacademic activities are subject to this equivalency requirement. Like IDEA, 504 requires that students with disabilities be thoroughly evaluated and periodically reevaluated, that they be educated to the maximum extent possible with nondisabled peers, and that parents be involved in the development of educational programs for their children. For the most part, for students who also qualify under IDEA, compliance with IDEA will usually satisfy the educational requirements of 504. 504 prohibits discrimination against students with disabilities in the provision of services and materials, requires that school facilities be made accessible to those students, mandates modifications in classrooms, "reasonable accommodations" in courses (e.g., teaching techniques, exam procedures), and the provision of auxiliary aids and devices. The Third Circuit has written that there is little difference between the affirmative obligations of IDEA and 504's prohibition against discrimination. Both laws require that students with disabilities be provided with a free appropriate public education (see sec. 6.3).[38]

Enforcement

School districts are required to establish and publicize grievance procedures to deal with alleged violations of 504. Individuals may also file a grievance against a school district with the Department of Education (ED) within 180 days of an allegedly discriminatory action. ED will investigate the allegation, and if a violation is found, the district must correct the violation or risk loss of all federal funds. Individuals can also sue for compensatory monetary damages for a violation of 504[39] or ADA but not for punitive damages.[40] A successful complainant can also be awarded attorney's fees under either law. ADA also prohibits retaliation, interference, coercion, or intimidation against individuals claiming rights under the law, assisting in investigating violations, or testifying in proceedings brought under the law.

6.3   THE INDIVIDUALS WITH DISABILITIES EDUCATION ACT

Congress enacted the first version of the IDEA[41] with 504 already in force to further define the obligations of schools to children with disabilities and to help meet part of the cost of educating them. IDEA is a grant program providing money to states that choose to participate—all states do—to help support the education of children with disabilities. To be eligible for federal funds under the IDEA, a state must develop a plan for providing all children with disabilities a "free, appropriate public education which emphasizes special education and related services designed to meet their unique needs." The plan must include a system for allocating funding to local school districts and must comply with the program requirements as spelled out in the law and implementing regulations. In turn, each local school district must submit an application to the state indicating how it will comply with IDEA requirements.

The basic mandate of the IDEA is that all children with disabilities must receive a free, appropriate public education (FAPE). FAPE means "special education and related services that are provided at public expense, under public supervision and direction without charge and are provided in conformity with the child's individual education plan (IEP)." The FAPE requirement extends to children with disabilities who have chosen to attend public schools, religious or other private schools, charter schools, or home schools and even to children with disabilities who have been suspended or expelled from school. IDEA also gives parents of children with disabilities the right to participate in the making of decisions regarding their children and to examine all records concerning their children.

Eligibility

IDEA mandates services for children ages three to twenty-one[42] who are determined to be within one or more of fourteen specified categories of disability and who, "by reason thereof," need special education and related services. Categories include autism, deafness, deafblindness, hearing impairments, mental retardation, multiple disabilities, orthopedic impairments, other health impairments, serious emotional disturbance, specific learning disabilities, speech or language impairments, Tourette syndrome, traumatic brain injury, and visual impairment. The law provides extended definitions of specific learning disability, mental retardation, other health impaired, autism, and traumatic brain injury. States have a certain amount of latitude in applying these definitions in accordance with their own statutes and regulations, so IDEA eligibility criteria may vary from state to state.[43] IDEA also permits school districts to service students ages three to nine who are experiencing physical, cognitive, communicative, social, emotional, or adaptive developmental delays and who by reason thereof need special education and related services.

In order to be eligible for services under IDEA, a child must both fall within one of the specified category of disability and be in need of special education and related services "by reason thereof." If the child's educational performance does not suffer because of the disability, the child is not eligible for services under IDEA. But what does it mean for a child's educational performance to suffer? *Mr. I. v. Maine School Administrative District No. 25*[44] concerned a student with Asperger's Syndrome (a form of autism) who excelled academically. Viewing education as more than just academic outcomes, the First Circuit ruled that the student was eligible for services under IDEA because her disability adversely affected her communication and social interaction and caused her to be inflexible and to self-mutilate during school. But, the Fifth Circuit ruled that a student with Attention Deficit Hyperactivity Disorder was not covered because it was proven that the student's educational performance without special education was adequate with passing grades and success on standardized tests.[45]

Identification, Evaluation, and Classification

IDEA requires state and local education agencies (school districts) to locate, identify, and evaluate children with disabilities, even those who have never enrolled in public school. A school district that fails to live up to this requirement, for example, by overlooking "clear signs of disability" in one of their students may be compelled later to provide compensatory services.[46] If possible, the evaluation should be completed early enough so that an IEP can be in place by the beginning of the school year. If a child with a possible or apparent disability is applying for initial admission to a public school, the child—with parental consent—will usually be placed in the regular public school program until the evaluation is complete.

Before a child is evaluated, written notice explaining the proposed evaluation and the reasons for it must be given to the child's parent. The notice must be in the parent's native language or, if the parent does not have a written language, it must be communicated orally. If the parents refuse consent for the evaluation, the parents may agree to enter into mediation with the district or the district may request an impartial hearing to seek authorization to proceed with the evaluation. Either the district or the parents may request review of the hearing officer's decision by the state's education agency and ultimately by a court. Similar procedures apply if parents initiate a request for an evaluation but the school district refuses. The district must provide the parents with written notice of its decision not to evaluate. Parents may then request mediation or a hearing, or avail themselves of the other dispute resolution procedures described later in this section.

Parents must also be given a copy of the procedural safeguards of IDEA, including the right to be informed of and to request a hearing if they disagree with the referral or with the results of the evaluation, the IEP, or placement. Parents also have a right to receive notice of these procedural safeguards once a year and in conjunction with any disciplinary action taken against the child and to examine "all records relating to" the child.

The evaluation must be in "in the child's native language or other mode of communication and in the form most likely to yield accurate information on what the child knows and can do academically, developmentally, and functionally, unless it is clearly not feasible to so provide or administer." The evaluation must be free of racial or cultural bias, conducted by a multidisciplinary team, and designed to assess a wide range of skills including sensory, manual, and verbal. Only validated tests tailored to assess specific areas of educational need may be used. No general IQ test nor any "single procedure is to be the sole criterion for determining an appropriate educational program." School districts are permitted to determine if a student has a specific learning disability by employing either a discrepancy model (comparing academic achievement to intellectual potential in specified basic-skill areas) or by a newer model based on the student's response to a research-based intervention (RTI). A child shall not be identified as disabled "if the determinant factor . . . is lack of appropriate instruction in reading or math, or limited English proficiency."

Overall, the evaluation must be designed to assess the child's strengths as well as weaknesses. At the conclusion of the evaluation, "a team of qualified professionals and the parent of the child" are to determine if the child has disabilities. Reevaluation of any child found to have disabilities must take place at least every three years or more frequently if requested by the child's parents. Parents also have a right to obtain an independent educational evaluation. The school district must reimburse the parents for independent evaluation if an impartial hearing finds the school's evaluation was incorrect. Regulations specify that "A parent is entitled to only one independent educational evaluation at public expense each time the [school] conducts an evaluation with which the parent disagrees."

Despite all the procedures and safeguards, schools and parents may disagree as to whether a child should be classified as having disabilities under the IDEA criteria. *Yankton School District v. Schramm*[47] concerned a high school student, Tracy, with cerebral palsy. Until she reached high school, Tracy had been classified as having disabilities and eligible for IDEA services. Tracy's last IEP, written for her ninth-grade year, specified "adaptive physical education" as Tracy's only "special education." The rest of her program consisted of participation in regular course work with nondisabled peers. Because Tracy was succeeding in all her regular course work and no additional physical education was required for graduation, the district reasoned that Tracy was no longer in need of special education and therefore no longer viewed as having disabilities within the meaning of IDEA. This meant that she was not eligible for the transitional services mandated by the IDEA to prepare students with disabilities for life after high school.

However, the hearing officer, the district court, and ultimately, the Eighth Circuit Court of Appeals all disagreed. The court pointed out that although it was true that Tracy's last IEP specified adaptive physical education as her only "special education," it was not true that this was the only service she had been receiving because of her disability. The school had also provided her with shortened writing assignments, assistance in passing from class to class, and a variety of other accommodations that the court characterized as special education and related services. Thus, the district's own actions indicated that Tracy had disabilities within the meaning of the IDEA.

Even when they agree that a child has disabilities, schools and parents may disagree as to the proper classification of the disability. In *Gregory K. v. Longview School District*,[48] the school's evaluation concluded that Gregory was mildly mentally retarded, but his parents argued that he had learning disabilities. To support their view, the parents presented an independent evaluation by a psychologist indicating that Gregory suffered from dyslexia. To settle the issue, the court turned to the definitions in the IDEA regulations for the terms "specific learning disabilities" and "mental retardation." The court noted that one of the necessary criteria for classification as having learning disabilities was "near average, average or above average intellectual ability." Then, looking at the results of various IQ tests, the court concluded that Gregory's intellectual functioning was too low to meet the definition of having learning disabilities. Therefore, the school district's classification of Gregory as mentally retarded was correct.

The Individualized Education Program

Once it has been determined that a child qualifies for services under IDEA, an IEP must be developed. The process used to develop the IEP must consist of one or more meetings attended by the child's teacher, another public school representative qualified to supervise the provision of special education, the child's parents, and, where appropriate, the child. The district must take all necessary steps to ensure that the parents are able to attend the IEP meetings and understand the evaluation results, the proposed IEP, and anything else discussed at the meetings. If the child has been evaluated for the first time, a member of the evaluation team or someone else familiar with the procedures and results of the evaluation must also be present. If a public school has placed or proposes to place a child in a private school or facility, a representative of the private facility must also attend. A member of the IEP team may be excused from attending a meeting if the parents agree in writing and the excused member submits in writing prior to the meeting input regarding the development of the IEP. In developing the IEP, the team must consider any special circumstances that may be affecting the child's educational performance such as behavioral problems or limited English proficiency. The IEP must be reviewed by the same process at least once a year and early enough so that the new IEP can be in force at the beginning of the next school year. The review should specifically address any lack of expected progress. Between annual reviews, the IEP may be modified if the parents and school agree. Modifications should be made in writing and the IEP team informed.

If parents are dissatisfied with the outcome of the IEP process, they may seek review from an impartial hearing officer, designated state agency, and ultimately from a court. Failure of a school to provide parents with a meaningful opportunity to participate in the formulation of a student's IEP or to follow the other procedural requirements of IEP formulation may persuade a court to reject the IEP.[49] However, parents who have been properly included in the process are unlikely to succeed with a claim that they did not understand what they had agreed to.[50] If parents ultimately refuse to consent to the initial delivery of services, after reasonable efforts have been made to obtain consent, the district may not seek authorization via the impartial hearing, and the district is relieved of its obligations to provide a free appropriate public education.

An IEP is a written statement that includes the child's present level of educational performance; annual goals; the special education and related services to be provided; any assistive technology to be provided; the extent to which the student will participate in the school's general program with nondisabled students; the dates for initiation and duration of services; criteria, procedures, and schedules for evaluating whether the objectives are being achieved; and a plan for informing the parents of the child's progress. The IEP of students classified as severely cognitively impaired must also include benchmarks or short-term objectives. IDEA regulations define special education as "specially designed instruction" to meet the unique needs of a child with a disability, including adapting "content, methodology or delivery of instruction."

Special education must include the same range of courses offered to nondisabled students including art, music, homemaking, vocational education, and physical education as well as extracurricular activities and nonacademic activities and services, such as lunch and recess as appropriate. Related services may include transportation, special equipment such as hearing aids and computers, and a variety of other forms of assistance necessary to make it possible for the child to benefit from special education. The IEP may also include behavioral interventions if necessary and, beginning no later than age fourteen, transition services. Behavioral interventions are programs designed to deal with conduct that impedes the child's learning or that of others. Transition services are programs designed to ease movement from school to post-school activities including work, higher education, and vocational training.

Providing an "Appropriate" Education

An IEP must specify a program of special education consistent with the child's evaluation. The program must meet the basic IDEA requirement of providing a free, appropriate public education. The program must be consistent with a myriad of applicable federal and state regulations that implement and supplement the IDEA. Yet, even with all these requirements and guidelines, the issue of what constitutes an appropriate education for a particular child is often difficult to resolve. Not surprisingly, given the realities of educational budgets, the imprecision of instructional methodologies, and the strong emotions involved, the program requested by parents sometimes does not coincide with the one offered by the school. In these instances, IDEA and the implementing regulations do not always provide a clear solution. Courts may be called upon to resolve the issue of whether a particular program or service is required under the IDEA or of whether a child's overall program of special education satisfies the law.

The Rowley Case

The Supreme Court provided a framework for deciding these issues in *Board of Education of Hendrik Hudson Central School District v. Rowley.*[51] The case concerned Amy Rowley, a deaf student with above average intelligence, minimum residual hearing, and an excellent ability to read lips. Following its evaluation, the school district placed Amy in a regular classroom and provided her with a hearing aid and the part-time services of a speech therapist and specially trained tutor. After a brief trial period during kindergarten, the district concluded that Amy did not need the full-time services of a sign language interpreter. Amy's parents disagreed and sued the school.

The district court that first heard the case ruled in favor of the parents. The court found that Amy had adjusted well to school and that she was "performing better than the average child in her class and advancing easily from grade to grade." Nevertheless, the court pointed out that Amy did not understand a significant amount of what was said in class, and, given her intelligence, she was not "learning as much or performing as well academically as she would without her handicap." Because of this "shortfall" in Amy's learning, the court concluded that the school was not living up to its responsibility under the law. The court ruled that the law required that Amy be given "an opportunity to achieve full potential commensurate with the opportunity provided to other children." In the lower court's view, it was the courts' job to make certain the program selected by a school for a child with a disability is the one most likely to maximize the child's potential.

In reversing the lower court's decision and ruling in favor of the school, the Supreme Court offered a different interpretation of both the meaning of an "appropriate" education and the role of the courts in ensuring that the requirements of the IDEA are met. The Court noted that Congress' purpose in adopting legislation providing funds for the education of children with disabilities was to provide a "basic floor of opportunity" consisting of "specialized instruction and related services which are individually designed to provide educational benefit to the handicapped child." In other words, the law does not require that an IEP be designed to maximize the potential of a child with a disability or even to confer educational benefit commensurate with the benefit provided other children, but only to confer "some educational benefit upon the handicapped child." In the case of a child like Amy, who was receiving "specialized instruction and related services" and "performing above average in the regular classrooms of the public school," it was clear to the Court that the requirement of some educational benefit was being met.

The ruling in the *Rowley* case was in keeping with the Court's view that "[t]he primary responsibility for formulating the education to be accorded a handicapped child, and for choosing the educational method most suitable to the child's needs, was left by the [IDEA] to state and local educational agencies in cooperation with the parents or guardian of the child." Therefore, courts, including the Supreme Court, "must be careful to avoid imposing their view of preferable educational methods" upon the schools. This is one of a number of instances in which the Supreme Court has cautioned all courts not to substitute their judgment for that of professional educators and policy makers.

Applying Rowley

Rowley provides a basis for deciding many disputes over what constitutes an appropriate education. *Rowley* makes it clear that IDEA does not require that students with disabilities be provided with all services that might benefit them or with any and all services that their parents might request. Subsequent cases have interpreted *Rowley* to mean that a child's program is appropriate if the program confers a "meaningful benefit" or if the child receives more than "barely minimal benefits" from the program.[52] The Third Circuit has said that a program confers the required meaningful benefit if the program is likely to produce educational progress, not "regression or trivial . . . advancement."[53] The Third Circuit has also said that a child's "untapped potential" may be one factor in assessing whether an appropriate education is being provided.[54] Overall, six circuit courts, the Second, Third, Fourth, Fifth, Sixth and Ninth use a "meaningful benefit" standard to determine if an appropriate education is being provided, while five, the First, Eighth, Tenth, Eleventh and D.C. Circuits, use an "adequate benefit" standard and the Seventh Circuit uses a mixture of the two standards.[55] Regardless of the standard employed, the school district bears the burden of showing that its program is beneficial. In *Rowley*, the Supreme Court viewed Amy Rowley's record of academic achievement as evidence of meaningful benefit. In other cases, courts may rely on the testimony of teachers and other professionals to determine whether educational progress is occurring.[56]

Even if a student with disabilities is receiving educational services that are potentially beneficial, the student's program may still be judged not to meet the appropriate education standard if the school fails to protect the student from harmful mistreatment by other students. In one case, a student who had been classified as having a perceptual impairment was subjected to peer harassment and bullying so persistent and severe that the student became depressed and attempted suicide. The school reclassified the student as emotionally disturbed and modified his IEP but was unable to protect him from continuing bullying and harassment. When the school district refused the student's parents' request to place the student in a school in a neighboring district, the parents unilaterally transferred the student. The Third Circuit affirmed the hearing officer's finding that the first school had failed in its duty to provide a beneficial education. The district was ordered to pay the out-of-district tuition, related costs, and attorneys fees.[57]

Rowley sets forth minimum standards for determining what constitutes an appropriate education for a student with a disability. Some states' statutes and regulations prescribe a higher standard than required under federal law. Both federal and state courts will hold schools in these states to the higher standard.[58] The No Child Left Behind Act also has the effect of requiring higher academic standards for some students with disabilities than *Rowley* (see sec. 6.4).

Defining appropriate education in terms of benefit raises the question of whether there are children with disabilities for whom no appropriate education is possible. Are there children who have such serious disabilities that no educational program is likely to benefit them? If so, does the IDEA permit schools to decline to provide services to these children? The First Circuit considered these issues in *Timothy W. v. Rochester School District.*[59] A lower court had ruled that Timothy, a "severely retarded and multiply handicapped child," was not eligible for services under the IDEA because he could not benefit from special education. Plaintiff's experts argued that despite the severity of his disability, Timothy might benefit from certain types of stimulation, therapy, and training and that under IDEA, the district was required to provide these services. Finding in favor of Timothy, the First Circuit stated its conclusions as follows:

> The statutory language of the Act [IDEA], its legislative history, and the case law construing it, mandate that all handicapped children, regardless of the severity of their handicap, are entitled to a public education. The district court erred in requiring a benefit/eligibility test as a prerequisite to implicating the Act. School districts cannot avoid the provisions of the Act by returning to the practices that were widespread prior to the Act's passage, and which indeed were the impetus for the Act's passage, of unilaterally excluding certain handicapped children from a public education on the ground that they are uneducable.
>
> The law explicitly recognizes that education for the severely handicapped is to be broadly defined, to include not only traditional academic skills, but also basic functional life skills, and that educational methodologies in these areas are not static, but are constantly evolving and improving. It is the school district's responsibility to avail itself of these new approaches in providing an education program geared to each child's individual needs. The only question for the school district to determine in conjunction with the child's parents, is what constitutes an appropriate individualized education program (IEP) for the handicapped child. We emphasize that the phrase "appropriate individualized education program" cannot be interpreted, as the school district has done, to mean "no educational program."

Thus, the IDEA does not recognize the existence of children who have too severe disabilities to benefit from some form of education broadly defined.

In *Rowley*, the Court permitted the school to avoid incurring an expense that would have provided additional educational benefit because the program the district did provide met the requirements of the law. Other cases have cited *Rowley* in refusing to order services that promised no additional educational benefit.[60] In general, it is permissible for a school to choose a less costly program over a more costly program promising greater benefit as long as the less costly program meets the *Rowley* standard.[61] However, districts may be required to provide very costly services such as residential placement or a full-time specialized tutor if the services are necessary to provide the student with the necessary opportunity for educational benefit.[62] Thus, the Supreme Court ruled in *Cedar Rapids Community School District v. Garret F.*[63] that a school must provide full-time "one-on-one nursing services" to a quadriplegic student because without the services the student could not attend school. The Court rejected the school's claim that the law did not require the provision of such an expensive service.

Related Services

The main issue in the *Garret F.* case was whether the requested nursing service was a related service within the meaning of IDEA. IDEA defines related services to include:

transportation, and such developmental, corrective, and other supportive services (including speech-language pathology and audiology services, interpreting services, psychological services, physical and occupational therapy, recreation, including therapeutic recreation, social work services, school nurse [and health] services designed to enable a child with a disability to receive a free appropriate public education as described in the individualized education program of the child, counseling services, including rehabilitation counseling, orientation and mobility services, and medical services, except that such medical services shall be for diagnostic and evaluation purposes only) as may be required to assist a child with a disability to benefit from special education, and includes the early identification and assessment of disabling conditions in children.

The statute explicitly states that the term related services "does not include a medical device that is surgically implanted" such as a cochlear implant or muscle stimulator. School districts do have the responsibility "to appropriately monitor and maintain medical devices that are needed to maintain the health and safety of the child, including breathing, nutrition, or operation of other bodily functions, while the child is transported to and from school or is at school." The regulations further require the routine checking of hearing aids and external components of surgically implanted devices to assure they are functioning properly.

Related services may include assistive technology devices and assistive technology services. The regulations define an **assistive technology devices** as a piece of equipment or product used "to increase, maintain, or improve functional capabilities of [children] with disabilities"; for example, a hearing aid or computer, but, again, not including medical devices that are surgically implanted. An **assistive technology services** is a service that assists a child in the selection, acquisition, or use of an assistive technology, such as training a child with a disability in the use of a computer. Related services is a very broad concept encompassing almost anything necessary to make it possible for a child to benefit from special education.

The Supreme Court provided the framework for deciding cases like *Garret F.* in *Irving Independent School District v. Tatro.*[64] The issue was whether a school was required to provide a student with clean intermittent catheterization (CIC), "a procedure involving the insertion of a catheter into the urethra to drain the bladder." In order to decide the case, the Court offered three guidelines for determining whether a school is obligated to provide "services that relate to both the health and education needs of handicapped students." First, such services must be provided only to children who require special education. Second, services must be provided only if they are necessary to permit the child to benefit from special education. Thus, "if a particular medication or treatment may be administered to a handicapped child other than during the school day, a school is not required to provide nursing services to administer it." Third, services must be provided only if they may be performed by a nurse or other qualified person but are not required if they must be performed by a doctor. Even services that require a doctor's prescription or order must be provided if the doctor's actual presence is not necessary and the other guidelines are met. Applying these guidelines to *Tatro*, the Court determined that the school was obligated to provide CIC. The student required special education, could not attend school without the service, and CIC could be performed by a nurse or trained layperson.

The same reasoning led to the conclusion that the very expensive nursing services requested in *Garret F.* were also required by IDEA. That Garret needed continuous monitoring and frequent interventions by a person with a significant level of medical training and skill did not release the district from its obligation to provide the services necessary to allow Garret to benefit from school. However, supportive medical services that require a doctor's presence, because they are beyond the capabilities of a trained nurse, need not be provided.[65] IDEA regulations do require that medical services for diagnosis and evaluation be provided even though they require a licensed physician if the services are necessary "to determine a child's medically related disability that results in the child's need for special education. . . ." The courts have split on the issue of whether psychotherapy is an excluded medical service or a supportive psychological service.[66]

In *Butler v. Evans*,[67] the Seventh Circuit ruled that parents were not entitled to reimbursement for the time their daughter stayed in a psychiatric hospital where she received medication, psychotherapy, and educational services. The child, Niki, had been diagnosed as suffering from a "mental disorder needing long-term education, structural, locked residential protective placement." The court concluded that Niki's situation was different from Garret's:

> Niki's hospitalization was not an attempt to give her meaningful access to public education or to address her special educational needs within her regular school environment. This is not a case in which the disabled student needed medical assistance to remain in a regular school; Niki was committed to a psychiatric hospital. Niki might have continued to receive school assignments and some tutoring while hospitalized, but education was not the purpose of her hospitalization. Unlike in-school nursing in [*Garret F.*], Niki's inpatient medical care was necessary in itself and was not a special accommodation made necessary only to allow her to attend school or receive education.

Like any related service, transportation must be provided only if and to the extent that it is necessary to permit a child with a disability to benefit from education.[68] In one case, a deaf child capable of using the same transportation services as hearing children was denied publicly supported transportation to a private school.[69] However, in another case, transportation was a required related service for a child who needed suctioning of his tracheostomy tube and repositioning of his wheelchair during transit.[70] Another court required the district to transport a student with a disability between the public school where she received some special education services and her parochial school and ruled that the requirement did not violate the Establishment Clause.[71]

Least Restrictive Environment

IDEA demands that the FAPE offered to a child with a disability meet the requirement of least restrictive environment (LRE), also known as **mainstreaming**: "[T]o the maximum extent appropriate" the child must be educated with children who do not have disabilities and special classes and schools and institutionalization should be used only "when the nature or severity of the [disability] is such that education in regular classes with the use of supplementary aids and services cannot be achieved satisfactorily." The child must also receive any supplementary aids and services that are necessary for the child's participation in nonacademic activities and must be placed "as close as possible" to home. In order to meet these requirements, school districts must maintain a continuum of possible alternative placements including general education classrooms, special classes, resource rooms, special schools, home instruction, and institutionalization. IDEA requires that the IEP include an "explanation of the extent, if any, to which the child will not participate with nondisabled students in the regular class. . . ."

Some schools have adopted a policy of "inclusion" or "full inclusion," meaning that all or most children with disabilities are educated in regular education classrooms all or most

of the time. However, IDEA does not mandate inclusion and in fact requires special placement if the regular classroom cannot provide an appropriate education.

Disputes between parents and schools over the issue of LRE are common. Sometimes,
the school advocates special placement, while parents favor education in the regular classroom, and sometimes the positions are reversed. The LRE requirement creates a presumption in favor of the regular classroom. The presumption can be rebutted by a
showing that education in the regular classroom offers no meaningful educational benefit
for a particular student or that a student with disabilities is so disruptive that the education of other students would be significantly impaired. More controversial are cases in
which both approaches offer educational benefit but one approach offers significantly
greater benefits, or when one approach offers greater benefit but at significantly greater
cost. Another common problem is how to balance the potentially greater academic benefits of out-of-class placement with the potentially greater social benefits of mainstreaming.

Many courts have considered this issue with somewhat varying results.[72] The Ninth
Circuit has adopted a balancing test encompassing four factors:

1. The educational benefits available in a general education classroom with supplemen-
    tary aids and services as compared to the benefits available in a more restrictive envi-
    ronment.
2. The nonacademic benefits of the general classroom compared to the more restrictive
    environment.
3. The effect of the presence of the student with a disability on the teacher and other stu-
    dents in the general classroom.
4. The cost of placement in the general education classroom (which may be either higher
    or lower than the more restrictive placement).

The district bears the burden of proving the appropriateness of its preferred placement in
light of these four factors.[73] The Fourth Circuit has said that mainstreaming is not required
when there are no educational benefits to be realized from placement in a general class,
any marginal benefits from placement in a general class would be significantly outweighed
by the benefits of a more restrictive placement, or the student would be too disruptive a
force in the general class. The court noted that under IDEA, social benefits are subordinate
to academic achievement.[74] In two separate cases the Seventh Circuit has ruled in favor of
school districts when they placed disruptive students in settings other than the regular
classroom.[75]

Residential Placements

Among the most controversial placement decisions are those that involve the question of
whether or not to place a child in a residential facility. Residential placements are both the
most restrictive and usually the most expensive option. Nevertheless, IDEA regulations
specify that "placement in a . . . residential program is necessary to provide special education and related services to a child with a disability, the program, including nonmedical
care and room and board, must be at no cost to the parents of the child."[76] One court
approached the issue of whether residential placement was required for a child with severe
physical and mental disabilities by asking whether "full-time placement may be considered necessary for educational purposes, or whether the residential placement is a
response to medical, social, or emotional problems." If institutionalization was the only
way a child could receive educational benefits, even if the placement was also needed to
provide noneducational services, then the full cost of the residential placement had to be

paid for by the state or local school district. Residential placement was ordered for this child because the child could not be educated without close full-time supervision.[77]

In cases of emotionally disturbed children requesting residential placement, the courts consider whether the placement is necessary to meet educational needs, whether the facility is a hospital or an accredited educational facility, whether the program provided is prescribed by physicians or educators, the intensity of the program, and the cost as compared to nonresidential educational programs.[78] Even when a major goal of residential placement is training in basic life skills, such as using a fork, getting dressed, and using the toilet, courts have required schools to pay for the placement unless an appropriate education could be provided in a nonresidential setting.[79] The issue, said the Third Circuit, is whether "full-time placement may be considered necessary for educational purposes, or whether the residential placement is a response to medical, social or emotional problems." If the residential placement is "part and parcel of . . . specially designed instruction . . . to meet the unique needs of a handicapped child," the school must pay for it.[80]

Using this approach, the Seventh Circuit concluded that a school district did not have to reimburse parents for the costs of placing a disruptive child with a growing criminal record in a boarding school that specialized in dealing with such children. Confinement in the boarding school, said the court, was not educationally necessary but primarily designed to keep him out of jail:

> Another way to put this is that Dale's problems are not primarily educational. He has the intelligence to perform well as a student and no cognitive defect or disorder such as dyslexia that prevents him from applying his intelligence to the acquisition of an education, without special assistance. His problem is a lack of proper socialization, as a result of which, despite his tender age, he has compiled a significant criminal record. His substance abuse interferes with his schooling; that is true; but it interferes with much else besides, such as ability to conform to the law and avoid jail.[81]

The Sixth Circuit has said that cost may be considered only when comparing two options that both meet the *Rowley* standard, but not if a particular program or service is necessary to assure the child a free, appropriate education. Thus, in one case, the court ordered a residential placement that in 1984 cost $88,000 per year.[82] Even year-round placements at public expense will be ordered if necessary to yield educational benefits.[83] However, IDEA does not require a state or local school district to pay for residential placements undertaken for wholly noneducational purposes; for example, placement of a comatose child in a hospital.[84] After a child has been placed in a residential facility, whether public or private, the child's home school district continues to be responsible for monitoring compliance with the IEP and for reevaluation.

Students with Disabilities and Private Schools

If a private school student qualifies for services under IDEA, the public school district may at its option either make the appropriate special education available at public school or if permitted by state law, pay for the services in the private school.[85] The services provided to students with disabilities in private schools must be comparable in quality to the services provided in the public school. States may deem a home school an IDEA-qualifying private school.[86]

If a school district makes a FAPE available to a child with a disability in a public school, but the child's parents elect to place the child in a private school, the district does not have to pay the child's tuition or for the special costs associated with the child's disability.[87] If, however, a private facility is necessary in order to provide an appropriate education, the district must pay the cost of the child's education. If parents place their child with a disability in private school because they do not believe the public school's proposed placement is appropriate, and the parents' position is ultimately upheld by a hearing officer or court, the public school must reimburse the parents for the private school tuition and related costs such as transportation.[88]

There is a split in the courts regarding the question of whether parents in effect waive their right to reimbursement when they unilaterally place their child in a private school either prior to giving the district an opportunity to address their concerns with the public school's program or prior to even enrolling their child in the public school. The Eighth Circuit denied reimbursement in one case because the parents had not given the school a chance to change the student's program prior to enrollment in private school.[89] Similarly another court ruled that a parent who refused to cooperate in the child's evaluation prior to moving the child to private school had forfeited the right to reimbursement.[90] Two First Circuit cases denied reimbursement to parents who, without notice to the public school, enrolled their children in private school and then sought reimbursement.[91] However, two Second Circuit decisions permitted parents to obtain reimbursement for private placement despite the fact their child had never participated in the public school program. In one case it was ultimately determined that the public school placement was inappropriate and the court found that the parents had met the notice requirements regarding their intent to reject the IEP and enroll their child in a private school. The court said that public schools do not have a "first bite" at failure: "We believe that it unreasonable to suggest that [the student's] parents were legally required to engage in the useless and potentially counterproductive exercise of trying out the proposed public placement."[92]

When a child is placed in a private school located in a district other than where the child's home is located, IDEA requires the local district in which the private school is located to assume the responsibility for provision of equitable services to the child.

The Supreme Court has ruled that the provision of a signer to a deaf student attending a parochial school does not violate the Establishment Clause.[93] Likewise, it is probably permissible for public schools to provide any related service specified by a parochial school student's IEP.[94] Nevertheless, it is doubtful whether it would be permissible for a public school district to pay a child's religious school tuition, even if the school was specially equipped to provide the child with an appropriate education. Public schools are responsible for monitoring and reevaluating students with disabilities placed in private schools.

Change of Placement

The question of what constitutes a "change of placement" for a student with a disability has been considered by a number of courts and several different definitions have resulted. The Second Circuit said that a change of placement occurs when there is a change in the "general educational program in which the child is enrolled, rather than mere variations in the program itself." Thus, in *Concerned Parents v. New York City Board of Education*,[95] the court ruled there was no change of placement when, after one school closed, the student was transferred to a similar but less innovative program. The Sixth Circuit said a change of placement occurs when a modified educational program "is not comparable to the plan set forth in the original IEP."[96] The Third Circuit said the question "has to be whether the decision is likely to affect in some significant way the child's learning experience." Thus, the court said a change in how the child was transported to school was not a change of placement.[97]

However change of placement is defined, IDEA requires parental notification before a change of placement can occur. Parents who object to a proposed change of placement may agree to mediation or demand an impartial hearing and invoke the **stay-put** requirement. The stay-put requirement is designed to maintain the status quo during the impartial hearing and any subsequent appeals. Unless both the school and the parents agree, the child must be left in the present educational placement even if one party believes that it is not an "appropriate" placement under the law. Whether the present placement is appropriate is often the subject of the dispute under consideration. If either party wants to temporarily change the present placement before the appeal process is over, that party must go to court to effect the change.[98] The public school district must bear the cost of funding the present placement pending the outcome of the appeal process even if the present placement is in a private setting.[99]

Sometimes determining the present placement is not difficult. If the child is in a school or program because of an IEP, by an agreement between the parents and school, because of an order of a court, or if this was the placement of the child prior to the first IDEA evaluation and placement, this is the present placement. However, sometimes in the midst of a dispute with school officials, parents unilaterally move the child to a private school. The question then arises whether the private school placement is the present placement pending final resolution of the dispute. It may be if a court concludes that the parent had justification to make the unilateral shift—if, for example, the school delayed unduly in making an IEP proposal.[100] Also, if it is later determined that the public school placement was not appropriate, the parents are entitled to reimbursement of the cost of the private school. To be eligible for reimbursement, parents must notify the district in a timely manner of the private school placement and their reason for moving the child.

If a child with an IEP moves with his parents from one state to another, must the new state implement the IEP of the first state? This question was raised in *Michael C. v. Radnor Township School District*,[101] a Third Circuit case in which the plaintiff claimed that the stay-put requirement mandated implementation of the original IEP. Michael's IEP had placed him in a residential school near where his family formerly lived. He argued that he should be placed in a comparable residential school in his family's new state pending the outcome of proceedings to decide what his new IEP would be. The court rejected this argument saying that it did not believe Congress intended the stay-put provision to impose a requirement on states to implement an IEP established in another state without considering how consistent that IEP was with their own laws and policies.

In *Pardini v. Allegheny Intermediate Unit*[102] the Third Circuit ruled that the stay-put requirement of Part B of IDEA were applicable to a child in transition from Part C (services for children with disabilities ages birth to three years) to Part B (ages three to twenty-one). The court ruled that the school district had to provide the child with a continuation of the services she had been receiving until the dispute over her initial IEP was resolved.

Discipline of Students with Disabilities

Discipline of children with a disability raises many issues including whether various forms of discipline constitute a "change of placement," whether a child may be excluded from school for disciplinary reasons, what procedures must be followed in disciplining a child with a disability, where the child is to "stay-put" pending disciplinary proceedings, and whether exceptions to the usual requirements may be made if a disruptive child is a threat to others. Central to the answer to all these questions is the principle that children with disabilities are not to be excluded from receiving special education for disciplinary reasons.

All children with disabilities must receive a FAPE "including children with disabilities who have been suspended or expelled from school."

The rules concerning the discipline of students with disabilities apply both to students with IEPs and to children not yet declared eligible for special education if the school district "had knowledge . . . that the child was a child with a disability before the behavior that precipitated the disciplinary action occurred." A school district is deemed to have such knowledge if a parent has expressed concern in writing to supervisory or administrative personnel of the district, or to the child's teacher, that the child needs special education; or the parent has requested an evaluation; or the teacher of the child or other district personnel have expressed specific concerns about a pattern of behavior possibly indicative of disability directly to the director of special education or other supervisory personnel. A district will not be deemed to have knowledge of disability if the parent of the child has not allowed an evaluation of the child for possible disability, or has refused services after an evaluation, or the child has been evaluated and it was determined that the child was not a child with a disability. If the district is not deemed to have knowledge, yet the child is in fact disabled, the child may be subjected to disciplinary measures applied to children without disabilities who engaged in comparable behaviors. If an initial request for an evaluation is made during this time, the evaluation must be conducted in an expedited manner (meanwhile the child remains in the placement determined by school officials); if the child is then determined to be disabled, the rights afforded by IDEA will now fully apply.

For children who already have an IEP or whom the district knows to have disabilities, disciplinary measures may be employed only to the extent that the same measures are employed with children without disabilities. Any lawful form of discipline that is not a change of placement may be used. These may include verbal reprimands, denial of privileges, and detentions of reasonable duration. Whether corporal punishment of children with disabilities may be employed in places where it is otherwise allowed is an unresolved issue. It is also permissible to relocate a misbehaving child with a disability to what the law calls an **"interim alternative educational setting"** (IAES), presumably including a more restrictive placement or in-school suspension for ten days or less or to suspend the student for ten days or less without employing change of placement procedures.

Removal of a child with a disability from the child's current educational placement is deemed a change of placement if the removal is for more than ten consecutive school days or the

> removals . . . constitute a pattern—because (i) the removals total more than 10 days in a school year; (ii) the child's behavior is substantially similar to the previous incidents that resulted in the removals; and (iii) because of additional factors such as the length of each removal, the total amount of time the child has been removed, and the proximity of the removals to one another.

If a school district wishes to discipline a child with a disability in a manner that constitutes a change of placement, the IEP team must first undertake an inquiry to determine if the student's misbehavior was a "**manifestation** of the disability." The manifestation inquiry may be undertaken while the child is being disciplined in a manner that does not constitute a change of placement such as a suspension of ten days or less. The IEP team's findings are subject to review by an impartial hearing officer at parental request. Misbehavior is a manifestation of a student's disability if the misbehavior and disability are directly related, such as, if the disability impairs the student's ability to understand the impact or consequences of the behavior or impairs the student's ability to control the behavior.

Misbehavior may also be deemed a manifestation of a student's disability if the behavior was a direct result of the student's IEP not being followed or being inappropriate.

If the behavior was a manifestation of the disability, the school must perform a **functional behavioral assessment** and develop a **behavioral intervention plan** as part of the student's IEP. Further disciplinary procedures involving relocation or exclusion from school require standard change of placement procedures including parental notification, IEP team deliberations, and possibly an impartial hearing and court review. If, however, a child with a disability brings a weapon to school or possesses or sells illegal drugs at school, the IEP team may place the student in an IAES for up to forty-five days during the manifestation determination and change of placement procedures. School officials may also report any crime committed by a child with a disability to the police. An impartial hearing officer can also place a student with a disability in an IAES if the school convinces the hearing officer that it is dangerous for the student to remain in the present placement. The IAES must permit the child to continue to participate in the general curriculum and to receive the services specified in the IEP. The school must perform a functional behavioral assessment and develop a behavioral intervention plan within ten days of the IAES placement.

If a student's misbehavior is found not to be a manifestation of the student's disability, the student may be subjected to the same disciplinary procedures, including long-term suspension, as nondisabled students. However, students with disabilities must always continue to receive a FAPE. This means that school districts must provide home tutors or other alternative arrangements that offer a meaningful opportunity for educational benefit to students with disabilities excluded from school for any reason. In-school suspensions must also provide a meaningful opportunity to benefit.

Dispute Resolution

Any substantive or procedural dispute between parents and school over any aspect of the IDEA is subject to mediation if both sides agree to mediation. Mediation must be confidential, at no cost to the parents, and conducted by a knowledgeable individual chosen from a state-maintained list.

If mediation is not desired or fails to produce an agreement, either side can request a hearing before an impartial hearing officer. Prior to the hearing, the district must convene a resolution meeting with the parents and others designated in the law in an attempt to reach agreement. The law does not specify the level of expertise that the hearing officer must possess, but "impartial" means that the hearing officer must not be a regular employee of the district or directly involved in the care of the child. Parents may demand a hearing to insist that their child be evaluated; to protest the process or outcome of an evaluation or IEP meeting; to challenge the adequacy of special education, related services, or other aspects of the program provided; to object to changes of placement or disciplinary actions; or to claim that their procedural rights as parents have been violated.

A school district may also initiate a hearing if the district believes that parents are preventing a child with a disability from receiving an appropriate education except that a school district may not initiate a hearing to contest parental refusal of an initial placement in special education. Either parents or school district may appeal an adverse decision by a hearing officer to a designated state agency and ultimately to a court. Courts will generally not consider complaints that have not exhausted the administrative hearing process. Violation of the procedural requirements of IDEA does not automatically mean that a child has been denied a FAPE. Only procedural inadequacies which result in the loss of educational opportunity are sufficient to constitute a violation of IDEA. An error such as missing a deadline or failure to include someone on the IEP team may in one case amount to a violation of IDEA and in another case, because of the circumstances, be viewed as harmless.[103]

The Supreme Court has ruled that under IDEA the burden of proof in an impartial hearing is on the party "seeking relief." Parents requesting a hearing to challenge their child's IEP would bear the burden of showing that the school's program is not appropriate.[104] However, some states have adopted legislation placing the burden of proof on the school district except in cases when parents want the district to pay for placement in a private school.[105] The situation changes when a case is appealed to a court. In *Rowley*, the Supreme Court warned that the federal courts lack expertise in the area of special education and therefore ought to give due weight to the decision of the experts. Courts have interpreted this comment to mean that the burden of proof is on the party who seeks to challenge an impartial hearing officer's ruling,[106] but a minority of courts have held that the burden of proof remains on the school district or, in placement disputes, on the party proposing the more restrictive environment.[107]

If parents prevail at an administrative hearing, the school district must take whatever action the hearing officer or state agency prescribes. Parents who prevail in a court case may be granted declaratory and injunctive relief—judicial orders to do what the law requires. Courts may also order remedial action such as an extended school year as a remedy for a school's failure to provide an appropriate education to a child with a disability.[108] In addition, parents may be reimbursed for expenses incurred in providing the necessary special education or related service.[109] Parents who successfully sue a school district in court for violation of IDEA may be awarded reimbursement of their attorney's fees but not fees for the services of expert witnesses[110] or attorney fees for representation at an impartial hearing[111] or for parents who represent themselves.[112] Compensatory and punitive damages are not available under IDEA[113] nor can Section 1983 (see sec. 10.10) be used to recover damages for violations of IDEA.[114]

6.4 NO CHILD LEFT BEHIND AND STUDENTS WITH DISABILITIES

There is a potential for conflict between IDEA and NCLB (see sec. 2.6) as it applies to students with disabilities. IDEA requires schools to provide individualized educational programs to students with disabilities based on learning goals designed to meet their unique educational needs. NCLB requires that there be statewide standards of proficiency in reading and math, in effect, uniform learning goals, for all students including students with disabilities. Under NCLB, students with disabilities are a designated subgroup whose performance must be assessed to determine if a school is making adequate yearly progress (AYP). NCLB requires that at least 95 percent of each statutorily designated subgroup participate in yearly statewide assessments and that schools be designated as needing improvement if any subgroup fails to make adequate yearly progress. This means that in any given year, the same percentage of the students with disabilities in a given school must score "proficient" on state assessments as is required of the school's student body as a whole and that by 2014 all of a school's students with disabilities must be proficient.

The Department of Education has granted states and school districts some flexibility in meeting NCLB requirements. States are permitted to develop modified assessment standards for students with severe cognitive disabilities. Up to 2 percent of students in any school district or state may be assessed using the modified standards, and scores on the modified assessment may be aggregated with scores on the standard assessment to determine whether a school has made AYP.[115] In *State v. Spellings*,[116] a federal district court ruled that the Department of Education's refusal to allow special education students to be tested out of grade level was not arbitrary and capricious.

IDEA requires that all special education teachers meet the NCLB criteria for highly qualified teachers. The highly-qualified-teacher standards are somewhat relaxed for special education teachers teaching two or more core subjects or teaching core subjects to severely cognitively impaired secondary students who will participate in the state's modified assessments. Teachers in private elementary and secondary school of parentally placed students with disabilities do not have to meet the IDEA highly-qualified-teacher standards.

IDEA requires that all students with disabilities be included in all statewide assessments including those mandated by NCLB. A federal district court ruled, however, that the enactment of NCLB did not change the requirements of IDEA regarding the provision of an appropriate education:

> Although the IDEA clearly conditions the States' receipt of IDEA funds on the inclusion of disabled children in the assessments mandated by [NCLB], it does not require that FAPE determinations be based on the results of those assessments, nor does it require that the IEP's prepared for disabled children be designed specifically to enhance their scores on standardized tests. While it is clear that both the IDEA and [NCLB] require recipient States to include disabled children in the assessments, with the modifications necessitated by their disabilities, neither statute indicates that FAPE determinations under the IDEA are controlled by the performance of disabled children on assessments required under the [NCLB].

The court also said, "The assessments required under the [NCLB], however, can be considered as one factor in the broader inquiry as to whether a given disabled child's education is meaningful."[117]

In *Board of Education of Ottawa Township High School District 140 v. Spellings*,[118] the Seventh Circuit ruled that the plaintiffs (parents and school districts) had not succeeded in showing that it was impossible to comply with both IDEA and NCLB. The court also said that if the two laws are shown to conflict, NCLB should take precedence because it is the newer law.

6.5 ENGLISH LANGUAGE LEARNERS

Educators and policy makers must deal with a variety of interrelated issues to meet their educational and legal obligations to children who are non-English proficient or limited English proficient, commonly referred to as English Language Learners (ELL). Some of the issues are phrased in the language of equity, discrimination, and civil rights. Is it equitable to provide all children with an education in the primary language of the country in which they live? Conversely, is it equitable to teach students in a language they cannot understand? Is it a moral or legal responsibility of public schools to provide special English proficiency programs for ELL students? Is it fair to spend more money on students who don't speak English than on those who do?

A second group of issues is pedagogical. What is the most effective way to help ELL children become English proficient? Should or may English as a second language (ESL) programs be used? Under this approach, students spend most of their day in regular classes but are pulled out to receive intensive instruction in English. Or might an immersion program work best? One type of immersion has students in classes where the bilingual teacher instructs in English but is capable of understanding students who ask questions in their mother tongue. The curriculum is organized in a way that does not presume the students are English proficient. Or is bilingual education the best method? Under this arrangement students are enrolled in subject matter classes taught in their own language and are provided with special instruction to learn English.

Bilingual education itself comes in several versions. Transitional bilingual programs employ subject matter instruction in the child's language only until the child is capable of learning in all-English classes. Bilingual-bicultural maintenance programs continue instruction in the child's mother tongue even after attainment of English proficiency. They aim to help the children to develop fluency in both languages and to appreciate both their own and mainstream U.S. culture.

Finally, there are social and political questions: Is it in children's best interest to help them maintain proficiency in their mother tongue or does this tend to limit their prospects later in life? Should decisions like this be made by families, students themselves, or society as a whole? Do bilingual programs foster language divisions within the United States that can lead to political instability? Is the effort to promote English as the dominant language an expression of cultural and racial bias? Will we as a nation be better off if our citizens speak but one language or if they are multilingual? Should major policy decisions, such as how best to educate ELL children, be centralized or left to the states or local school districts?

Given the range and complexity and lack of consensus on these issues, it is not surprising that federal law and policy have been tumultuous and inconsistent. The first federal effort to address the civil rights of ELL students was based on Title VI of the Civil Rights Act of 1964.[119] In 1970, six years after the law was passed, the Office for Civil Rights (OCR) issued a memorandum interpreting Title VI's prohibition against discrimination on the basis of "national origin": "[W]here inability to speak and understand the English language excludes national origin-minority group children from effective participation in the educational program offered by a school district, the district must take affirmative steps to rectify the language deficiency in order to open its instructional program to these students."[120]

OCR's interpretation did not require an intent to discriminate as a necessary element of a Title VI violation; rather, a violation would be found wherever a school's language policy had the effect of excluding ELL students from effective participation in its program. Districts in violation of Title VI could lose all their federal funds.

In 1974, OCR's interpretation of Title VI was tested in the courts. The plaintiffs in *Lau v. Nichols* were Chinese ELL students who were not receiving any special assistance to learn English and were enrolled in all-English subject matter classes. The plaintiffs claimed that lack of special language assistance was both a form of racial discrimination in violation of the Equal Protection Clause and a violation of Title VI. The students lost in the lower courts on both claims. The Ninth Circuit wrote that "[e]very student brings to the starting line of his educational career different advantages and disadvantages caused in part by social, economic and cultural background, created and continued completely apart from any contribution by the school system."[121] It simply was not the school district's fault if ELL students were not prepared, and no legal obligation required the schools to overcome their deficiency.

In reviewing the Ninth Circuit's decision, the Supreme Court did not address the students' constitutional claims. It did, however, find in the students' favor relying solely on Title VI as interpreted by the OCR. "There is no equality of treatment," wrote the Court, "merely by providing students with the same facilities, textbooks, teachers, and curriculum; for students who do not understand English are effectively foreclosed from any meaningful education." To require a child to have already acquired basic English skills before participating in the educational program, said the Court, is to make a mockery of public education. Following the logic of the OCR interpretation, the Court said it was not necessary to show any invidious motivation on the part of the school to establish a Title VI violation. As for the remedy, the Court wrote, "Teaching English to the students of Chinese ancestry who do not speak the language is one choice. Giving instructions to this group in Chinese is another. There may be others."[122]

It did not take Congress long to embrace the position taken by the OCR and accepted by the Supreme Court. In 1974, the same year that *Lau* was decided, Congress adopted the Equal Educational Opportunity Act (EEOA), which provides in part:

> [N]o State shall deny equal educational opportunity to an individual on account of his or her race, color, sex, or national origin, by . . . the failure by an educational agency to take appropriate action to overcome language barriers that impede equal participation by its students in its instructional programs.[123]

The U.S. Attorney General or students adversely affected by a school's language policy are empowered to file civil actions for denial of equal educational opportunity whether the school intended to discriminate or not.

In sum, both EEOA and Title VI require a school to provide ELL students with instruction designed to help them overcome language barriers that impede their equal participation in the school's program. Title VI prohibits intentional (de jure) discrimination against ELL students, but does not prohibit unintentional (de facto) discrimination unless the federal government has issued regulations extending Title VI to unintentional discrimination (see sec. 5.8).[124] The Department of Justice has in fact issued a policy guidance document interpreting Title VI to prohibit discriminatory impact (unintentional discrimination) based on national origin (including limited English proficiency), thus requiring recipients of federal aid (including schools) "to take reasonable steps to ensure meaningful access to the information and services they provide." The policy guidance lists factors to be considered in determining whether the steps taken are reasonable: number or proportion of limited English proficient individuals, their frequency of contact with the program, the nature and importance of the program, and the resources available.[125] Even though Title VI has been interpreted by the federal government to extend to unintentional discrimination, individual plaintiffs may not sue to seek enforcement based on this interpretation. Enforcement must be left to a federal or perhaps a state agency.[126]

The Supreme Court has never considered the substantive requirements of EEOA. In *Castaneda v. Pickard*,[127] the Fifth Circuit concluded that the EEOA was intended to require that schools "make a genuine and good faith effort, consistent with local circumstances and resources, to remedy the language deficiencies of their students. . . ." The language of the law speaks not of any specific program of bilingual education, but rather of taking "appropriate action . . . to overcome language barriers" that impede the "equal participation" of ELL children in the "regular instructional program." Based on this understanding, the *Castaneda* court prescribed what have become the generally accepted tests for determining whether a school is meeting its obligations to ELLs under EEOA:

1. The school must adopt a program "informed by an educational theory recognized as sound by some experts in the field or, at least, deemed a legitimate experimental strategy."
2. The actual programs and practices of the school must be "reasonably calculated to implement effectively the educational theory adopted by the school."
3. The school must be able to show that language barriers are actually being overcome.

Other courts have employed the *Castaneda* tests in deciding cases alleging violations of EEOA.[128]

Castaneda interpreted federal law to allow states and local school districts to decide whether to offer bilingual education or to employ some other method of assisting ELL students. The federal grant program that assists states and localities in educating ELL students (the English Language Acquisition, Language Enhancement, and Academic Achievement Act[129]) also takes this position, stating that the law shall not be interpreted "to require a State or a local educational agency to establish, continue, or eliminate any particular type of instructional program for limited English proficient children."

Federal law also requires that local school districts offering a federally supported program:

> shall not later than 30 days after the beginning of the school year, inform a parent or the parents of a limited English proficient child identified for participation in, or participating in, such program of—
>
> (1) the reasons for the identification of their child as limited English proficient and in need of placement in a language instruction educational program;
> (2) the child's level of English proficiency, how such level was assessed, and the status of the child's academic achievement;
> (3) the method of instruction used in the program in which their child is, or will be, participating and the methods of instruction used in other available programs, including how such programs differ in content, instruction goals, and use of English and a native language in instruction;
> (4) how the program in which their child is, or will be participating will meet the educational strengths and needs of the child;
> (5) how such program will specifically help their child learn English, and meet age appropriate academic achievement standards for grade promotion and graduation;
> (6) the specific exit requirements for such program, the expected rate of transition from such program into classrooms that are not tailored for limited English proficient children, and the expected rate of graduation from secondary school for such program if funds under this title [20 USCS §§ 6801 et seq.] are used for children in secondary schools;
> (7) in the case of a child with a disability, how such program meets the objectives of the individualized education program of the child; and
> (8) information pertaining to parental rights that includes written guidance—
>
>> (A) detailing—
>>
>>> (i) the right that parents have to have their child immediately removed from such program upon their request; and
>>> (ii) the options that parents have to decline to enroll their child in such program or to choose another program or method of instruction, if available; and
>>
>> (B) assisting parents in selecting among various programs and methods of instruction, if more than one program or method is offered by the eligible entity.[130]

ELL students must be included in the annual assessments required by the No Child Left Behind Act (see sec. 2.6). The assessment of any student who has attended school in the

United States for three or more consecutive years must be in English. (On a case-by-case basis, individual students may be exempted from this requirement.) The English proficiency of students of limited-English speaking ability must also be assessed annually.

In recent years, there has been a trend both at both the federal and state level away from advocating or offering bilingual education. Several states have formally adopted laws and policies prohibiting bilingual education. In 1998, California voters passed a referendum amending the California education code to require that "all children in California public schools shall be taught English by being taught in English. In particular, this shall require that all children be placed in English language classrooms."[131] California generally prohibits school districts from using bilingual education except for children who have obtained a waiver in accordance with criteria and procedures specified in the law.[132] The California statute has survived several constitutional challenges.[133]

Two other issues concerning language proficiency have also been litigated. In *Martin Luther King Jr. Elementary School Children v. Michigan Board of Education*,[134] a federal district court extended the reasoning of *Lau* to require schools to take special steps to address the needs of speakers of the dialect known as Black English. In *Jose P. v. Ambach*,[135] another federal court found that failure to provide bilingual education to ELL students with disabilities may violate the Rehabilitation Act of 1973 (see sec. 6.2).

6.6 CLASSIFICATION BY AGE AND ABILITY

When parents claim that a five-year-old should be permitted to start the first grade or that a precocious twelve-year-old ought to be able to skip a grade, they are objecting to age grouping. Similarly, parents may object to their child's placement in a particular ability group or academic track. Parents raising these objections usually argue that exclusion from the desired program violates their child's right to a generally available educational benefit and therefore to the "equal protection of the laws." School officials respond that age and ability grouping is an educationally sound practice that improves the efficiency of the school and helps to ensure, by and large, that children and program are appropriately matched.

Because differential treatment based on age and ability do not trigger the use of the more stringent tests, courts employ the rational basis test to resolve these disputes. Under this test, the plaintiffs must prove either that the age or ability grouping criteria do not serve any legitimate purpose or that the classification is wholly unrelated to its alleged purpose. Despite some evidence that ability grouping in particular is educationally ineffective and even counterproductive, plaintiffs do not usually win these suits. Age and ability grouping are long-standing practices intended to serve legitimate purposes, and despite the contrary evidence, courts do not consider it unreasonable for school officials to believe that these purposes relate to the criteria of classification.[136] The major exception is when tracking is used to create segregated programs within schools.[137]

Parents have the greatest chance of prevailing in a suit attacking ability grouping where the district is under court order to desegregate and the grouping has the effect of perpetuating racial segregation.[138] Similarly, parents may be successful if they can prove that tests and other procedures used to assign pupils to programs have a discriminatory impact on racial minorities and that the procedures were chosen because of this impact rather than in spite of it.[139]

State law and regulations may also provide a basis for objecting to a child's educational placement or program on equity grounds. For example, some states have laws mandating special educational services for gifted students. On the basis of one of these laws, parents in Pennsylvania were successful in establishing that their local school district had an obligation to provide their gifted child with an enrichment program, including advanced instruction in reading and math. The court made clear that the district's obligation was not to maximize the student's achievement nor to become a "Harvard or a Princeton to all who have IQ's over 130," but the district did have an obligation "to bring their talents to as complete fruition as our facilities allow."[140] However, courts have rejected claims that gifted children have a constitutional or statutory right to start school younger than state statute prescribes.[141]

6.7 SUMMARY

This chapter considered a number of pupil characteristics that justify the provision of an educational program that differs from the one most students receive. In all cases, differential treatment must meet the requirements of the Equal Protection Clause—that it at least be rationally related to a legitimate state goal. In most instances, classifications based on the characteristics considered in this chapter—certain physical and mental disabilities, limited English proficiency, age, and intellectual ability—do meet this requirement.

In addition, federal statutes and, arguably, the Equal Protection Clause as well require that students with disabilities or limited English proficiency receive an education from which they may reasonably be expected to benefit. The education of students with disabilities is regulated by four statutes: the Rehabilitation Act of 1973, the Americans with Disabilities Act, the Individuals with Disabilities Education Act, and the No Child Left Behind Act. The first two laws prohibit discrimination on the basis of disability, IDEA makes federal money available to states and districts that follow certain guidelines, and NCLB emphasizes achievement goals for children with disabilities.

The purpose of these laws is to provide children with disabilities with a free, appropriate public education designed to meet their individual educational needs. School districts must seek out children with disabilities within their jurisdiction; provide each with a nondiscriminatory, multidisciplinary evaluation of strengths and weaknesses; develop in accordance with each student's evaluation an individualized educational program consisting of special education and related services; and provide services in the least restrictive environment. Students with disabilities must be educated in a manner designed to meet measurable goals. Throughout the process, there must be parental participation and the observance of certain procedural safeguards.

The law regarding the treatment of limited-English proficient students is not nearly as extensive. However, Title VI of the Civil Rights Act of 1964 and the Equal Educational Opportunity Act of 1974 both require schools to take "appropriate action" to ensure that ELL students are not functionally excluded from meaningful participation in their programs. Appropriate action may include any locally chosen program that is supported by recognized educational theory and is effective in assisting ELL students in learning English. Some states prohibit the use of bilingual education.

Age grouping and most forms of ability grouping and tracking, although not mandated by considerations of equity, generally survive challenges based on the Equal Protection Clause. The major exception is when grouping or tracking leads to increased racial segregation in a district under court order to desegregate.

NOTES

1 State *ex rel.* Beattie v. Bd. of Educ. of Antigo, 172 N.W. 153 (Wis. 1919).
2 334 F. Supp. 1257 (E.D. Pa. 1971), and 343 F. Supp. 279 (E.D. Pa. 1972).
3 348 F. Supp. 866 (D.D.C. 1972).

4 29 U.S.C. §§ 701–796.

5 42 U.S.C. §§ 12101–12213.

6 20 U.S.C. §§ 1400–1485.

7 20 U.S.C. §§ 6311–6322.

8 *But see* City of Cleburne v. Cleburne Living Center, 473 U.S. 432 (1985).

9 N.M. Ass'n for Retarded Citizens v. New Mexico, 678 F.2d 847 (10th Cir. 1982).

10 29 U.S.C. § 701–796; except as otherwise noted, the discussion of RHA is based on the statutes and RHA regulations, Volume 34 C.F.R.

11 Rothschild v. Grottenthaler, 907 F.2d 286 (2d Cir. 1990).

12 42 U.S.C. §§ 12101–12213; except as otherwise noted, the discussion of ADA is based on the statutes and ADA regulations, Volumes 28, 29, 34, & 36 C.F.R.

13 Weixel v. Bd. of Educ. of City of New York, 287 F.3d 138 (2d Cir. 2002).

14 Sch. Bd. of Nassau County v. Arline, 480 U.S. 273 (1987).

15 Baird *ex rel.* Baird v. Rose, 192 F.3d 462 (4th Cir. 1999).

16 Costello v. Mitchell Pub. Sch. Dist. 79, 266 F.3d 916 (8th Cir. 2001).

17 McGuinness v. Univ. of New Mexico, 170 F.3d 974 (10th Cir. 1998).

18 Knapp v. Northwestern University, 101 F.3d 473 (7th Cir. 1996).

19 442 U.S. 397 (1979).

20 Campbell v. Bd. of Educ. of Centerline Sch. Dist., 58 Fed. Appx. 162 (6th Cir. 2003); Johnson v. Thompson, 971 F.2d 1487 (10th Cir. 1992); Pushkin v. Regents of the Univ. of Colorado, 658 F.2d 1372 (10th Cir. 1981); *compare*, Doe v. New York Univ., 666 F.2d 761 (2d Cir. 1981).

21 Monahan v. Nebraska, 687 F.2d 1164, 1171 (8th Cir. 1982).

22 Wright v. Columbia Univ., 520 F. Supp. 789 (E.D. Pa. 1981); Poole v. South Plainfield Bd. of Educ., 490 F. Supp. 948 (D.N.J. 1980); Grube v. Bethlehem Area Sch. Dist., 550 F. Supp. 418 (E.D. Pa. 1982); *see also* Doe v. Woodford County Bd. of Educ., 213 F.3d 921 (6th Cir. 2000); *but see* Kampmeier v. Nyquist, 553 F.2d 296 (2d Cir. 1977).

23 M.P. v. Indep. Sch. Dist. No. 721, 439 F.3d 865 (8th Cir. 2006).

24 K.M. v. Hyde Park Cent. Sch. Dist., 381 F. Supp. 2d 343 (S.D. N.Y. 2005).

25 Sandison v. Mich. High Sch. Athletic Ass'n, 64 F.3d 1026 (6th Cir. 1995).

26 Pottgen v. Mo. State High Sch. Athletic Ass'n, 40 F.3d 926 (8th Cir. 1994), *rev'd on other grounds*, 103 F.3d 720 (8th Cir. 1997); *see also* Mahan v. Agee, 652 P.2d 765 (Okla. 1982).

27 Denin v. Conn. Interscholastic Athletic Conference, 913 F. Supp. 663 (D. Conn. 1996), *vacated as moot*, 94 F.3d 96 (2d Cir. 1996); Univ. Interscholastic League v. Buchanan, 848 S.W.2d 298 (Tex. App. 1993); Johnson v. Florida High Sch. Athletic Ass'n, 899 F. Supp. 579 (M.D. Fla. 1995), *vacated as moot*, 102 F.3d 1172 (11th Cir. 1997).

28 McPherson v. Mich. High Sch. Athletic Ass'n, 119 F.3d 453 (6th Cir. 1997) (en banc).

29 Washington v. Indep. High Sch. Athletic Ass'n, 181 F.3d 840 (7th Cir. 1999).

30 Hoot v. Milan Area Schs., 853 F. Supp. 243 (E.D. Mich. 1994).

31 Alexander v. Choate, 469 U.S. 287 (1985).

32 28 C.F.R. § 35.130(b)(7).

33 34 C.F.R. § 104.33.

34 697 F.2d 179 (7th Cir. 1983).

35 Sullivan v. Vallejo City United Sch. Dist., 731 F. Supp. 947 (E.D. Cal. 1990).

36 480 F. Supp. 2d 610 (E.D.N.Y. 2007).

37 133 F.3d 141 (1st Cir. 1998).

38 Ridgewood Bd. of Educ. v. N.E., 172 F.3d 238 (3d Cir. 1999).

39 Pandazides v. Virginia Bd. of Educ., 13 F.3d 823 (4th Cir. 1994).

40 Barnes v. Gorman, 536 U.S. 181 (2002).

41 20 U.S.C. §§ 1400–1485; except as otherwise noted, discussion of IDEA is based on the statutes and IDEA regulations, Volume 34 C.F.R.

42 From birth to age three, children with disabilities are covered by Part C of IDEA, 20 U.S.C. § 1431.

43 *See* J.D. *ex rel.* J.D. v. Pawlet Sch. Dist., 224 F.3d 60 (2d Cir. 2000).

44 480 F.3d 1 (1st Cir. 2007).

45 Alvin Indep. Sch. Dist. v. A.D. *ex rel.* Patricia F., 503 F.3d 378 (5th Cir. 2007).

46 Bd. of Educ. of Fayette County, Kentucky. v. L.M., 478 F.3d 307 (6th Cir. 2007).

47 93 F.3d 1369 (8th Cir. 1996).

48 811 F.2d 1307 (9th Cir. 1987).

49 Indep. Sch. Dist. No. 283 v. S.D., 88 F.3d 556 (8th Cir. 1996).

50 Blackmon *ex rel.* Blackmon v. Springfield R-XII Sch. Dist., 198 F.3d 648 (8th Cir. 1999).

51 458 U.S. 176 (1982).

52 Polk v. Cent. Susquehanna Indep. Unit 16, 853 F.2d 171 (3d Cir. 1988); Mrs. B. v. Milford Bd. of Educ., 103 F.3d 1114 (2d Cir. 1997); Hall v. Vance County Bd. of Educ., 774 F.2d 629 (4th Cir. 1985).

53 Bd. of Educ. v. Diamond, 808 F.2d 987 (3d Cir. 1986); *see also* Ridgewood Bd. of Educ. v. N.E. *ex rel.* M.E., 172 F.3d 238 (3d Cir. 1999); M.C. *ex rel.* J.C. v. Cent. Reg'l Sch., 81 F.3d 389 (3d Cir. 1996).

54 M.C. *ex rel.* J.C. v. Cent. Reg'l Sch., 81 F.3d 389 (3d Cir. 1996).

55 Lester Aron, "Too Much or Not Enough: How Have the Circuit Courts Defined a Free Appropriate Public Education After *Rowley*?," 39 SUFFOLK U. L. REV. 1 (2005).

56 Cypress-Fairbanks Intermediate Sch. Dist. v. Michael F., 118 F.3d 245 (5th Cir. 1997).

57 Shore Reg'l High Sch. Bd. of Educ. v. P.S., 381 F.3d 194 (3d Cir. 2004); *see also* M.L. v. Federal Way Sch. Dist., 394 F.3d 634 (9th Cir. 2005).

58 Burke County Bd. of Educ. v. Denton, 895 F.2d 973 (4th Cir. 1990); Bd. of Educ. of E. Windsor Reg'l Sch. Dist. v. Diamond, 808 F.2d 987 (3rd Cir. 1986); David D. v. Dartmouth Sch. Comm., 775 F.2d 411 (1st Cir. 1985); *compare* O'Toole v. Olathe Dist. Sch. Unified Sch. Dist. No. 233, 144 F.3d 692 (10th Cir. 1998); *see also* Johnson v. Indep. Sch. Dist. No. 4, 921 F.2d 1022 (10th Cir. 1990) (holding that Kansas and Oklahoma law do not provide for a higher standard).

59 875 F.2d 954 (1st Cir. 1989).

60 Rettig v. Kent City Sch. Dist., 788 F.2d 328 (6th Cir. 1986); Johnson v. Lancaster-Lebanon Intermediate Unit 13, 757 F. Supp. 606 (E.D. Pa. 1991).

61 Clevenger v. Oak Ridge Sch. Bd., 744 F.2d 514 (6th Cir. 1984).

62 Johnson v. Indep. Sch. Dist. No. 4, 921 F.2d 1022 (10th Cir. 1990).

63 526 U.S. 66 (1999).

64 468 U.S. 883 (1984).

65 Detsel v. Bd. of Educ., 637 F. Supp. 1022 (N.D.N.Y. 1986), *aff'd*, 820 F.2d 587 (2d Cir. 1987) (per curiam).

66 *See* Max M. v. Thompson, 592 F. Supp. 1450 (N.D. Ill. 1984) (supportive psychological service); McKenzie v. Jefferson, 566 F. Supp. 404 (D.D.C. 1983) (excluded medical service).

67 225 F.3d 887 (7th Cir. 2000).

68 *See* Hurry v. Jones, 734 F.2d 879 (1st Cir. 1984); Alamo Heights Indep. Sch. Dist. v. State Bd. of Educ., 70 F.2d 1153 (5th Cir. 1986).

69 McNair v. Oak Hills Local Sch. Dist., 872 F.2d 153 (6th Cir. 1989).

70 Macomb County Intermediate Sch. Dist. v. Joshua S., 715 F. Supp. 824 (E.D. Mich. 1989).

71 Felter v. Cape Girardeau Pub. Sch. Dist., 810 F. Supp. 1062 (E.D. Mo. 1993).

72 *See* Daniel R.R. v. State Bd. Of Educ., 874 F.2d 1036 (5th Circ. 1989); Roncker v. Walter, 700 F.2d 1058 (6th Cir. 1983); Lachman v. Ill. State Board of Education, 852 F.2d 290 (7th Cir. 1988); Oberti v. Board of Educ. of Clementon Sch. Dist., 995 F.2d 1204 (3d Cir. 1993); Greer v. Rome City Sch. Dist., 950 F.2d 688 (11th Cir. 1991), *opinion withdrawn and remanded*, 956 F.2d 1025 (11th Cir. 1992).

73 Sacramento City Unified Sch. Dist. Bd. of Educ. v. Rachel H., 14 F.3d 1398 (9th Cir. 1994).

74 Hartmann v. Loudoun County Bd. of Educ., 118 F.3d 996 (4th Cir. 1997).

75 Bd. of Educ. of Twp. High Sch. Dist., 211 v. Ross, 486 F.3d 267 (7th Cir. 2007); Sch. Dist. of Wisconsin Dells v. Z.S., 295 F.3d 671 (7th Cir. 2002).

76 *See* Drew P. v. Clarke County Sch. Dist., 877 F.2d 927 (11th Cir. 1989).

77 Kruelle v. New Castle County Sch. Dist., 642 F.2d 687 (3d Cir. 1981).

78 Taylor v. Honig, 910 F.2d 627 (9th Cir. 1990); Clovis Unified Sch. Dist. v. California Office of Admin. Hearings, 903 F.2d 635 (9th Cir. 1990).

79 Abrahamson v. Hershman, 701 F.2d 233 (1st Cir. 1983); Battle v. Pennsylvania, 629 F.2d 269 (3d Cir. 1980).

80 Kruelle v. New Castle County Sch. Dist., 642 F.2d 687 (3d Cir. 1981).

81 Dale M. *ex rel.* Alice M. v. Bd. of Educ. of Bradley-Bourbonnais High Sch. Dist. No. 307, 237 F.3d 813 (7th Cir. 2001); *see also* Butler v. Evans, 225 F.3d 887 (7th Cir. 2000).

82 Clevenger v. Oak Ridge Sch. Bd., 744 F.2d 514 (6th Cir. 1984).

83 Alamo Heights Indep. Sch. Dist. v. State Bd. of Educ., 790 F.2d 1153 (5th Cir. 1986); Helms v. Indep. Sch. Dist. No. 3 of Broken Arrow, 750 F.2d 820 (10th Cir. 1984).

84 Parks v. Pavkovic, 753 F.2d 1397 (7th Cir. 1985) (dictum); Abrahamson v. Hershman, 701 F.2d 223 (1st Cir. 1983) (dictum).

85 KDM *ex rel.* WJM v. Reedsport Sch. Dist., 196 F.3d 1046 (9th Cir. 1999), *reh'g denied*, 210 F.3d 1098 (9th Cir. 2000); Jasa v. Millard Pub. Sch. Dist. No. 17, 206 F.3d 813 (8th Cir. 2000).

86 Hooks v. Clark County Sch. Dist., 228 F.3d 1036 (9th Cir. 2000).

87 Cefalu v. E. Baton Rouge Parish Sch. Bd., 117 F.3d 231 (5th Cir. 1997).

88 Burlington Sch. Comm. of Burlington v. Dep't of Educ. of Massachusetts, 471 U.S. 359 (1985); *see also* Florence County Sch. Dist. Four v. Carter, 510 U.S. 7 (1993).

89 Evans v. Dist. No. 17 of Douglas County, 841 F.2d 824 (8th Cir. 1988); *see also* Schonefeld v. Parkway Sch. Dist., 138 F.3d 379 (8th Cir. 1998); Tucker v. Calloway County Bd. of Educ., 136 F.3d 495 (6th Cir. 1998).

90 Patricia P. v. Bd. of Educ. of Oak Park and River Forest High Sch. Dist. No. 200, 8 F. Supp. 2d 801 (N.D. Ill. 1998).

91 Greenland Sch. Dist. v. Amy N., 358 F.3d 150 (1st Cir. 2004); Ms. M. *ex rel.* K.M. v. Portland Sch. Comm., 360 F.3d 267 (1st Cir. 2004).

92 Frank G. v. Bd. of Educ. of Hyde Park, 459 F.3d 356 (2d Cir. 2006); *see also* Bd. of Educ. of City Sch. Dist. of City of New York v. Tom F., 193 Fed. Appx. 26 (2d Cir. 2006), *aff'd by equally divided court*, 128 S. Ct. 1 (2007).

93 Zobrest v. Catalina Foothills Sch. Dist., 509 U.S. 1 (1993).

94 *See* Agostini v. Felton, 521 U.S. 203 (1997).

95 629 F.2d 751 (2d Cir. 1980).

96 Tilton v. Jefferson County Bd. of Educ., 705 F.2d 800 (6th Cir. 1983).

97 DeLeon v. Susquehanna Cmty. Sch. Dist., 747 F.2d 149 (3d Cir. 1984); *see also* Weil v. Bd. of Elementary & Secondary Educ., 931 F.2d 1069 (5th Cir. 1991).

98 Doe v. Brookline Sch. Comm., 722 F.2d 910 (1st Cir. 1983).

99 Saleh v. District of Columbia, 660 F. Supp. 212 (D.D.C. 1987).

100 Cochran v. District of Columbia, 660 F. Supp. 314 (D.D.C. 1987).

101 202 F.3d 642 (3d Cir. 2000).

102 420 F.3d 181 (3d Cir. 2005).

103 R.B. *ex rel.* F.B. v. Napa Valley Unified Sch. Dist., 496 F.3d 932 (9th Cir. 2007); W.G. v. Bd. of Trustees of Target Range Sch. Dist. No. 23, 960 F.2d 1479 (9th Cir. 1992).

104 Schaffer v. Weast, 546 U.S. 49 (2005).

105 N.Y. EDUC. LAW § 4404 (1)(c); MINN. STAT. ANN. § 125A.091.

106 Walczak v. Fla. Union Free Sch. Dist., 142 F.3d 119 (2d Cir. 1998); Fort Zumwalt Sch. Dist. v. Clynes, 119 F.3d 607 (8th Cir. 1997); Clyde K. v. Puyallup Sch. Dist., 35 F.3d 1396 (9th Cir. 1994); Roland M. v. Concord Sch. Comm., 910 F.2d 983 (1st Cir. 1990); Kerkam v. McKenzie, 862 F.2d 884 (D.C. Cir. 1988); Spielberg v. Henrico County Pub. Sch., 853 F.2d 256 (4th Cir. 1988).

107 Oberti v. Bd. of Educ. of Clementon Sch. Dist., 995 F.2d 1204 (3d Cir. 1993); Lascari v. Bd. of Educ. of Ramapo Indian Hills, 560 A.2d 1180 (N.J. 1989).

108 Jefferson County Bd. of Educ. v. Breen, 853 F.2d 853 (11th Cir. 1988); Miener v. Missouri, 800 F.2d 749 (8th Cir. 1986); *but see* Alexopulos v. San Francisco Unified Sch. Dist., 817 F.2d 551 (9th Cir. 1987).

109 Hurry v. Jones, 734 F.2d 879 (1st Cir. 1984); Burr v. Ambach, 863 F.2d 1071 (2d Cir. 1988).

110 Arlington Central Sch. Dist. Bd. of Educ. v. Murphy, 548 U.S. 291 (2006).

111 Buckhannon Bd. & Care Home, Inc. v. West Virginia Dep't of Health & Human Res., 532 U.S. 598 (2001); Smith v. Fitchburg Pub. Schs., 401 F.3d 16 (1st Cir. 2005).

112 Woodside v. The Sch. Dist. of Philadelphia Bd. of Educ., 248 F.3d 129 (3d Cir. 2001); Doe v. Bd. of Educ. of Baltimore County, 165 F.3d 260 (4th Cir. 1998).

113 Ortega v. Bibb County Sch. Dist., 397 F.3d 1321 (11th Cir. 2005).

114 A.W. v. Jersey City Pub. Sch., 486 F.3d 791 (3d Cir. 2007); Padilla v. Sch. Dist. No. 1, 233 F.3d 1268 (10th Cir. 2000); Sellers v. Sch. Bd. of Manassas, 141 F.3d 524 (4th Cir. 1998); *but see* W.B. v. Matula, 67 F.3d 484 (3d Cir. 1995).

115 34 C.F.R. 200.1(d) and (e); 34 C.F.R. 200.6; 34 C.F.R. 200.13.

116 549 F. Supp. 2d 161 (D. Conn. 2008).

117 Leighty v. Laurel Sch. Dist., 457 F. Supp. 2d 546 (W.D. Pa. 2006).

118 517 F.3d 922 (7th Cir. 2008).

119 42 U.S.C. § 2000(d).

120 Office for Civil Rights, *Identification of Discrimination of Denial of Services on the Basis of National Origin*, 35 Fed. Reg. 11,595 (May 25, 1970).

121 483 F.2d 791 (9th Cir. 1973), *rev'd*, 414 U.S. 563 (1974).

122 Lau v. Nichols, 414 U.S. 563 (1974).

123 20 U.S.C. § 1703(f).

124 Alexander v. Sandoval, 532 U.S. 275 (2001); Guardians Ass'n v. Civil Serv. Comm., 463 U.S. 582 (1983).

125 Civil Rights Div., Dep't of Justice, 65 Fed. Reg. 50,123 (August 16, 2000).

126 Alexander v. Sandoval, 532 U.S. 275 (2001).

127 648 F.2d 989 (5th Cir. 1981).

128 Gomez v. Ill. State Bd. of Educ., 811 F.2d 1030 (7th Cir. 1987); Teresa P. v. Berkeley Unified Sch. Dist., 724 F. Supp. 698 (N.D. Cal. 1989): *see also* Serna v. Portales Mun. Sch., 499 F.2d 1147 (10th Cir. 1974); Rios v. Read, 480 F. Supp. 14 (E.D.N.Y. 1978); Flores v. Ariz., 48 F. Supp. 2d 937 (D. Ariz., 1999), and 172 F. Supp. 2d 1225 (2000).

129 20 U.S.C. § 6845 (referring to 20 U.S.C. § 6811).

130 20 U.S.C. § 7012.

131 CAL. EDUC. CODE § 305. *See* California Teachers Ass'n v. State Bd. of Educ., 271 F.3d 1141 (9th Cir. 2001); Valeria G. v. Wilson, 12 F. Supp. 2d 1007 (N.D. Cal. 1998); *see also* ARIZ. REV. STAT. ANN. § 15–751 et seq.

132 McLaughlin v. State Bd. of Educ., 89 Cal. Rptr. 2d 295 (Cal. Ct. App. 1999).

133 California Teachers Ass'n v. State Bd. of Educ., 271 F.3d 1141 (9th Cir. 2001); California Teachers Ass'n v. State Bd. of Educ., 263 F.3d 888 (9th Cir. 2001); Valeria G. v. Wilson, 12 F. Supp. 2d 1007 (N.D. Cal. 1998).

134 451 F. Supp. 1324 (E.D. Mich. 1978).

135 3 E.H.L.R. 551:245 (E.D.N.Y. 1979).

136 Sandlin v. Johnson, 643 F.2d 1027 (4th Cir. 1981); Hammond v. Marx, 406 F. Supp. 853 (D. Me. 1975).

137 McNeal v. Tate County Sch. Dist., 508 F.2d 1017 (5th Cir. 1975); Morales v. Shannon, 516 F.2d 411 (5th Cir. 1975); Moses v. Wash. Parish Sch. Bd., 330 F. Supp. 1340 (E.D. La. 1971), *aff'd*, 456 F.2d 1285 (5th Cir. 1972) (per curiam); Hobson v. Hansen, 269 F. Supp. 401 (D.D.C. 1967), *aff'd sub nom*, Smuck v. Hobson, 408 F.2d 175 (D.C. Cir. 1969) (en banc).

138 McNeal v. Tate County Sch. Dist., 508 F.2d 1017 (5th Cir. 1975); Bester v. Tuscaloosa City Bd. of Educ., 722 F.2d 1514 (11th Cir. 1984).

139 Larry P. v. Riles, 793 F.2d 969 (9th Cir. 1984).

140 Centennial Sch. Dist. v. Dep't of Educ., 539 A.2d 785 (Pa. 1988).

141 Zweifel v. Joint Dist. No. 1, 251 N.W.2d 822 (Wis. 1977).

7 Federal Constitutional and Statutory Rights of Teachers

Now begins a series of three chapters discussing the legal framework of the relationship between schools and their employees. The law concerning the school's treatment of its employees emanates from many sources—state and federal constitutional provisions, state and federal statutes, and the common law. For example, the dismissal of a tenured teacher must be for reasons specified in state law and follow procedures required by state law, the teacher's contract, the collective bargaining agreement, and the Constitution's Due Process Clause. The dismissal may not violate the free speech or other constitutional rights of the teacher or federal or state statutes prohibiting various forms of discrimination in employment. This chapter examines the federal constitutional and statutory rights of teachers and other employees. Chapter 8 deals with employment and personnel issues like hiring, evaluation, and dismissal. Chapter 9 looks at collective-bargaining, contracts, and the role of professional unions.

Recall that the Constitution places limitations on the power of government to control the behavior of individuals. There are certain behaviors that under normal circumstances government may not regulate and certain laws that it cannot make. Viewed from the perspective of the individual, these limitations are the civil rights and liberties enjoyed by every member of society. School officials, as representatives of the government, are bound to respect these rights in their dealings not only with students but also with their subordinate employees.

However, as with students, there are times when the special circumstances of the school necessitate a balancing between the constitutional rights of employees and the promotion of important educational goals. In addition, the legal power of the government over its employees is greater than over ordinary citizens. Thus, there are circumstances when the school board may impose requirements and restrictions on its employees that government in general could not impose on the citizenry. At times, however, the school must accommodate its program to the constitutional rights of its employees.

This chapter examines these issues with regard to the constitutional provisions that have engendered the most conflict and litigation in education: freedom of speech, freedom of religion, the right to privacy, the Fourth Amendment's protection against unreasonable search and seizure, and the Fourteenth Amendment's guarantee of equal protection of the law. The discussion assumes knowledge of the constitutional principles and doctrines presented in earlier chapters.

In addition to the Constitution, a significant body of federal statutes regulates the employment practices of public schools. These statutes supplement and expand the requirements of the Equal Protection Clause by prohibiting discrimination in employment on the basis of race, ethnicity, gender, religion, disability, or age. Sections 7.4 to 7.7 examine the application of federal antidiscrimination statutes to employment practices in public education.

7.1 POLITICAL ACTIVITY AND NONCURRICULAR SPEECH

May school boards insist that employees embrace the board's political and educational views? Must school employees be permitted to publicly oppose the policies or to directly criticize the members of the school board that employs them? Must teachers be permitted to reveal or advocate their political or personal beliefs to a captive audience of students? Does not the school have the right to inculcate society's chosen values by controlling the speech of its teachers? Do not public school officials have the right and perhaps the duty to protect their pupils from viewpoints they consider undesirable or dangerous? To answer these questions, courts have had to strike a balance between educators' freedom of speech and a school's right to promote its educational goals. As with students, the balance depends in part on whether the speech occurs in school or out and whether the speech is part of the school's curriculum. This section deals with school employee speech that occurs outside the context of the school curriculum. The next section deals with curricular speech by teachers and other school employees.

Public school teachers have always occupied a sensitive and a visible role in the community. In the public schools of colonial New England people could not be teachers unless the town minister certified their religious and moral rectitude. Although states no longer impose a religious qualification on teachers, they have in more recent times employed ideological tests. Practices designed to enforce these qualifications have included political background checks, disqualification of members of political groups considered dangerous or subversive, and required loyalty oaths.

In keeping with the strong anticommunist sentiments of the time, the Supreme Court during the 1950s generally found these practices a constitutionally permissible way of protecting the government service from subversives. For example, in *Adler v. Board of Education of New York*,[1] the Supreme Court upheld a New York law disqualifying from employment in civil service or public schools any person who "advocates, advises or teaches" governmental overthrow by force or violence or who organizes or joins any group advocating such doctrine.

With the coming of the new decade, the Supreme Court changed its view of the constitutionality of these security measures. In 1960, in *Shelton v. Tucker*,[2] the Court prohibited school boards from requiring teachers to disclose all their associational ties and memberships. In 1964, in *Baggett v. Bullitt*,[3] the Court forbade the use of vaguely worded loyalty oaths.

Then, in 1967, in *Keyishian v. Board of Regents*,[4] the Court took a major step toward protecting the political rights of teachers by prohibiting states and school boards from dismissing teachers for membership in disfavored organizations, even those with violent or unlawful goals such as the Communist party. Such dismissals, reasoned the Court, would violate the teachers' right to freedom of association, a corollary of free speech (see sec. 3.6). It would be permissible to fire a teacher for "specific intent to further the unlawful aims of an organization" but not for "mere membership" or even knowledge of the organization's unlawful goals.

However, as much as *Keyishian, Baggett,* and *Shelton* stand against attempts to impose ideological qualifications on teachers, the Supreme Court continues to allow states or school boards to require an "affirmative oath," a pledge, for example, to uphold and defend the Constitution or oppose the overthrow of the government by illegal means.[5] (Negative oaths, for example, "I have never been a member of a subversive organization," are impermissible.) The Court has also upheld against a challenge based on the Equal Protection Clause a state policy denying teacher certification to aliens who were eligible but refused to apply for U.S. citizenship.[6] Thus, although no one may be excluded from teaching solely because of membership in a disfavored political organization, even one that advocates violent overthrow of the government, the Constitution permits requiring teachers to take a specifically worded positive loyalty oath or to hold or seek citizenship.

On a related issue, the Supreme Court has made it clear that public employees generally may not be dismissed, punished, or rewarded solely because of their party affiliation or political beliefs. Thus, the Court has sought an end to the traditional practice of political patronage, which in schools often meant the replacement of administrators and even teachers after municipal or school board elections. The major exception to this limitation is with regard to those positions for which "party affiliation is an appropriate requirement for the effective performance of the public office involved."[7] Based on these principles, teachers have been protected from dismissal because they either supported the recall or opposed the reelection of incumbent school board members.[8] One court ruled that the refusal to hire teachers for summer employment because they supported the losing candidates for school board was impermissible.[9] It is, however, arguably permissible for a school board to replace top central office administrators whose politics on issues relating directly to the operation of the schools differ from the board's.

In *Castle v. Colonial School District*,[10] a federal district court prohibited enforcement of a school board policy prohibiting employees from engaging in political activities on school property at any time. The purpose of the policy was to prevent off-duty teachers from soliciting votes at polling places located in the schools. The board argued that the prohibition was needed to limit disruption and to protect voters from undue influence from teachers. But there was also evidence that board members were "annoyed about teachers advocating the election of rival board candidates." The court ruled in favor of the teachers, finding that the very essence of free speech was at stake; teachers had a right to criticize the current board and were in a unique position to provide the public with information regarding the quality of the schools.

Because of the great potential for conflict of interest, school employees may be prohibited from becoming school board members in the district in which they are employed;[11] however, they may not be prohibited from serving on the school board of another district or from running for or holding other public office.[12] Mandatory leaves of absence for school employees who seek or hold public office are also impermissible except, possibly, as part of a general requirement of leave of absence[13] for any similarly time-consuming outside employment or activity.

Criticism of School Policies and Personnel

In a significant number of cases, a school district has sought to punish teachers for expressing personal opinions critical of school policies or practices or the performance of the school board or administrators. The district's rationale for punishing the teacher is usually that the communication did or had the potential to undermine public support for or damage working relationships within the school. Over the years, the Supreme Court has dealt with a series of cases in which teachers or other public employees have claimed that such punitive actions violated their right to freedom of speech. The outcome of these cases provides a *six-part framework* for dealing with such claims in any public employment context including a public school.

Employees objecting to the actions of a public employer on free speech grounds *first* bear the burden of showing that they were subjected to an **adverse employment decision.** Dismissal, demotion, negative job evaluations and forced unpaid leave qualify as adverse employment decisions, but lateral transfers generally do not. The *second* question is whether the employee spoke **pursuant to his official duties or as a citizen.** If the employee spoke pursuant to his official duties, the employee does not enjoy First Amendment protection. If the employee spoke as a citizen, the *third* question is whether the subject of the speech was **a matter of public concern**. If the speech was not a matter of public concern, the employee is not afforded First Amendment protection. If the speech was a matter of public concern, the *fourth* question is whether the public interest in what the employee had to say **outweighs the disruption**, if any, the speech has caused or might cause to the employer. If the employer's interest in avoiding the disruption outweighs the public interest in the speech, the employee again does not receive First Amendment protection. But if the public interest in the speech outweighs the disruption, the employee's speech falls into the category of *protected speech*. Now in order to prevail, the employee must establish the *fifth* element: that the protected speech was a **substantial factor** in the adverse employment decision. If the employee successfully meets this burden of proof, the burden now switches to the employer for the *sixth* and final part of the test. The employer must show that the **same** adverse employment decision would have been made in the absence of the protected speech. Otherwise the employee will win the case.

The *Ceballos* Case

Garcetti v. Ceballos[14] is the case in which the Supreme Court first developed the distinction between a public employee speaking "pursuant to his official duties" and a public employee speaking "as a citizen." The case concerned a disagreement between Ceballos, a deputy district attorney, and his superiors over the handling of a criminal prosecution. Ceballos not only expressed doubts about the case in a memo to his superiors but also testified for the defense that a police affidavit that had been used to gather evidence against a defendant was inaccurate. Ceballos was subsequently reassigned to a different position and denied a promotion.

After affirming that "the First Amendment protects a public employee's right, in certain circumstances, to speak as a citizen addressing matters of public concern," the Court went on to explain why, in this case, Ceballos was not protected:

> When a citizen enters government service, the citizen by necessity must accept certain limitations on his or her freedom . . . Government employers, like private employers, need a significant degree of control over their employees' words and actions; without it, there would be little chance for the efficient provision of public services . . .
>
> Ceballos did not act as a citizen when he went about conducting his daily professional activities . . . In the same way he did not speak as a citizen by writing a memo that addressed the proper disposition of a pending criminal case. When he went to work and performed the tasks he was paid to perform, Ceballos acted as a government employee. The fact that his duties sometimes required him to speak or write does not mean his supervisors were prohibited from evaluating his performance.

Ceballos does not "articulate a comprehensive formula" for determining when public employees may be regarded as having spoken pursuant to their official duties beyond suggesting that official job descriptions are not the determining factor. Several school-based circuit court cases have addressed this issue. The Tenth Circuit has said that speech may be considered pursuant to official duties if it is generally consistent with the type of activities the employee was paid to do even if it dealt with activities the employee was not expressly required to perform. Speech may be viewed as pursuant to official duties if "the speech reasonably contributes to or facilitates the employee's performance of the official duty." But, not all speech which occurs at work is expressed pursuant to official duties, nor is all speech about the subject matter of an employee's work necessarily made pursuant to official duties. "Instead, we must take a practical view of all the facts and circumstances surrounding the speech and the employment relationship." Based on this somewhat amorphous definition, the court sorted through a variety of statements made by teachers at a public charter school and concluded that some were expressed pursuant to their duties and some were not. Statements found to be made pursuant to their duties as teachers concerned student behavior, curriculum and pedagogy, and expenditures for instructional aids, furniture, and computers. Statements found to be made not pursuant to their duties as teachers concerned the resignation of other teachers, whether the school's code restricted their freedom of speech, staffing levels, spending on teacher salaries, the visibility of the principal at school board meetings and important events, lack of feedback by and poor communication with the principal, treatment of parents by the principal, favoritism by the principal, the renewal of the school's charter, and the upcoming board elections. (The question of whether any or all of these topics were matters of public concern is a separate issue.)[15]

In a Fifth Circuit case, the plaintiff was removed from his job as a school's athletic director after writing a letter to the office manager protesting the failure to provide him with information regarding the athletic account and writing a memorandum to the school principal regarding the handling and disbursements of gate receipts. In ruling in favor of the district, the court drew a distinction between the kind of speech activity engaged in by citizens and activities undertaken in the course of performing one's job. The plaintiff's statements were job related, said the court, because he was seeking information needed to operate the athletic department; because he wanted the gate receipts to pay for costs he was responsible for paying; and because his comments were based on special knowledge he had as athletic director.[16]

In *Casey v. West Las Vegas Independent School District*[17] the Tenth Circuit reached the conclusion that, in effect, there are circumstances when *Ceballos* dictates that whistle-blowing (reporting misconduct by a public official) is not protected speech. A school superintendent whose job included serving as CEO of the district's Head Start program reported to federal authorizes that as many as 50 percent of the children served in the program were not eligible. She previously had raised the same concern with the school board, which told her "not to worry about it, to leave it alone, or not to go there." On a separate matter, the superintendent also reported to the state's attorney general her belief that the school board was violating the state's open meeting law. After she was demoted to assistant superintendent she brought suit claiming the demotion was in retaliation for exercise of her free speech rights. Regarding the communication about Head Start, the court ruled that since as the CEO of Head Start, she was the person primarily responsible for administering the program in compliance with federal regulations and that she in fact risked civil and criminal liability for remaining silent, her communication to federal officials was part of her job responsibilities and thus pursuant to her official duties. Based on *Ceballos*, therefore, the court reached the ironic conclusion that although her speech was clearly a matter of public concern, it was not protected speech. The court also ruled that her report of the board's noncompliance with the open meetings law was not related to her job responsibilities and hence made as a private citizen.

After *Ceballos*, teachers can only hope to receive First-Amendment protection when they speak as private citizens and not pursuant to their official job responsibilities. A special education teacher who tells parents at an IEP meeting that her school district did not offer adequate services to students with disabilities would be speaking pursuant to her official duties. Her speech would not be protected. The same teacher making the same point at a meeting of a local advocacy group might be speaking as a private citizen. Her speech would then be protected if its subject was judged to be a matter of public concern and if the importance of what the teacher had to say was judged to outweigh any disruption the speech might cause.

The *Pickering* Case

In *Pickering v. Board of Education*,[18] the Supreme Court developed a framework for deciding these cases. Pickering, a teacher, wrote a letter to the local newspaper criticizing his board of education's allocation of funds and desire to raise additional funds through a bond issue and accusing the superintendent of schools of attempting to prevent teachers from opposing the proposed bond issue. Some of the alleged facts in the letter were erroneous. After a hearing, the board voted to dismiss Pickering for conduct "detrimental to the efficient operation and administration of . . . the district." As justification for their actions, the board cited the falsity of some of Pickering's statements, which they claimed unjustifiably damaged the reputations of the board and superintendent. In addition, the board argued that the letter would be disruptive of faculty discipline and tend to arouse "controversy, conflict, and dissension among teachers, administrators, the Board of Education, and the residents of the district." Pickering objected to the dismissal on the grounds that his actions were protected by the First Amendment.

In deciding the *Pickering* case, the Court was faced with the task of balancing the teacher's right to free expression with the board's legitimate expectation that the teachers in its employ would promote the valid educational goals and policies of the district. The Court began its analysis by stating that, despite the board's claims, Pickering's letter had no potential to adversely affect "either discipline by superiors or harmony among coworkers." The working relationships between a teacher and school board and between a teacher and superintendent "are not the kind of close working relationships for which it can persuasively be claimed that loyalty and confidence are necessary to their proper functioning." Furthermore, noted the Court, the board had produced no evidence of damage to anyone's reputation or of any controversy or conflict resulting from the letter.

Most significantly, the subject of Pickering's letter was

> a matter of public concern on which the judgment of the school administration, including the School Board, cannot, in a society that leaves such questions to popular vote, be taken as conclusive. On such a question, free and open debate is vital to informed decision-making by the electorate. Teachers are, as a class, the members of a community most likely to have informed and definite opinions as to how funds allotted to the operation of the schools should be spent. Accordingly it is essential that they be able to speak out freely on such questions without fear of retaliatory dismissal.

In evaluating the significance of the factual errors found in Pickering's letter, the Court again drew a distinction between issues of public debate and concern such as those discussed by Pickering and matters of the day-to-day operation of the schools. Whereas it might be difficult for a school administration to counter a teacher's false statements about what goes on daily in their schools, in Pickering's case there would be no assumption on the part of his readers that he possessed any special or insider knowledge, and the board had only to publish the true facts. There was no evidence that Pickering had set out to lie or to deceive, only that he had made mistakes. Based on all of these considerations, the Court concluded that "absent proof of false statements knowingly or recklessly made by him, a teacher's exercise of his right to speak on issues of public importance may not furnish the basis for his dismissal from public employment." Pickering's dismissal was unconstitutional.

Post-*Pickering* Cases

Four other Supreme Court cases help to clarify the issues raised in *Pickering*. In the first of these cases, *Givhan v. Western Line Consolidated School District*,[19] the Court held that speech need not be made in a public forum to be considered a matter of public concern. Thus, although a teacher's criticism of the school board's policies on racial issues was privately expressed to the principal, it still received the protection of the First Amendment.

The second and most significant of these cases, *Connick v. Myers*,[20] concerned an assistant district attorney, Myers, dismissed in part for circulating a questionnaire soliciting the support of her coworkers for her criticisms of the policies and practices of her superiors in the office. To decide the case, the Court, in accordance with *Pickering (Ceballos* had not yet been decided), first had to determine whether the questionnaire dealt with matters of public concern or public importance. "Whether an employee's speech addresses a matter of public concern," declared the Court, "must be determined by the content, form, and context of a given statement. . . ."

Analyzing the questionnaire, the Court concluded that most of the issues it raised were simply personal grievances. Most of the questions did not touch on ongoing issues already in the public realm. Nor did they attempt to inform the public directly of important issues or to bring to light wrongdoing or breaches of the public trust. In addition, Myers spoke out only in the context of her office and only after receiving an unwanted transfer notice, suggesting that her motivation was purely personal. The Court concluded that personal grievances expressed within the context of public employment do not qualify as matters of public concern: "[T]he First Amendment does not require a public office to be run as a roundtable for employee complaints over internal office affairs." Thus, the Court concluded that the questions that reflected purely personal grievances did not receive First Amendment protection.

However, in analyzing the questionnaire, the Court found one question that was not a purely personal grievance: The question asked if assistant district attorneys were ever pressured by superiors to work on political campaigns, thereby implicitly alleging wrongdoing on the part of high public officials. Because this allegation was a matter of public concern, it was necessary to determine whether it was permissible for this question to have contributed to Myers' dismissal. In making this determination, the Court sought to strike a balance between Myers' rights and the interest of her office "in promoting the efficiency of the public services it performs. . . ."

There is a limit, said the Court, to how much disruption need be tolerated by a public employer for the sake of freedom of speech. The limit must be determined on a case-by-case basis depending on such factors as the importance of the issue that was raised, the likelihood that the speech would result in disruption, and the degree and nature of disruption that actually occurred. Applying these criteria to Myers' actions, the Court found that the questionnaire addressed a matter of public concern only in "a most limited way," that the questionnaire was an act of insubordination that could and did cause a "mini-insurrection," and that the questionnaire damaged close working relations within the district attorney's office. Thus, the Court concluded that Myers' dismissal did not violate her right to freedom of speech.

In 1987, the Supreme Court provided further clarification of the *Pickering* and *Connick* doctrines. In *Rankin v. McPherson*,[21] the Court held that a clerical employee in a local constable's office could not be discharged for saying over the telephone, after hearing of the attempted assassination of President Reagan, "If they go for him again, I hope they get him." In finding that McPherson's remark dealt with a matter of public concern, the Court noted that the remark was made in the context of a conversation addressing the policies of the Reagan administration, and that the "inappropriate or controversial character of a statement is irrelevant to the question of whether it deals with a matter of public concern." The Court went on to conclude that the actual and potential disruptive effect of the remark was minimal because McPherson did not serve in a confidential, policy-making, or public-contact role, nor was there any showing that McPherson's statement had interfered with the effective functioning of the constable's office or that it was made in a context that would bring discredit upon the office. The Court ruled that McPherson had engaged in "protected speech" and that her dismissal was impermissible.

In 1994, in *Waters v. Churchill*,[22] the Supreme Court again used the *Pickering* and *Connick* doctrines to decide the case of a nurse at a public hospital dismissed after a private conversation at work with a trainee. The hospital claimed that the nurse's statements were personal grievances designed to prevent the trainee from working in a particular department of the hospital and to undermine the authority of the department's supervisor. The nurse claimed that her statements concerned the failure of her department to follow established procedures and thus were matters of public concern. In a plurality opinion, the Court ruled that the nurse's First Amendment rights had not been violated because the hospital had made a "reasonable, good-faith" effort to determine if the speech dealt with matters of public concern and had concluded that it did not. Even though a court might have found differently, "[g]overnment employers should be allowed to use personnel procedures that differ from the evidentiary rules used by courts, without fear that these differences will lead to liability." Furthermore, as stated in *Connick*, even speech addressing matters of public concern may be the basis of dismissal if the employer can make a substantial showing that the speech was likely to be disruptive. "Discouraging people from coming to work for a department," the Court noted, "certainly qualifies as disruption," as do negative comments that undermine the authority of a direct supervisor.

Applying these cases in the context of the public school requires careful analysis. In order to determine whether a speech that school employees engage in as private citizens (that is, not pursuant to their delivery of the curriculum or other official duties of their job) is protected, school officials must make a reasonable good-faith attempt to answer two questions. First, did the speech address a matter of public concern? If not, the speech is not protected and may constitutionally be the basis for disciplining the employee. However, if yes, then considering the content, form, and context of the speech, which was greater: the employee's interest in the speech or the actual or potential disruptive effect of the speech? If the former, then the speech is protected, but if the latter, then it is not.

Although there is no clear formula for answering the first question, the cases that have been decided so far indicate that courts will view comments on the following topics as matters of public concern: the school curriculum and program, the safety and physical well-being of students, issues raised in collective bargaining, alleged corruption by school or other public officials, and issues that are already the subject of widespread public discussion.[23] In one case, the alleged lenient treatment by a school board of a teacher who had viewed pornography on a school computer was judged to be a matter of public concern.[24] Also viewed as matters of public concern are any remarks made in a court trial or at a public hearing regarding issues placed on the agenda by a public agency.[25] However, the Seventh Circuit has ruled that speech regarding the effects of a school policy on an employee personally will not be viewed as addressing a matter of public concern. So, a teacher who discussed class size only in defense of criticism about her classroom performance was deemed not to have spoken on a matter of public concern.[26] Similarly the Fifth

Circuit ruled that a principal did not speak on a matter of public concern in a memo regarding allegations of the misuse of a student activity fund, because the content, form, and context of the memo showed it was only an effort by the principal to clear his name rather than to contribute to a public dialogue.[27] Purely private communications on issues of no importance to the public may also not be protected. In one case, the court upheld the dismissal of a teacher who told some of her colleagues at work that she was bisexual and had a female lover, ruling that private communication of this kind was not protected speech.[28]

Regarding the second question, at least this much can be said: The more important the issue raised by the employee and the more significant the information supplied by the employee (i.e., the more valuable the speech), the more the courts seem willing to insist that some disruption be tolerated. However, the more vituperative and abusive the language used by the employee and the more personal the attack, the less disruption need be tolerated. Speech that urges colleagues to engage in unlawful disruptive activities such as illegal strikes is less likely to receive protection than is speech that discloses the content of confidential or private files or speech that contains significant errors or deliberate falsehoods. Even an honest statement of opinion can be disruptive enough to warrant dismissal as in the case of a teacher dismissed from a predominantly Black school after expressing hatred of Blacks.[29]

In *Montle v. Westwood Heights School District*,[30] the court ruled in favor of a school district that declined to renew the contract of a probationary teacher who wore a T-shirt bearing the initials of the teacher's union and the statement "Working Without a Contract" and who confronted other teachers who declined to wear the shirt. The court found that the teacher's actions including the wearing of the T-shirt "caused or could have caused disharmony in the workplace," a disruption that outweighed the minimal value of the T-shirt in providing information to the public. Similarly, the Sixth Circuit ruled that a letter a principal wrote to the school board in the context of a dispute over a school dress code was too disruptive and not sufficiently important to be protected. The letter did not illuminate the dress code issue for the public but rather concentrated primarily on the relationship among the principal, the board, and the superintendent.[31]

Melzer v. Board of Education of City of New York[32] concerned the firing of a teacher with over thirty years of exemplary service in a "highly selective, science-oriented high school." The dismissal occurred after it became generally known that Melzer, "a self-described pedophile," was an active member of the North American Man/Boy Love Association. The Association's "stated primary goal is to bring about a change in the attitudes and laws governing sexual activity between men and boys." The school's Parents' Association had threatened to conduct "sitdown strikes," "boycott" the school and remove their children if Melzer were allowed to continue teaching. The court ruled that although the subject of Melzer's speech activities on behalf of the Association was a matter of public concern, he could still be dismissed because public knowledge of his membership had caused disruption, and it was safe to predict that his continued presence would compromise the learning environment. Although the protesting parents were in one sense external to the school, the court nevertheless found that they were internal to the operation of the school because their cooperation was needed to make the school work.

On issues relating to their "official responsibilities," school employees deemed to work in policy-making positions (most administrators) may have less protection of freedom of speech than non-policy-making employees (teachers and nonprofessionals). The Seventh Circuit permitted the demotion and ultimate dismissal of a principal who, against the orders of her superiors, publicly criticized the district's reformulation of a grant proposal. The court found that, as a policy maker in the district, the principal owed her superiors a "duty of loyalty" on this subject even though it was a matter of public concern: "[T]he First Amendment does not prohibit the discharge of a policy-making employee when that individual has engaged in speech on a matter of public concern in a manner that is critical of superiors or their stated policies." The court did not view its ruling as inconsistent with *Pickering*; rather, it found that the potential for disruption was self-evident in cases when a policy maker publicly expresses disagreement with policies that her job requires her to enforce. The principal's remarks had in fact created tension between the teacher's union and school board.[33] The Second Circuit has ruled that "high level employees are entitled to limited *Pickering* protection" because generally "the likelihood of disruption will outweigh the employee's right to speak."[34]

School officials may not seek to stifle open criticism by teachers of school policies by requiring that genuine issues of public concern be pursued exclusively through "channels."[35] Nor may regulations of employee speech be unconstitutionally vague or overbroad (see sec. 4.1); for example, prohibitions against "criticism" of colleagues or superiors.[36] School officials should also be aware that forty states have enacted whistleblower statutes that protect teachers and other public employees who in good faith report a violation of law, government waste, or specific dangers to public health and safety from adverse employment actions.[37]

School employees who succeed in establishing that they have suffered an adverse employment decision and that they have engaged in protected speech still bear the burden of showing that the protected speech was a substantial factor in the adverse decision. It is not enough that the protected speech occurred sometime before the adverse decision; the employee must show that the decision was motivated by or in retaliation for the protected speech. In one case, a fired bilingual coordinator's criticism of her supervisors, which occurred more than a year prior, was judged too remote in time to permit an inference of retaliatory discharge. The court noted that the plaintiff's job performance had declined during the intervening year.[38] In *Cox v. Miller County R-I School District*[39] the plaintiff claimed his dismissal as a substitute bus driver was based on his vocal opposition to the school district's proposed tax increases, speech that was deemed to be protected. But the court rejected the claim that his speech was a substantial factor in his dismissal. The court noted that other bus drivers had also voiced opposition to the tax increase but were not dismissed, the plaintiff had actually been rehired following one of his complaints about the tax increase, and there were numerous parental complaints regarding the driver's job performance.

If a teacher-plaintiff succeeds in establishing that protected speech was a substantial motivating factor in an adverse employment decision, the burden of proof then switches to the school district to establish by a preponderance of evidence that the same decision would have been reached regardless of the teacher's speech. That is, school officials must establish that the administrative action occurred for some other reason, such as because of the teacher's incompetence. Thus, a teacher cannot be disciplined for engaging in protected speech, but a teacher cannot avoid discipline just by engaging in protected speech.[40] This points to the usefulness of an adequate set of contemporaneous records to accompany any adverse administrative action taken against a teacher or other employee.

7.2 ACADEMIC FREEDOM AND CURRICULAR SPEECH

Chapter 2 showed that the school retains the power to control its own curriculum even in the face of most parental and student objections. But what about teachers? Do they have the right to exercise any control over what they teach in their own classrooms, or does the school have absolute control?

The doctrine that teachers have the right to control their own curriculum and instructional methodology is known as "academic freedom." Although U.S. university professors customarily enjoy a high degree of academic freedom, public elementary and secondary teachers have a much more modest claim. Although many cases have been brought by teachers claiming academic freedom, no court has recognized the constitutional right of a teacher to control basic course content or instructional methodology.

In *Cary v. Board of Education of Adams-Arapahoe School District 28–J*,[41] the court ruled against teachers who claimed their First Amendment rights were violated when their school board removed ten books from a large list of books approved for use in elective junior- and senior-level literature classes. The board decreed that any teacher who assigned these books, gave credit for reading the books, had the books read aloud in class, or discussed the books at significant length could be dismissed. Although upholding this policy, the court noted that teachers do have "some rights to freedom of expression" in junior and senior classrooms. Teachers "cannot be made to simply read from a script prepared or approved by the board . . . Censorship or suppression of expression of opinion, even in the classroom, should be tolerated only when there is a legitimate interest of the state which can be said to require priority." At the same time, the court said it was legitimate for the curriculum of the school to "reflect the value system and educational emphasis which are the collective will of those whose children are being educated and who are paying the costs." If the board has the power to not offer a particular elective course as it surely does, said the court, it also has the authority to select the major texts of the courses it does offer. The case would have been different, the court continued, if the removal had represented a systematic effort to exclude a particular system of thought or philosophy. However, because the teachers did not claim they were prohibited from studying an entire representative group of writers, their position amounted to a desire "to be freed from the 'personal predilections' of the board," and this wish, the court concluded, had no constitutional basis.

Similarly, in *Millikan v. Board of Directors of Everett School District*,[42] the court found against teachers who wished to offer a team-taught social studies course of their own design instead of the "conventional" course approved by the board. The majority of students in the school, when offered a choice between the two courses, had opted for the conventional course. In deciding the case, the court noted that the course the teachers wished to offer differed significantly from the conventional course in content as well as instructional methodology (the proposed course centered around the use of "discovery techniques"—small group work, independent reading and writing, and inquiry). "Course content," said the court, "is manifestly a matter within the board's discretion." The court's position regarding instructional methods was less absolute: "[T]eachers should have some measure of freedom in teaching techniques employed." Nevertheless, after reviewing a variety of related cases, the court endorsed the principle that "a school district has authority to prescribe both course content and teaching methods." Moreover, the court concluded that if the unconventional teaching methods detract from the scope of a conventional history course, the teachers "may be compelled to abandon their own preferred techniques and to teach history in a more conventional manner."

These cases do not mean that in classroom situations the school can always put whatever words it chooses into a teacher's mouth. In one case, a federal appeals court protected a teacher's refusal to participate in a school-mandated flag salute. The court found that the teacher's refusal did not disrupt her tenth-grade class, in part because another teacher was in the room to lead the exercise.[43] However, if the refusal had been viewed as part of a pattern of depriving the students of access to the prescribed curriculum, the teacher would probably have lost.[44]

Although the case involved student speech, a number of courts have relied on the basic doctrine of *Hazelwood v. Kuhlmeier* (see sec. 3.3)—that school officials may control "school-sponsored expressive activities so long as their actions are reasonably related to legitimate pedagogical concerns"—to reject teacher claims of academic freedom. One court cited *Hazelwood* in ruling against a teacher who was disciplined for permitting students to put on a play depicting a dysfunctional family in which one child was lesbian and another pregnant out of wedlock.[45] Another cited both *Hazelwood* and *Pickering* in denying a teacher's right to select a class reading list without first obtaining prior approval.[46] The Eighth Circuit allowed the dismissal of a teacher who violated board policy by allowing her students to perform in class student-written plays that contained a great deal of profanity.[47] A state court permitted the reassignment of a science teacher who would not teach the theory of evolution without including a criticism of the theory, which was not part of the curriculum.[48]

In *Kingsville Independent School District v. Cooper*,[49] a nontenured high school teacher used a role-playing simulation to teach the history of the post-American Civil War Reconstruction period. The school decided not to renew her contract because the school received numerous complaints about the controversial nature of the simulation. The court held that "classroom discussions" including the simulation are protected speech, and the discharge "cannot be upheld unless the discussions clearly overbalance her usefulness as an instructor." Another court protected a teacher who had invited speakers into the class to discuss industrial hemp even though state law prohibited its possession.[50]

In *Mailloux v. Kiley*,[51] a high school teacher wrote the word "fuck" on the blackboard, asked a student what the word meant, and explained that the definition, "sexual intercourse," is not a taboo word in our culture, but the word on the blackboard is. The teacher did this "to illustrate that to some extent a society and its ways are illustrated by its taboo words." This discussion was to help explain the meaning of a book legitimately assigned to the students. The district court found that the case involved "the use of teaching methods which divide professional opinion." The court found that in such a case "the state may suspend or discharge the teacher for using that method but it may not resort to such drastic sanctions unless the state proves he was put on notice either by a regulation or otherwise that he should not use that method." The district court found that no such warning had been given and therefore ordered the defendants to reemploy the teacher.

Not all courts have been as protective of teachers' choices as *Cooper* and *Mailloux*. *Krizek v. Cicero-Stickney Township High School District No. 201*[52] concerned a nontenured teacher whose contract was not renewed because she showed an R-rated movie containing nudity, "vulgarity," and "sexually explicit scenes" to her high school English class. The court determined that the issue under consideration was one of reasonableness: Was it reasonable for the school to refuse to renew the teacher's contract because she showed the film? The court based its answer to this question on two factors:

> The first is whether the school could reasonably find the showing of the film offended "legitimate pedagogical concerns" . . . given the school's right to establish the contents of the curriculum. The second factor is the severity of the sanction . . . It is not reasonable to fire a teacher for any indiscretion; the indiscretion must be of significant enough importance to justify such a severe sanction.

Applying this analysis to the facts of the case, the court decided that it was reasonable for the school to conclude that the teacher's actions raised legitimate pedagogical concerns about her judgment that were serious enough to justify nonrenewal.

Teachers are vulnerable to dismissal when, against school policy, they deliberately refuse to obtain prior approval for supplementary materials.[53] Teachers may also be dismissed if they proselytize or conduct religious activities in their class[54] or use their classroom as a platform to instigate specific political action by their students.[55] One court allowed the dismissal of a teacher who alluded in class to a rumor that two students had engaged in sexual intercourse on campus.[56]

Some courts have relied on the Due Process Clause of the Fourteenth Amendment to protect teachers from dismissal for using materials or methods that they had not been informed in advance were forbidden. These rulings are in keeping with the general procedural due process principle that forbids punishment without prior notice that the behavior was prohibited. For example, in *Webb v. Lake Mills Community School District*,[57] the court ruled that the due process rights of a drama teacher had been violated when she was dismissed because there was drinking and profanity in the plays she produced. The court found that the rule the district said it relied on was "vague and generally unarticulated" and did not absolutely prohibit drinking scenes or vulgarity. As such, the teacher had not received proper notice that her actions were prohibited. However, the First Circuit has written,

> ... while we acknowledge a First Amendment right of public school teachers to know what conduct is proscribed, we do not hold that a school must expressly prohibit every imaginable inappropriate conduct by teachers. The relevant inquiry is: based on existing regulations, policies, discussions, and other forms of communication between school administration and teachers, was it reasonable for the school to expect the teacher to know that her conduct was prohibited?[58]

The academic freedom cases have all been lower court decisions. The Supreme Court itself has never held that the First Amendment establishes a right of academic freedom for public school teachers. If the current Supreme Court were to rule on this issue, it is likely that at most a very narrow and limited right to academic freedom would be affirmed. We can infer this result from the Court's decisions in *Hazelwood* and in *Rust v. Sullivan*,[59] permitting Congress to bar physicians receiving federal funds from discussing abortion with their patients. However, in *Garcetti v. Ceballos* (see sec. 7.1) the Supreme Court wrote that "expression related to academic scholarship or classroom instruction [may] implicate additional constitutional interests."

In-School, Noncurricular Speech

Schools have broad latitude to determine what and how their teachers will teach; however, does this mean that schools can control the content of everything that teachers say while they are at work or in the presence of students? Or do teachers have the right to express their personal views to colleagues and students, for example, by wearing an armband or button or distributing literature on their free time?

A majority of the courts that have considered these issues have recognized the existence of in-school, noncurricular speech not subject to the same level of control as curricular speech. In deciding disputes over teacher in-school, noncurricular speech, most cases have applied the approach first developed for use with students in *Tinker v. Des Moines* (see sec. 3.4): A teacher's speech is protected as long as it does not materially and substantially disrupt the school and its operations. Thus, in *Texas State Teachers Association v. Garland Independent School District*,[60] the court agreed with the plaintiffs that it was unconstitutional for the school to prohibit teachers from engaging in discussions concerning any teacher union or organization "on school premises during school hours, even though those discussions occur during lunch hour or other non-class time." It was also unconstitutional for the school to forbid teachers to use the school's intramural mail system to distribute union-related information because there was no general prohibition against using the system for personal messages nor any material and substantial disruption of the school. However, the court did note that it would be a violation of the Texas constitution's prohibition against giving public funds to a private organization if the district were to permit employees to engage in union promotional activities on a "release time" basis.

James v. Board of Education of Central District No. 1[61] differs from *Garland* in that the teacher's speech took place in the classroom. Like *Tinker*, the case concerned an individual, but this time a teacher, who wore a black armband in school to protest U.S. involvement in the Vietnam War. When James refused his administrator's order to remove the armband, he was suspended and eventually fired by the school board. The board justified its action by arguing that all teacher speech occurring during a class is curricular speech over which the school has broad control.

The court, however, took a different view. Although agreeing with the board's claim of control over the curriculum and with the principle that teachers cannot claim the right to substitute political proselytizing or indoctrination for carrying out their assigned duties, the court nevertheless found the firing unconstitutional. The court noted that there was no hint of disruption caused by James' actions nor any reason to expect disruption. Most importantly, wearing the armband did not in any way interfere with James' ability to carry out his teaching functions. For the firing to be justified, said the court, "school authorities must demonstrate a reasonable basis for concluding that the teacher's conduct threatens to impair their legitimate interests in regulating the school curriculum." However, James had made no attempt to proselytize his students and since the mature eleventh graders whom James taught understood that the armband was only a symbol of the teacher's personal views, the curriculum was not disrupted. Furthermore, the board had engaged in viewpoint discrimination because it had permitted another teacher to display a slogan supportive of U.S. foreign policy and, in firing James, had cast a "pall of orthodoxy" over the classroom in direct violation of the principles announced by the Supreme Court in *Tinker*.

In a case whose facts bear some similarities to *James*, the Ninth Circuit ruled against a teacher who was prohibited from posting materials on his school bulletin board in opposition to Gay and Lesbian Awareness Month. The school had posted materials promoting observance of the event, and it had permitted other teachers to post their own supporting materials in favor of the school's position. The court ruled that the school had not created a public forum because the principal retained control over the bulletin board (that is the crucial difference between this case and *James*). In permitting some materials and prohibiting others, the school was deciding what it wished to say and what it wished not to say. Citing *Hazelwood*, the court noted that the school is not required to be content-neutral with regard to speech that bears the "imprimatur" of the school.[62] The case might have been different if the teacher had been prohibited from expressing his opposing view in a forum that was not school controlled, for example, in an after-school conversation with other teachers.

7.3 PRIVACY, MORALITY, AND LIFESTYLE

There are two types of privacy issues that can lead to conflict between a school and its employees. The first type of issue arises when schools seek to control the personal lifestyle choices and behaviors of their employees. The second arises when schools seek to acquire information about their employees that the employees do not wish the schools to have.

Many states' statutes authorize dismissing a teacher for "immorality" or "unprofessional" conduct (see sec. 8.4). These somewhat vague categories seem to authorize firing for behavior and lifestyle choices that the community or school board deems wrong or unfitting for teachers. However, some personal choices, no matter how a community might view them, are protected by the derived constitutional right to privacy.[63] This does not mean that the Constitution provides teachers absolute immunity from discharge for lifestyle choices. It does mean, however, that if the right of privacy is implicated, the school must have an especially good reason for the dismissal.

There is no firm definition or rule to draw a distinction between protected and unprotected lifestyle choices. One court upheld a school's dress code requiring that male teachers wear ties to class. A teacher objected claiming he had a First Amendment free speech right and a liberty right under the Fourteenth Amendment to do his job without a tie. In support of his First Amendment claim, the teacher said that his refusal to wear a tie "made a statement on current affairs which assists him in his teaching." The court found this claim of symbolic speech to be vague and unfocused and that the teacher had other more effective means of communicating his social views to his students: "He could, for example, simply have told them his views on contemporary America; if he had done this in a temperate way, without interfering with his teaching duties, we would be confronted with a very different First Amendment case." Balancing the teacher's First Amendment claim against the board's interest "in promoting respect for authority and traditional values, as well as discipline in the classroom, by requiring teachers to dress in a professional manner," the court found that the dress code was a rational means to promote these goals.

Regarding the Fourteenth Amendment claim, the court concluded that the liberty interest not to wear a tie was not of great constitutional weight. "As public servants in a special position of trust, teachers may properly be subjected to many restrictions in their professional lives which would be invalid if generally applied." The court noted that the rule did not affect teachers' appearance when they were off duty.[64] Likewise, most courts will uphold dress regulations for teachers unless they are arbitrary and unreasonable. Thus, the dismissal of a teacher who refused to stop wearing short skirts to school was upheld.[65]

A minority of courts has recognized a teacher's hairstyle as a protected interest and permitted regulation only if necessary to avoid disruption of the school or advance some other compelling educational purpose.[66] In one such case, three teachers brought a successful suit on privacy and equal protection grounds against a school rule controlling male hair styles and prohibiting facial hair.[67] However, most courts have said that hairstyle and grooming regulations are permissible unless the teacher can establish that the requirements are not rationally related to a legitimate purpose of the school—a burden that teachers usually cannot meet.[68]

A series of Supreme Court opinions has established the principle that government policies affecting family, marriage, and procreation are impermissible unless necessary to the achievement of a compelling state interest. Based on this principle, the Court has rejected laws prohibiting the use of contraception, banning all abortions, and barring people with unmet child-support obligations from marrying.[69] In general, schools may regulate employee behavior in these areas only if regulation is necessary to achieve a very important educational purpose. In one case, a federal court concluded that a school district could not refuse to rehire a teacher because of her divorce: "[M]atters involving marriage and family relationships involve privacy rights that are constitutionally protected."[70]

There are, however, some situations in which school regulation of employee marital relationships is constitutionally permissible. In one case, a federal court backed a school district's decision not to rehire a teacher whose wife had assaulted him violently and burst into his classroom to threaten his life. The court denied that the right to marry gave the teacher a right "to engage in domestic altercations in the classroom of a public high school," especially "potentially explosive and dangerous" altercations.[71] Another court permitted a school district to transfer a teacher who married her assistant principal. The district had a policy prohibiting any employee supervising a near relative, and the court concluded that the policy served to preclude the "perception of favoritism on the part of other members of the teaching faculty."[72] In another case, the school district went even further when it did not renew a high school principal's contract because he married a teacher in his school. Despite the fact that the district's effort to avoid conflicts of interest and favoritism deeply affected the right to marry, the court ruled the policy did not offend the Constitution.[73]

What then is the constitutionality of dismissing a teacher for committing adultery? Some courts have rejected dismissal for adultery even in disapproving communities but generally not on constitutional grounds.[74] However, in *Hollenbaugh v. Carnegie Free Library*,[75] the Supreme Court refused to review a case that had sustained the dismissal of two library employees for living together in open adultery.[76] Notorious or open adultery, it appears, is simply not a constitutionally protected right. The courts have, however, protected unwed mothers from dismissal, rejecting claims that the teachers' presence in the classroom would serve as a bad role model and encourage sexual activity on the part of the students.[77]

The constitutionality of dismissing a teacher for homosexuality is not fully decided. One court ruled that the Constitution permitted dismissal of a teacher who revealed her homosexuality to other school employees;[78] however, another court found impermissibly overbroad a state statute that permitted dismissing a teacher for "advocating, soliciting, imposing, encouraging or promoting public or private homosexual activity that creates a substantial risk that such conduct will come to the attention of schoolchildren or school employees."[79] Several cases have upheld the constitutionality of dismissing teachers for engaging in homosexual acts in public or making homosexual advances to other adults at school.[80] However, a federal district court in Ohio ruled that firing a teacher simply for being gay violated the teacher's Fourteenth Amendment right to equal protection of the law.[81]

In the absence of controlling federal court rulings, we can only speculate about the constitutionality of dismissing a teacher for homosexual orientation or actually practicing gay sex in a nonpublic, nonnotorious way. Regarding homosexual orientation, we believe it is clear that such a dismissal would be unconstitutional. As shown in Section 7.1, the Constitution affords broad protection to people's beliefs, feelings, preferences, and desires. The issue of dismissal for actually practicing gay sex is a little less clear, but the Supreme Court's 2003 ruling that states may not classify homosexual sex as a crime[82] suggests that dismissal might also be impermissible. At minimum, the 2003 ruling eliminates the possibility of schools dismissing gay teachers on the grounds that they are poor role models because they committed a crime (see sec. 8.4).

A number of school district regulations limiting employee lifestyle choices have been challenged on constitutional grounds: The Fifth Circuit upheld a school policy prohibiting substantial outside employment during the school year, finding it reasonably related to the school's interest in ensuring that teachers devote their professional energies to the education of children.[83] The Supreme Court allowed a school district policy requiring their employees to live in the district.[84] Several courts have prohibited the dismissal of public-school classified employees for enrolling their children in private segregated schools.[85] Another court reached the opposite conclusion.[86]

The **Family and Medical Leave Act**[87] seeks "to balance the demands of the workplace with the needs of families; and to promote national interest in preserving family integrity." The Act "entitles employees to take reasonable leave for medical reasons, for the birth or adoption of a child, and for the care of a child, or parent, who has a serious health condition." The term "child" includes biological, adopted, and foster children, stepchildren, and legal wards. The Act applies to public school districts and private schools with fifty or more employees at any one site. Employees are covered once they have worked for at least a year, provided that they worked at least 1,250 hours during the year prior to the leave. Employees may take up to twelve weeks of unpaid leave within a twelve-month period. The employee may take the leave intermittently (e.g., a day or two at a time), or as a reduced work week. The leave arrangement has to be coordinated with the employer unless it is a "medical necessity." Teachers or others whose absence would disrupt the instructional program of the school are subject to special provisions. When a teacher requests a leave that is "foreseeable based on planned medical treatment" and when the teacher would be on leave for more than 20 percent of the total work days during an instructional period, the school may require that the leave be taken for a particular time period not to exceed the planned medical treatment or require the employee to temporarily transfer to an alternative position.

Investigation, Surveillance, and Searches of Employees

Schools may have a variety of reasons for seeking information about their employees. In order to protect their students and avoid liability for negligent hiring or retention (see sec. 10.5), schools may wish to inquire into the behavior of current and prospective employees, particularly with regard to criminality and sexual or other misconduct involving children. In order to assess their fitness for work, schools may want to learn about the mental or physical health of or the use of drugs by current or prospective employees (see sec. 7.6). To make sure that employees are not shirking their duties or engaging in misconduct, schools may want to use open or hidden electronic surveillance techniques or monitor employee use of e-mail or the Internet on the school's computer system. The need for investigation may be particularly strong with regard to employee behaviors that the school is legally obligated to try to prevent such as racial and sexual harassment (see sec. 7.4) or for which schools may be held legally liable such as copyright infringements (see sec. 2.6) and inadequate supervision of students (see sec. 10.4), or when there has been an allegation of wrongdoing.

Whatever the motivation, the collection and disclosure by schools of information about their employees raises a variety of legal issues. The Fourteenth Amendment's protection of personal privacy (discussed earlier in this section) prohibits schools from inquiring into areas of personal behavior like marriage and sex unless they have a compelling reason to do so. The need to protect students from employee misconduct can provide the necessary reason as in *Flaskamp v. Dearborn Public Schools*,[88] in which a federal court allowed a school district to inquire into the post-graduation relationship between a female teacher and one of her former pupils. To be constitutional, inquiries such as these, as one court ruled, must be justified by the legitimate interests of the school district and narrowly tailored to meet those legitimate interests and the use of the information must be proper in light of the school's interests.[89]

In cases involving either the collection of information or its disclosure to the public, courts must balance the privacy interests of the employee against the needs of the school and public.[90] In *O'Connor v. Pierson*,[91] the court found that a school board's insistence on receiving a teacher's medical records regarding substance abuse treatment could serve no legitimate purpose because the "board was not competent to independently evaluate those records." The court also noted that revealing private medical information without consent may also violate due process. In *Fleming v. State University of New York,*[92] the court found that a doctor's due process rights had been violated by the release to a prospective employer of the fact that the plaintiff suffered from sickle cell anemia. In reaching this conclusion the court noted that this was the kind of private information that could expose the plaintiff to intolerance and discrimination.

Daury v. Smith[93] concerned a school principal ordered to submit to a psychiatric examination as a condition of being rehired. The principal had been involved in physical altercations with other administrators and with a child, had been the subject of numerous parental complaints, and had admitted to suffering from stress. In finding that the required examination did not violate the principal's right to privacy, the court emphasized that the school board's action was aimed at ensuring the safety of the students and teachers within the school. "A school [board]," wrote the court, "may justifiably compel a teacher or administrator to submit to a psychiatric examination as a condition of continued employment if the [board] has reason to believe that the teacher or administrator may be jeopardizing the welfare of students under his or her supervision." The court also noted that the psychiatrist's report had not been made public and that the principal had been reinstated upon receiving a favorable report. However, the court went on to suggest that had the school board attempted to obtain personal information about the principal from the psychiatrist for reasons unrelated to the welfare of the students, the principal's privacy rights would have been violated. In addition to the constitutional limitations discussed in *Daury*, the Rehabilitation Act of 1973 and the Americans with Disabilities Act place statutory limitations on the authority of schools to order their applicants and employees to undergo medical and psychiatric examinations (see sec. 7.6) as do the statutes of some states.[94]

All states have **Open Records** laws requiring that records of public entities like school districts be open to public scrutiny subject to certain exceptions. When a school district receives a request for information under an Open Records law, the district must either comply or assert that a specific exemption prohibits it from disclosing the information. Records regarding an ongoing investigation of employee misconduct may be subject to an exception that covers preliminary drafts and recommendations as opposed to completed documents and decisions. Some personnel files may be covered by a "personal privacy" exception.

As noted in Section 7.1, the First Amendment's protection of the right of freedom of association has been interpreted by the Supreme Court to prohibit school boards from requiring teachers to disclose their associational ties and memberships.[95] Schools may not retaliate against teachers who refuse to say whether they are a member of a particular group. Employees may also invoke their Fifth Amendment right against self-incrimination in refusing to answer employers' questions that might lead to criminal prosecutions against them.[96] An older Supreme Court case suggests that the invocation of the Fifth Amendment may be treated by the employer as the basis of a dismissal for insubordination;[97] however, subsequent Supreme Court decisions, although not explicitly overruling this precedent, suggest that employers may not dismiss employees for invoking their Fifth Amendment rights.[98] But if a teacher has been granted immunity from criminal prosecution, a refusal to answer questions on matters of legitimate concern to the school may be treated as insubordination (see sec. 8.4).

Search and Seizure

The Fourth Amendment protects individuals from unreasonable searches and seizures by the government. *New Jersey v. T.L.O.* established the principle that public schools may only search students if they have reasonable suspicion that the search will reveal evidence of wrongdoing (see sec. 4.3). But does the same principle apply to teachers and other school employees?

Although it occurred in a hospital rather than a school, the case most relevant to this issue is *O'Connor v. Ortega*.[99] In that case, a doctor objected to his employer's search of his office in a public hospital. Although the case produced no majority opinion, only a nonprecedent-setting plurality opinion, a majority of the justices did agree that the Fourth Amendment's protection against unreasonable search and seizure does extend to public employees. The plurality opinion suggests that the Fourth Amendment applies only to areas where an employee has a reasonable expectation of privacy, a determination that must be made on a case-by-case basis. Employees do have reasonable expectations of privacy with regard to personal closed containers such as handbags, luggage, and briefcases as well as lockers, desks, filing cabinets, and computers owned by the employer but used exclusively by the employee. However, an employee's expectation of privacy regarding lockers, desks, filing cabinets, and computers "may be reduced by actual office practices and procedures, or by legitimate regulation." The more other employees and supervisors have access to these areas, the less the expectation of privacy. But the Second Circuit has ruled that an employee does not lose the expectancy of privacy in a computer supplied by the employer because of infrequent and selective searches for maintenance purposes or to retrieve needed documents, justified by the "special needs" of the employer to pursue legitimate work-related objectives.[100] Another Second Circuit case ruled that whatever reasonable expectation of privacy a teacher may have had in his classroom as teacher in good standing no longer applied after the teacher was suspended, barred from his classroom, made to surrender the key to the classroom's locked file, and given an opportunity to remove personal items prior to the search.[101]

Even if a public employee has a reasonable expectation of privacy, said the *Ortega* plurality, the employer may still conduct a search if the search is "reasonable":

> Ordinarily, a search of an employee's office by a supervisor will be "justified at its inception" when there are reasonable grounds for suspecting that the search will turn up evidence that the employee is guilty of work-related misconduct, or that the search is necessary for a noninvestigatory work-related purpose such as to retrieve a needed file . . . The search will be permissible in its scope when "the measures adopted are reasonably related to the objectives of the search and not excessively intrusive in light of . . . the nature of the [misconduct]."

The plurality and concurring opinion in *Ortega* indicate that the majority of the Court would accept reasonable intrusions into a protected area for routine work-related purposes such as to hunt for needed supplies or to uncover evidence of work-related malfeasance. One case found that a state agency had reasonable grounds to search an employee's computer based on an anonymous tip that the employee spent the majority of his time at work on activities unrelated to the agency's work. The search revealed that the employee was carrying on a tax preparation service at work.[102]

Because *Ortega* occurred in a nonschool setting and because the case produced no majority opinion, it does not fully settle the application of the Fourth Amendment to educators. Nevertheless, it does seem clear that school employees have reasonable expectations of privacy in their handbags, briefcases, and other personal packages brought to school. To the extent that desks, filing cabinets, storage areas, and lockers are shared with other employees, no reasonable expectation of privacy would exist. Where an expectation of privacy does exist, the requirements of the Fourth Amendment apply so a search may only be conducted in accordance with the "reasonable grounds" test quoted previously.

School examination of employee e-mail sent or received on the school's computer system raises a number of legal issues, most not fully decided. Messages sent to or from a general school account as opposed to a personal, password-protected account may be deemed in "plain view" and therefore not entitled to Fourth Amendment protection, as may messages disseminated to a wide audience or chat room. Messages sent to a supervisor have been voluntarily disclosed so they also receive no Fourth Amendment protection.[103] Messages between individuals sent from or to an employee's personal account should be treated like telephone messages; schools can examine them only if the *Ortega* criteria are met.[104] It is probably not permissible for a school to require employees to waive Fourth Amendment rights if they wish to have access to their school's e-mail or computer system.[105] The federal statute known as the Electronic Communications Privacy Act of 1986 (ECPA)[106] generally prohibits the interception of messages sent by telephone or e-mail.[107]

The use of **electronic surveillance** also raises both Fourth Amendment and statutory issues. In one case, a school placed a hidden camera in a "break" room to determine if the custodians were slacking off. The court ruled there was no Fourth Amendment violation because the custodians did not have a reasonable expectation of privacy in a break room available to all. The court also said that even if the Fourth Amendment did apply, the search was reasonable because the school had evidence that the custodians were slacking during the hours when the cameras were in operation.[108] In another case, a custodian caught by a hidden camera stealing money from an envelope in a classroom argued unsuccessfully that the hidden camera violated his Fourth Amendment rights; the court ruled he had no reasonable expectancy of privacy in the classroom even at 5 a.m.[109] Employees have a legitimate expectation of privacy in private restrooms or private areas of public restrooms.[110] Devices that record sound are covered by ECPA, but when visibly placed in work areas, they do not violate the statute.

Drug testing of employees is a search for Fourth Amendment purposes. If school officials have reasonable grounds to suspect that an employee is intoxicated or possesses drugs or alcohol at school, required testing does not violate the Fourth Amendment. Thus, the Eleventh Circuit upheld the testing of a teacher after drug-sniffing dogs detected drugs in the teacher's car and a subsequent search of the car revealed marijuana in the ashtray.[111] Random drug testing of employees in the absence of individualized suspicion raises a much more difficult issue. In *Independent School District No. 1 of Tulsa County v. Logan*,[112] the court found that requiring school bus drivers to undergo annual "toxicological urinalysis" was not

> unreasonable under the fourth amendment . . . [T]he school district has a sufficient safety interest in maintaining a pool of bus drivers free from the effects of drug use to require drug screening as part of the annual physical examination without a particularized suspicion of drug use directed at any one individual employee. . . .[113]

The same reasoning might justify random testing of shop or driver education teachers, but do most teachers occupy "safety-sensitive" positions? The highest state court of New York concluded that a school district's mandatory drug testing of all probationary teachers was an impermissible infringement of their Fourth Amendment rights.[114] But after deciding that teaching is a safety-sensitive occupation with a diminished expectation of privacy, the Sixth Circuit upheld a school's program of random drug testing of teachers.[115] And the Fifth Circuit upheld a school's mandatory drug-testing requirement for custodians.[116]

The federal **Drug-Free Schools and Communities Act** Amendments of 1989[117] require that schools receiving federal assistance establish programs for both employees and students designed to prevent drug and alcohol abuse. Schools must annually distribute written materials specifying that it is unlawful to possess or distribute illicit drugs and alcohol, describing the legal sanctions for violation of the law, explaining the health risks associated with drugs and alcohol, listing available counseling programs, and warning that the school will impose its own sanctions for possession and use. The statute does not require districts to institute drug testing, but it does require enforcement of sanctions against those employees and students who violate drug and alcohol rules.

7.4 RACE, ETHNICITY, GENDER, SEXUAL ORIENTATION, AND SEXUAL IDENTITY

Adverse employment decisions may lead to claims of discrimination based on race, ethnicity, alienage, gender, sexual orientation, sexual identity (transgenderism), religion (see sec. 7.5), disability (see sec. 7.6), or age (see sec. 7.7). Plaintiffs may challenge an allegedly inequitable salary or benefit structure or an adverse decision regarding hiring, promotion, transfer, demotion, or dismissal. Most of these legal challenges are based on federal statutes, which are the primary focus of this section.

There are, however, some cases in which employees base their claims on the Equal Protection Clause. In *Chang v. Glynn County School District*,[118] the teacher-plaintiffs successfully relied on the Equal Protection Clause to block a school district from firing them based on a state statute prohibiting schools from employing "any alien for any purpose until a thorough investigation has been made and it is ascertained that there is no qualified American citizen available to perform the duty desired." In a Montana case, an unmarried same-sex couple successfully argued that the denial to them of fringe benefits provided to unmarried heterosexual couples violated the Equal Protection Clause of the state's constitution.[119] Another court refused to dismiss a transsexual's claim of denial of equal protection after an offer of employment was withdrawn because he was planning to undergo a sex change operation.[120] Some older cases have rejected claims that firing teachers who underwent sex change operations violated due process or privacy rights,[121] but given the Supreme Court's more recent protection of the privacy rights of gays and lesbians these decisions may no longer be sound precedent: "Liberty presumes an autonomy of self that includes freedom of thought, belief, expression, and certain intimate conduct."[122]

In *Schroeder v. Hamilton School District*,[123] a gay teacher was not successful in an equal-protection-based claim that the school district discriminated against him on the basis of his sexual orientation by not taking sufficient steps to stop a campaign of harassment brought against him by students, parents, and staff members. For five years the teacher endured taunts, slurs, libelous comments, harassing phone calls, and having his tired slashed, culminating in a mental breakdown and resignation from his teaching position. The teacher's equal protection argument was that the district failed to address his complaints about harassment in the same manner as it handled complaints of harassment of students based on race or gender. In evaluating this claim, the court relied on the rational-basis equal-protection test because differential treatment based on sexual orientation does not trigger strict scrutiny (see sec. 5.9). The court found that the higher priority placed on stopping other forms of harassment was rational: "[I]t is not irrational for school administrators to devote more time and effort to defusing racial tensions among many students than to preventing harassment of one homosexual teacher." The court noted that the teacher had not been treated differently from heterosexual teachers and that the district had taken some steps to address the harassment such as punishing students who used the term "faggot." This showed that the school had not been "deliberately indifferent" to the harassment, which the court said was all that was necessary to defeat the equal protection claim. (Note that, as discussed later in this section, the plaintiff was unable to base his case of discrimination based on sexual orientation on Title VII of the Civil Rights Act of 1964.)

Title VII of the Civil Rights Act of 1964 forbids discrimination in public and private employment on the basis of race, gender, color, religion, or national origin.[124] The **Civil Rights Act of 1991** supplements Title VII with additional antidiscrimination requirements.[125] **Title IX of the Education Amendments of 1972** also prohibits gender discrimination in employment in schools receiving federal financial assistance.[126] The **Pregnancy Discrimination Act of 1978**[127] prohibits employers from discriminating on the basis of pregnancy and specifies that Title VII's prohibition of discrimination on the basis of gender includes discrimination on the basis of "pregnancy, childbirth, or related medical conditions."[128]

The federal agency charged with enforcing federal laws prohibiting discrimination in employment is the **Equal Employment Opportunity Commission (EEOC)**. Employment discrimination complaints must be filed first with the EEOC or a related state fair-employment agency. If the EEOC ultimately fails to act or chooses not to take legal action, the employee may then go to court with a private suit.

Title VII states:

> It shall be an unlawful employment practice for an employer—(1) to fail or refuse to hire or to discharge any individual, or otherwise to discriminate against any individual with respect to his compensation, terms, conditions, or privileges of employment, because of such individual's race, color, religion, sex, or national origin. . . .[129]

There is disagreement as to whether Title VII prohibits discrimination on the basis of sexual orientation; most federal courts that have considered the issue hold that it does not.[130] Thus, in most jurisdictions it is not a Title VII violation to deny employment benefits to unmarried homosexual couples that are provided to unmarried heterosexual couples or, as two courts have said, to provide benefits to unmarried homosexual but not heterosexual couples.[131] (Note that some states have statutes that prohibit discrimination based on sexual orientation.) Discrimination based on failure to conform to a sex stereotype, whether in appearance or behavior, is covered by Title VII.[132]

Some courts have also ruled that Title VII protects transsexuals against discrimination either on the basis of gender nonconforming conduct or because of self-identification as a transsexual.[133] Yet most courts have ruled that Title VII does not prohibit discrimination based on transsexualism.[134] Not surprisingly these rulings have led to the conclusion that Title VII is not violated when a transgendered individual is denied the use of the restroom of the gender with which the individual identifies.[135] But the reasoning in these cases denying protection to transsexuals may be inconsistent with the Supreme Court's decision in *Price Waterhouse v. Hopkins*[136] extending Title VII protection to people who do not conform to a sexual stereotype.[137] Influenced by *Price Waterhouse*, a federal district court ruled that Title VII was violated when a biological woman with male genitalia was required to use the male restroom. The basis of the discrimination was that she failed to conform to the employer's (stereotypical) expectations regarding a woman's anatomy. The court also interpreted Title IX to extend the same protection.[138] On a related issue, the Eighth Circuit ruled that a school district's policy of allowing a transgendered male to use the woman's restroom did not create a hostile work environment (see discussion of sexual harassment later in this section). (Note that California, Minnesota, Rhode Island, and New Mexico have state laws prohibiting gender-identity discrimination.)

The outline that follows lists the major categories of cases—whether based on race, color, religion, sex, or national origin—that may be brought under Title VII. The subsections that follow the outline explain each category or case, including how the law allocates the burden of proof between the employee and employer and the kind of evidence each may be asked to produce.

    I. Disparate treatment of an individual
        A.   overt
            1.   bona fide occupational qualification
            2.   affirmative action
        B.   covert or hidden motive
        C.   mixed motive
   II. Pattern or practice
        A.   disparate treatment
        B.   disparate impact
  III. Sexual and racial harassment
        A.   quid pro quo
        B.   hostile environment

Disparate Treatment of an Individual (DTI)

The hallmark of DTI cases is that the employer acted with an intent to discriminate on the basis of race or gender.[139] DTI cases may involve either overt or covert discrimination. The Civil Rights Act of 1991 amends Title VII by allowing DTI plaintiffs to seek not only reversal of the discriminatory decision, costs, and attorney fees but also compensatory damages and to demand a jury trial.[140]

In **overt DTI** cases, the employer openly bases a difference in treatment on race or gender. A school might insist, for example, that a coach for girls' sports be female and thus, refuse to hire an otherwise qualified male. In cases like these, there is no need for the complaining party to establish that gender or race was a criterion in the employment decision because it is admitted. The crucial issue is whether the school has an adequate reason for using the criterion.

Title VII explicitly permits gender to be the basis of a hiring decision when gender is a **bona fide occupational qualification (BFOQ)**. Race can never be a BFOQ. The Supreme Court has said that the BFOQ exception is to be strictly limited to cases where an employee of a specific gender is "reasonably necessary to the normal operation of a particular business or enterprise."[141] In a case rejecting the exclusion of women from telephone line repair, the court said that the central question was whether the employer "had a factual basis for believing that all or substantially all women would be unable to perform safely and efficiently the duties of the job involved."[142] In another case, the court held that gender could be a criterion in the hiring of a night security officer at a university because rape victims would be more comfortable reporting an attack to a female counselor.[143] Analogous reasoning might justify same-sex counselors at a school birth control clinic. A few other school jobs such as positions requiring supervision of a locker room or lavatory might also have gender as a BFOQ.

Another important exception to the prohibition against discrimination on the basis of sex is that Title VII permits employers to impose different appearance and dress standards on men and women.[144] Sex-differentiated appearance regulations like different hair length requirements for men and women must not significantly deprive either sex of employment opportunities, and the employer must evenhandedly apply the policy to employees of both sexes.[145] Any unequal burden on one of the sexes must be justified as a BFOQ.[146] In *Barnes v. City of Cincinnati*,[147] a police officer was denied promotion because of his feminine appearance—he "had a French manicure, had arched eyebrows and came to work with makeup or lipstick on his face on some occasions." Under the *Price Waterhouse* doctrine, the Sixth Circuit extended Title VII protection to the officer, a male-to-female transsexual who lived as a male while on duty but often lived as a woman while off-duty. The court found that the employer violated Title VII by denying promotion to the plaintiff based on his failure to conform to a sex stereotype. If a school were to bar a male teacher from wearing make-up or women's clothes, presumably the school would have to establish that the prohibition was a BFOQ.

Another type of overt DTI case challenges the use of an **affirmative action** program. Affirmative action programs seek to remedy past discrimination by giving preference to a particular gender or race. Objections to an affirmative action employment program may be brought under Title VII or the Equal Protection Clause. In *McDonnell Douglas Corp. v. Green*,[148] the Supreme Court fashioned the following three-step framework for dealing with cases brought under Title VII:

1. The complainant . . . must carry the initial burden under the statute of establishing a prima facie case [proof that will suffice unless refuted by other evidence] of racial discrimination. This may be done by showing (i) that he belongs to a [protected class]; (ii) that he applied and was qualified for a job for which the employer is seeking applicants; (iii) that, despite his qualifications, he was rejected; and (iv) that, after his rejection, the position remained open and the employer continued to seek applications from persons of complainant's qualifications. . . .
2. The burden then must shift to the employer to articulate some legitimate, nondiscriminatory reason for the employee's rejection.
3. Once the employer has offered its explanation, the employee must show that the defense is pretextual for intentional wrongful discrimination.

In *Johnson v. Transportation Agency, Santa Clara County*,[149] the male plaintiff complained that he was more qualified than the female who was promoted and that he was denied the promotion because he was male. However, the Supreme Court upheld the affirmative action plan adopted by the Transportation Agency in order to increase the number of women employed as "skill craft workers." The Court agreed that there existed a "manifest imbalance" that reflected underrepresentation of women in a job category that was "traditionally segregated." The Court also noted that gender was but one factor in the hiring decision, that the plan was temporary, and that there were no quotas.

Wygant v. Jackson Board of Education[150] was an affirmative action case brought at about the same time as *Johnson*, but was based on the Equal Protection Clause rather than Title VII. In *Wygant*, a school district faced with the need to decrease the size of its staff had retained recently hired minority teachers while laying off more senior White teachers. Preference for job retention was given solely on the basis of race with no consideration of other criteria such as merit. The lower courts had approved the district's actions as a reasonable way to promote the legitimate goal of providing role models for minority pupils, but the Supreme Court reversed the decision. The Court noted that the standard of "reasonableness" applied by the lower courts was not the correct test for deciding this case. Rather, a race-based affirmative action plan, like any classification based on race, must be subjected to strict scrutiny. To pass constitutional muster, racial classification "must be justified by a compelling governmental interest" and "narrowly tailored to the achievement of that goal." (See chap. 5.)

Applying this standard to the facts in *Wygant*, the Supreme Court could find no compelling governmental interest to justify the affirmative action plan. Schools do not have a compelling interest in ensuring that the racial makeup of the staff is similar to that of the student body. If they did, an all-White school would be justified in rejecting Black teaching applicants solely on the basis of race. If a school has an obligation to remedy past discrimination in hiring, an affirmative action plan that favored the formerly disadvantaged race might pass strict scrutiny, but that was not the case in *Wygant*. Furthermore, the Court indicated that it would be more likely to accept an affirmative action plan related to hiring than one giving preferential treatment in lay-offs. In the former case, the "burden . . . is diffused to a considerable extent on society generally," while in the latter it is borne by specific "innocent individuals."

The reasoning in *Wygant* suggests that if the *Johnson* case had been brought under the Equal Protection Clause instead of Title VII, the result would have been reversed. This makes no legal sense because a statute cannot authorize a government action that is impermissible under the Constitution. The Supreme Court clarified the situation somewhat in *Richmond v. J. A. Croson Co.*[151] by ruling that public employer affirmative action plans are constitutionally permissible only when: (a) undertaken to correct identifiable past racial discrimination by the very employer adopting the plan (not to redress the effects of past societal racial discrimination), (b) necessary to correct the past discrimination because racially neutral policies will not work, and (c) narrowly tailored to correct the past discrimination without aiding people who have not been discriminated against or unnecessarily harming innocent people.

The Third Circuit applied these criteria to a Title VII case in ruling against a school district that, in response to a financial crisis, used race as the criterion for laying off a White teacher instead of a Black teacher with equal seniority. The court rejected the district's affirmative action plan because it was not designed to remedy past discrimination but rather as a way to achieve a desired level of faculty diversity, it was not sufficiently limited in time or scope, and the harm imposed on the innocent White teacher was substantial.[152] Although the case was never heard by the Supreme Court because the parties agreed to settle, we believe that the Court would have agreed with the Third Circuit that public employer affirmative action plans are permissible under Title VII only if they meet the *Richmond* criteria. In any case, public school affirmative action plans must comply with the *Richmond* criteria in order not to violate the Equal Protection Clause.

School affirmative action plans designed to achieve desired diversity in the teaching staff or to rectify a long history of racial discrimination in society in general now appear to be unconstitutional; however, affirmative action plans may be permissible in school districts that have been guilty of racial discrimination in their employment practices in the past. Affirmative action plans that include race-based transfers of teachers among schools may also be used as one element of a court-ordered desegregation plan; however, once desegregation has been achieved and the district declared "unitary" by a court, a school district may not continue to make employment decisions on the basis of race (see sec. 5.4).[153]

In affirmative action and other overt DTI cases, plaintiffs do not have to prove that employment decisions were based on race because it is admitted. In **covert or hidden motive DTI** cases, plaintiffs allege that considerations of race or gender affected hiring, firing, promotion, pay, or other employment decisions but there is no direct proof. Plaintiffs bear the burden of convincing the court that the employer intended to discriminate. The determination is made by using the three-part *McDonnell Douglas* framework introduced earlier. Plaintiffs bear the initial burden of making a prima facie case of discriminatory intent. Plaintiffs need only show that they suffered **an adverse employment decision**. Adverse employment decisions include rejection for a position for which one is qualified (but not necessarily as qualified as the person hired);[154] transfer to a job that a reasonable person would find less desirable (not merely a job that one personally feels is less desirable); or loss of job benefits or privileges. Even an unfavorable letter of reference can be an adverse employment decision.[155]

If the plaintiff succeeds, then the employer may attempt to refute the prima facie case by offering a **nondiscriminatory reason** for the decision. The employer need not persuade the court that it was actually motivated by the proffered reason but need only raise a genuine question regarding what motivated the action.[156]

If the employer does so, then the plaintiff may attempt to show that the employer's reason was a **pretext** to justify intentional discrimination. In 1993, the Supreme Court explained the application of the framework to covert DTI cases as follows:

> Assuming then that the employer has met its burden of producing a nondiscriminatory reason for its actions, the focus of proceedings . . . will be on whether the jury could infer discrimination from the combination of (1) the plaintiff's prima facie case; (2) any evidence the plaintiff presents to attack the employer's proffered explanation for its actions; and (3) any further evidence of discrimination that may be available to the plaintiff (such as independent evidence of discriminatory statements or attitudes on the part of the employer) or any contrary evidence that may be available to the employer (such as evidence of a strong track record in equal opportunity employment).[157]

The most common method of proving pretext is to show that similarly situated persons of a different race or gender than the plaintiff received more favorable treatment (e.g., if a school district dismissed a Black employee for improperly using sick leave but did not discipline a White employee guilty of similar conduct[158]). Pretext may also be established if the proffered reason is simply false (e.g., if a school district lays off a Hispanic teacher, claiming a budget short-fall that does not in fact exist[159]). A showing that the employer's reasons are pretextual is usually, but not always, sufficient to support a finding of discrimination depending on the overall strength of the plaintiff's case.[160]

In *Ridler v. Olivia Public School System No. 653*,[161] a male applicant turned down for a job as a school cook brought a sex discrimination suit against the school. Ridler made his prima facie case by showing that he was a member of a protected class (gender) and that he had sought the job, that he was trained as a cook and had had several jobs as a cook (including related large-scale cooking in the National Guard), that despite his qualifications he was not interviewed for the job (in fact none of the male applicants was interviewed), and that the job was offered to a woman. The woman who was ultimately hired had no formal training in cooking, and her experience was limited to substitute work at the school and volunteer work at her church. The school offered as its nondiscriminatory reason that it had chosen the woman based on considerations of previous experience as a cook (especially for a large number of people), previous employment in the school district, and the applicants' work record and dependability. The school claimed that in light of these criteria the male applicants were less qualified.

Ridler, however, was able to establish that this explanation was a pretext for intentional discrimination. The record showed that the district had never hired a male cook and that generally several other job categories in the district were segregated by sex. The head cook referred to a position in the kitchen as "sandwich girl." The requirement that candidates have experience in the district had an illegitimate discriminatory effect because the school had never hired a male cook and, in any case, was an "after-the-fact" rationalization: The application form did not request information regarding this criterion, one interviewed applicant had no substitute cooking experience with the school, and the district did not interview another applicant who did have such experience. Furthermore, the district had acted inconsistently regarding the work-record criterion: Ridler was not interviewed despite his work in the National Guard, but a female candidate with no work record outside the home was interviewed. The district also applied the reliability criterion inconsistently when it interviewed a female applicant with a record of job stability no better than Ridler's. So, the court found that the school had discriminated against Ridler on the basis of gender in violation of Title VII and awarded him damages and attorney fees.

Plaintiffs can cite many factors as evidence of intent to discriminate: (a) inconsistent application of employment criteria (e.g., asking women about family responsibilities but not men), (b) exclusive use of subjective criteria, (c) selective judgments made by evaluators of all one race or sex, (d) lack of objective proof that evidence was collected to support subjective judgments, (e) ad hoc tailoring of criteria in order to predetermine the outcome of a personnel decision, (f) establishment of job criteria that are not truly necessary job requirements, (g) proof that the plaintiff was objectively better qualified than the person selected, and (h) statistical evidence of a pattern in similar decisions.

This does not mean that Title VII requires an employer to hire or promote the objectively most qualified employee. Subjective criteria may enter into the decision-making process as long as they are legitimate, nondiscriminatory judgments related to the requirements of the job.[162] A school board is not restricted to hiring the candidates with the highest grades in college or the highest scores on a teacher's exam.

Title VII specifically forbids discrimination against employees because of opposition to practices made unlawful by Title VII, because the employee filed a suit charging the employer with discrimination, or because the employee participated in an investigation or proceeding dealing with employer discrimination. In *Crawford v. Metropolitan Government of Nashville and Davidson County*,[163] the Supreme Court ruled that protection against retaliation extended to an employee who did not speak out against harassment on her own initiative but answered questions posed to her during an employer's internal investigation of another employee. The Supreme Court has also ruled that the prohibition against retaliation even extends to former employees. In *Robinson v. Shell Oil Company*,[164] after the plaintiff had been fired he filed charges with the EEOC under Title VII. While those charges were pending he sought another job, and the prospective employer contacted the first employer for a reference. The plaintiff then filed suit claiming he got a negative reference for having filed his original charge with the EEOC. The Supreme Court ruled that even if the alleged retaliation of the negative reference took place after he was no longer an employee, Title VII still protected him. In **retaliatory discharge** cases, the plaintiff asserts that an adverse employment decision was made because the plaintiff asserted legal claims under Title VII. A modified version of the *McDonnell Douglas* framework is used in these cases. To make the prima facie case, plaintiffs must prove that they were engaged in a protected activity such as asserting rights under Title VII, they suffered adversely for it, and there was a causal link between the protected activity and the employment decision.[165] Plaintiffs may also rely on a federal statute known as Section 1981 to object to retaliation for asserting racial non-discrimination rights.[166]

In **mixed motive DTI** cases, the plaintiff establishes that an employment decision was made partially because of a discriminatory reason. For example, a school may have had a preference for a male science teacher, but the female plaintiff may also have been less qualified or experienced than the successful male applicant. According to the Civil Rights Act of 1991, "an unlawful employment practice is established when the complaining party demonstrates that race, color, religion, sex, or national origin was a motivating factor for any employment practice, even though other factors also motivated the practice." The demonstration may be by direct or circumstantial evidence,[167] but the evidence (e.g., derogatory racial comments) must be proven to be related to the challenged decision.[168] When the employer is able to demonstrate that the same action would have been taken in the absence of the impermissible motivating factor, the court may not order reversal of the challenged decision, only cessation of the impermissible practice and attorney fees.

Pattern or Practice (PP)

In PP cases, either the federal government brings a civil suit charging an employer with a pattern of discrimination against a particular race or gender or other protected group, or members of a protected group initiate a class action suit based on similar allegations. The alleged discrimination may consist of systematic **disparate treatment** of members of the group or of the use of policies that have a **disparate impact** on the group. PP cases are evaluated using the *McDonnell Douglas* framework. In disparate treatment PP cases, the plaintiff's prima facie case is usually based on statistics. For example, in a case alleging discrimination against Blacks in a school district's hiring policy, the plaintiff had to show "a statistically significant discrepancy between the racial composition of the teaching staff and the racial composition of the qualified public school teacher population in the relevant labor market."[169] In a case charging a pattern of discrimination in promotions and salary, the plaintiff had to show that with all other variables—such as credentials and experience—held constant, the salary differences between men and women could only be explained by gender discrimination.[170]

Disparate impact cases "involve employment practices that are facially neutral in their treatment of different groups but that in fact fall more harshly on one group than another and cannot be justified by business necessity."[171] For example, a racial or ethnic group might challenge the use of tests for hiring teachers that exclude a disproportionate number of minority candidates. Foreign-born candidates might challenge a preference for hiring teachers who speak unaccented English or who obtained their credentials in the United States. A woman might object to the practice—still found in some school districts—of seeking superintendents with nonworking spouses. (However, rules prohibiting the hiring of spouses of employees are permissible even if they have a disparate impact on one gender.[172]) The use of a selection committee disproportionately comprised of one race or gender might also lead to a disparate impact claim especially if the selection criteria are primarily subjective.[173] In disparate impact cases, unlike disparate treatment cases, intent to discriminate need not be proved. Disparate impact cases may not be brought under the Equal Protection Clause because the Supreme Court has said that disparate impact is not per se unconstitutional.[174]

According to Title VII, to make a prima facie disparate impact case, the plaintiff must establish that the employer uses a particular employment practice that causes a disparate impact on a protected group, for example, a preemployment test that "selects applicants for hire or promotion in a racial [or gender] pattern significantly different from that of the pool of applicants."[175] What counts as a significant difference is a matter of some controversy, but plaintiffs must demonstrate—often with statistics—a real difference that would have been unlikely to occur by chance. Once the prima facie case has been made, the employer may defend itself by showing that the challenged practice is "job related for the position in question and consistent with business necessity."[176] Although the precise meaning of this phrase is not clear, a plausible interpretation is that the challenged practice must have a significant, not just trivial, relation to the job. For example, an employer might argue for the validity of a strength test in a job requiring the loading of heavy packages by hand even though the test excluded most female candidates.

The third and final stage in disparate impact cases affords the plaintiff the opportunity to prevail by establishing pretext. The plaintiff must convince the court that the challenged practice unnecessarily disadvantages the protected group because it does not in fact aid the employer's business in any significant way. This can be done by showing that the challenged practice does not select the employees best able to serve the employer's legitimate (nondiscriminatory) business purposes, or by demonstrating the availability of other not excessively costly tests or selection devices that would serve the employer's legitimate interests equally well without the disparate impact and that the employer refuses to adopt.[177]

Disparate impact has been the basis of several cases challenging standardized testing of teachers for purposes of initial certification or job retention. Plaintiffs have often prevailed in these cases because either the test was misused or the test itself or the cut-off score was not properly validated.[178] However, in *United States v. South Carolina*,[179] the court upheld the use of the National Teacher's exam to certify teachers and set teacher pay scales.

Gender discrimination in compensation is illegal both under Title VII and under another federal statute, the **Equal Pay Act**.[180] This law is violated when unequal wages are paid to men and women for "equal work on jobs the performance of which requires equal skill, effort, and responsibility and which are performed under similar working conditions." A difference in pay, however, can be justified by four defenses: a seniority system, a merit pay system, a system that measures pay by quality and quantity of production, or any other factor not based on sex. The most common equal-pay issue in education is paying male and female coaches different salaries. Resolution depends on actual job content, not job descriptions, regarding such matters as amount of time worked.[181] Fringe benefits such as health and pension plans must also be provided on a nondiscriminatory basis.[182] The Supreme Court has ruled that employees have 180 days to file a complaint of gender wage discrimination with the Equal Employment Opportunity Commission from the time the discriminatory pay-setting decision is made. If they fail to do so, subsequent payments of discriminatory wages cannot be the basis of an EEOC complaint or lawsuit.[183]

Sexual and Racial Harassment

The regulations implementing Title VII define sexual harassment as follows:

> Unwelcome sexual advances, requests for sexual favors and other verbal or physical conduct of a sexual nature constitute sexual harassment when (1) submission to such conduct is made either explicitly or implicitly a term or condition of an individual's employment, (2) submission to or rejection of such conduct by an individual is used as the basis for employment decisions affecting such individual, or (3) such conduct has the purpose or effect of unreasonably interfering with an individual's work performance or creating an intimidating, hostile, or offensive working environment.[184]

As the regulations indicate, only behaviors of a sexual nature can constitute sexual harassment. The creation of a generally unpleasant or offensive work atmosphere or nonsexual practical jokes played on all faculty members regardless of gender would not violate Title

VII.[185] In order for behavior to constitute sexual harassment, it must be unwelcome. The harassed person must not have solicited the behavior and must have communicated to the harasser that the behavior was not desired. Either direct confrontation of the harasser or a persistent failure to respond to advances may be sufficient to communicate unwelcomeness.[186] That a person may have welcomed some sexual advances or conduct does not mean that all such behaviors are welcome. However, some courts do not view a supervisor's retaliation against an employee who terminates a consensual sexual relationship as sexual harassment.[187]

Behavior by a member of the same sex is covered by Title VII as long as it fits the definition of harassment.[188] So is harassment that is based on the victim's failure to conform to a sex stereotype;[189] for example, if a man is seen as effeminate by coworkers. Yet, as noted earlier, some courts do not view harassment based on sexual orientation as covered by Title VII. Thus, the issue in some cases is whether the harasser actually knew the sexual orientation of the victim. The same act may be impermissible under Title VII if motivated by sex stereotyping but not prohibited if based on sexual orientation.[190]

There are two different forms of sexual harassment. In **quid-pro-quo harassment**, an employee is asked to exchange sex for job benefits, continued employment, or promotion. Most courts require a showing of denial or loss of a tangible employment benefit as part of a prima facie case of quid-pro-quo harassment. Thus, in one case, a teacher lost a sexual harassment suit against her principal because she was not discharged or denied promotion or any other job benefit; she was dismissed only after refusing an offer to transfer to another school.[191] Employees who submit to unwelcome sexual advances must show that they were threatened with adverse consequences in order to make their prima facie case.[192] To defend against a charge of quid-pro-quo harassment, the employer may either present a legitimate reason for the adverse employment action or show that the person who committed the harassment was not involved in the adverse decision.[193] The employee may then show that the employer's reason is pretextual; for example, by proving that a supervisor rewarded those employees who submitted and punished those who did not.[194]

Hostile-environment harassment, either sexual or racial, entails the claim that an employee was subjected to an intimidating, hostile, or offensive working environment because of the employee's sex or race. Although there have been more lawsuits involving sexual than racial harassment, both generally and in schools, the principles controlling both kinds of cases are similar. Both verbal and nonverbal conduct may create a hostile environment but only if (a) the conduct is "sufficiently severe or pervasive to alter the conditions of the victim's employment and create an abusive working environment,"[195] (b) the conduct is offensive (but not necessarily psychologically harmful[196]) to the victim, and (c) a reasonable person would also have been offended by the conduct.

To determine whether conduct is sufficiently pervasive or severe to constitute harassment, courts consider the nature of the conduct (touching is worse than verbal abuse[197]), the frequency or repetitiveness of the conduct, and the period of time over which the conduct occurred.[198] Thus, isolated jokes, inappropriate remarks, or a single sexual proposition or lewd comment (including in one case, the remark, "My penis stretches from here to District 1") is not usually sufficient to establish a hostile environment.[199] However, repeated generalized sexist jokes or comments or gender- or race-based commentary about a person's appearance or behavior do constitute hostile-environment harassment.[200] One court ruled that a single stinging slap on the plaintiff's buttocks created a sexually hostile environment.[201] Another found that two incidents in which a noose was found hung over an employee's workstation could create a racially hostile environment.[202]

Because the statute is directed at employers, not individuals, educators harassed at work may sue their school district under Title VII but not the harassers themselves. This raises the issue of whether and under what circumstances a school district or other employer will be held responsible for the harassment of an employee by a supervisor or colleague. With regard to supervisors, the Supreme Court ruled that:

> An employer is subject to vicarious liability to a victimized employee for an actionable hostile environment created by a supervisor with immediate (or successively higher) authority over the employee . . . No affirmative defense is available . . . when the supervisor's harassment culminates in a tangible employment action, such as discharge, demotion, or undesirable reassignment . . . [However,] [w]hen no tangible employment action is taken, a defending employer may raise an affirmative defense to liability or damages, subject to proof by a preponderance of the evidence, . . . The defense comprises two necessary elements: (a) that the employer exercised reasonable care to prevent and correct promptly any sexually harassing behavior, and (b) that the plaintiff employee unreasonably failed to take advantage of any preventive or corrective opportunities provided by the employer or to avoid harm otherwise. While proof that an employer had promulgated an antiharassment policy with complaint procedure is not necessary in every instance as a matter of law, the need for a stated policy suitable to the employment circumstances may appropriately be addressed in any case when litigating the first element of the defense. And while proof that an employee failed to fulfill the corresponding obligation of reasonable care to avoid harm is not limited to showing any unreasonable failure to use any complaint procedure provided by the employer, a demonstration of such failure will normally suffice to satisfy the employer's burden under the second element of the defense.[203]

One court ruled that a teaching intern had been subjected to a "tangible employment action" when, because she rejected her principal's sexual advances, the principal took back art supplies that he had previously given her and wrote a mixed evaluation that caused her to fail her internship. The court also ruled that both the school district and the principal himself (see sec. 10.10) could be sued and forced to pay damages.[204] The Supreme Court has said that an employee who is constructively discharged (purposely forced by employer-created circumstances to resign) as a result of a supervisor's harassment may have suffered a tangible employment action.[205]

In order to minimize the possibility of liability for harassment by their supervisory employees, school districts should create, publicize, and enforce antiharassment policies with clearly defined complaint procedures and plans for dealing with allegations of harassment. A school should respond to allegations of harassment as quickly as possible, usually within hours or, at most, days. The investigation and any necessary remedial steps should be properly undertaken because a bungled investigation or ineffective remedial steps will not prevent liability.[206] School officials should also carefully document the prompt and appropriate remedial steps they take; not to do so may cause a jury to disbelieve the district's claims that it responded appropriately to a harassment complaint.[207]

The Supreme Court has not yet ruled on whether and when an employer is responsible for sexual or racial harassment of an employee by a colleague. Because one colleague cannot subject another to an adverse employment decision, the Fifth Circuit has ruled that harassment by a colleague does not fit the Title VII definition of harassment.[208] However, other circuits have ruled that employers may be liable under Title VII if supervisors knew about, acquiesced in, or orchestrated the harassment.[209] Because schools have been held liable for not dealing appropriately with known student-on-student harassment (see sec. 5.9), it seems likely that most courts would take the same position regarding employee harassment of colleagues. For this reason and as a matter of ethics, schools should include measures designed to prevent harassment by colleagues in their antiharassment policies. At the same time, in their investigations and responses to allegations of racial or sexual harassment of employees, whether by supervisors or colleagues, school officials should be careful not to violate the constitutional, statutory, or contractual rights of the accused.[210]

7.5 RELIGION

Teachers who wish to practice their religion, wear religious garb, or otherwise manifest their religious beliefs at school create a difficult constitutional problem. To permit publicly paid teachers in religious clothing to teach a captive audience of impressionable children runs the risk of violating the Establishment Clause's prohibition against government promotion of religion. Yet, to prohibit teachers from wearing such clothes or taking other actions that are a requirement of their beliefs runs the risk of violating their right to the free exercise of religion.

In *Cooper v. Eugene School District No. 4J*,[211] the court upheld the constitutionality of a state law prohibiting public school teachers from wearing "religious dress while engaged in the performance of duties as a teacher," and the revocation of the teaching certificate of teachers who violate the rule. The rule was challenged by a middle school teacher punished for wearing a white turban as part of her practice of the Sikh religion. The teacher claimed that the rule violated her free exercise rights, but, the court felt that the rule was a legitimate way for schools to maintain religious neutrality. The *Cooper* court was careful to point out that it would not be permissible to fire a teacher for wearing an unobtrusive religious symbol such as a cross on a necklace or for occasionally wearing religious clothes. Only when a teacher's overt and repeated display of religious garb or symbols might convey the message of school approval or endorsement does the court authorize dismissal. Nevertheless, one might still question whether the case was correctly decided. Is it true that children will perceive the wearing of a turban or yarmulke by a teacher as endorsement by the school of the religious beliefs of the teacher? In any case, how is Cooper's wearing of a white turban to express a religious belief different from the wearing of an armband to express a political belief?

Related issues arise when teachers seek to distribute religious materials on school grounds or to use school facilities for religious exercises prior to the start of the school day. Although these issues are not fully decided, courts seem likely to permit the prohibition of any activity likely to give the appearance of school endorsement of religion. Therefore, a general ban on the distribution of religious literature by teachers might be permissible under the Free Exercise Clause and under the Establishment Clause, would probably be required (see sec. 2.3). At least one court has suggested that a school that permits teachers to meet informally before school to discuss topics of their own choosing might not be permitted to prohibit teacher prayer meetings, especially if the students and community are unaware of the meetings.[212]

A different problem arises when teachers seek exemption from job requirements on free exercise grounds. In one case, a teacher refused to lead her kindergarten class in the pledge of allegiance, patriotic songs, or celebrations of holidays. Based its analysis on doctrine developed by the Supreme Court in *Wisconsin v. Yoder*,[213] the Seventh Circuit ruled that although the teacher's refusal was based on a sincere religious belief, it was not her right to reject the board's officially adopted curriculum.[214] In general, a teacher's free-exercisebased challenge to a school's rules or curriculum would be unlikely to succeed unless the rules or curriculum were adopted for the purpose of preventing the teacher from satisfying religious mandates. This principle follows from the Supreme Court's current view that the Free Exercise Clause does not relieve an individual of the obligation to comply with generally applicable valid laws.[215]

The desire to celebrate religious holidays sometimes puts teachers at odds with their employers. In one case, a Jewish teacher claimed that the school infringed upon his free exercise of religion when it required him to take personal leave or unpaid leave in order to observe his religious holidays. In contrast, Christian teachers could take their holidays without penalty because the school was closed. The court rejected the teacher's claim, reasoning that because the loss of a day's pay for time not worked did not constitute substantial pressure to modify behavior, the school's policy did not constitute an infringement of religious liberty.[216] In another case, the California Supreme Court ruled that it was a violation of the state constitution to dismiss a teacher for being absent without permission in order to observe a religious holiday. The court said that the district was required to accommodate the teacher's religious needs by allowing a reasonable amount of unpaid leave, five to ten days a year.[217]

In addition to the Constitution, Title VII of the Civil Rights Act of 1964 (see also sec. 7.4) also protects teachers against religious discrimination in employment. The term religion is not defined in Title VII, but the courts have given it a sufficiently broad definition to include not only traditional theistic religions but also a sincere and meaningful belief that plays a role analogous to belief in a god. The regulations of the EEOC state that the

> Commission will define religious practices to include moral or ethical beliefs as to what is right and wrong which are sincerely held with the strength of traditional religious views . . . The fact that no religious group espouses such beliefs or the fact that the religious group to which the individual professes to belong may not accept such belief will not determine whether the belief is a religious belief of the employee or prospective employee.[218]

One court held that Title VII protected an employee's atheistic beliefs and prohibited requiring her to attend employee meetings that included religious ceremonies.[219] However, employee beliefs will not be protected if they are merely personal lifestyle preferences[220] or if they are not sincerely held. An employee who claimed he should not work on Sundays lost his Title VII claim when it was shown that in the past he had worked on Sundays.[221] Nevertheless, the courts are willing to tolerate a degree of inconsistency, recognizing that a person's commitment to religion can grow over time.[222] The EEOC compliance manual includes as examples of religious practices the wearing of a head scarf by a Muslim and a forehead marking by a Hindu.[223]

Title VII permits religious schools to discriminate in hiring and other employment decisions on the basis of religion (but not on the basis of race or gender).[224] Title VII also recognizes that religion can be a bona fide occupational qualification (see sec. 7.4), which conceivably might justify religious discrimination in some private school employment but never in public schools. Cases alleging covert disparate treatment of individuals on the basis of religion are litigated using the *McDonnell Douglas* framework discussed in Section 7.4.

Title VII requires accommodation of "all aspects of religious observances and practices as well as belief, unless an employer demonstrates that he is unable to accommodate an employee's or prospective employee's religious observance or practice without undue hardship on the conduct of the employer's business." Furthermore, "an employer may not permit an applicant's need for a religious accommodation to affect in any way its decision whether to hire the applicant unless it can demonstrate that it cannot reasonably accommodate the applicant's religious practices without undue hardship." The Supreme Court has defined "undue hardship" as "more than de minimis costs to the employer."[225] In one case, the First Circuit ruled that it would have been an undue hardship to accommodate an employee who claimed that her religion required her to display all her facial jewelry so she could not replace the jewelry with clear plastic retainers as suggested by the company. The company, said the court, would lose control of its public image if it went along with the employee's demand.[226] But the EEOC compliance manual says an employer violated Title VII by refusing to permit a Sikh to wear a turban simply because his customers expressed discomfort. Other possible accommodations, assuming they do not entail undue hardship, include display of religious objects in private work spaces and use of unoccupied areas for prayer during scheduled breaks.[227] In some cases, a school may be able to reject a requested accommodation such as the display of religious objects in classrooms on the grounds that to grant it would violate the Establishment Clause.[228] An inference of discrimination will be drawn if an employer asks an otherwise qualified prospective employee about the need for accommodation and then rejects the applicant.

Ansonia Board of Education v. Philbrook[229] concerned a teacher whose religious obligations required him to miss approximately six days of school per year. The contract between the school district and its teachers permitted only three days per year of paid religious leave. The district was willing to accommodate the teacher's religious beliefs by allowing him to take the additional three days off without pay, but the teacher argued that he should be allowed to use days from another category of permissible paid leave and so receive pay for the missed days. The Supreme Court ruled that Title VII only requires an employer to make a reasonable accommodation to an employee's religious obligations, not necessarily the accommodation the employee would prefer. Furthermore, the Court said that unpaid leave will usually be a reasonable accommodation unless paid leave is available for all other purposes except religion. The Court explained its ruling as follows:

> In enacting [Title VII] Congress was understandably motivated by a desire to assure the individual additional opportunity to observe religious practices, but it did not impose a duty on the employer to accommodate at all costs. The provision of unpaid leave eliminates the conflict between employment requirements and religious practices by allowing the individual to observe fully religious holy days and requires him only to give up compensation for a day that he did not in fact work. Generally speaking the direct effect of unpaid leave is merely a loss of income for the period the employee is not at work; such an exclusion has no direct effect upon either employment opportunities or job status.

7.6 DISABILITY

Employees with disabilities are protected by two of the same federal laws that protect children with disabilities (see sec. 6.2). The older of these two laws, the Rehabilitation Act of 1973 (Section 504),[230] provides that "no otherwise qualified handicapped individual" shall be excluded from participation in a program receiving federal financial assistance "solely by reason of his handicap." This law applies only to programs receiving federal financial assistance.

However, the newer law, the Americans with Disabilities Act (ADA) of 1990,[231] is not qualified in this way. Replacing the term handicap with disability, ADA's central provision regarding employment is that no employer "shall discriminate against a qualified individual with a disability because of the disability of such individual in regard to job applications procedures, the hiring, advancement, or discharge of employees, employee compensation, job training, and other terms, conditions and privileges of employment."

Eligibility

Both of these laws apply to people who have "a physical or mental impairment which substantially limits one or more such person's major life activities," have a record of such an impairment, or are regarded as having such an impairment. ADA defines "major life activities" to include but not be limited to "caring for one's self, performing manual tasks, seeing, hearing, eating, sleeping, walking, standing, lifting, bending, speaking, breathing, learning, reading, concentrating, thinking, communicating, and working." The term also encompasses major bodily functions including, but not limited to, functions of the immune system, normal cell growth, and digestive, bowel, bladder, neurological, brain, respiratory, circulatory, endocrine, and reproductive functions.[232] The regulations further state that an "impairment is substantially limiting if it significantly restricts the duration, manner or condition under which an individual can perform a particular major life activity as compared to the average person." One court ruled that a man who had fractured his hip and subsequently walked with a limp, had trouble climbing stairs, and could walk only about a mile without a cane was not substantially limited with regard to the major life activity of walking.[233]

An impairment that substantially limits one major life activity need not limit other major life activities to be considered a disability. And an impairment that is episodic or in remission may still be a disability if it would substantially limit a major life activity when active. Consistent with these principles, a federal district court ruled that an art teacher who suffered from degenerative arthritis was covered by ADA even though she was essentially capable of performing her job without any accommodations. The teacher was substantially limited in performing the major life activity of walking.[234]

Only permanent or long-term impairments count as disabilities. "[T]emporary, nonchronic impairments of short duration, with little or no long term or permanent impact, are usually not disabilities. Such impairments may include, but are not limited to, broken limbs, sprained joints, concussions, appendicitis, and influenza. Similarly, except in rare circumstances, obesity is not considered a disabling impairment." The plaintiff in one case was five foot six inches tall and weighed 375 pounds. Depending on the temperature, she could walk about 500 yards, and a physician estimated she suffered a 50 percent disability. Nevertheless, the court found that she was not sufficiently substantially impaired to be covered, but it also noted that she might qualify under another facet of the definition—being regarded as having an impairment.[235]

The ADA also specifies that the determination of whether an impairment substantially limits a major life activity must be made without regard to the ameliorative effects of mitigating measures such as medication, eyeglasses, prosthetics, hearing aids, mobility devices, oxygen equipment, assistive technology, auxiliary aids (including interpreters), and learned behavioral or adaptive neurological modifications. However, an employer may refuse to hire or retain an employee with a disability in a job that would exacerbate the disability, thereby posing a direct threat to the employee's health or safety.[236]

As noted earlier, ADA protects people who, although they currently have no impairment of a major life activity, have a record of such an impairment or are regarded as having such an impairment. A person meets the requirement of being "regarded" as having an impairment if they have been subjected to an action prohibited by the ADA because of an actual or perceived physical or mental impairment whether or not the impairment limits or is perceived to limit a major life activity. But not everyone who has ever had a temporary disability or whom anyone regards as disabled is covered. In one case, a federal district court ruled that a teacher who had been hospitalized for breast cancer surgery did not have a record of impairment sufficient to establish eligibility under ADA.[237] Another federal district court ruled that the obese plaintiff was not able to prove she was regarded as having a disability because her evidence consisted only of isolated comments spread over time and one inquiry regarding her ability to walk; neither was she able to prove there was a perception that she was unable to do her job in the school library.[238]

In addition to prohibiting discrimination against employees who are themselves disabled, ADA also prohibits discrimination against employees "because of the . . . disability of an individual with whom the [employee] is known to have a relationship or association." This provision is violated if the employer declines to hire someone because the employer believes the applicant would miss work or leave work early to care for a family member with a disability or if the employer provides reduced health insurance benefits because the employee has a dependent with a disability. However, the law does not require reasonable accommodation—for example, a change in work schedule—of an employee without a disability in order to enable the employee to care for a dependent with a disability.

People currently engaged in the illegal use of drugs are not covered by Section 504 and ADA, but those participating in a drug rehabilitation program are. Alcoholics whose use of alcohol "prevents such an individual from performing the duties of the job in question or whose employment, by reason of such current alcohol abuse, would constitute a direct threat to property or the safety of others" are not covered. Nonstandard sexual orientations and preferences such as bisexuality and transvestitism are specifically excluded from coverage.

Regarding Section 504, the Supreme Court has said the definition of a "handicapped person" includes those with an infectious disease such as tuberculosis, and a lower court has included a teacher carrying the HIV virus but not suffering from AIDS.[239] ADA regulations provide that a person who poses a "direct threat" to the health and safety of others is not covered. The term "direct threat" means a significant risk of substantial harm that cannot be eliminated or reduced by reasonable accommodation. In deciding whether a teacher with AIDS could be excluded from the classroom and reassigned to an administrative position, the Ninth Circuit looked at four factors: (a) the nature of the risk—how the disease is transmitted, (b) how long the carrier is infectious, (c) the potential harm to third parties, and (d) the probability the disease would be transmitted and cause harm. After examining the scientific evidence, the court found that there was no apparent risk of HIV infection to individuals exposed only through the type of contact that occurs in the course of a teacher's job and so ordered the teacher returned to the classroom.[240]

Of course, the fact that a person has a disability does not mean that the person must be employed. The law only prohibits discrimination against people with disabilities who are "**otherwise qualified**"; that is, who despite their disability have the training, experience, abilities, and skills to perform the essential requirements of the job they seek or hold.[241] When interviewing job applicants, school officials may "inquire into the ability of an applicant to perform job-related functions, and/or may ask an applicant to describe or to demonstrate how, with or without reasonable accommodation, the applicant will be able to perform job-related functions." Job applications may not inquire whether an applicant is an individual with a disability, the nature or severity of an applicant's disability, or ask how often the individual will require leave for treatment or use leave as a result of a disability. Neither may school districts require an applicant to undergo a medical examination prior to making a job offer, but they may require a medical examination after making an offer.

Reasonable Accommodation

If an otherwise qualified job applicant or employee with a disability can perform the essential functions of a job with reasonable accommodation, a failure to provide reasonable accommodation is unlawful unless the school can demonstrate that the accommodation would impose an undue hardship on it.[242] (The reasonable accommodation requirement does not apply to people covered by the ADA solely because they are regarded as having an impairment.) The essential functions of a job are its fundamental duties as opposed to marginal functions, the elimination of which would not significantly alter the position as the employer has defined it. For example, being able to convey information orally is an essential function of most teaching jobs, but being able to type quickly usually is not. Undue hardship is determined by taking into account the costs and overall financial resources of the school district, the effect of the accommodation on other employees, and whether the accommodation would fundamentally alter the nature or operation of the education program. Reasonable accommodation may include modifying facilities, equipment, or work schedules; job restructuring; or the acquisition of special equipment. The Supreme Court has ruled, however, that when an employer has an established seniority system, employees with seniority have priority over less senior employees with a disability even if the particular position could uniquely accommodate the less senior employee.[243]

When designing reasonable accommodations, the law requires the employer to engage in an "informal interactive process" with the employee with a disability and to make a good faith effort to design accommodations that will make it possible for the employee to perform the essential functions of the job.[244] The Ninth Circuit has ruled that the required interactive process must involve more than a one-time offer of a single option.[245] If more than one set of accommodations would permit the employee to perform the essential functions of the job, the employer retains the ultimate authority to choose the accommodations that are the cheapest or easiest to provide. Relying on these principles, a federal district court ruled that a custodian who had sustained an injury and consequently could no longer do the heavy lifting his job required was not denied reasonable accommodation when his school district refused either to assign him to permanent light custodial duties or to give him a job as a food service manager. The court ruled that assignment to light duties exclusively would transform the essential functions of the job and impose a greater workload on the other custodians. Regarding the managerial position, the court concluded that the plaintiff's experience as a manager years earlier did not make him qualified for the position especially because he had no experience in food services.[246]

Violations of Section 504 and ADA

Schools may be accused of violating Section 504 and ADA for engaging in hidden motive **disparate treatment** of an employee with a disability, for adopting polices and practices with a **disparate impact** on such employees, for **failing to make reasonable accommodations** for otherwise qualified employees with disabilities, or for engaging in **retaliation** against employees for asserting rights under the statutes or aiding in investigations to enforce the statutes. Disparate treatment cases employ the *McDonnell Douglas* framework examined in Section 7.4. The plaintiff bears the initial burden of establishing a prima facie case of intentional discrimination: that the plaintiff was an otherwise qualified individual with disabilities who suffered an adverse employment decision. The school may then defend itself by showing that the adverse employment decision was taken for legitimate nondiscriminatory reasons.

Schools charged with adopting policies that have a disparate impact on qualified individuals with disabilities must show that the policies are job-related and consistent with business necessity and that reasonable accommodations are not possible. *Pandazides v. Virginia Board of Education*[247] concerned a probationary teacher who was not rehired because she was unable to pass a standardized test that was a requirement of permanent certification in her state. The teacher argued that she was an otherwise qualified person who was unable to pass the test because of a learning disability and that, as applied to her, the standardized test requirement was impermissible under Section 504. The Fourth Circuit ruled that in order to determine whether the teacher was "otherwise qualified" within the meaning of the statute, it was necessary to consider more than just whether the teacher could satisfy the state board of education's requirements for a teaching certificate (passing the test). Rather, it was necessary to consider whether the teacher could perform the essential functions of the job of school teacher and whether the test actually "measured those functions." Furthermore, even if it was determined that the teacher could not perform all the duties of the job, it would still be necessary to determine whether reasonable modifications could be made that would allow her to teach. The case was remanded to the district court to make the necessary determinations.

Schools charged with failing to make reasonable accommodations may defend themselves by demonstrating either that they did offer reasonable accommodations that were rejected or that any possible effective accommodations would impose undue hardship on the district. To successfully defend a suit charging retaliation, the school would have to show that the adverse employment decision was taken for legitimate reasons other than retaliation.

A person with a disability victimized by intentional discrimination may sue a school for compensatory damages, but the Supreme Court has ruled that ADA and Section 504 do not permit plaintiffs to sue entities that receive federal funds (such as public schools) for punitive damages.[248] The Equal Employment Opportunity Commission may pursue an employee's ADA claim even if the employee is personally prohibited by an arbitration agreement from doing so.[249]

7.7 AGE

Intentionally treating employees differently on the basis of age raises both constitutional and statutory issues. The Supreme Court dealt with the constitutionality of mandatory retirement in *Massachusetts Board of Retirement v. Murgia*.[250] Because age classifications do not trigger strict scrutiny, the Court rejected the plaintiffs' claim that a mandatory retirement policy violated the Equal Protection Clause because the policy was rationally related to the goal of assuring a physically fit police force. Applying this approach, the Second Circuit concluded that a mandatory retirement policy was constitutionally permissible in that it served, among other things, to foster employment of young people.[251] However, the Seventh Circuit has held that mandatory retirement might be unconstitutional.[252]

The uncertainty regarding the constitutionality of mandatory retirement of teachers is a moot point in light of the **Age Discrimination in Employment Act of 1978 (ADEA)**. This federal statute protects people above the age of forty from discrimination on the basis of age with regard to hiring, firing, and other terms and conditions of employment.[253] Thus, mandatory retirement for teachers is prohibited by law. Disparate treatment litigation brought under ADEA follows the same framework as other disparate treatment cases.[254] Although ADEA recognizes that age may sometimes be a bona fide occupational qualification, it is unlikely that this narrowly defined exception would ever apply to a teaching position. Thus, a school charged with disparate treatment age discrimination must defend itself by showing that the adverse employment decision was based on legitimate factors other than age.[255]

In *Smith v. City of Jackson*[256] the Supreme Court settled a dispute among the circuit courts by ruling that ADEA permits disparate impact suits. However, the Court also said that the scope of disparate impact liability under ADEA was narrower than under Title VII. The plaintiff bears the burden of isolating the specific practice of the employer that has a disparate impact on older workers. Even if the plaintiff meets this burden, the employer might still prevail by showing that the disparate impact "is based on reasonable factors other than age discrimination."[257] The statute also permits an employer to defend itself by showing that it was observing a bona fide seniority system or employment benefit plan that was not a subterfuge to evade the law.

This framework was used by a court to decide whether a school district's seniority-based salary schedule was permissible under the ADEA. Because the salary schedule made experienced teachers more expensive, the district had adopted a hiring policy that favored hiring less experienced teachers, a policy that had a discriminatory impact on older applicants. Nevertheless, the court concluded that the pay system was a bona fide seniority-based system and had not been adopted with a discriminatory intent.[258]

Early retirement plans and reductions in force may raise difficult issues under the ADEA. Truly voluntary early retirement plans are permitted;[259] however, when incentives are offered for early retirement, the employer must demonstrate legitimate, nondiscriminatory reasons for the plan.[260] Retirement benefits may also be keyed to the age of retirement as long as the differences in benefits are based on non-age-related reasons like cost.[261] Layoffs in accordance with a legitimate seniority system are permitted, but laying off older workers first in order to save money is not.[262]

The Supreme Court has interpreted ADEA's prohibition against age discrimination to include protection against retaliation for complaining of age discrimination.[263]

7.8 SUMMARY

The school has both a right and an obligation to ensure that all of its employees perform the legitimate duties of their jobs. However, the school's power over its teachers and other employees is limited because they retain the same constitutional rights as any citizen. Many cases require balancing an employee's constitutional rights against a school's need to promote its goals.

Freedom of speech protects a teacher's right to advocate any political belief, either by symbolic or actual speech or through membership in a political party or organization. When acting as private citizens, teachers may speak freely on any matter of public concern including education issues, if their speech is not excessively disruptive to their school's educational mission, but the airing of private gripes (e.g., about supervisors) may be prohibited even if not disruptive. Even on matters of public concern, speech that materially and substantially disrupts the school may be barred.

Within the classroom, freedom of speech affords only limited protection to teachers. K–12 teachers, unlike university professors, have little academic freedom; they may be required to adhere closely to the curriculum and instructional methods chosen by the school.

The right of privacy affords school employees some protection in matters of lifestyle and morality. Although some issues such as the right to use contraception or to become pregnant are well settled, others are not. Before allowing dismissal for personal lifestyle choices, most courts require a proven connection between the behavior and the ability to do the job. Teachers enjoy Fourth Amendment protection against unreasonable searches and seizures. Mandatory drug testing may be permissible for bus drivers and other employees whose impairment would pose a direct and significant threat to the safety of students; however, random drug testing of all teachers is questionable.

Although schools must make reasonable accommodations to a teacher's religious beliefs, freedom of religion does not provide an exemption from the essential duties of the job. In particular, a teacher may not claim a religion-based right to modify the curriculum, a practice that would violate the Establishment Clause. In accommodating employees' religious beliefs, schools must avoid appearing to endorse them. Thus, the Free Exercise Clause does not give teachers the right to recite prayers openly within the classroom or, at least according to some courts, to dress in religious garb. Free exercise does protect a teacher's right to take a reasonable number of days off for religious observance, not necessarily with pay, or to wear unobtrusive symbols of faith.

Discrimination is a very active and complex area of employment law. The Equal Protection Clause and a number of federal statutes including the Civil Rights Acts of 1964 and 1991 protect both employees and prospective employees of schools from discrimination based on race, gender, religion, disability, or age. Although summarizing the thrust of these laws is difficult, employment decisions must not be based on any of these characteristics unless there is an extremely compelling rationale. Race must never influence employment decisions, except possibly in certain carefully crafted affirmative action programs designed to remedy past discrimination by a particular employer. Gender may perhaps be a bona fide occupational qualification for a few education jobs, but the justification must be strong. Schools must make reasonable accommodations for employees with disabilities but are not obliged to employ persons with disabilities who are unable to perform the essential functions of the job. Mandatory retirement or gearing salary or benefits directly to age is illegal. Schools must not permit employees to be subjected to racial or sexual harassment.

NOTES

1 342 U.S. 485 (1952).
2 364 U.S. 479 (1960).
3 377 U.S. 360 (1964).
4 385 U.S. 589 (1967).
5 Cole v. Richardson, 405 U.S. 676 (1972); Connell v. Higginbotham, 403 U.S. 207 (1971).
6 Ambach v. Norwick, 441 U.S. 68 (1979).
7 Rutan v. Republican Party of Illinois, 497 U.S. 62 (1990); Branti v. Finkel, 445 U.S. 507 (1980); Elrod v. Burns, 427 U.S. 347 (1976).
8 Childers v. Indep. Sch. Dist. No. 1, 676 F.2d 1338 (10th Cir. 1982); Guerra v. Roma Indep. Sch. Dist., 444 F. Supp. 812 (S.D. Tex. 1977).
9 Solis v. Rio Grande City Indep. Sch., 734 F.2d 243 (5th Cir. 1984).
10 933 F. Supp. 458 (E.D. Pa. 1996).
11 Haskins v. State *ex rel.* Harrington, 516 P.2d 1171 (Wyo. 1973; *see also* Rutan v. Republican Party of Illinois, 497 U.S. 62 (1990); Branti v. Finkel, 445 U.S. 507 (1980); Elrod v. Burns, 427 U.S. 347 (1976).
12 Minielly v. State, 411 P.2d 69 (Or. 1966).
13 Allen v. Bd. of Educ., 584 S.W.2d 408 (Ky. Ct. App. 1979).
14 547 U.S. 410 (2006).
15 Brammer-Hoelter v. Twin Peaks Charter Academy, 492 F.3d 1192 (10th Cir. 2007).
16 Williams v. Dallas Indep. Sch. Dist., 480 F.3d 689 (5th Cir. 2007) *see also* United States *ex rel.* Battle v. Bd. of Regents for Ga., 468 F.3d 755 (11th Cir. 2006).
17 473 F.3d 1323 (10th Cir. 2007).
18 391 U.S. 563 (1968).
19 439 U.S. 410 (1979).
20 461 U.S. 138 (1983).
21 483 U.S. 378 (1987).
22 511 U.S. 661 (1994).
23 *See, e.g.,* Morfin v. Albuquerque Pub. Sch., 906 F.2d 1434 (10th Cir. 1990); Jeffries v. Harleston, 52 F.3d 9 (2d Cir. 1995); Levin v. Harleston, 770 F. Supp. 895 (S.D.N.Y. 1991).

24 Fisher v. Wellington Exempted Village Sch. Bd. of Educ., 223 F. Supp. 2d 833 (N.D. Ohio 2002).

25 Piver v. Pender County Bd. of Educ., 835 F.2d 1076 (4th Cir. 1987).

26 Cliff v. Bd. of Sch. Comm'rs of Indianapolis, 42 F.3d 403 (7th Cir. 1994).

27 Bradshaw v. Pittsburg Indep. Sch. Dist., 207 F.3d 814 (5th Cir. 2000).

28 Rowland v. Mad River Local Sch. Dist., 730 F.2d 444 (6th Cir. 1984).

29 Anderson v. Evans, 660 F.2d 153 (6th Cir. 1981).

30 437 F. Supp. 2d 652 (N.D. Mich. 2006).

31 Sharp v. Lindsey, 285 F.3d 479 (6th Cir. 2002).

32 336 F.3d 185 (2d Cir. 2003).

33 Vargas-Harrison v. Racine Unified Sch. Dist., 272 F.3d 964 (7th Cir. 2001).

34 McCullough v. Wyandanch, 187 F.3d 272 (2d Cir. 1999).

35 Brocknell v. Norton, 732 F.2d 664 (8th Cir. 1984).

36 Westbrook v. Teton County Sch. Dist. No. 1, 918 F. Supp. 1475 (D. Wyo. 1996).

37 Tim Barnett, *Overview of State Whistleblower Protection Statutes*, 43 LAB. L.J. 440 (1992).

38 Deschenie v. Bd. of Educ. of Central Consolidated Sch. Dist. No. 22, 473 F.3d 1271 (10th Cir. 2007).

39 951 F.2d 927 (8th Cir. 1991).

40 Mt. Healthy City Sch. Dist. Bd. of Educ. v. Doyle, 429 U.S. 274 (1977).

41 598 F.2d 535 (10th Cir. 1979).

42 611 P.2d 414 (Wash. 1980) (en banc).

43 Russo v. Cent. Sch. Dist. No. 1, 469 F.2d 623 (2d Cir. 1972).

44 Palmer v. Bd. of Educ. of Chicago, 603 F.2d 1271 (7th Cir. 1979).

45 Boring v. Buncombe County Bd. of Educ., 136 F.3d 364 (4th Cir. 1998).

46 Kirkland v. Northside Indep. Sch. Dist., 890 F.2d 794 (5th Cir. 1989).

47 Lacks v. Ferguson Reorganized Sch. Dist. R-2, 147 F.3d 718 (8th Cir. 1998), *reh'g and reh'g en banc denied*, 154 F.3d 904 (8th Cir. 1998); *see also* Erskine v. Bd. of Educ., 207 F. Supp. 2d 407 (D. Md. 2002).

48 LeVake v. Indep. Sch. Dist. No. 656, 625 N.W.2d 502 (Minn. Ct. App. 2001).

49 611 F.2d 1109 (5th Cir. 1980).

50 Cockrel v. Shelby County Sch. Dist., 270 F.3d 1036 (6th Cir. 2001).

51 323 F. Supp. 1387 (D. Mass.), *aff'd*, 448 F.2d 1242 (1st Cir. 1971).

52 713 F. Supp. 1131 (N.D. Ill. 1989).

53 Fisher v. Fairbanks N. Star Borough Sch. Dist., 704 P.2d 213 (Alaska 1985).

54 Breen v. Runkel, 614 F. Supp. 355 (W.D. Mich. 1985); Marchi v. Bd. of Coop. Educ. Servs. of Albany, 173 F.3d 469 (2d Cir. 1999).

55 La Rocca v. Bd. of Educ. of Rye City Sch. Dist., 406 N.Y.S.2d 348 (N.Y. App. Div.), *appeal dismissed*, 386 N.E.2d 266 (N.Y. 1978); Birdwell v. Hazelwood Sch. Dist., 491 F.2d 490 (8th Cir. 1974).

56 Miles v. Denver Pub. Sch., 944 F.2d 773 (10th Cir. 1991).

57 344 F. Supp. 791 (N.D. Iowa 1972); *see also* Keefe v. Geanakos, 418 F.2d 359 (1st Cir. 1969).

58 Ward v. Hickey, 996 F.2d 448 (1st Cir. 1993).

59 500 U.S. 173 (1991).

60 777 F.2d 1046 (5th Cir. 1985), *aff'd*, 479 U.S. 801 (1986).

61 461 F.2d 566 (2d Cir. 1972).

62 Downs v. Los Angeles Unified Sch. Dist., 228 F.3d 1003 (9th Cir. 2000).

63 Griswold v. Connecticut, 381 U.S. 479 (1965).

64 E. Hartford Educ. Ass'n v. Bd. of Educ. of E. Hartford, 562 F.2d 856 (2d Cir. 1977).

65 Tardif v. Quinn, 545 F.2d 761 (1st Cir. 1976).

66 Finot v. Pasadena City Bd. of Educ., 58 Cal. Rptr. 520 (Cal. Ct. App. 1967).

67 Conard v. Goolsby, 350 F. Supp. 713 (N.D. Miss. 1972).

68 Domico v. Rapides Parish Sch. Bd., 675 F.2d 100 (5th Cir. 1982).

69 Griswold v. Connecticut, 381 U.S. 479 (1965); Roe v. Wade, 410 U.S. 113 (1973); Zablocki v. Redhail, 434 U.S. 374 (1978).

70 Littlejohn v. Rose, 768 F.2d 765 (6th Cir. 1985).

71 Mescia v. Berry, 406 F. Supp. 1181 (D.S.C. 1974), *aff'd*, 530 F.2d 969 (4th Cir. 1975).

72 Solomon v. Quinones, 531 N.Y.S.2d 349 (N.Y. App. Div. 1988).

73 Keckeisen v. Indep. Sch. Dist. No. 612, 509 F.2d 1062 (8th Cir. 1975).

74 Erb v. Iowa State Bd. of Pub. Instruction, 216 N.W.2d 339 (Iowa 1974).

75 439 U.S. 1052 (1978).

76   *See also* Johnson v. San Jacinto Junior Coll., 498 F. Supp. 555 (S.D. Tex. 1980).

77   Avery v. Homewood City Bd. of Educ., 674 F.2d 337 (Former 5th Cir. 1982); Andrews v. Drew Mun. Separate Sch. Dist., 507 F.2d 611 (5th Cir. 1975).

78   Rowland v. Mad River Local Sch. Dist., 730 F.2d 444 (6th Cir. 1984).

79   National Gay Task Force v. Bd. of Educ. of Oklahoma City, 729 F.2d 1270 (10th Cir. 1984), *aff'd by an equally divided Court*, 470 U.S. 903 (1985).

80   Sarac v. State Bd. of Educ., 57 Cal. Rptr. 69 (Cal. Ct. App. 1967); Stephens v. Bd. of Educ., Sch. Dist. No. 5, 429 N.W.2d 722 (Neb. 1988).

81   Glover v. Williamsburg Local Sch. Dist. Bd. of Educ., 20 F. Supp. 2d 1160 (S.D. Ohio 1998).

82   Lawrence v. Texas, 539 U.S. 558 (2003).

83   Goseny v. Sonora Indep. Sch. Dist., 603 F.2d 522 (5th Cir. 1979).

84   McCarthy v. Philadelphia Civil Serv. Comm'n, 424 U.S. 645 (1976).

85   Fyfe v. Curlee, 902 F.2d 401 (5th Cir. 1990); Brantley v. Surles, 718 F.2d 1354 (5th Cir. 1983).

86   Cook v. Hudson, 511 F.2d 744 (5th Cir. 1975).

87   29 U.S.C. § 2601.

88   232 F. Supp. 2d 730 (E.D. Mich. 2002); *see also* Hughes v. N. Olmsted, 93 F.3d 238 (6th Cir. 1996).

89   Thorne v. City of Segundo, 726 F.2d 459 (9th Cir. 1983).

90   Sterling v. Minersville, 232 F.3d 190 (3d Cir. 2000); Kallstrom v. Columbus, 136 F.3d 1055 (6th Cir. 1998).

91   426 F.3d 187 (2d Cir. 2005); *but see* Thompson v. City of Arlington, Texas, 838 F. Supp. 1137 (N.D. Texas 1993).

92   502 F. Supp. 2d 324 (E.D.N.Y. 2007); *see also* Powell v. Schriver, 175 F.3d 107 (2d Cir. 1999).

93   842 F.2d 9 (1st Cir. 1988); *see also* Lyons v. Sullivan, 602 F.2d 7 (1st Cir. 1979).

94   Sch. Dist. No. 1 v. Teachers' Retirement Fund Ass'n, 95 P.2d 720 (Or. 1939); Cude v. State, 377 S.W.2d 816 (Ark. 1964).

95   Shelton v. Tucker, 364 U.S. 479 (1960).

96   Garrity v. New Jersey, 385 U.S. 493 (1967); Albertson v. Subversive Activities Control Bd., 382 U.S. 70 (1965).

97   Beilan v. Bd. of Educ., 357 U.S. 399 (1958).

98   Gardner v. Broderick, 392 U.S. 273 (1968); Lefkowitz v. Cunningham, 431 U.S. 801 (1977).

99   480 U.S. 709 (1987).

100   Leventhal v. Knapek, 266 F.3d 64 (2d Cir. 2001).

101   Shaul v. Cherry Valley-Springfield Cent. Sch. Dist., 363 F.3d 177 (2d Cir. 2004).

102   Leventhal v. Knapek, 266 F.3d 64 (2d Cir. 2001).

103   Smyth v. Pillsbury Co., 914 F. Supp. 97 (E.D. Pa. 1996).

104   United States v. Charbonneau, 979 F. Supp. 1177 (S.D. Ohio 1997); United States v. Maxwell, 45 M.J. 406 (C.A.A.F. 1996).

105   *Compare* Wyman v. James, 400 U.S. 309 (1971).

106   18 U.S.C. §2510–2522, *amended by* the Electronics Communication Privacy Act of 1986, Pub. L. No. 99–508, 100 Stat. 1848.

107   Steve Jackson Games, Inc. v. United States Secret Serv., 36 F.3d 457 (5th Cir. 1994); United States v. Reyes, 922 F. Supp. 818 (S.D.N.Y. 1996).

108   Brannen v. Kings Local Sch. Dist. Bd. of Educ., 761 N.E.2d 84 (Ohio Ct. App. 2001).

109   State v. McLellan, 744 A.2d 611 (N.H. 1999).

110   People v. Triggs, 506 P.2d 232 (Cal. 1973).

111   Hearn v. Bd. of Pub. Educ., 191 F.3d 1329, *reh'g denied*, 204 F.3d 1124 (11th Cir. 1999).

112   789 P.2d 636 (Okla. Ct. App. 1989).

113   *See also* Skinner v. Ry. Labor Executives' Ass'n, 489 U.S. 602 (1989).

114   Patchogue-Medford Congress of Teachers v. Bd. of Educ. of Patchogue-Medford, 510 N.E.2d 325 (N.Y. 1987).

115   Knox County Educ. Ass'n v. Knox County Bd. of Educ., 158 F.3d 361 (6th Cir. 1998); *see also* Crager v. Bd. of Educ. of Knott County, Ky., 313 F. Supp. 2d 690 (E.D. Ky. 2004).

116   Aubrey v. Sch. Bd. of Lafayette Parish, 148 F.3d 559 (5th Cir. 1998).

117   20 U.S.C. § 1145g.

118   457 F. Supp. 2d 1378 (S.D. Ga. 2006).

119   Snetsinger v. Montana Univ. System, 104 P.3d 445 (Mont. 2004).

120   Doe v. United States Postal Service, 1985 U.S. Dist. LEXIS 18959.

121 Ashlie v. Chester-Upland Sch. Dist., 1979 U.S. Dist. LEXIS 12516; *see also* Grossman v. Sch. Dist. of Twp. of Bernards, 316 A.2d 39 (N.J. Super. Ct. App. Div. 1974).

122 Lawrence v. Texas, 539 U.S. 558 (2003).

123 282 F.3d 946 (7th Cir. 2002).

124 42 U.S.C. § 2000(e).

125 42 U.S.C. § 1981.

126 N. Haven Bd. of Educ. v. Bell, 456 U.S. 512 (1982).

127 42 U.S.C. § 2000(e).

128 *See* Mitchell v. Bd. of Trustees of Pickens County, 599 F.2d 582 (4th Cir. 1979).

129 42 U.S.C. § 2000e–2(a)(1).

130 Simonton v. Runyon, 232 F.3d 33 (2d Cir. 2000) (holding sexual orientation is not covered under Title VII); Bibby v. Philadelphia Coca-Cola Bottling Co., 260 F.3d 257 (3d Cir. 2001) (same); Spearman v. Ford Motor Co., 231 F.3d 1080 (7th Cir. 2000) (same); Williamson v. A.G. Edwards & Sons, 876 F.2d 69 (8th Cir. 1989) (same); Desantis v. Pac. Tel. & Tel. Co., 608 F.2d 327 (9th Cir. 1979) (same); United States Dep't of Hous. & Urban Dev. v. Federal Labor Relations Auth., 964 F.2d 1 (D.C. Cir. 1992) (same); *but see* Rene v. MGM Grand Hotel, Inc., 305 F.3d 1061 (9th Cir. 2002) (en banc) (plurality opinion) (holding sexual orientation is covered under Title VII); Nichols v. Azteca Rest. Enterprises, Inc., 256 F.3d 864 (9th Cir. 2001) (same).

131 Foray v. Bell Atlantic, 56 F. Supp. 2d 327 (S.D.N.Y. 1999); Cleaves v. City of Chicago, 21 F. Supp. 2d 858 (N.D. Ill. 1998), *amended on reconsideration*, 68 F. Supp. 2d 963 (N.D. Ill. 1999).

132 Price Waterhouse v. Hopkins, 490 U.S. 228 (1989); Rene v. MGM Grand Hotel, Inc., 305 F.3d 1061 (9th Cir. 2002) (en banc); Nichols v. Azteca Rest. Enters., Inc., 256 F.3d 864 (9th Cir. 2001).

133 Smith v. City of Salem, 369 F.3d 912 (6th Cir. 2004); Schroer v. Billington, 424 F. Supp. 2d 203 (D.D.C. 2006).

134 Holloway v. Arthur Andersen & Co., 566 F.2d 659 (9th Cir. 1977); James v. Ranch Mart Hardware, 881 F. Supp. 478 (D. Kan. 1995); Dobre v. Nat'l R.R. Passenger Corp. (AMTRAK), 850 F. Supp. 284 (E.D. Pa. 1993); Powell v. Read's, Inc., 436 F. Supp. 369 (D. Md. 1977); Voyles v. Ralph K. Davies Medical Center, 403 F. Supp. 456 (N.D. Cal. 1975).

135 Sommers v. Budget Mktg., Inc., 667 F.2d 748 (8th Cir. 1982).

136 490 U.S. 228 (1989).

137 Schwenk v. Hartford, 204 F.3d 1187 (9th Cir. 2000).

138 Kastl v. Maricopa County Cmty. Coll. Dist., 2004 U.S. Dist. LEXIS 29825.

139 Tex. Dep't of Cmty. Affairs v. Burdine, 450 U.S. 248 (1981).

140 42 U.S.C. § 10201.

141 Dothard v. Rawlinson, 433 U.S. 321 (1977); UAW v. Johnson Controls, Inc., 499 U.S. 187 (1991).

142 Weeks v. Southern Bell Tel. & Tel. Co., 408 F.2d 228 (5th Cir. 1969); *see also* Hayes v. Shelby Mem'l Hosp., 726 F.2d 1543 (11th Cir. 1984).

143 Moteles v. Univ. of Pennsylvania, 730 F.2d 913 (3d Cir. 1984).

144 Barker v. Taft Broad. Co., 549 F.2d 400 (6th Cir. 1977); Earwood v. Cont'l Southeastern Lines, Inc., 539 F.2d 1349, 1351 (4th Cir. 1976); Longo v. Carlisle DeCoppet & Co., 537 F.2d 685 (2d Cir. 1976).

145 Jespersen v. Harrah's Operating Co., 444 F.3d 1104 (9th Cir. 2006).

146 Frank v. United Airlines, Inc., 216 F.3d 845 (9th Cir. 2000).

147 401 F.3d 729 (6th Cir. 2005); *but see* Oiler v. Winn-Dixie Louisiana Inc., 2002 U.S. Dist. LEXIS 17417 (E.D. La. Sept. 16, 2002).

148 411 U.S. 792 (1973).

149 480 U.S. 616 (1987).

150 476 U.S. 267 (1986).

151 488 U.S. 469 (1989).

152 Taxman v. Bd. of Educ. of Piscataway, 91 F.3d 1547 (3d Cir. 1996), *cert. granted*, 521 U.S. 1117 (1997), *cert. dismissed*, 522 U.S. 1010 (1997).

153 Kromnick v. Sch. Dist. of Philadelphia, 555 F. Supp. 249 (E.D. Pa. 1983).

154 Mitchell v. Baldrige, 759 F.2d 80 (D.C. Cir. 1985); Abrams v. Johnson, 534 F.2d 1226 (6th Cir. 1976).

155 Robinson v. Shell Oil Company, 519 U.S. 337 (1997); Smith v. St. Louis Univ., 109 F.3d 1261 (8th Cir. 1997).

156 Texas Dep't of Cmty. Affairs v. Burdine, 450 U.S. 248 (1981).

157 St. Mary's Honor Ctr. v. Hicks, 509 U.S. 502 (1993); *see also* Fisher v. Vassar Coll., 114 F.3d 1332 (2d Cir. 1997).

158 *See, e.g.,* Abasiekong v. City of Shelby, 744 F.2d 1055 (4th Cir. 1984).

159 *See, e.g.,* Hallquist v. Local 276, Plumbers, 843 F.2d 18 (1st Cir. 1988), *aff'g* Hallquist v. Max Fish Plumbing & Heating Co., 46 Fair Empl. Prac. Cases (BNA) 1855 (D. Mass. 1987).

160 Reeves v. Sanderson Plumbing Prods., Inc., 530 U.S. 133 (2000).

161 432 N.W.2d 777 (Minn. Ct. App. 1988).

162 McCarthney v. Griffin-Spalding County Bd. of Educ., 791 F.2d 1549 (11th Cir. 1986).

163 129 S. Ct. 846 (2009).

164 519 U.S. 337 (1997).

165 Ruggles v. Cal. Polytechnic State Univ., 797 F.2d 782 (9th Cir. 1986); Murray v. Sapula, 45 F.3d 1417 (10th Cir. 1995).

166 CBOCS West, Inc. v. Humphries, 128 S. Ct. 1951 (2008).

167 Desert Palace, Inc. v. Costa, 539 U.S. 90 (2003).

168 Rayl v. Fort Wayne Cmty. Schs., 87 F. Supp. 2d 870 (N.D. Ind. 2000), *citing* Emmel v. Coca-Cola Bottling Co. of Chicago, 95 F.3d 627 (7th Cir. 1996).

169 Hazelwood Sch. Dist. v. United States, 433 U.S. 299 (1977).

170 Craik v. Minn. State Univ. Bd., 731 F.2d 465 (8th Cir. 1984).

171 Int'l Bhd. of Teamsters v. United States, 431 U.S. 324 (1977).

172 Sine v. Trustees of Cal. State Univ., 11 Fair Empl. Prac. Cases (BNA) 334 (E.D. Cal. 1974), *aff'd*, 526 F.2d 112 (9th Cir. 1975).

173 *See, e.g.,* Rowe v. Cleveland Pneumatic Co., 690 F.2d 88 (6th Cir. 1982).

174 Washington v. Davis, 426 U.S. 229 (1976); Personnel Adm'r of Mass. v. Feeney, 442 U.S. 256 (1979).

175 Albemarle Paper Co. v. Moody, 422 U.S. 405 (1975).

176 42 U.S.C. § 2000e–2(k)(1)(B)(ii).

177 Albermarle Paper Co. v. Moody, 422 U.S. 405 (1975).

178 Richardson v. Lamar County Bd. of Educ., 729 F. Supp. 806 (M.D. Ala. 1989), *aff'd*, 935 F.2d 1240 (11th Cir. 1991); United States v. Texas, 628 F. Supp. 304 (E.D. Tex. 1985), *rev'd on other grounds*, 793 F.2d 636 (5th Cir. 1986); York v. Ala. State Bd. of Educ., 581 F. Supp. 779 (M.D. Ala. 1983); United States v. North Carolina, 400 F. Supp. 343 (1975), *vacated*, 425 F. Supp. 789 (E.D.N.C. 1977).

179 445 F. Supp. 1094 (D.S.C. 1977), *aff'd mem.*, 434 U.S. 1026 (1978).

180 20 U.S.C. § 206(d).

181 Brock v. Georgia Southwestern Coll., 765 F.2d 1026 (11th Cir. 1985); EEOC v. Madison Cmty. Unit Sch. Dist., 818 F.2d 577 (7th Cir. 1987); Perdue v. City Univ. of N.Y., 13 F. Supp. 2d 326 (E.D.N.Y. 1998).

182 Ariz. Governing Comm. for Tax Deferred Annuity & Deferred Compensation Plans v. Norris, 463 U.S. 1073 (1983); Los Angeles v. Manhart, 435 U.S. 702 (1978).

183 Ledbetter v. Goodyear Tire and Rubber Company, 550 U.S. 618 (2007).

184 29 C.F.R. § 1604.11(a).

185 *See, e.g.,* Vermett v. Hough, 627 F. Supp. 587 (W.D. Mich. 1986).

186 Lipsett v. Univ. of P.R., 864 F.2d 881 (1st Cir. 1988).

187 Keppler v. Hinsdale Twp. Sch. Dist. 86, 715 F. Supp. 862 (N.D. Ill.1989); Succar v. Dade County Sch. Bd., 229 F.3d 1343 (11th Cir. 2000).

188 Oncale v. Sundowner Offshore Servs. Inc., 523 U.S. 75 (1998).

189 Price Waterhouse v. Hopkins, 490 U.S. 228 (1989).

190 *See* Dandan v. Radisson Hotel Lisle, No. 97-C-8342 2000 WL 336528 (N.D. Ill. March 28, 2000); Spearman v. Ford Motor Co., 231 F.3d 1080 (7th Cir. 2000); Carrasco v. Lenox Hill Hosp., No. 99-C-927 2000 WL 520640 (S.D.N.Y. April 28, 2000).

191 Trautvetter v. Quick, 916 F.2d 1140 (7th Cir. 1990).

192 Karibian v. Columbia Univ., 14 F.3d 773 (2d Cir. 1994).

193 Anderson v. Univ. Health Center, 623 F. Supp. 795 (W.D. Pa. 1985).

194 Priest v. Rotary, 634 F. Supp. 571 (N.D. Cal. 1986).

195 Meritor Savings Bank v. Vinson, 477 U.S. 57 (1986).

196 Harris v. Forklift Sys., Inc., 510 U.S. 17 (1993).

197 Redman v. Lima City Sch. Dist. Bd. of Educ., 889 F. Supp. 288 (N.D. Ohio 1995).

198 Ross v. Double Diamond, Inc., 672 F. Supp. 261 (N.D. Tex. 1987).

199 Cohen v. Litt, 906 F. Supp. 957 (S.D.N.Y. 1995); *see also* Clark County Sch. Dist. v. Breeden, 532 U.S. 268 (2001).

200 Smith v. St. Louis Univ., 109 F.3d 1261 (8th Cir. 1997); King v. Bd. of Regents of Univ. of Wis. Sys., 898 F.2d 533 (7th Cir. 1990); *but see* Becker v. Churchville-Chili Cent. Sch., 602 N.Y.S.2d 497 (N.Y. Sup. Ct. 1993).

201 Campbell v. Kansas State Univ., 780 F. Supp. 755 (D. Kan. 1991); *but see* Collins v. Baptist Mem. Geriatric Center, 937 F.2d 190 (5th Cir. 1991).

202 Vance v. Southern Bell Tel. & Tel. Co., 863 F.2d 1503 (11th Cir. 1989).

203 Burlington Indus., Inc. v. Ellerth, 524 U.S. 742 (1998); *see also* Faragher v. City of Boca Raton, 524 U.S. 775 (1998).

204 Molnar v. Booth, 229 F.3d 593 (7th Cir. 2000).

205 Pennsylvania State Police v. Suders, 542 U.S. 129 (2004).

206 Carr v. Allison Gas Turbine Div., 32 F.3d 1007 (7th Cir. 1994).

207 Hathaway v. Runyon, 132 F.3d 1214 (8th Cir. 1997).

208 Mattern v. Eastman Kodak Co., 104 F.3d 702 (5th Cir. 1997).

209 Knox v. Indiana, 93 F.3d 1327 (7th Cir. 1996); Gunnell v. Utah Valley State Coll., 152 F.3d 1253 (10th Cir. 1998).

210 *See, e.g.*, Lyons v. Barrett, 851 F.2d 406 (D.C. Cir. 1988).

211 723 P.2d 298 (Ore. 1986), *appeal dismissed*, 480 U.S. 942 (1987); *see also* United States v. Bd. of Educ. for Sch. Dist. of Philadelphia, 911 F.2d 882 (3d Cir. 1990).

212 May v. Evansville-Vanderburgh Sch. Corp., 787 F.2d 1105 (7th Cir. 1986).

213 406 U.S. 205 (1972).

214 Palmer v. Bd. of Educ. of Chicago, 603 F.2d 1271 (7th Cir. 1979).

215 Employment Div., Dep't of Human Resources v. Smith, 494 U.S. 872 (1990).

216 Pinsker v. Joint Dist. No. 28J of Adams & Arapahoe Counties, 735 F.2d 388 (10th Cir. 1984).

217 Rankins v. Comm'n on Prof'l Competence, 593 P.2d 852 (Cal.), *appeal dismissed*, 444 U.S. 986 (1979).

218 29 C.F.R. § 1605.1.

219 Young v. Southwestern Savings & Loan Ass'n, 509 F.2d 140 (5th Cir. 1975).

220 Brown v. Pena, 441 F. Supp. 1382 (S.D. Fla. 1977), *aff'd*, 589 F.2d 1113 (5th Cir. 1979).

221 Hansard v. Johns-Manville Prod. Corp., 5 Fair Empl. Prac. Cases (BNA) 707 (E.D. Tex. 1973).

222 *See, e.g.*, Cooper v. Oak Rubber Co., 15 F.3d 1375 (6th Cir. 1994).

223 http://www.eeoc.gov/policy/docs/religion.html.

224 Corp. of Presiding Bishop of Church of Jesus Christ of Latter-Day Saints v. Amos, 483 U.S. 327 (1987); Little v. Wuerl, 929 F.2d 944 (3d Cir. 1991).

225 TWA v. Hardison, 432 U.S. 63 (1977).

226 Cloutier v. Costco Wholesale Corp., 390 F.3d 126 (1st Cir. 2004).

227 http://www.eeoc.gov/policy/docs/religion.html.

228 Helland v. South Bend Cmty. Sch. Corp., 93 F.3d 327 (7th Cir. 1996).

229 479 U.S. 60 (1986).

230 29 U.S.C. §§ 701–796.

231 42 U.S.C. §§ 12101–12213.

232 42 U.S.C. § 12102.

233 Kelley v. Drexel Univ., 94 F.3d 102 (3d Cir. 1996).

234 Gordon v. Dist. of Columbia, 480 F. Supp. 2d 112 (D.D.C. 2007).

235 Nedder v. Rivier Coll., 944 F. Supp. 111 (D.N.H. 1996).

236 Chevron U.S.A., Inc. v. Echazabal, 536 U.S. 73 (2002).

237 Treiber v. Lindbergh Sch. Dist., 199 F. Supp. 2d 949 (E.D. Mo. 2002).

238 Ridge v. Cape Elizabeth Sch. Dep't, 77 F. Supp. 2d 149 (D. Me. 1999).

239 Sch. Bd. of Nassau County v. Arline, 480 U.S. 273 (1987); Chalk v. United States Dist. Court & Orange County Superintendent of Schs., 840 F.2d 701 (9th Cir. 1988).

240 Chalk v. United States Dist. Court & Orange County Superintendent of Schs., 840 F.2d 701 (9th Cir. 1988).

241 *See* Strathie v. Dep't of Transp., 716 F.2d 227 (3d Cir. 1983).

242 Southeastern Cmty. Coll. v. Davis, 442 U.S. 397 (1979).

243 U.S. Airways, Inc. v. Barnett, 535 U.S. 391 (2002).

244 Taylor v. Phoenixville Sch. Dist., 9 Am. Disabilities Cas. (BNA) 311 (3d Cir. 1999)

245 Humphrey v. Mem'l Hosp. Ass'n, 239 F.3d 1128 (9th Cir. 2001).

246 Hinson v. U.S.D. No. 500, 187 F. Supp. 2d 1297 (D. Kan. 2002).

247 946 F.2d 345 (4th Cir. 1991).

248 Barnes v. Gorman, 536 U.S. 181 (2002).

249 EEOC v. Waffle House, 534 U.S. 279 (2002).

250 427 U.S. 307 (1976).

251 Palmer v. Ticcione, 576 F.2d 459 (2d Cir. 1978).

252 Gault v. Garrison, 569 F.2d 993 (7th Cir. 1977).

253 29 U.S.C.A. §§ 623, 631.

254 Western Air Lines v. Criswell, 472 U.S. 400 (1985).

255 Kaufman v. Kent State Univ., 815 F. Supp. 1077 (N.D. Ohio 1993); Wooden v. Bd. of Educ. of Jefferson County, 931 F.2d 376 (6th Cir. 1991); Shook v. St. Bede Sch., 74 F. Supp. 2d 1172 (M.D. Ala. 1999).

256 544 U.S. 228 (2005)

257 *See* Meacham v. Knolls Atomic Power Lab., 2008 U.S. LEXIS 5029 (2008).

258 United States EEOC v. Newport Mesa Unified Sch. Dist., 893 F. Supp. 927 (C.D. Cal. 1995).

259 Henn v. Nat'l Geographic Soc'y, 819 F.2d 824 (7th Cir. 1987).

260 Cipriano v. Bd. of Educ. of North Tonawanda, 785 F.2d 51 (2d Cir. 1986).

261 Karlen v. City Colls. of Chicago, 837 F.2d 314 (7th Cir. 1988).

262 29 C.F.R. § 1625.7(f).

263 Myrna Gomez-Perez v. Potter, 128 S. Ct. 1931 (2008).

8   Teacher Employment

Chapter 7 examined the federal constitutional and statutory law that forms the foundation of a school's relationship to its teachers and other employees. This chapter focuses directly on teacher personnel issues: certification, hiring, job assignment, transfer, evaluation, nonrenewal, and dismissal. The primary source of law for the topics examined in this chapter is the statutes of the fifty states, although the Constitution is also relevant, particularly the Due Process Clause of the Fourteenth Amendment. Although the principles and cases presented are consistent with the law of most states, it must be remembered that personnel statutes and interpretations do vary across states, sometimes considerably. Therefore, practitioners should supplement the materials in this chapter with the relevant statutes of their state.

8.1 ELIGIBILITY FOR EMPLOYMENT

Eligibility for a particular teaching position in a public school requires a state-issued certificate or license. State certification requirements may include a requirement of good moral character, a college degree, specified courses, practice teaching, and, in more than half of the states, passing one or more examinations. Most states have "alternative" certification programs for people with demonstrated expertise in areas of teacher shortage such as science and math. Many states require a background check and fingerprinting and deny certification to anyone with a record of a serious criminal offense or any wrongdoing with a child.[1] A California court upheld the denial of certification to an applicant who had been convicted six times for public drunkenness and drunk driving.[2] Some states require citizenship for certification, sometimes with specified exceptions.[3] In *Ambach v. Norwick*,[4] the Supreme Court upheld a New York state regulation denying certification to non-U.S. citizens who had not shown an intention to apply for citizenship.

Obtaining a certificate grants only eligibility for, not entitlement to, employment and it does not automatically signify competence. In the absence of a state-authorized waiver, schools may not hire a candidate without the proper certificate. Thus, a West Virginia court held that a school district abused its discretion when it hired a person certified in general education and mathematics as a teacher of the gifted instead of someone certified in gifted education.[5]

Because teaching certificates have value, the law protects people against wrongful denial or revocation. The Due Process Clause prohibits arbitrary and capricious denial of a certificate to a candidate meeting all specified requirements.[6] A number of states require that the grounds for revocation be connected to teaching effectiveness. In *Erb v. Iowa State Board of Public Instruction*,[7] the Supreme Court of Iowa prohibited the state board from revoking a high school teacher's certificate on the grounds of adultery. The court wrote:

We emphasize the board's power to revoke teaching certificates is neither punitive nor intended to permit exercise of personal moral judgment by members of the board. Punishment is left to the criminal law, and the personal moral views of board members cannot be relevant . . . The sole purpose of the board's power . . . is to provide a means of protecting the school community from harm . . . [A] certificate can be revoked only upon a showing before the board of a reasonable likelihood that the teacher's retention in the profession will adversely affect the school community.

Nevertheless, obtaining a certificate does not guarantee the right to retain it. Because certificates are not contracts (see sec. 9.6), states may change retention requirements without violating constitutional prohibitions against the impairment of contracts.[8] In addition, certificates can be revoked for good cause after following the procedures spelled out in state law. In *Boguslawski v. Department of Education and Professional Standards and Practices Commission,*[9] the court upheld the revocation of the plaintiff's teaching certificate for the improper sexual touching of students despite the fact that the plaintiff had been acquitted in a criminal trial of the same charges. The court found that there was "substantial evidence" of wrongdoing, and said that the resolution of criminal charges in favor of the plaintiff did not bar subsequent civil or administrative proceedings concerning the same conduct. In another case, Florida unconditionally revoked the certificates of two teachers found in possession of marijuana plants.[10]

A person eligible for a teaching job by virtue of the requisite state certificate may still face additional requirements such as residency in the district or passing a physical examination. Courts have upheld these requirements against constitutional challenges.[11] Continuing education requirements may also be imposed on teachers as a condition of retaining their jobs.[12] The highest court of New York, however, struck down a school district requirement that probationary teachers pass a urine drug test to be eligible for tenure.[13]

The No Child Left Behind Act requires that schools receiving financial assistance under the Act ensure that all teachers supported by these funds are "highly qualified" as defined by the state.[14] The law further mandates that steps be taken to ensure "that poor and minority children are not taught at higher rates than other children by inexperienced, unqualified, or out-of-field teachers." States are required to report

the percentage of . . . teachers teaching with emergency or provisional credentials, and the percentage of classes in the State not taught by highly qualified teachers, in the aggregate and disaggregated by high-poverty compared to low-poverty schools which, for the purpose of this clause, means schools in the top quartile of poverty and the bottom quartile of poverty in the State.

Districts must inform parents that they may request certain information about their children's teachers including "timely notice that the parent's child has been assigned, or has been taught for four or more consecutive weeks by, a teacher who is not highly qualified."[15] The law also requires that paraprofessionals working in programs supported by NCLB funds meet certain requirements including two years of study at an institution of higher education.[16]

8.2 ASSIGNMENT, TRANSFER, AND DEMOTION

Hiring practices must comply with all constitutional and statutory antidiscrimination requirements (see chap. 7). Even the appearance of illegal discrimination such as in the questions asked at interviews and the make-up of selection committees should be avoided.

Once teachers have been hired, the board enjoys considerable discretion in assigning them to specific schools, classes, and extra duties. Like all personnel actions, however, assignments may not be discriminatory, violate state seniority or other statutory requirements, be done in retaliation for the legitimate exercise of a constitutional right, violate the terms of the teaching certificate, or violate either the teacher's contract or the collective-bargaining contract.[17]

Refusal to accept an assignment within the teacher's certification area is grounds for dismissal.[18] Similarly, unless there is a state statute to the contrary, refusal to accept lawful extra-duty assignments reasonably related to their job exposes teachers to dismissal for insubordination.[19] In judging the reasonableness of an extra-duty assignment, the courts consider such factors as the degree to which the assignment relates to the educational function of the school, the number of hours of the assignment, the relation of the assignment to the teacher's expertise, and the degree of impartiality in the assignment of extra duties.[20]

Extra duties may, however, be so removed from the basic responsibilities of a teacher that they cannot be required except by a supplemental contract that provides extra pay. Teachers who refuse to take on these extra-pay duties are not subject to dismissal.[21] However, teachers who perform extra duties do not obtain an entitlement to these jobs, so districts are free to remove teachers from, for example, coaching positions.[22]

Schools also enjoy broad discretion to transfer teachers. Unless a teacher can establish that the transfer was unlawful, not exercised in good faith for the best interests of the district, or an abuse of discretion, the refusal to accept the assignment is insubordination.[23] Transferring a teacher outside the area of the teacher's tenure may be prohibited unless the teacher consents. However, tenure does not give a teacher a vested right in a particular class or school. In *Thomas v. Smith*,[24] the Fifth Circuit ruled against a teacher who claimed he should have been given due process rights before being transferred to another school within the district and stripped of coaching duties.

Depending on state law, a transfer may constitute a demotion if it involves loss of pay, rank, reputation, or prestige. Demotions are permissible when, like dismissals, they are done for reasons specified in state law such as insubordination or budget cutbacks (see sec. 8.4 and 8.6). A demotion may entail the loss of a constitutionally protected interest and hence trigger constitutional due process protections (see sec. 8.5). State law may also specify a hearing or other procedures that must be followed when demoting a teacher.[25] Demotions must also conform to the requirements of the collective bargaining contract.

8.3 PROBATIONARY TEACHERS: EVALUATION, RENEWAL, AND TENURE

States are not constitutionally required to create a system of probation and tenure for teachers, but most have chosen to do so. In most states, a teacher with less than three years of continuous service in the same school district is a probationary teacher. Upon receiving a fourth consecutive annual contract, a teacher achieves nonprobationary or "permanent" status, which some states call "tenure." States may modify or eliminate their tenure system[26] but must honor the terms of previous tenure commitments.[27] In states that have a tenure system, local school boards may not refuse to grant tenure because they oppose the system itself or require their employees to waive their right to earn tenure.[28]

Some states place requirements on the evaluation of teachers, such as specifying the number of times that a teacher's class must be observed, and others permit school boards to design their own procedures. Some states require each school district to design a teacher evaluation plan within the boundaries set by state law and to submit the plan to the state board of education. Evaluation requirements for probationary teachers are often more extensive than for tenured teachers. A few states including Iowa require elaborate "induction" and comprehensive evaluation procedures for beginning teachers and condition the issue of a permanent teaching license on the results of the evaluation.[29] Alaska requires that probationary teachers be evaluated twice a year and that students, parents, community members, teachers, and administrators be given the opportunity to "provide information on the performance of the teacher." A teacher whose performance does not meet district standards must be provided a plan of improvement unless the teacher's performance warrants immediate dismissal.[30] Many school districts' collective-bargaining agreements also regulate the evaluation of teachers, both probationary and tenured.

School boards annually face the question of whether to renew the contract of probationary teachers and, ultimately, whether to grant tenure. Until fairly recently, these decisions were not subject to many procedural requirements. All states' statutes drew a sharp distinction between the procedures required for a nonrenewal decision and a decision to dismiss for cause. This distinction still exists in many states. In those states, school boards may decide not to rehire a probationary teacher for any constitutionally permissible reason. Statutes generally require only that the teacher be notified by a specified date of the decision not to renew. No hearing or other due process is required by either state statute or the Constitution (see sec. 8.5). State courts are split on the question whether a probationary teacher automatically achieves tenure if the school board fails to notify the teacher by the specified date.[31] However, today, almost half the states require that any teacher, tenured or not, whose contract is not to be renewed be given a statement of reasons as well as other significant procedural protections.[32] Failure to follow these procedures could result in the teacher automatically obtaining tenure by default.[33]

An Ohio statute illustrates the procedural rights probationary teachers now enjoy in many states. In the year prior to nonrenewal, a probationary teacher must be evaluated twice. Each evaluation must be based on two thirty-minute observations and specific criteria regarding expected job performance in the teacher's field. A required written report on the evaluation must contain recommendations for improvement regarding any deficiencies noted. The board must notify the teacher by April 30 of its intention not to renew. The teacher may demand a hearing. If the hearing affirms the decision not to renew, the decision may be appealed to a court, but the court's review is limited to determining whether the board complied with the statutory procedures. The court may not review the grounds for nonrenewal.[34]

Thus, even in states where nonrenewal of probationary teachers requires due process, boards still retain considerable discretion. The Rhode Island Supreme Court upheld a rule that said that probationary teachers who missed twenty-seven days or more during any one of their three probationary years would not be renewed or granted tenure.[35] An Alaska statute explicitly states that nontenured teachers are subject to nonretention "for any cause that the employer determines to be adequate."[36] The law even permits a school board not to renew a teacher's contract simply on the grounds that it believes a better teacher could be found. The teacher's only recourse is to prove that the decision not to renew violated a constitutional or statutory right (e.g., that the nonrenewal occurred because of race, religion, age, or other discriminatory reasons). Probationary teachers dismissed during a contract year as opposed to nonrenewal at the end of a contract year receive the same due process protection as tenured teachers (see sec. 8.5).

8.4 DISMISSAL FOR CAUSE

The contract of a post-probationary or tenured teacher must be renewed from year to year unless the teacher is dismissed for cause. State statutes protect tenured teachers by limiting the permissible grounds for dismissal. Tenured teachers may not be dismissed for engaging in constitutionally or statutorily protected behavior or because the school board believes that a better teacher could be found or even if a better teacher is found. When dismissing a tenured teacher, the school board bears the burden of showing by substantial evidence that it has statutory grounds for dismissal. In some states, the grounds for dismissal may be subject to a time limitation; for example, in New York, dismissal may not be for an act that occurred more than three years prior unless the act was the commission of a crime.[37] Many states also require that teachers be given the opportunity to remediate their deficiencies prior to dismissal. Dismissal is allowed only if remediation fails or if there is a finding of irremediability.[38] Failures in maintaining classroom discipline or performance of instructional duties are typically viewed as remediable, but serious misconduct that may do permanent harm, such as having sex with students, is not.[39]

Although the wording varies from state to state, statutory grounds for dismissal can be grouped into five general categories. Each category has been given a descriptive label, which may differ from the terms actually used in state statutes. None of these grounds is precisely defined in statute or case law, and each has been the issue in a significant amount of litigation.

Incompetence: grounds relating to expertise as a teacher. Some instances of incompetence may be referred to as "unprofessional conduct" or "inefficiency" in the statutes of some states. Factors such as a lack of knowledge of the subject matter; inability or failure to impart the designated curriculum; failure to work effectively with colleagues, supervisors, and parents; and failure to maintain adequate discipline or to supervise students have been recognized as indicative of incompetence. One court upheld the dismissal of a teacher whose students were disruptive, daydreamed, and left class without permission.[40] However, in another case, a teacher who was unable to establish rapport with his students was found not incompetent.[41] The Pennsylvania Supreme Court permitted the dismissal of a teacher whose classroom was filthy and who failed to plan lessons or keep order.[42] The Connecticut Supreme Court allowed the dismissal of a teacher who was competent in one of the two subject areas that she taught but incompetent in the other.[43] In some states, teaching out of certificate is proof of incompetence.[44]

Sometimes, the issue arises whether a teacher can be found incompetent for one instance of what the school board considers to be a serious instructional mistake. For example, a South Dakota case challenged the dismissal of a teacher for frankly answering a student's question about homosexuality. In disallowing the dismissal, the Supreme Court of South Dakota emphasized that incompetence usually must involve a pattern or course of conduct displaying

> a habitual failure to perform work with the degree of skill or accuracy displayed by other persons . . . Nevertheless, there are times when only one incident may be of such magnitude or of such far reaching consequences that a teacher's ability to perform his or her duties will be permanently impaired and a finding of "incompetence" would be proper.

In this case, however, there was no showing that the teacher's ability to teach had been impaired or that students were detrimentally affected. The court also concluded that it was unlikely the teacher would repeat the prohibited behavior.[45]

Student performance on standardized tests and other measures of student performance such as grades may play a role in determining a teacher's competence. A Minnesota court upheld the dismissal of a teacher based on evidence of lack of student progress, poor rapport with students, insufficient communication with parents, and unwillingness to follow administrative directives.[46] A Florida statute provides that teacher assessment should consider knowledge of subject, skill in discipline, and ability to plan and deliver instruction, evaluate instructional needs, and maintain "positive collaborative relationships with students' families . . ." but that evaluation of both teachers and school administrators "must be primarily based on the performance of students assigned to their classrooms or schools . . ."[47] Based on this statute, Florida courts have overturned the dismissal of teachers for "deficient performance" when the primary consideration was other factors besides student performance.[48]

School citizenship: grounds relating to in-school behavior and performance of duties other than actual teaching. Some instances may be referred to as "insubordination" or "neglect of duty" in the statutes of some states. Insubordination refers usually to willful, but sometimes even to inadvertent, disobedience either to an officially adopted school rule or to the legitimate order of a supervisor. In one case, the firing of a teacher who refused to execute normal duties associated with a teaching position such as going to faculty meetings and meeting with parents was allowed.[49]

However, a Kentucky court held that a teacher could not be dismissed for insubordination when merely charged with having failed to "cooperate" with the principal. To prove insubordination, the school had to point to a refusal on the part of the teacher to follow a specific school rule or a specific order.[50] In *Howard v. West Baton Rouge Parish School Board*,[51] a teacher was successful in overturning his dismissal for "willful neglect of duty" for having a wholly concealed handgun in his car parked on school grounds. The court ruled that in the absence of a school policy on the subject and in the absence of any specific order to the plaintiff, the school failed to establish that the teacher had "willfully or deliberately neglected his duties or acted in contravention of an order or school policy."

Teachers may not be dismissed for disobedience when the school rule or order violates their constitutional or statutory rights or the order was beyond the authority of the person issuing it. Thus, the Supreme Court ruled that the dismissal of a competent teacher for publicly criticizing the school board's budgetary policies was an impermissible violation of the teacher's right of free speech.[52]

To find a teacher insubordinate, it is not necessary to prove a pattern of behavior; a single instance may suffice. For example, a Pennsylvania teacher was dismissed for using sick leave to take a skiing vacation.[53] A finding of "neglect of duty" may also be based on a single incident. In *Flickinger v. Lebanon School District*[54] the court upheld the dismissal of a principal who failed immediately to respond to several requests from the assistant principal for assistance in dealing with a report that a specific student possessed a gun. Refusal to take a new teaching assignment is insubordination[55] as is violating rules against using corporal punishment[56] or employing certain teaching materials.[57] However, some courts will not permit dismissal for minor acts of disobedience that result in no harm to the school.[58]

Acts of academic dishonesty such as helping students cheat on tests or obtain a diploma under false pretenses are also generally upheld as causes of dismissal.[59] But the charges must be supported by substantial evidence. The case of *Altsheler v. Board of Education of the Great Neck Union Free School District*[60] involved the dismissal of a teacher based on the charge that she had prepared her students for the Stanford Achievement Test by revealing to them in advance vocabulary words that were to appear on the test. The case began after five students reported to their parents that some words on the test had been the subject of review in class. The students in the plaintiff's sixth-grade class increased their scores over the previous year by an average of 26 percentile points, and her fifth-grade class by over 20 points. The fifth-grade scores dropped significantly the following year. Of 285 "key words" on the test, 41.4 percent appeared on the teacher's vocabulary drill cards, but only 2 to 3 percent of the words on the cards appeared on other standardized tests. Nevertheless, the teacher won the case because the court believed the testimony of experts who said that test scores could jump if a teacher employs rote instruction and extensive drills and that because the teacher's drill cards were derived from "content" reading in science and social studies it was no surprise that her vocabulary list better matched the Stanford than the other tests, which drew upon basic reading textbooks. Of the 999 words on the drill cards, only 11.8 percent were on the Stanford test, and there was no evidence the teacher had seen the Stanford test before it was administered. The court concluded that the dismissal—for "conduct unbecoming a teacher and insubordination"—was not backed by "substantial evidence."

Incapacity: grounds relating to the mental or physical inability of the teacher to perform the job (but see sec. 7.6 on employment of persons with disabilities). In some instances, incapacity may be referred to as "unfitness" or "neglect of duty." One case upheld the firing of a teacher with a severe personality disorder,[61] but another case blocked dismissal of a teacher suffering from temporary mental illness.[62]

Role model: grounds relating to the teacher as an example for students. Some instances may be referred to as "immorality," "conduct unbecoming" a teacher, or "unfitness" in the statutes of some states. Cases in this category are of three types: teachers convicted or accused of violating a criminal law, teachers engaging in noncriminal extramarital sex, and teachers committing other noncriminal acts condemned by the school board such as lying.

In general, any serious criminal behavior is grounds for dismissal, especially if it involves violence[63] or stealing. Courts have permitted the dismissal of teachers convicted of theft, welfare fraud, income tax evasion, mail fraud, and sometimes even shoplifting.[64] Other cases have supported teacher dismissals for public intoxication, fighting, battery of a fiancée at a nightclub, negligent homicide arising out of an automobile accident, and driving under the influence of alcohol.[65] A Pennsylvania court ruled that a teacher at a school for students with drug and alcohol problems could be dismissed as a bad role model after three DUI convictions.[66] Teachers caught possessing illegal drugs or growing marijuana have also been subject to dismissal.[67] In Missouri, a teacher was successfully dismissed following an arrest for indecent exposure for masturbating in a public restroom, exposing himself, and making a homosexual advance to an undercover policeman.[68]

Despite these cases, many courts do not permit dismissal for a nonviolent or relatively minor crime unless the school board can establish a connection between the criminal behavior and teaching effectiveness. The West Virginia Supreme Court has ruled that in order for a teacher to be fired for any act committed away from the job, either the conduct must have directly affected the teacher's job performance or the notoriety surrounding the teacher's conduct must have significantly affected the teacher's ability to perform teaching duties. In the latter case, the notoriety must have been caused by the act itself, not by the school board's consideration of the act.[69]

Other courts have adopted positions similar to West Virginia's. A Washington state court disallowed the dismissal of a teacher convicted of grand larceny for purchasing a stolen motorcycle, stating that "simply labeling an instructor a convicted felon will not justify a discharge."[70] An Ohio court protected a teacher from dismissal even though he had been convicted of leaving the scene of a traffic accident.[71] A Montana court ruled that a teacher who had been found guilty three times of driving under the influence could not be dismissed because his crime was not "tantamount to immorality" and there was no proof that the convictions affected his performance as a teacher.[72] A New Mexico court reached the same conclusion even though this driver-education teacher was arrested not only for driving under the influence but also for resisting arrest and for battery. The court found that there was no relationship between the teacher's ability to teach and coach and his arrest for DUI and not cooperating with the police. The court noted that the teacher had used the incident as a lesson with his students and players.[73]

Dismissals for noncriminal sexual conduct raise both the statutory issues considered here and the constitutional issues considered in Section 7.3. An Ohio court barred the dismissal of an associate superintendent, ruling that his adulterous affair with a married school employee could not be considered immoral under state law in the absence of proof that it created hostility in the school community or had a serious impact on his professional duties. The court specifically rejected reliance on the fact that his colleagues had a negative perception of him and the argument that he was a "bad role model." To rely on the role model argument, said the court, "would open the door to allow other teachers to be terminated because of race, religion, political beliefs, and/or sexual orientation simply because the teacher was not 'the type of role model parents want their children to have.'"[74]

Other courts have taken a similar approach, rejecting dismissal and certificate revocation for consensual unwed sex and for notorious adultery in a disapproving community.[75] The major exception is for public performance of intimate sex acts; in one case, a tenured elementary school teacher was successfully dismissed for immorality following her arrest for openly engaging in sexual activities with three men at a "swinger's club."[76] Federal law does not permit dismissal of unwed mothers on the grounds of immorality or being a bad role model for students.[77]

In light of *Lawrence v. Texas*,[78] the Supreme Court's 2003 decision prohibiting states from classifying homosexual sex as a crime, earlier cases upholding the dismissal of teachers for merely being gay[79] would undoubtedly be decided differently today. It is no longer possible to dismiss homosexual teachers on the grounds that they have engaged in criminal behavior by violating state sodomy laws. Even prior to *Lawrence*, the California Supreme Court ruled that state law did not permit revocation of the certificate of a teacher who had engaged in homosexual sex with a consenting adult many years earlier. The court said that certificate revocation would be warranted only if the teacher posed a significant danger to either students or school employees or if there were a proven connection between the teacher's conduct and the teacher's effectiveness.[80] (In some jurisdictions, Title VII may also protect against dismissal for being gay, see sec. 7.4.)

In *Walthart v. Board of Directors of Edgewood-Colesburg Community School District*,[81] an Iowa school district was permitted to dismiss a teacher for "just cause" based on noncriminal, off-campus behavior. The case involved a teacher who permitted students to camp on her property on a Saturday and later realized that the students were drinking. Her failure to attempt to stop the drinking and adequately to monitor the students arguably contributed to a fatal accident. The court wrote,

> The board concluded this damaged her reputation as a teacher and was detrimental to her ability to be an effective role model. It found she lacked support from other faculty members, indicating her effectiveness as a teacher was greatly diminished. The board concluded that "for the Board to retain her on the faculty would render its anti-alcohol policy meaningless and subject to utter disregard by the student body and perhaps even the faculty."

Lying to school officials might sometimes be the basis for a finding of immorality. In one case, a tenured teacher who had been denied permission to attend a conference went anyway and upon returning submitted a request for an excused absence based on illness. The court upheld the dismissal of the teacher saying that immoral behavior was not limited to sexual conduct.[82] However, in another case, the court ruled that a teacher could not be dismissed for writing two letters to a recently graduated student, letters that the court said contained gross, vulgar, and offensive language. The court could find no connection between these private letters and the teacher's fitness to teach.[83]

In general then, despite some cases to the contrary, most courts insist that school boards wishing to fire teachers for immorality demonstrate a connection between the allegedly immoral conduct and teaching effectiveness. If the teacher has committed a serious crime involving violence or a significant theft, a connection—that the teacher's presence in the school poses a danger to persons or property—may be assumed. For less serious crimes, the connection must be established affirmatively. If the alleged connection is that notoriety surrounding the teacher's conduct has led to a loss of respect from students or community members, the notoriety must have occurred as a result of the conduct itself and not because the board publicized the conduct.

Posing a threat to pupils: behavior that harms or endangers students may be referred to as "immorality," "unprofessional conduct," or "unfitness to teach" in the statutes of some states. Drinking or using drugs[84] or engaging in illegal, dangerous, or reckless behavior with students is grounds for dismissal as is the physical or verbal abuse of students.

Teachers may be dismissed for subjecting students to vulgar or racial invective in or out of class.[85] Inappropriate classroom commentary may also be dangerous enough to justify dismissing a teacher. One twelfth-grade teacher was dismissed for explaining the operation of houses of prostitution including minimum age requirements for admission, discussing the size of a penis, and telling stories about intercourse with virgins and sex with a cow.[86] An Iowa court upheld the dismissal of a ninth-grade English teacher who used sarcasm with his students and said to one student who had written a paper on suicide that "for extra credit, why don't you try it."[87]

Dismissal of teachers who have sex with minors is always upheld. It does not matter whether the minor was currently enrolled in the teacher's school or even in the same school district. Thus, the Maine Supreme Court upheld the dismissal of an elementary teacher who had sexual intercourse with a fifteen-year-old even though she and the boy did not live in the town where she taught.[88] Nor does it matter if the sexual relationship took place prior to the teacher's current employment. When a twenty-three-year-old man established that his former elementary school teacher had sexually abused him many years before, the teacher's dismissal was allowed.[89] Another case upheld the dismissal of a teacher twelve years after having a sexual relationship with a fifteen-year-old student while employed in another school district.[90] There is some question as to whether a legal sexual relationship with a student, that is, a consensual relationship with a student who had reached the legal age of consent, is cause for dismissal. Dismissal would almost surely be upheld if the student attended the same school where the teacher taught.

Dismissal of teachers who engage in sex with minors is not only permissible, but may be legally prudent or even mandatory in some cases. School districts that hire or retain teachers with a history of sexual relationships with minors may be vulnerable to lawsuits for negligent hiring if the behavior is repeated (see sec. 10.5). School districts that fail to act on instances of sexual involvement between teachers and students, even involvement that falls short of sexual intercourse, may be vulnerable to lawsuits under Title IX (see sec. 5.9). However, schools must be careful to differentiate between sexual abuse and harassment and well-intentioned, nonsexual touching.[91]

Making a Case for Dismissal

A case for dismissal becomes stronger when it contains any of the following elements: documented observations of the teacher according to a formalized and properly followed evaluation procedure, establishment of a connection between the behavior and teaching effectiveness in the classroom, evidence of incompetence or other grounds based on more than the subjective evaluation by a single school official (but subjective impressions may be part of a properly executed evaluation[92]), proof that formal steps of remediation were undertaken and failed, proof that the teacher's behavior undermined the educational goals of the school, evidence of specific harms or disruption of the school's educational mission, proof of the violation of a written school rule or policy, the establishment of a pattern of offending behavior, evidence of notices and warnings provided to the teacher, the absence of any sound educational justification for the teacher's behavior, evidence of notoriety over the teacher's behavior diminishing the school's or teacher's effectiveness (but not notoriety resulting primarily from the school board's actions), the absence of mitigating circumstances explaining or excusing the teacher's behavior, or evidence that the continuing presence of the teacher in the school poses an educational or physical risk to the students.

The testimony of students may be used in making a case for dismissal, as may the results of a polygraph test.[93] A California court has ruled that even illegally obtained evidence—evidence that could not be used in a criminal proceeding against the teacher—may be used in a dismissal proceeding.[94] Some courts may exclude hearsay evidence from teacher dismissal hearings or require that hearsay be given very little weight.[95]

Few things can diminish a school's effectiveness more than a teacher who cannot perform adequately; yet, far fewer teachers are actually dismissed than are considered incompetent by their supervisors. Reasons for the discrepancy include reluctance to cause harm to the incompetent person, fear of litigation or other unpleasant repercussions, and the belief that incompetence can more easily be dealt with through other methods such as forced resignation. The latter approach—forcing resignation by making working conditions intolerable—is known as "constructive discharge." Although it may be desirable to give an unsatisfactory employee the opportunity to resign before instituting formal proceedings, courts often view constructive discharge as a violation of due process. Employees who voluntarily resign will usually find courts unsympathetic if they try to rescind their action unless they can show a significant degree of coercion.

Whereas failing to fire an incompetent teacher rarely results in litigation, dismissals for constitutionally or statutorily impermissible reasons often do. Typically, these cases arise when administrators act out of anger or personal animosity toward a teacher, in the face of community pressure, or when the teacher lives an unorthodox lifestyle. School officials serve their students, teachers, and community best and are far less likely to find themselves on the losing side of a lawsuit when they act on the basis of professional standards and statutory requirements and not out of personal pique or political pressure.

8.5 PROCEDURAL DUE PROCESS

As with students, rules that govern the behavior of teachers must meet the basic due process requirement that they not be vague or overbroad (see sec. 4.1). In one case, a Nebraska teacher disciplined by his school board for violating the state law against corporal punishment of students argued that the law was impermissibly vague. The teacher had either "tapped" or "slapped" the student on the back of the head in frustration when the student repeatedly ignored his orders. Citing Supreme Court precedent, the court stated that

> due process requires that [a rule] supply (1) a person of ordinary intelligence a reasonable opportunity to know what is prohibited and (2) explicit standards for those who apply it . . . The test is whether the defendant could reasonably understand that his conduct was proscribed by the statute.

Although the court agreed that corporal punishment might have been more carefully defined in the law, it nonetheless ruled that the term was not so vague as to violate due process. The court did agree with the teacher's contention that

> that portion of the board's order requiring that [the teacher] "obtain adequate professional counseling" is so vague as to be virtually unenforceable. Without a minimum of objective standards setting forth the duration of the counseling, or the payment provisions or nature of the mandatory counseling, this portion of the order is subject to the most arbitrary kind of enforcement by the board.[96]

In making a case for the dismissal of a teacher, the school board must follow certain procedures. The Constitution, as the supreme law of the land, lays down the minimum procedural requirements that all dismissals must satisfy. State statutory law and local policy must at least comply with these minimum requirements, but states and school districts may and often do adopt additional or stronger procedural requirements than the Constitution requires. Local school district procedures regarding teacher firings may be found in individual teacher contracts, collective-bargaining agreements, or the policy statements of local school boards. Whatever their source, school district procedures must be consistent with state requirements.

Two Supreme Court cases, decided at the same time, deal with the issue of when the Constitution requires due process for teacher dismissals. Although these are higher education cases, the same principles apply in the lower schools. The first case, *Board of Regents of State Colleges v. Roth*,[97] involved a teacher who was not rehired after his first year of teaching at a public college. He was not given a hearing or any statement of reasons, but was simply informed that his contract would not be renewed. The second case, *Perry v. Sindermann*,[98] also involved a state college's nonrenewal without a hearing of a nontenured teacher, but this time one who had been working in the system for ten years. Both teachers claimed that they should have been entitled to a hearing under the Due Process Clause of the Fourteenth Amendment.

In finding against Roth but in favor of Sindermann, the Supreme Court drew important distinctions between the two cases. The Fourteenth Amendment only requires due process when the state seeks to deprive a person of property or liberty. But Roth had been given no promise of employment beyond the duration of his contract or any reason to expect that he would be rehired. Nor had the nonrenewal been handled in such a manner as to jeopardize Roth's reputation or his prospects for employment elsewhere. Thus, he had no property or liberty interest at stake and no constitutional claim to due process.

By contrast, Sindermann's school had a written policy and longstanding practice of rehiring its teachers as long as their "teaching services are satisfactory." Furthermore, although Sindermann had not been formally notified of the reasons for his nonrenewal, the college had issued a press release "setting forth allegations of [his] insubordination," thus damaging his reputation as a teacher. Unlike Roth, Sindermann did have a property interest in continued employment and a liberty interest in restoring his reputation and, therefore, a constitutional right to due process. All teachers have a property interest in continued employment for the duration of their contracts. In addition, the effect of state tenure and continuing contract statutes is to grant a legally enforceable expectation of continued employment to teachers who have been hired beyond the probationary period.

However, *Roth* and *Sindermann* indicate that not every personnel action entails a constitutional right to due process. Unless due process is specifically mandated by state statute, the nonrenewal of a probationary teacher's contract usually does not require a formal hearing or even notification of reasons (see sec. 8.3). By contract, custom, statute, and even definition, probationary teachers do not have a legal expectation of continued employment or reemployment; probationary teachers do not have a property interest in their jobs beyond the expiration date of their contract. As the Court said in *Roth*, "abstract need or desire" or "unilateral expectation" is not enough to establish a property right. Unless state law or district policy specifically grants them due process, probationary teachers usually succeed in establishing a property right to employment only if they are dismissed in the middle of their contract or, as in *Sindermann*, if there exists a de facto policy that creates the equivalent of tenure.

As discussed in *Roth*, personnel actions taken in retaliation for speech activities require due process, "whether or not the speech or press interest is clearly protected under substantive First Amendment standards." *Roth* also suggests that actions that might seriously damage a teacher's reputation or standing within the community or impair prospects for future employment also may be viewed as deprivations of liberty requiring due process. Thus, teachers, whether tenured or not, have occasionally succeeded in claiming that transfers, demotions, failure to provide salary increases, failure to grant tenure, or temporary suspensions should have been accompanied by procedural protections. This is most likely to occur when an adverse decision is based on publicly made charges. Charges of intoxication, racism, and mental instability have been found sufficiently stigmatizing to require due process.[99] In other cases, however, allegations of poor job performance such as incompetence, inadequacy, and insubordination have not been found to require due process.[100]

Once it is decided that a teacher has a right to procedural due process, the question becomes: What process is due? In *Cleveland Board of Education v. Loudermill*,[101] the Supreme Court considered the issue of whether the Constitution requires specific due process procedures for tenured public employees such as teachers in addition to the due process rights that may be specified by state law. Although the Court recognized that the government may have a significant "interest in quickly removing an unsatisfactory employee," it nevertheless ruled that a tenured employee's interest in avoiding unwarranted dismissal was important enough to require at least a minimal opportunity for a pretermination hearing. The minimum constitutional requirements for the hearing are similar to those afforded to a student prior to suspension from school: "The tenured public employee is entitled to oral or written notice of the charges against him, an explanation of the employer's evidence, and an opportunity to present his side of the story."

Loudermill makes clear that the Constitution imposes due process procedures independent of the requirements of state law. Where state law specifies post-termination procedures adequate to "definitively resolve the propriety of the discharge," pretermination proceedings need not be elaborate. All that is required is some notice of the charges and supporting evidence and an opportunity to refute them. An investigation, no matter how thorough, cannot substitute for a hearing. Thus, a teacher who was suspended for four days and then transferred following an investigation for possible child abuse, but without a hearing, successfully claimed that his due process rights had been violated. The court ruled that the suspension and transfer implicated both property and liberty interests thereby requiring an opportunity to present evidence and cross-examine adverse witnesses.[102]

Loudermill does not fully specify the level of due process required when educational employment contracts are terminated. In teacher dismissal cases, state statutes generally require advanced notice of the charges and a hearing before an impartial tribunal. To satisfy constitutional and statutory requirements, the notice must be given sufficiently in advance of the hearing and be sufficiently precise to allow the preparation of a defense.[103] In one case, a notice informing a teacher being charged with "insubordination based upon the fact you refuse to cooperate with the principal of your school" was found to be inadequate.[104] Similarly, merely charging a teacher with "incompetence" is not adequate notice.[105] To satisfy due process requirements, the notice should support its charges with indications of the specific unacceptable behaviors and deficiencies. Careful crafting of charges is important also because the hearing may not consider charges not listed in the notice or evidence not relevant to those charges.

Due process requires that the outcome of the hearing be determined by impartial decision makers. Impartiality may be questioned if the decision maker has a conflict of interest, harbors personal animosity toward the employee, prejudges the case, acts as both judge and "prosecutor," meets with the "prosecutor" or others with interests opposed to the employee outside the hearing, or considers evidence not presented at the hearing. In *Hortonville Joint School District No. 1 v. Hortonville Education Ass'n*,[106] a group of teachers fired while engaging in an illegal strike claimed that their due process rights had been violated. To support their claim, the teachers argued that the board of education, which had made the decision to fire them, could not be impartial because the board and the teachers were on opposite sides of the strike. In rejecting the teachers' argument, the Supreme Court noted that "the Board is the only body vested by [state] statute with the power to employ and dismiss teachers." The Court concluded that simply because the board was "involved in the events" preceding the firing was not enough "to overcome the presumption of honesty and integrity in policymakers with decisionmaking power."

Hortonville allows that decision makers may hold prejudgments on what constitutes sufficient grounds for dismissal or other policy matters, but prejudgment of the facts or the outcome of a specific case violates due process.[107] Courts will disqualify decision makers when there is proof of actual bias or prejudice. Bias on the part of one member of a dismissal hearing panel is enough to taint the entire process.[108] In one case, a member of a teacher dismissal hearing panel asked for and received extra compensation from the school board. The court ruled that the extra compensation created an appearance of impropriety sufficient to indicate a violation of the teacher's right to an impartial hearing.[109] A history of heated exchanges between the employee and decision maker is not usually enough to prove bias.[110]

Some states permit or require local school boards to conduct teacher dismissal hearings, but others require an independent hearing officer or panel selected according to specified procedures. Ohio permits a teacher to demand a hearing either before the board itself or by a referee chosen by mutual consent between the teacher and board from a list of three chosen by the superintendent. New York requires that the hearing panel be made up of three nondistrict employees picked by the school board and the teacher from a list of state-approved hearing officers. Other states allow the teacher and school board each to designate one member of a three-member panel. The first two members must then jointly choose the third. Another method is to have the state provide a list of qualified hearing officers. The list is passed back and forth between teacher and school board, each in turn crossing out one name until the last remaining name is designated to hear the case.

One potentially conflictive aspect of the hearing process is the role of the prosecutor. Plaintiffs sometimes question the impartiality of the school board when the case against the teacher is presented by the board's own regular attorney, but courts have rejected this claim.[111] More troublesome for the courts is when the school's attorney or other official involved in prosecuting the case joins the board in its deliberations. When this occurs, the prosecution gets a second chance to influence the board without the defense being given an equivalent opportunity. As unfair as this practice may seem, the courts have split regarding its permissibility.[112]

State statutes may grant teachers the right to an attorney or other representative in dismissal hearings. Where no statute exists, a majority of the few courts that have considered the issue have concluded that teachers do have a right to counsel.[113]

Courts also protect an accused teacher's right to confront and cross-examine witnesses including witnesses who testify by written affidavit, to receive a tape or transcript of the hearing, and to receive a written or oral statement of reasons for the decision.[114] Many states' laws grant the right to appeal the decision of the local board or hearing panel to the state commissioner of education or some other administrative agency. Subject to certain conditions, appeals may also be taken to the courts. The most important condition is that courts will not usually hear appeals unless all administrative remedies afforded by state law or local policy have been exhausted.

The No Child Left Behind Act (see sec. 2.6) and some state statutes permit or require the involuntary transfer or dismissal of teachers in schools repeatedly designated as failing.[115] Teachers dismissed pursuant to these statutes may bring a variety of legal challenges including violation of procedural due process, violation of substantive due process (if the tests on which the dismissal was ultimately based lack curricular validity), and violation of contract or the collective bargaining agreement (see chap. 9).

8.6 REDUCTION IN FORCE

Reduction in force (RIF) refers to dismissal because of financial exigency, declining enrollment, or a decision to discontinue a particular program or service. Realignment of the workforce, including transfers and demotions for economic reasons, is governed by different statutes than those governing nonrenewal of probationary teachers, dismissals for cause, and disciplinary transfers and demotions. Many states' statutes require RIF dismissals in reverse order of seniority.

Other states take different approaches. Nebraska law provides that before a school board may dismiss a teacher as part of a RIF, the board must have proof that a change in circumstances necessitated the reduction, the change in circumstances is specifically related to the affected teacher, and there are no vacancies for which the teacher is qualified.[116] The West Virginia Supreme Court rejected the view that state law required that a RIF be done strictly according to seniority. The court ruled that the board must also consider years of teaching experience in a given subject area.[117] Collective-bargaining agreements may also affect RIF policies and procedures.

Legal challenges to RIFs include claims that:

- Economic circumstances or drops in enrollment did not justify the RIF.[118]
- Abolition of a position did not in fact occur; instead, the same position was retained under a different title.[119]
- The RIF prevented the provision of mandated services or improperly affected the quality of the education program.[120]
- The order of dismissal violated seniority or other statutory mandate.[121]
- A demotion as part of the RIF plan was arbitrary and violated seniority rights.[122]
- The statutorily prescribed order of reinstatement and recall was violated.[123]
- RIF procedures violated statutory due process requirements.[124]
- RIF procedures violated contractual requirements.[125]
- The RIF policy was racially discriminatory.[126]

8.7 LEAVES OF ABSENCE

School boards have the authority to grant leaves of absence for personal reasons such as illness, for professional reasons such as to pursue additional training, or for public service such as military or jury duty. Boards also have the authority to impose involuntary leave on teachers who are physically or mentally unfit if the teachers' procedural due process rights are satisfied.[127] Boards may not, however, grant a leave that constitutes a gift of public money to a private individual.

Litigation concerning a leave of absence may involve the claim that a school board violated its own policy, the collective-bargaining agreement, state statute, federal antidiscrimination law, or the Constitution. In 1974, the Supreme Court ruled that mandatory pregnancy or postpartum leaves of absence violate the teachers' right of privacy.[128] Federal antidiscrimination laws prohibit treating pregnancy differently from other disabilities, such as not allowing pregnant teachers to use sick leave.[129] Federal law also prohibits religious discrimination in the administration of a personal leave policy (see sec. 7.5).

8.8 WORKERS' COMPENSATION

Teachers injured on the job have two possible paths to compensation from their school district. If the teacher's injury results from careless, reckless, or intentionally wrongful behavior on the part of the district or another of its employees, the teacher may be able to sue the district for negligence or another tort (see chap. 10); however, such suits may only be brought for injuries that are not eligible for redress under the system known as "workers' compensation."

In most, but not all, states, teachers are covered by workers' compensation statutes. Although workers' compensation laws vary from state to state, all are designed to provide compensation to employees for on-the-job injuries regardless of whether their employers were negligent. The idea is that employers should be responsible for the harm suffered by employees in the course of conducting their employer's business. In most states, an employee's injury resulting from the intentionally wrongful behavior of the employer or a coworker (see sec. 10.1) is not covered by workers' compensation, but workers' compensation is the exclusive remedy for injuries caused by simple negligence (see sec. 10.4) on the part of an employer.

To be eligible for compensation, a teacher or any employee must prove the existence of three elements: (a) an injury by accident, (b) arising out of, and (c) in the course of, employment.

At one time, the accident requirement meant that the employee had to prove the occurrence of a sudden impact related to something other than routine work. Occupational diseases and back injuries or hernias suffered during routine lifting were excluded from coverage. This narrow notion of an accident has given way to a broader interpretation so that now teachers may also seek compensation for injuries that developed slowly over time or are caused by routine tasks, such as lifting books. Teachers are also covered if preexisting conditions are aggravated by their work. Thus, an on-the-job heart attack may be compensable even if it results in part from years of unhealthy living. However, some states will not require workers' compensation to cover heart attacks unless caused by work stress greater than most people experience during normal daily living.

Once the accident element is proven, a teacher claiming workers' compensation must next show that the injury arose out of the job of teaching. In most states, to satisfy this element, the teacher must show that the act of doing the job increased the probability of the injury. For example, this element can usually be proven in the case of a teacher injured by a student's assault because teaching increases the likelihood of being assaulted.

Under some conditions, job-induced mental illness and even stress may be compensable. Harassment of any kind—sexual, racial, or just personal animosity—is a common source of compensable stress. In one case, a teacher successfully claimed workers' compensation after being falsely accused of sexually harassing a student.[130] However, unless the employer acts unreasonably, claims for compensation for stress arising from overwork, discipline, denial of promotion, layoff, or discharge are usually denied. For example, one court refused to allow a claim for work-related mental stress because there was no proof that the claimant's particular working conditions were uniquely stressful (she supervised bus routes and other transportation-related matters). The court noted that there was no evidence to suggest that the stress the claimant experienced was the result of anything other than her own mismanagement of the position.[131]

North Carolina's highest court denied workers' compensation to a teacher who claimed her general anxiety disorder arose when the students in her class were disrespectful and disobedient and verbally and physically harassed her. To win her case, said the court, the plaintiff had to establish that her anxiety disorder "arose due to stresses and conditions unique to her employment." But the court found that,

> There is substantial evidence . . . to show that, although the environment in plaintiff's classroom was certainly stressful, such stress was not created by defendant, nor was it characteristic of plaintiff's particular employment. Rather, the evidence showed that the stressful classroom environment was caused by plaintiff's inability to effectively manage her classroom. Other teachers at plaintiff's school who taught the same students did not experience the disciplinary problems encountered by plaintiff. Defendant did not require plaintiff to do anything other than perform her job duties as a teaching professional. Such duties included maintaining control of the classroom learning environment, a task plaintiff unfortunately was unable to perform. Defendant attempted to intervene and assist plaintiff in her endeavors to better manage her classroom, but such attempts were ultimately unsuccessful. We conclude there was substantial evidence to support the . . . findings that plaintiff was responsible for the stressful work environment, and that such stress was not characteristic of the teaching profession.[132]

The final element of a workers' compensation claim is to show that the injury occurred in the course of employment. This element focuses on where the injury occurred and what the employee was doing at the time. Hence, a teacher who is injured in a car accident while commuting to work would not be covered, but once the teacher crosses the school's property line the commute is over and coverage begins. Teachers injured while driving off-campus on school business would also be covered. A teacher may lose coverage by engaging in willful misconduct, such as being drunk or disobeying the law or the school's rules.

In most states, the workers' compensation system operates outside the regular court system. Claims must be prosecuted through an administrative agency created specifically for that purpose. Some states have a separate agency for public employees like teachers. In most states, a claim is first decided by a hearing officer, and both sides have the option of appealing to the full agency. The agency's decisions may then be appealed to a court on either procedural or substantive grounds.

All states' workers' compensation systems require the employee to promptly notify the employer of any injury and establish time limits and procedures for filing claims. Failure to satisfy these requirements will result in a denial of claims. Successful claims may result in compensation for medical expenses, rehabilitation, lost wages, disability or disfigurement, or death benefits to surviving dependents, but there is a limit to the amount that may be awarded, and no punitive damages are allowed. Monetary damages under workers' compensation are usually less than they would have been if a successful tort suit could have been brought.[133]

8.9 SUMMARY

Most of the law relevant to the hiring and firing of professional school employees is found in state statutes. States are free to set whatever teacher certification requirements they wish, except that standards may not be arbitrary, racially discriminatory, or otherwise violative of constitutional rights. Because certification does not amount to a contractual agreement, states may also set new standards for certification retention even by "life-certificated" employees.

For their part, schools are free to offer employment to whomever they deem most qualified, provided that the candidate meets state eligibility requirements, including certification, and that the hiring process does not violate federal constitutional or statutory provisions. Once hired, teachers may be assigned to any school, grade level, or subject matter for which they are qualified unless their contract says otherwise. They may also be assigned extra duty and tasks reasonably connected to the legitimate educational goals of the school and their job, again subject to contractual constraints.

Schools also have wide latitude in the evaluation and contract renewal decision concerning probationary teachers. In many states, a school may decide not to renew the contract of a teacher in the first three years of employment for any constitutionally permissible reason and without granting a hearing or following any specific procedures. It may not even be necessary to reveal the reasons for the decision to the teacher. About half of the states do have some guidelines regarding the decision not to renew a beginning teacher. Generally, these amount to requirements that the teacher receive at least a minimal evaluation, that the reasons for the nonrenewal be given, and that the teacher have an opportunity to provide a rebuttal. Even in states with these requirements, districts are generally free to nonrenew for any constitutionally permissible reason, provided statutory procedural requirements are met.

The situation regarding tenured teachers is quite different. Each state's statutes establish a list of the only acceptable bases for termination or nonrenewal of the contract of a teacher who has passed the probationary period. Although the wording varies considerably from state to state, acceptable causes for dismissal can be grouped into five categories: incompetence, violation of role model obligations, poor citizenship within the school, posing a threat to students, and incapacity. The law places the burden of proof on the school to show, in many states through a prescribed evaluation process, that the teacher falls into one of the dismissible categories. Unlike with probationary teachers, the law does not permit the firing of a tenured teacher to hire someone who is cheaper or better.

In addition to the requirement that dismissal be for a specified cause, both the Constitution and state statutes impose significant procedural due process requirements on tenured-teacher firings. In general, the Constitution requires an impartial hearing including a statement of charges and a reasonable opportunity to refute them. Most states' statutes specify additional procedures, often granting a right to counsel, to call and cross-examine witnesses, to receive a transcript of the proceedings, and to appeal. Because a great deal is at stake and the risk of litigation is very high, firings should comply with both the letter and spirit of all relevant law.

Reduction in force—dismissal of teachers because funds are lacking or programs eliminated—is also primarily controlled by state statute. Most of the litigation challenging a specific RIF is resolved by comparing the specific procedures employed with the requirements of state statutes. A common but not universal feature of these statutes is that more recently hired teachers be let go before those with greater seniority.

School boards may grant voluntary leaves of absence or impose involuntary leaves consistent with federal and state law and their own policies and contractual agreement.

Leave-of-absence policies may not discriminate on the basis of race, religion, or pregnancy. Teachers injured at work may receive payment in accordance with the workers' compensation laws of their state. To be eligible for workers' compensation, a teacher must sustain an injury by accident arising out of and in the course of employment.

NOTES

1   *See, e.g.*, A.C.A. § 6–17–410.
2   Watson v. State Bd. of Educ., 99 Cal. Rptr. 468 (Cal. Ct. App. 1971).
3   *See, e.g.*, 105 ILCS 5/21–1 (2008); N.J. STAT. § 18A:26–1; NEV. REV. STAT. ANN. § 391.060; 24 P.S. § 11–1109.
4   441 U.S. 68 (1979).
5   Johnson v. Cassell, 387 S.E.2d 553 (W. Va. 1989); *see also* Bradford Cent. Sch. Dist. v. Ambach, 436 N.E.2d 1256 (N.Y. 1982).
6   Commonwealth v. Great Valley Sch. Dist., 352 A.2d 252 (Pa. Commw. Ct. 1976).
7   216 N.W.2d 339 (Iowa 1974).
8   State v. Project Principle, Inc., 724 S.W.2d 387 (Tex. 1987).
9   837 A.2d 614 (Pa. Commw. Ct. 2003).
10   Adams v. State Prof'l Practices Council, 406 So. 2d 1170 (Fla. Dist. Ct. App. 1981).
11   Pittsburgh Fed'n of Teachers Local 400 v. Aaron, 417 F. Supp. 94 (W.D. Pa. 1976).
12   Harrah Indep. Sch. Dist. v. Martin, 440 U.S. 194 (1979).
13   Congress of Teachers v. Bd. of Educ. of Patchogue-Medford Union Free Sch. Dist., 510 N.E.2d 325 (N.Y. 1987).
14   20 U.S.C. § 6319(a)(1).
15   20 U.S.C. § 6311.
16   20 U.S.C. § 6319(c).
17   Gibbons v. New Castle Area Sch. Dist., 500 A.2d 922 (Pa. Commw. Ct. 1985); Adelt v. Richmond Sch. Dist., 58 Cal. Rptr. 151 (Cal. Ct. App. 1967); Appeal of Santee, 156 A.2d 830 (Pa. 1959).
18   Commonwealth *ex rel.* Wesenberg v. Sch. Dist. of Bethlehem, 24 A.2d 673 (Pa. Super. Ct. 1942); Shiers v. Richland Parish Sch. Bd., 902 So. 2d 1173 (La. App. 2d Cir. 2005).
19   Harrisburg R-VIII Sch. Dist. v. O'Brian, 540 S.W.2d 945 (Mo. Ct. App. 1976); Dist. 300 Educ. Ass'n v. Bd. of Educ. of Dundee Cmty., 334 N.E.2d 165 (Ill. App. Ct. 1975).
20   Bd. of Educ. of Asbury Park v. Asbury Park Educ. Ass'n, 368 A.2d 396 (N.J. Super. Ct. Ch. Div.), *aff'd in part and appeal dismissed in part*, 382 A.2d 392 (N.J. Super. Ct. App. Div. 1977).
21   Swager v. Bd. of Educ., Unified Sch. Dist. No. 412, 688 P.2d 270 (Kan. Ct. App. 1984).
22   Lexington County Sch. Dist. 1 Bd. of Trustees v. Bost, 316 S.E.2d 677 (S.C. 1984).
23   Goodwin v. Bennett County High Sch. Indep. Sch. Dist., 226 N.W.2d 166 (S.D. 1975).
24   897 F.2d 154 (5th Cir. 1989).
25   Candelori v. Bd. of Educ. of New Britain, 428 A.2d 331 (Conn. 1980).
26   State *ex rel.* McKenna v. District No. 8, 10 N.W.2d 155 (Wis. 1943).
27   Indiana *ex rel.* Anderson v. Brand, 303 U.S. 95 (1938).
28   Lambert v. Bd. of Educ. of Middle Country Cent. Sch. Dist., 664 N.Y.S.2d 422 (Sup. Ct. 1997); *see also* Conetta v. Bd. of Educ. of Patchogue, 629 N.Y.S.2d 640 (Sup. Ct. 1995).
29   IOWA CODE § 284.5; ILL. REV. STAT. ch. 105 § 5/21A-20.
30   ALASKA STAT. § 14.20.149.
31   *Cases granting tenure*: Harrodsburg Bd. of Educ. v. Powell, 792 S.W.2d 376 (Ky. Ct. App. 1990); Day v. Prowers County Sch. Dist. RE-1, 725 P.2d 14 (Colo. Ct. App. 1986); Fucinari v. Dearborn Bd. of Educ., 188 N.W.2d 229 (Mich. Ct. App. 1971). *Contra* Bessler v. Bd. of Educ. of Chartered Sch. Dist., 356 N.E.2d 1253 (Ill. App. Ct. 1976), *modified*, 370 N.E.2d 1050 (Ill. 1977); Snell v. Brothers, 527 S.W.2d 114 (Tenn. 1975).
32   State v. Bd. of Educ. of South Point, 339 N.E.2d 249 (Ohio 1975); Hedrick v. Pendleton County Bd. of Educ., 332 S.E.2d 109 (W.Va. 1985).
33   Farrington v. Sch. Comm. of Cambridge, 415 N.E.2d 211 (Mass. 1981).
34   OHIO REV. CODE ANN. § 3319.111.
35   Asadoorian v. Warwick Sch. Comm., 691 A.2d 573 (R.I. 1997).
36   ALASKA STAT. § 14.20.175.

37 DeMichele v. Greenburgh Cent. Sch. Dist. No. 7, 167 F.3d 784 (2d Cir. 1999).

38 Gilliland v. Bd. of Educ. of Pleasant View, 365 N.E.2d 322 (Ill. 1977).

39 Grissom v. Bd. of Educ. of Buckley-Loda Cmty. Sch. Dist. No. 8, 388 N.E.2d 398 (Ill. 1979); Weissman v. Bd. of Educ. of Jefferson County Sch. Dist. No. R-1, 547 P.2d 1267 (Colo. 1976) (en banc).

40 Bd. of Dir. of Sioux City v. Mroz, 295 N.W.2d 447 (Iowa 1980).

41 Powell v. Bd. of Trustees of Crook County Sch. Dist. No. 1, 550 P.2d 1112 (Wyo. 1976).

42 Bd. of Educ. of Philadelphia v. Kushner, 530 A.2d 541 (Pa. 1987).

43 Sekor v. Bd. of Educ. of Ridgefield, 689 A.2d 1112 (Conn. 1997).

44 Chambers v. Bd. of Educ. of Lisbon Cent. Sch. Dist., 391 N.E.2d 1270 (N.Y. 1979).

45 Collins v. Faith Sch. Dist. No. 46–2, 574 N.W.2d 889 (S.D. 1998).

46 *In re* Proposed Termination of James E. Johnson, 451 N.W.2d 343 (Minn. 1990); Whaley v. Anoka-Hennepin Indep. Sch. Dist. No. 11, 325 N.W.2d 128 (Minn. 1982).

47 FLA. STAT. § 1012.34.

48 Sherrod v. Palm Beach County Sch. Bd., 963 So. 2d 251 (Fla. 4th Dist. App. 2006); Young v. Palm Beach County Sch. Bd., 968 So. 2d 38 (Fla. 4th Dist. App. 2006).

49 Meckley v. Kanawha County Bd. of Educ., 383 S.E.2d 839 (W. Va. 1989).

50 Osborne v. Bullitt County Bd. of Educ., 415 S.W.2d 607 (Ky. Ct. App. 1967).

51 793 So. 2d 153 (La. 2001).

52 Pickering v. Bd. of Educ., 391 U.S. 563 (1968) (see sec. 7.1).

53 Riverview Sch. Dist. v. Riverview Educ. Ass'n, 639 A.2d 974 (Pa. Commw. Ct. 1994).

54 898 A.2d 62 (Pa. Commw. Ct. 2006).

55 Thomas v. Mahan, 886 S.W.2d 199 (Mo. App. 1994).

56 Fisher v. Fairbanks N. Star Borough Sch. Dist., 704 P.2d 213 (Alaska 1985).

57 Ware v. Morgan County Sch. Dist. No. RE-3, 748 P.2d 1295 (Colo. 1988) (en banc).

58 Rust v. Clark County Sch. Dist., 683 P.2d 23 (Nev. 1984).

59 Carangelo v. Ambach, 515 N.Y.S.2d 665 (N.Y. App. Div. 1987).

60 441 N.Y.S.2d 142 (N.Y.A.D.2d 1981).

61 Fitzpatrick v. Bd. of Educ. of Mamaroneck, 465 N.Y.S.2d 240 (N.Y. App. Div. 1983).

62 Smith v. Bd. of Educ. of Fort Madison, 293 N.W.2d 221 (Iowa 1980).

63 *In re* Thomas, 926 S.W.2d 163 (Mo. Ct. App. 1996); Skripchuk v. Austin, 379 A.2d 1142 (Del. Super. Ct. 1977).

64 Bd. of Dir. of Lawton-Bronson v. Davies, 489 N.W.2d 19 (Iowa 1992); Startzel v. Commonwealth, Dep't of Educ., 562 A.2d 1005 (Pa. Commw. Ct. 1989); *In re* Shelton, 408 N.W.2d 594 (Minn. Ct. App. 1987); Perryman v. Sch. Comm. of Boston, 458 N.E.2d 748 Mass. App. Ct 1983); Logan v. Warren County Bd. of Educ., 549 F. Supp. 145 (S.D. Ga.1982).

65 Watson v. State Bd. of Educ., 99 Cal. Rptr. 468 (Cal. Ct. App. 1971); Williams v. Sch. Dist. No. 40 of Gila County, 417 P.2d 376 (Ariz. Ct. App. 1966); Purvis v. Marion County Sch. Bd., 766 So. 2d 492 (Fla. Dist. Ct. App. 2000); Ellis v. Ambach, 124 A.D.2d 854 (N.Y. App. Div. 1986); Scott v. Bd. of Educ. of Alton, 156 N.E.2d 1 (Ill. App. Ct. 1959).

66 Zelnov v. Lincoln Intermediate Unit 12 Bd. of Dirs., 786 A.2d 1022 (Pa. Commw. 2001).

67 Chicago Bd. of Educ. v. Payne, 430 N.E.2d 310 (Ill. App. Ct. 1981); Adams v. State Prof'l Practices Council, 406 So. 2d 1170 (Fla. App. 1981); Dominy v. Mays, 257 S.E.2d 317 (Ga. Ct. App. 1979); Gedney v. Bd. of Educ., 703 A.2d 804 (Conn. App. Ct. 1997).

68 C.F.S. v. Mahan, 934 S.W.2d 615 (Mo. Ct. App. 1996).

69 Golden v. Bd. of Educ., 285 S.E.2d 665 (W. Va. 1982); *see also* Rogliano v. Fayette County Bd. of Educ., 347 S.E.2d 220 (W.Va. 1986).

70 Hoagland v. Mount Vernon Sch. Dist. No. 320, 623 P.2d 1156 (Wash. 1981).

71 Hale v. Bd. of Educ. of Lancaster, 234 N.E.2d 583 (Ohio 1968).

72 Lindgren v. Bd. of Trustees, High Sch. Dist. No. 1, 558 P.2d 468 (Mont. 1976).

73 *In re* Termination of Kibbe, 996 P.2d 419 (N.M. 1999).

74 Bertolini v. Whitehall City Sch. Dist. Bd. of Educ., 744 N.E.2d 1245 (Ohio Ct. App. 2000).

75 Sherburne v. Sch. Bd. of Suwannee County, 455 So. 2d 1057 (Fla. App. 1984); Erb v. Iowa State Bd. of Pub. Instruction, 216 N.W.2d 339 (Iowa 1974).

76 Pettit v. State Bd. of Educ., 513 P.2d 889 (Cal. 1973); *see also* Bd. of Educ. v. Calderon, 110 Cal. Rptr. 916 (Cal. Ct. App. 1973); Sarac v. State Bd. of Educ., 57 Cal. Rptr. 69 (Cal. Ct. App. 1967); Stephens v. Bd. of Educ., Sch. Dist. No. 5, 429 N.W.2d 722 (Neb. 1988).

77 Avery v. Homewood City Bd. of Educ., 674 F.2d 337 (Former 5th Cir. 1982); Andrews v. Drew Mun. Separate Sch. Dist., 507 F.2d 611 (5th Cir.), *cert. granted*, 423 U.S. 820 (1975), *cert. dismissed*, 425 U.S. 559 (1976).

78 539 U.S. 558 (2003).

79 Gaylord v. Tacoma Sch. Dist. No. 10, 559 P.2d 1340 (Wash. Ct. App.), *aff'd*, 535 P.2d 804 (Wash. 1975) (en banc).

80 Morrison v. State Bd. of Educ., 461 P.2d 375 (Cal. 1969).

81 694 N.W.2d 740 (Iowa, 2005).

82 Bethel Park Sch. Dist. v. Krall, 445 A.2d 1377 (Pa. Commw. Ct. 1982).

83 Jarvella v. Willoughby-Eastlake City Sch. Dist., 233 N.E.2d 143 (Ohio 1967).

84 Bd. of Educ. of Hopkins County v. Wood, 717 S.W.2d 837 (Ky. 1986).

85 Ware v. Morgan County Sch. Dist., 748 P.2d 1295 (Colo. 1988); Bovino v. Bd. of Sch. Dir. of the Indiana Area Sch. Dist., 377 A.2d 1284 (Pa. 1977); Clarke v. Bd. of Educ. of Omaha, 338 N.W.2d 272 (Neb. 1983).

86 State v. Bd. of Sch. Dir. of Milwaukee, 111 N.W.2d 198 (Wis. 1961), *appeal dismissed*, 370 U.S. 720 (1962).

87 Sch. Dist. Bd. of Dir. v. Lundblad, 528 N.W.2d 593 (Iowa 1995).

88 Elvin v. City of Waterville, 573 A.2d 381 (Me. 1990).

89 Fisher v. Indep. Sch. Dist. No. 622, 357 N.W.2d 152 (Minn. Ct. App. 1984).

90 Toney v. Fairbanks N. Star Borough Sch. Dist., 881 P.2d 1112 (Alaska 1994).

91 Youngman v. Doerhoff, 890 S.W.2d 330 (Mo. App. 1994).

92 Iverson v. Wall Bd. of Educ., 522 N.W.2d 188 (S.D. 1994).

93 Libe v. Bd. of Educ. of Twin Cedars, 350 N.W.2d 748 (Iowa Ct. App. 1984).

94 Governing Bd. of Mountain View Sch. Dist. v. Metcalf, 111 Cal. Rptr. 724 (Cal. Ct. App. 1974).

95 *See* Youngman v. Doerhoff, 890 S.W.2d 330 (Mo. App. 1994).

96 Daily v. Bd. of Educ. of Morrill County Sch. Dist. No. 62–0063, 588 N.W.2d 813 (Neb. 1999).

97 408 U.S. 564 (1972).

98 408 U.S. 593 (1972).

99 McKnight v. Southeastern Pennsylvania Transp. Auth., 583 F.2d 1229 (3d Cir. 1978); Wellner v. Minnesota State Junior Coll. Bd., 487 F.2d 153 (8th Cir. 1973); Bomhoff v. White, 526 F. Supp. 488 (D. Ariz. 1981).

100 Gray v. Union County Intermediate Educ. Dist., 520 F.2d 803 (9th Cir. 1975); Beitzell v. Jeffrey, 643 F.2d 870 (1st Cir. 1981).

101 470 U.S. 532 (1985).

102 Winegar v. Des Moines Indep. Cmty. Sch. Dist., 20 F.3d 895 (8th Cir. 1994).

103 Staton v. Mayes, 552 F.2d 908 (10th Cir. 1977); Benton v. Bd. of Educ. of Winnebago, 361 N.W.2d 515 (Neb. 1985); Hawkins v. Bd. of Pub. Educ. in Wilmington, 468 F. Supp. 201 (D. Del. 1979).

104 Osborne v. Bullitt County Bd. of Educ., 415 S.W.2d 607 (Ky. Ct. App. 1967).

105 Bd. of Educ. of Clarke County v. Oliver, 116 So. 2d 566 (Ala. 1959).

106 426 U.S. 482 (1976).

107 Staton v. Mayes, 552 F.2d 908 (10th Cir. 1977).

108 Crump v. Bd. of Educ. of Hickory Admin. Sch. Unit, 392 S.E.2d 579 (N.C. 1990).

109 Syquia v Bd. of Educ., 579 N.Y.S.2d 487 (N.Y. App. Div. 1992).

110 Simard v. Bd. of Educ. of Groton, 473 F.2d 988 (2d Cir. 1973).

111 Niemi v. Bd. of Educ., 303 N.W.2d 105 (Mich. Ct. App. 1981).

112 Kinsella v. Bd. of Educ. of Amherst & Towanda, 378 F. Supp. 54 (W.D.N.Y. 1974), *aff'd*, 542 F.2d 1165 (2d Cir. 1976); White v. Bd. of Educ., 501 P.2d 358 (Haw. 1972); Miller v. Bd. of Educ. of Sch. Dist. No. 132, Cook County, 200 N.E.2d. 838 (Ill. App. Ct. 1964).

113 Cochran v. Chidester Sch. Dist. of Ouachita, 456 F. Supp. 390 (W.D. Ark. 1978); Doe v. Anker, 451 F. Supp. 241 (S.D.N.Y. 1978), *remanded*, 614 F.2d 1286 (2d Cir. 1979); Frumkin v. Bd. of Trustees, Kent State Univ., 626 F.2d 19 (6th Cir. 1980).

114 McGhee v. Draper, 564 F.2d 902 (10th Cir. 1977), *appeal after remand*, 639 F.2d 639 (10th Cir. 1981); McClure v. Indep. Sch. Dist. No. 16, 228 F.3d 120 (10th Cir. 2000).

115 *See, e.g.*, N.C. GEN. STAT. § 143B–146.7.

116 Nickel v. Saline County Sch. Dist. No. 163, 559 N.W.2d 480 (Neb. 1997).

117 State *ex rel.* Melchiori v. Bd. of Educ., 425 S.E.2d 251 (W. Va. 1992).

118 Laird v. Indep. Sch. Dist. No. 317, 346 N.W.2d 153 (Minn. 1984).

119 Baron v. Mackreth, 260 N.E.2d 554 (N.Y. 1970).

120 Geduldig v. Bd. of Educ. of N.Y., 351 N.Y.S.2d 167 (N.Y. App. Div. 1974).

121 Peck v. Indep. Sch. Dist. No. 16, 348 N.W.2d 100 (Minn. Ct. App. 1984).

122 Green v. Jenkintown Sch. Dist., 441 A.2d 816 (Pa. Commw. Ct. 1982).

123 Massey v. Argenbright, 683 P.2d 1332 (Mont. 1984).
124 Palone v. Jefferson Parish Sch. Bd., 306 So. 2d 679 (La. 1975).
125 Law v. Mandan Pub. Sch. Dist., 411 N.W.2d 375 (N.D. 1987).
126 Taxman v. Bd. of Educ. of Piscataway, 91 F.3d 1547 (3d Cir. 1996).
127 Newman v. Bd. of Educ. of N.Y., 594 F.2d 299 (2d Cir. 1979).
128 Cleveland Bd. of Educ. v. LaFleur, 414 U.S. 632 (1974).
129 42 U.S.C. § 2000(e).
130 Crochiere v. Bd. of Educ., 630 A.2d 1027 (Conn. 1993).
131 King v. Bd. of Educ., 716 A.2d 1077 (Md. Ct. Spec. App. 1998).
132 Hassell v. Onslow County Bd. of Educ., 641 S.E.2d 324 (N.C. 2007).
133 Dudley v. Victor Lynn Lines, Inc., 161 A.2d 479 (N.J. 1960).

9 Collective Bargaining, Unions, and Teacher Contracts

Many facets of the relationship between a board of education and its teachers are regulated by the Constitution and federal and state statutes. Within the boundaries set by these laws, the terms and conditions of a teacher's employment are set by a contractual agreement. For more than three-fourths of teachers today, most of the terms of the agreement are determined through a process of collective bargaining in which a union represents and negotiates for all of a district's teachers simultaneously. Ultimately, whether or not collective bargaining takes place, each teacher must enter into a contract with the employing board of education. This chapter considers the legal framework for collective bargaining and contract formation in education.

9.1 COLLECTIVE BARGAINING FOR TEACHERS: AN OVERVIEW

Since the late nineteenth century, collective bargaining has been politically and legally controversial in the United States. Until the 1930s, collective bargaining did not enjoy legal protection. In fact, private employers were able to use the law to suppress strikes, picketing, and even the formation of unions. However, following the 1932 election of President Franklin Roosevelt, a series of federal laws was enacted limiting the power of federal courts to issue injunctions against union activities, authorizing the formation of unions, and imposing on employers the legal duty to bargain collectively. Many states made similar changes in their own laws.

For several reasons, the emergence of collective bargaining in the public sector occurred more slowly. First, collective bargaining was seen as incompatible with the concept of government sovereignty and the principle that government decision making should be democratically controlled. Second, collective bargaining was viewed as a form of unlawful delegation of government authority. Third, collective bargaining in the public sector was criticized for skewing the normal political process in favor of one interest group to the disadvantage of others. Even today, some would argue that collective bargaining in education gives teachers too much power relative to parents and the community at large.

Even the authority of local school districts to engage in collective bargaining was in doubt. No statutes expressly authorized school districts to engage in collective bargaining, and the courts were split on the question of whether school districts could engage in collective bargaining without express statutory authorization. When the authority to bargain was found, the courts concluded only that school boards were permitted to engage in collective negotiations, not that they were required to.[1]

Public sector collective bargaining slowly gained recognition beginning in 1949 when Wisconsin enacted legislation permitting it. In 1962, President Kennedy issued an executive order giving federal employees some limited rights to bargain collectively. Today, most states have statutes authorizing some form of collective negotiations between teachers and school boards. In more than two-thirds of the states, actual collective bargaining is now required in districts where teachers have formed a union. Missouri joined this group as recently as 2007 when its highest court overruled longstanding precedent and said that a clause in the state constitution gave school employees the right to bargain collectively.[2] Other states require only that the board meet and confer with the representative union. Collective bargaining by public school teachers is prohibited by statute in North Carolina.[3] Note that private school teachers are not covered by state public sector collective-bargaining laws but by the National Labor Relations Act (NLRA).[4] Whether charter school teachers are covered by the NLRA or state public sector collective-bargaining laws depends on the terms of state law and the specific school's charter.[5]

There are important variations in the provisions of public sector collective-bargaining laws. For example, some states designate a wider range of topics as negotiable than others. Some states permit or require arbitration, whereas others prohibit arbitration. In short, some state legislatures have been more willing than others to encourage or force local school boards to share power with teacher unions.

Nevertheless, many states' collective-bargaining laws have certain key features in common. At the heart of the standard public collective-bargaining law are provisions specifically giving public employees the right to join a union and prohibiting public employers such as school boards from transferring or disciplining employees for engaging in union activities. These statutes also impose on the employer a duty to bargain with the union in good faith. This means, among other things, that the employer may not take unilateral action on certain categories of issues if the employee union wants to negotiate them.

Not every employee, however, may join a collective-bargaining unit. State statutes often exclude supervisors, those in managerial positions, and even confidential employees who work for supervisors and managers.[6] Depending on the authority delegated to the faculty, school site management arrangements—such as those found in some charter schools—have the potential to turn a school's entire faculty into managers prohibited from joining a union.[7]

To get to the point of actually bargaining, several steps need to be taken. First, the bargaining unit must be defined. Different categories of employees have different interests in common, so more than one union may be necessary in one school district. The standard state law provides for a formal process to officially designate and recognize the bargaining units. Although these laws vary regarding the criteria for defining an appropriate bargaining unit, two criteria are generally used: Employees should be divided into as few separate bargaining units as possible and a bargaining unit should include only members who share a "community of interests." Too many different unions place an undue burden on the school district to engage in multiple collective-bargaining processes. But to combine employees with very different interests risks persistent internal union strife and compromises the union's ability to represent all its members fairly.

Many states' statutes establish **a public employment relations board (PERB)** with power to resolve disputes relating to union representation in education. Nevertheless, disputes over the makeup of education employee unions sometimes end up in court. A Michigan case decided that nonteaching coaches should not form a separate bargaining unit.[8] A Wisconsin court concluded that student teachers should be placed in the same unit with full- and part-time professional employees.[9] A federal court in Indiana rejected the claim that a school district's noncertified employees had a constitutional right to hold an election to see if they wanted to form a separate union from the district's teachers.[10]

Once the number and makeup of bargaining units have been decided, employees must be given an uncoerced opportunity to decide if they want to be collectively represented by a union, and, if so, which union. The school board may not unilaterally select the union.[11]

Rather, state statutes typically establish several methods for making these decisions. One method, certification by the PERB without an election, can be used when there is no serious dispute over unionization. However, if there is any question regarding whether the employees want a union or which union they prefer, the PERB will supervise an election.

Although school officials may have a preference in these elections, state laws prohibit board domination, interference, or assistance in the formation, administration, or affairs of the employee union. Also, once a union has been victorious in an election, most states' statutes create a moratorium period during which its status as the exclusive representative of the unit may not be challenged or decertification sought. The purpose of this moratorium is to assure both employees and employer some period of labor peace and stability.

A minority of states permit certain arrangements to help protect what is called "union security." For example, some states permit an agency-shop arrangement under which, as a condition of continued employment, teachers must either be dues-paying union members or pay a service charge to the union. A few states permit the union-shop arrangement, where teachers must actually be union members to retain employment. The closed-shop arrangement requires prospective employees to be union members at the time of application for employment. In contrast, about twenty states have enacted right-to-work laws prohibiting employers and unions from compelling employees to become union members or pay any fee. The relation between agency-shop arrangements and right-to-work laws was addressed in *North Kingstown v. North Kingstown Teachers Association*.[12]

In exchange for the privilege of becoming the exclusive representatives of the employees in the bargaining unit, state law imposes on the union a duty of fair representation. It must represent all the employees in the unit, members or not, and may not sacrifice the interests of those who have chosen not to join for the sake of its members.

When bargaining begins, both parties are obligated to bargain in good faith. This difficult-to-define concept imposes on the parties a duty to bargain with a sincere desire to reach an agreement but no obligation to make concessions. Legal mechanisms are established by statute for bringing and resolving charges that a party is not bargaining in good faith.

If the negotiators manage to come to an agreement, the contract must be ratified by a majority vote of both the school board and the teachers who will work under it. State law does not allow school boards to delegate to a negotiator the power to actually make a contract, so the board must act formally to ratify any agreement. Assuming ratification, which usually occurs, each teacher may then choose to accept the agreement or not. The only option for a teacher unwilling to work under the agreement is to resign. No teacher may negotiate a separate agreement with the board, except for supplemental contracts as permitted by statute and the collective-bargaining agreement itself. No penalty may be imposed on a teacher who chooses to resign within a statutorily designated period after negotiation of the collective-bargaining agreement.

In cases where negotiations do not produce a contract agreeable to both sides, states designate a variety of procedures designed to break the impasse. Again, depending on the specific provisions of state law, dispute-resolution schemes may include mediation, fact-finding, or arbitration (also called "interest arbitration"). All these involve the naming, either by a state official or jointly by the parties themselves, of an individual or board to help create a contract. A mediator's powers are limited to bringing the two sides together for continued talk and using human-relations skills to facilitate or coax agreement.

A fact finder may hold hearings where both sides are required to submit whatever information they possess regarding their contract proposals. The fact finder then issues a report containing recommendations of what the final contract should be. Although it is hoped that the view of a neutral labor relations expert, which in most cases is made public, will exert pressure on both sides to accept the proposed settlement, fact finders' reports may be and often are rejected by one or both sides.

An arbitrator has all the power of both mediator and fact finder, with the very important difference that the arbitrator's findings are binding on both sides. In other words, the arbitrator has the power to dictate a contract that may not be rejected by either the union or board. In some schemes, arbitrators are limited to accepting the position of either one side or the other; other arbitration schemes allow the arbitrator to fashion a compromise. The legality of arbitration has been upheld against claims that it involves an unlawful delegation of power to private individuals and that it denies due process or equal protection to public employees.[13]

Arbitration is also controversial from a policy standpoint because it takes from the school board and ultimately from the people the board represents the final decision about how much they are willing to pay the teachers they employ. For this reason, arbitration has been adopted by only a few states. Arbitration may not be employed as part of the negotiation process in states where it has not been specifically authorized by statute.

Many states' statutes permit school boards to issue unilateral contracts if they are unable to come to terms with their teachers. In these states, after all other procedures have failed, the board will issue a contract that the union has no opportunity to ratify or reject as a group. Individual teachers still have the choice of working under the contract as offered, resigning, or, in some states, continuing to work under the previous year's contract.

State laws also contain provisions regarding the obligations of the parties when bargaining or impasse resolution continues beyond the termination date of the previous contract. Some courts have ordered employers to meet their obligations under the old contract, such as providing salary step increases, in order to maintain the status quo pending a new agreement.[14]

In sum, state laws establish a set of rights and duties regarding union representation of school employees and collective bargaining. Violation of these laws is an unfair or improper labor practice that may result in an injunction, firing, or other penalty against the offending side. Unfair labor practices include: dismissal, transfer, or discharge of employees for engaging in union activities; denial by the employer of the use of facilities for proper union activities; attempts by the union or employer to coerce an employee to vote a certain way in a certification election; antiunion intimidation and harassment; unilateral changes by the employer in terms and conditions of employment; refusal to bargain or failure to bargain in good faith; union violation of the duty of fair representation; refusal to execute or implement a written agreement embodying the results of the bargaining process; refusal to enter into a legally mandated dispute resolution procedure; and engaging in an unlawful strike.

9.2 RIGHTS OF UNION MEMBERS

In the absence of state statutory authorization, do public employees have a constitutional right to join a union? In 1968, in *McLaughlin v. Tilendis*,[15] the Seventh Circuit ruled that the First Amendment prohibits any state or school district to forbid its teachers from joining a union or to dismiss those who do. The court explained its decision as follows:

> It is settled that teachers have the right of free association, and unjustified interference with teachers' associational freedom violates [their constitutional rights]. Public employment may not be subjected to unreasonable conditions, and the assertion of First Amendment rights by teachers will usually not warrant their dismissal. Unless

there is some illegal intent, an individual's right to form and join a union is protected by the First Amendment.

The court rejected the argument that because some of the activities that unions often advocate and engage in, such as collective bargaining and teacher strikes, were (at that time and in that state) illegal, it was permissible for the state to prohibit union membership and even advocacy of union membership as well. The court relied on the important distinction between membership in an organization and participation in the illegal activities that the organization may advocate or even sponsor:

> It is possible of course that at some future time plaintiffs may engage in union-related conduct justifying their dismissal. But the Supreme Court has stated that, "Those who join an organization but do not share its unlawful purposes and who do not participate in its unlawful activities surely pose no threat, either as citizens or as public employees." Even if this record disclosed that the union was connected with unlawful activity, the bare fact of membership does not justify charging members with their organization's misdeeds. A contrary rule would bite more deeply into associational freedom than is necessary to achieve state interests, thereby violating the First Amendment.

In previous discussions of the rights of students and teachers, it was noted that freedom of association and assembly are corollaries of free speech. By joining with others of like mind, people seek to amplify their voices and to increase their influence. The *McLaughlin* decision recognizes that insofar as they are expressive acts, forming and joining a union are constitutionally protected. Would not the same reasoning then apply to collective bargaining? After all, collective bargaining is a way for a group of people (employees) to speak as one.

The courts that have considered the issue say that it does not: Collective bargaining is more than a form of expression for union members because it also compels the government (employer) to participate in the process. Unions and their members are free to exercise their constitutional rights to try to influence their employer, but there is no free speech or other constitutional provision that requires a government employer to engage in collective bargaining (or any other communication) with a union of its employees. Nor is there any federal statute giving public sector employees the right to bargain collectively. Thus, states may prohibit collective bargaining by public school teachers, and in states where public sector collective bargaining is not required by statute, school boards are free to refuse to negotiate with unions.[16] Even in states where statutes do give teachers the right to bargain collectively, there is no constitutional right for individuals to select the union that will represent them.[17]

Freedom of speech does protect the right of teachers to promote unionization during nonclass time. As long as the effort to persuade other faculty members does not materially and substantially disrupt the school, one court said, school officials may not restrict it.[18] Another court said that teachers could not be precluded from using the school mail system and bulletin boards for the same purposes, but upheld school rules limiting the access to school grounds by union organizers who were not school employees to the time before and after school. The court reasoned that school grounds were not a public forum, so school authorities could impose reasonable regulations on the use of the school's property.[19] A California court said that under a provision of the state's collective-bargaining law giving employee organizations "the right of access at reasonable times to areas in which employees work," teachers had the right to wear union buttons at school during noninstructional time. But the court also said that under a provision of the state education code authorizing school districts to prohibit employees from "engaging in political activity during working hours," a school may prohibit the buttons during instructional time.[20]

The First Amendment also protects the right of employees publicly to criticize school officials regarding union issues that are a matter of public concern.[21] As with all political speech by teachers, whether any particular example of such speech is protected will depend on the factors discussed in Section 7.1, in particular, whether the speech is made as a private citizen or pursuant to the teacher's official duties. Ironically, teachers who serve as union leaders as part of their official duties might enjoy less protection when they speak out on union issues than teachers who do not. Picketing also enjoys an important degree of free speech protection,[22] but courts are likely to allow prohibition of picketing when done with force, violence, or intimidation or for illegal purposes such as to promote an illegal strike.[23]

Teacher Strikes

Public employees do not have a constitutional right to strike. Courts have denied claims that laws prohibiting teacher strikes are a form of involuntary servitude, violate the right of freedom of speech or assembly, or deny due process.[24] In rejecting the argument that prohibiting public school teacher strikes where private sector strikes are permitted violates equal protection, one court cited the crucial function that education plays in promoting the welfare of the state:

> The state has a compelling interest that one of its most precious assets—its youth— have the opportunity to drink at the font of knowledge so that they may be nurtured and develop into the responsible citizens of tomorrow. No one has the right to turn off the fountain's spigot and keep it in a closed position. Likewise, the equal protection afforded by the fourteenth amendment does not guarantee perfect equality. There is a difference between a private employee and a public employee, such as a teacher who plays such an important part in enabling the state to discharge its constitutional responsibility. The need of preventing governmental paralysis justifies the "no strike" distinction we have drawn between the public employee and his counterpart who works for the private sector within our labor force.[25]

State statutes vary with regard to the definition of a strike. Kansas defines a strike as any "action taken for the purpose of coercing a change in the terms and conditions of professional service or the rights, privileges or obligations thereof, through any failure by concerted action with others to report to duty including, but not limited to, any work stoppage, slowdown, or refusal to work."[26] Where such broad and vague definitions apply, courts may consider organized refusals to perform extracurricular duties or work-to-rule actions as strikes.[27]

About half the states do not permit any organized work stoppages by teachers. In these states, a variety of penalties is possible against the union and individual teachers who defy the law. These penalties include loss of pay, fines, and even dismissal of striking employees; fines and jail terms for union leaders who defy a court order to return to work; and union reimbursement of the board for substitute teachers, legal fees, and other expenses incurred in dealing with a strike.[28]

In states where statutes or common law give teachers the right to strike, the board may not retaliate against strikers, provided the strike is conducted according to law. Only about ten states grant teachers a full right to strike equal to that of private sector employees. In the remaining states that allow strikes, the board may still seek a court injunction ordering striking teachers back to work if the board can show that the strike creates a significant threat to public safety or is otherwise seriously detrimental to the public welfare.[29]

Statutes vary regarding the procedures to be followed in obtaining an injunction to end a strike, the penalties faced by striking employees, the extent to which these penalties are mandatory or subject to procedural rights or to modification by mitigating circumstances, the procedural rights of teachers before they may be dismissed or otherwise punished for illegal strike activity, the penalties that may or must be imposed upon the union itself such as fines or loss of the dues deductions or other privileges, and the authority of the courts to issue antistrike injunctions and to impose penalties for disobeying the court's order.

A majority of state courts have held that a hearing prior to dismissal of illegally striking teachers is not constitutionally required. These courts generally view illegally striking teachers as having abandoned their contracts, thus giving up any property rights to their jobs and any claims to procedural due process. A prompt hearing following dismissal to consider a case in which a teacher claims not to have been on strike is required.[30]

9.3 RIGHTS OF NONUNION MEMBERS

Is it permissible to deny participation in the collective-bargaining process to teachers who decline to join the union? May nonunion teachers be forced to pay union dues or fees? May schools adopt rules that make it easier for the officially designated union than for rival unions or individuals to communicate with teachers? The central issue in these questions is how to protect the rights of nonunion members without violating the rights of union members or damaging the effectiveness of the collective-bargaining process.

Two Supreme Court cases have considered the issue of whether and under what circumstances a school board may give a teacher union and its members more opportunity to speak to the board than is granted to nonunion members. In *Madison Joint School District No. 8 v. Wisconsin Employment Relations Commission*,[31] a school board was accused of an unfair labor practice for allowing a nonunion teacher to speak at a public meeting in which the board was considering its position regarding an issue being negotiated with the union. The president of the union was also permitted to speak and to present a petition signed by union members. The Supreme Court ruled that it would have been impermissible to deny the nonunion teacher the right to speak:

> Regardless of the extent to which true contract negotiations between a public body and its employees may be regulated—an issue we need not consider at this time—the participation in public discussion of public business cannot be confined to one category of interested individuals. To permit one side of a debatable public question to have a monopoly in expressing its views to the government is the antithesis of constitutional guarantees. Whatever its duties as an employer, when the board sits in public meetings to conduct public business and hear the views of citizens, it may not be required to discriminate between speakers on the basis of their employment, or the content of their speech.

Minnesota State Board for Community Colleges v. Knight[32] concerned a Minnesota statute requiring public employers to engage in "meet-and-confer" sessions with their professional employees to exchange views on policy issues outside the scope of collective bargaining. The statute further specified that if an agency's professional employees were unionized, only representatives of the union could participate in the meet-and-confer sessions with the agency administration. Nonunion teachers argued that permitting unionized teachers to express their views to supervisors while denying nonunion members the right to express theirs in the same forum was a violation of their right of free speech.

In considering this claim, the Supreme Court was careful to distinguish the *Knight* case from *Madison*. Whereas the school board meeting in *Madison* was a traditional forum for the expression of public views, the meet-and-confer sessions in *Knight* were not. "It is a fundamental principle of First Amendment doctrine that for government property to be a public forum, it must by long tradition or by government designation be open to the public at large for assembly and speech." No one, explained the Court, has a constitutional right to speak in a nonpublic forum, even people directly affected by the issues under consideration. To hold otherwise would require revision of the procedures of every government body from Congress to school boards. Minnesota's law did not restrict employees from speaking or from joining with others of like mind. It simply restricted access to the formal meet-and-confer sessions to the duly elected representatives of the majority of an agency's professional employees. This, concluded the Court, was neither unconstitutional or unreasonable.

Mandatory Union Fees

The issue under consideration by the school board in the *Madison* case was whether to force nonunion members to pay a service or "agency-shop" fee to the union. Some states do not permit mandatory agency-shop fees, while others do. The Supreme Court has considered constitutional issues relating to agency-shop fees in five cases.

In the first case, *Abood v. Detroit Board of Education*,[33] the Court agreed with teachers who objected to paying fees that were used by a union for political and "ideological activities." The Court reasoned that compelling teachers to support the promotion of views with which they did not agree was a violation of their rights of freedom of association and speech. However, the Court did not prohibit all agency-shop arrangements. Instead, it ruled that it was permissible for nonunion teachers to be charged a fee to compensate the union for its collective-bargaining activities. The Court reasoned that nonunion members reap the same benefits from these services as members, that the state had a legitimate interest in preventing "free riders," and that any infringement on First Amendment rights related to the collective-bargaining fee was justified by the contribution of the single bargaining unit system to "labor peace." Thus, it is permissible, in states with agency-shop laws, for nonunion teachers to be required by their contracts to pay the percentage of union dues used to support collective bargaining.

In *Ellis v. Railway Clerks*,[34] the Court invalidated, as a violation of a federal statute, a rebate scheme that "allowed the union to collect the full amount of a protesting employee's dues, use part of the dues for objectionable purposes, and only pay the rebate a year later." The Court said that given the availability of alternative arrangements, such as the reduction of dues in advance or the use of interest-bearing escrow accounts, "the union cannot be allowed to commit dissenter's funds to improper uses even temporarily." The *Ellis* Court also held that the union could not charge dissenting employees for the costs of general organizing efforts and for costs of litigation not involving the negotiation of agreements or the settlement of grievances. However, the union could charge these employees their share for the union's quadrennial convention, union publications, and social activities. The Court drew a distinction among these charges using the following test: "whether the challenged expenditures are necessarily or reasonably incurred for the purpose of performing the duties of an exclusive representative of the employees in dealing with the employer on labor-management issues."

In *Chicago Teachers Union, Local No. 1 v. Hudson*,[35] the Court unanimously ruled against another union dues rebate procedure. The procedure was unconstitutional for three reasons: First, it permitted the temporary use of nonmember contributions for ideological purposes. Second, it did not provide dissenting employees enough information to gauge the propriety of the union's calculation of the mandatory service fee. Third, it did not provide for a reasonably prompt decision by an impartial decision maker for employees who disputed the amount of the service charge. The Court also required that an escrow account be set up for the amount of the charge reasonably in dispute pending resolution.

In *Lehnert v. Ferris Faculty Association*,[36] the Court announced three guidelines for deciding what charges to nonunion members were permissible. To be included in an agency fee, an activity must be "germane" to collective bargaining, be justified by the need for labor peace or to avoid "free riders," and not significantly add to the burden on free speech already imposed by the agency-shop agreement. Applying these guidelines, the Court concluded that employees could be charged a pro rata share of the local union's payments to the state and national affiliate of the local union including support of the parent union's general collective-bargaining activities; a union publication concerning professional development, unemployment, job opportunities, award programs, and education generally; sending delegates to the state and national conventions of the parent union; and expenses incurred preparing for a strike that would have been illegal under state law.

Most recently, in *Davenport v. Washington Education Association*,[37] the Court rejected a union's claim that a state statute barring the union from using the agency shop fees of a non-member for "election-related purposes . . . unless affirmatively authorized by the individual" violated the union's First Amendment right of freedom of association. The Court said that federal law gives states the right to regulate agency-shop arrangements.

Some states' laws permit individuals who object on religious grounds to union membership or the activities of a given union to in effect pay the equivalent of union dues to a charity of their choice in lieu of paying the money to the union.[38] Depending on the precise phrasing of such a law, it may be open to challenge as a violation of the Establishment Clause.[39] In agency-shop states without such a law, a teacher might be able to argue that failure to accommodate religious objection to union dues violates Title VII (see sec. 7.5). A California teacher who objected on religious grounds to paying union dues was unsuccessful in arguing that the accommodation provided by state law violates Title VII. Under California statute, a religious objector must pay full union dues, which are donated to a designated charity, but a political objector must pay only a lower "representation" fee. The court also ruled that this arrangement does not violate the Establishment Clause or the Equal Protection Clause.[40]

The agency-shop arrangement may be coupled with an administrative device called "dues check-off." Under this arrangement the union and employer agree that union dues and nonmember service fees will be deducted by the employer from the employee's paycheck and forwarded to the union. This arrangement saves the union the time and expense of collecting dues and helps prevent employees from engaging in dues avoidance. State laws vary with regard to dues check-offs, with some states making it a mandatory subject of bargaining, some making it a permissive subject of negotiations, and others actually prohibiting the arrangement. The states are split on whether dues check-off can be granted exclusively to the incumbent union.

Relying on the principles established in the Supreme Court agency-shop-fee decisions, the Ninth Circuit upheld a dues-deduction system under which the fee paid by nonunion members was placed in an independently managed interest-bearing escrow account. No later than October 15th, nonmembers had to be informed how they could obtain a rebate of the portion of the fee that was not mandatory. Non-members who wanted rebates had to submit letters by November 15th. They could either accept the union's calculation of the amount of the rebate and receive it promptly or request an independent calculation by an arbitrator, in which case the rebate would be paid by mid-February. The court found this scheme to be a reasonable way of preserving the constitutional rights of nonmembers without imposing an undue administrative burden on the union.[41]

In addition to agency shops and dues deduction, incumbent unions have sought other protections against the activities of rival unions. Some states permit the incumbent union to be given exclusive access to school facilities. The constitutionality of a union's exclusive access to teacher mailboxes and internal mail delivery system was addressed by the Supreme Court in *Perry Education Association v. Perry Local Educators' Association*.[42] The Court began its analysis by noting that the school's internal mail system was not a public forum. Rather, it was created and employed for specific purposes relating to the conduct of the school's business. "Implicit in the concept of the nonpublic forum," said the Court,

> is the right to make distinctions in access on the basis of subject matter and speaker identity. These distinctions may be impermissible in a public forum but are inherent and inescapable in the process of limiting a nonpublic forum to activities compatible with the intended purpose of the property. The touchstone for evaluating these distinctions is whether they are reasonable in light of the purpose for which the forum at issue serves.

Furthermore, said the Court, the differential access in this case was reasonable:

> The differential access provided PEA [the official union] and PLEA [the rival union] is reasonable because it is wholly consistent with the District's legitimate interest in preserving the property . . . for the use to which it is lawfully dedicated. Use of school mail facilities enables PEA to perform effectively its obligations as exclusive representative of all Perry Township teachers. Conversely, PLEA does not have any official responsibility in connection with the School District . . . Moreover, exclusion of the rival union may reasonably be considered a means of insuring labor peace within the schools. The policy serves to prevent the District's schools from becoming a battlefield for inter-union squabbles.

Finally, the Court noted that the school had made no attempt to prevent the rival union from communicating with teachers by other means, either in or out of school. Thus, the official union's exclusive access to the internal mail system was upheld.

9.4 RIGHTS AND DUTIES IN COLLECTIVE BARGAINING

The question of the **scope of bargaining**—which subjects must be negotiated—has implications for the balance of power between teachers and school board. In most states, possible subjects of negotiation are divided into three categories: First, mandatory subjects must be bargained over if either party wishes. A refusal to negotiate over a mandatory subject of bargaining is a violation of the duty to negotiate in good faith and an improper or unfair labor practice. Second, permissive subjects may be bargained over if both parties agree. Sometimes, a state statute specifies a policy that must be used, for example, to carry out a reduction in force (RIF), unless the union and school board agree to negotiate a different policy.[43] Refusal to bargain over a permissive subject is not a violation of the duty to negotiate in good faith. Third, illegal subjects may not be bargained over; the board must decide these issues unilaterally.

State laws regarding which issues are mandatory, permissive, and illegal subjects of negotiation vary significantly, so the law of each state should be consulted. In general, issues relating to the terms and conditions of teachers' employment are mandatory subjects of negotiation. These include hours of employment, length of the work year, workload, extra duties, salary, sick leave and other fringe benefits, grievance procedures, and issues of teacher safety.[44]

Issues of educational policy and school management such as who shall be hired and fired (sometimes referred to as "managerial prerogatives") are generally illegal subjects of negotiation.[45] Other subjects ruled nonnegotiable by some courts or designated as nonnegotiable by some state statutes include promotions, curriculum, length of school year, transfer and assignment, staff size, academic freedom, outsourcing, use of volunteers, and adoption of experimental programs.[46] Also nonnegotiable are issues controlled by constitutional or statutory law such as which categories of employees are eligible for tenure.[47] A Wisconsin court ruled that a race-conscious layoff provision was unconstitutional and thus, an illegal subject of negotiation.[48]

The line between mandatory, permissive, and illegal subjects of negotiation is often not clearly drawn. For example, in some states, class size is a mandatory subject of negotiations, but in most it is permissive. Even in states where class size is not mandatory, the impact of class size on teacher workload may be.[49] The school calendar may also be mandatory or permissive. Curriculum is at most a permissive subject of negotiations, but the workload effects of the curriculum adopted by the board are a mandatory subject. A Tennessee court ruled that dress code is not a mandatory subject of negotiations, but the enforcement of a dress code, for example, the penalties for noncompliance, is.[50] In most states, the criteria for the evaluation of teachers are nonnegotiable, but the procedures for evaluation are mandatory. An Iowa court ruled that not only the procedures of evaluation but also the substantive criteria of evaluation are mandatory subjects of negotiation.[51] Conversely, a Connecticut court ruled that even the procedures of evaluation are not a mandatory subject of negotiation.[52]

Most states take the position that an initial decision to carry out a RIF is a nonnegotiable management prerogative, but that RIF procedures and the impact of a RIF on staff are mandatory. An Illinois court, however, ruled that even the initial decision to lay off teachers was a mandatory subject of negotiation.[53] Conversely, a New Jersey court ruled that both the initial RIF decision and the impact of the decision were illegal subjects of negotiation.[54] Another New Jersey court ruled that the decision whether to hold school on recess days to make up for snow days was not a mandatory subject, but the impact of the decision was negotiable unless negotiations would significantly interfere with managerial prerogatives. The court said that only if the impact of the decision could be severed from the basic decision were negotiations over the impact mandatory.[55]

Some states' statutes seek to avoid confusion by specifying a list of subjects in each category. Whatever the level of specificity of the statutes, disputes over the negotiability of specific subjects may arise because many educational issues involve both teacher working conditions and questions of policy and school management.[56] A further complication is that the statutory language defining the scope of bargaining must be reconciled with other state statutes such as those addressing the promotion and evaluation of teachers.[57]

State statutes impose a duty of **fair representation** on the union. One of the requirements of this duty is that the union not enter into a contract that discriminates against any of its members. A New York court explained the union's obligation as follows:

> The bargaining agent has the duty to serve the interests of all members of a unit without hostility or discrimination toward any, to exercise its discretion with complete

good faith and honesty, and to avoid arbitrary conduct . . . The deliberate sacrifice of a particular employee as consideration for other objectives must be a concession the union cannot make.[58]

Thus, in another New York case, a court concluded that a union had breached its duty of fair representation when it failed to bargain vigorously on behalf of female coaches. In settling for an unfair salary for these union members because the burden of representing them became onerous, the union discriminated as surely as if it had proposed the inadequate salary.[59]

The duty to bargain in **good faith** is imposed by law on both the school and the teachers' union, but good faith is hard to define. Good-faith negotiating means making a sincere attempt to come to an agreement. It requires cooperating in the bargaining process by scheduling and attending mutually convenient meetings, listening to and considering proposals made by the other side, and trying to resolve differences in a way both sides can accept. Good faith does not, however, require compromise or even revising one's original position, although as a matter of tactics and for the sake of public relations, both sides virtually always move from their original positions. Good-faith bargaining also requires sticking to one's word by not later vetoing a contract previously offered to the other side. Behaviors that can lead to a finding of a violation of the duty to bargain in good faith include: repeated postponement of meetings, taking unilateral action regarding a mandatory or agreed upon subject of negotiation, refusal to schedule regular meetings, repeated backing away from agreements reached on specific items earlier in the negotiations process, unwillingness to supply arguments and information to support proposals, and employing a negotiator who lacks the authority actually to engage in bargaining. Missouri's highest court has ruled that school boards are under no obligation to accept the proposals of a teacher union, but that once they agree to a contract, they may not unilaterally rescind the agreement.[60]

In *Montgomery County Council of Supporting Services Employees, Inc. v. Board of Education*,[61] the court discussed the difficulty of determining whether one party is simply a hard bargainer or comes to the table with no subjective intent to reach an agreement:

> The requirement of good faith is a subjective measure which can be applied only in light of the totality of the circumstances. It is not required that the parties reach agreement; nor is it even necessary that concessions be made . . . Somewhat paradoxically, perhaps, the cases suggest that a "desire to reach agreement" constitutes good faith bargaining, and conversely that a "desire not to reach an agreement" is bad faith; condemned is a "predetermined resolve not to budge from an initial position," and required is a "serious attempt to resolve differences and reach a common ground." . . .
>
> The difficulty . . . is trying to legislate a state of mind. The task in applying the good faith standard is to distinguish, upon the facts of each case, between a party genuinely participating in negotiations, listening to and evaluating proposals made by the other side and attempting to explain its own position, with willingness to persuade and be persuaded, and a party merely "going through the motions" with a "predetermined resolve not to budge from an initial position."

9.5 GRIEVANCE PROCEDURES

Most collective-bargaining agreements include grievance procedures for dealing with alleged contract violations and settling differences in contract interpretation. Depending on the terms of the agreement and state law, even allegations of violations of antidiscrimination statutes, constitutional rights, and other state and federal laws may be subject to grievance procedures.[62] In about twenty states, the law permits submitting teacher contract disputes to **grievance arbitration**, in which a neutral third party is empowered to make a decision that both sides must accept. Courts have affirmed the legality of grievance arbitration with regard to subjects within the scope of bargaining.[63] The Supreme Court has ruled that contractual agreements to submit disputes over rights granted by employment statutes to arbitration are legally permissible.[64]

Usually the law requires exhausting all available grievance procedures before submitting a dispute to a court; however, there may be times when state law and the collective-bargaining agreement give teachers two separate options for contesting what they believe to be a contractually impermissible action by their employer. For example, a dismissed teacher might seek review of the decision through the grievance mechanism of the contract or through the procedures spelled out in state law. Courts are in agreement that where these options exist, teachers may choose either of them.[65] Election of one procedure sometimes, but not always, has been held to bar the use of the other.[66] New York permits a teacher to pursue the grievance procedure and statutory procedure simultaneously even if this creates the possibility of inconsistent results.[67] Once a particular procedure has been pursued to its final step and a final decision rendered, the other procedure can no longer be used.[68]

Collective-bargaining contracts often give the union the exclusive power to decide whether a grievance will be filed. A teacher whose union refuses to prosecute a grievance could not use this avenue of redress. In exercising the power to decide whether to prosecute a grievance, private sector unions are under a federal statutory obligation to act fairly.[69] State courts have found a similar duty under state public sector bargaining laws as part of the union's duty of fair representation.[70] On the same basis, when two members of the same union are in conflict regarding which one will be retained and which one let go, the union may not hire an attorney to defend only one of them.[71]

An issue that frequently arises in conjunction with the use of grievance procedures is whether the board has the authority to submit a particular issue to arbitration. For example, is it permissible for the board to agree to submit a teacher dismissal to arbitration or must the board reserve the ultimate decision to itself? The answers to questions like this vary from state to state depending on statute.[72]

Assuming the board has the authority to submit a particular issue to arbitration, a school board and teacher can still disagree on whether the contract requires submitting the issue to arbitration. In other words, disputes can arise concerning the scope of the negotiated arbitration agreement itself. State courts have taken divergent approaches to resolving these issues.[73]

State courts are also divided over the related issue of whether the arbitrator or the courts decide whether an issue may be decided by arbitration. New York courts assert that they have the primary authority to interpret a contract's arbitration clause and that "it must be taken, in the absence of clear, unequivocal agreement to the contrary, that the board of education did not intend to refer differences which might arise to the arbitration forum."[74] Minnesota courts take a position somewhat more favorable to arbitration. In that state, if the arbitrability of a dispute is subject to "reasonable debate," the arbitrator must first make the determination of arbitrability. After arbitration, this decision may be appealed to the courts, which will consider the question of arbitrability independently.[75] Wisconsin's approach is the most favorable toward arbitration. The arbitrator must first decide arbitrability. On appeal, the court must defer to the arbitrator's decision "as long as it is within the bounds of the contract language, regardless of whether we might have reached a different result under that language, [provided the decision] does not violate the law."[76]

Once a grievance has been settled by arbitration, most courts take the decision of the arbitrator as valid and binding and will not review or overturn the decision unless it is totally unreasonable[77] or violates state or federal law or policy such as by contradicting a legitimate school board decision concerning a nonnegotiable issue.[78] The remedy granted by the arbitrator to the winning party such as reinstatement or damages must conform to the contract and not violate state law.[79] In 2007, a Pennsylvania court upheld an arbitrator's ruling that a custodian could not be dismissed for having used marijuana off the job. The court said that in reviewing the decision of the arbitrator it had to "determine: (1) whether the issue presented is encompassed by the terms of the collective bargaining agreement, and (2) whether the arbitrator's interpretation can be rationally derived from that agreement." In this case, the contract permitted dismissal for "just cause," but the term was undefined so it was left to the arbitrator to define it. The arbitrator concluded there was no just cause to dismiss the employee because her behavior did not violate any school district policy and did not have any effect on any school district function. Accordingly, the court ruled that the arbitrator's decision was rationally derived from the contract.[80]

9.6 INDIVIDUAL TEACHER CONTRACTS

As seen in Chapters 7 and 8, many aspects of the relationship between teachers and their employers are controlled by federal and state constitutional and statutory law. School boards and teachers—either collectively or individually—may not enter into contracts that contradict state law; for example, by allowing teachers to make personnel decisions that the law reserves to school boards.[81] State law may even permit school boards to make decisions that have the effect of modifying the contract between the board and its teachers; for example, by revising the school calendar to make up for days missed because of weather. Teachers may be required to follow the modified calendar, even to attend school on days specifically designated by the contract as vacations.

As discussed earlier in this chapter, in school districts with collective bargaining, many of the terms of employment of all of a school district's teachers are set by an agreement between a teacher union and school board. The collective-bargaining agreement is a mandatory part of the contract of each individual teacher within a school district, so school boards and teachers may not enter into contracts that contradict the collective bargaining agreement even if both wish to do so. For example, where the collective bargaining agreement specifies a single salary schedule for all teachers, the school board may not agree to a higher than scheduled salary for a teacher it considers particularly valuable.

However, the collective-bargaining agreement is not by itself specific enough to constitute an enforceable contract between the school board and any individual teacher. Teachers must still have individual contracts spelling out, among other things, the specific positions they are to hold, the hours they are to work, and the salary and benefits they are to receive. Teachers may also have separate or supplementary contracts regarding coaching or other extra-duty assignments. The collective-bargaining agreement may be viewed as setting the framework of the agreement between a teacher and school board with the individual contract filling in the details.

In school districts without collective bargaining, each teacher is theoretically free to negotiate the entire contract from scratch. In practice, however, the board generally insists on fairly similar general terms for all of its teachers with only variations similar to those in collective-bargaining districts.

Whether an individual teacher's contract emanates from a collective-bargaining agreement or not, an extensive and complex set of statutory and common laws regulates its formation and implementation. Employment contracts in education are usually bilateral, meaning that each party makes promises in advance to the other, and are express rather than implied, meaning that the promises are made in words rather than inferred from actions. Where permitted by law, teaching contracts or, more frequently, supplemental duty contracts, may be oral. Oral contracts are difficult to enforce because it is hard to prove what was said. Even where there is no written contract, an employee is entitled to reasonable compensation for services performed at the request of and for the benefit of an employer.

The five essential elements of a binding employment contract in education are: (a) manifestation of mutual assent, (b) consideration, (c) competence of the parties, (d) legality of subject, and (e) satisfaction of statutory requirements for formation of a contract.

Manifestation of mutual assent is accomplished by the making of an offer and its acceptance. An offer is a specific proposal with definite terms communicated by one person to another that creates in the mind of a reasonable person the perception of an invitation to assent. An offer and acceptance lacking definite terms do not create an enforceable contract. Courts will not supply missing terms or provide definitions for vague terms like "good wages."[82]

A properly formulated and communicated offer confers on the person to whom the offer is made (offeree) a power of acceptance until the offer terminates. An offer can terminate by lapse of time, revocation, rejection, counteroffer, death or insanity of either party, destruction of the specific subject matter to which the offer relates, or subsequent illegality of the type of contract contemplated by the offer. Offers may contain specific dates by which the acceptance must be made. If there is no such express time limit, the offer is said to be open for a reasonable time or until revoked or otherwise terminated. Offers, rejections, and counteroffers are effective when received.

An acceptance of an offer is some overt act by the offeree, usually written or oral, that manifests an intent to assent to the terms of the offer. The acceptance must be positive and may not change any of the terms of the offer, so counteroffers operate as a rejection of the original offer. In one case, a teacher who deleted from her contract the condition that she update her certificate was held not to have executed a contract.[83] In another case, a principal who added to the contract the stipulation that he be given rent-free housing was held to have made a counteroffer that did not create a contract.[84]

A late or defective acceptance does not create a contract; however, a late or defective acceptance does operate as a new offer that the original offeror may accept. Acceptances are generally effective when dispatched, not just when received, unless the offer specifically provides otherwise or the offeree uses an unauthorized means of communication. An authorized means of communication is one that has been expressly authorized by the offeror or, if none is authorized, the means used by the offeror. Thus, if the offer came by mail, the offeree should use the mails, and the acceptance is effective the moment the offeree mails the properly stamped and addressed acceptance.

Mistakes arising from a failure to read a document are not a basis for avoiding contractual liability. With very few exceptions, parties are held to what they sign; however, no binding contract is formed if one party makes an offer containing a serious mistake (e.g., a misplaced decimal point in a proposed salary) and the other accepts knowing of the error or with good reason to suspect it.

Consideration is whatever is given in exchange for something else provided. Two requirements must be met: The parties must intentionally enter into a bargained exchange and the promises or performance of both parties must meet certain tests of legal sufficiency. The concept of a bargained exchange means that the parties negotiated and mutually agreed on what is to be exchanged.

The tests of legal sufficiency are technical. What one party, either offeror or offeree, gives to the other must either be a legal detriment to that party or provide a legal benefit to the other party. **Legal detriment** means doing or promising to do something that the person making the promise was under no legal obligation to do or refraining or promising to refrain from doing something that could have been legally done. **Legal benefit** is obtaining from the other party something that one had no prior legal right to obtain. These technical requirements are easily satisfied in employment contracts: The school board promises salaries and benefits, something it was not previously obligated to offer, and gets in return a promise of services, something the teacher was not previously obligated to provide. When the board gives remuneration, it suffers a legal detriment and the teacher gets a legal benefit. Likewise, the teacher providing services suffers a legal detriment and the board gets a legal benefit.

Both parties to the contract must be of legal age and mentally competent to undertake the terms of the contract. This is not usually an issue in education employment contracts.

No employment contract may commit the board to undertake an act that is illegal or contrary to public policy. For example, the board and Mr. Jones could not strike a deal under which Jones stays on as principal of the high school in exchange for the board contracting with Jones's son for a school renovation.

Education employment contracts must also satisfy a variety of **state statutory requirements**. Most states' laws specify that only the board, acting as a corporate body at a properly convened meeting, can contractually bind the district. The board may not delegate its power to make contracts to its administrators or other employees, and contracts not formally approved by the board may not be enforced.[85] Nor are contracts enforceable if they exceed the board's statutory authority. Most states also require that school district employment contracts be in writing. In some states, the failure to issue a notice of nonrenewal automatically constitutes an offer of employment for the subsequent year.[86]

Occasionally, the issue arises whether a contract has been formed even though some aspect of the statutory requirements has not been satisfied. Courts insist that major requirements such as school board approval be satisfied, but contracts are sometimes upheld even if minor technical requirements are not met.[87] In any event, improperly processed contracts can be ratified by the board after the fact, thereby rectifying the earlier error.

Termination of Contract

The duties and obligations of a contract may be **discharged**, thus terminating the agreement in several ways. Exact performance of the contractual duties discharges both parties from further obligation. A breach of the contract by one party that is material and goes to the essence of the contract discharges the other party's duties. A breach that is not material still gives rise to a cause of action for breach of contract (discussed later) and provides an excuse for nonperformance by the aggrieved party. A nonmaterial breach does not, however, discharge the aggrieved parties from further duties under the contract. Interference by one party that prevents performance by the other constitutes a material breach that discharges the contract.

Repudiation in advance by one party of the contract is treated as a breach, and the nonrepudiating party may bring suit as if it were a breach. Mutual agreement by the parties rescinds the contract. An agreement to substitute a new performance for the duty originally owed under the contract terminates the original agreement. Performance is discharged when a subsequent change in the law makes the contract illegal. The death or debilitating illness of an employee under contract to perform personal services discharges the contractual duties. In this situation, known as **impossibility of performance**, an employer's duties are also discharged, and the person may be let go. Impossibility also encompasses **impracticality**, meaning that the contract could be fulfilled only with extreme and unreasonable difficulty, expense, injury, or loss. Thus, in one case, a teacher could be dismissed when his deteriorating eyesight led him to seek extended sick leave and his diminished ability to read made it increasingly hard to meet normal teaching duties.[88] However, federal and state law prohibiting discrimination against people with disabilities should be taken into account before dismissals are undertaken in such situations (see sec. 7.6).

Contracts may include **conditions** or **contingencies**. A contractual condition is any event the happening or nonhappening of which affects the duties in the contract. There may be conditions that must be satisfied before any duty to perform exists. For example, approval of the contract by the school board is necessary to the creation of contractual duties. Other conditions terminate any duties to perform. For example, a teacher's job might be subject to the condition that the federal government renew the grant funding the position.[89]

Breach of Contract

When one party fails to live up to the terms of the contract, the disappointed party can sue for breach of contract. The law seeks to provide a remedy that places the injured party in the same position as if the contract had been fulfilled. Sometimes, this only requires a court to issue an order prohibiting continued violation of a contractual term or requiring specific execution of a provision of the contract such as the procedures governing teacher dismissal. Most often, the remedy for breach of contract is the awarding of monetary damages to compensate the aggrieved party for what would have been gained had the breach not occurred and for expenses incurred because of the breach. Employees who fail to complete the term of their contracts might have to compensate their employers for expenses incurred in obtaining a replacement. Aggrieved employees may be awarded salary and any other expenses incurred as a result of an employer's breach, such as the cost of seeking and moving to a new job.[90]

In fairness to the defaulting party, the law says the injured party cannot recover damages that could have been avoided through the exercise of reasonable diligence and without incurring undue risk, expense, or humiliation. The injured party is expected to take reasonable steps to **mitigate damages** by, for example, seeking another job, but the injured party does not have to take a job inferior to the one lost. In one case, a principal dismissed in violation of his contract was not required to accept a job as a teacher that paid as much as the principalship.[91]

In some employment contracts, the parties agree that an employee who breaches the contract will pay a specified amount of money in lieu of damages based on actual loss. These **liquidated damage** clauses are enforceable when it is difficult for the contracting parties to determine the exact monetary value of the contract breach, provided the amount is reasonable and not punitive.[92] State statutory law may require that individual contracts contain a damages provision and specify the kinds and limits of the damages to be awarded. The highest court in Colorado interpreted a statutory provision limiting damages to "ordinary and necessary expenses" not to include salaries paid to employees who would have been paid anyway when those employees helped to search for a replacement teacher after the plaintiff resigned without giving sufficient notice.[93] A Montana court upheld as consistent with a state statute a liquidated damage clause that required the plaintiff to pay 20 percent of his salary. The court found the 20-percent requirement not unduly oppressive or a penalty as opposed to a true damages provision. And the fact that the district found a replacement teacher at a lower salary than was paid to the plaintiff did not preclude enforcement of the liquidated damage clause.[94]

Contract Interpretation

Unless there is a statute to the contrary, the law permits teachers to work without a contract, but when there is no contract the issue may arise regarding the salary owed to the teachers. When a statute is available to govern the noncontract situation, its terms control the level of payment owed, but when there is no statute, courts resolve such questions in a manner designed "to assure a just and equitable result."[95] In one case, the court ruled that teachers who did agree to a new contract would be paid retroactively under the new salary schedule, whereas teachers who did not agree were to be paid under the terms of the previous year's salary schedule, including the experience increment due to them under that schedule.[96]

Contracts are not formed by statements of intention to hire or to work in the absence of a definite agreement between the parties on terms of the employment. Even where there is a definite agreement, a contract may not be formed if one of the parties lacks the authority to enter into a contract.[97] Thus, a teacher's acceptance of a public school principal's offer of employment would not create a contract because only school boards have the statutory authority to enter into contracts with teachers.[98] Employment contracts may also fail to be formed when a teacher does not return an acceptance by the stated deadline[99] or if the acceptance is not delivered by the required mode (e.g., if a school district's written offer required a written acceptance but the acceptance was oral[100]).

In a Florida case, a teacher told her principal that she was inclined to apply for an additional year of leave; however, before she filed any leave forms, but after the principal had hired a replacement, the teacher told the principal she had changed her mind. The court ruled that the teacher had not relinquished her position.[101] In an Oklahoma case, a faculty member signed the annual letter setting the salary and wrote the words "under protest" on the letter. The court ruled that his signing was a valid acceptance and not a counteroffer that terminated the original offer. Therefore, an enforceable contract had been formed.[102]

Several cases have considered the issue of whether a teacher with coaching or other paid supplemental duties is working under one contract or two. These cases usually involve teachers who wish to resign from coaching but continue to teach or school boards that wish to fire a coach with tenure as a teacher. Some state statutes require that supplemental duty agreements be separate from the basic teacher contract even if they are written on a single document.[103] However, where no such statute exists, the divisibility of a contract depends primarily on the intentions of the parties. One court ruled that a teacher who had a three-year contract to teach and coach had the right to continue to teach and to be paid the full agreed-upon salary for the entire period even if the school district no longer wished him to coach.[104]

Questions sometimes arise over whether a teacher's contract may include more than what is written on the document both parties signed. Specifically, cases have addressed the question of whether school rules, a teachers' handbook, or a school publication is part of the contract. The courts have said that such materials may be part of the contract if their terms are sufficiently specific, the employee is aware of them, and the materials are part of the bargained exchange.[105] Courts in several states, however, have ruled that if there is evidence that the employer reserved the right to unilaterally change the handbook, then it is not considered part of the contract.[106] Also, if the handbook specifically contains a statement that it does not constitute a contract, then the courts will not enforce it.[107]

Courts are in general agreement that state law is part of the contract.[108] The power of legislatures to change the terms of the contract by changing the law may be implied or an express provision of the contract. Some states permit school boards to unilaterally change employment contracts under exigent circumstances. In 1991, in response to a severe budget crisis, the City of Baltimore decided to pay its teachers approximately 1 percent less than the salary specified in their contracts. The teachers sued the city, claiming that the unilateral contract modification violated Article 1, Section 10 (the Contract Clause) of the Constitution. The Contract Clause prohibits states from passing any law "impairing the obligation of contracts." In rejecting the claim, the Fourth Circuit noted that the Contract Clause is not an absolute bar to modification of a state's own financial obligations. Unilateral contract modifications must be "reasonable and necessary to serve an important public purpose." The salary reduction was permissible because Baltimore had made concerted but unsuccessful efforts to find alternative solutions, the reduction was no greater than necessary, and the plan was abandoned at the first opportunity.[109]

Sometimes, the parties to a contract have expressed themselves in both a specific document and other oral or written statements, known as **parol evidence**. When this happens, there are several possibilities: There are two separate contracts, the basic written document and the other statements comprise one contract, or the written document constitutes the entire and only contract, unaffected by the other statements. The general rule is that when the basic written contract is an integrated agreement, the parol evidence will not be permitted to modify it in any way. A written contract is an integrated agreement when the parties so intended. To manifest this intention, many contracts contain a clause affirming that the contract constitutes the entire agreement between the parties.[110]

Even when the parties know what words constitute their contract, they may disagree on their meaning. Carefully worded contracts are less likely to engender these disputes. When disagreements do arise, the courts may be asked to interpret the contract. Although there is no procedure that guarantees discovery of the true meaning of a contract, certain rules of interpretation serve as guidelines. Contracts are interpreted in accordance with the purpose and intentions of the parties insofar as these are ascertainable. Ordinary words are given their usual meaning and technical words their technical meaning. Separately negotiated terms are given greater weight than standardized terms and specific terms greater weight than general terms. Interpretations that make the contract and all its provisions reasonable, lawful, meaningful, and consistent are preferred.

9.7 SUMMARY

Within the boundaries of federal and state law, the terms and conditions of a teacher's employment are set down in a contract. In most school districts, the contract is developed through a process of collective negotiations between a union representing all the district's teachers and the school board. Teachers have a constitutional right to join a union, but collective bargaining is at the discretion of the legislature and courts of each state. Most states do allow some form of collective bargaining for teachers.

The process for selecting the union, the terms of the relationship between the union and its members and between the union and the school board, and the duties and obligations of both sides in collective bargaining are established by state law. The union is required to fairly represent all teachers within the district, even those who choose not to join. Both sides are obliged to bargain in good faith, (i.e., with an intention of reaching a mutually satisfactory agreement) over issues specified or implied by state law as mandatory subjects of negotiation. Generally, these issues relate to teacher well-being and working conditions. Certain other issues may be bargained at the discretion of both sides.

Collective-bargaining agreements often include an agreement to submit certain employment disputes to arbitration by a neutral third party.

In addition to the collective-bargaining agreement, each teacher has an individual contract detailing the specific terms of employment. To be enforceable, a teacher's contract must meet certain conditions. The most important of these is that both parties must come to an understanding of the duties and obligations that each will assume. Even so, legal disputes sometimes arise concerning the meaning and interpretation of a contractual provision. The more clear and detailed the contractual language, the less likely that these disputes will arise.

NOTES

1 Norwalk Teachers Ass'n v. Bd. of Educ. of Norwalk, 83 A.2d 482 (Conn. 1951); Virginia v. County Bd. of Arlington County, 232 S.E.2d 30 (Va. 1977).
2 Independence-National Educ. Assoc. v. Independence Sch. Dist., 223 S.W.3d 131 (Mo. 2007).
3 N.C. GEN. STAT. §§ 95–98.
4 *In re* Pinkerton Academy, 920 A.2d 1168 (N.H. 2007).
5 *See* 2002 WL 1880478 (NLRB A.L.J. July 31, 2002).
6 Michigan Educ. Ass'n v. Clare-Gladwin Intermediate Sch. Dist., 396 N.W.2d 538 (Mich. Ct. App. 1986); Missouri Nat'l Educ. Ass'n v. Missouri State Bd. of Mediation, 695 S.W.2d 894 (Mo. 1986) (en banc).
7 *See* N.L.R.B. v. Yeshiva Univ., 444 U.S. 672 (1980).
8 Michigan Coaches Ass'n v. Warren Consol. Sch., 326 N.W.2d 432 (Mich. Ct. App. 1982).
9 Arrowhead United Teachers Org. v. Wis. Employment Relations Comm., 342 N.W.2d 709 (Wis. 1984).
10 Indiana State Teachers Ass'n v. Bd. of Sch. Comm'rs, 918 F. Supp. 266 (S.D. Ind., 1996), *aff'd*, 101 F.3d 1179 (7th Cir. 1996).
11 Fayette County Educ. Ass'n v. Hardy, 626 S.W.2d 217 (Ky. Ct. App. 1980).
12 297 A.2d 342 (R.I. 1972).
13 City of Biddeford v. Biddeford Teachers Ass'n, 304 A.2d 387 (Me. 1973).
14 Indiana Educ. Employment Relations Bd. v. Mill Creek Classroom Teachers Ass'n, 456 N.E.2d 709 (Ind. 1983).
15 398 F.2d 287 (7th Cir. 1968); *see also* Am. Fed'n of State, County & Mun. Employees v. Woodward, 406 F.2d 137 (8th Cir. 1969).
16 Winston-Salem/Forsyth County Unit of the N.C. Ass'n of Educators v. Phillips, 381 F. Supp. 644 (M.D.N.C. 1974).
17 Indiana State Teachers Ass'n v. Bd. of Sch. Comm'rs, 918 F. Supp. 266 (D. Ind. 1996), *aff'd*, 101 F.3d 1179 (7th Cir. 1996).
18 Georgia Ass'n of Educators v. Gwinnett County Sch. Dist., 856 F.2d 142 (11th Cir. 1988).
19 Texas State Teachers Ass'n v. Garland Indep. Sch. Dist., 777 F.2d 1046 (5th Cir. 1985).
20 Turlock Joint Elementary Sch. Dist. v. Pub. Employment Relations Bd., 5 Cal. Rptr. 3d 308 (Cal. App. 5 Dist. 2003).
21 Hickman v. Valley Local Sch. Dist. Bd. of Educ., 619 F.2d 606 (6th Cir. 1980).
22 Pittsburg Unified Sch. Dist. v. California Sch. Employees Ass'n, 213 Cal. Rptr. 34 (Cal. Ct. App. 1985).
23 Teamsters Local 695 v. Vogt, 354 U.S. 284 (1957); Bd. of Educ. of Martins Ferry City Sch. Dist. v. Ohio Educ. Ass'n, 235 N.E.2d 538 (Ohio Ct. Common Pleas 1967).
24 City of New York v. DeLury, 243 N.E.2d 128, *remitter amended*, 244 N.E.2d 472 (N.Y. 1968); United Fed'n of Postal Clerks v. Blount, 325 F. Supp. 879 (D.D.C.), *aff'd*, 404 U.S. 802 (1971).
25 Sch. Comm. of Westerly v. Westerly Teachers Ass'n, 299 A.2d 441 (R.I. 1973).
26 KAN. STAT. ANN. § 72–5413.
27 Bd. of Educ. of Asbury Park v. Asbury Park Educ. Ass'n, 368 A.2d 396 (N.J. Super. Ct. Ch. Div. 1976).
28 Passaic Township Bd. of Educ. v. Passaic Teachers Ass'n, 536 A.2d 1276 (N.J. Super. Ct. App. Div. 1987); Nat'l Educ. Ass'n v. S. Bend Cmty. Sch. Corp., 655 N.E.2d 516 (Ind. App. 1995).

29 Jersey Shore Area Sch. Dist. v. Jersey Shore Educ. Ass'n, 548 A.2d 1202 (Pa. 1988).
30 Sanford v. Rockefeller, 324 N.E.2d 113 (N.Y. 1974), *appeal dismissed*, 421 U.S. 973 (1975); Farrelly v. Timberlane Reg'l Sch. Dist., 324 A.2d 723 (N.H. 1974).
31 429 U.S. 167 (1976).
32 465 U.S. 271 (1984).
33 431 U.S. 209 (1977).
34 466 U.S. 435 (1984).
35 475 U.S. 292 (1986).
36 500 U.S. 507 (1991).
37 551 U.S. 177 (2007).
38 *For example*, 115 ILCS 5/11; ALM GL ch. 150E, § 12.
39 Katter v. Ohio Employment Relations Bd., 492 F. Supp. 2d 851 (S.D. Ohio 2007).
40 Madsen v. Associated Chino Teachers, 317 F. Supp. 2d 1175 (C.D. Cal. 2004).
41 Grunwald v. San Bernardino City United Sch. Dist., 994 F.2d 1370 (9th Cir. 1993).
42 460 U.S. 37 (1983).
43 Bd. of Educ. of Cmty. Unit Sch. Dist. No. 201-U v. Crete-Monee Educ. Ass'n, 497 N.E.2d 1348 (Ill. 1986).
44 Lorain City Sch. Dist. v. State Employment Relations Bd., 533 N.E.2d 264 (Ohio 1988); Local 195 IFPTE, AFL. CIO v. State, 443 A.2d 187 (N.J. 1982).
45 Bd. of Educ. of North Bergen v. North Bergen Fed'n. of Teachers, Local 1060, 357 A.2d 302 (N.J. Super. Ct. App. Div. 1976).
46 Boston Teachers Union, Local 66 v. Sch. Comm. of Boston, 434 N.E.2d 1258 (Mass. 1982); Unified Sch. Dist. No. 501 v. Kansas Dep't of Human Resources, 685 P.2d 874 (Kan. 1984); MICH. COMP. LAWS § 423.215.
47 Spiewak v. Bd. of Educ. of Rutherford, 447 A.2d 140 (N.J. 1982).
48 Milwaukee Bd. of Sch. Dir. v. Wis. Employment Relations Comm., 472 N.W.2d 553 (Wis. 1991).
49 Decatur Bd. of Educ. No. 61 v. Illinois Educ. Labor Relations Bd., 536 N.E.2d 743 (Ill. App. Ct. 1989); Beloit Educ. Ass'n v. Wisconsin Employment Relations Comm'n, 242 N.W.2d 231 (Wis. 1976).
50 Polk County Bd. of Educ. v. Polk County Educ. Ass'n, 139 S.W.3d 304 (Tenn. Ct. App. 2004).
51 Aplington Cmty. Sch. Dist. v. Iowa Pub. Employment Relations Bd., 392 N.W.2d 495 (Iowa 1986).
52 Wethersfield Bd. of Educ. v. Connecticut State Bd. of Labor Relations, 519 A.2d 41 (Conn. 1986).
53 Cent. City Educ. Ass'n v. Illinois Educ. Labor Relations Bd., 557 N.E.2d 418 (Ill. App. Ct. 1990), *appeal granted*, 561 N.E.2d 687 (Ill. 1990), *modified*, 599 N.E.2d 892 (Ill. 1992).
54 Maywood Bd. of Educ. v. Maywood Educ. Ass'n, 401 A.2d 711 (N.J. Super Ct. App. Div.), *appeal denied*, 405 A.2d 836 (N.J. 1979).
55 Piscataway Twp. Educ. Ass'n v. Piscataway Twp. Bd. of Educ., 704 A.2d 981 (N.J. Super. Ct. App. Div. 1998).
56 *See, e.g.*, Chee-Craw Teachers Ass'n v. Unified Sch. Dist. No. 247, Crawford County, 593 P.2d 406 (Kan. 1979).
57 Bethlehem Twp. Bd. of Educ. v. Bethlehem Twp. Educ. Ass'n, 449 A.2d 1254 (N.J. 1982).
58 Union Free Sch. Dist. No. 6 Babylon v. N.Y. State Div. of Human Rights, 349 N.Y.S.2d 757 (N.Y. App. Div. 1973), *appeal dismissed*, 309 N.E.2d 137 (N.Y. 1974).
59 United Teachers of Seaford v. N.Y. State Human Rights Appeal Bd., 414 N.Y.S.2d 207 (N.Y. App. Div. 1979).
60 Independence-Nat. Educ. Assoc. v. Independence Sch. Dist., 223 S.W.3d 131 (Mo. 2007).
61 354 A.2d 781 (Md. 1976).
62 Gray v. Caddo Parish Sch. Bd., 938 So. 2d 1212 (La. App. 2 Cir. 2006).
63 West Fargo Pub. Sch. Dist. No. 6 of Cass County v. West Fargo Educ. Ass'n, 259 N.W.2d 612 (N.D. 1977).
64 Gilmer v. Interstate/Johnson Lane Corp., 500 U.S. 20 (1991); E.E.O.C. v. Waffle House, 534 U.S. 279 (2001); Wright v. Universal Maritime Service Corp., 525 U.S. 70 (1998).
65 Bd. of Educ. of Huntington v. Associated Teachers, 282 N.E.2d 109 (N.Y. 1972); Pub. Employees Relations Comm'n v. Dist. Sch. Bd. of DeSoto County, 374 So. 2d 1005 (Fla. Ct. App. 1979).
66 Pedersen v. S. Williamsport Area Sch. Dist., 677 F.2d 312 (3d Cir. 1982).

67 *In re* Susquehanna Valley Teachers Ass'n, 429 N.Y.S.2d 741 (N.Y. App. Div. 1980), *aff'd*, 420 N.E.2d 400 (N.Y. 1981); *but see* Bd. of Educ. Cattaraugus Cent. Sch. v. Cattaraugus Teachers Ass'n, 447 N.Y.S.2d 51 (N.Y. App. Div. 1981), *aff'd*, 434 N.E.2d 262 (N.Y. 1982).

68 Bd. of Educ. of Huntington v. Associated Teachers, 282 N.E.2d 109 (N.Y. 1972).

69 Vaca v. Sipes, 386 U.S. 171 (1967).

70 Baker v. Bd. of Educ. of West Irondequoit, 514 N.E.2d 1109 (N.Y. 1987).

71 Jacobs v. Bd. of Educ. of East Meadow, 405 N.Y.S.2d 159 (N.Y. Sup. Ct. 1977), *rev'd*, 409 N.Y.S.2d 234 (N.Y. App. Div. 1978).

72 Acting Super. of Sch. of Liverpool Cent. Sch. Dist. v. United Liverpool Faculty Ass'n, 369 N.E.2d 746 (N.Y. 1977); Sch. Comm. of Danvers v. Tyman, 360 N.E.2d 877 (Mass. 1977); Bd. of Educ. of Philadelphia v. Philadelphia Fed'n. of Teachers Local No. 3, 346 A.2d 35 (Pa. 1975).

73 Wyandanch Union Free Sch. Dist. v. Wyandanch Teachers Ass'n, 397 N.E.2d 384 (N.Y. 1979); Sch. Dist. of Erie v. Erie Educ. Ass'n, 447 A.2d 686 (Pa. Commw. Ct. 1982).

74 Acting Super. of Sch. of Liverpool Cent. Sch. Dist. v. United Liverpool Faculty Ass'n, 369 N.E.2d 746 (N.Y. 1977).

75 Minnesota Educ. Ass'n v. Indep. Sch. Dist. No. 495, 290 N.W.2d 627 (Minn. 1980).

76 Fortney v. Sch. Dist. of West Salem, 321 N.W.2d 225 (Wis. 1982); *see also* Scranton Fed'n of Teachers, Local 1147 v. Scranton Sch. Dist., 444 A.2d 1144 (Pa. 1982); Sch. Dist. of Erie v. Erie Educ. Ass'n, 447 A.2d 686 (Pa. Commw. Ct. 1982).

77 Niagara Wheatfield Adm'r Ass'n v. Niagara Wheatfield Cent. Sch. Dist., 375 N.E.2d 37 (N.Y. 1978).

78 Buffalo Council of Supervisors & Adm'r v. City of Buffalo Sch. Dist., 626 N.Y.S.2d 623 (N.Y. App. Div. 1995).

79 Kennewick Educ. Ass'n v. Kennewick Sch. Dist. No. 17, 666 P.2d 928 (Wash. App. Ct. 1983).

80 Loyalsock Twp. v. Loyalsock Custodial, 931 A.2d 75 (Pa. Commw. 2007).

81 *In re* Brighton Cent. Sch. Dist., 505 N.Y.S.2d 522 (N.Y. Sup. Ct. 1986); Bd. of Educ. v. Round Valley Teachers Ass'n, 914 P.2d 193 (Cal. 1996); Oak Harbor Sch. Dist. v. Oak Harbor Educ. Ass'n, 545 P.2d 1197 (Wash. 1976).

82 McCutcheon v. Chicago Principals Ass'n, 513 N.E.2d 55 (Ill. App. Ct. 1987); Ayer v. Bd. of Educ. of Cent. Sch. Dist. No. 1, 330 N.Y.S.2d 465 (N.Y. Sup. Ct. 1972); Fairplay Sch. Twp. v. O'Neal, 26 N.E. 686 (Ind. 1891).

83 Nelson v. Doland Bd. of Educ., 380 N.W.2d 665 (S.D. 1986).

84 Morton v. Hampton Sch. Dist. No. 1, 700 S.W.2d 373 (Ark. Ct. App. 1985).

85 Big Sandy Sch. Dist. No. 100-J v. Carroll, 433 P.2d 325 (Colo. 1967); Bd. of Educ. of D.C. v. Wilson, 290 A.2d 400 (D.C. 1972).

86 Enstad v. N. Cent. of Barnes Pub. Sch. Dist. No. 65, 268 N.W.2d 126 (N.D. 1978).

87 Sch. Bd. of Leon County v. Goodson, 335 So. 2d 308 (Fla. Dist. Ct. App. 1976); Lynch v. Webb City Sch. Dist. No. 92, 418 S.W.2d 608 (Mo. Ct. App. 1967).

88 Oneal v. Colton Consol. Sch. Dist. No. 306, 557 P.2d 11 (Wash. Ct. App. 1976); Fisher v. Church of St. Mary, 497 P.2d 882 (Wyo. 1972).

89 Parliament v. Yukon Flats Sch. Dist., 760 P.2d 513 (Alaska 1988).

90 McBeth v. Bd. of Educ. of DeValls Bluff Sch. Dist. No. 1, 300 F. Supp. 1270 (E.D. Ark. 1969).

91 Williams v. Albemarle City Bd. of Educ., 508 F.2d 1242 (4th Cir. 1974).

92 Bowbells Pub. Sch. Dist. No. 14 v. Walker, 231 N.W.2d 173 (N.D. 1975).

93 Klinger v. Adams County Sch. Dist. No. 50, 130 P.3d 1027 (Colo. 2006).

94 Arrowhead Sch. Dist. No. 75 Park County v. Klyap, 79 P.3d 250 (Mont. 2003).

95 Bradkin v. Leverton, 257 N.E.2d 643 (N.Y. 1970).

96 Davis v. Bd. of Educ. of Aurora Pub. Sch. Dist. No. 131, 312 N.E.2d 335 (Ill. App. Ct. 1974).

97 Bottineau Pub. Sch. Dist. No. 1 v. Currie, 259 N.W.2d 650 (N.D. 1977); Knipmeyer v. Diocese of Alexandria, 492 So. 2d 550 (La. Ct. App. 1986); Bd. of Educ. of D.C. v. Wilson, 290 A.2d 400 (D.C. 1972); D'Ulisse-Cupo v. Bd. of Dir. of Notre Dame High Sch., 520 A.2d 217 (Conn. 1987).

98 Brown v. Caldwell Sch. Dist. No. 132, 898 P.2d 43 (Idaho 1995).

99 Niedbalski v. Bd. of Educ. of Sch. Dist. No. 24 of Platte Ctr., 418 N.W.2d 565 (Neb. 1988); Corcoran v. Lyle Sch. Dist. No. 406, 581 P.2d 185 (Wash. Ct. App. 1978); *but compare* California Teachers Ass'n v. Governing Bd. of Mariposa County Unified Sch. Dist., 139 Cal. Rptr. 155 (Cal. Ct. App. 1977).

100 *See* Foster v. Ohio State Univ., 534 N.E.2d 1220 (Ohio Ct. App. 1987).

101 Gainey v. Sch. Bd. of Liberty County, 387 So. 2d 1023 (Fla. Dist. Ct. App. 1980).

102 Price v. Oklahoma Coll. of Osteopathic Med. & Surgery, 733 P.2d 1357 (Okla. App. Ct. 1986).

103 Swager v. Bd. of Educ., Unified Sch. Dist. No. 412, 688 P.2d 270 (Kan. Ct. App. 1984).

104 George v. Sch. Dist. No. 8R of Umatilla County, 490 P.2d 1009 (Or. 1971).

105 Law v. Mandan Pub. Sch. Dist., 411 N.W.2d 375 (N.D. 1987); Pine River State Bank v. Mettille, 333 N.W.2d 622 (Minn. 1983).

106 Heideck v. Kent Gen. Hosp., Inc., 446 A.2d 1095 (Del. 1982); Jackson v. Action for Boston Cmty. Dev., Inc., 525 N.E.2d 411 (Mass. 1988); Johnson v. McDonnell Douglas Corp., 745 S.W.2d 661 (Mo. 1988).

107 Castiglione v. Johns Hopkins Hosp., 517 A.2d 786 (Md. Ct. Spec. App. 1986).

108 Haverland v. Tempe Elementary Sch. Dist. No. 3, 595 P.2d 1032 (Ariz. Ct. App. 1979); Bump v. Union High Sch. Dist. No. 3, 24 P.2d 330 (Or. 1933).

109 Baltimore Teachers Union v. Mayor of Baltimore, 6 F.3d 1012 (4th Cir. 1993).

110 See Chandler v. Lamar County Bd. of Educ., 528 So. 2d 309 (Ala. 1988).

10 TORTS

A student throws a pencil striking another in the eye. A visitor trips in a pothole on the school grounds and injures his knee. An intruder forces a student into a school closet and rapes her. A student severs his finger on a saw in shop class. Another student sneaks out of school during school hours and is injured by a speeding motorist. A teacher sues the school because her supervisor's evaluation described her lesson plans as unprofessional. Cases like these are the province of the body of law known as torts.

Unlike criminal law, which deals with wrongs against society in general, torts deals with harm inflicted by one party on another whether by intentional wrongdoing, recklessness, or simple carelessness. Whereas the primary purpose of criminal law is to punish the wrongdoer, tort law seeks to provide restitution to the injured party. Tort law provides a way to sue for compensation for wrongful harm to, among others, one's body, property, or reputation. The usual remedy is monetary damages, although courts may also issue an injunction to prohibit the continuation of a harmful activity.

A typical tort suit involves one private individual suing an individual, a corporate body, an agent of the government, or the government itself for harm done either intentionally or negligently. Children may be plaintiffs in lawsuits against their schools and school districts or against individual educators. Children may also be defendants in tort suits, although, in practice, it may be difficult to prove the elements of a tort case against a young child, particularly a tort that requires a showing of intentional wrongdoing, such as battery. It also may be difficult to collect damages from children, many of whom have few assets of their own. As a result, individuals injured or damaged as a result of a tort committed by a student at school often seek to hold the school liable (e.g., for failing to adequately supervise the child).

Whereas schools and their employees once enjoyed protection from tort suits under principles of government and government officer immunity, these immunities have been severely curtailed or eliminated in most states. As a result, tort suits may be brought against individual educators as well as the school board or district itself, and, occasionally, individual school board members. Individual teachers and principals may be held personally responsible for their tortious acts. Principals may also be held liable for failing to properly train or supervise a teacher who commits a tort as a result of the principal's failure. School boards and districts may be held liable regarding such matters as the failure to provide a sufficient number of teachers to supervise school activities or for the faulty maintenance of the school's buildings and grounds. School districts may also be held "vicariously" liable for the tortious acts of their employees or anyone else authorized to act on behalf of the district (see sec. 10.5).

Because of the variety of activities schools undertake and the immature and active nature of their clientele, school boards and personnel are particularly vulnerable to certain kinds of tort suits. Yet, school districts of similar size, programs, and demographics often vary greatly with regard to the number of suits filed against them, suggesting that a high rate of tort litigation is not inevitable. With attention to legal principles and care, the risk of incurring a tort suit can be greatly reduced. This chapter presents an overview of the law relating to the types of torts that are most common in schools. A principal goal of the chapter is to provide an understanding of the principles of tort law sufficient to form the basis of a program of preventive law.

10.1 INTENTIONAL TORTS: BATTERY, ASSAULT, FALSE IMPRISONMENT, AND INTENTIONAL INFLICTION OF MENTAL DISTRESS

Intentional means that a person desires to bring about the consequences of an act or believes that the consequences are almost certain to result from it. If X, believing he is alone on the desert, fires a gun, and the bullet strikes and injures Y, X intended to fire the gun but not to injure Y. If, however, X throws a bomb into Y's office with intent to injure him, knowing that Z is also there and will almost certainly be injured too, then X intended the injury not only to Y but also to Z. X's intent to injure Y applies to Z as well. Motive is distinguished from intent. Motives are the reasons for bringing about the consequences of an act. Minors are liable for their intentional acts; however, a minor's age, knowledge, and intelligence are important in determining if the minor was capable of forming an intent to harm.

Battery is the intentional, unwanted, and offensive or harmful touching of another person's body with the intent to cause the other to suffer the contact. Battery can involve direct bodily contact such as a punch or the use of an object such as a stick. A contact is viewed as offensive if it would be offensive to a hypothetical reasonable person. However, consent to some bodily contact is assumed in normal situations where contact is inevitable, such as a crowded elevator.

Assault is distinct from battery. An assault is an action that has the intent to place another in reasonable apprehension of imminent bodily harm or offensive contact. The apprehension must be one that would be aroused in the mind of a reasonable person. Words accompanying an action can add to the apprehension. Whereas battery protects bodily integrity, assault protects peace of mind. Thus, in assault, the person in danger of immediate bodily contact must have knowledge of the danger. An assault typically precedes a battery, but, even if no battery occurs, the assault is still actionable. Both battery and assault may be crimes as well as torts and can lead to both a civil lawsuit and a separate criminal prosecution.

False imprisonment is the intentional confining of a person within a fixed space. The person must be conscious of the confinement or harmed by it. The restraint can be accomplished by physical barriers, threats of force, false assertion of legal authority, or indirect methods such as confiscating a purse to prevent the departure of the owner. The tort of false imprisonment protects people's interest in freedom from restraint. Although rare in school contexts, false imprisonment claims may be brought in cases of the unjustified confinement of a student.

The tort of **intentional infliction of mental distress** permits people who have been subjected to extreme and outrageous conduct to sue for damage done to their peace of mind. Discomfort arising out of ordinary everyday insults, indignities, profanity, or even threats is not actionable, and only distress that a reasonable person of ordinary sensibilities would feel in the circumstances may be compensated. In one case, a coach played a trick on a kindergarten student by telling the student that the coach had hanged two of the student's friends. The coach showed the student one of the friends lying on the floor pretending to be dead. When the student began to cry, the coach admitted the joke. Subsequently, the student, previously a well-adjusted five year old, began to experience psychological difficulties: he refused to go to the bathroom alone and to wipe himself, he was afraid the coach was going to jump out of the mirror at him, he would not sleep in his own room, and he became overly dependent on his mother. The student won an award of $100,000 and his parents won an additional $10,000 for **loss of consortium**, damage to the relationship between parent and child.[1]

Besides cruel pranks such as this, repeated, severe verbal and physical abuse (including racial and sexual harassment, see sec. 5.9) may result in a claim of intentional infliction of emotion distress, but these cases are often difficult to win. The Eighth Circuit denied a claim of intentional infliction of emotional stress brought against a band teacher who publicly humiliated a student in a variety of ways including regularly and publicly calling the student "retarded," "stupid," and "dumb." The teacher belittled the student in front of the class for poor performance on a written assignment, threw the student's notebook in her face, and told her she could no longer play in the band "because she was too stupid." The court ruled that although the teacher's behavior was "unprofessional" and "intemperate" (and despite the fact that the student became depressed and suicidal), it did not meet the legal requirements for intentional infliction of emotional distress: "To constitute intentional infliction of emotional distress," explained the court,

> a plaintiff must show (1) that there has been intentional or reckless conduct; (2) that the conduct was so outrageous in character and so extreme in degree as to go beyond all possible bounds of decency and is to be regarded as atrocious and utterly intolerable in a civilized community; and (3) that the conduct caused emotional distress so severe that no reasonable person should be expected to endure it.[2]

The Defense of Privilege

A defendant is not liable for an intentional tort if the defendant's act was privileged. Tort law recognizes that certain actions are socially so important that the defendant is protected from liability despite injury to the plaintiff. The privileges most often relevant in education cases are the authority of certain adults to discipline children, consent, self-defense, and defense of others. Although the plaintiff carries the burden of persuading the court that a tort has occurred, the defendant has the burden of establishing the existence of one of the privileges.

The **privilege of discipline** allows parents and teachers to use reasonable force including corporal punishment for the discipline and control of children. For example, school officials may seize pupils who refuse lawful orders and physically compel them to move.[3] However, there are limits to what constitutes reasonable force, and tort suits charging school personnel with assault and battery are not uncommon. Whether the force used on a child was reasonable is determined in light of the age, sex, physical and mental condition of the child, the nature of the child's wrongdoing, the reasons for the child's actions, the influence of the child's example on other children, whether the force was necessary to compel the child's obedience, whether the force was proportionate to the child's offense, and the harm inflicted. Findings of abuse of the privilege of discipline are most common if the child suffers permanent or long-term harm, especially physical injury, or if the teacher acts out of ill-will or malice. The courts have also found liability when the force was unnecessarily degrading, as in the case of a teacher who used a cattle prod to discipline his pupils.[4]

In states where corporal punishment is illegal by statute, educators may still use reasonable force to control students but not in retribution for wrongdoing. Even in states where corporal punishment is legal, its use is generally limited to statutorily specified purposes and must be reasonable under the circumstances. For example, a Texas court found that under that state's law, corporal punishment may only be used when

> necessary (1) to enforce compliance with a proper command issued for the purpose of controlling, training or educating the child, or (2) to punish the child for prohibited conduct; and, in either case, the force or physical conduct must be reasonable and not disproportionate to the activity or offense.

Based on this principle, the court found that a football coach was not privileged to use "physical violence against a child" for purposes of "instruction and encouragement." Such use of violence, concluded the court, might constitute assault, even though the coach had no intent to injure the child (see sec. 4.5).[5]

Consent by the plaintiff to the tortious conduct of the defendant generally precludes the liability of the defendant. Consent may be expressed explicitly or implied by the plaintiff's conduct. The defendant can show that the plaintiff consented by presenting evidence demonstrating that a reasonable person would have understood the plaintiff as consenting. The privilege extends only to the specific conduct to which the plaintiff consented, not related acts. The consent is not effective if not given voluntarily or if the plaintiff lacked capacity to consent. There is no specific age when a minor acquires the capacity to consent, so the issue must be evaluated on a case-by-case basis. The general rule in tort is called the "rule of sevens": minors younger than 7 are unable to give consent; from 7 to 13 there is a rebuttable presumption of inability to consent; and from 14 on there is a rebuttable presumption of capacity to consent. In general, the more serious the invasion of a minor's interest, the less likely that the minor has the capacity to consent. State *criminal* laws vary in setting the age at which minors have the capacity to consent to sex, with half setting the age at 18, and some courts apply the state criminal age of consent to sex in tort cases.[6] In some states the age of consent to sex is increased when the partner is a teacher. The defense of assumption of risk, closely related to consent, is discussed in Section 10.4.

The privilege of **self-defense** and the privilege of **defense of others** allow the use of reasonable force to defend oneself or someone else against unprivileged battery or other bodily harm that one reasonably believes is about to be intentionally inflicted by another. In some cases, a person may reasonably believe there is danger, even if no danger actually exists. The past conduct, reputation, words, and gestures of the plaintiff can be taken into account in determining if an apprehension of danger was reasonable. The question is whether, for example, a reasonable teacher would have believed that a pupil was about to intentionally inflict harm. If so, the privilege of self-defense or defense of others applies, but the act of defense must be proportionate to the threat. In one case, a teacher successfully claimed self-defense when he pulled a gun from the glove compartment of his car and brandished it at a student who had been chasing him with a thirty-inch two-by-four.[7]

A majority of the states allow a person to stand and fight when threatened even if flight is possible. The privilege of self-defense ends when the assailant has been disarmed or defeated, withdraws, or gives up. Revenge and retaliation are not self-defense.[8] Students are not privileged to use force to resist teachers physically enforcing lawful orders. For example, if a teacher orders a student to leave the classroom, the student refuses, and the teacher forcibly escorts the student from the class, the student is not privileged to use self-defense against the teacher. One may use self-defense only against unprivileged uses of force.[9]

10.2 DEFAMATION AND EMPLOYEE LETTERS OF REFERENCE

When people spread gossip about teachers or students, write reference letters or perform-ance reviews, publish articles in the school newspaper or yearbook, make comments about school administrators at public meetings, answer questions about someone else in the course of an investigation, or write statements about students for inclusion in their per-manent file, the possibility of saying something defamatory arises. Defamation occurs when one person makes a false statement about another that causes damage to the per-son's reputation or standing within the community. Generally speaking, **libel** is written defamation and **slander** is spoken defamation, although this distinction has undergone some modification in recent years.

To support a legal finding of defamation, a certain specific set of conditions or elements must be present. The six elements of defamation are: false facts, harm, publication, clear reference, standard of fault, and no privilege. Although the law of defamation varies somewhat from state to state, the principles presented are applicable in most jurisdictions.

The first element of defamation is that the defendant must have conveyed **false facts** about the plaintiff. There must be a significant misrepresentation or inaccuracy, some-thing more than a minor error or technical untruth.[10] A statement by a principal that teacher X had missed class more than once a week for a year or by a teacher that students Y and Z had had sexual relations would satisfy this element if the alleged events had not occurred. False facts can be communicated by implication as in the case of a former employer who told a prospective employer he "couldn't go into" the reasons for a dis-missal. The statement was made in a way that implied that the employee had been termi-nated for serious misconduct.[11]

Statements of pure opinion, such as "I don't like teacher Jones," cannot be the basis of a defamation suit because they do not state a fact that can be disproved. Subjective judg-ments based on true facts and conclusions from facts assumed to be generally known, such as "Jones is the worst teacher in the school," cannot be defamatory even if unreasonable or unfair.[12] Courts have viewed an accusation that a principal was a racist[13] and, in another case, a student's writing that a professor's in-class statements made her believe that the professor was homophobic[14] as opinion and therefore not defamatory. Also gen-erally immune from defamation because they convey opinions rather than alleged facts are verbal abuse, hyperbole, and humor. Thus, in one case, the caption, "Not tonight Ms. Salek. I have a headache," under a teacher's photo in the "Funny Pages" of the school yearbook was ruled nonactionable.[15]

On the other hand, statements of **mixed opinions** may satisfy the first element of defamation. Mixed opinions are statements apparently based on facts not expressly stated nor assumed to exist; the statement thus implies that the speaker or writer possesses facts that justify the opinion. A statement such as "In my opinion, teacher Jones is an alco-holic" may be defamatory because it implies a set of facts that may be false. So may state-ments like "I feel that teacher Jones does not turn the students on" and "I believe that Jones is unwilling to go the extra mile" because they imply a lack of effort and success in teaching.[16]

Whether the burden of proof regarding the truth or falsity of an allegedly defamatory statement lies with the plaintiff or defendant varies with the type of case. The Supreme Court has ruled that when the statement involves a matter of public concern, the plaintiff must prove that it was false.[17] In cases involving nonmedia defendants, many states require the defendant to prove the truth of the statement; however, the law is changing on this point, with an increasing number of jurisdictions placing the burden on the plaintiff to prove falsity.

The second element of defamation is that the defendant's statement must have caused **harm** to the plaintiff's reputation or standing within the community. Another way of saying this is that the statement must have been defamatory. Some statements are considered defamatory **per se**, meaning that they are assumed to have caused harm. Accusations of criminal behavior, adultery, or that a person is suffering from a sexually transmitted disease are defamatory per se.[18] Courts are split on whether falsely stating that a person is homosexual is defamatory per se.[19] Statements that are not defamatory per se can still be defamatory **per quod** if the defendant can show that the statement caused actual harm.[20] Accusations of intoxication at a public dinner, that a teacher let students "pet" in the hallways, and that a teacher stole books from the school were all found to be defamatory per quod.[21] Accusations by an employer or supervisor that an employee abused drugs or committed sexual harassment at work may be defamatory per quod.[22]

The third element of defamation is **publication**. The statement must have been intentionally communicated by the defendant to someone other than the plaintiff, such as by sending a letter of reference to a prospective employer. In one case, dictation to a secretary of a dismissal letter counted as publication.[23] A person who repeats a statement has satisfied the element of publication even if the original source is cited; so has anyone assisting in communicating a statement to others, such as the publisher of a book or a school that sponsors a student newspaper. However, if someone eavesdrops on a statement by the defendant to the plaintiff or someone copies and distributes a letter from the defendant to the plaintiff, the defendant is not liable.

Employers sometimes seek to avoid liability for defamation by orally informing only employees themselves of reasons for their dismissal and subsequently refusing to write anything other than the confirmation of dates of employment in letters of reference. Employees seeking new employment then may face the dilemma of having either to lie or to repeat false defamatory statements about themselves when asked what reasons their former employer gave for dismissing them. To deal with this situation, the legal theory of **compelled self-publication** has recently emerged. The doctrine holds that when defamatory statements are made to a terminated employee, publication will be assumed because the employee will be forced to repeat the reasons for the dismissal when seeking reemployment.[24]

The fourth element of defamation, **clear reference**, means that it must be reasonably apparent that the statement was about the plaintiff. The plaintiff does not have to be specifically named in the statement; the reference can be by inference, even as part of an alleged work of fiction in which the plaintiff is recognizable as one of the characters. Statements regarding a group of people—for example, "All teachers in school X smoke pot"—can satisfy this element if plaintiffs can show that the statements referred to them as part of the group. Even a reference to "some" teachers in the building might satisfy this element for plaintiffs who prove that their reputations were damaged.[25]

The fifth element, **standard of fault**, varies from case to case depending on the status of the plaintiff within the community, the topic of the allegedly defamatory communication, and the specifics of state law. If the plaintiff is a public official and the topic relates to the official's performance of duty or fitness for office, defamation can be found only if the defendant knew of the falsity of the statement or spoke with reckless disregard of the truth.[26] A school newspaper sued for accusing the superintendent of schools of embezzling district funds would fall into this category. This same standard, known as **actual malice**, also applies in cases involving public figures such as movie stars and communications by individuals who voluntarily involve themselves in matters of public concern.

At the other end of the spectrum, in cases involving private individuals, most states require only a showing of **negligence**, meaning that the defendant was careless about whether the statement was true. A suit against a school newspaper for writing that a student had sexual relations with numerous partners fits in this category. The fault standards for cases falling between these established categories are still somewhat in question, but, in general, cases involving public matters invoke the actual malice standard, and private matters call for a lesser standard of fault.

Public officials and figures have a much heavier burden of proof of defamation than private citizens. Although several Supreme Court cases have defined these categories,[27] the definitions have proved difficult to apply in education cases. Most courts would probably agree that a state or local superintendent of schools is a public official. In one case, a Maryland court ruled that a high school principal was a public official, a classification that most courts would also probably follow.[28] Courts are split regarding teachers and coaches; some consider them private persons[29] and others classify them as public officials.[30]

There is even more uncertainty as to what constitutes a matter of public concern and which matters of public concern are related to an official's performance of duties or fitness for office. To date, courts have not provided clear definitions of these concepts. The most that can be said is that a topic is more likely to be judged a matter of public concern if it is the sort of issue that should be open to wide public debate.[31]

Even when the first five elements of defamation can be proved, there are certain situations when, as a matter of law, defendants are immune from a finding of defamation. The sixth and final element of defamation, no privilege, means that defamation can only be found when no such immunity or privilege exists.

An **absolute privilege** protects from liability for defamation even for false, defamatory statements made with malice or intent to harm. An absolute privilege of speech obtains concerning statements made in judicial or legislative proceedings; statements made by certain government executive officers, including superintendents of schools in some states, in the course of their duties; statements made with the consent of the person spoken about; and statements made between husband and wife when they are alone. Broadcasters are also immune from suit when a candidate for public office makes a defamatory comment over the air.

Qualified privileges, also called conditional privileges, can be forfeited if the speaker goes beyond the scope of the privilege, uses it for reasons other than for which it was created, speaks with the intent of causing harm,[32] or otherwise abuses the privilege. A commonly used standard finds the privilege to have been abused when the defendant knew the defamatory statement to be false or had no reasonable grounds for believing it to be true.[33] Thus, a qualified privilege may be lost because of actual malice, or a reckless or callous disregard for the truth.[34] In all cases, the defendant has the burden of invoking the privilege, but the plaintiff must establish that it was abused.

Of the various categories of qualified privilege, the ones most relevant to education are those that protect communications to someone who may act in the public interest, protect fair comment on matters of public concern, and protect communications made in the interest of a third party. The first category includes statements made by one public official to another regarding official duties, employee evaluations within an organization,[35] and statements by private citizens about the conduct of public officials. In one case, a school board member was protected by the first category of qualified privilege when the board member said that marijuana cigarettes had been found in a student's car.[36] Another case that fell into the first category involved a principal who incorrectly informed the guidance office that the plaintiff had suffered a mental breakdown.[37] A parental report to school officials and other interested parties regarding the allegedly harmful behavior of a teacher would fall into the first and second categories of qualified privilege.[38] A New York court ruled that under that state's law, allegedly libelous articles concerning an assistant principal's treatment of teachers written by a teacher in a union newsletter were entitled to qualified privilege because of "the common interest shared by the union and the employer in preventing mistreatment of teachers in the workplace and ensuring compliance with the [district's] rules." The privilege would not apply if the articles were written with "actual malice, specifically, that the teacher published the statements while highly aware that they were probably false."[39]

In some states, common law includes post-employment letters of reference in the third category of qualified privilege.[40] In addition, about half the states have adopted employee reference statutes that specifically extend a qualified privilege to employers and supervisors in the writing of letters of recommendation.[41] These statutes vary somewhat, but they generally permit employers who have received a request from a former employee for a reference to reveal job performance information about the former employee. The privilege is lost if the employee can show by preponderance of evidence that false and defamatory information was conveyed with actual malice or with reckless disregard for the truth.

As executive officers, superintendents may enjoy absolute privilege regarding false and defamatory statements made in the performance of their job. One court found that a superintendent could not be held liable for defamatory statements contained in a letter of reprimand placed in a teacher-coach's personnel file.[42] However, in the same case, the court extended only qualified immunity to the superintendent regarding a statement he issued to the press. The current trend in most states is to extend only qualified immunity to local government bodies and officials such as school board members and superintendents of schools.

In some states, parents enjoy absolute immunity when airing complaints about a teacher at a school board meeting. Thus, a New York court ruled that parents enjoyed absolute immunity from a libel suit regarding a petition filed with the school board. In that petition, the parents claimed that the teacher had missed classes, struck a student, threatened bodily harm to a student's mother, accused a student of being a liar without justification, and insulted a student with an ethnic slur.[43] However, some states extend only a qualified privilege to parents.[44]

A privilege that may be invoked regarding school board meetings and other forums of debate of educational issues is known as the **fair report** privilege. The fair report privilege protects fair and accurate reports of governmental proceedings, official actions, and even nongovernmental proceedings that deal with matters of public concern.[45] The value of the privilege is that it protects a defendant against liability even when the defendant repeats a defamatory statement that was made during a proceeding and even if the defendant knows the reported assertions are false; the privilege is not limited to reporting on public officials or public figures. Once the defendant has made a prima facie case for the fair report privilege, the burden shifts to the plaintiff to establish that the privilege should not operate because of substantial inaccuracy or unfairness of the report.[46] The privilege is not lost if the report of the proceedings is substantially accurate.

The most common defamation suits in education involve reference letters written by administrators to prospective new employers. Generally, plaintiffs will not win these suits unless the recommender acts with malice or otherwise abuses the qualified privilege.[47] Thus, to avoid the possibility of an adverse finding of defamation, a recommender need only make a good faith effort to accurately convey relevant information. Minor inaccuracies, inadvertent errors of fact, and honestly offered adverse evaluations of performance will not support a finding of defamation. In cases when a recommender knowingly and maliciously distorts the truth to prevent a former employee from securing a new job, damages may be awarded to compensate the employee for harm done to reputation, loss of earnings, and mental anguish. In severe cases, punitive damages may also be awarded. False and malicious recommendations that prevent an applicant from securing a job can also lead to liability under another tort known as **intentional interference with prospective contractual relations** and, in some states, criminal liability under antiblacklisting statutes.

Despite the considerable protection built into the law for recommenders who act in good faith, many school districts have become overly cautious about the recommendations they provide for former employees. Some schools refuse to provide any recommendations at all, and others provide only positive recommendations whether deserved or not. Although effectively eliminating possible lawsuits for defamation, the no-recommendations policy is extremely unfair and detrimental both to praiseworthy former employees and to prospective future employers of ineffective former employees. To combat this trend, thirteen states have enacted "service-letter" statutes giving employees the right to receive written confirmation of employment from former employers; however, most of these statutes are of limited use as they only require the provision of dates of employment and positions held.

The policy of providing falsely positive recommendations even to employees fired for serious incompetence or wrongdoing, although educationally and morally indefensible, seems in most states to entail little legal risk. A New York court expressly rejected a negligence claim (see sec. 10.4) against a school that failed to disclose that a teacher had a record of sexual misconduct.[48] However, at least in theory, an employer who either fails to disclose negative information or misrepresents an employee in a positive way could be held liable for **negligent nondisclosure** or **negligent misrepresentation.**[49]

The California Supreme Court has actually applied this theory in one extreme case: Three school districts, former employers of Robert Gadams, wrote extremely positive letters of reference containing such comments as "I wouldn't hesitate to recommend Mr. Gadams for any position." None of the letters mentioned Gadams' long history of improper sexual contact with students in all three school districts. Gadams was hired by a fourth district where he sexually assaulted the plaintiff. The plaintiff brought suit against the former employers. The court found that the letters recommending Gadams without reservation or qualification "constituted affirmative representations that strongly implied Gadams was fit to interact appropriately and safely with female students. These representations were false and misleading in light of defendants' . . . knowledge of charges of Gadams' repeated sexual improprieties." Having undertaken to provide some information about Gadams' fitness as a teacher, said the court, the former employers had an obligation to disclose all other facts that materially qualified the facts disclosed: "[T]he writer of a letter of recommendation owes to third persons a duty not to misrepresent the facts in describing the qualifications and character of a former employee, if making these misrepresentations would present a substantial foreseeable risk of physical injury to third persons."[50]

10.3 INVASION OF PRIVACY, STUDENT RECORDS, AND THE DUTY TO REPORT CHILD ABUSE

Closely related to defamation, **invasion of privacy** is a multifaceted tort that can be committed in four different ways: (a) appropriation or use of a person's name or likeness for gain, such as using the name of a movie star to promote a product without permission; (b) unreasonable intrusion on the seclusion of another; (c) unreasonable publication of private facts about another—the unreasonable publication must involve public disclosure of private facts, and the matter made public must be highly offensive and objectionable to a reasonable person of ordinary sensibilities (the truth of the private facts is not a defense); and (d) unreasonable publication that places another in a false light in the public eye.

Although unusual in school contexts, invasion of privacy may occur if school officials disclose information about teachers or students concerning sexual behavior, medical history, family problems, school performance, substance abuse, socioeconomic status, or other private matters for reasons not supported by legitimate educational concerns. For example, school officials should be careful to inform only those who have a need to know that a teacher or student has AIDS. However, not everything that a person wishes to keep secret is considered a private matter by the law. In one case, school officials spoke with the media about an incident in which three teachers were in an alcohol-related accident following a retirement party. An Oregon appellate court reversed a verdict of invasion of privacy against the school officials because the accident and the school district's campaign to stop drinking were public knowledge and the disciplinary record of the teachers was public information under state law.[51]

Invasion of privacy may also be claimed in connection with unjustified searches, including drug testing, of students or teachers: "One who intentionally intrudes, physically or otherwise, upon the solitude or seclusion of another or his private affairs or concerns, is subject to liability to the other for invasion of his privacy, if the intrusion would be highly offensive to a reasonable person."[52] A Texas court ruled that an employer's search of an employee's locker and of a purse found in the locker could create liability for invasion of privacy.[53] The West Virginia Supreme Court ruled that random drug testing of employees was an unwarranted invasion of privacy, but testing upon reasonable suspicion was not.[54] Recall that unjustified drug testing and other unreasonable searches can also violate the constitutional rights of students (see sec. 4.3) and teachers (see sec. 7.3).

Employees have had little success in claiming invasion of privacy when employers read e-mails sent or stored on the employer's e-mail system. Courts typically rule that the employee does not have a reasonable expectation of privacy even in the face of the employer's assurance that their e-mails would not be intercepted.[55] Similarly, school employees are unlikely to succeed in claiming invasion of privacy because of surveillance cameras in classrooms or offices. In one case, a school set up a video camera in the private office two employees shared in order to determine who was improperly using computer equipment in the office after the workday had concluded. Considering all the facts relating to the videotaping including its scope, location, and purpose, the court decided that the taping was not "highly offensive to a reasonable person." The court noted that the employees did not have a reasonable expectation of privacy in the office because the custodian had a key and that "the computer office was not a location where employees would ordinarily be expected to attend to [personal] bodily matters."[56]

In some situations, the law recognizes a **privilege to disclose private facts** as a defense against invasion of privacy. The privilege may be absolute (e.g., when one is a witness at a trial) or qualified, as when an employer makes internal disclosures of private information about an employee.[57] Similarly, educators have a qualified privilege to disclose private information about a student to another educator or to a former student's new school on a need-to-know basis.

Student Records

Concerns about the privacy and contents of student records engendered considerable litigation and state legislative activity during the 1960s and early 1970s.[58] Critics complained that school records often contained unfounded, erroneous, or irrelevant information and that records were kept secret from parents and children but routinely released without permission to police, employers, creditors, and anyone else who asked. Several state and federal courts held that parents had a common law or due process right to inspect their children's school records under certain conditions and about half of all states granted parents access to records by statute.

In 1974, Congress enacted the **Family Education Rights and Privacy Act (FERPA)**, sometimes called the **Buckley Amendment**.[59] The Act is designed to protect the privacy of students and assure fairness in the keeping and use of school records. School records include most materials directly related to a student and maintained by the school district. However, certain types of records are not included: personal instructional records of teachers kept in the teachers' sole possession and shown only to substitute teachers; records of a law enforcement unit of a school district; and records of a physician, psychiatrist, psychologist, or other recognized health-care professional or paraprofessional, made, maintained, or used only in connection with the treatment of a student. The Supreme Court has ruled that FERPA is not violated by the practice of letting students grade each other's tests.[60]

All rights conferred by the Act belong to parents until the child reaches eighteen years of age, after which they belong to the former child and no longer to the parents. The Act requires that parents, including noncustodial natural parents,[61] be granted access to all records maintained by the school concerning their child within a reasonable period of time, in no case more than forty-five days after requesting it. After inspecting the records, parents have a right to request the modification of any portion they believe false, misleading, or violative of privacy or other rights of their child. If the school refuses to modify the record, parents must be given a full and fair hearing before an impartial hearing officer to decide whether the record will be changed. At the hearing, each side may be represented by counsel, present evidence, call witnesses, and cross-examine the other's witnesses. The hearing officer must render a decision in writing based solely on the evidence and testimony presented at the hearing with nothing outside the record considered. Should the parents prevail, the school must modify the record in accordance with the hearing officer's findings. Even if the school prevails, parents must still be allowed to add a statement to the record presenting their side of the story.

In addition to making school records available to parents, FERPA requires that they be kept confidential from all others, with certain specified exceptions. Records may be shown to educators within the school system who have a legitimate educational interest in them, but a log must be kept of all those viewing the record. Records may be sent to other schools in which the student seeks to enroll or in response to a subpoena, but in both cases parents must be notified. Schools may disclose personally identifiable information to appropriate parties in connection with an emergency if the information is necessary to protect the health or safety of the student or other individuals. Records may also be shown to state and federal education agencies for research and statistical purposes. Otherwise, records must not be released without written permission of the parents, except that the school may, if it wishes, provide "directory" information such as names, addresses, fields of study, activities, and awards.

The Supreme Court has ruled that FERPA does not create a private right of action, meaning that an individual may not sue a school either directly or by using the federal law known as Section 1983 (see sec. 10.10) to redress a violation of FERPA.[62] However, school districts that fail to comply with FERPA may have their federal funds withheld by the Secretary of Education, and educators may be liable if statements contained in student records are libelous or invasive of privacy.

Reporting Child Abuse

Although exact figures on the incidence of child abuse are unavailable, conservative estimates conclude that a million or more children are abused each year. In response to this social tragedy, all fifty states have enacted statutes requiring that cases of actual or suspected child abuse be reported to various authorities. Although these laws vary among the states, they tend to embrace a broad definition of child abuse, including physical and emotional abuse, neglect and abandonment, incest, sexual molestation, and sexual exploitation, including using children for pornographic purposes.

The duty to report suspected incidents of child abuse generally extends to health practitioners and those who work in positions involving child care, including teachers, school administrators, and other school personnel. In addition to those required to report suspected child abuse, any person with reasonable cause to suspect that a child was abused may make a report. Reports must be made to a specifically designated state agency responsible for child protective services. In some states, the law also requires that school employees notify the person in charge of the school or a designated agent, who then becomes responsible for making the report. The law thus anticipates that each school will have a properly developed internal system for processing child abuse reports. The law may also impose a duty on the school to provide all current and new employees with written information explaining the reporting requirements.

If there is an initial oral report, it must typically be followed by a written report that includes the name and address of the child; the name and address of the child's parent or guardian; the child's age, sex, and race; the nature and extent of the suspected abuse; information regarding prior injuries or abuse; information regarding the abuse of siblings; the name of the person allegedly responsible for the abuse; the name and address of the person making the report; and actions taken by the reporting source.

Because of the great importance of protecting children from abuse and to allay fears of legal reprisals, the law grants immunity from civil and criminal liability to people who report child abuse. In some states, the immunity is absolute, meaning there is no liability even for maliciously and knowingly submitting a false report.[63] In other states, immunity is only granted for reports made in good faith. Good faith will be presumed if the reporters were "acting in discharge of their duties and within the scope of their employment," and if the report did not result from "willful misconduct or gross negligence."[64]

Despite the availability of legal immunity, educators often hesitate to make child abuse reports. The failure to make a report that the law requires is a misdemeanor that exposes the educator to the possibility of criminal prosecution. There is also the possibility of civil liability; for example, for harm done to a child by an abuser that might otherwise have been prevented. It is, therefore, legally imperative that educators file a report whenever they have reasonable cause to suspect that child abuse has occurred. In addition to actual observations of abuse and of its consequences, such as a pattern of poorly explained bruises and other injuries, a reasonable suspicion of abuse might be based on conversations with the child, the parents or other suspected abuser, or the child's friends. A professional assessment of the child by the school psychologist may provide further supporting evidence, as would knowledge of prior abusive behavior by the suspected abuser. When making a report, an effort should be made to repeat accurately what the child and other people interviewed actually said.

10.4 NEGLIGENCE

The single most common type of litigation in education is students suing school districts and educators because they were injured at school. These suits raise the issue of negligence. Negligence can be defined as the failure to exercise reasonable care resulting in harm to another person. Ordinary negligence is not a crime, but some negligent acts expose a person both to a civil tort suit for negligence and separate criminal charges. An example is a car accident caused by driving while intoxicated that seriously injures another person.

A finding of negligence requires the plaintiff to prove the existence of each of four elements. The failure of the plaintiff to establish any of the elements precludes a finding of negligence:

1. **Duty and standard of care.** The defendant owed a legal duty to the plaintiff to conform to a standard of care established by law.
2. **Breach of duty.** The defendant failed to live up to the standard of care.
3. **Legal cause.** The defendant's behavior resulted in harm to the plaintiff.
4. **Injury and damages.** The plaintiff sustained an actual injury, one that can be measured in monetary terms.

Duty and Standard of Care

Despite the fears of many educators, not all accidents or injuries create liability for negligence. Negligence can be found only in connection with behavior that "falls below the standard established by law for the protection of others against unreasonable risk of harm."[65] The generally applicable standard of behavior established by statute or common law in most situations is that of a reasonable person acting prudently in light of the circumstances. Thus, in order to avoid a finding of negligence, every person has a duty always to act as would a hypothetical reasonable person.

If a person fails to live up to this duty and injury or other harm to another person results, there may be liability for negligence. No one is liable, however, for accidents that were unavoidable, not foreseeable, or not preventable by reasonable precautions. Thus, a school bus driver would be liable for injuries caused by careless driving, but a bus driver with no history of heart trouble would not be liable for an accident resulting from a sudden heart attack.

Because of the responsibilities inherent in their jobs and the special skills teachers are supposed to possess, educators in most states are held to a different and generally higher standard of behavior than ordinary citizens.[66] Teachers are expected to do a better job of protecting students from injury than an average reasonable and prudent person would. For example, if a visitor to a school sees students throwing ice balls at each other on the playground, ignoring the students would not fall below the required standard of care. However, if a teacher assigned to supervise the playground ignored the ice ball fight, the teacher's behavior would be below the applicable standard.[67]

States vary regarding the duty of care imposed by law on school officials. Some states' tort laws hold educators to the standard of a "reasonably prudent parent"; however, Illinois teachers are liable only for willful and wanton misconduct. Regarding the furnishing of equipment to students, however, Illinois imposes a stronger standard—"ordinary prudence."[68] As in Illinois, in some states, the standard of care applicable to school personnel may vary depending on the specific job or activity the employee is performing. A Michigan statute holds that when disciplining students, a school official is liable only for gross abuse and disregard of the student's health and safety.[69] By contrast, regarding the operation of school buses, a few states impose an extraordinary duty of care.[70] Nebraska has specified the duty owed by a coach in dealing with an injured football player as "that of the reasonably prudent person holding a Nebraska teacher certificate with a coaching endorsement."[71] Educators who establish a "special relationship" with a student—for example, by promising to protect a student who has been threatened—may be held to an especially high standard of care.[72]

The reasonable and prudent teacher is a fictitious person who sets an objective standard of behavior. What the judge or jury determines this hypothetical person would have done in a given situation is the standard against which the behavior of an educator charged with negligence is measured. If the teacher has a physical disability, the standard of conduct is that of a reasonable teacher with a like disability. Expert testimony from other teachers and educators can help to establish the professionally expected norms of conduct.[73]

In general, the higher standard of care expected of educators obtains only when they are on the job. With the exception of school-sponsored events, there is usually no duty to supervise or protect students off school grounds or outside school hours beyond that of an ordinary citizen.[74] Courts have generally not held schools liable for criminal assaults on students by third parties on nonschool property contiguous to the school unless school officials had specific knowledge of imminent criminal activity or prior incidents suggested that a criminal assault was foreseeable.[75] However, a Louisiana court found a school liable for a shooting on contiguous property, ruling that the district had assumed the affirmative duty of protecting its pupils on contiguous property when it hired a security counselor who was stationed outside the school during the noon hour.[76] A district also may be held liable for injuries to a student off school grounds if the student was able to leave the school because of negligent supervision.[77] But the Idaho Supreme Court has ruled that a school district does not have a duty to provide crossing guards at all intersections even if the district has undertaken to provide guards at some intersections and even if the city has designated an intersection as a school crossing.[78]

Generally schools and teachers are only responsible for supervising students during the school day and at other times when students are under their direct control.[79] There are some circumstances when the duty to supervise extends to before or after school or off the school campus such as while the child is on the school bus, as the child disembarks from the school bus, and, in some states, as the child crosses the street after leaving the school bus.[80] Some courts have said that, depending on circumstances, educators may be held liable for failing to supervise students just before or just after formal school hours.[81] If educators voluntarily undertake supervision of students who arrive early or stay late, the applicable standard of care is that of an educator, not an ordinary citizen.[82]

In *Ernest v. Red Creek Central School District*[83] the highest New York court established a rule "that a school district's duty of care requires continued exercise of control and supervision in the event that release of the child poses a foreseeable risk of harm." In this case the court found a possible breach of duty when students were released before all school busses had left the vicinity of the school, and a student was severely injured as he crossed a busy street because his view of an on-coming truck was blocked by a departing school bus. In a case in which a pedestrian was hit by a student "peeling" out of a school parking lot, a California court held that a school district had a duty to nonstudents to supervise students as they drove out of the school parking lot.[84] In *Hoyem v. Manhattan Beach School District*,[85] the district was held responsible for the injury of a student that occurred off school grounds after the student wrongfully left school grounds during the school day.

The highest court of New Jersey has provided guidelines regarding the policies school districts in that state must adopt regarding the handling of dismissal from school. Districts, said the court, must have a "reasonable policy concerning dismissal" including specific procedures for adult supervision and patrols during dismissal. Parents must be notified of the dismissal policy including information about the time of dismissal, the supervision provided, the existence of supervised after-school services, if any, and how a student can enroll in those services. Parents must also be told that it is their obligation to inform the district if the child is not to be allowed to walk home alone if the parent is not present. If so informed, the district must continue supervision of the child while the child waits for the parent or other designated escort or transportation.[86]

Under certain circumstances, principals and other school administrators may owe a duty to students to ensure that teachers are properly supervising them. In one case, the Supreme Court of Minnesota ruled that a principal was legally liable to a student who sustained quadriplegic paralysis as a result of the faulty execution of a gymnastic exercise. The student was being supervised by a recently hired physical education teacher who was also held legally responsible for his negligent supervision. The principal was found liable on the grounds that he was negligent in entrusting the physical education program to an inexperienced teacher without providing closer supervision, for failing to instruct the teacher to refer to a bulletin on physical education published by the state department of education, and for failing either to require the former teacher to develop a plan for the new teacher or to require the new teacher to develop a detailed plan.[87]

Courts have generally held that schools do not have a duty to protect teachers from attacks by students.[88] However, there are some exceptions. In a New York case, a principal assigned a student with violent propensities to a class being taught by a substitute teacher. The teacher sued the school after being assaulted by the student. The court ruled that the school had a duty to inform the teacher of the student's tendency to violence.[89] A duty to protect teachers may also exist if a school district establishes a special relationship with its teachers; for example, if the district's contract with the union requires the district to establish a security system to protect teachers from assaults by students. Most injuries to teachers at school, whatever the cause, are covered by workers' compensation, which usually precludes a suit for negligence (see sec. 8.8).[90]

Breach of Duty

Generally, the key to determining whether an educator's conduct fell below the required standard of care turns on the question of whether the educator should have foreseen the resulting injury. The mere existence of an injury is not proof that the standard of care has been breached. School officials are not expected to prevent every conceivable injury, only to take reasonable precautions designed to prevent foreseeable injuries. Nor is the absence of a teacher when an injury occurs in itself proof of breach of duty. Schools are not ordinarily required to supervise every student every minute of the school day, although the longer students are left alone, the more likely a finding of breach of duty.

Different school activities pose different sets of known dangers, and appropriate precautions must be taken accordingly. Students must be properly instructed in the performance of potentially dangerous activities in advance. Supervision and precautions must increase if past occurrences indicate an increased likelihood of danger. The age, capacity, and past behavior of students are also relevant to the foreseeability of danger. The likelihood of a finding of breach of duty is increased if a state law, regulation, or a school's own policy is violated. Ultimately, however, the determination of foreseeability and breach of duty occurs on a case-by-case basis.

The following are examples of cases where students were injured and educators were found to have breached their duty of care:

- A regular classroom teacher left a lighted candle on her desk, and a child whose costume came in contact with the flame was badly burned.[91]
- A teacher left a classroom of mentally retarded teenagers unattended for a half hour, and one student threw a wooden pointer, injuring the eye of another.[92]
- A student was abducted from school by an intruder and raped. The doors of the

school were not locked, and there was a history of sexual assaults and other violent crimes in the neighborhood.[93]

- A student was pushed out of a bathroom window by other students in a school with racial tensions.[94]

- On the school playground, students engaged in slap boxing for five to ten minutes until one student fell, mortally fracturing his skull.[95]

- A student was injured when permitted to wear mittens while playing on the jungle gym.[96]

- Students were required to play a game of line soccer in the gym with little experience or technical instruction in soccer skills. A melee occurred as the students kicked for possession of the ball, and one student was hurt.[97]

- In shop, a student was injured using a drill press while the instructor, who had not properly instructed students in use of the press or provided safety warnings, was absent from the shop.[98]

- A fifteen-year-old student employee stole chemicals from an unlocked chemistry lab and left them in bushes outside the school. The chemicals were found by an eight-year-old boy who was burned when he put a match to them.[99]

- On a school-sponsored field trip, a child unsupervised while swimming in the ocean was hurt by a rolling log.[100]

- After classes, a student had an accidental run-in with another student who then threatened her with death. Plaintiff informed a teacher and sought help in the security office, but there were no security personnel in the office or in their assigned locations at the time students were leaving school. When the plaintiff and her sister were attacked in the school building, there was no assistance available to them.[101]

- A student who was attending a school event in a park near the school was given permission to leave the park to obtain lunch at a nearby pizzeria. While the student was in the pizzeria, her class left the park. When she returned to the park and could not find her class, she proceeded to walk home alone, at which time she was accosted and raped.[102]

- Two school counselors were informed by a student's friends that the student intended to kill herself. After the student did kill herself, a court held the counselors had a duty to use reasonable means to prevent the suicide and that they breached that duty when they failed to warn the student's parents.[103]

Legal Cause

In all states, the law imposes liability only for harms that are reasonably closely associated with negligent conduct. Generally, a finding of legal cause requires that two conditions be met: (a) **causation in fact**, that the injury be a result of the negligent party's act and (b) **proximate cause**, that the act be sufficiently connected to the injury to be considered its cause. (The term "proximate cause" is often also used synonymously with "legal cause" to encompass both requirements.) Different states seem to interpret the notion of legal cause differently, and it is not always easy to reconcile cases even within the same state.

A widely used test for causation in fact is the **but-for** requirement: A person's behavior is the cause of an injury if the injury would not have occurred but for the behavior. An act or omission is not a but-for cause of an injury if it would have happened regardless of what the defendant did. For example, a school fails to erect a fence around the school yard. A truck driver loses control and enters the school yard, killing a student. The failure to install the fence is not the proximate cause of the death if the truck would have crashed through the fence had it been there and still killed the student.

Even when the but-for requirement is met, courts sometimes fail to find proximate cause for reasons of fairness or public policy when an injury is separated from its but-for cause by time, space, or intervening events. Consider the following example: John is walking around the chemistry lab with a glass container filled with an explosive liquid. The teacher, Miss Smith, is in the supply closet for a half hour. Jim, a student with rough-housing tendencies, pushes John. The container falls and sets off an explosion. The impact of the explosion knocks a large vase off a shelf in another room across the hall. The vase hits the floor, breaks, and fragments of glass embed in Ellen's eye. Ellen sues Smith for negligence.

Arguably Smith's absence is a but-for cause of the accident. Had she been present, she might have prevented John from walking around with the dangerous liquid or might have controlled Jim's rough-housing. But should Smith's actions be considered a proximate cause of Ellen's injury? As a matter of public policy and fairness, are people to be held liable for any bizarre chain of events their behavior might set into motion? How proximate does a cause have to be?

Generally, courts do not find proximate cause in cases like the one described;[104] however, there is no set rule for determining when an act is sufficiently closely connected to a consequence to be considered a proximate cause. Among the tests courts have employed are to find defendants responsible for the but-for consequences of their acts that are foreseeable harms, directly traceable harms, or, in retrospect, not highly extraordinary. Using any of these tests would appear to absolve Smith from negligence in connection with Ellen's injury.

The Smith hypothetical also raises the issue of **intervening causes**. Suppose a defendant's carelessness contributes to an injury but so does another independent cause arising subsequent to the defendant's behavior. For example, the defendant sets a fire and afterward a wind springs up spreading the fire. The question is whether the defendant is not liable because of the subsequent event. Generally, the courts hold the defendant liable even in the face of an intervening cause if the intervening cause was foreseeable. Thus, a teacher who leaves a lighted candle on her desk can foresee that a misbehaving child might push another child into the candle. Similarly, a teacher who fails to fulfill assigned hall duty in a school in a high-crime neighborhood could foresee that an intruder might enter the school and harm a student. However, a teacher who sends students to the playground without proper supervision could not foresee they might be injured by an earthquake.

In the following instances, the courts concluded that legal cause had not been proven:

- A fourteen-year-old student left school in the middle of the day and went joyriding. A high-speed police chase resulted in a serious car accident in which the boy was hurt. The parents used the school claiming negligence regarding, among other things, the failure of the school to notify them of their son's truancy. The court ruled that failure to notify of the truancy was not a legal cause of the student's injury.[105]
- At the noon recess, a student threw a small rock that hit a larger rock on the ground and bounced up to strike another student in the eye. The supervising teacher had just walked past this group of boys when the incident occurred. The court ruled that "[w]here the time between an act of a student and injury to a fellow student is so short that the teacher had no opportunity to prevent injury, it cannot be said that negligence of the teacher is a proximate cause of the injury."[106]

Injury and Damages

In addition to establishing a breach of a standard of care and legal cause, the plaintiff must establish the existence of an injury and the monetary value of the injury. If a previous injury of the plaintiff is aggravated by the defendant, the defendant is liable only for the additional loss. The plaintiff generally can collect monetary compensation for losses such as damage to property, physical injury (including past and future medical expenses), lost earnings, pain, and emotional distress. Most courts do not permit recovery for emotional distress unaccompanied by physical injury, illness, or other physical consequences.

Affirmative Defenses

Even if all four elements of negligence are proven, a defendant's liability may be eliminated or reduced by the existence of one or more factors. The most common of these defenses are contributory negligence, comparative negligence, and assumption of risk. The burden is on the defendant to raise and prove an affirmative defense.

Contributory Negligence

Contributory negligence is conduct on the part of the plaintiff below a reasonable standard of care for self-protection that contributes along with the defendant's behavior to the plaintiff's injury. The principles of proximate cause apply to the contributory negligence defense. Historically, and still in a few states today, if the defendant could prove contributory negligence on the part of the plaintiff, the plaintiff could not recover any damages. This was true whether the plaintiff's own negligence was slight or extensive.

The standard of care children owe themselves depends on their age, experience, and capacities. Thus, the same behavior by a seventeen-year-old and ten-year-old might be viewed differently, with the elder being held contributorily negligent but not the younger. In some states, children below a certain age, often seven, are presumed by law to be incapable of being contributorily negligent. The contributory negligence defense may be effective in cases where older students disobey express instructions regarding the use of dangerous equipment in shop or dangerous maneuvers in gym,[107] or if older students mix chemicals just to see what might happen or with the deliberate intention of building a bomb.[108]

Comparative Negligence

The contributory negligence doctrine can produce an unfortunate outcome: Slight negligence on the part of the plaintiff can let a more negligent defendant off the hook. Hence, an increasing majority of states have substituted the comparative negligence doctrine. Comparative negligence holds that plaintiffs whose negligence contributes to their own injuries can recover damages only for the portion of the injury attributable to the defendant's negligence. Comparative negligence does not totally bar recovery by the plaintiff, but it reduces the damages in proportion to the plaintiff's fault. Some states have modified comparative negligence rules to bar recovery if the plaintiff's negligence was more than 50 percent or greater than the defendant's.

In one case where the comparative negligence defense was used, a seventh grade student broke his leg playing a pick-up game of tackle football in violation of school rules. The teacher was ruled negligent for not seeing and stopping the game, but the court also ruled the boys were old enough to know that tackling could cause injury. Thus, the court reduced the percentage of fault attributable to the teacher and school board to 5 percent. The plaintiff was allowed to recover $10,000 rather than the $200,000 awarded by the trial court.[109]

Assumption of Risk

A plaintiff can relieve the defendant of liability by expressly or implicitly recognizing a danger and voluntarily assuming the risk. Voluntary participants in athletic contests assume the risk of the normal hazards of the sport. Spectators who sit near the sidelines of a playing field assume the risk of being hurt by players crashing into them in the normal course of the game.

To successfully employ the defense of assumption of risk, the defendant must establish that the plaintiff knew the risk was present. The plaintiff's age and level of experience will be considered. It must also be shown that the plaintiff understood the nature of the risk and that the assumption of the risk was voluntary. A person may not consent to assume a risk if confronted with a choice of evils, under duress, or given no choice. Even valid assumptions of risk are limited to the normal risks associated with the activity. For example, a football player does not consent to deliberate infliction of injury by other players in violation of the game's rules or assume the risks of substandard equipment or poorly maintained fields.[110]

Schools often try to protect themselves from potential lawsuits by asking parents to sign forms indicating an awareness of the dangers connected with an activity, assuming the risk, and releasing the school form liability. But are these forms legally effective? For example, is a school district immune from suit if parents sign a consent and waiver of liability enabling their child to participate in a school field trip? One court held that release forms signed by a parent do bar an injured student from suing for negligence even when the student upon reaching the age of majority sought to repudiate the release.[111] Other courts have held that for releases from liability to be effective, they must be voluntarily and knowingly executed[112] and specifically indicate what fault is being waived. Even when these conditions are met, a number of courts have ruled that waivers by schoolchildren or their parents are contrary to public policy.[113] In a significant number of jurisdictions, any ambiguity in a waiver will be interpreted against the school district.[114] Other courts have said that although waivers may be valid as to the parents, they do not block suits by the injured children themselves.[115] Thus, release forms often do not block redress for a school's negligence, but they do serve the useful purpose of showing that parents agreed to expose their children to the dangers normally associated with an activity.[116]

* * *

In sum, the law of negligence does not require that schools be insurers against all harms that may come to students. Constant and unremitting vigilance and supervision are not required. What is always required, however, is the care that a reasonable and prudent person would take in the circumstances. When unusual dangers exist, such as the presence of students with a known propensity for violence, special caution must be employed. This duty extends to principals, teachers, bus drivers, and all other personnel placed in a position of supervising students.

Furthermore, school boards and school administrators have a duty to ensure adequate levels of supervision depending on the circumstances and the age and capacities of the pupils. Similarly, they have a duty to provide safe shop, laboratory, and gym equipment and proper instruction and warnings regarding the performance of potentially dangerous tasks. State health and safety regulations must be enforced as well as the school's own rules. Appropriate medical care should be provided in the case of accidents. If supervision is undertaken when not required by law, it must still meet legal standards of adequacy.

10.5 NEGLIGENT HIRING AND VICARIOUS LIABILITY

When school employees intentionally cause harm to pupils, colleagues or other people, their school or school district may be held legally responsible under either or both of two separate and distinct legal theories, **negligent hiring** and **respondeat superior**. Under the doctrine of negligent hiring, an employer is held responsible for having acted negligently in the hiring or retention of an employee who harms someone else. Under the doctrine of respondeat superior, an employer is held vicariously liable for wrongful acts committed by an employee within the scope of the employee's job.

Negligent Hiring

To establish that a school district should be held responsible for negligent hiring or negligent retention, an injured plaintiff must establish three points: that the person who caused the injury was unfit for hiring or retention or was only fit for the position if given more supervision than was actually provided, that the hiring or retention was the legal cause of the injury, and that the employer knew or should have known of the employee's lack of fitness. Because employers are often unaware of an employee's lack of fitness, liability typically turns on whether an employer should have become aware of an employee's unfitness through more careful investigation or closer supervision of the employee. For example, in a nonschool case, the employer of an apartment manager was held liable after the manager assaulted a female tenant. The assault was clearly outside the scope of the manager's employment, yet the employer was liable because the employer had made only a cursory investigation into the background of the manager, and a more thorough investigation would have uncovered the fact that the manager had been convicted of violent crimes. Legal cause was established because the employer's negligence was the only reason the manager was on the premises and had a passkey.[117]

On the other hand, an employer will not be held responsible if it cannot be established that the employer should have known about an employee's propensity for wrongdoing. In one case, a court ruled that a school district could not have known about a principal's history of sexual abuse when the principal had resigned from his previous position ostensibly for health reasons and none of the principal's references had mentioned his previous history. Telephone interviews with former employers did not reveal any history of allegations against the principal and letters of reference referred to him as "one of the most promising men in education" and lamented having "lost a very valuable educator."[118]

Some states have statutes dealing with inquiries about the arrests and convictions of prospective employees. California requires applicants for noncertified school employment to submit fingerprint cards prepared by a local law enforcement agency so the applicants may be screened.[119] California law also prohibits the hiring of people convicted of a violent or serious felony for positions requiring certification.[120] Some state laws prohibit employers from asking about arrests or detentions that do not result in convictions, whereas others specifically allow such inquiries subject to certain restrictions regarding who in the company has access to the records.[121] Illinois exempts local governments and school districts from restrictions imposed on other employers and permits convictions to be used in evaluating employees.[122] New York permits an employer to deny employment based on criminal convictions only if the conviction is related to the job at issue.[123] Texas law requires school districts to "obtain criminal history record information." Federal regulations permit the use of arrest record information in hiring where it is related to the position and is relatively recent even if there is a disparate impact on a class protected under Title VII (see sec. 7.4).[124]

Vicarious Liability

Under the doctrine of respondeat superior, school districts may be held vicariously liable for the negligent and, sometimes, the intentional wrongdoing of their employees and anyone else authorized to act on their behalf. Respondeat superior holds the ultimate employer, not the supervisor, liable for the tortious acts of its "servants," even if the employer was not at fault, provided the tortious act was committed within the scope of employment. Thus, teachers who negligently supervise the playground may expose not only themselves but also the school district to liability. Students and parent volunteers who negligently perform services for the school under the school's direction and control, even if they are not compensated, may also expose the district to vicarious liability.

Whether a district will be held liable under the doctrine of respondeat superior depends on a number of factors that vary somewhat from state to state. Often, the main issue is whether the employee's act was committed within the scope of employment. Whether an act was within the scope of employment is determined case by case, considering the time, place, and purpose of the act; its similarity to what was authorized or required of the employee; and a host of other factors. However, a school or other employer cannot avoid vicarious liability by forbidding in advance what was done or by ordering the employee to act carefully.

A California case required the court to decide whether a school should be held vicariously liable for a custodian sexually molesting an eleven-year-old student in the custodian's office after school. The court said that for the assault to be considered within the scope of the custodian's employment it was necessary that the act was required or "incident" to his duties or the misconduct was reasonably foreseeable. The court concluded that sexual molestation was "in no way related to mopping floors, cleaning rooms, or any of the other tasks that are required of a school custodian." The employee was motivated by his personal ends, not the purposes of the job; the mere fact that he was on the job and used school facilities was not a basis for liability. It might have been different if the tortious act was done in connection with carrying out his assigned duties (e.g., a security officer who uses excessive force in controlling students). The court defined foreseeability to mean

> that in the context of the particular enterprise an employee's conduct is not so unusual or startling that it would be unfair to include the loss resulting from it among other costs of the employer's business . . . The test is not whether it is foreseeable that one or more employees might at some time act in such a way . . . but rather, whether the employee's act is foreseeable in light of the duties the employee is hired to perform.

The court had no difficulty in concluding that the sexual assault was nothing other than "highly unusual and very startling"; it was not the kind of conduct that was likely to occur in the conduct of the school district's business. Hence, the court concluded the district would not be held vicariously liable.[125]

Many courts will not hold a school district liable under respondeat superior for a teacher's sexual abuse of students if the school district was justifiably unaware of the abuse because sexual relations with students are completely outside the scope of teachers' job-related duties.[126] Recall, however, that a school district may be liable for sexual abuse under Title IX (see sec. 5.9), Title VII (see sec. 7.4), or other federal statutes (see sec. 10.10).

A school district may be held vicariously liable for acts outside the scope of a teacher's employment if the school district permits the teacher to act with apparent authority. Thus, in one case, a court held the school district liable when a girl was negligently injured during a "powder puff" football game held at halftime of the regular game, even though the game's sponsoring teacher had acted outside the scope of his employment. Because the powder puff team used the school's field and locker room, and the school helped publicize the game, the court reasoned that the school had a duty to ensure that the players were furnished with proper safety equipment.[127]

Vicarious Liability of Parents

If school districts can be held vicariously liable for the tortious acts of their employees, may parents be held vicariously liable for torts committed by their children? For the most part, they may not, although most states have adopted statutes imposing a modest level of liability (no more than several thousand dollars) on parents for the willful and wanton torts of their child. Parents may also be held legally responsible for the torts of the child that the parent directed or encouraged, or if the parent entrusts the child with a dangerous instrument such as a gun, leaves a gun where it is accessible to a child, or fails to take a gun from a child.

> More broadly, the parent who has notice of a child's dangerous tendency or proclivity must exercise reasonable care to control the child for the safety of others, and the parent who ignores the child's tendency to [for example] beat other children . . . may be held for his or her own negligence in failing to exercise control.

Parents will not, however, be held responsible "for general incorrigibility, a bad education and upbringing, or the fact that the child turns out to have a nasty disposition." The parent may be under a duty to warn others of their child's disposition.[128]

These principles were applied by the Wisconsin Supreme Court in finding parents legally liable for the harm their son did to a teacher. The parents of Jason, who had attention deficit hyperactivity disorder, stopped providing him with his prescribed medication without informing themselves of the consequences of doing so by consulting with their physician and without informing school officials. Several months later, while a teacher was attempting to remove Jason from the classroom for misbehavior, Jason grabbed the teacher's hair with such force that she fell, herniating a disk in her neck; the teacher required an operation and the curtailment of almost all her activities outside of work. The court found the parents negligent, not for removing him from the medication, but for not taking reasonable steps to control their son—failing to inform themselves about the consequences of stopping the medication and about alternative forms of treatment, and failing to inform school officials that Jason's disruptive behavior might return. The court noted that if school officials had been notified, their approach to handling Jason would have been different, and the injury to the plaintiff might have been averted.[129]

10.6 LIABILITY FOR DANGEROUS BUILDINGS AND GROUNDS

Owners of land and buildings, including school districts, owe duties to all who enter their property. Traditionally and in somewhat more than half the states today, the law divides those who enter property into three categories: trespassers, licensees, and invitees. The duty of owners to inspect, repair, and maintain their property and to warn entrants of possible hazards varies according to the category of entrant; the highest duty is owed to invitees and the lowest to trespassers. About twenty states have adopted an alternative system which, in effect, extends the standard rules of negligence to property liability cases. This approach imposes a standard of reasonable care on owners with the status of the entrant as one factor in deciding whether the owner should be held liable for an entrant's injury. A few states have systems of property liability that combine elements of both approaches.[130] Property liability cases in schools have involved many kinds of hazards: jagged edges on equipment, failing equipment, falling ceilings, slippery floors, pot holes on playgrounds, unsafe electrical equipment, icy sidewalks, badly illuminated passageways, defective playground and gym equipment, and attacks on visitors attending school events.

Trespassers, Licensees, and Invitees

A **trespasser** is a person who enters the property of another without permission or privilege to do so. One also becomes a trespasser by leaving that part of a property to which one has been admitted and entering another part without permission. A person who breaks into a school at night to use the gym is a trespasser, but someone who uses an outdoor playing field on school grounds that is readily accessible and regularly used by the public for recreation is not. Trespassers must take care of themselves, even in encounters with inherently dangerous conditions such as an open pit with no railing or warning sign. Hence, the owner is not liable to the trespasser for failure to exercise reasonable care to make the property safe or to conduct business on the property in a way that would be safe for the trespasser. The owner, however, is not permitted intentionally to inflict injury on the trespasser; for example, by deliberately setting a trap. The owner must refrain from willful and wanton harmful conduct toward the trespasser. Although the law is interested in protecting property rights, it recognizes even a trespasser's interest in safety.

An important exception to the rules regarding trespassers is the **attractive nuisance** doctrine applicable to child-trespassers. The idea of the doctrine is that if a child is "attracted" onto property by a condition such as playground equipment or a swimming pool, the owner is responsible for the safety of the trespassing child. The attractive nuisance doctrine holds that an owner is liable for harm to trespassing children if the owner knew or should have known that children were likely to trespass on the place where the harm occurred, the owner knew or should have known that conditions on the property posed an unreasonable risk to children, the children because of their youth were not aware of the risk, the usefulness to the owner of maintaining the risk and the cost of eliminating it were slight as compared to the risk to children, and the owner failed to exercise reasonable care to eliminate the risk or protect the children.[131] Some states adhere to the additional requirement that the owner is only liable if the child was attracted on to the property by the same condition that injured the child.[132]

Schools are therefore responsible for taking reasonable steps to keep trespassing children away from potentially dangerous areas of the school and campus. However, some courts will not hold schools responsible for injuries to trespassing children caused by risks that children can understand and appreciate such as the risk of falling off a roof.[133] The classic attractive nuisance is an unguarded accessible swimming pool, but school grounds often contain other attractive nuisances like power tools, trampolines, lab equipment, and driver education cars.

A **licensee** is anyone who has a privilege—tacit or explicit consent—to enter on property. Licensees include social guests, salespeople calling at a private home, and people who have personal business dealings with employees of the owner or possessors of the land. Outside groups meeting at a school would generally fall into the category of licensees as would employee spouses entering the school for legitimate reasons. Most courts treat trespassers similarly to licensees if the trespasser's presence is known to the owner. The duty owed to licensees is to warn or otherwise protect them from unreasonable risks of which the owner is aware but the licensees are not. Licensees generally must assume the risks associated with hazards unknown to the owner.

An **invitee** may enter land as a business visitor or as a public invitee. Business visitors include customers and clients of businesses, drivers picking up and delivering goods, people seeking employment, independent contractors and their employees doing work on the premises, and others invited to do work. People using public playgrounds or attending free public lectures and others on land by reason of a general invitation to the public are public invitees. Students, school employees, and, at times, even the public are invitees to schools.[134] Invitees have a legal expectation that the property will be made safe for them. Owners must protect them not only from hazards that the owner knew about, but also from hazards that the owner could have discovered by careful inspection of the property.

The duty owed the invitee is not that of an insurer of absolute safety. Nor is the possessor of land expected to discover all hazards instantly. What is required is reasonable prudence under the circumstances (e.g., taking steps to warn people away from floors made slippery by mopping).

Invitees and licensees are expected to take some care in protecting themselves from obvious hazards. The standard rule has been that the owner has no duty to protect the invitee against hazards that are known or obvious to entrants. However, many courts have in recent years found this rule unsatisfactory in cases where invitees are legitimately distracted and thus unable to protect themselves against known or obvious dangers. Thus, an increasing number of jurisdictions now embrace a different rule: "A possessor of land is not liable to his invitees for physical harm caused to them by any activity or condition on the land whose danger is known or obvious to them, unless the possessor should anticipate the harm despite such knowledge or obviousness."[135] A hole in a school playground may be obvious, but the school district should anticipate that running students may not pay attention to the hole.

Regarding the child invitee, the duty of self-care will depend on the child's age, maturity, and experience. In some cases, school officials may invoke the defenses of contributory or comparative negligence or assumption of risk (see sec. 10.4), but the child plaintiff may counter by claiming distraction, youthful lack of judgment and capacity, or inadequate warning of the hazard. In one case, a Missouri court ruled that a junior high school student injured in a long-jump competition had not assumed the risk of a dangerous condition created by the school district.[136] If players voluntarily continue to play even after becoming aware of dangerous conditions on a field, they may be found to have assumed the risk.[137]

Some states have adopted recreational use statutes that protect landowners from liability when the landowner invites members of the public to use the land for recreational purposes without charging a fee. The landowner will only be held liable for willful or wanton negligence. Even where such laws exist, they may not apply to schools.[138]

Injuries caused by accumulations of ice and snow on school property present an especially slippery issue. Courts in more than half the states, relying on either common law or statute, hold there is no duty to protect entrants against natural accumulations of snow and ice as long as the accumulation was not "artificial" (created by human activity), the hazard was not aggravated by the owner, and the owner did not voluntarily attempt to deal with the hazard but did so negligently. In states without this "natural accumulation" rule, snow and ice cases are treated like other premises liability cases. In deciding these cases, courts consider a number of factors including the fierceness of the storm, the length of the interval between the end of the storm and the accident, the obviousness of the hazard, whether the plaintiff could be expected to be carrying vision-obscuring objects, efforts undertaken to alleviate the hazard (e.g., spreading sand or salt), the adequacy of lighting, and whether a warning was provided.[139]

The Negligence Approach to Property Liabiity

In the more than twenty states that have abolished the traditional categories of entrants on to property, property liability cases are decided in a manner similar to other negligence cases (see sec. 10.4). Liability is determined based on the reasonableness of the owners' actions in light of the foreseeability of the injury. When making this determination, the courts look at a variety of factors including the expected use of the premises; the reasonableness of the inspection, repair, and warning; and the burden on the owner to provide adequate protection. Schools in these states may face a heightened risk of premises liability especially with regard to entrants who traditionally would have been classified as licensees. For example, a student voluntarily using a school's athletic field for a summer workout would be considered a licensee in some states. The student would therefore be unable to collect damages for injuries sustained as a result of a hazardous condition at the field of which the school was unaware. However, in states that take the new approach, the student could collect damages if the school's inspection and maintenance of the field was not adequate given its likely use.

Kurshals v. Connetquot Central School District[140] illustrates the use of the negligence approach to property liability with regard to a child injured while playing at a school:

> The 15-year-old plaintiff, Matthew Kurshals, was playing handball when the ball was hit onto the roof of the Peconic Street Junior High School in Ronkonkoma. This plaintiff had attended the school and knew that there were skylights on the roof. When he climbed up to the first level of the roof, he observed the skylights, which were four-foot by four-foot plastic domes. He then climbed up to the second level of the roof, where he stepped on a skylight and fell through to the gym floor below.
>
> A landowner has a duty to exercise reasonable care in maintaining his property in a safe condition under all of the circumstances, including the likelihood of injury to others, the seriousness of the potential injuries, the burden of avoiding the risk, and the foreseeability of a potential plaintiff's presence on the property. Encompassed in this duty is a duty to warn of potentially dangerous conditions. There is, however, no duty to warn against a condition which is readily observable or an extraordinary occurrence, which "would not suggest itself to a reasonably careful and prudent person as one which should be guarded against."
>
> The skylight was not defective in any way. It was not an unobservable dangerous condition. Rather, it is clear that the accident was the result of the injured plaintiff's misuse of the skylight, which was an extraordinary occurrence that need not have been guarded against.
>
> The plaintiffs rely on evidence that the misuse was foreseeable, because the defendant was aware that children sometimes climbed up onto the roof. "However, foreseeability of misuse alone is insufficient to make out a cause of action."

Based on this reasoning, the child's property liability claim against the school district was dismissed.

Finally, a brief note on federal legislation requiring public and private schools to inspect for and take appropriate steps to eliminate asbestos from their premises. Failure to comply with these requirements exposes the school district and school officials to monetary civil penalties. Individual school officials may be fined up to $25,000 per day for noncompliance with the law.[141]

10.7 EDUCATIONAL MALPRACTICE

Malpractice, whether in education, medicine, law, or another enterprise, is a specialized form of negligence arising out of a professional practice. The basic claim in a malpractice case is that a professional practitioner has caused harm by failing in the duty to competently provide services in accordance with the standards of the profession. Because malpractice is a category of negligence, all four elements of negligence must be proven. Thus, in medicine, the profession whose malpractice litigation has been the most widely publicized, successful suits do not arise simply out of undesirable results or even mistakes in medical treatment. A finding of medical malpractice requires proof that a doctor had a professional duty to treat a patient in a certain manner; that the doctor failed to live up to that duty, thus placing the patient at unreasonable risk of injury; and that the failure of performance was the legal cause of actual injury.

In education, two types of malpractice claims have been brought. The first type, brought by pupils who have failed to learn (usually to read), alleges a breach of duty in the provision of an instructional program. The argument is that from the student's failure to learn and from facts relating to the education given the student, a failure to teach properly can be inferred. Sometimes, plaintiffs also make the related claim that the school was negligent in certifying learning that did not in fact take place—either by assigning passing grades or granting a diploma.[142] A second type of malpractice case alleges the provision of an inappropriate education or other harm as a result of a failure to properly assess or classify.[143]

Courts have rejected educational malpractice claims in both categories on the grounds that educators have no statutory or common law duty to their students to perform up to a professional standard and that in any case, considerations of public policy preclude recognition of educational malpractice as a cause of legal action. However, some instances of educational wrongdoing—for example, a teacher intentionally and maliciously furnishing false information to parents about a child's disability[144] or a guidance counselor misinforming a student about the requirements for eligibility for college athletics[145]—may be actionable based on other legal theories.

10.8 GOVERNMENTAL IMMUNITY AND STATUTES AFFECTING TORT SUITS

In the old common law, the doctrine of **sovereign immunity** protected state governments from tort suits. This decision by government to prohibit its laws and courts from being used against itself was descended from a principle of English law that "The King can do no wrong." The doctrine of sovereign tort immunity has been extended from the state itself to its municipalities and school districts. As agencies of the state, they are said to partake in the sovereignty of the state. This immunity of local government from suit is often called "governmental" or "municipal immunity."

Governmental immunity has never been a complete bar to all tort suits. One of the most common exceptions permits liability regarding activities deemed **proprietary**, done as an owner, as opposed to **governmental**. However, the criteria used for distinguishing between the proprietary and governmental activities of local government are not very precise, leading to many difficulties in classification. Some states consider all school district activities governmental, whereas others classify certain fee-charging activities, such as football games, as proprietary.

Another traditional common law distinction is between **discretionary** and **ministerial** acts. Discretionary acts involve planning, goal setting, evaluation, and the exercise of judgment; ministerial acts are performed in a prescribed manner not requiring judgment. In some jurisdictions, governments may be immune from liability for discretionary but not ministerial acts. For example, under these doctrines, a school district could not be liable regarding the formulation of its snow removal policy but could be liable for the negligent execution of the policy.[146]

In any case, the doctrine of governmental immunity has undergone significant changes by reason of both legislative and judicial action. The often tortuous history and nature of these modifications vary from state to state. For example, in Michigan, governmental immunity was at first abolished by judicial action. Subsequently, it was restored by statute, but the statute was held unconstitutional on procedural grounds. Finally, the statute was reenacted, with the newly enacted law abolishing immunity only regarding proprietary functions and the creation and operation of nuisances that result in injury to property or people. Immunity for governmental functions was retained.

Today, there is considerable variation in state law on the question of governmental immunity. The doctrine has served to block a number of suits alleging school-district negligence in a child's suicide.[147] In a few states, governmental immunity protects school districts from liability for the tort of negligent hiring or retention (see sec. 10.5). Some states allow suits regarding nondiscretionary functions only. Others limit the dollar amounts that may be collected. Still others permit suits only for personal injury or death or only regarding dangerous conditions of property.[148] Illinois generally allows tort suits against teachers only for "willful and wanton" misconduct, but this rule is subject to exceptions that make schools vulnerable to certain other kinds of suits. Despite these variations, the trend is to limit governmental immunity, thus increasing the likelihood of school districts being held liable for tortious acts.[149]

Government Officer Immunity

In addition to governmental immunity, a second type of immunity protects certain government officers from tort liability. Judges and legislators enjoy absolute immunity from tort suits regarding judicial or legislative acts even if performed in bad faith, with malice, or with corrupt motives. School board members as individuals traditionally enjoy absolute official immunity.[150]

Under traditional common law, school officials and employees may also enjoy qualified immunity for acts performed without bad faith or malice and only for discretionary not ministerial acts. This distinction has been difficult for the courts to apply with any consistency. A Georgia court ruled that the placing of a mat at the door of the school was discretionary.[151] A Minnesota court said that a guidance counselor was immunized against a suit brought by parents of a student who committed suicide; the court ruled that the decision whether or not to tell parents about the student's contemplation of suicide was a matter of professional discretion and thus was subject to immunity.[152] However, another Minnesota court decided that a principal's supervision of a gym teacher's gymnastics class was ministerial. The exercise of judgment, said the court, did not make it a discretionary act.[153] Concerning matters relating to the prevention of school violence, the trend in case law seems to be that school policies regarding the supervision of students, the hiring and assignment of security guards, and school safety generally are matters of discretion that enjoy immunity.[154] School officials may still be liable for the negligent execution of school safety policies.

In recent times, many states have enacted statutes revising common law official immunity doctrines. These statutes may draw distinctions regarding the scope of immunity in terms of discretionary acts versus ministerial acts, acts within the scope versus outside the scope of employment, or curricular versus noncurricular functions, among others.[155]

A Connecticut statute provides that the qualified immunity doctrine will not protect an official in circumstances when it is apparent that a failure to act would be likely to subject an identifiable person to imminent harm. Based on that exception, the Connecticut Supreme Court ruled that a superintendent did not enjoy immunity from a suit brought by a child who slipped and broke his elbow on a sheet of ice that had not been sanded or salted and with regard to which no warnings had been posted.[156]

A federal statute, the Teacher Liability Protection Act,[157] is designed to protect teachers from liability if they accidentally injure a student in the course of maintaining order and discipline at school. The Act provides that "no teacher in a school shall be liable for harm caused by an act or omission of the teacher on behalf of the school if" they were acting within the scope of employment "in furtherance of efforts to control, discipline, expel or suspend a student or maintain order or control in the classroom or school"; they are licensed or certified; "[t]he harm was not caused by willful or criminal misconduct, gross negligence, recklessness misconduct, or a conscious, flagrant indifference to the rights or safety of the individual harmed by the officer or employee"; and the injury was not caused by operating a vehicle, aircraft, or vessel. The exemption from liability does not apply to criminal misconduct for which the teacher was convicted including violent crimes and sexual offenses; acts done under the influence of alcohol or drugs; or conduct that violates a federal or state civil rights law. In cases where a teacher is guilty of "willful or criminal misconduct, or a conscious, flagrant indifference to the rights or safety of the individual harmed," the Act allows the awarding of punitive damages. The law also does not protect teachers from suits initiated by their school or another government entity and does not affect state or local laws or policies concerning corporal punishment.

Statutes of Limitation and Notice of Claims

The failure of the plaintiff to comply with a statute of limitations or a notice of claim statute can effectively bar a tort suit. Statutes of limitation establish deadlines for the initiation of suits usually from the date of discovery of injury. Notice of claim statutes require a plaintiff to give written notice to the defendant within a specified period of time, in some states as short as three months. The notice is intended to inform the defendant of the accident, and, thereby give the defendant an opportunity to investigate and prepare a defense, as well as to take steps to prevent repetition of the accident.[158]

Indemnity

Statutes in many states either authorize or mandate that local school districts indemnify their employees from personal monetary liability for torts committed in the scope of their employment. Educators may still be sued for tortious behavior, but the school is responsible for paying any damages. These laws usually indemnify both discretionary and ministerial acts but exclude malicious and unauthorized conduct.

10.9 SUBSTANTIVE DUE PROCESS

The other sections of this chapter concentrated on the application of state tort law to education. This section concerns two federal constitutional rights, the **right to be free of state-created danger** and the **right to bodily integrity,** rooted in the Due Process Clause of the Fourteenth Amendment. These rights do not emanate from the procedural sense of due process discussed in Sections 4.4, 8.5, and elsewhere throughout this book. Rather they emanate from substantive due process, a complex and elusive concept that demands that government have adequate justification before depriving an individual of life, liberty, or property. Violation of substantive due process rights exposes a school to the possibility of a lawsuit for monetary damages.

State-Created Danger

DeShaney v. Winnebago County Department of Social Services[159] concerned a four-year-old boy severely injured by his father after a County Department of Social Services failed to act on repeated reports that the father was abusing the child. The Supreme Court, in denying claims against the Department and its employees, ruled that government does not have a duty to protect people from harm inflicted by other people. Analogous reasoning has been used in some cases to protect schools from liability for failing to seek medical attention for students who appeared ill while under the school's care.[160] In *DeShaney*, the Court noted two circumstances when the government is responsible for protecting people from harm by others: if they are in the physical custody of the government or if it is the government itself that created the danger of harm. Injuries that occur under either of these circumstances are the result of state-created danger.[161]

Courts have been unwilling to accept claims of school liability for a student's injury based on the first of the *DeShaney* circumstances—that students are under the "physical custody" of the school. The physical-custody requirement is only met, say the courts, when an individual is involuntarily placed under the complete custody and care of the state; for example, confined to a state mental hospital. Under such circumstances, individuals are placed at a disadvantage in caring for themselves, so they must rely on the government to care for them. Despite the existence of compulsory education laws, this condition is not met at school because students are only there part-time and have the option of transferring to another school, and primary custody remains with the parents.[162]

Courts have been more willing to accept claims against schools based on the second *DeShaney* circumstance, but it is still often difficult for a plaintiff to prevail. The elements necessary to sustain a claim of state-created danger vary across jurisdictions.[163] In *McQueen v. Beecher Community Schools*,[164] the Sixth Circuit was faced with a state-created-danger claim on behalf of a first-grade student who was shot dead by another first-grade student after the teacher left the classroom. The shooter had a reputation for disruptive and sometimes violent behavior. The court said that in order to prevail the plaintiff had to establish that there was (a) an affirmative act by the school which created or enhanced the risk that the plaintiff would be exposed to a private act of violence; (b) the risk was specific to the plaintiff as distinguished from the general public; and (c) the school knew or should have known that its action specifically endangered the plaintiff, i.e., that the school was deliberately indifferent. In dismissing the case, the court said regarding point (a) that,

> The danger to [the plaintiff] was created by [the other student's] possession of a gun and [plaintiff's] presence in the classroom with him. This danger existed irrespective of [the teacher's] location. If [the teacher] had been in the room, there is no guarantee that, upon seeing the gun, she would have gotten to [the killer] in time to prevent the shooting; indeed, in a busy classroom, she may not have even noticed [the killer's] actions until the fatal moment. . . . Also there is no reason to believe that [the teacher's] presence in the room would have discouraged [the killer] from drawing the weapon, as [the killer's] behavioral issues indicate that he did not shy away from misbehaving directly in [the teacher's] view.

As to point (b), the court agreed that with only five students left behind in the classroom (the teacher took the rest of the students with her) the danger here was greater for the plaintiff than for the general public. Regarding point (c), the matter of deliberate indifference, the court found that, despite the reputation of the killer, there was no evidence the killer had ever threatened the dead student or any other student, that he had ever brought a gun or other weapon to school, or that the teacher suspected the killer had a gun. Without this evidence, the plaintiff could not show that the risk was so obvious that the teacher should have known about it.

In *D.R. by L.R. v. Middle Bucks Area Vocational Technical School*,[165] the Third Circuit rejected a state-created-danger claim in a case involving persistent sexual abuse of the plaintiff by other students in a unisex bathroom at the back of an art classroom. The court found that the assigning of an inadequately trained and supervised student-teacher to the class and failure of the student-teacher to report the abuse to parents or other authorities were not the kind of affirmative acts needed to win the case. All that the plaintiff proved was "nonfeasance" in the face of a purely private wrong.

The plaintiff in *Maxwell v. School District of the City of Philadelphia*[166] was a special education student in a locked classroom presided over by a substitute teacher, May Chu. When, at one point during the day, the students became disruptive, Chu said, "I don't care what you do as long as you do not bother me." Subsequently, Chu observed two students seize a female student, take her to the back of the classroom and attempt to rape her. The student managed to escape and returned to her seat. Chu did nothing. Then, in full view of Chu, students seized the plaintiff, took her to the back of the room, and raped her. To decide if the victim's state-created-danger claim could succeed, the court employed a framework created by the Third Circuit in an earlier case:

> (1) the harm ultimately caused was foreseeable and fairly direct; (2) the state actor acted in willful disregard for the safety of the plaintiff; (3) there existed some relationship between the state and the plaintiff; [and] (4) the state actors used their authority to create an opportunity that otherwise would not have existed for the third party's crime to occur.

Applying this framework to the facts of this case, the court had no trouble in finding liability. (1) The rape was not merely foreseeable, it was known to Chu as it was occurring; (2) Chu demonstrated her indifference by announcing that she did not care what the students did, doing nothing about the prior attempted rape, and passively sitting by as the plaintiff was raped. (3) There was a specific relationship between the plaintiff and Chu. And, (4), the school had locked the classroom door preventing escape, and Chu had made clear she was going to do nothing.

In another case, the Tenth Circuit refused to dismiss a state-created-danger claim in a case in which a district suspended a sixteen-year-old special-education student and then transported him to his empty home in the middle of the school day without notifying his parents. The student, who had emotional problems and a history of violence and suicide threats, committed suicide while home alone.[167]

Bodily Integrity

Corporal punishment that is administered in accordance with applicable laws and policies and is not excessive does not violate the substantive due process right to bodily integrity (see sec. 4.5). However, courts have said that the right to bodily integrity is violated by punishment that is arbitrary, egregious, and shocking to the conscience.[168] In a case involving not physical punishment but repeated humiliation of seventh-grade student by a teacher, the Eighth Circuit said that to establish a substantive due process claim, a plaintiff must show that the school's actions "either shock the conscience or offend judicial notions of fairness or human dignity."[169] Usually courts will not find a constitutional violation unless a teacher's actions are purposely injurious and result in significant harm; grabbing or hitting students to control them will not suffice even if it results in minor injury.[170] However, in *Johnson v. Newburgh Enlarged School District*,[171] the Second Circuit found that "the line had been crossed": The court summarized the facts of the case as follows:

On February 20, 1996, after T.J. and his classmates had finished playing dodge ball, [gym teacher] Bucci asked T.J. to hand in the ball. T.J. threw the ball towards Bucci from a distance of about twenty feet. The ball landed near Bucci without hitting him. In response, Bucci threw two balls back at T.J. and then yelled "you think that's funny, you think that's funny!" as he walked over to T.J. Bucci grabbed T.J. by the throat, shouted "I'll kick the shit out of you!," lifted him off the ground by his neck and dragged him across the gym floor to the bleachers. Bucci then choked T.J. and slammed the back of T.J.'s head against the bleachers four times. Bucci also rammed T.J.'s forehead into a metal fuse box located on the gym wall and punched him in the face. During much of the attack, Bucci prevented T.J. from escaping by placing one of his arms across the boy's chest. Bucci only stopped his assault after another student threatened to intervene.

Next the court listed the factors to be considered in evaluating alleged due process violations by the excessive use of force:

the need for the application of force, the relationship between the need and the amount of force that was used, the extent of injury inflicted, and whether force was applied in a good faith effort to maintain or restore discipline or maliciously and sadistically for the very purpose of causing harm. With respect to the last factor, if the force was "maliciously or sadistically [employed] for the very purpose of causing harm" in the absence of any legitimate government objective and it results in substantial emotional suffering or physical injury, then the conduct is presumptively unconstitutional. This presumption follows from the fact that the substantive due process guarantee of the Fourteenth Amendment protects individuals from "conscience-shocking" exercises of power by government actors. . . . [M]alicious and sadistic abuses of government power that are intended only to oppress or to cause injury and serve no legitimate government purpose unquestionably shock the conscience. Such acts by their very nature offend our fundamental democratic notions of fair play, ordered liberty and human decency.

Based on these principles, the court had no trouble ruling that a constitutional violation had occurred:

Bucci's alleged assault on T.J. is conscience-shocking because it constitutes conduct (1) maliciously and sadistically employed in the absence of a discernible government interest and (2) of a kind likely to produce substantial injury. First, the force Bucci used far surpassed anything that could reasonably be characterized as serving legitimate government ends, such as student discipline, classroom control or self-defense. Second, the alleged assault was extremely violent. Bucci's conduct was of a kind likely to cause substantial physical injury or emotional suffering and a need for medical treatment. It is alleged that T.J. suffered head trauma, lacerations, and bruising, that his injuries required hospital treatment, and that various emotional injuries were inflicted. Accordingly, we easily find the alleged assault to be conscience-shocking in violation of T.J.'s substantive due process right to be free of excessive force.

10.10 SECTION 1983 AND TORTIOUS VIOLATIONS OF FEDERAL LAW

Enacted as part of the Civil Rights Act of 1871, the federal law known as "Section 1983" states:

> Every person who, under color of any statute, ordinance, regulation, custom or usage of any State or Territory or the District of Columbia, subjects or causes to be subjected, any citizen of the United States or other person within the jurisdiction thereof to the deprivation of any rights, privileges, or immunities secured by the Constitution and laws, shall be liable to the party injured in any action at law, suit in equity, or other proper proceeding for redress.[172]

Section 1983 does not itself create any substantive rights; it only authorizes suits for money damages for the violation of rights that other bodies of law establish. Many cases in which students or teachers allege violations of their constitutional rights (e.g., free speech, freedom from unreasonable searches, procedural due process, substantive due process (see sec. 10.9), or equal protection) rely on Section 1983. For example, one teacher succeeded in collecting damages under Section 1983 from his superintendent and principal for the violation of his procedural due process and free speech rights. The administrators had concocted false negative evaluations regarding the plaintiff, delayed the hearing the plaintiff requested to rebut the charges, and dismissed him in part for defending another educator who had been fired.[173]

Section 1983 also applies to violations of rights protected by federal antidiscrimination and other statutes.[174] However, some federal statutes include their own system of remedies that preclude use of Section 1983.[175]

Liability of School Officials

Section 1983 can only be used to bring suit against people whose actions are "fairly attributable" to the state. This means that the statute cannot be employed against a private wrongdoer such as parents who abuse their children[176] or one student who racially or sexually harasses another even if the harasser happens to be receiving state benefits.[177] But what about a teacher or other school employee who violates the rights of a student or another employee? Is the wrongdoing employee to be viewed as a state actor subject to a Section 1983 lawsuit or as a private person? Asked in the language of the statute, under what circumstances are the actions of a school employee to be viewed as performed "under color" of the state?

The answers to these questions are not fully resolved. It is reasonably clear that school employees who act in furtherance of their job-related duties or the goals of the school are acting under color of the state. Thus, a principal who strip searches a class of students for drugs without a reasonable suspicion that a particular student has drugs (in furtherance of the goal of maintaining a safe school) is subject to a Section 1983 suit. But what about school employees who act for private purposes unrelated to school goals such as teachers who molest students (recall that some courts have said that respondeat superior (see sec. 10.5) does not apply to employee molestation of students because the act occurred outside of the scope of employment). The Fifth Circuit ruled that a custodian who raped a student was subject to a Section 1983 suit because the act occurred on school grounds when the custodian was "on the clock."[178] A successful Section 1983 suit against a school employee is less likely for acts committed away from school at a time when the employee is not being paid.

Even when school officials are acting under color of the state, they can only be held liable under Section 1983 for the deprivations of rights that they actually cause. Thus, the Second Circuit ruled that a principal could not be held liable under Section 1983 for a racially discriminatory dismissal of a teacher because the dismissal had been ordered by other school officials.[179]

Based on Supreme Court precedents, public officials, including school board members and school employees, have a qualified immunity from judgments under Section 1983.[180] The immunity applies as long as the official acted in good faith and did not violate a clearly established statutory or constitutional right that a reasonable person in that position would have known.[181] Any request for qualified immunity in Section 1983 lawsuits must be raised by the official claiming its protection,[182] and the official bears the ultimate burden of proving that the immunity applies.[183]

Obviously, whether a particular point of law is sufficiently clear that a school official should have known of it will often be debatable. In one case, school officials conducted a search, without individualized suspicion, of all nineteen students in a class in order to look for a pair of stolen shoes. The district court concluded that the search was impermissible under the Fourth Amendment and that the plaintiff's constitutional rights were violated when he was suspended for refusing to consent to the search. However, the court noted that notwithstanding the *T.L.O.* case (see sec. 4.3), the legality of a search without individualized suspicion had not been specifically ruled upon by the Supreme Court or the Fourth Circuit in which the district court was located. Therefore, the court found that a reasonable school official would not have known that the search violated clearly established rights and, therefore, that the defendant principal was immune from monetary damages.[184] By contrast, the Eleventh Circuit held that reasonable school officials could not have believed that the Fourth Amendment would allow two eighth graders to be strip searched twice in an attempt to find some stolen money. The school officials were denied qualified immunity.[185]

In *Jefferson v. Ysleta Independent School District*,[186] the court considered the issue of whether a teacher should be immune from a Section 1983 lawsuit for tying a second grader to a chair for almost two full days of school. The procedure was not imposed as punishment, but was "part of an instructional technique imposed by school policy." In other words, the teacher's actions were authorized by her employer. Nevertheless, the court pointed out that the teacher was not immune from liability under Section 1983 if she "violates a clearly established statutory or constitutional right of another person known to or knowable by a reasonable person." Because the court agreed that the child's constitutional rights had been violated ("the right to be free of state-occasioned damage to a person's bodily integrity is protected by the fourteenth amendment guarantee of due process"), the outcome depended on whether the teacher should have been aware of this constitutional principle. The court ruled as follows:

> We are persuaded that in January 1985, a competent teacher knew or should have known that to tie a second-grade student to a chair for an entire school day and for a substantial portion of a second day, as an educational exercise, with no suggested justification, such as punishment or discipline, was constitutionally impermissible. A young student who is not being properly punished or disciplined has a constitutional right not to be lashed to a chair through the school day and denied, among other things, the basic liberty of access to the bathroom when needed.

This result shows the importance of teachers being aware of the general principles of education law and, in particular, of the rights of their students.

In addition to Section 1983, another federal statute, Section 1985, can be used to sue school officials for conspiracy to deprive others of their rights to equal protection of the laws.[187] This happened to a group of school officials who worked together to prevent parents from pursuing a suit for the sexual molestation of their daughter by lying to the parents, misinforming them that bringing charges would expose them to a suit for defamation, and telling them that pursuing the case could cause problems for their other child.[188] Under yet another federal statute, Section 1986, school officials who have the power to prevent a conspiracy prohibited under Section 1985 may be held liable for damages if they deliberately or negligently fail to prevent the conspiracy.[189]

Liability of Supervisors

In the Jefferson case, the plaintiff sued not only the teacher who mistreated her but also the school principal and the school district itself. Under what circumstances may plaintiffs in a Section 1983 lawsuit prevail against the supervisor or employer of the person who violated their constitutional rights?

The Supreme Court has said that supervisors can be held accountable under Section 1983 but not simply for being the supervisor of a wrongdoer. Rather, it is necessary that the supervisors themselves also committed a wrong that in some way aided, encouraged, or permitted the violation of a right.[190] When the necessary conditions are met, supervisors may be held liable either for inadequate supervision or for the inadequate training of subordinates.[191]

The lower courts, however, are divided regarding the standard for determining whether a supervisor may be held responsible under Section 1983. A number of circuits require a showing of "deliberate indifference" by the supervisor to the wrongdoing although the meaning of this standard varies somewhat from circuit to circuit.[192] By contrast, the First Circuit says that supervisory liability requires a finding of "supervisory encouragement, condonation or acquiescence" or "gross negligence."[193] The Second Circuit uses a gross negligence standard.[194] No matter how the standard is phrased, the chances of a supervisor being found liable increase with: evidence of prior similar incidents and that the supervisor was aware of the prior incidents, the recency of prior incidents and the shortness of the time period over which they were spread, the inadequacy of the supervisor's response to the prior similar incidents, the inadequacy of the response to the incident that is the subject of the litigation, efforts to cover up or suppress complaints, and the strength of the proof that the supervisor's inadequate response is causally linked with the plaintiff's injury.[195]

Liability of School Districts

In *Monell v. Department of Social Services of New York*[196] and *Owen v. Independence*,[197] the Supreme Court held that Section 1983 could be used to bring suit against local government bodies like school districts and that government immunity cannot bar these suits. However, the *Monell* Court held that a local government unit cannot be held liable solely because it employs a wrongdoer. The doctrine of respondeat superior does not operate under Section 1983. Thus, unless an employee's wrongdoing meets one of the conditions listed later, the school district will not be liable. Nor as a general proposition will government agencies be held responsible for a failure to take affirmative steps to protect individuals from wrongdoing by other private individuals; in instances where students violate the rights of other students, the school district again will not be liable unless the case meets one of the conditions listed next.

A school district may be held liable under Section 1983 for wrongs committed under its supervision or auspices if any of the following conditions are met:

1. Either (a) the wrongdoing was undertaken pursuant to a custom or formal policy of the district, (b) the individual who committed the wrongful act was an official with

final policy-making authority, or (c) an official with final authority ratified a subordinate's wrongful act.[198] The idea here is that if any of these circumstances is proven, the wrongdoing can fairly be said to have been caused by the district's policy.

The failure to have a formal policy for dealing with sexual harassment might expose a district to Section 1983 liability because the lack of a formal policy indicates a custom of tolerating sexual harassment.[199] (Recall that under Title IX, districts are expected to have a policy for dealing with sexual harassment.) In one case, a principal and an assistant principal over a period of four years discouraged students from pressing charges of sexual assault by their teachers, expressed doubt regarding the validity of reported incidents, took no steps to confront the teachers, and kept only secret notes of the accusations rather than placing anything in the teachers' files. The Third Circuit ruled that evidence such as this could be sufficient for a jury to conclude that the principal and assistant principal had established a custom or policy of reckless indifference to sexual abuse by teachers and that this climate was a cause of the sexual assault on the plaintiff by her teacher.[200] The principal and assistant principal exposed not only themselves personally but also the school district to liability under Section 1983.

2. A school official with authority to take corrective action had actual notice of wrongdoing actionable under Section 1983 and was deliberately indifferent. This is the standard recently developed by the Supreme Court to decide whether school districts are liable in Title IX cases,[201] and it can be applied in Section 1983 cases as well. Inadequate hiring policies[202] or the inadequate training of employees may be viewed as forms of indifference.[203] Inadequate training combined with deliberately indifferent supervision is a potent formula for district liability. A school district was found liable for a strip search of students because a previously widely publicized strip search of students had not resulted either in a policy against such searches or training of school employees.[204]

3. Affirmative acts of the school district expose plaintiffs to dangers to which they would not otherwise have been exposed or increase the risk of preexisting dangers.[205] The mere fact that students' rights have been violated at school or that the violator is a teacher does not mean that this "state-created danger" condition has been met.[206] Rather, the plaintiff must show that the school district exposed the plaintiff to people with a known propensity to harm the plaintiff or provided such people with the means or increased opportunity to injure the plaintiff.[207] Assigning a student of known violent propensities to the class of an inadequately trained teacher is the kind of affirmative step that could lead to liability.[208]

4. A school that is part of a state-run correctional facility or other involuntary custodial arrangement fails to protect a student against injury by another student or other third party.[209] Several federal courts have said that this "special relationship" condition does not apply in ordinary public schools.[210]

Damages

Plaintiffs suing under Section 1983 are entitled to recover only nominal damages unless they can show actual loss. The damage award is not based on the value or importance of the violated right, but only on the actual injuries suffered. Plaintiffs may also be able to obtain punitive damages against individual defendants who act with malice.[211] Punitive damages against a school district itself are not permitted because the Supreme Court reasoned that punitive damages against a government entity would only punish the taxpayers and that only individuals, not government entities, can act with malice.[212] Even with these limitations, individuals who win Section 1983 lawsuits can sometimes receive large awards.

10.11 SUMMARY

Tort law allows individuals to sue for compensation for injuries caused by the wrongful acts or carelessness of others. The injury can be to the individual's body, property, reputation, or emotional well-being. Depending on the circumstances, school districts, individual school board members, administrators, and teachers may all be held liable for the commission of torts; however, a variety of common law and statutory immunities and other limitations on tort suits against governmental bodies and their employees may apply. Like many aspects of tort law, these immunities and limitations vary considerably from state to state.

Intentional torts are either acts designed to produce harm or acts that the actor realizes were likely to cause harm to another. In education, they are: battery, assault, false imprisonment, and intentional infliction of mental distress. Educators may use reasonable force in self-defense or to enforce legitimate orders or school rules. Also, except where prohibited by statute, educators have a common law privilege to administer corporal punishment to students, but students may still sue for assault and battery if the corporal punishment is excessive or otherwise unreasonable.

Defamation refers to false communications that harm an individual's reputation and good name. Libel is written defamation, and slander is oral defamation. The law of defamation varies depending on whether the communication deals with a matter of public concern and whether the person defamed was a public official, public figure, or private individual. School officials and school boards may be held liable for defamatory statements in the school newspaper. Educators may also be liable if they knowingly write false and damaging letters of recommendation.

Invasion of privacy protects individuals including students and teachers from the unreasonable publication of private facts. The privacy of student records is further protected by a federal law, the Family Educational Rights and Privacy Act. The Act requires that parents have access to their children's educational records, that specified procedures be followed if parents request modification of their child's records, and that, with certain specified exceptions, access to a child's records be granted to individuals outside the school only with parental consent.

Negligence is careless or reckless behavior that causes injury to another person. It is by far the most common tort in education. School districts and individual educators can be found negligent for injuries to students, employees, or visitors to the school if they had a duty to live up to a standard of care recognized in law, they failed to live up to the duty, another person was injured as a result of their failure, and the extent and value of the injury can be measured. Teachers have a general duty to behave in all situations as would a reasonable and prudent teacher with similar training and physical capacity. The exact level of supervision and care that is required in any particular situation depends on the circumstances, but the school is not expected to guarantee that accidents will never occur.

School districts may also be held liable for injuries caused by hazards on their property. These cases generally turn on the adequacy of the design of buildings and equipment, maintenance, and whether conditions adhere to local building codes. In most states, liability is greater with regard to invitees to the school as opposed to trespassers; however, the school is still likely to be held liable if a child trespasser is injured by an encounter with an attractive nuisance like an unattended accessible swimming pool.

Malpractice is professional negligence. Two types of educational malpractice claims have been brought: the failure to learn caused by improper instruction and harm caused by misclassification. Virtually no cases have been won by plaintiffs. Courts have rejected claims of educational malpractice for failing to prove the elements of negligence and for reasons of public policy.

Under a federal law known as Section 1983, individuals may bring suit against government agencies and their officers and employees for violations of federal constitutional or statutory rights. School districts with policies that violate the constitutional or federal statutory rights of students, parents, or employees are vulnerable to these suits. Individual educators may also be sued and required to pay monetary damages if they personally violate the civil rights of others or, under certain circumstances, if they permit their subordinates to do so.

NOTES

1 Spears v. Jefferson Parish Sch. Bd., 646 So. 2d 1104 (La. Ct. App. 1994).
2 Costello v. Mitchell Pub. Sch. Dist. 79, 266 F.3d 916 (8th Cir. 2001); *see also* Stamper v. Charlotte-Mecklenburg Bd. of Ed., 544 S.E.2d 818 (N.C. Ct. App. 2001).
3 People *ex rel.* Hogan v. Newton, 56 N.Y.S.2d 779 (City Ct. of White Plains 1945).
4 Rolando v. Sch. Dir. of Dist. No. 125, County of LaSalle, 358 N.E.2d 945 (Ill. App. Ct. 1976).
5 Hogenson v. Williams, 542 S.W.2d 456 (Tex. App. 1976); *see also* Tinkham v. Kole, 110 N.W.2d 258 (Iowa 1961).
6 Wilson v. Tobiassen, 777 P.2d 1379 (Ore. App. 1989).
7 Landry v. Ascension Parish Sch. Bd., 415 So. 2d 473 (La. Ct. App. 1982).
8 Thomas v. Bedford, 389 So. 2d 405 (La. Ct. App. 1980).
9 *Compare* Andreozzi v. Rubano, 141 A.2d 639 (Conn. 1958).
10 Masson v. New Yorker Magazine, Inc., 85 F.3d 1394 (9th Cir. 1996).
11 Frank B. Hall & Co. v. Buck, 678 S.W.2d 612 (Tex. Ct. App. 1984).
12 *See* Moyer v. Amador Valley Joint Union High Sch. Dist., 275 Cal. Rptr. 494 (Cal. Ct. App. 1990).
13 Stevens v. Tillman, 855 F.2d 394 (7th Cir. 1988).
14 Lester v. Powers, 596 A.2d 65 (Me. 1991).
15 Salek v. Passaic Collegiate Sch., 605 A.2d 276 (N.J. 1992).
16 True v. Ladner, 513 A.2d 257 (Me. 1986).
17 Milkovich v. Lorain Journal Co., 497 U.S. 1 (1990).
18 *See* Baskin v. Rogers, 493 S.E.2d 728 (Ga. App. 1997).
19 *Per se*: Manale v. New Orleans, 673 F.2d 122 (5th Cir. 1982); Mazart v. State, 441 N.Y.S.2d 600 (N.Y. Ct. Cl. 1981); *contra* Hayes v. Smith, 832 P.2d 1022 (Colo. Ct. App. 1992); Moricoli v. Schwartz, 361 N.E.2d 74 (Ill. 1977).
20 *See* Rocci v. Ecole Secondaire Macdonald-Cartier, 755 A.2d 583 (N.J. 2000).
21 Ford v. Jeane, 106 So. 558 (La. 1925); Larive v. Willitt, 315 P.2d 732 (Cal. Ct. App. 1957); Angel v. Levittown Sch. Dist. No. 5, 567 N.Y.S.2d 490 (N.Y. App. Div. 1991).
22 Houston Belt & Terminal Ry. v. Wheery, 548 S.W.2d 743 (Tex. App. 1976), *appeal dismissed*, 434 U.S. 962 (1977); Gonzalez v. CNA Ins. Co., 717 F. Supp. 1087 (E.D. Pa. 1989).
23 Frankson v. Design Space Int'l, 380 N.W.2d 560 (Minn. Ct. App.), *rev'd in relevant part*, 394 N.W.2d 140 (Minn. 1986).
24 Lewis v. Equitable Life Assurance Soc'y, 389 N.W.2d 876 (Minn. 1986).
25 W. P. KEETON, ED., PROSSER AND KEETON ON TORTS § 111 (5th ed. 1984).
26 New York Times Co. v. Sullivan, 376 U.S. 254 (1964); Harte-Hanks Communications, Inc. v. Connaughton, 491 U.S. 657 (1989).
27 Gertz v. Robert Welch, Inc., 418 U.S. 323 (1974); Time, Inc. v. Firestone, 424 U.S. 448 (1976); Curtis Publ'g Co. v. Butts, 388 U.S. 130 (1967); New York Times Co. v. Sullivan, 376 U.S. 254 (1964).
28 Kapiloff v. Dunn, 343 A.2d 251 (Md. Ct. Spec. App. 1975).
29 Moss v. Stockard, 580 A.2d 1011 (D.C. 1990); Detsel v. Auburn Enlarged Sch. Dist., 672 N.Y.S.2d 591 (N.Y. App. Div. 1998); Nodar v. Galbreath, 462 So. 2d 803 (Fla. 1984); Richmond Newspapers, Inc. v. Lipscomb, 362 S.E.2d 32 (Va. 1987); Franklin v. Benevolent &

Protective Order of Elks, Lodge 1108, 159 Cal. Rptr. 131 (Cal. Ct. App. 1979); Milkovich v. News-Herald, 473 N.E.2d 1191 (Ohio 1984); True v. Ladner, 513 A.2d 257 (Me. 1986).

30 Basarich v. Rodeghero, 321 N.E.2d 739 (Ill. App. Ct. 1974); Grayson v. Curtis Publ'g Co., 436 P.2d 756 (Wash. 1967); Elstrom v. Indep. Sch. Dist., 533 N.W.2d 51 (Minn. App. 1995); Johnston v. Corinthian Television Corp., 583 P.2d 1011 (Okla. 1978).

31 Dun & Bradstreet v. Greenmoss Builders, Inc., 472 U.S. 749 (1985).

32 Karnes v. Milo Beauty & Barber Shop Co., 441 N.W.2d 565 (Minn. Ct. App. 1989); Manguso v. Oceanside Unified Sch. Dist., 200 Cal. Rptr. 535 (Cal. Ct. App. 1984).

33 Gardner v. Hollifield, 549 P.2d 266 (Idaho 1976).

34 Moss v. Stockard, 580 A.2d 1011 (D.C. 1990).

35 McCone v. New England Tel. & Tel. Co., 471 N.E.2d 47 (Mass. 1984).

36 Morrison v. Mobile County Bd. of Educ., 495 So. 2d 1086 (Ala. 1986).

37 Peters v. Baldwin Union Free Sch. Dist., 320 F.3d 164 (2d. Cir. 2003).

38 Segall v. Piazza, 260 N.Y.S.2d 543 (N.Y. Sup. Ct. 1965).

39 Santiago v. United Federation of Teachers, 833 N.Y.S.2d 80 (A.D. 1 Dept. 2007).

40 Hett v. Ploetz, 121 N.W.2d 270 (Wis. 1963); RESTATEMENT (SECOND) OF TORTS § 596 (1977).

41 Alex B. Long, *Note: Addressing the Cloud over Employee References: A Survey of Recently Enacted State Legislation*, 39 WM. & MARY L. REV. 177 (1997).

42 Santavicca v. City of Yonkers, 518 N.Y.S.2d 29 (N.Y. App. Div. 1987).

43 Weissman v. Mogol, 462 N.Y.S.2d 383 (N.Y. Sup. Ct. 1983).

44 Desselle v. Guillory, 407 So. 2d 79 (La. Ct. App. 1981).

45 RESTATEMENT (SECOND) OF TORTS, § 611 (1977); Warren v. Pulitzer Publ'g Co., 78 S.W.2d 404 (Mo. 1934) (church proceeding).

46 RESTATEMENT (SECOND) OF TORTS §§ 613(1)(h), 619(2) (1977).

47 *See* Hett v. Ploetz, 121 N.W.2d 270 (Wis. 1963).

48 Cohen v. Wales, 518 N.Y.S.2d 633 (N.Y. App. Div. 1987); *see also* Richland Sch. Dist. v. Mabton Sch. Dist., 45 P.3d 580 (Wash. Ct. App. 2002).

49 W.P. KEETON, ED., PROSSER AND KEETON ON TORTS, Chap. 18 (5th ed. 1984).

50 Randi W. v. Muroc Joint Unified Sch. Dist., 929 P.2d 582 (Cal. 1997); *see also* Davis v. Bd. of County Comm'rs of Dona Ana County, 987 P.2d 1172 (Ct. App. N.M. 1999).

51 Trout v. Umatilla County Sch. Dist., 712 P.2d 814 (Or. 1985).

52 RESTATEMENT (THIRD) OF TORTS § 625B.

53 K-Mart Corp. v. Trotti, 677 S.W.2d 632 (Tex. Ct. App. 1984).

54 Twigg v. Hercules Corp., 406 S.E.2d 52 (W. Va. 1990).

55 Smyth v. Pillsbury Co., 914 F. Supp. 97 (E.D. Pa. 1996); McLaren v. Microsoft Corp., 1999 WL 339015 (Tex. Ct. App. 1999).

56 Crist v. Alpine Union Sch. Dist., 2005 Cal. App. Unpub. LEXIS 8699 (September 26, 2005).

57 Bratt v. Int'l Bus. Mach. Corp., 467 N.E.2d 126 (Mass. 1984).

58 *See, e.g.*, Van Allen v. McCleary, 211 N.Y.S.2d 501 (N.Y. Sup. Ct. 1961).

59 20 U.S.C. § 1232h; 34 C.F.R. § 99.1–99.8.

60 Owasso Indep. Sch. Dist. No. I–011 v. Falvo, 534 U.S. 426 (2002).

61 Matter of Unido R., 441 N.Y.S.2d 325 (N.Y. Fam. Ct. 1981).

62 Gonzaga Univ. v. Doe, 536 U.S. 273 (2002).

63 Storch v. Silverman, 186 Cal. App. 2d 671 (Cal. Ct. App. 1986).

64 N.Y. SOC. SERV. LAW § 419.

65 RESTATEMENT (SECOND) OF TORTS § 282 (1965).

66 *But see* Albers v. Cmty. Consol. No. 204 Sch., 508 N.E.2d 1252 (Ill. App. Ct. 1987).

67 Cioffi v. Bd. of Educ. of N.Y., 278 N.Y.S.2d 249 (N.Y. App. Div. 1967).

68 Albers v. Cmty. Consol. No. 204 Sch., 508 N.E.2d 1252 (Ill. App. Ct. 1987).

69 Atkinson v. DeBraber, 446 N.W.2d 637 (Mich. Ct. App. 1989).

70 Norris v. American Casualty Co., 178 So. 2d 662 (La. 1965).

71 Cerny v. Cedar Bluffs Junior/Senior Pub. Sch., 628 N.W.2d 697 (Neb. 2001).

72 Greene v. City of N.Y., 566 N.Y.S.2d 875 (N.Y. App. Div. 1991); Gammon v. Edwardsville Cmty. Unit Sch., 403 N.E.2d 43 (Ill. App. Ct. 1980); *compare* Logan v. City of N.Y., 543 N.Y.S.2d 661 (N.Y. App. Div. 1989); Dickerson v. N.Y. City, 258 A.D.2d 433 (N.Y. 1999).

73 Lehmuth v. Long Beach Unified Sch. Dist., 348 P.2d 887 (Cal. 1960).

74 Bennett v. Bd. of Educ. of N.Y., 226 N.Y.S.2d 593 (N.Y. App. Div. 1962), *aff'd*, 196 N.E.2d 268 (N.Y. 1963); Palella v. Ulmer, 518 N.Y.S.2d 91 (N.Y. Sup. Ct. 1987); Cobb v. Fox, 317 N.W.2d 583 (Mich. Ct. App. 1982).

75 Brownell v. Los Angeles Unified Sch. Dist., 5 Cal. Rptr. 2d 756 (Cal. Ct. App. 1992).

76 Peterson v. Doe, 647 So. 2d 1288 (La. Ct. App. 1994).

77 Hoyem v. Manhattan Beach Sch. Dist., 585 P.2d 851 (Cal. 1978).

78 Martin v. Twin Falls Sch. Dist. No. 411, 59 P.3d 317 (Idaho 2002); Rife v. Long, 908 P.2d 143 (Idaho 1996).

79 Bowers v. City of New York, 742 N.Y.S.2d 659 (N.Y. App. Div. 2002); Winter v. Bd. of Educ. City of New York, 704 N.Y.S.2d 142 (N.Y. App. Div. 2000).

80 Pratt v. Robinson, 384 N.Y.S.2d 749 (N.Y. 1976).

81 Toure v. Bd. of Educ. of N.Y., 512 N.Y.S.2d 150 (N.Y. App. Div. 1987).

82 Titus v. Lindberg, 228 A.2d 65 (N.J. 1967); Barnes v. Bott, 571 So. 2d 183 (La. Ct. App. 1990)

83 93 N.Y.2d 664 (N.Y. 1999).

84 Hoff v. Vacaville Unified Sch. Dist., 68 Cal. Rptr. 2d 920 (Ct. App. 1997).

85 585 P.2d 851 (Cal. 1978).

86 Jerkins *ex rel.* Jerkins v. Anderson, 922 A.2d 1279 (N.J. 2007).

87 Larson v. Indep. Sch. Dist. No. 314, 289 N.W.2d 112 (Minn. 1979).

88 Krakower v. City of N.Y., 629 N.Y.S.2d 435 (N.Y. Sup. Ct. 1995).

89 Ferraro v. Bd. of Educ. of New York, 212 N.Y.S.2d 615 (N.Y. App. Div. 1961), *aff'd*, 221 N.Y.S.2d 279 (N.Y. App. Div. 1961).

90 Scionti v. Bd. of Educ. of Middle County Cent. Sch. Dist., 638 N.Y.S.2d 748 (N.Y. App. Div. 1996).

91 Smith v. Archbishop of St. Louis, 632 S.W.2d 516 (Mo. Ct. App. 1982).

92 Gonzalez v. Mackler, 241 N.Y.S.2d 254 (N.Y. App. Div. 1963).

93 District of Columbia v. Doe, 524 A.2d 30 (D.C. 1987).

94 Lauricella v. Bd. of Educ. of Buffalo, 381 N.Y.S.2d 566 (N.Y. App. Div. 1976).

95 Dailey v. Los Angeles Unified Sch. Dist., 470 P.2d 360 (Cal. 1970) (en banc).

96 Ward v. Newfield Cent. Sch. Dist. No. 1, 412 N.Y.S.2d 57 (N.Y. App. Div. 1978).

97 Keesee v. Bd. of Educ. of New York, 235 N.Y.S.2d 300 (N.Y. Sup. Ct. 1962).

98 Roberts v. Robertson County Bd. of Educ., 692 S.W.2d 863 (Tenn. Ct. App. 1985).

99 Kush v. Buffalo, 449 N.E.2d 725 (N.Y. 1983).

100 Morris v. Douglas County Sch. Dist. No. 9, 403 P.2d 775 (Or. 1965) (en banc).

101 Mirand v. City of New York, 637 N.E.2d 263 (N.Y. 1994).

102 Bell v. Bd. of Educ. of New York, 687 N.E.2d 1325 (N.Y. 1997).

103 Eisel v. Bd. of Educ. of Montgomery County, 597 A.2d 447 (Md. 1991); *see also* Grant v. Bd. of Trustees of Valley View Sch. Dist., 676 N.E.2d 705 (Ill. App. Ct. 1997); *but see* Carrier v. Lake Pend Oreille Sch. Dist. No. 84, 134 P.3d 655 (Idaho 2006).

104 Palsgraf v. Long Island R.R. Co., 162 N.E. 99 (N.Y. 1928).

105 Palella v. Ulmer, 518 N.Y.S.2d 91 (N.Y. Sup. Ct. 1987).

106 Fagan v. Summers, 498 P.2d 1227 (Wyo. 1972).

107 Izard v. Hickory City Sch. Bd. of Educ., 315 S.E.2d 756 (N.C. Ct. App. 1984).

108 Wilhelm v. Bd. of Educ. of New York., 227 N.Y.S.2d 791 (N.Y. App. Div. 1962); Hutchinson v. Toews, 476 P.2d 811 (Or. Ct. App. 1970).

109 Marcantel v. Allen Parish Sch. Bd., 490 So. 2d 1162 (La. Ct. App. 1986).

110 *See* Benitez v. New York City Bd. of Educ., 541 N.E.2d 29 (N.Y. App. 1989).

111 Sharon v. City of Newton, 769 N.E.2d 738 (Mass. 2002).

112 Whittington v. Sowela Technical Inst., 438 So. 2d 236 (La. Ct. App. 1983).

113 Wagenblast v. Odessa Sch. Dist. No. 105–157–166J, 758 P.2d 968 (Wash. 1988) (en banc).

114 Doyle v. Bowdoin Coll., 403 A.2d 1206 (Me. 1979).

115 Fedor v. Mauwehu Council, Boy Scouts of Am., 143 A.2d 466 (Conn. Super. Ct. 1958); *see also* Scott v. Pacific West Mountain Resort, 834 P.2d 6 (Wash. 1992); *but see* Zivich v. Mentor Soccer Club, Inc., 696 N.E.2d 201 (Ohio 1998).

116 *See* Hohe v. San Diego Unified Sch. Dist., 274 Cal. Rptr. 647 (Cal. Ct. App. 1990).

117 Ponticas v. K.M.S. Inv., 331 N.W.2d 907 (Minn. 1983); *see also* DiCosala v. Key, 450 A.2d 508 (N.J. 1982); Garcia v. Duffy, 492 So. 2d 435 (Fla. Ct. App. 1986).

118 Medlin v. Bass, 398 S.E.2d 460 (N.C. 1990).

119 Cal. Educ. Code §§ 45125, 33129.

120 Cal. Educ. Code § 44830.1.

121 *See, e.g.*, Conn. Gen. Stat. § 31–511.

122 Ill. Rev. Stat. Ann., ch. 68, § 2–103.

123 N.Y. Human Rights Law § 296(15).

124 *See* Green v. Missouri Pac. R.R. Co., 523 F.2d 1290 (8th Cir. 1975).

125 Alma W. v. Oakland Unified Sch. Dist., 176 Cal. Rptr. 287 (Cal. Ct. App. 1981).

126 Godar v. Edwards, 588 N.W.2d 701 (Iowa 1999); John R. v. Oakland Unified Sch. Dist., 769 P.2d 948 (Cal. 1989).

127 Lynch v. Bd. of Educ. of Collinsville Cmty., 412 N.E.2d 447 (Ill. 1980).

128 W. P. KEETON, ED., PROSSER AND KEETON ON TORTS § 123 (5th ed. 1984); RESTATEMENT (SECOND) OF TORTS § 316 (1977).

129 Nieuwendorp v. Am. Family Ins. Co., 529 N.W.2d 594 (Wis. 1995).

130 See, e.g., Nelson v. Freeland, 507 S.E.2d 882 (N.C. 1998).

131 RESTATEMENT (SECOND) OF TORTS § 339 (1965).

132 Ambrose v. Buhl Joint Sch. Dist., 887 P.2d 1088 (Idaho App. 1994).

133 Barnhizer v. Paradise Valley Unified Sch. Dist. 69, 599 P.2d 209 (Ariz. 1979) (en banc); but see Stahl v. Cocalico Sch. Dist., 534 A.2d 1141 (Pa. Commw. Ct. 1987).

134 McIntosh v. Omaha Pub. Sch., 544 N.W.2d 502 (Neb. 1996).

135 Ward v. K-Mart Corp., 554 N.E.2d 223 (Ill. 1990).

136 Sheppard v. Midway R-1 Sch., 904 S.W.2d 257 (Mo. Ct. App. 1995).

137 Compare Maddox v. City of New York, 487 N.E.2d 553 (N.Y. 1985).

138 Rankey v. Arlington Bd. of Educ., 603 N.E.2d 1151 (Ohio Ct. App. 1992); contra McIntosh v. Omaha Pub. Sch., 544 N.W.2d 502 (Neb. 1996).

139 Gregory G. Sarno, Annotation, Liability for Injuries in Connection With Ice or Snow on Nonresidential Premises, 95 A.L.R.3d 1 (1979 & Supp.); Michael J. Polelle, Is the Natural Accumulation Rule All Wet? 26 LOYOLA U. CHI. L. REV. 631, 647–648 (1995).

140 643 N.Y.S.2d 622 (N.Y. App. Div. 1996).

141 Asbestos Hazard Emergency Response Act of 1986, 15 U.S.C.A. § 2641–2656; 20 U.S.C. §§ 4014, 4021–4022; 40 C.F.R. § 763; see also Asbestos School Hazard Detection & Control Act of 1980, 20 U.S.C. §§ 3601–3611.

142 Donohue v. Copiague Union Free Sch. Dist., 391 N.E.2d 1352 (N.Y. 1979); Peter W. v. San Francisco Unified Sch. Dist., 131 Cal. Rptr. 854 (Cal. Ct. App. 1976).

143 Snow v. State, 475 N.E.2d 454 (N.Y. 1984); Doe v. Bd. of Educ. of Montgomery County, 453 A.2d 814 (Md. 1982); Hoffman v. Bd. of Educ. of New York, 400 N.E.2d 317 (N.Y. 1979); B.M. v. State, 649 P.2d 425 (Mont. 1982); Rick v. Kentucky Day, Inc., 793 S.W.2d 832 (Ky. App. 1990).

144 Hunter v. Bd. of Educ. of Montgomery County, 425 A.2d 681 (Md. Ct. App. 1981), aff'd in part and rev'd in part on other grounds, 439 A.2d 582 (Md. Ct. App. 1982).

145 Sain v. Cedar Rapids Cmty. Sch. Dist., 626 N.W.2d 115 (Iowa 2001).

146 Lostumbo v. Bd. of Educ. of Norwalk, 418 A.2d 949 (Conn. Super. Ct. 1980).

147 Brooks v. Logan, 944 P.2d 709 (Idaho 1997); Grant v. Bd. of Trustees of Valley View Sch. Dist., 676 N.E.2d 705 (Ill. App. Ct. 1997); Killen v. Indep. Sch. Dist. No. 706, 547 N.W.2d 113 (Minn. Ct. App. 1996); Fowler v. Szostek, 905 S.W.2d 336 (Tex. App.—Houston [1st Dist.] 1995); Nalepa v. Plymouth-Canton Cmty. Sch. Dist., 525 N.W.2d 897 (Mich. Ct. App. 1994).

148 See Stahl v. Cocalico Sch. Dist., 534 A.2d 1141 (Pa. Commw. Ct. 1987).

149 Ayala v. Philadelphia Bd. of Pub. Educ., 305 A.2d 877 (Pa. 1973).

150 Holloway v. Dougherty County Sch. Sys., 277 S.E.2d 251 (Ga. Ct. App. 1981).

151 Hennessy v. Webb, 264 S.E.2d 878 (Ga. 1980).

152 Killen v. Indep. Sch. Dist. No. 706, 547 N.W.2d 113 (Minn. Ct. App. 1996).

153 Larson v. Indep. Sch. Dist. No. 314, 289 N.W.2d 112 (Minn. 1979).

154 Mosley v. Portland Sch. Dist. No. 1J, 843 P.2d 415 (Or. 1992); Coyle v. Harper, 622 So. 2d 302 (Ala. 1993).

155 See, e.g., Kimpton v. Sch. Dist. of New Lisbon, 405 N.W.2d 740 (Wis. Ct. App. 1987).

156 Burns v. Bd. of Educ. of Stamford, 638 A.2d 1 (Conn. 1994).

157 Paul D. Coverdell Teacher Protection Act of 2001, 20 U.S.C.A. §§ 6731–6738.

158 Plumeau v. Yamhill County Sch. Dist., 907 F. Supp. 1423 (D. Or. 1995).

159 489 U.S. 189 (1989); see also Town of Castle Rock v. Gonzales, 545 U.S. 748 (2005).

160 472 F.3d 1026 (8th Cir. 2007).

161 See Bowers v. DeVito, 686 F.2d 616 (7th Cir. 1982).

162 Wyke v. Polk County Sch. Bd., 129 F.3d 560 (11th Cir. 1997); Doe v. Hillsboro Indep. Sch. Dist., 113 F.3d 1412 (5th Cir. 1997); J.O. v. Alton Cmty. Unit Sch. Dist. 11, 909 F.2d 267 (7th Cir. 1990); D.R. v. Middle Bucks Area Vocational Technical Sch., 972 F.2d 1364 (3d Cir.1992).

163 See Jones v. Reynolds, 438 F.3d 685 (6th Cir. 2006); Kennedy v. City of Ridgefield, 439 F.3d 1055 (9th Cir. 2006); Hart v. City of Little Rock, 432 F.3d 801 (8th Cir. 2005); Pena v.

DePrisco, 432 F.3d 98 (2d Cir. 2005); Mark v. Borough of Hatboro, 51 F.3d 1137(3rd Cir. 1995).

164 433 F.3d 460 (6th Cir. 2006).

165 972 F.2d 1364 (3d Cir. 1992).

166 53 F. Supp. 2d 787 (E.D. Pa. 1999).

167 Armijo v. Wagon Mound Pub. Schs., 159 F.3d 1253 (10th Cir. 1998).

168 Peterson v. Baker, 504 F.3d 1331 (11th Cir. 2007).

169 Costello v. Mitchell Pub. Sch. Dist. 79, 266 F.3d 916 (8th Cir. 2001).

170 Gonzales v. Passino, 222 F. Supp. 2d 1277 (D.N.M. 2002).

171 239 F.3d 246 (2d Cir. 2001); see also Preschooler II v. Clark County Sch. Bd., 479 F.3d 1175 (9th Cir. 2007); P.B. v. Koch, 96 F.3d 1298 (9th Cir. 1996).

172 42 U.S.C. § 1983.

173 Burnaman v. Bay City Indep. Sch. Dist., 445 F. Supp. 927 (S.D. Tex. 1978).

174 Seamons v. Snow, 84 F.3d 1226 (10th Cir. 1996); Lillard v. Shelby County Bd. of Educ., 76 F.3d 716 (6th Cir. 1996); Williams v. Sch. Dist. of Bethlehem, 998 F.2d 168 (3d Cir. 1993).

175 Owasso Indep. Sch. Dist. No. I–011 v. Falvo, 534 U.S. 426 (2002).

176 DeShaney v. Winnebago County Dep't of Social Serv., 489 U.S. 189 (1989).

177 Mentavlos v. Anderson, 249 F.3d 301 (4th Cir. 2001).

178 Doe v. Hillsboro Indep. Sch. Dist., 81 F.3d 1395 (5th Cir. 1996); compare Doe v. Rains County Indep. Sch. Dist., 66 F.3d 1402 (5th Cir. 1995); but see Doe v. Hillsboro Indep. Sch. Dist., 81 F.3d 1395 (5th Cir. 1966) (Garza J., dissenting); Doe v. Taylor Indep. Sch. Dist., 15 F.3d 443 (5th Cir. 1994) (Garwood J., dissenting).

179 Taylor v. Brentwood Union Free Sch. Dist., 143 F.3d 679 (2d Cir. 1998).

180 Wood v. Strickland, 420 U.S. 308 (1975); Scheuer v. Rhodes, 416 U.S. 232 (1974).

181 Harlow v. Fitzgerald, 457 U.S. 800 (1982).

182 Gomez v. Toledo, 446 U.S. 635 (1980).

183 Harlow v. Fitzgerald, 457 U.S. 800 (1982).

184 DesRoches v. Caprio, 974 F. Supp. 542 (E.D. Va. 1997).

185 Jenkins v. Talladega City Bd. of Educ., 95 F.3d 1036 (11th Cir. 1996).

186 817 F.2d 303 (5th Cir. 1978).

187 42 U.S.C. § 1985(3).

188 Larson v. Miller, 55 F.3d 1343 (8th Cir. 1995).

189 42 U.S.C. § 1986.

190 Monell v. Dep't of Social Serv., 436 U.S. 658 (1978); Rizzo v. Goode, 423 U.S. 362 (1975).

191 Oona R.-S. v. Santa Rosa City Sch., 890 F. Supp. 1452 (N.D. Cal. 1995), aff'd, 122 F.3d 1207 (9th Cir. 1997).

192 Larson v. Miller, 55 F.3d 1343 (8th Cir. 1995); Doe v. Taylor Indep. Sch. Dist., 15 F.3d 443 (5th Cir. 1994); Gates v. Unified Sch. Dist. No. 449, 996 F.2d 1035 (10th Cir. 1993); Stoneking v. Bradford Area Sch. Dist., 882 F.2d 720 (3d Cir. 1989).

193 Hegarty v. Somerset County, 53 F.3d 1367 (1st Cir. 1995).

194 Black v. Coughlin, 76 F.3d 72 (2d Cir. 1996).

195 Kit Kinports, The Buck Does Not Stop Here: Supervisory Liability in Section 1983 Cases, 1997 U. ILL. L. REV. 147 (1997).

196 436 U.S. 658 (1978).

197 445 U.S. 622 (1980).

198 Gillette v. Delmore, 979 F.2d 1342 (9th Cir. 1992); see also Jett v. Dallas Indep. Sch. Dist., 491 U.S. 701 (1989); St. Louis v. Praprotnik, 485 U.S. 112 (1988); Pembaur v. Cincinnati, 475 U.S. 469 (1986).

199 Doe v. Estes, 926 F. Supp. 979 (D. Nev. 1996).

200 Stoneking v. Bradford Area Sch. Dist., 882 F.2d 720 (3d Cir. 1989).

201 Gebser v. Lago Vista Indep. Sch. Dist., 524 U.S. 274 (1998).

202 Doe v. Hillsboro Indep. Sch. Dist., 81 F.3d 1395 (5th Cir. 1996); Benavides v. County of Wilson, 955 F.2d 968 (5th Cir. 1992).

203 City of Canton v. Harris, 489 U.S. 378 (1989); Doe v. Estes, 926 F. Supp. 979 (D. Nev. 1996).

204 Kennedy v. Dexter Consol. Sch., 955 P.2d 693 (N.M. Ct. App. 1998).

205 Johnson v. Dallas Indep. Sch. Dist., 38 F.3d 198 (5th Cir. 1994); Leffall v. Dallas Indep. Sch. Dist., 28 F.3d 521 (5th Cir. 1994).

206 D.R. by L.R. v. Middle Bucks Area Vocational Technical Sch., 972 F.2d 1364 (3d Cir. 1992) (en banc).

207 Plumeau v. Yamhill County Sch. Dist., 907 F. Supp. 1423 (D. Or. 1995).

208 *Compare* Cornelius v. Town of Highland Lake, 880 F.2d 348 (11th Cir. 1989).

209 DeShaney v. Winnebago County Dep't of Social Serv., 489 U.S. 189 (1989); Griffith v. Johnson, 899 F.2d 1427 (5th Cir. 1990); *compare* Walton v. Alexander, 44 F.3d 1297 (5th Cir. 1995).

210 Sargi v. Kent City Bd. of Educ., 70 F.3d 907 (6th Cir. 1995) (citing supporting cases from the 3d, 7th, and 10th Circuits).

211 Carey v. Piphus, 435 U.S. 247 (1978); Memphis Cmty. Sch. Dist. v. Stachura, 477 U.S. 299 (1986).

212 City of Newport v. Fact Concerts, Inc., 453 U.S. 247 (1981).

The Constitution of the United States of America

[Parts of the Constitution pertinent to education law.]

We the People of the United States, in Order to form a more perfect Union, establish Justice, insure domestic Tranquillity, provide for the common defence, promote the general Welfare, and secure the Blessings of Liberty to ourselves and our Posterity, do ordain and establish this Constitution for the United States of America.

ARTICLE I.

SECTION 1. All legislative Powers herein granted shall be vested in a Congress of the United States, which shall consist of a Senate and House of Representatives.

SECTION 8. The Congress shall have Power To lay and collect Taxes, Duties, Imposts and Excises, to pay the Debts and provide for the common Defence and general Welfare of the United States; . . .

To promote the Progress of Science and useful Arts, by securing for limited Times to Authors and Inventors the exclusive Right to their respective Writings and Discoveries; . . .

To make all Laws which shall be necessary and proper for carrying into Execution the foregoing Powers, and all other Powers vested by this Constitution in the Government of the United States, or in any Department or Officer thereof.

SECTION 10. No State shall pass any . . . Law impairing the Obligation of Contracts . . .

ARTICLE II.

SECTION 1. The executive Power shall be vested in a President of the United States of America.

ARTICLE III.

SECTION 1. The judicial Power of the United States, shall be vested in one supreme Court, and in such inferior Courts as the Congress may from time to time ordain and establish. The Judges, both of the supreme and inferior Courts, shall hold their Offices during good Behaviour, and shall, at stated Times, receive for their Services, a Compensation, which shall not be diminished during their Continuance in Office.

SECTION 2. The judicial Power shall extend to all Cases, in Law and Equity, arising under this Constitution, the Laws of the United States, and Treaties made, or which shall be made, under their Authority;—to all Cases affecting Ambassadors, other public Ministers and Consuls;—to all Cases of admiralty and maritime Jurisdiction;—to Controversies to which the United States shall be a Party;—to Controversies between two or more States;—

between a State and Citizens of another State;—between Citizens of different States;—between Citizens of the same State claiming Lands under Grants of different States, and between a State, or the Citizens thereof, and foreign States, Citizens or Subjects.

In all Cases affecting Ambassadors, other public Ministers and Consuls, and those in which a State shall be Party, the Supreme Court shall have original Jurisdiction. In all the other Cases before mentioned, the Supreme Court shall have appellate Jurisdiction, both as to Law and Fact, with such Exceptions, and under such Regulations as the Congress shall make.

ARTICLE VI.

This Constitution, and the Laws of the United States which shall be made in Pursuance thereof; and all Treaties made, or which shall be made, under the Authority of the United States, shall be the supreme Law of the Land; and the Judges in every State shall be bound thereby, any Thing in the Constitution or Laws of any State to the Contrary notwithstanding.

* * *

ARTICLES IN ADDITION TO, AND AMENDMENT OF, THE CONSTITUTION OF THE UNITED STATES OF AMERICA, PROPOSED BY CONGRESS, AND RATIFIED BY THE SEVERAL STATES, PURSUANT TO THE FIFTH ARTICLE OF THE ORIGINAL CONSTITUTION.

AMENDMENT I [1791].

Congress shall make no law respecting an establishment of religion, or prohibiting the free exercise thereof; or abridging the freedom of speech, or of the press; or the right of the people peaceably to assemble, and to petition the Government for a redress of grievances.

AMENDMENT IV [1791].

The right of the people to be secure in their persons, houses, papers, and effects, against unreasonable searches and seizures, shall not be violated, and no Warrants shall issue, but upon probable cause, supported by Oath or affirmation, and particularly describing the place to be searched, and the persons or things to be seized.

AMENDMENT V [1791].

No person shall be held to answer for a capital, or otherwise infamous crime, unless on a presentment or indictment of a Grand Jury, except in cases arising in the land or naval forces, or in the Militia, when in actual service in time of War or public danger; nor shall any person be subject for the same offence to be twice put in jeopardy of life or limb; nor shall be compelled in any criminal case to be a witness against himself, nor be deprived of life, liberty, or property, without due process of law; nor shall private property be taken for public use, without just compensation.

AMENDMENT VI [1791].

In all criminal prosecutions, the accused shall enjoy the right to a speedy and public trial, by an impartial jury of the State and district wherein the crime shall have been committed, which district shall have been previously ascertained by law, and to be informed of the nature and cause of the accusation; to be confronted with the witnesses against him; to have compulsory process for obtaining Witnesses in his favor, and to have the Assistance of Counsel for his defense.

AMENDMENT VII [1791].

In Suits at common law, where the value in controversy shall exceed twenty dollars, the right of trial by jury shall be preserved, and no fact tried by a jury, shall be otherwise re-examined in any Court of the United States, than according to the rules of common law.

AMENDMENT VIII [1791].

Excessive bail shall not be required, nor excessive fines imposed, nor cruel and unusual punishments inflicted.

AMENDMENT IX [1791].

The enumeration in the Constitution, of certain rights, shall not be construed to deny or disparage others retained by the people.

AMENDMENT X [1791].

The powers not delegated to the United States by the Constitution, nor prohibited by it to the States, are reserved to the States respectively, or to the people.

AMENDMENT XI [1798].

The Judicial power of the United States shall not be construed to extend to any suit in law or equity, commenced or prosecuted against one of the United States by Citizens of another State, or by Citizens or Subjects of any Foreign State.

AMENDMENT XIV [1868].

SECTION 1. All persons born or naturalized in the United States and subject to the jurisdiction thereof, are citizens of the United States and of the State wherein they reside. No State shall make or enforce any law which shall abridge the privileges or immunities of citizens of the United States; nor shall any State deprive any person of life, liberty, or property, without due process of law; nor deny to any person within its jurisdiction the equal protection of the laws.

AMENDMENT XV [1870].

SECTION 1. The right of citizens of the United States to vote shall not be denied or abridged by the United States or by any State on account of race, color, or previous condition of servitude.
SECTION 2. The Congress shall have power to enforce this article by appropriate legislation.

AMENDMENT XIX [1920].

SECTION 1. The right of citizens of the United States to vote shall not be denied or abridged by the United States or by any State on account of sex.

SECTION 2. Congress shall have power to enforce this article by appropriate legislation.

AMENDMENT XXVI [1971].

SECTION 1. The right of citizens of the United States, who are eighteen years of age or older, to vote shall not be denied or abridged by the United States or by any State on account of age.

SECTION 2. The Congress shall have power to enforce this article by appropriate legislation.

Table of Cases

Cases cited in the notes are listed by page number followed by note number. Numbers in italics indicate the page where the note and complete citation are found.

Index

eBooks – at www.eBookstore.tandf.co.uk

A library at your fingertips!

eBooks are electronic versions of printed books. You can store them on your PC/laptop or browse them online.

They have advantages for anyone needing rapid access to a wide variety of published, copyright information.

eBooks can help your research by enabling you to bookmark chapters, annotate text and use instant searches to find specific words or phrases. Several eBook files would fit on even a small laptop or PDA.

NEW: Save money by eSubscribing: cheap, online access to any eBook for as long as you need it.

Annual subscription packages

We now offer special low-cost bulk subscriptions to packages of eBooks in certain subject areas. These are available to libraries or to individuals.

For more information please contact webmaster.ebooks@tandf.co.uk

We're continually developing the eBook concept, so keep up to date by visiting the website.

www.eBookstore.tandf.co.uk